Fundamental Problems of the Sociology of Thinking

Historical Materialism Book Series

Editorial Board

Loren Balhorn (*Berlin*)
David Broder (*Rome*)
Sebastian Budgen (*Paris*)
Steve Edwards (*London*)
Juan Grigera (*London*)
Marcel van der Linden (*Amsterdam*)
Peter Thomas (*London*)

VOLUME 265

The titles published in this series are listed at *brill.com/hm*

Fundamental Problems of the Sociology of Thinking

By

Konstantin Megrelidze

Translated by

Jeff Skinner

Edited, with an introduction and editorial apparatus, by

Craig Brandist

BRILL

LEIDEN | BOSTON

This translation was supported by a grant from the Transcript Program of the Mikhail Prokhorov Foundation.

The Library of Congress Cataloging-in-Publication Data is available online at https://catalog.loc.gov
LC record available at https://lccn.loc.gov/2022042141

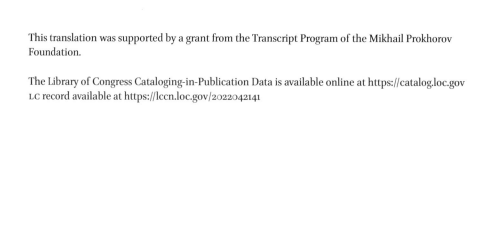

Typeface for the Latin, Greek, and Cyrillic scripts: "Brill". See and download: brill.com/brill-typeface.

ISSN 1570-1522
ISBN 978-90-04-30008-8 (hardback)
ISBN 978-90-04-52590-0 (e-book)

Copyright 2023 by Koninklijke Brill NV, Leiden, The Netherlands.
Koninklijke Brill NV incorporates the imprints Brill, Brill Nijhoff, Brill Hotei, Brill Schöningh, Brill Fink, Brill mentis, Vandenhoeck & Ruprecht, Böhlau, V&R unipress and Wageningen Academic.
All rights reserved. No part of this publication may be reproduced, translated, stored in a retrieval system, or transmitted in any form or by any means, electronic, mechanical, photocopying, recording or otherwise, without prior written permission from the publisher. Requests for re-use and/or translations must be addressed to Koninklijke Brill NV via brill.com or copyright.com.

This book is printed on acid-free paper and produced in a sustainable manner.

Contents

Introduction: Konstantin Megrelidze and His
  Fundamental Problems of the Sociology of Thinking   IX
    Craig Brandist
Acknowledgement   XXVIII
From the Editor of the Russian Edition   XXIX

Fundamental Problems of the Sociology of Thinking

Foreword   3

General Exposition of the Question of Thinking   8
A Critique of Naturalistic Precepts (§§ 1–3)   8

PART 1

1   **Material Conditions and Social Preconditions Necessary for the Rise of the Human Level of Consciousness**   18
    Working Life Activity (§ 4)   18
    Relations of Consumption and Production (§ 5)   20
    Labour and the Product of Labour (§§ 6, 7)   24
    The Product of Labour: Material Mediator of Social Relations (§ 8)   29
    Labour and Society: Mutual Dependence (§ 9)   34

2   **From the Animal Level of Consciousness to Human Thinking**   40
    The Biological Roots of Consciousness (§ 10)   40
    Instincts and Reflex Responses (§§ 11, 12)   42
    The Intellectual Activity of Animals (§ 13)   48
    Shortcomings of Physiological Psychology and Classical Psychology (§ 14)   59
    On Gestalt Psychology (§ 15)   62
    The Manifestation of Consciousness in Animals (§§ 16, 17)   66
    Distinguishing Characteristics of Human Consciousness (§ 18)   71
    Interaction in the Animal World and Social Interaction (§ 19)   78
    The Ideational Content of Consciousness (§ 20)   85
    The Essential Particularities of Human Consciousness (§ 21)   91
    Preliminary Results (§ 22)   94

3   **Material Culture and Thinking** 97
     Labour Activity and Thinking (§§ 23, 24) 97
     The Materialisation of Ideas in the Process of Labour Activity and
     the Acquisition of Ideational Content by Things (§ 25) 102
     Embodied Reason and Its Social Significance (§ 26) 106
     The Qualitative Particularity of Social Relations (§ 27) 112
     The Instrument of Labour – the Hand – Reason (§§ 28, 29) 115
     The Cognitive Significance of Mediated Activity (§§ 30, 31) 124
     The Tale of How 'the Transcendental Is Made Immanent' and
     'the Immanent Is Made Transcendental' (§ 32) 132

4   **The Problem of Perception in the Field of Marxist Philosophy** 134
     The Perspective of Classical Psychology and Philosophy (§ 33) 134
     Sensation Is Not the Basic Mental Atom (§ 34) 138
     Sensation Is Not a Symbol, but the Reflection of Reality (§§ 35, 36) 139
     The Relational Dependence of Sense Data (§§ 37–42) 143
     From the History of the Perception of Colours (§§ 41, 42) 154
     The Marxist Perspective on the Question of Sensory Perception
     (§ 43) 169

5   **The Question of a Subject's Self-Awareness** 173
     Objects Are Perceived Primarily according to Their Social Significance
     (§ 44) 173
     Self-Awareness Is Historically a Much Later Phenomenon Than
     the Perception of Objects of Activity (§ 45) 173
     An Individual Subject's Perception Was Historically Preceded
     by the Perception of the Collective Subject (§ 46) 175

     PART 2

6   **The Rise of the Idea** 178
     Comprehension. The Concept (§ 48) 179
     The Concept and the Notion [*predstavlenie*] (§ 49) 182
     The Particular and the General (§ 50) 188
     The Doctrine of Existence and Concept (§ 51) 190
     The Doctrine of the Concept in the Empiricists and in Kant (§ 52) 191
     The Place of the Concept in the System of Rationalist Views (§§ 53,
     54) 192
     Chance and Necessity (§ 55) 201
     Three Pictures of the World (§ 56) 206

Concept and Reality (§ 57)   208
The Self-Contained Structure (§ 58)   217
Self-Contained Structure and the Concrete Concept (§§ 59, 60)   219
On Mathematical Concepts (§§ 61, 62)   224
Generalisation and General Concepts (§ 63)   234
The Formation of Concepts (§§ 64, 65)   238

7 **The Sociogenesis of Ideas**   245
The Social Character of Individual Thinking (§ 66)   245
On the Question of Parallelisms and Convergences (§ 67)   248
The Theory of Dispersion (§ 68)   249
The Theory of Borrowing (§ 69)   251
The Theory of the Identity of the Human Mind (§ 70)   254
The Geographical Theory (§ 71)   257
Shortcomings of the Existing Hypotheses (§ 72)   258
Questions of Parallelisms in the Marxist Interpretation (§ 73)   259
On the Origin of the Tinderbox (§ 74)   263
Parallelisms in the Sphere of Calculating Time (§ 75)   269
Convergences in the Realm of Types of Thinking (§ 76)   272
Social Existence and Social Consciousness (§ 77)   274
The Individual and Society (§§ 78, 79)   277
The Social Genesis of Ideas (§ 80)   282

8 **The Process of the Social Circulation of Ideas**   285
The Propagation of Ideas (§ 81)   285
Social Circulation of the Products of Mental Creativity (§ 82)   288
On Popular Creativity (§ 83)   289
On Borrowing (§ 84)   293
Social Consciousness (§ 85)   296
The Composition and Content of Social Consciousness (§§ 86, 87)   300

9 **The Social Implementation of Ideas**   308
The Material Support of Ideas (§§ 88, 89)   308
Needs and Interests (§ 90)   311
The Construction of Social Interests (§ 91)   313
The Domination of Fetishistic Relations (§ 92)   318
Surplus Product and Private Property (§ 93)   321
Proprietary Alienation and Its Liquidation (§§ 94, 95)   325
The Concept of the Collective Social Field of History (§§ 96, 97)   332
Class Interests (§ 98)   339

Ideas Are Derivatives of Social Interests (§§ 99, 100)   342
The Character of Conformity to the Laws of History in an Antagonistic Society (§§ 101, 102)   346
The Social Implementation of Ideas (§§ 103–106)   353
Class Consciousness (§ 107)   360
Ideological Changes and Social Changes (§ 108)   363

10   **Testing Ideas in the Process of Their Implementation**   365
What Is an Experience (§ 109)   365
Testing Ideas by Experience, Practice (§§ 110–113)   366
Pragmatism and Marxism (§ 114)   370
A Thesis on Practice in Its General Philosophical Meaning (§ 115)   372
Concluding Observations (§ 116)   373

Supplement: Nikolai Iakovlevich Marr and the Philosophy of Marxism (1935)   375
Translated by Craig Brandist
Glossary of Names   398
References   413
Index   422

INTRODUCTION

Konstantin Megrelidze and His *Fundamental Problems of the Sociology of Thinking*

Craig Brandist

Konstantin Romanovich Megrelidze's book *The Fundamental Problems of the Sociology of Thinking* is a remarkable and rare type of work: a comprehensive and subtle work of Marxist philosophical thought which engages extensively with contemporary European philosophy, psychology and social science, dating from the height of the Stalin period. The book is far from a dogmatic rebuttal of various schools of thought, which predominated at the time, but a much more creative and critical engagement from the perspective of someone trying to develop a holistic form of Marxism that could account for the many dimensions of the human activity of thinking. In this project the erudition and judiciousness of the author remains clear to the reader, and it is notable that this survives in a text that was subject to many changes, first adopted by the author under duress, and then compounded by excisions some decades after his death. The text we present here in English translation was therefore not that which could be regarded as the author's own version, but is translated from the edition that was published in the USSR in 1965 and reissued in 1973 and, most recently, in 2007. A putative second volume of the work was allegedly written while Megrelidze was held in one of the camps of Stalin's GULAG system, but seems to have been lost.[1] In common with the work of many thinkers of the time, therefore, the text remains problematic in a number of ways, but the contents are significant enough to make its appearance in English for the first time worthwhile and timely. In what follows we shall present information about the biography of the author and the complicated history of the work before moving on to a discussion of how the work relates to the debates of the time and finally, the relevance of the work today.

---

1 Vitzthum 1993, p. 210.

A Biographical Sketch[2]

Konstantin (Kita) Romanovich Megrelidze was born the son of a village priest in Khrialeti, Georgia, on 30 December 1900. He attended the village school from 1906 before enrolling in the boy's grammar school in the Georgian port city of Poti. On graduation he for a time worked as a teacher of German, and of mathematics, at the Supsa-Ozurgeti College of Higher Education. In 1919 he enrolled at the newly formed (1918) Tiflis (from 1936 Tbilisi) State University (now the Ivane Javakhishvili Tbilisi State University), graduating in philosophy and psychology in 1923. He stayed on at the University to work towards the title of Professor of Philosophy, simultaneously teaching political economy and the history of materialism at the Central Party School, the pedagogical section of which he headed, and teaching courses of general and child psychology at the Higher Pedagogical Institute.

In 1924 the Central Committee of the Communist Party and the Commissariat of Enlightenment sent Megrelidze to Germany to continue his education. He spent two semesters at Baden Albert Ludwigs University in Freiberg (1924–25) and then shifted to the Friedrich Wilhelms University in Berlin, where he spent a further four semesters. While in Germany he attended lectures by some of the leading German intellectuals of the time, including phenomenologist Edmund Husserl, Gestalt psychologists Wolfgang Köhler and Max Wertheimer, and the neo-Kantian philosopher Arthur Liebert (1878–1946). While resident in Berlin, Megrelidze joined the German Communist Party (KPD) under the name of Hans Schlosser, where he was a member of the Bureau of Communist Students of the Central Committee. When a German Union of Soviet Students was formed, Megrelidze was selected as Chair of its Central Executive Committee, in which capacity he attended the Second All-Union Conference of Proletarian Students in Moscow. He also proved to be a talented linguist, developing a command of German, French, English and Turkish in addition to his native Georgian and Russian. Meanwhile Megrelidze worked as a correspondent for the Tblisi newspapers *The Communist* and *Dawn of the East*, where he published surveys of the political situation in Germany.

On returning to Tiflis in June 1927 Megrelidze served as Deputy Head of the Agitation and Propaganda Department of the Central Committee of the Georgian Party for two years, followed by a term as Head of the Scientific Department of the Georgian Commissariat of Enlightenment (1929–31) and, from 1931,

---

[2] Information for this section was derived from the following sources: Megrelidze 1989; Dzioev 1989; Vitzthum 1993; Friedrich 1993; Shilov 1995.

as Deputy Head of the section of Language and the History of Material Culture at the Institute of Marxism-Leninism. Throughout this period, he lectured on philosophy, dialectical and historical materialism at various higher education institutes in Tiflis (the Transcaucasian Communist University, the Chemistry Institute and the Institute of Communication) first as a docent and, from 1930, as a professor. He was also Chair of the Georgian State Film Industry and Rektor of the Academy of Art.

In 1933 Megrelidze visited the Institute of Language and Thinking (*Institut iazyka i myshleniia*, IIaM), of the Academy of Sciences in Leningrad, where from 1 February 1934 he was confirmed as a permanent 'Scientific Specialist' and, from January 1935, he was the institute's Party Organiser.[3] In February of the same year he was appointed the head of the Department of Nationalities at the Leningrad State Public Library. The Institute of Language and Thinking granted him a Kandidat (roughly equivalent to a PhD) degree without the need to defend a dissertation, and in 1935 he submitted his doctoral dissertation (akin to a D. Litt) *Social Phenomenology* to the Academy's Institute of Philosophy, where it was to be examined by Abram Moiseyevich Deborin (1881– 1963) and Grigorii Samuilovich Tymianskii (1893–1941). The defence did not take place, however, because Megrelidze unexpectedly was expelled from the Communist Party for allegedly concealing the fact that he had been arrested in 1923 for participating in his wife's Menshevik organisation (he had actually only met his future wife, the economist Aleksandra Fedorovna Kartsivadze [1905–1960] in 1929). The publication of the monograph scheduled for 1937 was halted when the responsible editor, Leon Georgievich Basindzhagian (1893– 1938), was arrested by the NKVD. Even though Head of the Institute, academician Ivan Ivanovich Meshchaninov (1883–1967) cleared the book for release the following year, the entire edition was confiscated when Megrelidze was arrested and charged with having connections to a counter-revolutionary Dashnak (Armenian Revolutionary Federation) group, a Trotskyist-Zinovievite terrorist group and with foreign intelligence agencies.

After a lengthy trial, a seriously ill Megrelidze was released, returned to Tblisi in December 1939 and took up a position as Senior Research Fellow at the Institute of Language, History and Material Culture of the Georgian branch of the Academy of Sciences. A number of academicians again recommended the publication of the book, but this was again thwarted when, in December 1940, Megrelidze was arrested once more on visiting Leningrad to support his wife who had herself been arrested when she tried to change apart-

---

3 Kazanskii (ed.) 2013, pp. 362, 397.

ments. Charged with anti-Soviet propaganda, Megrelidze was sentenced to ten years of correctional labour in a camp in the Kirov region, where he died in 1943. His wife was only released from a prison camp following Khrushchev's 'secret speech' in 1956, at which point she joined their daughter Manana Konstantinova Megrelidze to petition for the posthumous rehabilitation of Konstantin Romanovich. This was granted in September 1958 on the grounds that there was no evidence of guilt.

The Published Text

Megrelidze's cousin, the philologist Iosif Varfolomeevich Megrelidze (1909–1996), managed to extract a copy of Megrelidze's monograph from his already sealed office at the Institute of Language and Thinking, and this became the basis of the text published in 1965. A special commission was established at the Academy of Sciences of the Georgian SSR to consider publication in 1956, eventually leading to publication in 1965. There seems little doubt that Megrelidze adjusted the text before his initial attempts to publish the book, not least changing the title from *Social Phenomenology* to *Fundamental Problems of the Sociology of Thinking* so that it no longer foregrounded phenomenology.[4] Giga Zedania, professor and rector of Ilia State University, Tbilisi, claims the 1965 edition involved a number of excisions of references to Stalin and abridgements of considerations of the work of the prominent and controversial philologist and archaeologist Nikolai Iaklovlevich Marr. Unfortunately such editorial incursions are not uncommon: references to Marr, whose ideas had been denounced by Stalin in his comments on Marxism and linguistics in June 1950, were missing from the publication of Mikhail Bakhtin's now famous essays on the novel of the 1930s when they were published posthumously in 1975, while references to these same comments by Stalin were removed from the publication of Bakhtin's 1953 essay 'Problems of Speech Genres' when it was published in 1978, 1979 and 1996.[5]

Such interventions obscure both the political and intellectual contexts in which the works in question were written. It is hard to imagine how a work on Marxist theory written for publication in in the USSR in 1937 could not have included references to Stalin, however much they may have represented instances of obligatory genuflection. It is even less likely given that Megrelidze

---

4 Dzhioev 1989, p. 88.
5 Bakhtin 1996, p. 536.

was the Party organiser in the Institute of Language and Thinking. Considerations of the work of Nikolai Marr were also to be expected since Marr was the founding director of the institute, the leading figure in the field, especially from 1932, and that there were numerous commemorative publications about Marr appearing at the very time the book was being prepared for publication following his death in 1934. The extremely and disproportionately short Chapter 5 of the published book introduces the question of early forms of social consciousness before moving on and it is here discussion of Marr was most likely located. Fortunately, we can glean a sense of the contents from Megrelidze's article 'N. Ia. Marr and the Philosophy of Marxism', which was originally delivered as a lecture in memory of Marr at the Academy of Sciences in February 1935 and published in a special issue of *The Problems of the History of Pre-Capitalist Societies*, the journal of Marr's State Academy for the History of Material Culture (GAIMK) to mark Marr's death. It was republished, with a few minor changes, in the Party journal *Under the Banner of Marxism* the same year. The article considered the importance of Marr's work for the philosophy of Marxism and a translation of this article is appended to the translation of the current book. The article helps us to reconstruct where Marr's ideas were significant to Megrelidze's approach, and it gives a flavour of the publishing conventions of the time, not least in the invocation of Stalin in the final sentence.

While not wishing to exaggerate the ethnic dimension, there was undoubtedly a close community of Georgian and other Caucasian scholars at IIaM, including the Georgians Marr, Konstantin and Iosif Megrelidze, Basindzhagian, Karpez Darispanovich Dondua (1891–1951) and the Armenian Iosif Abgarovich Orbeli (1887–1961). Study of the languages and cultures of the Caucasus region was central to the activity of the institute, which began as the 'Japhetic Institute', based on Marr's earlier theory that the languages and cultures of the Caucasus constituted a Japhetic group, which were related to Semitic languages and cultures by virtue of them having a common 'Noetic' ancestor.[6] Georgians Marr and Stalin had an interesting correlation of ideas and interests, and even some correspondence in 1932, while it was under the influence of another Georgian linguist, Arnold Stepanovich Chikobava (1898–1985), that Stalin composed his work attacking the legacy of Marr in linguistics in 1950.[7] Marr's ideas proved controversial among Georgian scholars for a number of reasons, both scholarly

---

[6] This was Marr's subversive variation on the 'Mosaic ethnology' that dominated Indo-European philology. See Trautmann 1997, pp. 28–61.

[7] See Ilizarov 2012 for an interesting consideration of the question.

and ideological.[8] Megrelidze clearly believed, however, that at least one aspect of Marr's thought was an important contribution to the development of the philosophy of Marxism.

Megrelidze's Social Phenomenology

The title of Megrelidze's book *Fundamental Problems of the Sociology of Thinking* may appear a little unusual in English since the 'sociology of thought' seems a little more natural. There is, however, an important reason for the translation. Megrelidze specifically uses the term *myshlenie* (thinking) rather than thought (*mysl'*) to foreground *activity* and *process*. The book presents a comprehensive consideration of the social nature of human thinking, arguing that the Marxist approach to the question is sharply distinguished from all previous approaches and that characteristic of modern bourgeois philosophy. Marxist philosophy requires a socio-historical approach to thinking and knowledge, based on the understanding of the active, social, and practical essence of humanity. Marxism anticipated methodological innovations that came to the fore in various areas of scientific thinking later: a holistic approach to thinking, as well as to other objects of study; the need to consider the structural connections between thinking and other aspects of human activity; the need for complex study of phenomena, which, in turn, implies the denial of rigid boundaries between branches of science. He concluded that 'in the history of the formation and development of human society, labour, tools, material culture, language and thinking are components of the whole as inextricably linked and mutually conditioning each other; and if we want to study thinking, we need to take this complex whole in its totality and unity with the general historical process of human development'.

The two closely related tendencies in bourgeois philosophy that Megrelidze considered in need of being completely eradicated from Marxism were naturalistic reductionism and empiricism. The first could be viewed in attempts to take studies of animal behaviour as given and then to extrapolate their findings to human behaviour. While recognising the importance of developments in physiology, Megrelidze held that an excessive focus on the nervous system and the physiology of the brain obscures such fundamental problems as why social conditions make one and the same nervous-neurological apparatus work in a certain way in one era and in a different way in another. Reducing man

---

8 On the Georgian reception see Cherchi and Manning 2002 and Tuite 2011.

to a natural being fails to study what is specifically human in human beings, in its place substituting the animal. Physiology and psychology need therefore to be restructured in fundamental ways in order to study what is specifically human. The essence, composition and structure of human consciousness, the forms and ways of thinking, are formed and developed primarily under the influence of social forces, which operate according to social and historical laws.

The fundamental innovations of Marxism had, Megrelidze held, still not adequately restructured the study of human consciousness. The irreducible nature of sociality was still too often interpreted as a relatively minor feature of thinking; the qualitative uniqueness of human consciousness often overlooked. While the early Soviet period saw a rise in studies of the relationship between machines and humans, the social nature of consciousness was too often ignored. The creative nature of human labour, on which Marx placed particular emphasis as manifesting essential human powers, was too often considered narrowly as an external relationship to utility. Megrelidze aimed to give them full consideration as manifestations of the essence of the human.

This failure fully to account for the social essence of the human leads to naturalism, and when this social nature and the specificity of human activity is removed from the theory of knowledge the result is empiricism. Sensations are now regarded as natural data and from them the empiricist tries to explain the essence of human knowledge. Megrelidze claims the connection of this position with naturalism was rarely realised, since the main features of the philosophy of empiricism became embedded in scientific dogmas and prejudices. The persistence of these dogmas constitutes a great danger for Marxist philosophy. In opposition to these narrow perspectives, Megrelidze argues that it is not only the highest functions of the psyche that are products of the history of society, but even its most elementary functions such as sensations and feelings. Sensations, feelings and the data derived therefrom are not a direct source of knowledge for Marxism, which recognises that a person learns certain ways of perceiving by means of the senses.

The naturalistic and empiricist point of view identifies objectivity with the material, and the latter with the natural. As a result, the specific objectivity of social formations, their necessity and regularity, is distorted. Objective value is identified with the natural and material existence of the objects to which value is attributed. Similarly, by regarding the aesthetic aspects of perception as dependent on social factors and so not having a natural character leads many thinkers to regard aesthetic factors as merely subjective. All this suggests that both empiricist and naturalistic interpretations of Marxist philosophy have not yet been completely overcome.

Recognition of the social aspects of the person and of human thinking is crucial in overcoming empiricism and naturalism. However, mere recognition of the social determination of human consciousness without an explanation of human activity essentially reproduces empiricism and naturalism in a new, collectivist form. Society becomes merely an external determinant of human activity. This approach Megrelidze calls 'sociologism': the direct derivation of human consciousness from the organisational forms of a given society.[9] Durkheim and others (Megrelidze ascribes Saussure to this company, as was common at the time) are the chief representatives of this approach which, Megrelidze complains, turns consciousness into a dead apparatus, meaninglessly reproducing alien forms. Thinkers such as Durkheim, Saussure and Lucien Lévy-Bruhl do not understand that the individual is not only forced to think as others think, in traditionally established forms, but may also compel others to think in his/her own way. The individual not only perceives the traditionally developed forms, but also participates in the creation and re-creation of these forms. Here Megrelidze anticipates, by several decades, an argument advanced by Roy Bhaskar in arguably his most significant work, *The Possibility of Naturalism* (1979).[10]

For thinking to be necessary, and for it to be determined socially, it must have a certain function, it must be inherent in social activity; to conceive of thinking as a passive reflection of social reality means to consider it useless, merely accidental for the social process. Consistent determinism is compatible only with the recognition of the potency of human activity. 'Thinking does not just reproduce a particular social system – it would be useless, but acts each time according to the meaning of these objects and makes mental constructions that solve these problems'.

This activity manifests itself already at the stage of sensory cognition: sensory representations are not recognised as 'simple mirror images of objects'. Here, in particular, we can see the influence of Megrelidze's study under Husserl and the Gestalt psychologists, and we can begin to understand why his study was initially entitled *social phenomenology*. According to Husserl's doctrine of intentionality, consciousness is not only consciousness *of* something, but an *act* of seeing, hearing and so on directed *towards* something. Objects of perception are therefore *presented* to consciousness according to these acts; we perceive things in a particular way. What are presented to consciousness in

---

9   A similar argument is advanced by Medvedev 1983 [1926]. Comparison of Megrelidze's position with that of members of the Bakhtin Circle such as Voloshinov and Medvedev would be worthwhile.
10 Bhaskar 1998 [1979], pp. 25–44.

these acts are not atomic sensations, but structured wholes that are objects (or states of affairs, *Sachverhalten*) which can only be broken down into their constituent parts through analytical processes. This is because, as Husserl outlines in his second and third *Logical Investigations*, perception always involves some level of interpretation of sensations. Interpretation is here not in the Kantian sense of imposing concepts on a formless 'manifold', for reality is already structured and interpretation is not always conceptual. Thus, when we recognise x as a part of whole a rather than whole b, there is no progression via concepts, but an act of perception involving sensory interpretation. Only later, in his 1913 book *Ideas: General Introduction to Pure Phenomenology*, does Husserl seek to distinguish fundamentally between perception of putative objects and separate *noema*, that is correlated elements of the structure of any intentional act, which lead him to embrace idealism.[11]

While by the time Megrelidze studied under Husserl the latter had made his decisive transition to transcendental idealism, a generation of thinkers inspired by the same tradition of Austrian philosophy were working to retain and develop the earlier ontological realism.[12] Megrelidze encountered these ideas directly when he moved to Berlin and worked with Köhler, Wertheimer and others.[13] The Berlin School argued that the structured wholes or *Gestalten*, that were the primary objects of the perceiving consciousness, were not ideal entities but could be established experimentally and were repeatedly observable. Perception is a matter of direct relations to reality rather than a detour via ideal entities. Perhaps the most famous example of their experimental work was the so-called 'phi-phenomenon' discovered by Wertheimer when he noted that under certain conditions two subjects (in actual fact his two colleagues Köhler and Kurt Koffka) were exposed to two alternately flashing lights a short distance apart, they perceived movement back and forth between them. The movement perceived was not the product of any intellectual production but sensory interpretation. Some of the theoretical implications of this were developed by both Koffka and Wertheimer, of which particularly significant was the idea that perception is a result of the state of readiness or 'mental set'

---

11   For a discussion see Dummett 1983, pp. 61–83; Philipse 1995.
12   On this intellectual trend see, *inter alia*, Schuhmann and Smith 1985; Mulligan (ed.) 1987; Rollinger (ed.) 1999.
13   It is questionable whether Megrelidze imbibed Husserl's idealism to the extent suggested by Zedania (2014), not least given the absence of ideas or terms specifically derived from his later works, and the presence of significant ideas from Gestalt theorists fundamentally hostile to Husserl's idealist turn. On Gestalt psychology in Germany see especially Ash 1998. For a survey of the wider theories of *Gestalt* at the root of these perspectives see Smith 1988.

(*Einstellung*) of the perceiver towards the stimulus.[14] Successive presentations are integrated according to this 'mental set', psychologically grounded states which reflect 'materially determinate knowledge and habits of mind acquired through time by the organism in question and which may be further dependent on social factors, institutions, authorities, language and so on'.[15] Perceived structures, *Gestalten*, are therefore correlations between objective and subjective factors, which include bodily phenomena such as feelings.[16]

Particularly important for Megrelidze's development of these ideas was Husserl's contention that perceptual states form parts of wider 'psychological and behavioural wholes, and only an analysis of the role of perceptual acts within such contexts will allow us to make sense of the perceptions of a subject in motion, of perceptions of dynamic objects and of the connection between perceptual states and the sets appropriate to different types of activity'.[17] These innovative perspectives about dynamic perception were not fully to be developed in experimental psychology until the 1950s, when Koffka's student James Jerome Gibson developed what would come to be known as 'ecological psychology' according to which an animal's sensory apparatus constituted a perceptual system with which the dynamic and mobile organism discerned the structures of the physical world through interaction with it.[18] For Gibson, the animal seeks 'affordances' or the opportunities for action that the environment affords the animal, and humans similarly perceive the object's affordances rather than its particular qualities.

As we have already seen, Megrelidze's sociological development of the ideas of Husserl and the Gestalt psychologists did not, like Gibson, work on the basis of continuity between the animal and human, but the qualitative difference between them. This is clear from Megrelidze's scepticism towards the conclusions about alleged human-like intellectual behaviour in apes that Köhler draws from his experiments (see especially Chapter 2). Instead, Megrelidze insists on the fundamental distinction between apes and man, following the then recently published texts that became known as Marx's *German Ideology* and Engels's unfinished essay 'The Part Played by Labour in the Transition from Ape to Man', published as part of *The Dialectics of Nature*. Conscious

---

14 This principle was outlined in a number of articles from around 1915, but most clearly stated in Koffka 1935. The notion of *Einstellung*, rendered in Russian as *ustanovka*, was commonly invoked in a range of disciplines including philosophy, psychology and literary theory by the early 1920s.
15 Smith 1994, p. 264.
16 See, particularly, Wertheimer 1961.
17 Mulligan 1995, p. 169.
18 The most developed argument is in Gibson 1979.

human labour is the socially coordinated activity that enables and embodies the perceptual states that lead to fundamentally different forms of consciousness: thinking. While Engels had raised the general idea that collective human labour is the means through which language and reason arise and develop, Megrelidze's development of this idea drew upon some rather more specific arguments which he derived from the work of Ludwig Noiré and Marr.

Noiré took as his point of departure 'Spinoza's monism, Kant's criticism and Schopenhauer's theory of will' and proceeded to combine reason, language and will on the basis of human activity.[19] It is the 'percepts [obscure ideas – CB] connected with the will' that are 'the most natural and primitive of all', and it is in '*practical* thinking ... thinking guided by interest and founded on the subjective basis of will' that one needs to search for the origins of human reason.[20] It is worth citing the following passage at length:

> The emancipation of our thought from our desires and wants constitutes every advance towards theoretical knowledge, and it certainly follows thence, that originally thought was wholly coalesced with will; that percepts, accordingly, in the consciousness of primitive men, were not arranged in any causal, genetic, or intellectual connection, but simply in the order in which through instinctive impulses and emotion they had entered their various incidental or natural connections. The will for a long time remained absolute autocrat; all speech aimed at practical effects, *sympathetic* agreement, and incitation to common action. From the earliest, instinctive utterances of will, which, in the shape of sounds simultaneously uttered, encouraged men to perform the primitive acts of digging, plaiting, etc. up to the kindling eloquence of the popular orator who fired the souls of his audience with martial enthusiasm ... – throughout the same law unceasingly operates, the action of will upon will through the sympathetic frame of mind and its attendant percepts. Everywhere we find imitation, everywhere will, everywhere activity.[21]

The emancipation of thought from the tyranny of will first begins when the 'active causality of our will' produces effects, that are perceived and 'converted into percepts'. Will is made conscious when made visible in some object of the outside world. The collective nature of such activities leads to the next stage,

---

19 Noiré 1917, p. 94.
20 Noiré 1917, p. 43.
21 Noiré 1917, pp. 43–4.

when percepts are combined freely and regularly, 'guided and irradiated by the light of cognition, in a word, the *Logos*'.²²

> Causality gained freedom solely through the rise of concepts and words. The oldest words, *dig, plait, bind, separate*, have no other content than that of causal relation – the connection of two sensually perceptual percepts that constitute their causal members, the *Logos*.²³

This 'union of percepts with percepts, of concepts with concepts, of judgements with judgements constitutes ... the essential character of thought'.²⁴

Megrelidze combines Noiré's 'percepts' with Husserl's 'presentations' and the Gestalt theorists' *Einstellungen* into the Russian term *predstavlenie*, which simultaneously means presentation (of something), representation (in the psychological sense) and notion (see especially § 49).²⁵ However, for Megrelidze, will loses its metaphysical character as something impelling humans, and becomes simultaneously a product and component of human development. Here he draws upon Marx's now famous distinction between human and animal labour in chapter seven of *Capital* volume one:

> A bee puts to shame many an architect in the construction of her cells. But what distinguishes the worst architect from the best of bees is this, that the architect raises his structure in imagination before he erects it in reality. At the end of every labour-process, we get a result that already existed in the imagination of the labourer at its commencement.²⁶

Even the most primitive acts of will in the proper sense, Megrelidze tells us in § 21, are peculiarly human in being an 'aspiration towards a conscious goal' and so 'liberated from direct dependence of the sensory field'. In § 19 we learn a 'rupture of the natural bonds uniting the organism with nature and with other organisms' is necessary for such acts and this ensues 'when the objective mediator of relations ... between the subject and nature, and between the subject and other subjects' becomes firmly established. That mediator is the product of

---

22 Noiré 1917, pp. 44–5.
23 Noiré 1917, p. 45.
24 Noiré 1917, p. 46.
25 The term literally denotes standing (something) before oneself (*pered* – before; *stavit'* – to stand). Bukharin 2005 [1937], pp. 214–23 appears to attempt a similar recasting of the notion of presentation in his prison writings.
26 Marx 1996 [1887], p. 188.

labour: material culture. The dialectic of will and activity in labour establishes a spiral of development through which herd-like behaviour ascends to human thinking. It is the concept (*poniatie*) that manifests the full, active nature of human consciousness, the understanding, comprehension of things and their relations. The concept conveys the semantic expressions of an object, its role, its meaning, the structure and internal law of objects.

Semantic Palaeontology

Megrelidze's exploration of this development ranges widely through psychology, the history of science, mathematics, anthropology and philology, and draws upon thinkers writing in a wide range of languages. While one finds important engagements with some of these areas in the work of Lev Vygotskii and his associates (Aleksandr Romanovich Luria, Alexei Nikolaevich Leont'ev), and in the works of the thinkers now known as members of the Bakhtin Circle (*inter alia* Mikhail Mikhailovich Bakhtin, Pavel Nikolaevich Medvedev and Valentin Nikolaevich Voloshinov), Megrelidze is probably the most wide-ranging, and the most thoroughly versed in the ideas of Marx. An introduction could not hope adequately to prepare the reader for the range of material adduced in the book and so a glossary of proper names has been appended to allow the reader to explore these figures as appropriate. However, more needs to be said regarding the specific contexts of composition and the material likely to have been expunged from the Russian publication of 1965, and that brings us to the vexed question of the legacy of Nikolai Marr.

While very little of Marr's voluminous work has appeared in English translation, there is a significant amount of reliable secondary material that describes his fundamental ideas in linguistics and their sources.[27] Discussion of the various ways in which many thinkers engaged with Marr's ideas, deriving significant principles of analysis while avoiding some of their mentor's more eccentric and extravagant formulations, has gradually been appearing in recent years, but this is still far from exhaustive.[28]

---

[27] In English see Matthews 1950; Thomas 1957; Cherchi and Manning 2002; Brandist 2015, pp. 193–220. There is a much wider scholarship in Russian, such as Vasil'kov 2001; Alpatov 2004; Iliazarov 2012. It is worth noting that Marr has recently begun to be recognised as a thinker among whose ideas were those that anticipated perspectives later developed under the rubric of Orientalism and postcolonial studies.

[28] In English see, for instance, Moss 1984; Perlina 2002; Brandist 2011; Tihanov 2012. Little specifically relating Megrelidze's work to that of Marr has been published, with the exception of Nikonova 2003 and Friedrich 2005.

Megrelidze's 1935 essay on Marr focuses entirely on the significance of semantic palaeontology for Marxism, and steers clear of Marr's disputed ideas about the kinship of Kartvelian and Semitic languages, and from the notorious and often derided contention that all words in all languages derived from the four primordial syllables *sal, ber, ion* and *rosh*. Indeed, Marr's linguistic speculations take a back seat to the palaeontology of fundamental philosophical concepts that are traced back to pre-Socratic, Vedic and folkloric motifs. Methodologically, Marr is celebrated for those features he had adopted from Noiré: the rise of language in the process of collective human labour, and its development according to shifts in technology and social relations. Noiré had followed Lazar Geiger to argue that the first specifically linguistic phenomena were verbal roots, and that things marked out by the human action performed on them received their names from the action of which they were made object.[29] This Marr developed into the principle of functional semantics, according to which the function something plays in social life determines the way that object is perceived, interpreted and designated. Thus, at early stages of social history, if the camel came to serve the function previously played by the horse then the word that previously designated horse came to designate camel since the social significance of the animal overrides the zoological distinction. This was to undergird Marr's archaeological approach to language which, he insisted, must be studied along with the history of material culture.

Tracing the history of words according to these principles provides evidence of previous modes of thinking, with the result that as the earliest modes of consciousness are approached then items that served the same function were treated identically even if they shared nothing else in common. As the researcher moves deeper into prehistory, we see 'one appellation signified a whole series of concepts and objects, and consequently, was distinguished by multiple meanings (polysemanticism)'.[30] This is not for any rational or analytical reasons, but because the relevant objects were encountered together. This earlier stage survives in the semantic clusters or nests (*puchki*) that form the bases of poetic metaphors and plot formations as things previously perceived as identical are rethought as analogous or similar. The specifically poetic dimensions were explored at depth by Megrelidze's colleagues Izrail' Frank-Kamenetskii and Ol'ga Freidenberg, while Megrelidze concentrated on the emergence of abstract and philosophical terms from cultic identity. Poetic metaphor and the concept are phenomena that develop in unison from the

---

29 Noiré 1917, p. 149.
30 Meshchaninov 2010 [1929], p. 177.

common world of myth. Focusing on early philosophical terms, Megrelidze traces the emergence of semantic series – the connection between ideas such as fire, soul, mind and spirit are given as examples. Meshchaninov explains this idea as follows:

> In the process of the continuing development of human speech a series of words were connected to each other according to their meanings as semantic derivatives, as they emerged from previous appellations of a range of concepts and objects. Later they also emerged from such separate appellations, forming a series of words with their distinct meanings (*semantic series*), united by successive changes of meaning (semantic links) and ascend to one common basis for the whole semantic series (the beginning or the first link of the semantic series).[31]

These series, for Megrelidze, are also evidence of the social basis of perception, of social phenomenology, through which the Marxist contention about the humanisation of the senses are provided with historical evidence.

The progressive liberation of human thinking from the common engagement in natural processes through the mediation of cultural phenomena is a thread that runs throughout Megrelidze's work and one can only speculate how this may have been developed in the putative second volume of his book. Some clues may be found in two further articles written while he was working at the Institute of Language and Thinking, only one of which has been published. Megrelidze develops his work on semantic palaeontology further, dealing with the nature of human superstitions (a critical response to Lévy-Bruhl's notion of prelogical thinking) and a discussion of the wider significance of Marr's linguistic ideas.[32] It appears Megrelidze was continuing to explore these ideas in his work after completion of the first volume of his book, as is evidenced by the theses of a paper delivered orally at the Institute of Language and Thinking in January 1938 on 'The Problem of the origin of numbers and numerals', focused on Marr's ideas about the origin of grammatical categories.[33] Here he further explores Marr's idea that at the earliest stage of the evolution of human speech the name of the totem incorporated all grammatical persons within a

---

31 Meshchaninov 2010 [1929], pp. 177–8.
32 Megrelidze 1935. The second is an undated 119-page typescript entitled 'Novye dostizheniia iazykoznaniia' (New Achievements of Linguistics) which is held in Marr's archive PFA RAN 800/6/E349. The authorship of this typescript is not certain, but seems likely to have been by Megrelidze.
33 'K voprosu o proiskhozhdenii chisla i chislitel'nykh'. PFA RAN 77/1/18/5–6.

single third person, thus rendering any distinction between subject and object impossible. Subject, object and grammatical persons become differentiated with the development of tribal society, and transformation from matriarchy to patriarchy.[34]

There seems little doubt that Megrelidze overstates the extent to which Marr's ideas developed in connection with Marxism. In the wake of Stalin's debunking of Marr's ideas in 1950 a range of scholars had little difficulty showing that Marr's central ideas were formed under the influence of romanticism and positivism of the nineteenth century, and that he and his collaborators rather opportunistically connected them to Marxist terminology only subsequently.[35] Indeed, the sources of Marr's ideas have proven fairly easy to trace, and the extent to which they were compatible with Marxism is a matter of some debate, but what is certain is that many early Soviet Marxists were engaging with the same ideas, and seeking in various ways to combine them with Marxism and adapt them to their own agendas.

Moreover, it should be remembered that it was at this very time that some of the most significant texts of Marx and Engels that ventured into questions of language, culture and science were appearing in published form. Thus, it was in 1932 that three fragments were combined and published as *The German Ideology*, while Engels's various fragments on natural science were combined and published as the *Dialectics of Nature* in 1927 and then in a fuller version in 1935. Scholars of Megrelidze's generation were therefore some of the first to engage with these aspects of the work of Marx and Engels, and they did so with editions of texts that we now know were products of extensive editorial incursion. Where the first generation of Russian Marxists, exemplified by Plekhanov, had sought to fill in the gaps in what was then known as Marxism by drawing upon philosophical materialism, physiology and positivism in order to develop what they regarded as compatible ideas about anthropology, literature and science, this generation had more texts by Marx and Engels to draw upon. They were therefore seeking to make sense of these ideas in a specific intellectual and political environment, and in order to advance the fields in which they worked they were seeking correspondences with ideas in circulation as best they could. Continuities with the previous generation continued – Noiré had been a significant influence on Plekhanov, Bogdanov and Bukharin,[36] for instance, but

---

34 See also Frank-Kamenetskii 1932, p. 274.
35 Brandist 2015, pp. 215–20.
36 Plekhanov 1969 [1908], pp. 57–8 refers to Noiré in his influential *Fundamental Problems of Marxism* and adopts most of his argument. Noiré appears throughout Bogdanov's work, but most insistently in Bogdanov 2010 [1910]. Bukharin 1926 [1922] adopts Noiré's argu-

new perspectives were now added, and Megrelidze's text is a particularly good example of this change. The specificities of the Stalinist environment are particularly important in this regard, not least since positive reference to Bogdanov was risky and Plekhanov's rather mechanical materialism was achieving canonical status. In this perspective it is all the more regrettable that the published text of Megrelidze's book was separated from some of the important intellectual and ideological coordinates of the time. It makes it more difficult to judge the extent of the obligatory genuflection of the time from more substantial engagement.

Megrelidze shows extensive familiarity with the works of Marx and Engels published at the time, and with Lenin's recently published *Philosophical Notebooks*, which significantly complicated the somewhat psychologistic reflection theory of knowledge of his earlier anti-Bogdanov tract *Materialism and Empiriocriticism* (1909). This allowed Megrelidze creatively to employ lessons from phenomenology and Gestalt theory in recasting the Marxist theory of knowledge as an active and intersubjective process. There are areas, however, where Megrelidze appears less sure-footed in employing Marxist terminology, such as in his discussion of economics in §91, where he uses the term 'labour power' (*rabochaia sila*) to mean labour as a general force in the productive process, coupled with the 'means of production', and then employs the same term to signify labour specifically *as a commodity*. This tendency to treat labour as an essence, independent of the specific form it takes in various modes of production, was a common feature of the time (one may find variants in Bogdanov, Marr and elsewhere) and it facilitated the treatment of labour as the manifestation of *will* in the Schopenhauer sense. Like Foucault's employment of 'power' as a category separate from its historically determinate forms and structures, it is in danger of becoming a metaphysical category, albeit one that facilitates some interesting analyses. On the other hand, the clarity of Megrelidze's discussion, in §98, of class as an objective relationship, dependent on a person's place within the relations of production, is perhaps unrivalled in its time and runs quite contrary to then official Soviet definitions of class.[37]

As we become more familiar with the various fragments and notebooks on ethnography and natural science among others in the still incomplete second

---

ment in his textbook on historical materialism, which was required reading at most institutes of higher education in the late 1920s, and he appears again, along with Marr in his final prison writings 2005 [1937], pp. 207–8. For a discussion see Brandist 2015, pp. 43–9.

[37] It would perhaps not be until Geoffrey de Ste Croix's work of the 1980s that a similar analysis was developed, though as part of a study of ancient history. See Ste Croix 1981, p. 43.

Marx-Engels-Gesamtausgabe (MEGA2, 1975–) we will certainly be in a more advantageous position to judge the extent to which the attempts of early Soviet thinkers to develop an overall social phenomenology of thinking converge with those of Marx and Engels. Whatever the results of this, however, we can see already that much in Megrelidze's work can help us think through a range of problems that have concerned Marxists for many decades. It also helps us to understand that the received and long-ingrained idea that Soviet Marxism by the 1930s was devoid of any creative impulses and that these were pursued only within the realms of what became known as Western Marxism needs serious revision. The complexities of early Soviet engagements with Marxism and other perspectives are still being explored, but the fate of Megrelidze's text reminds us of the obstacles that are still encountered.

A Note on Some Translation Issues

A number of specific translation issues have been discussed above. Here we mention certain generic issues.

There are a number of instances where the gendered nature of Russian grammar causes specific issues for the translator. Where the author speaks of the 'individual' [*individ*] person [*chelovek*] or the 'subject' [*sub'ekt*] these terms are grammatically masculine and would normally result in subsequent employment of the pronoun 'he'. Unfortunately, this would give the reader today the wrong impression of the authorial position, rather like the translations of Marx's use of '*Mensch*' as 'man' and consequent use of 'he'. One alternative would be to replace such instances with the third person plural, 'they', but this results in grammatical distortion. In order to avoid imposing any gendered or binary distinctions not present in the Russian text I have chosen to impose the somewhat cumbersome 's/he' and 'his/her' where necessary.

Megrelidze draws extensively on German-language material and leaves some quotations in the original language in the Russian edition without translation. This reflects the assumption of the time that the readers engaging with these areas of scholarship would be familiar with the German language, an assumption that cannot be made among an anglophone audience today. I have therefore provided basic English-language renderings of the most significant of these in addition to reproducing the German originals.

Like German, Russian is a language that allows the writer to build words that would not normally be combinable in English. Where this proves significant, or where specific terms may be rendered differently in different contexts but carry important connotations, the original Russian term has been appended in square brackets. In cases where the transliterated Russian has been provided, we have followed the convention of the Library of Congress system (without diacritics).

Acknowledgement

Translated from: Konstantin Romanovich Megrelidze, *Osnovnye problem sotsiologii myshleniia* / Ed. and foreword by A.T. Bochorishvili, 3rd edn, Moscow: URSS, 2007, 488pp. (From the legacy of Soviet philosophical thought: social philosophy)

From the Editor of the Russian Edition

The book now being submitted for readers' attention is the posthumous publication of a work by Konstantin (Kita) Romanovich Megrelidze, *Fundamental Problems of the Sociology of Thinking*.

Megrelidze was born in 1900, in the village of Khrialeti in the *uyezd* of Ozurgetskii. He received his secondary education at the preparatory school in Poti.

Having graduated from Tblisi State University in 1923, Megrelidze was sent to Germany by the Central Committee of the RKP(b) and the Georgian People's Commissariat for Education to advance his knowledge.

By the time of his return to the Soviet Union in 1927, having already established the range of questions that would occupy him for the rest of his life, he began working on the problems of the development of thought while giving lectures in universities and working in the Central Committee of the Georgian KP(b); in 1929 he became the head of the Board of the Central Administration for Scientific, Scholarly-Artistic, and Museum Institutions of the Georgian SSR.

From 1932, he continued his work in Leningrad, at the Institute for Language and Thinking in the USSR Academy of Sciences. He was also director of the National Office of the Leningrad Public Library (now the Russian National Library). During these years, his articles on scientific and political questions were published in our periodicals in Russian and in Georgian, and sometimes in German in foreign periodicals.

In Leningrad, Megrelidze worked primarily on the questions of the psychology and sociology of thought, and the philosophy of language. His research was printed in academic periodicals from 1935 to 1937, and in the special periodical press. Much of the work of this period is lost; only the articles 'On popular superstitions and "ur-logical" means of thought (a reply to Lévy-Bruhl)' and 'From animal consciousness to human' are preserved. The latter article is one of the chapters of *Fundamental Problems of the Sociology of Thinking*, on which the author worked for many years.

This work was published in February 1938 by the publishing house of the USSR Academy of Sciences under the editorship of I.I. Meschaninov, but before its release the author became a political prisoner and the print run was withdrawn. Iosif Megrelidze, who at that time was working at the Institute of Language and Thinking, managed to save and preserve the copy that had been signed off for printing.

At the end of 1939, the spurious charges against Konstantin were dropped; he was freed and restored to his former posts in Leningrad, but his broken health necessitated his return to Georgia where he continued his scientific work in the Georgian branch of the USSR Academy of Sciences.

In Tblisi, he began elaborating new problems. Having familiarised themselves from Megrelidze's reports with chapters of his work, *Fundamental Problems of the Sociology of Thinking*, academician I.A. Djavakhishvili, active member of the USSR Academy of Sciences D.N. Uzdnadze, and academician S.N. Djanashia considered publication of this book in Tblisi to be desirable, but publication of the book was not carried through owing to the start of the war. Megrelidze died in 1943 at the age of 43, having been unsuccessful in realising and developing his extensive scientific projects. A new endeavour, on which he had been working at the end of his life, has also been lost.

In 1956, the question of publishing the book arose again. A special commission had been created at the USSR Academy of Sciences consisting of Professors Sh. Dzidziguri, S. Narikashvili, S. Tsereteli, G. Chitaia, T. Sharadzenidze and the author of these lines, to whom the book had been handed over for reference. The commission found that the endeavour had not lost its scientific significance and topicality. We polished the text, factoring in all the reviewers' fundamental remarks.

Megrelidze's work draws attention first and foremost through the topicality of its theme and the importance of the point of view employed by its author. The sociological study of thought is a relatively new field. If we have a great deal of valuable research in the area of the psychology and logic of thought, this cannot be said about the sociology of thought. In bourgeois science, thought was examined in a two-fold manner: as a purely subjective phenomenon or as a fact of a completely objective, supraindividual nature. Correspondingly, it was considered to be a subject of study for psychology or metaphysics; moreover, the social factor in the origin and development of thought was ignored in both cases. Only recently has serious, systematic philosophical research of this problem begun from the point of view of 'pure idealism' (Scheler et al.). It is unlikely that there is any work in Marxist-Leninist literature that explores the sociology of thought in this aspect with such completeness as does the present work. It goes without saying that no single human mental phenomenon can be correctly explained and understood without including the social factor. This pertains first and foremost to thought. Given this premise, the topicality of the theme of this work is completely self-evident.

What the author did for a solution to this problem is no less significant. Broad erudition, a profound knowledge of the scientific disciplines called up to have their say on the question, and the synthetic point of view they employ give the author the resources to ensure the necessary comprehensiveness in examining the question and to achieve persuasive results.

Resting only on the most important merits of this work, we wish to point out the following:

1. Megrelidze's work has indisputably brought about a revival of interest in similar research. It must be said that at one time this interest among us was stronger than it is now – which, of course, should not be welcomed.
2. The fact that not one of the fundamental questions of this problem that have thus far been brought to light has escaped the author's field of vision must be classed among the merits of his work. And this is one of the necessary conditions for a correct solution to the problem.
3. It must also be noted that the principle of sociological research in the work is constructed with logical consistency from beginning to end. If the impression sometimes arises that this principle is being carried to extremes, it is only because the habit towards the psychological examination of thought, and towards ignoring the social factor in the process of its study, is too great.
4. The merit of the author must be seen in that his work not only does not restrict the possibility of examining thought from other points of view, in terms of other sciences, but – on the contrary – defines their place in a unifying, general philosophical construct.
5. The defining attribute of the book is also the fact that in examining individual questions, the author expresses completely original propositions and critically re-examines several common tenets (e.g. Spinoza's attributes).
6. At this juncture, it is difficult to name a work that embraces such broad-ranging scientific data and uses it so systematically.

All of us who promoted the printing of this book are certain that it will provide the benefit that we expect of it.

A. Bochorishvili

*Fundamental Problems
of the Sociology of Thinking*

∴

Foreword

> The science of thought is therefore, like every other, a historical science, the science of the historical development of human thought.
> FRIEDRICH ENGELS

∴

For whom is the meaning of Engels' words incomprehensible – or who among us, engaged in scientific thinking, would begin to deny their correctness? Meanwhile, it is difficult to name anyone among the number of philosophers, psychologists, and even linguists – that is, among scholars obliged by their profession to study thought – who would observe this elementary requirement and consistently implement it in their research.

What would all the other specialists in thought be occupied with, if their science were not a historical science? What would psychology, logic, philosophy, and even linguistics be engaged in?

Owing to the conditions of time and place for his work, the author of this book – being a Marxist in his worldview – had to go through a philosophical school that was, in essence, old (although in the Soviet period). It was also his lot to diligently go through the school of classical psychology, hammering assiduously away at the doctrine of perceptions, representations and associations, engaging in laboratory research of stimulation thresholds, differential thresholds, scope of attention, the laws of memory, and so on.

What were they interested in, in these laboratories of psychology? Living humans were broken down into the basic particle types there, into the mental atoms of perceptions, representations, elementary senses, volitional impulses, and so on. Then, with the help of the 'omnipotent' concept of associations – that most universal resource of classical psychology – we tried to 'glue together' a human analogue from these atoms and molecules.

If the author had had to go through the school of physiological psychology or reflexology, he would obviously have studied the breakdown of living beings into the basic elements of another type: nerve pathways, neural links, the connection and disconnection of receptor and motor pathways; and he would have sought to reconstruct a poor likeness of a human being through the composition of basic reflexes.

Human psychology was regarded as a branch of the natural sciences. We believed humans to be a variety of animal, and their sense organs to be receptacles open to external influences; the human psyche and human thinking were products of a purely biological process of development. At the same time, sure of our correctness, we continued to think of ourselves as consistent Marxists. We knew a thing or two about dialectical and historical materialism, having more audacity than positive knowledge in this field, however; we knew, for example, that the development of humans as social beings is subject to social and historical laws, but we believed all this to the purview of another science – the social sciences – and believed that it did not in the least concern those of us studying the psychology of humans, whose thinking (we thought) was the natural product of the composition of perceptions – or, as the disciples of gestalt psychology spoke of it, the particular case of the universal law of constitution.

The questions of thought and cognition were studied in a somewhat different manner, and from the perspective of ingrained traditions, in bourgeois philosophy. It saw its main task in constructing a purely abstract, but 'logically flawless' design. So, for example, in the opinions of nineteenth- and twentieth-century philosophers, three things were necessary for every act of cognition: firstly, a cognised object (*Erkenntnisobjekt*); secondly, a cognising subject (*Erkenntnissubjekt*); and thirdly, a link between them. Three basic spheres of philosophical problematics, which became traditional for European philosophical thought, were therefore outlined: 1. The problem of the object (*Gegenstandsproblem. Problem der Gegenständlichkeit*); 2. The problem of the subject (the 'empirical ego', the 'transcendental ego', consciousness in general, and so on); and 3. The problem of givenness ('how an object external to consciousness can become immanent to it', 'how a definition immanent to consciousness is made transcendental', and so on). On the basis of these purely logical dispositions arose a long range of other, equally abstract questions, for example of the following type: each concrete entity necessarily implies the existence of objects in space, in time, in a certain relation, and so on. It follows that the categories of space, time, causality and others are the a priori conditions for each reality, each experience and act of cognition. Philosophical research was written, books were compiled, and belief systems arose according to this model.

Abstract logical reasoning of a similar type could not, of course, lead to a *historical* formulation of the question, and nearly all European philosophy was reduced to occupying itself solely with searching for the limits of cognition and defining general a priori conditions of thought, which were considered to be eternal and unchanging.

In the majority of cases, pre-Marxist philosophy did not realise that the norms of thought and the forms of cognition, being social products, change in the process of the historical development of society. If any bourgeois thinker noticed this, they did not draw from it the necessary conclusions for a real reconstruction of the methods and experiences of the study of thought.

When the existence of thinking of a structure other than ours was revealed (primarily through the work of ethnographers), theoreticians were caught in a rather awkward situation; some of them (Edward Tylor, James Frazer) tried to fit these facts into known forms of religious thinking with the goal of somehow or other subordinating them to the norms of prevailing European thought (the theory of 'animism'), others (Emile Durkheim, Lucien Lévy-Bruhl), detecting the idiosyncrasies of primitive thought in these facts, ascribed them to pre-logical forms of thought. In both cases, the ancient opinion that there is only one logic, universally binding for all times and peoples, and that any deviation from it is either inconceivable or belongs to 'pre-logical' thought, remained unshakeable.

The question of 'primitive' thinking interests us, of course, not only from the point of view of this or that terminology (participation mystique, prélogique and so on, which we considered incorrect), but also in essence. We are convinced that the hundreds of thousands of years of development of tribes and peoples in the most variegated living conditions, and the aboriginal revolutions in the development of their language and thought, presuppose not one eternal identical logic but different forms of thinking – that is, a range of *different* logics preceding ours. Each of them was no less relevant for their time than medieval formalistic logic for bourgeois society, no less well-formed and every bit as good.

From his past lessons in psychology and philosophy, the author nonetheless derived one benefit: the conviction that he is doing not what he must and is looking not where he ought to, that the questions of thought must be approached from some other angle. The trends of psychology and philosophy prevailing in Europe do not provide answers to these questions and cannot, according to their precepts. This obliged the author to study more concrete questions from the history of the development of the idea of number, time, space, causality and so on. In the process of their elaboration he first understood where the mistake lay, and the situation set before us by this epigraph was first filled out (for him) by the point, by specific content: *studying thought in isolation from other aspects of life is useless, impossible, and senseless*. Let us explain our thinking.

The disciples of idealist philosophy believe that thought develops and moves by its own agency, growing from itself, and therefore can also be explained exclusively from itself (thought). All other fields, in the idealists' opinion, are characterised by the same completely independent development: economy, technology, law, language, religion, philosophy, and so on. Each of them conducts its own line of development, independent of the other spheres. The ideas of law, they say, can flow from legal ones; religious ideas from religious ones, philosophical ideas from the philosophical views that preceded them, and so on. As a result, the world breaks down into a range of parts that are not linked to each other. Each of them, it is supposed, has its own separate history with its own laws, allegedly not linked with the others' history and laws of development. The idea of the unity of the historical process is absent. From this naturally flows the negation of conformity to the laws of history and the endeavour to replace history with the description of unconnected facts (the requirement of 'idiographic' science as opposed to 'nomothetic').

From these ideas about a splintered historical process flowed the other requirement of traditional philosophical science: once each of these branches (technology, economy, law, religion, aesthetics) has its own internal principles of consistent development that are not shareable with the others, then amalgamation (of these principles) threatened general confusion and the failure of scientific thought. This explains the anxious concern of bourgeois thinkers with establishing firm boundaries between the sciences, with a ban on violating them. For example, Kant's concerns that the boundaries of science should never be mixed up together are well-known. We, however, are not inclined to see the great misfortune in this and do not think that we will be deprived of the opportunity to understand what relates to what without the establishment of firm boundaries between the sciences.

Our standpoint differs fundamentally from these views. *Time-worn scientific boundaries, separating the sciences from each other like the Great Wall of China, must be demolished.* Moving beyond the narrow horizons of a self-contained category must be the watchword in our research praxis, if we do not want to box scientific thought into the suffocating frame of a formalism doomed to eternal sterility.

We must start from the fact that for a Marxist, the problem of thought (and cognition) presents only a part of a more general question about the process of social and historical development.

With the collection and processing of material on the history of thought, new questions arose within the author and a review of a range of old concepts was required. These new problems, together with the old ones presented in a new light, dovetailed together by degrees and formed a kind of unified chain of ideas, the missing links of which were gradually filled in.

Throughout the entire work the ideas of Marx and Engels served the author as a foundation and guide; the deeper he studied their works, the more strongly they captivated and astounded him with their grandeur. The whole of this work grew out of their ideas.

The general conclusion we arrived at, which later served as the guiding thread of research, consists of the following: in the history of establishing and developing human society, labour, the instruments of labour, material culture, language and thought represent the elements of a whole as indissolubly linked and mutually conditioning each other; and if we want to study thought, it will be necessary to take this whole intricate social complex in its entirety and its unity with the general historio-creative process of humanity's development.

General Exposition of the Question of Thinking

A Critique of Naturalist Precepts

§ 1

If we are to actually begin the history of consciousness from its very seed and go backwards, into the depths of the past towards the beginning of organic existence, then we would have to attribute the origin of consciousness to those primary adaptive movements of the simplest organism, which permit a protoplasmic bubble to move to locations more favourable to it and to move away from less favourable ones.

From the standpoint of the searches for the biological roots of consciousness, we could consider as indisputable the position of the naturalists that consciousness, thought, will and humanity's entire mental world represents only the highest level of development of those physiochemical forces of matter that in the simplest organism manifest themselves as the primary reflexes of adaptation (food reflexes, phototropism, galvanotropism, geotropism, and other similar phenomena).

The works of the biologists and physiologists played a decisive role in the elucidation of these questions, and the successes of the naturalists in this field are truly colossal; but in most cases the naturalists (physiologists, biologists, and even subjectivist psychologists) – enraptured with the study of the natural processes of the manifestation of consciousness and occupied with the direct observation of physiochemical and neuromuscular processes, the description of reflexes, the reflex acts themselves of an organism, and so on – are inclined to see the ultimate foundations and the essence of all the manifestations of human consciousness in these processes. It has begun to seem to them that the study of consciousness can be limited to the study of the biological and physiological side of the question; they are convinced that the problem of human behaviour and of the human mode of thought is settled by them.

The naturalist viewpoint reduces all questions of consciousness, including human thought, to the natural processes of neurocerebral activity and to receptor and motor processes. Naturalists only see a quantitative difference in the degree of complexity between the behaviour of an amoeba and the behaviour of a human being, and not a difference in essence. They believe that human consciousness is the same work of nature, the same biological fact, as the consciousness of an animal.

'They saw this individual', says Marx, '… not as something evolving in the course of history, but posited by nature, because for them this individual was in conformity with nature, in keeping with their idea of human nature. This delusion has been characteristic of every new epoch hitherto'.[1]

The naturalistic view finds expression in the fact that human consciousness is considered to be the direct continuation of animal consciousness, only a complicated form of the latter. No fundamental qualitative distinction is observed between them, no difference in essence because both of them (human consciousness and animal consciousness) are places on the same plane of study. They are examined with the same methods, measured with one scale, and studied identically; the conclusions reached in one field are usually extended to the other.

The naturalists try to explain human consciousness starting from those same principles applied for explaining the behaviour of animals. They want to explain an entire varied, immense history, a whole world of ideological superstructures, all of humanity's globus intellectualis starting from the biological foundations of consciousness.

'There are people', Heine said, 'who think they know all about a bird just because they looked at the egg it came from'.

If we actually travel along that path, it is easy to arrive at a conclusion that abrogates a range of sciences occupied with the study of humanity and its social and economic life, for the biological prototypes of all this can always be found (with the aid of a certain strained interpretation) in the world of animals. Thus biology, covering all the social sciences with itself, would become universal. Going even further along this path, we would in the end have to reduce everything to one sole progenitor science: physics.

Physiology, like any other science, is valid only in its application to a definite range of phenomena and within certain limits. There exist objects, however, relating to the world of living beings, that do not enter into the scope of physiology. No-one starts insisting, for example, on the possibilities of the physiology of commodity prices, the physiology of right or the state; the physiology of grammar or of the rules of logarithmic calculation are likewise impossible. Although this does not in the least lessen the significance of physiology, these objects lie on another plane of reality, relating neither to physiology, nor to biology, nor to the experimental sciences in general. 'Land', Marx says, 'has nothing to do with land rent, and the machine has nothing to do with profit. For the landed proprietor, land has the significance only of rent of land; he leases his plots of land and receives rent; this is a feature which land can lose without losing a single one of its inherent features, without, for example, losing any part

---

1 Marks 1931a, p. 51.

of its fertility'.[2] These features are not inherent in things, as such. No chemical analysis reveals them in things. The physical sciences cannot study profit, rent, and so on, as these objects do not have an existence in the physical sense although they exist objectively and materially.

These objects also do not relate to the field of psychology, and are not the products of mental or cerebral activity. No analysis of people's minds or physiology can disclose these objects. They are rooted neither in people's consciousness nor in the physical shell of things. They exist as fully developed social relations (being the products of social life). All the arguments of the naturalists are mistaken in their attitude where, in touching on societal questions, they equate social formations with natural biological processes, trying to see the initial forms of social phenomena in biology.

Marxist science cannot adopt the position that *human* thinking is a product of nature, similar to a clover blossom. Marxism asserts that human consciousness and thought are phenomena not of a natural biological, but of a social order. Human consciousness does not relate to the field of natural history but to the field of history proper, and therefore requires a different approach to it – other methods and means of study than those applied to the behaviour of animals.

Human consciousness ultimately traces its ancestry from animal consciousness, but only to the extent and only in the sense that humanity traces its history from the animal state to the human. As that existence took root after the emergence of industrial activity and the formation of a social complex (labour relations, exchange, distribution, etc.) different in essence from physical and biological reality, to speak of human consciousness as of a variety of animal consciousness is as impossible as seeing the origin and prototype of capitalist accumulation in the instinctive collection of nuts by a squirrel is unthinkable.

'The statement that claims there is one basis for life, and another for consciousness, is already flagrantly false' (Marx). An animal's environment is an innate, natural one. An animal's consciousness therefore takes shape under the influence of innate causes and natural factors. Animal consciousness as a whole, with all its structure and all its functions, represents just an innate *phenomenon* (if you exclude, of course, the intervention of humanity in the life of nature and the processes of domestication, where nature stops being only nature). Animal consciousness is actuated and governed by natural, biological causes and laws. In studying the behaviour of animals, we find ourselves in the field of natural history and rarely go beyond its borders.

---

2 Marks i Engel's 1933, p. 209.

At the human level of development, consciousness represents the formation of a socio-historical order. Human consciousness is the product not of biological, but of *social* conditions of existence.

At this level of development, the general formula of consciousness – an individual's means of orientation in their environment – takes on a completely new meaning. A human's environment is not an innate and natural, but a productive and social environment. In accordance with this, their consciousness is formed not by natural forces, causes and laws, but first and foremost by social conditions. And, more importantly, the material conditions of culture and of social relations are created by the activity of people themselves.

§ 2

Physiology originates from the obvious position that without the elements of the neural system, mental life does not exist, and that thought is impossible outside of the activity of the neuro-cerebral apparatus. From this, they draw the conclusion that, in order to study the essential features of thought, it is enough to expose the internal mechanism of the neuro-cerebral apparatus.

As much as the former position is indisputable, the conclusions drawn from it are mistaken.

Clearly, without the neuro-cerebral apparatus, or more simply without a living subject, thought as such is impossible. Physiologically considered, every thought is of course the function of cerebral activity. But are we in the right, on these grounds, to place an equals sign between the work of a neural substance and the world view, convictions and aspirations of individuals, between the physiological structure of the neural system of the people of a certain epoch and their structure of thought and ideological formations?

In the majority of cases, physiologists do not ask themselves why the same neuro-cerebral apparatus, under specific conditions, works in such a way and forms such-and-such thoughts and convictions, and under other conditions thinks in a different way. Perhaps the reasons for the various workings of the cerebral apparatus only lie in itself, and not in the conditions and factor that in certain cases compel this apparatus to think in one direction, and in others to think and desire something else, often even something contrary.

In order for people's neuro-cerebral organisation to be able to produce certain thoughts, merely having a brain – even if the most perfect and brilliant – is insufficient. Beyond the existence of a specific neural organisation, it is necessary for an individual to be surrounded by the relations of things, to be placed objectively in conditions that compel him to act in a certain direction, that nourish cerebral functioning, that orient individuals towards certain tasks and goals, and that consequently compel the brain to work in a specific direction.

It is indisputable that no thought exists outside of neural activity. But does this mean that studying the functioning of the neural apparatus settles the problem of the study of thinking? Even if we succeed in precisely establishing which neural functioning is produced in the cerebral apparatus, what displacements occur and what neuron links are established in it, will it really become clear to us why such thoughts – and not others – arise? Will we know why people's neuro-cerebral apparatus started functioning just this way and in just this direction? Will we then succeed in understanding why humans of the Paleolithic thought differently than we do?

It is not too difficult to note than in the given case, we are dealing with some sort of error. Here is the same elementary *petitio principii* in which Socrates, in Plato's words (in *Phaedo*) 'unmasked' Anaxagoras: blindly seeking an explanation as to why he – Socrates – is sitting at the given moment (the conversation occurred in the prison where the philosopher had been incarcerated) in the fact that Socrates had legs consisting of bones connected to each other by joints, muscles tendons in such a way that they could bend and allow the man to sit. If the existence of flexible joints still somehow explains how a person can sit in general, then it certainly in no way helps in explaining why at this moment they prefer to sit and not stand, and certainly not asking why he 'chose' just that place for it.

Without a neural apparatus, of course, thinking is impossible; this does not mean, however, that the direction and content of thought is defined by it. On the contrary, every mental functioning (and, consequently, thought as well) are primarily defined by objective factors, under which conditions the bearer of this neural apparatus must orient themselves.

The circumstance of a human having a stomach of a definite physiological construction differing, for example, from the stomach of ruminants is also one of the components of history that conditioned the definite composition of human society, the character and several particularities of their economy. But can even the most detailed study of the structure of the stomach help with anything in explaining a social order?

The solution to the human mode of thinking lies, of course, not in the neural system and not in the brain, but in those *social conditions that compel the brain to perceive, think and function in such a way in one epoch, and differently in another; and that – compelling neural activity of people to function in a certain direction, created just this neuro-cerebral apparatus and no other*. In itself, the neuro-cerebral apparatus nothing and demonstrates nothing – what is more, it itself requires an explanation of its origins. Consequently, it is impossible to argue based solely on the definite structure of the apparatus.

'If you want to understand why people think in a given way, study the links and relations of the subjective processes of consciousness', the subjectivist psychologists tell us.

'If you want to divine the essence of people's thinking, study the physiology of their neural activity', say the physiologists.

It is difficult to understand how it is possible to rest on these assertions, when the new, essentially fundamental question that follows them – why are the subjective processes and cerebral functioning of our time one way, and the people from the epoch of prehistoric society completely different? – is so clear.

Or, perhaps, 'neural activity' is not permitted to present any questions? Absolutes were overthrown by the development of scientific thinking: Are spirit, soul, *logos*, the Absolute Ego and similar categories from the arsenal of authoritative metaphysical principles really only for clearing the throne for a new absolute – neural activity?

Do people really think differently because of the different physiological structure of their brains – and on the contrary, does solidarity in the convictions and aspirations of people indicate an identical constitution of their neuro-cerebral system? If we examine people from the side of the general state of their neural system, then it is possible to find a large quantity of individuals who are very close to each other in their psychophysical constitution but who belong to different social layers, and therefore who think differently and strive for contrary things. Neurasthenics and phlegmatics can be found among the aristocracy, among the capitalists, and among the working class. Within the same group of like-minded people, it is possible to find any number of people with completely opposite physical and mental constitutions. This does not prevent them, however, from thinking, having similar aspirations and convictions, and worshipping the same principles and ideals.

It is indisputable that a general neural and mental constitution also reveals itself and makes itself felt in the mental activity of people, but in the formation of the manner of thought, of world-view, of the direction of consciousness and behaviours it plays not a principal but an insignificant role, as people's thoughts and views are formed not in an individual manner but are produced by social relations that condition the functioning of any individual head taken separately, however badly it was constructed physiologically (with the exception, of course, of pathological cases).

Change individuals' general social conditions of life and you will then see what changes are produced in their world-views and convictions, with the same neural and physical constitution.

Herbert Spencer (1820–1903) – one of the radical representatives of the biosocial doctrine – tried to explain the difference between the psychology of the 'savage' and the 'cultured' person using a biological hypothesis. In Spencer's opinion, the development of thought and human feelings – like society itself – is subject to biological laws. For example, according to Spencer, the proprietary sentiment is motivated by purely biological reasons: 'The proprietary sentiment', he says, 'arises as a consequence of experiencing the gratifications that possession brings, continued through successive generations'.[3] Declaring in this way the 'proprietary sentiment' to be a biological category, rooted – so to speak – in the blood of the civilised person, Spencer proclaimed the tastes and psychology of the bourgeois proprietor to be fatal, universal qualities from which it is impossible to be liberated other than through the physical degeneration of the human race. The facts, however, demonstrate the complete opposite to what the adherents of the biological point of view taught.

If a change to human thinking occurred only by way of the hereditary evolution of the neuro-cerebral apparatus, then it would be impossible to explain – for example – how a 'savage' member of an aboriginal nation (at a young age), under the influence of a suitable environment and upbringing over the course of several years, could become a 'cultured' person, master the complex ideas of scientific thought, mathematical physics, and so on. It is impossible to explain such a rapid leap in intellectual development with the help of a biological, racial evolution requiring the regeneration of cerebral tissue over a number of generations.

A certain method of thought and behaviour based on a certain physical and neural constitution is not inherent in the human organism once and for all, as takes place in animals in the majority of cases – and that not at the highest, only at the lowest, primitive level of biological life.

Consequently, in studying consciousness and the system of human thought, the fundamental thing does not lie so much in the investigation of its physiology as it does in defining those conditions of the social order that compel the bearer of this or that physiological constitution to have identical or differing thoughts, aspirations, and convictions.

If we ask the question why the cerebral activity of people from different epochs and different social layers is different and is directed differently – that is, 'if we ask ourselves ... why the given world views and the given principles manifested themselves exactly in the eleventh or eighteenth centuries, and not in some other one' (Marx), then there is no possibility of explaining it by means of studying the physiology and neural systems of the citizens of that

---

[3] Spenser 1898, Vol. 1, pp. 38, 39. (Passage tentatively identified as that found in Spencer 1912, p. 62 – Translator.)

century. This cannot be done not only because the people of those times are no longer among the living, but specifically because their physiology in essence differed little from ours and would have provided no support for the elucidation of the questions occupying us: in what way, and why, did the views of those epochs differ. And therefore we will be constrained 'to investigating what the people of the eleventh century were like ... what were their needs, their productive forces, their means of production, the raw materials of their products, in the end what the relations of person to person, which flowed from all these conditions of existence, were like'.[4] Therefore, we will be constrained to elucidating the social conditions that created the soil for these thoughts and compelled the brains to function in a certain manner. And does investigating such questions not mean investigating the actual world history of people and their thoughts?

§3

Moreover, it should be noted that human reason and thought do not have *only an internal subjective existence*. In the process of labour activity, of setting and fulfilling goals, human reason acquires an *objective* reality in the objects of material culture and in formations such as language, religion, folklore, and so on; here, thoughts exist not only in the form of an immediate subjective process, in the form of the work of a neural substance, but in the form of *objectively existing formations of material culture and of the deposited forms of ideology*.

This objective reality of thoughts, as we will see further on, constitutes the most important condition for their subjective existence. Were it not for the objective world of reified ideas, no thoughts whatsoever would subjectively arise in a person.

Psychology and physiology do not take this circumstance into account.

If we stand on the path of physiological psychology and of reflexology, or on the path of a biological interpretation of the facts of human consciousness and of a vulgar materialism, then there is no guarantee that we will ever reach the actual study of the most essential aspects of human consciousness and thought.

On the question of whether the essence of thinking is settled through the study of physiological processes, Engels answered in the negative: 'One day we shall certainly 'reduce' thought experimentally to molecular and chemical motions in the brain; but does that exhaust the essence of thought?'[5]

---

4 Marks i Engel's, 1927–1935, Vol. v, pp. 368–9.
5 Engel's 1933, p. 18.

Even if physiologists succeed in precisely determining the function of a neural substance that occurs during the process of thought, it will be a great achievement for science, but at the same time it will not take us even a step towards understanding where the essence of human thought lies, what its role is, what forces and laws govern the work of consciousness and the development of thinking, and why the neurocerebral apparatus works precisely in a given direction.

The resources of physiologists on the one hand, and of subjectivist psychologists on the other, with which they attempt to measure and study a historical formation such as thinking – developed over hundreds of thousands of years – are insufficient as well as extremely limited in scope.

In textbooks on dialectical materialism for high schools, one often meets definitions of the following sort: 'Thinking is the product of the development of material reality, the product of the development of nature'. When Engels and Lenin spoke about 'the creation of the brain, and of humanity itself' being 'the products of nature', they had in mind the phylogeny of the human individual, and the biological prototype of humans and the organ of their thought. The authors of our textbooks often forget about this and, in interpreting the forms of human consciousness as the biological products of nature and not the products of social relations, they distort Marxism.

Marxism bases itself on the stance that the essence, the composition and the structure of human consciousness – and the forms and means of people's thought – take shape, change, and develop under the influence not of the forces of nature, but above all social forces. People's thinking does not move according to natural and biological laws, but in conformity with the laws of society and history. The human mode of thought is above all the phenomenon of a social order. 'Consciousness is, therefore, from the very beginning a social product, and remains so as long as men exist at all'.[6]

---

6   Marks i Engel's 1933.

PART 1

CHAPTER 1

Material Conditions and Social Preconditions Necessary for the Rise of the Human Level of Consciousness

Working Life Activity

§ 4

The classical scholars of Marxism believed that the cause that forms the human mental constitution, that creates the particular forms of their consciousness, the particular world of their perception and understanding, is above all human social reality, their productive activity in the broadest sense of the term. 'Die Menschengeschichte unterscheidet sich dadurch von der Naturgeschichte, dass wir eine gemacht und die andere nicht gemacht haben', says Marx, citing the words of Giambattista Vico.[1]

Marx regards 'productive, working life activity' as of paramount importance everywhere that the matter concerns the essential questions of human life and activity; for him, the analysis of working life activity is one of the main weapons of his philosophical criticism. If, on the basis of logical exposition, we are able to develop all the richness of the theoretical problems lying at the bottom here, it could become the best key to understanding all of Marxist philosophy and the sociology of thinking.

What does Marx mean by 'productive'? Above all, it is the production by individuals themselves of the means and conditions of their existence – hence, the production of their own lives. This constitutes the earliest precondition of human existence, and consequently of any history – and it is precisely that precondition, that people must have the possibility of living, in order to be in a condition to 'make history'.

'But life involves before everything else eating and drinking, a habitation, clothing and many other things. The first historical act is thus the production of the means to satisfy these needs, the production of material life itself. And indeed this is an historical act, a fundamental condition of all history, which today, as thousands of years ago, must daily and hourly be fulfilled merely in

---

[1] Marx 1923a, p. 317. '[H]uman history differs from natural history in that we have made the former, but not the latter'.

MATERIAL CONDITIONS AND SOCIAL PRECONDITIONS   19

order to sustain human life. Even when the sensuous world is reduced to a minimum, to a stick as with Saint Bruno [Bauer], it presupposes the action of producing the stick. Therefore in any interpretation of history one has first of all to observe this fundamental fact in all its significance and all its implications and to accord it its due importance'.[2]

'This activity ... this production serves as the basis for the sensuous world, as it now exists, to such a degree that if it were stopped even for only one year, then Feuerbach would not only find colossal changes to the physical world, but very soon he would not find the whole physical world, his own ability for contemplation, or even his own existence'.[3]

'This mode of production must not be considered simply as being the production of the physical existence of the individuals. Rather it is a definite form of activity of these individuals, a definite form of expressing their life, a definite *mode of life* on their part. As individuals express their life, so they are. What they are, therefore, coincides with their production, both with what they produce and with *how* they produce. The nature of individuals thus depends on the material conditions determining their production'.[4]

Thus 'in producing the necessary means for their existence, people indirectly also produce their own material life', produce their own social *modus vivendi*, and create their own history and their form of thinking.

'... all human history is nothing more than the formation of humanity through human labour'.[5]

The premises from which Marxism starts are not arbitrary; they are *not* doctrines, 'but real premises from which abstraction can only be made in the imagination. They are the real individuals, their activity and the material conditions under which they live, both those which they find already existing and those produced by their activity. These premises can thus be verified in a purely empirical way'.[6]

'Men can be distinguished from animals by consciousness, by religion or anything else you like. They themselves begin to distinguish themselves from animals as soon as they begin to *produce* their means of subsistence'.[7]

Animals never, under any conditions, conduct industrial activity; they do not know working life activity in the proper sense of the word, and therefore do not have a social life.[8]

---

2 Marks i Engel's 1933, p. 18.
3 Marks i Engel's 1933, p. 34.
4 Marks i Engel's 1933, pp. 10–11.
5 Marks i Engel's 1927–1935. Vol. III, p. 632.
6 Marks i Engel's 1933, p. 10.
7 Marks i Engel's 1933, p. 11.
8 All debate about 'industrious' animals, about the 'economic' and 'labour' activity of ants, bees,

The existence of animals differs from the existence of people in that the former live in a *natural* environment, and the latter live in an environment created by themselves – in *an environment that is the result of conscious labour activity*.

Relations of Consumption and Production

§5

The exchange of matter between an organism and the environment constitutes the general precondition of any organic existence. In this relation, both humans and animals are equally linked with the surrounding environment by material and physical bonds. The final task in both cases is the transfer, by the organism, of the material energy necessary for it from nature. But in relation to the *means* of appropriation of these gifts of nature, humanity differs in an essential way from the animals:

1. The exchange of matter between animals, and plants, in the environment occurs *immediately*. Animals take the ferments of nature in the form that they are given. Plants, being in direct contact with their environment, also immediately take the necessary juices (chlorophyll, and so on) from it via their roots and leaves. Animals also immediately obtain and appropriate the finished products of nature, running down their prey and tearing at it with their teeth.

2. Animals and plants are *only consumers* of what nature gives, or themselves serve as the objects of consumption for other organisms. In the general life of nature, animals participate as one of its blind components of power. They do not take part in the production of the objects consumed by them. Animals are limited by the fact that they devour the ready-made supplies of food from nature and destroy the objects necessary for them, but do not deliberately reproduce them.

In this sense, animals always remain only consumers, and never cross the boundaries of this elementary relation.

It should be observed that the relation of direct consumption in its essence is elementary, and does not produce new, sufficient impulses for development. It rather annihilates and destroys what is given rather than creating something new out of it. The negative aspect is strong and the reconstructive aspect is weakly expressed in it; the creative principle is lacking.

---

beavers, and so on, as well as the descriptions of the 'social' life of animals (beehives, anthills, herds, etc.), lack foundation and seriousness. The actions of animals, insofar as they represent instinctive reflex responses, are not labour and cannot be called such.

In any process of consumption, we are dealing not only with the annihilation and consumption of what is given, but also with regeneration. The substances consumed do not disappear completely; they are preserved and reproduce the energy of the organism. If, on the one hand, consumption signifies the destruction of the object consumed, on the other it signifies the regeneration of the organism 'just as in nature the production of a plant involves the consumption of elemental forces and chemical materials' (Marx).[9]

But this type of relation to nature (a relation of direct consumption) never draws the process out of the sphere of natural biology. The mutual relation of animals with the natural environment is characterised by the fact that each new act of consumption *only qualitatively repeats the same process*. Reproduction is always only equal to consumption. Animals appropriate the finished products of nature and assimilate them, and the same process begins anew – that is, once again with immediate acquisition and immediate consumption. Nothing new arises in the repetition of this process; nothing new appears except natural changes to nature itself (growth and propagation of the consuming biological species and elemental changes to the natural environment). At the end of every such act of consumption, as at the beginning of every act, we are dealing only with the same two members of an elementary relation: with a specific biological species and the natural environment – somewhat changed, of course, but changed in accordance with a blind natural process. No *new* reality arises between these two elementary members; no *new relations*, different from the previous ones, is created. The action always moves on the same plane, and the process constantly remains within the boundaries of natural and biological relations.

3. The relation of people to the environment is of an essentially different kind. The exchange of matter between people and nature does not occur directly and immediately, but through the medium of the forces of production. A whole range of mediating elements develop between people and nature – an entire world of new relations (all social reality), which is met with nowhere in the zoological world.

First, humans do not consume products in the form in which nature provides them. They must initially adapt these products to their own needs. Sociohistorical conditions have changed humans, and their needs and their organisms, so much that the materials of nature in their pristine form cannot satisfy them.

The development consisted of the fact that instead of direct natural relations, humans have established mediated, artificial (cultural) connections.

---

[9] Marks 1931b, p. 59.

They now appropriate and consume almost nothing immediately natural. The plants, fruits, and so on that humans use are the products of millennia of cultivation and domestication. The water they use is mediated by a plumbing system or – at the very least – a simple vessel. The only exception to this sphere consists – as it were – of air, inasmuch as it is not used industrially but for breathing, but technological development is already raising the question of the artificial purification and ozonisation of consumed air. Humans have become human insofar as their relation to the environment has become a relation mediated by labour, production, and industrial activity.

Second, mediation through labour calls forth yet another whole range of other mediating elements of a social character: the economic and legal connections of individuals, distribution, exchange and so on – relations that are completely unknown in the biological world.

Marx, in his *Contribution to a Critique of Political Economy*, classifies the mediating elements from the products of nature to the act of their consumption by people as follows: 1) the process of production, in which the members of a society adapt the products of nature to human needs; 2) distribution, which apportions the products in accordance societal laws; 3) exchange, which delivers to each the required objects – that is, redistributes what has already been distributed in accordance with specific needs; and, finally, 4) consumption, in which the product is taken out of general circulation and immediately becomes the servant of a specific need, satisfying the wants of individuals.

Humans are therefore also the consumers of the gifts of nature, but their consumption *is preceded by and is predicated upon the production* of these gifts. In their relation to the environment and to themselves, social humans appear above all as producers. 'Humans themselves create the conditions of their existence', 'they produce their material life themselves' (Marx). It is this circumstance that has created the separate world of history – the world of social, economic, class, legal (and so on) norms.

If no new links have arisen and no new reality has been created in the relations of consumption between animals and the environment, then *newer and newer* forms develop in the relations of production between a subject and nature, and new members of the relation appear: the products of previous labour, technology, a whole world of material culture and societal connections forming around the conditions of production and forming for the control of them. The process of production and consumption is cyclical, but each time the action begins anew, namely from production.

This entire world of technology, and all the systems of interpersonal relations, that arose as a result of labour activity are not natural; nature as such does not produce them but they are created by people themselves and are placed between themselves and nature. This new world of cultural values and social relations is absent in the lives of all living creatures besides humanity.

'The complex work of humans, which ploughs up the rocks and lays upon them a road for the transportation of foodstuffs, differs from the primitive seizure by animals of the food lying before them only in the variety of mediating elements', said L. Geiger.[10]

4. The relation of immediate consumption is an elementary 'hedonistic' relation, representing a low degree of activity. The abilities of animals extend only to appropriating what is given. If the objects consumed are not given ready-made, then the animal species ceases to exist or undergoes modification and degenerates. Animals are constantly in direct dependence on natural conditions.

The relations of production are characterised by a high degree of activity. Humans are not helpless in the face of nature's arbitrariness. If nature in its finished form does not provide humanity with the objects necessary to it, they themselves intervene in the life of nature and compel it to produce – or, taking materials from nature, they modify it and create new products for their own consumption.

5. And, finally, every consumption is in its essence individual, insofar as this is in reference to immediate consumption. Consumption of one and the same thing (or one and the same portion) by two different individuals is inconceivable. On the basis of an immediate consumptive relation, the formation of a social complex is therefore impossible. This relation is unable to bring organisms beyond the boundaries of natural and biological aggregative behaviour, of swarming.

Conversely, the nonsocial basis is in principle excluded in a productive relation. In its essence, production is a social act; the social complex is constantly recreated in it (see §§ 6–10).

Thus animals, being in relation to the environment only a part of nature and its consumer, preserve their biological species; humans, being a productive creature, externalise their activity in products of labour and create a new reality – a new world of articles of material culture and of social relations – they create a history different from the history of nature.

---

10   Geiger 1872, p. 85. The limitations of this observation from one of the shrewd thinkers of the nineteenth century consists of the fact that Geiger only has in mind the technology of mediation, and pays no attention to social relations.

Labour and the Product of Labour

§6

Marx calls the relationship of humans, as subject, to the environment, as object, *labour*.

'Labour is, first of all, a process between man and nature, a process by which man, through his own actions, mediates, regulates and controls the metabolism between himself and nature. He confronts the materials of nature as a force of nature. He sets in motion the natural forces which belong to his own body, his arms, legs, head and hands, in order to appropriate the materials of nature in a form adapted to his own needs. Through this movement he acts upon external nature and changes it, and in this way he simultaneously changes his own nature'. 'We are not dealing here with those first instinctive forms of labour which remain on the animal level'. 'An immense interval of time separates the state of things ... from the situation when human labour had not yet cast off its first instinctive form. We presuppose labour in a form in which it is an exclusively human characteristic'.[11]

At the end of expended labour efforts, people obtain an object that constituted the goal of their activity – a product that is able to satisfy some human need.

'Labour, then, as the creator of use-values, as useful labour, is a condition of human existence which is independent of all forms of society; it is an eternal natural necessity which mediates the metabolism between man and nature, and therefore human life itself'.[12]

Labour, as a relationship of humans to the objects of labour, as a process that takes place between humans and nature, can always be regarded as a two-sided process.

First, it is an objective process insofar as we examine the changes the object undergoes as the object of labour; it is this object that acquires another form and other properties.

Second, this activity of the subject is a subjective process insofar as we examine this process from the side of the action performed by the subject, of the

---

[11] Marx 1923, p. 133.
[12] 'Als Bilderin von Gebrauchswerten, als nützliche Arbeit, ist die Arbeit eine von allen Gesellschaftsformen unabhängige Existenzbedingung des Menschen, ewige Naturnotwendigkeit, um den Stoffwechsel zwischen Mensch und Natur, also das menschliche Leben zu vermitteln'. Marx 1923a, p. 10.

expenditure of the individual's internal subjective energy and of the subjective goal whose realisation the labour activity serves.

The labour process, examined from the side of the subject, represents the *externalisation* of the individual's subjective energy. 'During the labour process', Marx says, 'the worker's labour constantly undergoes a transformation, from the form of unrest into that of being, from the form of motion into that of objectivity'.[13]

Examined from the point of view of the object, labour is the overcoming of this object and its subordination to human needs – the 'humanisation of nature' (Marx).

The two-sidedness of this process is reflected in the product as the result of labour, in the form of its twofold character: the product simultaneously represents something *objective* and something *subjectivised*.

On the one hand, it (the product) – insofar as it has already been produced – is an object with all its objective properties, independent of our will and our desires, a definite materially substantive formation unquestionably belonging to objectively existing physical reality, but at the same time it represents not simply a natural object. Bread, paper, dishware or an internal combustion engine are not found immediately in nature; it does not produce them. In these objects, the materials of nature have lost their natural innocence and acquired other content thanks to the labour applied to them. They constitute not a natural, but an *artificial* reality which, according to the linguistic analysis given by Nikolai Marr, is designated in the majority of languages as 'manual' [*ruchno*] – that is, a hand-made reality [*ruchnotvornia deistvitel'nost'*].

Moreover, this reality is created not only by the hand, but also by the *mind*. The things that exist in it are not the result of the play of the blind forces of natural elements, but represent the deliberate realisation of consciously envisioned ideas; they are the products of purposeful activity, and hence goal-defined things.

'At the end of every labour process', Marx writes, 'a result emerges which had already been conceived by the worker at the beginning, hence already existed ideally. Humans not only effect a change of form in the materials of nature; they also realise their own purpose'.[14]

The properties inherent in the products of labour are essentially different from the qualities and properties of natural things. For the material of the pro-

---

13 Marx 1923, p. 144.
14 Marx 1923, p. 134.

duce these properties are not innate, nor are they accidentally acquired by it. These properties are purposefully imparted to the object by humans.

The product of labour is an object that becomes the bearer of useful properties intentionally given to it by humans, thus performing work useful to humans – that is, social functions.

From this point of view, of course, the product does not have its own significance independent of humanity. It acquires significance and meaning only in relation to humanity. The product does not belong to natural reality, but in essence relates to social reality and constitutes a part of it.

In short, a product is an object that is subordinate to human goals and to humanity's own subjective needs. It is a *subjectivised object*.

The subjective aspect of the product is displayed in its ability to satisfy a particular human need. This ability – that is, the usefulness of the product – turns it into a use value, a boon for humanity, no matter what need it satisfies – whether it goes to immediate consumption as an object of nourishment, to the production of the means of production, or to idle amusement.

§7

How is a product formed – this object with social functions inherent in it?

In the process of production, an individual consumes (requires): 1) material which, in this process, loses its original nature; 2) the implements of production, which gradually wear out or break down (e.g. in the application of chemical agents or burning); and 3) labour power – the energy of the worker.

The transfer of the first two components into the body of the product of labour are evident to simple observation: the part of the material necessary for the product is placed in it, and the part that is of no use to it is discarded as waste. The implements gradually wear down in the production of a product and also form part of this product. Both are transferred into the product.

As regards the third component – that is, expended labour – being the purposeful expenditure of muscular, neuro-cerebral (and so on) energy, it does not 'go missing'; otherwise, the object of labour would remain unchanged.

Labour activity enters into the body of the product; it is transferred into the product and remains in it in the form of those changes that the object underwent in the labour process. Labour subsides into the product and is preserved in it.

If in purposeless activity, human energy – like all energy that does not have a direction – is dissipated, then in goal-directed activity, energy is accrued in the object of activity.

Thus, in the process of production, humans pass their activity outwards, transfer a part of their individuality into the object and leave it behind in this product. A separation of a certain part of subjective activity from the subject occurs – an *alienation* by the individual of a part of their individuality, which subsides into the product, producing within it the corresponding changes and constructing it in conformity with the desires and skills of the subject. In a word: in the process of labour, humans transform a part of the subject into an objectively existing object.

Marx called this process the 'objectification of man' (*Vergegenständlichung*) and described it with the mastery distinctive to him alone in Chapter 7 of *Capital*:

> In the labour process, therefore, man's activity, via the instruments of labour, effects an alteration in the object of labour which was intended from the outset. This process is extinguished in the product. The product of the process is a use-value, a piece of natural material adapted to human needs by means of a change in its form. Labour has become bound up in its object: labour has been objectified, the object has been worked on. What on the side of the worker appeared in the form of unrest now appears on the side of the product, in the form of being ... The worker has spun, and the product is a spinning.[15]

From this point of view, in a certain sense, the product represents 'objectified personality'. It is the manifestation of subjective human energy and activity, having taken the form of objective existence in things, works, and so on. The product is the realisation of subjective human intentions, insofar as it is the bearer of human goals as well as the prime witness to the experience, mastery and skills of its producer.

If, from the side of the object, the product appeared before us as a *subjectivised object*, then now, observed from the side of the subject and their activity, it exists for us as objectified personality, an *objectivised subject*.

In the first volume of Capital, Marx analyses the objectification of labour from the point of view of developing questions linked to the formation of use value, surplus value, economic relations, and so on. Here, we are attempting

---

15 'Im Arbeitsprozess bewirkt also die Tätigkeit des Menschen durch das Arbeitsmittel eine von vornherein bezweckte Veränderung des Arbeitsgegenstandes. Der Prozess erlischt im Produkt. Sein Produkt is ein Gebrauchswert, ein durch Formveränderung menschlichen Bedürfnissen angeeigneter Naturstoff. Die Arbeit hat sich mit ihrem Gegenstand verbunden. Sie ist vergegenständlicht und der Gegenstand ist verarbeitet. Was auf seiten des Arbeiters in der Form der Unruhe erschien, erschient nun als ruhende Eigenschaft, in der Form des Seins, auf seiten des Produkts. Er hat gesponnen und das Produkt ist ein Gespinst'. Marx 1923, p. 136.

to use the same analysis with regard to problems concerning the origin and development of the human means of thought.

At the same time, labour is characterised by the passing of a part of the individual from the sphere of the subjective to the sphere of the objectively existing, and the changeover of the object from the sphere of the objectively natural to the sphere of the subjectively human – that is, the social.

Labour is the *alienation* by the subject of itself into an objective reality independent of it, and the *subjectivisation* of the object.

That the product is not simply an object, but also to a certain degree a part of the subject, is confirmed by the fact that in returning to the subject in the act of consumption, the product is nullified as an object; recombining with the subject and satisfying their needs, it renews the subject's existence. Marx very eloquently calls this process 'the personification of things'.

'It is obvious that man produces his own body, though eating, for example, one form of consumption. But this holds for every kind of consumption that, in one way or another, produces human beings in some specific aspect ... In the former (that is, in production – K.M.) the producer objectifies him or herself,[16] in the latter (that is, in consumption – K.M.) the object is personified'.[17]

In the act of consumption, the process comes back to where it started and begins anew, again with production. Consequently, a social person is a being who him or herself produces the means of one's existence, 'objectifying him or herself in them', and consumes what is produced; and in 'consuming themselves' thus create their own history. Converting themselves into the products of their own labour, 'humanising nature', creating human riches from it and consuming what has been created – in the process of such production and such consumption, humanity grew and enriched itself through both new material and spiritual needs, and the means and methods of satisfying them.

'The greatness of Hegelian 'phenomenology' and its final results', Marx says, 'consists of the fact that Hegel regards the self-generation of humanity as a

---

16   [Editor's note: the Russian reflexive pronoun used here is not gender specific, though 'person' (*chelovek*) is a masculine noun. Consequently, such forms are henceforth rendered as 'him or herself' and corresponding grammatical derivatives.]

17   Marx 1931b, p. 59. In subsequent discourses (§§ 94, 95) we will see that in the process of production, properly speaking, it is not the individual who objectifies themselves, but society itself. The phenomenon of alienation finds completely different expression in the further development of this form of alienation, in proprietary relations, regarding which Marx says: 'Property is only the material expression of humans becoming objective for themselves and at the same time becoming foreign, inhuman objects for themselves; that their manifestation of life becomes a removal from life, that their realisation becomes a loss of their reality, an alien reality'. Marks i Engel's 1927–1935, Vol. III, p. 625.

process, and regards externalisation (*Vergegenständlichung*) as objectification [*raspredmechivanie*] (*Entgegenständlichung*), as a dismissal and a withdrawing of this dismissal; in the fact that he perceives the essence of *labour* and understands objective humanity, truly existing humanity, as the result of its *own labour*. The true, active relationship of humanity to itself as a tribal (that is, social – K.M.) being, or the realisation of itself as an actual generic being, that is, as a human being, is possible only because humanity actually creates its own generic forces – and this is again possible only thanks to the collective activity of humanity, possible only as the result of history – and relates to them as it does to objects, which is possible at first only in the form of alienation'.[18]

The Product of Labour: Material Mediator of Social Relations

§ 8
The product of labour is thus not only an object, but something bigger – namely, a *subjectified* object. But it is not a subject, because it exists in the form of an object.

The product of labour has the advantage over the solid object in that it includes something human; it has been worked up in accordance with a person's goals and is thus functional, justified by a purpose, and possesses a meaningful definition. A natural object, being the product of natural elements, is entirely objective, and as such is devoid of message and purpose – a 'meaningless' existence.

On the other hand, the product of labour as 'part' of the subject differs from the subject. It has the 'advantage' over the organic parts of the subject in that it is able to be physically separated from the subject and can exist just as successfully, and to the benefit of any other person.

This two-sidedness, which finds its expression in the fact that the product of labour combines both principles – the subjective and the objective – in itself, explains the *role it plays in the formation of the social complex*.

As the objective realisation of a person's subjective goals, the product of labour is characterised by:
1) the fact that insofar as it is produced, it becomes materially external in relation to the producer, and is thus feasible;

---

18   Marks i Engel's 1927–1935, Vol. III, p. 639. But, as Marx notes earlier, Hegel remained on the positions of idealism, insofar as he 'only recognizes one aspect of labour, namely, the abstract spiritual'.

2) its *alienation* from its direct producer;[19] and
3) its transfer to the command of another person. Thus, the individual becomes accessible and useful to other individuals – not through the direct route of physical and material relations, but through the product of labour and the relations of production, appropriation, and so on (see §19).

The labour of the individual, embodied in the product of labour, becomes accessible to others only through this product. And in the product of labour, the individual can make its capabilities the property of others. Animals are deprived of this opportunity for the mutual use of their talents.

Labour and the product of labour are the only possibilities for socialising the individual energy of the subject; the only path for the constant collectivisation of persons who themselves, however, are the product of society and social relations.

The objective aspect of the product (i.e. the embodiment of the labour of individuals in the implements of labour and in products) makes possible the *collaboration* of individuals, the exchange of labour energy among them, the appropriation [*otsuzhdenie*] of labour, the distribution and exchange of products, the appropriation of the labour of others, and so on, and makes possible the relationships of individuals as social relations.

We say 'makes possible', but in order for the possible to become the actual – for alienation, appropriation, and so on to actually take place, it is necessary for someone to *want* to have that product, that the product be *desirable* to others. The subjective aspect of the product plays this role – namely those properties and functions that form the intended goal of a person's labour activity and produce a consumer value from things. Owing to these qualities, a thing is a useful, necessary, essential thing, and thus desirable for appropriation. The desire for alienation, for exchange, or – to take a particular case of this – the desire to purchase as well as the desire to sell is created precisely by the subjective aspect of the product, that is, its consumer value.

From this it follows that by virtue of its two-sidedness (its objective character and its subjective properties), the product of labour makes the real, material, and social relations of people possible.

Thanks to the product of labour, alienation as a social fact, and the relations of production, exchange, appropriation of the labour of others, and so on all become possible. Alienation, exchange, or the division of the individual

---

19 This condition remains in force in relation to an action that may appear absolutely inalienable, for example the activities of a teacher. The product of labour in this case is another individual who acquires the experience, knowledge, and mastery of the teacher – they do not adhere to the teacher as a natural 'offshoot' but remain an independent person whose knowledge in turn can be used by any third person.

itself as such are absurdities – but all these relationships of people can begin through the products produced by them. Even in the case where the object of giving, exchange, or 'alienation' is a person itself (for example in a slave-owning society), this is possible only to the degree that property relations have already become firmly established in society and that the slave implies the sum total of products or services that they are able to, and must, produce.

Owing to its useful properties acquired in labour, the ability to become *the material mediator* of the relationships between people is inherent in the product. All productive relations and the relations of appropriation, distribution, and exchange, all the relations of dominance and subordination, of violence and of agreement, of exploitation, of equality, and so on are possible only thanks to the product. The living relations of people are accumulated on the basis of production and by means of the appropriation of these material goods – that is, the products.

In short, with the help of and by *means* of the product of labour, all the real, material relations between people (i.e. human relationships in the proper sense, as opposed to biological) come to be.

The product, being the bearer of the social substance of labour, becomes at the same time the material mediator of the communication of individuals and of all social relations in general.

The product of labour is the material substrate by which all the relations of individuals come to be in society: '*the object, as reality for a person, as the objective existence of a person, is at the same time the personal existence of that person for others, their human relationship to other people, the social behaviour of a person in relation to people*' (Marx).

Lenin especially emphasised this thought of Marx, commenting: 'This point is highly significant, because it shows how Marx approaches the basic idea of his entire 'system', if one can call it that – namely, the idea of the social relations of production'.[20]

Social relations and social life become possible thanks to human labour activity. Humans as *zoon politikon* (a social animal) are only possible through 'reified humans' (i.e. through labour activity).

Certain theoreticians suppose that things become the mediators of social relations only in capitalist society. Rudolf Hilferding defended this view in his article 'Formulation of the Problem of Theoretical Economy in Marx' in *Neue Zeit*, 1904–1905, vol. I. But this is fundamentally mistaken. In all epochs the conditions of production have united or separated people, and every social

---

20   Lenin 1931, p. 43.

relation begins on the basis of production and appropriation only by means of things (i.e. the material gifts of labour). These social functions of things, however, are different in various epochs, and in different social structures the object of labour – as well as the product of labour – appears in different forms, being the bearer of different content, meaning, and social functions.

The essence of fetishism does not consist of the fact that things are supposed to be the bearers of social functions (they actually perform a necessary social service; all Marx's studies on productive forces and productive relations show this). Marx objects not to the social functions of things, but to believing these properties to be inherent in the things themselves from nature – thinking that the social functions of things are their natural properties – and on the other hand believing that social relations even to some degree can be relations of a physical order.

All these properties and social functions are inherent in things *per se*, but are the expression and reflection in them of social relations. This is obvious even from the fact that in the event of their withdrawal from the social complex and their isolation from people, these things ('human things' – the products of labour) immediately lose all their function and meaning.

With its two-sided aspect, the product of labour serves not only as the cause and means (the mediator) of communication between people; appearing in the form of the instruments of labour, utensils, artificial lighting, heating, and so on – in a word, in the form of the sum total of material goods that humans use – it is also the means of human communication with nature, serving as a material bearer mediating the relationship of humans to the natural environment.

Humans separate themselves from nature with the products of their labour; they communicate with nature and conquer it by means of these products.[21]

If animals are immediately subordinate to the influences of the natural environment, if they make up one part of this natural element and are subject to the natural laws of adaptation and selection, then social humans oppose nature *not with their organism*, not with their biological aspect, but with the

---

21   It may seem strange that from the very first chapter of this book, so much attention is being paid to the *product*, and not the *instrument* of labour, which had initiated actual humanisation. But the instrument of labour – as is not difficult to understand from the current account – must also be regarded as a product. We would thus have to preface an analysis of the question of the role of the instrument (which Chapter 3 of this book is dedicated to) with an analysis of more general problems, the conclusions of which apply to the instrument of labour as well.

entire world of technology and appropriation that they themselves create, partitioning themselves off from nature and advancing against it.

Humans create a *new* 'nature around them – a rationally organised world of things, technology, and so on – placing it between themselves as the subject in principle and nature as the absolute object'.[22]

Humans set artificial nature against wild nature, setting 'culture' against 'nature'.

'Humanity, as subject, and nature, as object', Marx says, 'exist in all stages of history',[23] but if between this subject in principle and the absolute object there arose no third party or mediators, if no mediating elements were generated in the form of the products of labour – these material equivalents of the activity of humans, which impart to them such colossal strength in their subjugation of nature – then the history of humanity would never have gone beyond the limits of natural history.

The entire history of humanity is essentially the history of the development of these middle elements (the aggregate of social goods), between 'humanity as subject and nature as object'.

Everything that grows, accumulates, and is deposited in historical reserves gives rise to something new, moves the history of humanity forward, and represents these mediating elements that are historically established between humans and nature, and also between humans and other humans – the world of material goods, spiritual culture, and social relations created by humanity.

The history of material culture is only the history of the development of and the changes to the forms of this mediation and the history of the real and material technical activity of humanity; the latter defines at the same time the history of human thinking, its language, and of all spiritual culture in general.

'All human history', Marx says, 'is nothing more than the formation of humanity through human labour, the formation of nature for humanity'.[24]

If the animal world adapts biologically to the natural environment, then humans, on the contrary, adapt nature to their own needs.

The manner of living and the production by people of the means necessary for their lives does not depend directly on nature, but above all on the means

---

22   In relation to nature, humans always remain the subject. Of course, they are in the position of object, but only in relation to other people and never in relation to nature. The loss by humans of their quality of subject in relation to natural forces simply means their death. In relation to humans, nature is an object in principle and nowhere appears as the subject.
23   Marks 1931b, p. 53.
24   Marks i Engel's 1927–1935, Vol. III, p. 632.

of production at people's disposal and created by them. The development of human society is defined not by natural forces, but by social forces. Therefore the laws of the development of human society are not simple reiterations of natural and historical laws.

Together with reorganising nature and producing the material conditions of its own existence, human society creates a particular new pattern of its own development – not a biological one, but a social one.

Marx repeatedly pointed out that reality such as cost, profit, capital, and so on could not be investigated using the microscope or chemical analysis. It is rooted not in the physical structure of substances; it is the expression of social relations, existing only in them. The same must be said about consciousness, thinking, reason, and the entire spiritual world. Humanity's thinking, its ideology, and its world view have nothing to do with the natural physical world or the biological world, but only with the social world.

Labour and Society: Mutual Dependence

§9

Up to now we have argued that labour and the products of labour create a particular means of people's communication with nature and with other individuals and constructs a particular sphere of relations different from biological ones – namely, a social complex and social relations.

These assertions are correct insofar as labour, by producing the conditions of human existence, actually historically created humans themselves and human society;[25] but these arguments are insufficient insofar as they only express half of this complex process.

The other, no less important side of the matter lies consists of the fact that this world of the products of human labour and material goods, like labour itself, is only possibly under the conditions of definite social relations of people and not otherwise.

Labour is always collaboration, and every labour activity is possible when individuals do not exist separately but form a coherent whole.

If earlier we were certain that social connections and relations began with the assistance and by means of the products of labour and material goods created by humans, and that labour first creates the social relations of individuals, then it must now be proven that society itself is the condition for the appear-

---

25 See Engel's 1933 ('The Role of Labour in the Transition from Ape to Man').

ance of labour, that labour is unthinkable without a social complex and outside of it, and that labour is a social category from the beginning.

In other words, it must be proven that a social formation as such first makes possible the form of activity called labour.

The question has been formulated with sufficient clarity so that the reader can go past without noticing the so-called 'vicious circle fallacy' (*circulus vitiosus*): on the one hand, labour is the condition for the origin of society; on the other, society is the condition for the origin of labour activity.

Undoubtedly, we are dealing with a *closed circle*: the condition and the conditions mutually enclose each other. But this shows that 'labour' and 'society' are not two different agents, but only components of a unified whole – moments of one and the same formation; in essence, genetically they make up *the same thing, the one gives rise to the other, mutually establishing the whole*. If the circle were not closed, this complex – like any other that does not have to do with a *closed formation* – would be unable to develop according to the internal laws of the struggle of interpenetrating opposites.

The social formation makes labour activity possible. But labour and the products created by it in turn connect and unite individuals in society, and provide an impulse towards the reproduction of the new and the consolidation of what has been acquired. If labour activity and the products created by it were in essence external and neutral in relation to social links, then the social formation as a particular spontaneously developing whole would be in principle impossible.

There is certainly a circle here – but why is it 'vicious'? Why is it 'vitiosus'? Does it actually not develop? On the contrary, we are dealing here with a circle that is continually developing and constantly reproducing new things.

A vicious circle would appear here only to a scholastically inclined mind; in fact, this is not a *circulus vitiosus*, but rather a *circulus vitalis* – a circle of life, a vital circle.[26]

Hegel saw the solution to this seeming antinomy in 'mutual interaction'. 'Cause, passing into effect, has in the final instance again a reverse causal action, owing to which the first cause in turn becomes the effect, or the state

---

26 The proposition of a 'vicious circle', generally speaking has no force in relation to the real and the existing. It remains within its rights only in the field of abstract intellectual constructions – such as mathematics, for example – so as not to consider what has not yet been proven as valid and proven. As a consequence of the excessive zeal of the rationalists, this determination – like many other principles of formal logic – has often gone far outside the bounds of its limited field and confused people, creating a mirage of some kind of problematics and empty conundrums.

(*gesetzt*). At the same time, this mutuality contains the fact that neither of the components of causality are absolute for themselves, but only this closed circle of the whole exists in itself and for itself' (Hegel, *Philosophical Propaedeutic*, §84).

Only formations where condition and conditioned, closing up, mutually urge each other on, moving and not leaving the complex in a condition of stagnation and rest, and constantly leading it outside the range of every level of development achieved can have their own laws of development and develop from within by means of the struggle of opposites.

The problem of closed formations, as the problem of mutual interaction, was first brought forward on a materialist basis by Marxist philosophy.[27]

Regarding people who are unable to understand the full depth of the questions arising here, Engels said: 'These gentlemen lack one thing – the dialectic. They look everywhere: here is the cause, there is the effect. They do not notice that this is an empty abstraction, that such diametrically opposed metaphysical abstractions do not exist in reality … They do not understand, that this entire colossal process progresses in the form of mutual interaction'.[28]

Lenin provided the following definition of the dialectic:

> The identity of opposites (their 'unity' …) is the recognition (discovery) of the contradictory, *mutually exclusive*, opposite tendencies in *all* phenomena and processes of nature (*including* mind and society). The condition for the knowledge of all processes of the world in their '*self-movement*', in their spontaneous development, in their real life, is the knowledge of them as a unity of opposites. Development is the 'struggle' of opposites.[29]

In Lenin's words, the division of a unity into mutually exclusive opposites and their struggle constitutes the 'source' of *self-movement*, providing the key to the 'leaps', the 'interruption of graduality', the 'transformation into opposites', and the 'destruction of the old and the rise of the new'.[30] This 'self-motion', this development from within, as a living dialectical process, is possible only if things objectively form known wholes – that is, closed formations. The social complex represents one such integral formation: people themselves create the conditions of their existence, and these conditions in turn define the character and direction of people's activity – that is, they define the development of

---

27 On these problems in more detail, see §§ 58 and 59.
28 Marx and Engels 1934, p. 382.
29 Lenin 1931, p. 323.
30 Lenin 1931, p. 324.

MATERIAL CONDITIONS AND SOCIAL PRECONDITIONS 37

society; that is why it is only possible to speak about a particular social pattern. 'It (the understanding of history – K.M.) shows that conditions create people to the same degree in which people create conditions' (Marx).[31]

We will often meet such processes that close in on themselves in Marxism's system of theoretical constructions: 'productive forces and relations of production', 'labour and consciousness', 'instruments of labour – hand – mind', 'language and thinking', and so on. We will have numerous opportunities to return to this theme.

At the present level of development, every labour is possible only on the basis of accumulated social material, whether by this we mean the objects or instruments of labour, the needs or habits and skills of the worker.

As regards both the material and the means and instruments of labour – as well as from the standpoint of habits and skills – it is impossible today to find any branch of labour that would represent the product of a single individual's activity with all these elements.[32]

But is labour ever possible as an individual activity, even at the very initial stages of its origin?

Ludwig Noiré showed[33] that primitive humans, in possessing a very labile attention span, could not work and their minds could not consolidate the achievements of labour if labour did not represent the movement of people in a collective rhythm, as homogeneous mass activity in which a certain mental emanation unites many individuals and makes them move and act uniformly on the basis of rhythm and imitation. These observations of Noiré are far too arbitrary to be taken seriously. Such elemental mass action itself is not justified by anything; placing it at the foundation of proof is equally as impossible as specifically pointing to the automatic and instinctual character of these actions. Labour as purposeful conscious activity could not be the result of instinctive, spontaneous movements, and even if such herd instinct actions took place at some point, they could not have acquired the character of consciously premeditated activity. On the contrary, such actions facilitate the transfer of conscious behaviour into the sphere of unconscious reflections rather than its realisation (see pp. 21–23).

---

31   Marks i Engel's 1933, p. 29.
32   'Even when I am occupied with scientific and other activities – activities that I can perform myself, without direct communication with others – I nonetheless act *socially*, for I am acting as a *person*. Not only is the material for my activity given to me as a social product – including the language with whose help the activity of the thinker is manifested – but my *own* existence is social activity; therefore what I do outside of myself, I do outside of myself for society'. Marks i Engel's 1927–1935, Vol. III, p. 624.
33   Noiré 1877; Noiré 1880.

Forming a complete conception of the 'first' rational act of primitive humans' conscious activity and drawing a visual map of the behaviour of the primitive stage of anthropoids is difficult, and there is no necessity in it.

In all probability, fully conscious behaviour – as well as labour in the form of a regular process – is the fruit of much later development.

It will be sufficient for our purposes if we show that labour is possible only as social – but never as individual – activity. This is confirmed if only by the fact that the data nowhere, in any epoch, discloses the nonsocial character of human labour.

On the other hand, we point to the important fact that that through any labour – even private and individual labour – humans, insofar as they are producing something, *constantly socialise their individual energy in the products of labour created by them; consequently, their social character is recreated in every act of labour.*

'The individual is the social being', Marx says. 'His manifestations of life – even if they may not appear in the direct form of *communal* manifestations of life carried out with others – *are* therefore an expression and confirmation of *social life*.

Man's individual and species-life are not *different*, however much – and this is inevitable – the mode of existence of the individual is a more *particular* or more *general* mode of the life of the species'.[34]

If we are still haunted by the evil question – which came first? Does labour precede the social formation and create it, or does the social formation give birth to labour? – then it must be said that this is not at all evil, but simply an incorrectly formulated and empty question analogous to the other, more trivial 'question' about the chicken and the egg. It is clear that every chicken is produced from an egg, and that every such egg is laid by a chicken, and not by a goat. But if the question about the original descent of the chicken and the means of reproduction is asked, then we are not looking for the first egg from which the first chick burst into the world, nor do we need to look for a certain ur-chicken that gladdened the world with the first egg. We reject this boring series of useless questions and search for a biological aspect that precedes chickens – or birds in general – that was neither egg nor chicken, but a third something that was characteristic of another, more general means of reproduction.

If we seek to ask the question about the origins of human industrial activity – to find the path by which humanity passed from an animal condition to

---

34 Marks i Engel's 1927–1935, Vol. III, p. 624.

the production of the instruments of labour, and so on – we must of course pass beyond the boundaries of social activity and the sociological formulation of the question and turn to causes, factors, and forces that are not social, but biological.

The most basic foundation of a beast's human nature beginning to utilise instruments and starting to work must be sought in the biological past: 'This was a step conditioned by the organisation of the body', Marx says. But once humanity began its productive life of labour, they put an end to their natural and biological life, rising to the level of social existence and leaving the zoological sphere of conformity to natural laws.

'When humanity left the hands of Nature, they were the children of Nature and not human at all. Humans were created by humans, by culture, by history' (Feuerbach).

At the conclusion of this chapter, we note as a thesis – in part disclosed in the preceding chapter, in part subject to disclosure in the following statement: the conditions for the appearance of the human means of consciousness are the material conditions and prerequisites of the appearance of society itself as conformity to socio-historical laws, in contrast to conformity to natural historical laws.

The two different states of life elucidated in this chapter – the animal aspect of *immediate* biological existence on the one hand, and the human means of *mediated* social life on the other – also correspond to two different types of consciousness: 1) animal consciousness and 2) human consciousness.

CHAPTER 2

From the Animal Level of Consciousness to Human Thinking

The Biological Roots of Consciousness

§ 10

'My relationship with my environment is my consciousness', Marx said. This formulation covers the entire history and prehistory of consciousness over a period of hundreds of thousands of centuries. It embraces consciousness at all stages of its development starting from the lowest forms, which cannot properly be called by this name (for example, the various tropisms and reactions of the protozoa), to the highest forms of development of the perspicacious mind in abstract mathematical analysis, in poetry, and in humour.

Human consciousness most probably did not come about through pure spontaneous generation, but developed gradually from other, lower form, as the history of the formation of people from an animal state to a human one generally ran.

The ability and inclination of an organism to occupy a position in its environment that is more advantageous for life evidently forms the initial natural and historical (that is, biological) basis from which the various forms of consciousness developed. Animal consciousness is a higher stage of development, and human consciousness has also generally preserved these attributes, undoubtedly in a more refined, more sophisticated, qualitatively altered form.

Even with this completely general attribute, consciousness is not entirely passive. At the lowest stages of development, it carries within it the beginnings of a certain alertness, though very weak. As is known, animals are not indifferent to their environment and to all the objects surrounding them; they display the rudiments characteristic of a subject and – as Hegel said – do not stand helpless before the reality of nature but seize and devour prey, revealing by this their active relationship of the subject,[1] but not being at all conscious that they are an agent.

---

1 Hegel 1921, p. 73. This thought is repeated in Hegel several times in his *Philosophy of Right*; for example, in § 44 of his *Encyclopedia of Science* and in other places.

The manifestation of animal consciousness represents a very primitive and as yet undeveloped form of the active relation of the subject to its environment; it is only the manifestation of an immediate and natural relation of consumption of a *biological* subject.

Two types of action are distinguished in the behaviour of an animal: 1) actions inherited phylogenetically by a specific animal type, performed automatically, without preparatory experience and training; and 2) actions acquired through individual experience. The first type concerns 'unconditioned' reflexes and instincts; the second type concerns all other actions and all habits acquired by the animal by way of individual experience.

'Everything', says Auguste Forel, one of the great experts on the life of animals,[2] 'that instinctive automatic actions were acquired and accumulated hereditarily by means of natural selection and other hereditary factors'. But secondary automatic actions are based on the ability of the neurocerebral apparatus to receive and retain impressions and to automate learned activity by means of practice.

Physiologists sought the manifestation of conscious activity primarily in the field of acquired, 'secondary' reflexes. It should be noted, however, that acquired reflexes are not conscious actions. If they are supported in their original appearance by the contribution of consciousness – and that not always – then as they are automated and begin to run according to the primary reflex type, consciousness contributes to them as little as it does to primary and hereditary reflexes. It can be said that manifestations of a conscious condition are not observed in either the field of hereditary reflexes or the field of acquired reflexes.

The results of seriously formulated studies of the behaviour of animals show that in the life of animals, precisely this type of automatic actions occupies a predominant place. Consciousness in the animal stage of development is expressed in the prevalence of automated reflex reactions, both acquired and hereditary; cases of *rational* behaviour are encountered relatively seldom and episodically. Consciousness is manifested only for a short while and quickly dies out.

In contrast to animals, the *conscious condition of consciousness predominates*. 'Humanity', says Marx, 'differs from the ram in that consciousness replaces their instinct, or that their instinct is conscious'.[3]

It would possibly be more correct as regards reflex responses and instinctive actions not to use the word 'consciousness', as there is not yet genuine aware-

---

2 Forel 1910.
3 Marks i Engel's 1933, p. 21.

ness in these phenomena. What is found here in reality is rather a stage preceding consciousness proper, as reflexes and instincts also serve the organism, playing the same role in the stage preceding consciousness of preserving the organism in the environment that consciousness plays at a subsequent, higher state; in both, this role consists of orienting the organism in its environment.

In order to avoid confusion and misunderstanding, we will settle on terminology. We will use the general term 'consciousness' or 'psyche' to mean any manifestation of the animal orienting it in the given situation, regardless (correctly or incorrectly) of whether it is by means of hereditary or acquired reflexes. Consciousness proper, or 'conscious condition' will be the orientation of an individual in which it anticipates the final results of its behaviour and in which this behaviour is constructed on the basis of the point of a task to be solved or the predicted result in accordance with it.

Instincts and Reflex Responses

§ 11

The impulses toward and capabilities of behaviour belonging to the hereditary characteristics of the organism are called instincts. The majority of these actions are complex, but are essentially performed identically in all normal persons of a kind or type.

Despite the fact that the question of instincts in ancient times occupied the attention of philosophers, physiologists, psychologists, and biologists, science can today admit that the nature of the instinct still represents a puzzle in many aspects.

In the majority of cases, physiologists consider instinctive actions to be produced from reflexes. Some of them generally recognise no difference between what they call reflex and instinct. Academician I.P. Pavlov said, 'I would prefer to use the word *reflex*, allowing others to substitute the word *instinct* for it as desired'.[4] Other physiologists – for example Thorndike, Watson, and the American school behaviourists in general, following the Spencerian theory of instinct – interpret instinct as the goal of reflexes, as a 'series of chain conditioned reflexes'.[5]

---

4 Pavlov 1923, p. 204.
5 Thorndike 1913; Watson 1914, p. 106. Similar interpretations to this are found among the vitalists. Driesch talks about instincts as 'aufeinander folgende Kette einzelner Reflexen' (Driesch 1921, pp. 321–30).

Characteristic of the physiological interpretation is the fact that basic instinctive actions are recognised as facts of an exclusively internal order. In the majority of cases, physiologists take only the nervous processes and links that make up neurons and ganglionic cells ('cleronomic paths', according to Ziegler) into account. A mistaken opinion – that instinctive actions are put in motion thanks only to the internal links of neural matter – emerges. Meanwhile, in the majority of cases an encounter with a definite *external* situation that arouses – or, more accurately, stimulates – these actions is necessary for this.

After the publication of the present article, Professor Peter Manteifel' made some interesting observations in this field from his practice in the Moscow Zoo: 'Barnacle goose, those beautiful polar birds, previously did not breed in the zoo until we put piles of rocks on the shores of the ponds. Until recently, these 'external' stimuli had nowhere been taken into consideration. Formerly indifferent to the springtime sun, these geese now make a fuss around the rocks, fighting each other off. Only there did the barnacle goose start hatching goslings ... In general, the significance of a habitual nest for certain birds is very great ... This trait manifests itself especially clearly in observing the common Australian parakeet. In zoos, where thousands of parakeet nestlings are hatched, we have repeatedly tested this startling attachment to a certain type of nest. We only had to put out hive-like nesting boxes in the cages, and the males and females who were previously uninterested in each other quickly broke up into pairs. Testicles in the males and eggs in the females matured not in a matter of days, but of hours. But the breeding period was cut short as soon as the nests were taken away: testicular function ceased, and even eggs in the oviducts dissolved' (*Izvestiia*, 10 March 1937).

In the majority of cases, instinctive actions are not spontaneous but develop depending on external conditions. To a certain extent, instinctive actions also adapt themselves to the properties of the objects they apply to. The construction of a certain type of nest is instinctive for birds. Moreover, they require various materials and their use of each type of material is particular. A bird does not pick up and carry straw the same way it does with down, and places it differently. If it comes across cotton wool, then it will use the material another way.

In a purely subjective approach to instincts as the sum of cleronomically generated neural circuits, one of the important aspects of instinctive actions remains outside our field of vision. The basic function and biological sense of the instincts consists in its creating the possibility for an animal of orienting itself in its environment. According to the mechanistic theory cited, all the actions of an animal are the sum of the internal functioning of motor paths, while these latter deal not with the objects themselves, but only with stimuli and receptor fibers. It appears that the animal does not orient itself in the objective environment, but only in its perceptions and the internal conditions of neural matter (!).

American behaviourists are proud, as is known, of the 'objective study' of the behaviour of animals and humans, insisting on absolute objectivism. Meanwhile, it is scarcely possible to imagine a more subjective theory than the one that bases all its constructions exclusively on the internal mechanical links of neurons, ganglionic centres, and so forth.

Other physiologists, rejecting the mechanical interpretation of instinct as the sum of reflexes, fall into a narrow extreme. They place instinct at the foundation of the interpretation of the behaviour of animals and apply this to reflexes. Thus, Erich Becher, in rejecting the mechanistic interpretation of instinct, advances a psychovitalistic one in its place.[6]

The question of whether the instinctive actions of animals are conscious or unconscious arouses comparatively less dispute. Currently, opinions that the instinctive actions of animals run unconsciously are not gathering much speed – if we do not take into account the vitalists[7] who place the question of the conscious and the unconscious on a completely different plane and essentially repeat what Scholastic doctrine asserted about instinct in the sixteenth and seventeenth centuries.

Spencer, Darwin, and others noted the unconscious character of instinctive actions. Certain scientists who ascribed memory, will, and even the capacity for ideas to animals, nevertheless believed as regards instinctive actions that animals were not able to anticipate the final result. Being subject to unconscious motives, and animal performs very complex and rational actions without consciously guiding them and knowing nothing about the results. It is impossible, for example, to think that a squirrel burying nuts in the ground has future needs in mind.

An instinct is a motive whose link with the goal is conspicuous, while the action itself of the animal is blind. There is much evidence for the lack of consciousness in the instinctive actions of an animal. This concerns, firstly, the sudden manifestation of certain instincts upon reaching the appropriate age or period of life of the animal; secondly, the perfection and completeness with which these actions are carried out without training and without any prior knowledge; and thirdly the confidence and permanency with which

---

6 Becher 1911, p. 401.
7 Müller 1840, pp. 107, 515; Driesch 1903; Driesch 1905.

they are carried out every time by the animal, and so on. The most striking fact of the absence of conscious premeditation in instinctive actions is the 'useless actions' of the animal. Placed in conditions under which a certain action proves to be useless, the animal repeats the action in the form it used under normal circumstances, that is, it displays full ignorance of what it is doing.

Lloyd Morgan reports[8] that a newborn squirrel taken from the nest, raised indoors, and fed on milk and biscuits, cracked nuts it saw for the first time, taking out and eating the contents like any forest squirrel. At the age of two months it had acquired the instinctive motive to hide nuts, similar to the way squirrels in the wild do, burying nuts two centimetres under the ground and subsequently finding them by scent and digging them up. Under indoor conditions, the squirrel grabbed the nut and, looking around, hid it under the protection of the couch leg, then making the movements that accompany a burial and the tamping down of earth on the buried object. Having carried out all that, the animal calmly went back to its usual activities, untroubled by the fact that the nut remained in plain sight.

'In the New Guinean scrubfowl (a chicken-like bird)', Ziegler reports, 'the male carries in a large pile of plant remains, on which the female then lays her eggs; if it happens that there are no brooding females, the male still accumulates a completely useless pile ... If eggs are taken out from under a brooding female who has prepared herself to hatch chicks, she will continue to sit on the empty nest for several days'.[9]

Instincts are adapted to the *animal's natural conditions* and function appropriately under normal conditions. With a change in normal conditions these actions lose meaning, but the animal still persistently repeats them. Of course, if the action were conscious and foreseen, the animal would not mechanically repeat the same movements without success, but would act every time according to the content of the conditions.

§12

Instinct represents the direct and immediate reaction of the organism to the needs necessary for the type or individual. There are no mediated actions here even when this is necessary for the saving of life. If direct action does not lead to the desired result, instinct will never help find a detour. More than that, instinct always urges the animal to direct action, even in those cases where

---

8 Lloyd Morgan 1909, p. 136.
9 Tsiegler 1914, p. 74.

it is useless and fatal. The same can also be said as regards habits acquired in individual experience, the secondary reflexes of the animal, and about all automated actions in general. They all spur to direct action and disrupt the selection of an indirect path, that is, they disrupt the creation of a conscious decision.[10]

A situation resolved directly does not require comprehension, and therefore neither provokes nor gives rise to a conscious decision. For an animal directly to catch prey, it does not require the special work of consciousness; it does so on the basis of inherited or acquired reflexive habits, similar to how humans keep their balance while walking, swimming, and so on.

If an animal is also active to a certain degree in relation to the objects necessary for it, then this activity only manifests itself in the direct striving for the target. Insofar as the target is not immediately present in the field of perception or is not directly accessible, the animal is unable either to 'imagine' and set their mind on a more distant target or to manage a solution. The animal will notice danger and take measures to avoid it only in those cases when that danger directly and immediately threatens it. But in general, it never notices indirect danger. Instinctive and reflexive actions help the animal orient itself in a situation that is resolved via direct and immediate actions; in an indirect situation, animals are able to orient themselves to an extremely small degree.

This direct dependence of animal consciousness on an immediate situation, this immediate dependence between the sensory field and the direct feedback response of the organism represents the predominant means and the basic form of animal behaviour in which the life of animal consciousness flows.

We consider the predominance of instinctive and reflex responses to be the condition of an organism corresponding to the relationship of an animal as consumer to the natural environment: these are essentially two sides of the same direct and immediate relationship to the environment.

Reflexes and instinctive actions are characterised by the absence of mediating processes between the circumstances of the environment and the reactions

---

10   When, for example, a dog was led by the experimenter into a dead end where it is separated from food by grating, it quickly found the exit, turned out of the dead end and reached the food via a circuitous route. When the experiment was repeated with the difference that the food was placed quite close to the grating, the dog pressed its face against the grating multiple times, not moving from the spot and not attempting to find a detour. See Köhler 1921, p. 10. Faced with this seemingly simplest of tasks, the dog remained helpless. Even more striking is the fact that before this, it had immediately solved the exact same task of a shortcut. It should be clear to us, however, that direct orientation on the

of the organism. In the majority of cases of environmental conditions, the given situation immediately provokes the specifically directed actions of the animal *without the mediating work of consciousness*, which could be expressed as 'being aware of the conditions of the situation and the form of one's own actions'. This analytic work of consciousness, so to speak – the work of mediating processes – is not observed here.

On the contrary, in the case of instinctive action, for example, only a single encounter between a definite initial situation (available nuts) and a living creature (a squirrel that is not hungry) is sufficient for the apparatus of action to be set in motion and to work through to the end an apparently previously determined portion, after which the action concludes as if automatically (despite the nut remaining unburied, the squirrel was satisfied with having performed the usual burying movements and rested content).

Reflexive and instinctive actions are characterised by direct orientation on the object of action and the absence of mediating elements both subjectively phenomenal (the absence of 'checks', 'inhibitions', 'internal reflexes') and objective – the absence of mediating actions aiding in the indirect attainment of the goal, the absence of 'work on the means'.

Consciousness represents precisely this middle moment, the mediating element between the objective situation and the reaction of the organism. Consciousness is a subjective process, mediating the relationship between the subject and the objective environment and, on the other hand, mediating the interaction between the subject and another subject. As we will subsequently see, this mediating function of consciousness is developed together with the breakdown of the biological relation of immediacy and with the establishment of the social form of mediating interaction both with the natural environment and with other individuals.

Putting aside for the moment the question of what proper consciousness (perception) could develop from, we will note the following: in any case, instinctive and reflexive actions could not lead to it. On the contrary, they are rather the dead ends of consciousness; not only are they not conducive to perception, they hamper its rise by transferring what is perceived into the field of unconscious actions.

---

target (the food), lying right in front of the dog's nose but on the other side of the grating and conditioned by its extreme proximity and the powerful input of its scent, defeated the impulse to find a detour and pushed the dog into direct action, impeding comprehension of the situation.

The Intellectual Activity of Animals

§13

Besides these instinctive and reflective actions, can such manifestations of deliberate conscious behaviour be observed in animals? Can cases of rational behaviour be found in animals, and under what conditions do they take place?

In directing the reader's attention towards two scientifically quite serious attempts at settling this question, we have in mind on the one hand the experiments of the American scientist Edward Thorndike,[11] and on the other the experiments of German psychologist Wolfgang Köhler.[12] On the whole, these two experiments contradict each other in the sense of both their initial methodological positions and their results.

In Thorndike's experiments, hungry animals (cats and dogs) were placed in specially constructed cages. Food was placed in front of the cage, and they observed how the animal succeeded in freeing itself from the cage and getting out to the food, how much time this operation took, and at what point the animal learned by heart the definite method that would free it from the cage. The door of the cage was opened by a system of complex mechanical devices that ended inside the cage with only the final part – a cord to be pulled, a handle to be turned, or a plate to be pressed. From inside it was impossible to see how the mechanism as a whole worked. The animal was required to open the door the cage by pulling or pressing a certain part of the mechanism. After thus having freed itself, the animal was rewarded with food and was again placed in the cage; the experiment started over, repeating until the animal completely mastered the specific method of freeing itself and accomplish this without unnecessary movements.

Thorndike reported that sometimes, in order to foster specific conditioned responses in the animals, the experimenter released them when they began to scratch the floor, to scratch themselves, or to clean themselves.

The first manifestation of an animal placed into Thorndike's situation consisted of rushing in the direction of the desired target and colliding with an obstacle. It repeated the same unsuccessful movement several times, sometimes scratching itself bloody on the obstacle.[13] In the intervals between the futile direct attempts it would become anxious, pointlessly rushing about to

---

11 Thorndike 1898.
12 Köhler 1922.
13 It is characteristic of animals placed in a situation where they are separated from the desired target by an obstacle to always begin with attempts at a direct path, even in those cases where this path is obviously impassable.

and fro until it accidentally brushed against one of the devices inside the cage, as a consequence of which the door automatically opened, giving the animal an open path to the food. But does that mean the animal was able to find a solution? Of course not. When it was immediately placed once again into the same conditions, it resumed its whole ordeal instead of using the solution achieved and setting the handle or plate into motion.

In the setting of Thorndike's experiments, the animal casting about in a disorderly manner were not movements directed towards the resolution of a task.[14] For the animal, the 'task' itself does not even exist: it is striving for the food, and not at all searching for a path to reach it. In their objective sense, the anxious, bustling movements that characterise the behaviour of an animal in the given situation have nothing in common with rational searches for a path. The animal is not looking for detours and a rational exit from the situation with these movements, but is urging itself forward again and again towards direct – that is, pointless – actions. During these spontaneous, clamorous, and pointless movements, which Karl Bühler calls 'overproduction of movement' (*Überproduktion von Bewegungen*) and 'aimless attempts' (*zielloses Probieren*),[15] the animal will sometimes in passing brush against the requisite handle or plate. The solution is achieved unexpectedly for the animal, and entirely accidentally as a *collateral result of its chaotic reactions*. After this the process of training begins, with the goal of consolidating these accidentally successful movements as 'secondary reflexes' and eliminating the rest.

Such setups of the experiment led Thorndike to the conclusion that no rudiments of rational behaviour and understanding are observable in animals, and nearly to the conclusion that animals are automatons. This is not surprising, as the principles on which Thorndike's experiments were based – as can easily be seen – assume *a priori* that animals are unconscious automatons whose every action is constructed exclusively on mechanically acquired, blind associative links and on the basis of the frequent repetition of stimulus and reaction.

The conditions of Thorndike's experiments were such that the animals were deprived of the possibility of understanding anything: there was no dependence or meaningful link between action and result; this dependence was purely external and accidental. The situation itself was meaningless, so demanding the manifestation of an intelligent solution from the animal was impossible.

---

14   This is obvious, if only from the fact that animals in this situation repeat the same unsuccessful movements several times until they wear themselves out or accidentally free themselves, having unintentionally engaged the necessary point.
15   Bühler 1918, p. 6.

The meaninglessness of the link between action and result is particularly obvious where, during the course of the experiment, the door was opened for the animal when it started scratching or cleaning itself. Where is the meaningful link here?!

Although the existence of a barrier to the target forms one of the necessary conditions for a conscious solution to arise, this alone is of course insufficient. If there is no barrier to the target, then the situation presents no task to the animal, which solves it directly without the particular work of consciousness and on the basis of hereditary and acquired reflexes. In other words, the actions of the animal will run along the channel of unconscious actions without provoking the work of perception. On the other hand, the existence of a barrier is not a sufficient condition for perception. More is necessary for the meaning of the barrier to somehow be accessible to the animal, that is, for the subject to be equal to the demands of the task. Animals placed in Thorndike's conditions are deprived of the possibility of displaying intelligent behaviour, since the situation is completely inaccessible and unobservable for its intellectual abilities, or the situation itself is meaningless and requires action that is 'on the off chance' (i.e., meaningless). Rational actions cannot, of course, arise under such conditions.

Perception and an ensuing rational decision require:

1) The existence of an obstacle to the target. The situation must be so complex that it does not give way to the usual direct solution by way of habitual automated action. Consequently, it is essential that this be the true state of the task. The task must be so new that it requires another approach and provokes a different means of resolution than the usual reflexive and unconscious one.
2) Furthermore, it is essential that the situation be entirely observable for the animal and so simple and accessible for the aspect being tested that it is capable to some extent of actually solving the task.

These conditions are not observed in Thorndike, and therefore in the experiments there can be no question of the detection of intellectual work in the animal. The work of consciousness begins only when an organism that is generally capable of it is put into the situation of the task that actually contains the possibility of an intelligent solution and is accessible to the intellectual abilities of the aspect being tested. In the experiments of German psychologist Wolfgang Köhler, conducted by him on the anthropoids of Tenerife from 1914 to 1917, these conditions were observed most precisely.

The difficulty of the task lay in creating the conditions of the experiment such that it would be manifestly possible to observe the moment of the *onset of perception*, the *comprehension of the situation*.

The best psychology of thinking, it is said, would be the good psychology of the 'aha!' (i.e., the moment of the onset of understanding). At this exact moment it is possible to observe the boundary that clearly separates the inert, passive, unconscious, blind condition of consciousness (a 'consumer' reflex consciousness) from the understanding, creative consciousness (the living, sharp, clear, perceptive condition of consciousness), when understanding illuminates consciousness all at once like lightning and the situation is embraced by thought and acquires meaning, and understanding begins.

Köhler succeeded in creating the most suitable experimental conditions for observing such an 'aha!' moment in animals, his experiments therefore clearly show when and to what degree animals manifest actual intellectual behaviour. It is here we first encounter the manifestation of the rudiments of resourceful, 'figurative' consciousness in the animal world.[16]

When an animal goes directly and reaches a desired object unhindered, there is no 'intelligence' here – or, rather, we have no evidence of the manifestation of this intelligence. An animal's rational understanding is observed only in those conditions where the work of consciousness is not directly and immediately aimed at the target but at something else that could in turn aid in the attainment of the desired object. In any case, we have the only evidence of the manifestation of an animal's intelligence in indirect actions where attention is directed towards another thing which, as a means, obtains a new meaning other than the one it had up until then.

Köhler creates a setup for the experiment in which the direct path to the target is impassable, and the indirect one – a detour, a roundabout action – remains open. The animal (a chimpanzee) is locked in a cage. A desirable object (fruit or some other food) is placed in front of the cage, at a distance beyond the reach of an extended arm. No practical link exists between the cage and the fruit. However, the situation includes the only means of the link: a stick, lying there in the cage, with which it is possible to drag the fruit closer.[17] The situation is fully observable and accessible to the animal's solution, as the chimpanzee is generally acquainted with the use of a stick. The criterion of intelligence is the ability of an animal independently to find the means for achieving a goal, to

---

16   Köhler set forth the results of his animal research primarily into of his works: 1) *Intelligenzprüfungen an Antropoiden*, Abh. d. kön. Preuss. Akad. d. Wiss. 1917, No. 1 (we use the above-mentioned second edition of this book) and 2) *Nachweis einfacher Strunturfunktionen beim Schimpansen und beim Haushuhn*. Abh. d. Preuss. Akad. d. Wiss., 1918, No. 2. (See the Russian translation, Wolfgang Köhler, *Issledovanie intellekta chelovekopodobnykh obez'ian*, 1930).

17   Köhler 1922, p. 22.

find a mediating, indirect route to a solution (i.e., in this case to use the stick). Change the situation and give the obstacle different forms, and the corresponding variations of possible detours will follow. With this, it is possible to create a gradual accumulation of the difficulties such a task contains for the test subject.

How does a chimpanzee behave in a similar situation? Let us cite Köhler's data.

Nueva, new arrival to the chimpanzee biological station, is put to the test. She was not familiar with the methods of such an experiment and was not brought into contact with the other apes at the station. As a preliminary she was given a stick in the cage, which she scraped on the floor, raked together a pile of banana skins, and then let fall approximately three quarters of a metre from the grating of the cage. Ten minutes later, fruit was placed in front of the cage at a distance beyond the reach of the chimpanzee's long hands. The animal unsuccessfully tried to grab the fruit and began to 'mourn' in the manner characteristic of chimpanzees, producing sounds similar to crying and finally, despairing, rolled around angrily on the ground. Approximately seven minutes of begging and complaining had passed, when upon catching sight of the stick the animal grew quiet, then immediately grabbed the stick and went immediately in the direction of the target, pushing the stick beyond the grating and drawing the fruit to her.[18] *In repeating the experiment the stick was used without any unsuccessful trials* if it was only laying on the floor, observable together with the area of the target.

Köhler's experiments observed all the conditions that aided and enabled a conscious solution and rational behaviour.

1) The animals being tested were preliminarily acquainted in general with the use of a stick, a box, or a rope with whose help the situation was resolved. They had skills in handling these things, both natural (climbing, grasping) and artificial (pushing, transporting boxes, etc.).
2) The situation was accessible to solution by the animal's methods since it was reduced to the operations of grasping, movement, and transportation (i.e., to movements freely performed by the ape).
3) the experiments were organised so that the situation, despite the novelty, was completely observable to the animal and to a certain extent suggested the solution.
4) The experiments were arranged logically by the degree of difficulty and complexity of their execution.

---

18   Köhler 1922, p. 23.

By observing these conditions, the results of the experiments turned out differently than Thorndike's, and the map of animal behaviour looks completely different.

In Köhler's experiments it was always clearly obvious when the animal was 'searching' and 'thinking', and when it was not doing so but simply erratically rushing about from side to side and solved the task accidentally, as with Thorndike. The point is that unpremeditated movements and accidental solutions look different than actual intellectual solutions with comprehension. 'In an accidental solution we have and agglomerate of solitary movements that appear, end, and spring up again; moreover, these separate movements are completely independent of each other in movement and speed'.[19] It is obvious that such erratic movements, independent of and opposed to each other, are not the manifestation of conscious behaviour in relation to a goal. If we depict the trajectory of such movements, then the following diagram is obtained (see Fig. 1, p. 54.)

If a chicken, placed in a dead end fenced off by a grating, sees the target (C) in front of it through the grating and tries to get it, it will always run into the obstacle. If on the path of such a trajectory of erratic movements the animal reaches the target, as happened in Thorndike's experiments, we would say that the solution was accidental and not rational.

The map of conscious behaviour and trajectory of movements in conscious action (fig-01) is completely different than it is in unconscious and accidental action. 'Genuinely rational action flows as a single process, completely closed in on itself both in a spatial and in a temporal relationship',[20] – in our case, as an uninterrupted run, without the slightest stop, from the point where the solution (B) took place to the target (C) itself. On this trajectory of the animal's movement the point where the solution arises and conscious behaviour begins (point B) is even clearly seen topographically. Starting from here, the crooked movement looks different; it does not consist of separate segments but represents one smooth line of movement that reaches the target. It is typical that the moment of solution begins in time not as a simple continuation of these nervous reactions of the animal, but independently of them and along another path. These chaotic reactions and nervous movements do not enable, but hinder the rise of a conscious solution.

The animal usually fills the time before the start of the solution itself with movements and actions that have no connection to the solution or with pauses

---

19   Köhler 1922, p. 12.
20   Köhler 1922, p. 12.

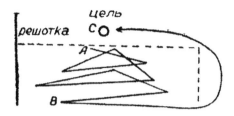

Fig-01

for rest; it is precisely these pauses – for example the pause in which 'Sultan scratched his head and produced no movements apart from the movements of the eyes and slow movements of the head, examining the situation attentively'[21] – that prepare a solution. This shows explicitly what kind of behaviour we are dealing with here. In the majority of cases, a rational solution begins immediately after such pauses and typically runs in one go. Sometimes, after aimless trials, a real solution arrives and then the difference between unpremeditated actions (chaotic reactions) and *conscious* behaviour is especially clearly noticeable. In the latter case the animal suddenly stops, as if puzzled, turns around, and finds the solution to the task in a completely different direction.

In Köhler's experiments, the moment intelligence arises was marked by a particular intensity in the animal, the suppression of purposeless movements, and some kind of momentary freeze. In the majority of cases, the onset of understanding is marked by an unfeigned joy that the individual displays in the moment of 'Eureka!' Köhler shows, that in children the moment of resolution can be determined by their faces: they literally beam. He also observed this change of expression in apes.

In one case when the animal thus solved the task and reached the target, and in another case when it resolved a situation through unpremeditated, secondary movements. The behaviour of the animal in these two occurrences were completely different, and at the base of this difference, of course, lie dissimilar subjective processes.

How does the solution occur? What factors enable it? Typically, the situation itself and its construction are not the least of these. It is as if the situation itself must aim at a solution; if there is none, then it can completely hinder the advent of a solution. When, for example, the stick lay in front of the ape in the same field of vision as the target object, in every case the apes solved the task of using the stick. But the solution came even more easily and smoothly when the stick lay in line with the desired object.

---

21 Köhler 1922, p. 138.

The farther away the stick was from the critical spot, the more difficult its use; it often happens that the stick, not being in use by the animal, loses its value if it is placed sufficiently far away from the target. If the stick is placed so that it does not fall in the field of vision when viewing the target, this could entirely deprive the animal of the possibility of using it. The animal sees the stick, but as it does not see the target simultaneously it is unable to use the stick.[22] According to this theory, the transformation of the stick into a tool and a means – as Koffka correctly notes – is in a sense the function of the geometrical arrangement of the field in which the stick lies and how it lies in the field.

Comprehension of the object – in this case, the stick – consists of the fact that the stick ceases to be perceived as something indifferent, even as a separate object, and becomes a component of the field that resolves the situation. Moreover, perception of the object (the stick) changes entirely. Even the nature of the object perceived changes. What was previously a 'neutral thing' – or represented an object 'for biting', 'for throwing', and so on – now acquires the nature of 'an object for dragging fruit'. The thing that up until then was neutral to the animal (the stick) jumps in as a 'bridge' to the desired situation, resolving it.[23]

From here it is not difficult to see why the spatial distance of the stick hampers resolution of the situation. 'It is natural that a separate thing located in proximity to the target that is causing excitement, and simultaneously visible with it, jumps into and is harnessed to the context more easily than an object spatially more distant – and even more so, if it belongs to another complex that it needs to be taken out of'.[24]

Chaotic reactions displayed by the animal as an indicator of general agitation have nothing in common with conscious behaviour, and do not aid in the rise of a conscious solution – with the exception of cases when such movements accidentally lead the animal to an advantageous position in relation to the situation. When a chicken, as a result of unpremeditated, nervous movements (represented in Fig. 1, p. xx, as the sum of crooked lines from A to B) accidentally finds itself in a more advantageous position that suggests a solution – that is, at point B, opposite the open door – the solution ensues immediately, and further behaviour from this critical point to the target (as the smooth, unbroken curved path from B to C indicates) represents a unified,

---

22   Köhler 1922, p. 26.
23   Koffka 1921, p. 153 (see Russian translation, K. Koffka, *Osnovy psikhicheskogo razvitiia*, 1934).
24   Köhler 1922, p. 136.

integral process. It is clear here that pointless, nervous movements did not so much solve the task as prepared its solution (i.e. arranged the situation favourably).

We will cite a few more examples showing that accidental movements can unexpectedly arrange the situation in favour of a correct solution. A piece of fruit is attached high up to the ceiling. In the cage there is a box that the ape frequently had occasion to deal with: carrying it from place to place, sitting on it, and so on – but never having occasion to use it as a stand. Having used the box, the ape could get the fruit. In this case, however, the box was located to the side of the target, at a distance of three metres. The ape (Koko) tried several times, unsuccessfully, to grab the fruit by leaping off the ground and throwing rope at it; after a number of attempts in vain entirely unrelated to the box, Koko moved away from the target, then returned, and again moved away from the target – and in the course of these wanderings ran into the box. Koko cast a glance at the hanging fruit and gave the box a quick shove – not moving it from its spot, however – and moved away from the box only to return and shove it again ... This was repeated four times, and the box had now been moved ten centimetres closer to the target. Koko again stood by the box and, while looking at the fruit, suddenly took the box and in one movement placed it under the target, leapt up onto it and plucked the fruit.[25]

The point is that the accidental shoves, in a completely unpremeditated fashion, moved the box closer to the target and brought it to a position in which the solution to the task was facilitated. It is as if the box itself suggested this solution; thanks to its proximity to the area of the target, the box was easily inserted into the context as a stand that could resolve the situation. This is particularly clear from the fact that, upon repeating the same experiment with the box somewhat further away from the target than the first time, Koko could not solve the task at all, despite the fact that it seemed that the ape must have acquired experience in such an operation several minutes earlier.

In order for the solution to take place, it was necessary that 'the box tended toward the situation' (*die Kiste tendiert in die Situation hinein*), as Koffka aptly put it.

The solution is even more strongly delayed if the necessary object is part of another complex and needs to be removed from it in order for it to be part of the necessary context for a solution. In these cases, individuals often become unable to use even methods of solution that are well known to them.

---

25   Köhler 1922, pp. 29–30.

These cases are even more significant for describing the structured work of consciousness and for describing the internal changes of the object of perception itself.

Hika (one of the chimpanzees) had perfectly mastered the methods of using the box as a stand, but having worn herself out in trying to reach the high-hanging fruit, did not put the box sitting right there in the middle to use. The box was not something the ape did not notice; on the contrary, she often sat on it when she was tired out from excessive rage. The entire point is that during the experiments, another ape (Tercera) was lying on the box. As soon as she by chance jumped down from the box, Hika immediately solved the task – she took the box, placed it under the target, and plucked the fruit.[26]

Koffka explains this fact as follows: 'When Tercera was lying on the box, the box was not 'an object for reaching the target' but specifically 'an object for lying on'. Under these conditions, the box was not linked with the target. It (the box) was sitting firmly in another situation, in another context, and therefore could not be freely brought into this context as a tool and a means. Removing an object from a given complex and switching it over to another, newly forming context – this relates to especially high-level intellectual activity'.[27] If, for example, the box had been standing against the wall, this would significantly hamper its use. If the box had been standing in the corner, closely abutting both walls, forming as it were an organic part of the corner, no ape could have arrived at the conclusion to use it.

With regard to this problem, Köhler notes: 'a certain optical permanency exists that hampers intellectual activity in pulling parts out of it, similar to how the strongest nails hamper practical attempts at separation. Moreover, the optical permanency does not operate as if the chimpanzee said to itself 'it's no use trying, this board is stuck – it's impossible to tear it away' (in order to use it as a means. K.M.). On the contrary, this permanency of the complex operates in such a way that the chimpanzee in general *does not see the board, does not notice it as a separate part*'[28] (Italics mine. K.M.).

Let us say that you need a flat, round object and spend some time looking for one; with some difficulty, you suspect you could successfully use the lid from a saucepan. The lid is something that belongs to the saucepan itself, forming a single whole with it. But the solution occurs more easily if the lid is not sitting

---

26   Köhler 1922, p. 128.
27   Koffka 1921, p. 140.
28   Köhler 1922, p. 78.

exactly on the saucepan but is hanging off the side (Koffka), and even more so if it is sitting separately from the saucepan.

By their position, things – and by its structure, a situation – often lead people to involuntary thoughts and stimulate them to certain actions. We have had occasion to test this more than once. There were three windows in my apartment that looked out onto the street. The casings of the windows, bound in sheet iron, stood at a height of 1.5 metres from the sidewalk; people passing by the windows automatically struck all three windowsills. Children and teenagers especially excelled at this. I came upon the idea of removing the tiresome iron coverings and took one off the middle window, but this required so much work that I left my venture at that. However, to my surprise and pleasure, the tiresome knocking ceased almost completely. The blows were heard only occasionally, as a very rare exception. The absence of the middle striking point in the series broke up the involuntary impulse so much that the action was in general not produced. The situation, as a result of the loss of this point, underwent such a change that it no longer imposed any involuntary ideas. The objects stopped stimulating mild hooliganism.

What Köhler expressed as: 'By its position in the visual field, the stick acquires definite functional significance for a certain situation',[29] what Koffka tried to say with '*die Kiste tendiert in die Situation hinein*',[30] what Wertheimer formulated as 'the field of perception itself tends towards becoming a semantic whole',[31] we can express in more generalised terms: By their position, it is as if objects themselves are invited into a definite context of understanding; by its composition, the situation itself aspires to thought. Strictly speaking, observing these relationships of things to each other and their relationships to the goal pursued by the subject is comprehension, reasoning, and understanding.

Constructing a field of consciousness thus depends to a significant degree on the composition and structure of the situation itself, subjected to comprehension. Thought is a function that not only depends on the subject (its neurocerebral apparatus), it is at the same time a function that depends on the disposition of the objective situation and the relationships of objects. Objective conditions, the relationships of objects arising in a definite manner, affect consciousness and ultimately lead it to a certain solution – and, in the course of time, to the best of all possible solutions; but again, *the situation does not*

---

29   Köhler 1922, p. 26.
30   Koffka 1921, p. 139.
31   Wertheimer 1925, p. 13.

suggest the necessary solution to every consciousness, only to one that disposed in favour of a definite apperception and can rise to the level of this understanding.

Material conditions and objective relationships are thus also the conditions of thought. Marx expressed this dual conditionality of thought brilliantly: '*It is not enough for thought to strive for realisation, reality* (i.e. the relationship of things – K.M.) *must itself strive towards thought*'.[32]

The basis of thought is not only in the head, but somehow also in the objects, because the conditions for the emergence of these thoughts lie in the objective construction of the environment in which consciousness has occasion to live and act. 'To have one basis for life and one for science is *a priori* a lie'.[33]

Shortcomings of Physiological Psychology and Classical Psychology

§14

Reflexologists, physiologists and the entire physiological school of psychologists adhere to one preconceived assumption: that consciousness is conditioned only by internal neural connections and physiological processes. The neurocerebral apparatus is assumed to be the sole factor defining the forms of consciousness. From this originates the opinion that if the internal workings of this apparatus are studied precisely, then all the secrets of thinking, consciousness and behaviour will be revealed. This is mistaken.

Though consciousness (and also behaviour) is the function of the subject, it is at the same time a function dependent on the objective surroundings. Behaviour is an absurdity, if it is not an indicator of a relationship with the environment. Consciousness and thought without an object of consciousness is nonsense.

Behaviour emerges not only in accordance with neurophysiological and psychological laws, but also vice versa – these laws are formulated in accordance with the conditions of life and the behaviour of a living subject. The neurocerebral apparatus is not only the cause of the function, but most likely also the consequence of these functions. Proving anything based on the apparatus would therefore be extremely one-sided.

---

32   *Aus dem literarischen Nachlass von K. Marx und F. Engels Herausgegeben von F. Mehring*, Stuttgart, 1920, Vol. I, p. 394.
33   Marks i Engel's 1927–1935, Vol. III, p. 629.

'In order to study behaviour', the behaviourists, reflexologists and other physiologists say, 'we have to observe it in extreme detail and adhere to the facts that can be recorded and measured'. The ideal of study is considered to be a full account of the secretions of every gland, the curve of respiration, the pulse; and the knowledge of all the separate movements produced in the organism as the result of the action of a specified stimulus. If this goal (a full account of the sum of movements and the condition of all the parts of the body) were attainable, then as a result of such grandiose work the behaviour of an individual would be no more understood than if someone who wanted to understand a sage proverb began looking for its meaning in a mathematical formula defining the oscillations of the air when articulating it.

How could this be, if it turns out that the same neurophysiological processes, in different cases, bring about different states of consciousness, and vice versa – the same subjective experiences can be brought about as a result of the actions of different neurophysiological processes? There are known cases of sound being absorbed in paints.[34]

If the entire essence of the matter is reduced to the question of the neural apparatus, then the difference between animals and humans is presented as a quantitative difference in the degree of complexity of this apparatus, in the complexity of the integration of receptor and motor paths, and so on. Thus it turns out that the difference in the behaviour of a human and an animal is only one of degree, and not of essence. Typically, with nearly all physiologists it unavoidably comes out like this: a human is an animal like all the others, only at a much higher *biological* level of development; human behaviour is governed by the same natural laws that govern animals in general. From this arises the requirement that the same methods of study be applied to humans as to animals. Only one care is taken: not to ascribe human qualities to animals (anthropomorphism). But no one sees to it that animal qualities are not ascribed to humans. On the contrary, this transfer of zoopsychological data onto humans is considered to be in the order of things, is encouraged, and is recommended. N.A. Ridec places people in almost the same exact experimental conditions as Thorndike placed his cats and dogs.

Human behaviour should never be assessed from the point of view of a 'conditional stimulant'. The societal conditions for the rise of social ideas should never be called 'stimuli', even provisionally. The idea and social ideology should

---

34   One physiologist who is not entirely unknown could find nothing better than to respond to me that this was idealism. That is, if a physicist confirms that the same thermal state is brought about by completely different arrangement of the movement and velocity of (gas) molecules, then it could be objected that this was idealism and obscurantism. But

never be accepted as 'a reaction to a specific stimulus' or as 'an inhibitory reflex'. In general, applying the terminology of animal behaviour – 'irritation', 'stimulus', 'reflex' – to human social existence and human consciousness is impossible. 'A human differs from a ram in that consciousness replaces instinct for them, or rather that their instinct is conscious' (Marx).

It must be understood that if a scientist devotes their entire life to the painstaking study of rats, this does not occur because rats 'stimulated' them or that they are a 'social stimulant'. Very likely, the behaviour of a bureaucrat cannot be explained by any 'stimuli'. This unfortunate terminology, based on neural theory, must be left behind. Humans, though they are animals, are only partly so. What interests us in them is not the animal, but what remains in addition to this 'partly' – precisely that aspect that can only be studied in them alone: they are social creatures, and therefore rational; creative, and not only passively consuming, with consciousness.

There is a debate – a long-running one – between physiologists and psychologists: who is to study the laws of behaviour and of the mind? Each of the sides, in questioning the other's claims, assert their own exclusive right. On the question of acknowledging the principal matters in the formation of consciousness, subjectivist psychologists insist on what they call the 'mental factor', allegedly the defining immanent psychical laws of the life of consciousness. Physiologists demand that all psychic processes be explains purely psychologically, based on physiological causes. 'Cerebral and neural processes', says zur Strassen, one of the better-known representatives of this school, 'can in no way be made simpler and more comprehensible through joining the mental processes of consciousness to them. In the role of the subjective reflection of physical and chemical neural processes, consciousness falls completely out of the picture of our study of causes and does not affect its results'.[35]

There are theoreticians who recognise both these 'factors'.

But in fact neither mental nor physiological causes are factors. The true factors forming the human means of consciousness are the social conditions and the social relations among which consciousness has to live and act.

---

in our opinion, idealism does not consist of the fact that the same neural processes can bring about different states of consciousness, but of the fact that when the monstrous Cartesian-era theory of psychophysical parallelism is taken as a prerogative, it is as if a specific neural process corresponds fully with each state of consciousness and vice versa. That is incontrovertible idealism. In different general states and different general orientations of consciousness, the same neuroreceptor processes can produce completely different subjective experiences.

35   Zur Strassen 1908.

With all their psychic make-up, humans should above all be the object of the social sciences. Physiologists and psychologists, insofar as the touch on human nature, must reconstruct their work in accordance with the social essence of humanity, or else they will study not what is human in humans, but what is animal – which is much easier to do on other kinds of animals.

Such was the demand of Marx and of Lenin, the strikingly prescient thinkers who could outpace the current state of our sciences by centuries.

On Gestalt Psychology

§ 15

Traditional psychology, for the explanation of mental reality, had a systematic outline of rubrics at the ready with the prepared labels 'perception', 'idea', 'memory', 'attention' and so on according to which it distributed all the phenomena of consciousness. Psychologists considered themselves fully satisfied if they succeeded in laying out a mental act, even if nominally, in a series of the simplest mental atoms ('perceptions', 'elementary senses', 'volitional impulses') and in mixing these elements according to the stereotypical systematic outlines.

The shortcomings of such a method – carelessly cutting up a living human into the most basic elements and seeing in the human only 'a sack of stimuli and perceptions' – together with the lack of detail of the ideas of this radificational outline for explaining the whole, rich, living psyche of a human are experienced by many, and this lay at the foundation of the feeling of disappointment that anyone who had occasion to go through the school of classical psychology and to patiently study the lessons on all the differential thresholds of perception, of the senses, of memory, of will and so on. Gestalt psychology and its champions are valuable in that they first expressed these doubts and showed, on the basis of splendidly constructed experiments, the naïve and groundless concepts with which classical psychology was operating and the inertness of a psychological thought that had been distorted for decades on arbitrary, untested and completely improbable assumptions.

But Gestalt psychology, as far as we are able to judge, has two essential shortcomings: first, extreme objectivism, and second, the historical positions it occupied in relation to human psychology. Gestalt psychology is too 'objective'. According to its tenets, behaviour is exclusively defined by the objective relationship of things and the objective structure of the field in which consciousness has to orient itself. This is only partially correct, and that only in relation to the animal level of consciousness. The inaccuracy and incorrectness

FROM THE ANIMAL LEVEL OF CONSCIOUSNESS TO HUMAN THINKING

of this position consists of the proposition that the construction of the field of consciousness is entirely a function dependent on the arrangement of the situation. Undoubtedly, the structure of the situation here plays a significant role, but this alone is still far from sufficient for a given solution to take place. The same situation could be resolved by other means: it could suggest different thoughts to different consciousnesses. Which of these possible solutions will be put into effect depends not only on the objective composition of the environment and the properties of the situation, but also on *the predisposition of the consciousness*.[36]

Four beads scattered on a table do not by themselves form a triangle plus one bead

Object 1

or a quadrilateral

Object 2

or two triangles joined at the base;

Object 3

it is simply bead plus the rubber band and the pencil lying next to them. Or, if you like, these beads simultaneously form *any of these shapes*. It depends

---

36 At the same time, it should not be forgotten that humans, in their thinking and in their behaviours are formed not only by an immediately perceived situation (like animals) but also conceivable and imagined ones.

on the subject and the tendency of their consciousness which constructions they take these items in and what they perceive in these objects – that is, what change the field of consciousness undergoes in encountering such a situation. Perception, consciousness, and thinking essentially do not represent anything other than a change of this kind in the field of consciousness.

Which solution 'chooses' the ape – applying the stick or manufacturing a universal skeleton key! – depends not only on the objective arrangement of the situation at hand and on objective conditions in general, but above all on the qualities of the subject themselves and the level of their development. In this experimental moment the onset of the solution depends on the general orientation of consciousness, for example when the animals were not interested (e.g. not hungry), all the observer's efforts were in vain; the animals manifested no intelligence and found no solutions. The onset of a given solution is consequently the function not only of the arrangement of objects, but of *the predisposition of the subject* (e.g. the state of consciousness itself).

That side of the matter, according to which objective relations define the consciousness and the behaviour of a subject, is fully and fruitfully developed in Gestalt psychology. But then the other, more essential side is forgotten (especially when the question is *human* consciousness) – the side of the subject, who is not simply subordinate to the dictates of the situation but who as an active being builds and creates this situation themselves. In any case, it is not involved in either the theoretical or the experimental constructions of the adherents of Gestalt psychology; its significance is not explained despite the facts insistently pointing this out. It cannot to be said that this moment is completely lost in the constructions of Gestalt psychology, but that it is not favoured with the necessary attention and elaboration befitting it – this is indisputable. At the same time, this side of the matter ought to be placed at the very head of the line in all those cases where the question is the creative consciousness and the goal-oriented activity of a human in contrast to the inert consciousness of an animal, limited to the narrow sphere of the fields of perception immediately at hand.

Obviously, the one-sidedness just mentioned has to do with the number, so to speak, of discipline-specific shortcomings (e.g. conditioned by the nature of the field of work with which these scientists were primarily occupied): the psychology of infancy, the psychology of animals, in which the situation at hand, defining the behaviour of the individual, plays a predominant role.

In the constructions of Gestalt psychology, the subject (the ego) is part of the general field of the environment. This is not bad thinking, but as the subject is the most essential part – insofar as the matter concerns the study of the human means of consciousness and human behaviour – and as the human environment is not a natural but above all a social and cultural one created by humans themselves, this side of the issue is left in the shadows. In Gestalt psychology, the subject and their active role are ignored.

Marx said: 'It is not enough for thought to strive for realisation, reality must itself strive towards thought'. If classical psychology, reflexology and behaviourism failed to take into account the second part of this formula, then Gestalt psychology ignores the first part. If reason and understanding are the judgement of the relationships of things and events to one another, then the degree and quality of this judgement still depend on the subject, on their maturity in relation to these problems and on the predisposition of their consciousness at the given moment. If the subject is not disposed towards a given perception, then despite the existence of a situation with a specific tendency they will remain unsuccessful, they will not perceive and they will not find a solution. It follows from this that Köhler's thesis on the 'visibility' of the situation requires a more precise clarification. But if the specifically tending objective relationships of things continue to surround the subject, playing a certain role in their life, then with the appropriate disposition of consciousness a solution to the situation will arise. Consequently, insofar as objective relations emerge more frequently with a certain orientation, continually stimulating consciousness in a given direction, then, ultimately, they will impose their solution onto consciousness – and over time the best solution. But again – not just onto any consciousness, but only a motivated consciousness equal to these tasks. The foundation of thought is neither located only within the neurocerebral apparatus, nor in mere objects and objective conditions.

There is undoubtedly a grain of psychological truth in the widely known saying about a 'poorly placed thing' that has been stolen – which, however, does not justify theft. Objects, of course, provoke those who indiscriminately yield to the provocation. But the main thing is that the provocation is *merely the self-provocation of the subject*. Ultimately, in theft the object as such actually has nothing to do with it! Gestalt psychology has another, even more material shortcoming, which consists of the fact that the mental constitution of a human is regarded as a *natural* formation, supposedly exclusively subordinate to its own *internal natural laws, and not as a historical formation*. In almost all its theoretical constructions, Gestalt psychology leans on the narrow field of physical and mental correspondences and uses intrapsychical motives, failing to account for the fact that human consciousness, both in its origins and in its content and construction, is of *social* origin and of a historical makeup. Gestalt psychology regards the life of consciousness as a particular case of the universal law of constitution, and forgets that the construction and the mechanisms of human consciousness are formed under the influence of social forces and causes, not natural conditions. The aim of Gestalt psychology – attempting to embrace the entire mental development of animals and humans with a single principle – is fundamentally mistaken.

The Manifestation of Consciousness in Animals

§ 16

In unusual situations, two means of orientation can be observed in animals: training and rational behaviour. We have already examined the latter. As regards training, it must be said that when an animal is placed in Thorndike's conditions or in conditions of training in general, receiving food only in connection with a definite response, it is clear that there is no semantic dependence between the food as a target and the 'stimulus', or even the action itself, except a purely mechanical one arbitrarily assumed by the experimenters themselves. The animal has to learn to 'choose' a certain 'stimulus' and not to react to others, and to respond only to that stimulus (i.e. the one 'after which it is fed').

In such conditions, the animal solves the task – as has already been shown – purely by accident, inadvertently hitting the desired spot during its blind responses. Subsequent training tasks consist of imprinting the inadvertently successful action as a 'conditioned reflex' in the animal with the help of a multitude of *repetitions*.

This training process has been given a purely mechanistic interpretation, according to which the elimination of 'incorrect' reactions and support of the 'correct' (i.e. 'rewarding') reactions occurs without any involvement and assistance from the consciousness of the animal itself. It was assumed that the links between certain actions and their results are established purely mechanically owing to the *multitude of repetitions*.

On this point, Köhler makes a substantive correction. He shows that even these means of the most incoherent instruction require a certain observancy on the part of the animal; that in training, we have the manifestation of a certain element of *understanding*. Köhler drew attention to an extraordinarily important 'detail' in the process of training, usually omitted by other researchers from the statistics of the distribution of the animal's correct and mistaken responses in the training experiments to choose from. It turned out, that if at first the correct and mistaken choices followed each other purely by chance in roughly equal quantities, then after a certain amount of time the moment of breakthrough came almost immediately, clearly evident by the fact that afterwards the mistaken reactions were scarcely repeated. Out of 50 acts of choice, the ape Hika made 25 mistakes up to the turning point, and afterwards only four. From this, Köhler drew a fully valid conclusion: 'finding the essential material for training (*herausfinden des eigentlichen Dressurmaterials*) is the basic task of the animal in training a selection'.[37]

After the animal differentiates the material on which it is being trained (a sign, a signal or an action), the number of incorrect actions falls sharply. This means that a change has occurred in the animal's field of consciousness and that specific phenomena have received a certain meaning (i.e. have turned into the 'central point of orientation'). The animal has learned to perceive objects and phenomena that were until then meaningless to it and that it could not perceive. We say 'it understood what was required of it'. New actions leading to success are retained in the animal's consciousness only when its significance is somehow noted – when the animal 'guesses' how to make some sort of connection between the action and the successful result (i.e. understanding after which specific action it will be fed).

These facts decisively refute the ideas of the adherents of classical psychology – the physiologists, associationists, and so on – on the role of multiple repetitions for imprinting of 'associative links'; here, we have only one repetition (specifically the last one), in terms of quantity entirely the same as all the preceding ineffective repetitions, but as a result a sudden and complete change in the whole state of consciousness and in the course of training.

Consequently, it must be admitted that even in training – this most absurd and senseless teaching – animals (despite the callousness of the experimenters) nonetheless display an element of rational behaviour, an element of consciousness.

§17

By way of a preliminary summary, we can say that in isolated cases, acts of rational behaviour can be observed in animals. This occurs in a combination of condition, for example when the animal is placed in the situation of a task where surmounting it is within reach of its mental abilities.

Is the problem of consciousness solved by this? Although perception arises in these cases, does it persist? Are these actions conscious in subsequent repetitions?

---

37   Köhler 1918, p. 51.

It is generally known that such actions, being repeated, become automated and run along the lines of reflex responses (i.e. unconsciously): the animal moves towards the target from its original location, avoiding obstacles automatically but, however, manifesting no work of perception. A significant number of such automated actions also partly characterise human behaviour: walking, riding a bicycle, swimming, writing and so on. We learn how to swim with a great deal of difficulty and consideration, but once we have learned – the action runs its course without our intentional assistance. These actions are performed unconsciously, and focusing attention on them disrupts their orderly flow. When you think about which hand to stretch out now and how to push off with your feet, proper swimming is disrupted and you inevitably swallow some water. When you stop to consider which foot to step forward with and how to take each step, your walking will constantly be disrupted.

Köhler's experiments showed that in a somewhat changed situation, the animals' movements, which had become automatic to them, were disrupted. They hindered the emergence of a correct resolution and led to 'absurd' mistakes. Consequently, these actions do not help a state of awareness to persist; on the contrary, the latter is led back into a state of being unaware.[38]

At the moment it arises – as experiments show – the resolution of a situation is indeed a conscious action. But furthermore, this occurs: with multiple repetitions, these processes – forming a pattern – begin running automatically, as if as a result of training. The conscious apparatus is not set into motion and the individual is not aware of whether or not it is an action, in the given case. If, for example, a chimpanzee rationally resolved the situation on the first try, then after multiple repetitions that same action would have become involuntary. The ape employed a process that had become habitual for it, disregarding the state of the situation in every individual case. When the situation changed in such a way that application of the acquired action could not lead anywhere, the animal nonetheless reached for the solution it had learned while the possibility of a much easier solution lay much closer.[39] The uniformity of the situation, the uniformity of conditions and the repetition of the exact same actions do not enable the emergence of a conscious state, just as direct

---

38   As soon as a normal situation in which an automated process (walking, riding, etc.) customarily runs its course is disrupted, consciousness immediately intervenes in the matter and changes the action in accordance with the demands of the situation. This fact is completely remarkable. It shows that consciousness requires continually renewing conditions around it – constantly problematic circumstances, so to speak.

39   See Köhler 1922, pp. 140, 141.

and habitual action does not enable it. These conditions prevent the ascent of a conscious state and lead it back to automated actions and a state of being unaware.

Thus we see that in both cases – in the case of learning through training and in the case of independent rational action – the conscious process in animals *returns once again to unconscious reflexes; the conscious state* switches back to a state of being unaware.

Johannes Lindworsky, in one of the principal objections to Köhler, advances the argument that the behaviour of apes cannot be conscious, intellectual action based on the fact that anthropoids, as opposed to humans, have displayed a continual and insurmountable moral vegetation at the exact same level of development for millennia.[40]

Lindworsky draws a mistaken conclusion from a correct position on the stagnation in the intellectual development of animals: that for this reason animals do not possess the rudiments of understanding. The facts cited by Köhler are too intelligible to be doubted. Without a doubt, animals manifest an element of consciousness. Proceeding from this, some believe that once the spark of consciousness has flared up, fed by an internal flame, it must never be extinguished but burn ever brighter, reshaping both life and itself according to the commands of consciousness.

Lindworsky reasons thus: if animals have consciousness and reason, then where are the results? Where is the development? Since there are no results, there is therefore no consciousness. Obviously, other facts have mistakenly appeared to us as the facts of consciousness.

Here is where the error begins. A single emergence of consciousness, or its episodic existence, is insufficient. Its persistence – and, moreover, its development – require the existence of the necessary basis and the proper conditions surrounding it that can continually feed it, support it, and facilitate its development. Otherwise, the splendid tree of consciousness will wither every time; consciousness will die out, arise again and fade again and possibly remain forever at the lowest level, never exceeding the boundaries of the natural elements and never leading its bearer beyond the borders of the 'enchanted' kingdom of biology.

The reason that animal consciousness does not lead its bearer beyond the boundaries of animal life is that consciousness in general does not do that. On the contrary, it itself takes shape in conformity with the objective circumstances of an individual's life.

---

40   *Stimmen der Zeit*, No. 97, 1919, p. 66. See also Lindworsky 1922.

The reason for this lies in the absence of *social* conditions and productive life among the animals, which first create the solid basis for the persistence of consciousness and for its development. Lindworsky's mistake is in his basic premise: consciousness develops out of itself, conditions life and moves it. This mistake is not a particular mistake of Lindworsky's, but a general mistake of the entire concept of idealism.

Conscious action does not arise even when the subject is capable of it, if there is not some novelty of situations, if there is no necessity for indirect action – if there is no condition of a task. But after consciousness arises, it does not persist if the situation is not constantly renewed and if ever newer tasks do not arise before it. Insofar as action is immediately directed at an object and obstacles that are either in the way or capable of arising are not taken into account every time, there is no continual anxiety about 'whether the exact same action will lead to the desired result'; insofar as there is no mediating act between the subject and the object of action (i.e. if there are no continual searches for new means, and hence conditions for new reflections are absent), there is therefore no regularity of consciousness and a consciousness state does not persist.

For consciousness not to fade out, two things are necessary:

1) the existence of an objective environment that continually stimulates consciousness in a certain direction; and
2) the existence of a task situation (i.e. conditions that continually hamper direct habitual action and that every time compel new mediation); the existence of conditions that continually *perplex* consciousness.

In order for a conscious state to persist, continual renewal of the conditions around the subject and new acts of mediation are required. This means: however complex the range of reflections between the basic target object and the subject, the action of the subject – even a mediated one – must give rise to an impulse towards new mediation. This properly forms the living progress of cognition, the essential deepening of reality, and the movement of cognition from phenomenon to essence.

Conditions in nature and the natural environment for the existence of the animal, of course, cannot create such conditions, either objectively or subjectively. These conditions are given only in social reality, where industrial life and social relations create the world of ideas, and ideas – being converted into objects – receive an objective existence in material and spiritual culture.

Distinguishing Characteristics of Human Consciousness

§ 18

The conscious activity of humans, called 'labour', cannot be regarded as a more sophisticated form of the activity of animals – Köhler's apes, for example. Will, ability, acumen, and an 'orientation' in the objective environment of tools, soils, forests and minerals alone are insufficient for an individual to perform labour: above all, they must have the conditions for labour or be given access to them. Here, the 'will' of the owners of the material conditions of labour (in the conditions of a capitalist economy, feudal landed property or communal property, etc.) plays a decisive role.

On the other hand, the environment surrounding humans and the objects they deal with represent not the gifts of nature but the products of human activity, the objects of some form of ownership. If the subject is human activity, this is where the essential point lies. At the same time, it is the decisive force in the process of formation of human consciousness and thought. Human activity, the types and branches of activity, the means of production and so on depend on these social conditions, alien to the nature of biological activity.

The conditions that create human consciousness intrinsically differ from the conditions of animal consciousness in the surroundings of natural elements.

In this chapter, we will take up clarification of the issue of the role played by labour as such in the process of the composition and development of human thinking, leaving the consideration of the social conditions of labour and the social conditions of consciousness – these most essential questions of thinking – for the following chapters.

Marx said: 'A spider conducts operations that resemble those of a weaver, and a bee puts to shame many an architect in the construction of her cells. But what distinguishes the worst architect from the best of bees is this, that the architect raises his structure in imagination before he erects it in reality. At the end of every labour process, a result emerges which had already been conceived by the worker at the beginning, hence already existed ideally. He not only effects a change of form in the material on which he works, but he also realises a purpose of his own that gives the law to his modus operandi, and to which he must subordinate his will'.[41]

Labour activity consequently presupposes the existence of an idea, of imagination. In the conventional language of psychology, this is called a reproduced representation or an internal image, in contrast to the visual represent-

---

[41] Marx 1923, p. 134 (Marx 1996, p. 134).

ation of an object located in the field of immediate perception. We will retain this terminology, understanding it to mean the representation of objects, situations or events located beyond the limits of the immediate sensory field.

We say that a reproductive representation or internal image of a visual sequence is the advantage of humans: animals, evidently, do not possess them.

Experimental data does not confirm the existence of reproductive representations in animals. In any case, the results of the experiments say that they do not play an appreciable role in the lives of animals. We have in mind only the reproductive forms of visual sequences; nothing is known to us about the representations of instinct, taste, hearing and the other senses. The materials from observations in this area are extremely weak, and too poor for it to be possible to express a definite opinion.

In all probability, the ability for representation only becomes apparent at a significantly higher level of mental development. Humans possess this ability in quite a limited range. They obviously cannot reproduce every sensory quality in their memories. Rare is the person who can successfully revive the representations of the senses of taste or smell in their consciousness as clearly and as vividly as a visual form. There are a great many people who are unable to reproduce auditory impressions – for example, singing an elementary melody in their mind. The representational ability in humans extends primarily to the area of visual – and to a lesser degree, auditory – impressions. Visual representations are absent in animals. It is possible that they have other representations – instinctual, for example – but for us, that remains unknown. We only know one thing: that animals can manage completely without them (i.e. having generally no reproductive representations); they are able to orient themselves in their environment.

Objects that are not located in an animal's field of immediate sensory perception do not appear in its consciousness as clear forms. As soon as the stick, which had many times before been in use by the animal (a chimpanzee), was moved further away from the target so that when surveying the area of the target it did not fall into the field of vision and when looking at the stick, the target was not visible (for example, if the stick lay against the rear wall behind the chimpanzee so when turning towards it, the target disappeared from the field of vision), then in no case were the apes able to make use of the stick.

Köhler gave the following description of these experiments: 'By any means I could, I drew the attention of Chego (one of the apes) to the sticks lying by the rear wall of her cage. She looked at them, but since she could not see the area of the target at the same time, the sticks remained useless and meaningless to her; she did not touch them. Even when, one morning, we forced her to take the stick from that location and put it to use – in the repeat experiment, when the sticks were lying in the same place, the ape proved to be unable to use them, despite the fact that when pacing about the cage in search of a solution, she often approached the sticks and looked at them. At the same time, any stick and any of its substitutes (a bunch of straw, a piece of wire, and so on) located in the field being surveyed together with the area of the target, was put to use without delay or hesitation'.[42] However, Chego even ran into her sleeping box to fetch a blanket. She pushed the material through the grating, hit the fruit with it and whipped them towards her.[43] At first glance it could appear that the work of a reproductive representation is present – that the ape revived the form of the blanket in her mind. But in Köhler, we find the following note on this point: 'The open door to the sleeping box is located right next to the grating, in the foreground and off to the side, so that Chego, being opposite the target, could – with an insignificant shift of her gaze, still keeping the area of the target in her field of vision – see the blanket through the open door, no closer to the target than the stick by the rear grating. But if the ape turned her face to the sticks, the area of the target left her field of vision'.[44]

This role of the sensory field in the intellectual activity of animals is particularly obvious in those cases when the stick is gradually moved, without the animal noticing, closer to the field that is observable together with the target. *As soon as the stick passes a definite, critical boundary, it is immediately perceived and used by the ape; up until that line, it remains useless.*[45]

K. Bühler, attempting to analyse the data from Köhler's experiments about the use of sticks as a means by chimpanzees, says: 'It is unsurprising ... in any case, the link between a branch and fruit should be well known to the inhabitant of a tree. Now that it is sitting in a cage, behind a grating beyond which there is fruit without a branch, and inside the cage a branch (i.e. the stick) without fruit, then from a psychological point of view the main task consists of *uniting these two experiences in an idea* into one; the rest is self-evident'.[46]

Such reasoning is highly unsound. The visual forms of past experiences of life in the forest and the astounding reasoning of a wild animal – 'this stick, essentially, is a branch, only without fruit', and 'this is fruit, but it lacks a branch' – change into the even more staggering conclusion of the animal 'to unite them in an idea, and then in action'. (?) If an ape used visual representations so freely and so broadly, then it would have no difficulty imagin-

---

42   Köhler 1922, p. 27.
43   Köhler 1922, p. 25.
44   Köhler 1922, p. 27.
45   Köhler 1922, p. 27.
46   Bühler 1921, p. 22.

ing the application of a stick in any situation. The precise form of memory about what has been seen even a minute beforehand does not usually remain with an animal. Objects and phenomena not located in the field of immediate sensory perception do not exist in the animal's representation as distinct images.

One specialist academic objected to me on this point: 'So how does a dog recognise its owner by appearance, seeing them from a distance? A clear image of its owner must have been retained in the dog's brain'. We will venture to unroll this inference as follows: consequently, the dog compares the form of this human placed before its eyes with its internal reproductive representation of its owner and finds a correspondence(?!).

Such an objection cannot be regarded as well-founded. The existence of an internal image is not required in order to recognise something familiar. When, for example, we detect some kind of odour, we are able to identify it correctly – a rose, or a violet – but we cannot freely reproduce odours in our conception. In any case, the reproduction of instinctual experiences never succeeds with such clarity and demonstrativeness as, for example, the reproduction of the face of an acquaintance or of any melody at all, which anyone can convince themselves of by their own experience. Odours, sensations of taste, physical pain, and even tactile experiences are very difficult to reproduce in the memory with living clarity, while we freely recognise them. The feeling of 'familiarity' is far from a witness to the existence of a reproductive image. Recognising an acquaintance occurs without an internal image.

Of course, it cannot be said that animals do not sense the absence of objects or people who constitute objects of interest to them. The absence of food is sharply felt by an animal, but neither an internal image of a food box nor an idea of what the food itself looks like arises in its consciousness. A puppy senses the absence of its mother, but her image does not figure in its consciousness. The animal senses the absence of something as a *gap*, as the lack of something, but never as the concrete, explicit image of a definite object. The experience in this case is much closer to the general feeling that 'something is not there' – the sensation of something missing and the striving to meet that lack. There is a major difference between the two states of consciousness: a diffuse general feeling – 'there is something edible in that direction' – and a clear visual representation – 'in that place, on the right, in the corner by the black stove there is, by appearance and odour, some kind of food on some kind of platter'.

In its imagination, of course, a carrier pigeon does not have a living map of what the path or place before it looks like, or of where it is flying; otherwise we would have to be amazed at why this bird did not pass ahead of humanity and did not create a better world of culture and better science.

Fish can also recognise familiar things. L. Edinger showed that fish were able to recognise places that were previously known to them. They could be tamed, 'remember' the place they were fed, and even the appearance of the person feeding them. Nonetheless, it would be absurd to suppose the existence of visual representations of memory in fish. The data of physiological attributes completely exclude the possibility of such a hypothesis. The function of the cerebrum (which in fish is so thin that for a long time it completely escaped observation) differs drastically from the functions of the human brain, and it would be meaningless to ascribe to fish the same consciousness as that in humans. Edinger correctly noted that fish were not required to have conscious memories in order to recognise the feeding place and the appearance of the feeder.

In the life of animals, we encounter the phenomenon of 'striving towards a goal' in those cases where the goal is not located in the field of immediate perception – the search for food or lying in wait by a predator to capture prey, for example – but this does not mean that the image of the victim figures in the imagination of the predator. This can take place on the basis of instinct, and the only thing the animal realises – without even being aware of it – is the general feeling of hunger, and not a living representation of an object able to satisfy that hunger.

If, in order to resolve the situation and achieve the goal it is necessary to *think of* a means – even the most elementary – and use it, however, then in these cases even the most developed animal proves to be helpless. They are incapable of inducing representations in their memories.

The following could be objected: we have just proven that animals are capable of displaying rational activity; how can they produce such activities without having an idea of the result (i.e. what will come out of them)?

Koffka provides all such doubts with a fully satisfactory explanation. The rational activity of animals (i.e. the comprehension of a situation) are in no way events taking place in the field of representation. This process can play out in its entirety in the field of perception, in the phenomenon of perception itself. The material itself (and consequently, after perception) often undergoes changes with lightning speed and is composed of a definite semantic whole. The perception itself, thus changed, influences the motor centres. The activity adapts itself to new impressions, conforming to the changed field. The specific organisation of the perceptive and motor aspect of behaviour takes place as a single act.[47]

---

47 Koffka 1921, p. 127.

This means that the field of perception is reorganised in such a way that the material of perception appears in a new light. The perception, not passing through the apparatus of representation and reproductive images that animals do not possess, and not undergoing conscious analysis, immediately lead to a corresponding action of the motor system and induce definite reactions. The entire affair plays out 'not in the field of representations, but in the field of perception itself'.[48]

As a result of his long observations, Köhler came to the conclusion that chimpanzees – these highly developed animals – did not possess living forms of visual memory. Despite the fact that vision in the apes is better developed than in other members of the animal world, reproduced visual representations play no role whatsoever in the mental activity of anthropoids.

If we admit that animals possess visual representations of memory, it would place us before two insoluble questions. How could animals manage with these representations, when very simple optical complexes are inaccessible for their mental abilities? The operation of images requires a highly sensitive and developed intellect, which animals do not have. Representations and images would remain a dead, useless burden, hindering – and not helping – the animal's orientation. There is no doubt that a 'dreaming animal' would not long survive.

On the other hand, if we admit that animals can use representations, make completely intellectual constructions and compose imaginary dispositions, then it would remain completely incomprehensible why wild animals do not change their way of life on the basis of conscious memory and purposeful activity, or why they do not develop and pass beyond the animal state. The reproductive image is the great advantage of the human level of consciousness. Not only is the animal consciousness incapable of retaining living optical images of recollection, but even human consciousness is often compelled to vigorously exert itself in order to retain living images in memory and prevent their blurring and decay.

In the development of children from the ages of 10 months to 2 years, it is possible to observe how the memory image gradually becomes stronger and how the time of its retention in consciousness gradually lengthens. At ages up to one year, whatever disappears from the child's field of vision immediately vanishes from their memory. At the age of two, the image lasts for a few hours before it becomes blurred and disappears.

It is known that children (from 10 to 12 months) who for some reason evidenced a liking for some object – a ball, for example – do not agree to any kind of

---

48 Koffka 1921, p. 152.

substitution if it is located within their field of vision. But if the ball disappears from the optical field, the child accepts a substitution of a box, a bottle, a stick, and so forth.

An eleven-month-old girl on whom we conducted our observations, had taken a liking to a comb. As soon as the comb entered her field of vision, she began reaching out for it and would not be enticed by anything else.

Once, while tramping around the room holding a ball in one hand and the comb in the other, the girl dropped the comb, which without her noticing was replaced by a matchbox, having briefly covered the object she dropped. As soon as the girl 'succeeded in freeing herself', she rushed to pick up what she had dropped and – though somewhat confused – nonetheless took the box instead of the comb and was as satisfied as if she were in possession of her beloved comb. Any attempt to take the comb away from her and to placate her with another toy, so long as the comb was visible to her, put the girl in a state of fury and she began to cry frantically.

The comb, having unexpectedly disappeared from her field of vision, left in the child's consciousness not its distinct image, but a general sensation of a *gap*, the feeling that 'something is missing'. And only owing to the not clearly defined character of this gap, owing to the fact that in the consciousness this space was not occupied by the concrete image of a definite item, could this gap be filled with another object.[49]

From the age of 12 to 18 months, the child retains the image perhaps for only a few minutes. From the age of two to two and a half, the memory image remains over the course of several hours. Everyone has had occasion to observe at that age how quickly children forget about the people nearest to them.

On the first day after parting, they cry bitterly; on the second day even a reminder evokes no dramatic affects. Living images of these people grow dim and blurry, and quickly decay in the child's consciousness. In these cases, we say 'the child soon forgets'. At roughly the age of three years, children are extremely affected by the first dreams they remember when, upon waking, they do not find around them what they saw in their sleep.

Experiments, as we have already noted, have not yet provided intelligible proof that animals have a figurative memory – but such a possibility, generally speaking, is not completely excluded. It is possible that animals have representations. However, the existence of even very distinct representations does

---

49   It ought to be noted, however, that not every 'gap' can always successfully be indifferently filled with any object whatsoever. When it is a question of things that are very 'dear' to the child, the gap formed by the disappearance of such an item can be filled only with an object extraordinarily close to the first one, and that not always.

not signify the ability to use them. It is one thing to have reproductive representations, and another to be able to break them down and combine them, and to build from this material imaginary semantic dispositions (or compositions). Just such operations of the free construction of imaginary semantic combinations is the characteristic feature of thinking. This act is incomparably more complex and difficult than simply invoking an image in memory, and only beings gifted with hands and having practical experience of the voluntary dissection and fragmentation of things in the process of labour can possess such an ability.

Interaction in the Animal World and Social Interaction

§ 19

To the extent that humans have become human, instead of the *natural* conditions of the environment they have created through their industrial activity, an artificial environment around them as the condition of their existence. The products of labour and the material culture produced by humans and placed by them between themselves and the natural environment become the mediator in relations between individuals. This objective equivalent of labour mediates the relationship of humans to nature and, in addition, serves as a means of interaction for individuals among themselves.

Where there is no mediator of interaction, the relationship of a subject to the environment – like the relationship between subjects – *is only possible as direct bodily relations*. In the absence of objective equivalents (in the form of the products of labour) *around which relationships begin* and the alienation and appropriation by the means of which interaction between individuals is realised, the only possible thing remaining is only purely animal relations of direct *bodily* use.

Needless to say, the sum of jointly existing organisms – microorganisms, for example – is an elementary formation where relationships are expressed in mutual consumption or existence through mutual isolation, and the relationships of much more highly developed animals are expressed only in the form of *bodily* relations, and the mutual interaction among them occurs exclusively on instinctual and biological grounds.

The animal's immediate interactions of consumption with its environment underlie the same immediacy of the manifestation of the animal's consciousness, to which the objects of its life interest are available according to instinct. On the other hand, as a consequence of the fact that in the animal world an objective mediator of relations does not arise among individuals and the material substrate in the form of the products of labour is absent, biological relations cannot emerge through tertiary (objective) things. Animal relations are direct relations, they are given as the elementary result of natural history, as a natural phenomenon, as a biological fact. The mutual relations of animals – this direct *bodily* relationship of mutual consumption or direct bodily relations of mutual benefit, is realised by them without their conscious intent.

The interaction of animals with each other occurs on the grounds of *organic reciprocity*. All relations – hostile, sympathetic, and so on – here have only a biological foundation and a biological meaning.

Cats feud with dogs not by reason of the antagonism of objectively material interests and not on the basis of personal grievance, but rather on the basis of some sort of 'phylogenetic grievance'. Scent alone incites their animosity and urges them to battle. And this war is never ending, is 'eternal'.[50]

The life of an animal is solidly joined with its environment. The animal's habitat is such a home to it that it is almost a continuation of its organism. Therefore, for animals in this environment there is nothing 'incomprehensible'. Everything that does not immediately concern their animal interest falls absolutely out of the field of their senses and does not exist for them; they are completely indifferent to the infinite diversity of concrete reality. But they are surprisingly keenly sensitive to everything that to some extent affects their direct interests, and they know how to react correctly – but again, not consciously

---

50 Proceeding from this, the famous American scholar William McDougall, in his work *An Introduction to Social Psychology* (Mak-Daugol 1916, p. 207) draws the conclusion, 'remarkable' in its own way, that states also fight with each other by reason of the 'instinct of pugnacity'. 'Wars', he says, 'are conditioned entirely by the immediate manifestation of the instinct of pugnacity ... In our own age the same instinct makes of Europe an armed camp occupied by twelve million soldiers, the support of which is a heavy burden on all the peoples; and we see how, more instantly than ever before, a whole nation may be moved by the combative instinct – a slight to the ... flag, or an insulting remark in some foreign newspaper, sends a wave of angry emotion sweeping across the country ... and two nations are ready to rush into a war that cannot fail to be disastrous to both of them. The most serious task of modern statesmanship is, perhaps, to discount and to control these outbursts of collective pugnacity'. Nevertheless, he intends to explain all other social phenomena and institutes by directly inferring them from animal instincts. For example, in the growth of cities and the accumulation of the population towards urban centres, McDougall sees exclusively 'the manifestation of the herd instinct' of people. He explains religion by 'the instinct of fear', the development of science by 'the instinct of curiosity', the concentration of capital by 'the instinct of acquisition' and so forth. This is the kind of picture obtained when animals are mixed up into history. Similar biological theories, however, having of course severed every link with science, presently adorn the most vulgar ideological stock of the fascistic racist theoreticians, serving as a weapon of unbridled propaganda for new imperialist wars.

but instinctively. For example, the keen sense felt by some animals – completely inaccessible to us – to the state of the weather is generally well known. Animals feeling the forces of nature and 'knowing' with surprising accuracy is a phenomenon for which science has not yet found an explanation.

For animals, there is nothing secret or 'unknown' not only in nature: there is nothing hidden or inaccessible as well for them in relations between them. Animals feel instinctively: the condition of a neighbouring organism and of the entire swarm is almost as directly and immediately accessible to them as their own. The beehive, as a known accumulation of insects, lives a fully organised life. The activities of individual bees are somehow so remarkably interrelated and coordinated with each other that up to now it has misled many scholars, compelling them to defend the opinion that these insects, in many ways, surpass humans with their intellectual abilities.

There is nothing hidden and 'mutually unknown', in all probability, in the relations among the inhabitants of an anthill. Ants immediately, organically and physically perceive and feel the condition of each of their kin. The remains of similar immediate interactions are partially preserved in humans in the exact area that has to do with bodily experiences. We feel and understand the pain or fear of those close to us without the aid of language and without the process of deduction and reasoning, and often – without particular external manifestations – we completely correctly perceive the hostile relations or mood of another person towards us.[51]

---

51   Many psychologists and philosophers, having placed the problem of the perception of the other 'self' and having written special monographs on 'the proof of other animacy', have excessively philosophised measures showing that regarding the subjective phenomena of other people, we supposedly infer only according to analogies with ourselves via the following argument: 'When I was in pain, I made such-and-such a grimace. He just now made a grimace that is similar to mine. Consequently, he is in pain'. It appears that people have to thoroughly study their own grimaces in a mirror and remember them well in order to be capable of understanding the basic feelings of another person. There is a multitude of people of such intellectual development who in no way realise the adduced inference: there are entire societies who generally do not make inferences according to the rules and laws of Aristotelian logic, but there is not a single primitive tribe in any single epoch, or even a single idiot who does not understand what the laughter and tears of another person means. Children at the age of two months respond to laughter with a smile, and the sight of a frowning person can make them cry. Who would get it into their head to talk about the inferences of infants at that age? 'There is nothing more offensive than the vulgar philosopher (*homo loci*)', Marx said in these cases. It should be said in general that the position about 'the analogue', where we would not have encountered it (in psychology, logic, or linguistics), is rather a convenient refuge for those who wish to cover up incomprehensible phenomena with words. Nothing in reality occurs on the basis of an analogue and owing to only one analogue.

'Consciousness', says Marx, 'like language, arises from the necessity of intercourse with other people'.[52] When, and how, does this necessity arise? It must be assumed that animals, even those standing at the highest level of development, never feel such a necessity. Instinctive sounds and movements, being unconscious reactions and immediately expressing the condition of the animal organism, are perceived by other animals in the same instinctive way and arouse the corresponding reactions in them. Proper consciousness as perception, however, does not function.

Animals, lacking language and reasoning, mutually 'understand' each other more fully than humans, who both think and possess the most perfect means of interaction! This is hardly surprising, since this 'understanding' does not exceed the boundaries of the organic and bodily sensation of the condition of another being. An animal also immediately senses the 'mood' and condition of the swarm just as we, for example, sense the general condition of our own organism without thinking about it or realising it.

'Where there exists a relationship, it exists for me: the animal does not enter into 'relations' with anything, it does not enter into any relation at all. For the animal, its relation to others does not exist as a relation'.[53]

Interaction in the world of the animals *does not present any problems. It is given to them directly from nature; therefore, the necessity for interaction does not arise.*

In order for the necessity for interaction to arise, *the violation of immediate interaction on instinctive and organic grounds* would be necessary.

The actual interaction and mutual understanding of individuals assumes a certain element of their alienation from each other and the existence of *differing* content of consciousness within them. *The objective content of consciousness* of a single individual must be immediately *inaccessible* to another. *Interaction must become a problem in order for the necessity for it to arise.* This necessity can arise only in creatures who have alienated themselves from each other so that they have stopped mutually understanding each other *by instincts*. A rupture of the natural bonds uniting the organism with nature and with other organisms is required.

This rupture ensues when the objective mediator of relations (i.e. the product of labour) becomes firmly established between the subject and nature, and between the subject and other subjects as well. As a result of this, the relations of individuals to the environment becomes something other than natural and

---

52   Marks i Engel's 1933, p. 20: 'die Sprache entsteht wie das Bewustsein, erst aus dem Bedürfnis, der Notdurft des Verkehrs mit anderen Menschen'.
53   Marks i Engel's 1933, p. 2.

elemental relations. They become purposeful, technological relations of influence, of setting and realising goals – the relations of labour, of production, and so on. Between the subject and nature arises an entire *historical* world of culture – a material, technological, and ideological world: in a word, instead of biological relations, relations of a *social and historical order* become firmly established.

Even the relations between individual change owing to labour and the products of labour. They are no longer biological and physical relations, but become relations that take shape *around* labour, production, acquisition, distribution, and exchange (i.e. *social and historical*). Here the social relations of production, of exchange, of distribution, of agreement and contract, of alienation and so on first arise.

From this moment of the rupture of natural relations and of the rise of mediated communication, *development* and modification of thinking first become possible; hence, from this moment the human level of consciousness and the human means of thinking arise.

After this rupture, consciousness – which exists at the animal level as well, but does not play a predominant role there inasmuch as all vital relations occur on the basis of the biological laws of heredity and adaptation, and run as the *natural processes* of an instinctive and reflexive order – *gradually acquires a dominant position and a defining role in the behaviour of the subject.*

Since the natural bonds linking the individual with the environment and other individuals have been ruptured, now consciousness must take on the task of the link with the environment, the orientation of the subject, and other functions that until then were performed automatically and unconsciously. To an increasing degree, the behaviour of the subject falls under the control of consciousness; it becomes the organisational centre of behaviour and the orientation of the subject becomes conscious. 'Humanity', says Marx, 'differs from the ram in that consciousness replaces their instinct, or that their instinct is conscious'.[54]

The work of consciousness thus acquires its own field of activity and conditions in which it can expand in manifold ways as conscious activity. Between the subject and nature, and between separate individuals as well, an objective mediator of relations arises – in the form of industry, the instruments of labour and products – that ruptures the natural biological bonds of the individual and cuts the natural umbilical cord that linked the subject via organic bonds with nature and with other individuals. The relations of individual to

---

54   Marks i Engel's 1933, p. 21.

individual *are transformed into a problem*. And this problem is solved not by natural means (since the immediate links have been ruptured) but by *intentional relations* and conscious activity, by labour and the social relations of production, exchange, agreement, and so on – in a word, by *social and historical relations*.

Thinking, in this sense of the word, arises and is firmly established together with industrial life.

The first reason for the disintegration of the organic unity of the subject and the environment, and for the violation of immediate biological relations of individuals among themselves is thus labour activity.

Labour, and the division of labour, create a difference in individuals, rupture the natural and biological bonds that unite individuals, establish a world of material culture among them, alienate individuals from each other and created different content of consciousness in them. The subjective conditions of such a difference in the objective content of consciousness of individuals is the ability for representation, the existence of reproductive images, which in turn is the result of a life of work and the division of labour.

The reproductive image first creates the *psychological* possibility of independent goal-setting, the possibility of pursing a goal that is inaccessible to immediately direct perception.

When the content of consciousness is limited only by the general sense of the bodily state of one's own organism, understanding the condition of another is not that difficult; this occurs on the grounds of the biological sense of mutuality. It is expressed in bodily movements, by sounds – cries or mimicry – and finds a response in another, similar organism. Such immediate interaction exists, for example, between a mother and her infant.

Hence, when consciousness is limited by the general organic sense of a bodily condition, this condition of the other is accessibly to another organism by direct and immediate means. Engels says: 'The little that even the most highly developed animals need to communicate to each other does not require articulate speech. In a state of nature, no animal feels handicapped by its inability to speak ...'.[55]

The bark of a dog is different, and a definite condition is expressed by each nuance. Animal experts understand well which nuance expresses fury, joy, fear, pain and so on. This provided the basis for many scholars to consider similar types of expressive activities to be the language of these animals. The 'languages' of dogs, apes, and chickens have more than once been

---

55   Marks i Engel's, 1925, p. 93.

honoured with research in monographs. The 'language' of animals – apes in particular – is considered to be the predecessor of human speech. This, of course, is the result of an obvious misunderstanding. It is true that language is a means of expression, but this does not necessarily mean that it is only the expression of the condition of an organism. The natural expressive movements of animals cannot be considered language. In this case, the boiling of water must be considered language, since the turbulent evaporation and gurgling of the boiling water also express the fact that the temperature of the water has reached a certain limit! Language begins where the subject reveals not the condition of their own organism, but the *objective ideational contents of their consciousness*. Only after that, as a result of the long development of consciousness, does the subject gradually begin to express their own condition in ways other than immediate grimaces – that is to say, through objective vocal means.

Organisms immediately and mutually 'understand' each other up until the point where they have passed out of an animal state and are in possession of *objective content of consciousness* – the world of ideas. With the rise of a differentiated world of ideas, with the manifestation of independent objective content of consciousness, individuals acquire an internal world of ideas and representations, completely inaccessible to the *direct perception of another person's consciousness*. We can perceive the condition of another person's organism (joy, pain or sorrow) immediately, but the ideational content of another person's consciousness is not immediately accessible to us. It is not possible to transmit the objective ideational content of consciousness (i.e. what we think of tertiary objects) by any natural means of expressiveness – grimaces, affective movements, and so on.

Language arises at the stage of development where the subject begins to acquire its own content of consciousness, the world of images and representations; where a certain difference between individuals becomes firmly established – a difference in the ideational content of consciousness; where the mutual 'incomprehension' necessary for the manifestation of real understanding (i.e. for the rise of the means and forms of expressiveness different from natural and biological means) sets in.

The conditions and premises for the rise of such differences between individuals are first created owing to labour and the use of the instruments of labour, which first made possible the heterogeneity of human activity and consequently laid the foundation for the difference in their consciousness.

The Ideational Content of Consciousness

§20

The capability for imagination arises and is imprinted in consciousness as a result of the labour activity of individuals (i.e. the conditions of life when objects necessary to the subject are not given to them in finished form).

Labour and the instruments of labour, being interposed between a need and its satisfaction, burst the purely animal immediacy that exists between the two – separating them from each other, creating intermediate links and packing them with a vast arsenal of means: the world of material culture, social relations and so on. As a consequence, biological needs and the means for their satisfaction are reorganised into definite social formations.

On one plane, the violation of biological and instinctive mutuality and a certain alienation of individuals from each other also takes place by this process.

Consciousness, as the mentally represented plane of behaviour, is unnecessary while the orientation of the organism depends directly on the environment at hand (i.e. results from the construction of the sensory field or is the result of instinctively coordinated movements of an accumulation of organisms, or 'swarm'). In that case, consciousness would be rather a hindrance and a burden for the animal, rather than an aid. A uniform field of the animal community such as a swarm or a herd does not create even the minimal degree of any circumstances for the rise of consciousness.

Back at the beginning of the nineteenth century, Nicolas Sadi Carnot formulated the principle: for any work, a difference in the states of the surroundings is necessary (in the case that interested him, the difference in thermal states). Something similar could be proposed in relation to the work of consciousness. In a homogeneous environment, nothing can happen. Intentional, conscious relations between individuals can arise only in a community, but as a result of a certain isolation of these individuals from each other, as a result of the isolation of the organism from the swarm and from the forces of nature.

While an organic unity and a biological wholeness exists between the organism and its environment, and in the relations between 'individuals', there is no necessity for subjective intellectual operations as the mediators of orientation:

1) Intellectual constructions in relation to objects are not necessary, since all the actions of an animal (including conscious ones) flow immediately from the situation being perceived at the given moment.

2) Intellectual constructions as mediators of mutual interaction are also not required in relation to other individuals, since interaction is immediate and individuals are mutually accessible to each other.
3) At this level of development, the content of consciousness does not have the elements available that are free from direct dependence on the sensory field; free representation is absent and there is no mental (ideational) content.

The freely perceived content of consciousness first arises under the conditions of labour, where the desired object is given to the subject not as a finished object, but is rather *specified* to them (i.e. this object needs to be produced); consequently, when it is necessary to work on the reproduction of the object that is constantly straining the consciousness.

The first objects of human perception, and of naming them as well, it must be supposed, were not the sky, the stars, the sun and other objects indifferent to them, but ultimately the objects of a goal: products created by people and the instruments of labour used by them. The reproduction of ideas was exercised and excelled at owing to labour as a purposeful activity in which the result of the labour had to be in the imagination before work began. In the process of labour the objects of activity, as a consequence of the constant exertion around them, are repeatedly 'hammered into' the consciousness of individuals.

On the other hand, the strengthening of this ability for the free reproduction of ideas *facilitated the formation of the elements of language to a tremendous extent.* Speech makes possible the arbitrary and free evocation of ideas in the field of lucid consciousness and strengthens the ability for reproduction. Owing to language, the reproduction of ideas and the work of the imagination become extraordinarily easy. The process of reproducing mental content becomes fluent, consciousness is liberated from the tyranny of the sensory field and acquires the freedom of the imagination. The imagination becomes active and flexible in the highest degree, and its scope can be continuously broadened.

The enormous role played by speech in the formation of the conscious field of memory, with its particular clearness, is revealed in the example of childhood development. Over time, the strengthening of a child's visual memory occurs in league with the process of acquiring speech. The interruption of these sequences is not accidental, if we take into consideration the fact that verbal associations in children are rapidly automated and can serve as a firm basis for practicing the ability to reproduce ideas. Drawing the reverse parallel, however, is highly risky. In primitive humans, speech arose and developed on the basis of the development of their consciousness; the consciousness of a child warms up primarily and precisely under the influence of speech and owing to it. In the intellectual development of a child, speech is the colossal instrument by means of which – as an already finished social and historical product – the child's consciousness rapidly ascends to the cultural heights contemporary to them.

The life of consciousness, in the proper sense of the word, begins after the rudiments of the internal world of ideas arise that enable consciousness to then have the prefigurations of things when they are not immediately given sensorily (i.e. to have its own ideational content).

Consciousness first illuminates the internal image with objective content, raising it to the level of lucid, precise perception, thinking and reasoning. The elaboration of the elements of language first become possible on the basis of ideation. Possession of the word, of the vocal substitute of representation, makes the ideational content of consciousness easily translatable for other types of intellectual comparison. In the majority of cases, figurative representations of things and situations are so durable and inelastic that disorganising them or otherwise regrouping them represents immense difficulties for mental operations. Having linguistic signs in the broad sense (or in general the semantic means of substitution) available, we often not do not need to recall the visual images of objects at all; we use their semantic replacement, directly relating our intellectual operations to the things themselves and not carrying all this out through the apparatus of figurative representations.

Thought never exists under its own power; it can exist only as the thought of something, as the thought of an object. Thought without an object cannot be, the same way as a body without gravitation cannot be. *The object is the body of thought.* Consciousness acquires this objective content owing to ideational ability. Consciousness deprived of objective content can only be the general sense of the state of an organism. Animals possess this sense.

Genuine consciousness is present where its content is filled with the objective structure of reality, where it can use images and the representations of things or their substitutes and compose imaginary dispositions. Essentially, mental operations are imagining formations, phenomena and events that do not yet exist (i.e. future) or no longer exist (i.e. past).

Human consciousness acquires freely conceivable and reproducible content; it ceases being linked to the situation at hand and subordinate to it, like an animal consciousness that is incapable of any sort of mental operations that do not flow directly from the perceived situation. In their intellectual activity, animals are the slaves of their own sensory field. Their consciousness is firmly limited by the field of perception at hand.

Human consciousness, having freely reproducible images and representations, is not limited only to the sensory field of the current moment. In their imagination, they can freely move forward and backward along the vector of time from the current point. Human behaviour is defined not so much by the situation at hand as it is by the conceivable and imaginable one. Their consciousness is a response not only to impressions perceived at that given second; human consciousness and behaviour constantly bears in mind those objects and circumstances located beyond the sensory field in both the temporal and the spatial sense. Briefly put, the free ideational content of consciousness is, in *psychological respects*, that essential trait that distinguishes human consciousness from animal consciousness.

In those cases where a person loses the ability to freely reproduce representations, they return to a condition very close to an animal state.

From this point of view, pathological cases of memory loss are of no small interest, especially those where the individual loses the ability to reproduce past representations and cannot reconstruct anything in their consciousness except what is immediately at hand in their sensory field. Such cases, which have been observed and described again and again, represent a particular type of amnesia and are called 'psychic blindness'. We will cite several places in the records of Wolfgang Hochheimer, who had the opportunity to study one such patient. The results of his observations were published in the German journal *Psychologische Forschung*.[56]

At the age of thirty, the subject (whom we will call S) suffered a head wound in the war, after which he lost the ability to visually reproduce in his memory – to whatever degree – images of the past and also to imagine the immediate future.

His speech centres were not affected by the wound, and S retained the capability of speech. Upon careful analysis, however, it was revealed that S's speech was characterised by pure automatism and the complete absence of freely reproduced ideas (i.e. it was an automatic verbal flow, and not the expression of intentions planned in advance). In S, thoughts did not lead to words; rather, verbal automatism directed the process of comprehension. For example, he could discuss republics and monarchies like an ordinary burgher; he knew which countries were located in Asia but was completely incapably of visually reproducing a geographical map in his memory. When asked which countries were located in Asia, he replied without thinking: 'Japan, China, Mongolia, Russian Central Asia'.

---

56   Hochheimer 1932, pp. 1–69.

'Do you imagine a map of Asia when you're answering?' they asked him. 'No, I know it by heart', S answered, showing how he could count them on his fingers.[57]

The majority of people are normally unable to vividly reproduce odours and tastes in their memories, but S was generally unable to revive any representations, even visual ones.

'If you close your eyes, can you imagine the colour green?' 'When my eyes are closed, I can only say: trees are green, but it's impossible to imagine it. I can say what something is called, but it's impossible to imagine anything', S said on the subject.

For S; 'saying what something is called' signified only the automatic links between words. It was especially obvious in the cases where S attempted to characterise optical qualities such as colours. In these cases, he could only react verbally:

Q. 'Can you imagine colours?'

S. 'Colours? Green, red, blue – the number 19! Green-red'. It should be noted here that 19 the number of his trolley line, whose signal was green and red. As soon as he said 'green' and 'red', this automatically brought '19' along with it. In the field of consciousness, the visual representations of these objects were absent.

Q. 'Can you imagine the colour red?'

S. 'Red? Blue – red!'

Q. 'Can you imagine glass?'

S. 'Glass? Caution – glass!'

When asked which months were in winter, S first answered 'October, November, December'. 'Is October really in winter?' they asked him.

'Oh no, that's autumn ... January, February, March', S said, correcting himself.

Having corrected himself in one automatic definition, S here includes March, as once the series began with January, the involvement of March was automatically unavoidable.

When asked about the taste of pasta in comparison to potatoes, S answered 'Obviously, pasta is softer than potatoes. Pasta is a dish made from flour, it must have a floury taste'. *S does not remember the taste of pasta, but discusses it.* He could not evoke either the visual or the taste impressions of pasta in his memory.

---

57   Hochheimer 1932, p. 17.

S was unable to remember even the faces of the people closest to him. 'Can you remember what your parents look like?' 'If I meet them on the street, I recognise them. But it's impossible to imagine their appearance'.[58]

When S was given a letter he had written the week before, he read through it attentively but did not notice that it was his own letter; only when his attention was drawn to his signature did he cheerfully exclaim. 'But that's my signature. That means I wrote this letter to you. But I don't remember it'.[59]

When asked, 'Could you recognise your own letter without looking at the signature?' he responded, 'How could I recognise it without reading the signature?' It is clear that S had no vivid memories. He could never answer the question, 'What did we do last time?' – his consciousness was limited exclusively to the current moment.

'When the next thing happens, whatever was before that disappears',[60] S said.

In his consciousness, S was unable either to revive the past or to imagine the future. His consciousness was limited to the narrow band of the immediate moment at hand: 'only what is current (*bloss was momentan ist*)', he said about his ideas.

What we call 'the past' appeared thus to S: 'Something new is always happening, and then what was, disappears permanently'. The 'future' for S was also something curled up around the point of the present. Our view along the vector of time, back to the past and forward to the future, was completely inaccessible to S.

'They say that other people can do it', he complained; 'I can't even try it'. 'When you feel badly, do you hope that things will get better for you at some point? Or do you simply state: "I feel badly"?' they asked him. 'It's like this: every minute, you're thinking that in a moment it will all be over, and then it's not over'.

Seeing as how S lacked any function of internal imagination, he was unable to display any sort of independent initiative; for example, he could not initiate a conversation. 'He continually had to be nudged, if we wanted to get something out of him', Hochheimer reported. When asked to tell a story about something, S answered: 'I can't. Ask me, and I'll answer. I can't speak, if someone doesn't ask me questions'. 'But you can't independently start a conversation – for example,

---

58 Hochheimer 1932, p. 33.
59 Hochheimer 1932, p. 35.
60 Hochheimer 1932, p. 32.

with your children? You really never do that?' 'For my kids, I have a few rote phrases. I ask them 'How did you behave today' and so on'.[61]

Thus, we see that the absence of consciousness in no way signifies the existence of previously planned intentions and the capability of imagination. It is possible to consciously orient oneself in the situation at hand and at the same time be unable to have visual representations of the past or the future.

Despite the fact that S was incapable of having any ideas about either the past or the future, he lived and acted consciously – though his consciousness was limited exclusively to the present moment. He did, of course, have a tremendous advantage over animals: this was his speech apparatus, which was preserved only in the form of verbal automatisms, but this apparatus in no way functioned for him as a linking moment between the past, the present, and the future.

In cases where psychic blindness is accompanied by aphasia, the subject loses completely the capability for any goal-setting whatsoever and begins to live only in the current moment, reacting only to what immediately affects their senses; all the rest falls outside the field of their consciousness. Humans are transformed into the slaves of their sensory fields, like animals. The state of consciousness of people thus afflicted is close to an animal state.

The Essential Particularities of Human Consciousness

§ 21
The capability of ideation is the psychological advantage of humans without which they would differ in few ways from the animals. Their consciousness would be continually limited to the narrow band of the present moment. The past would not exist for such consciousness; consequently, conscious experience would not exist. All experience acquired by animals, for example, is automated habit and action, and from the point of view of consciousness is unconscious, dead experience.

On the other hand, without this capability for free representation the future would also not exist for the individual, and any sort of goal-setting would be impossible. All the aspirations, behaviour and thought of an individual would be defined by the sensory environment at hand in the given moment. Consequently, there would be no acts of will. Will is not an empty urge to action; it is the aspiration towards a conscious goal. In order to have a will, the sub-

---

61   Hochheimer 1932, p. 17.

ject must be able freely to reproduce a definite goal in their consciousness. A real act of will exists only where the individual can spontaneously imagine a goal and consciously strive towards it. And this is possibly only in cases where consciousness has ideational content and is capable of freely reproducing representations.

Acts of will, in the proper sense of the phrase, are nowhere observed in the behaviour of animals. All their actions and behaviour – including rational ones – are defined and dictated by the situation at hand. Anything that does not flow from the situation at hand at that given moment is not realised and is not performed by the animal. An act of will and voluntary behaviour are inherent to humans; they are possible only at the human level of development where consciousness, liberated from direct dependence on the sensory field, can attract imagined objects and set itself a conceptual goal. There is no doubt that humans developed this ability in the process of their working life.

The capability of free reproduction of representations is the necessary psychological condition for the growth and the enrichment of consciousness. Thanks to this capability, consciousness acquires independent ideational content – its own internal world of representations, ideas and thoughts that liberate humanity from direct subordination to the sensory environment. This freedom of the content of consciousness and independence of consciousness, however, is only apparent. The conceptual world of consciousness, though liberated from direct dependence on the sensory field, is extraordinarily dependent on other conditions – specifically the social conditions of human existence, which is why we will call it a quasi-independent conceptual world.[62]

---

62   The Moscow psychologist Alexander Luria, in a review he wrote of the second chapter of this book (*Vestnik Akademii Nauk SSSR*, 1936, No. 8–9, pp. 55–8), raises the objection that animals also possess the ability of preserving and reproducing the sensory field, which 'varies depending on the ecological peculiarities of the animal and in some aspects reaches the maximum'. He poses the question 'Should we look for the peculiarities of human consciousness in such a relatively simple quality as reproduction?' Further on, he points out that in the transition from animal to human consciousness, the important issue is not the reproduction of representations, but the capability of 'generalisation', of the 'general reflection of reality'. This reproach does not seem quite correct to us, if we take into account the fact that we assigned the main role in the formation of human consciousness not to 'reproduction' but to labour, which 'grants' this ability. Throughout this study we have tried to explain the peculiarities of human thinking not by psychological means, but by social causes and have emphasised several times that the reproduction of representations is only the *psychological* expression of the advantage of human consciousness over the animals. As regards 'generalisation', for us it represents a problem solved only on the basis of the existence of the ability for representation (i.e. of elementary figurative memory). *We do not consider a representation to be a simple reflection of objects*. On the

The conclusions we came to may seem questionable from the point of view of the logical correctness of the construction. We said that the capability for reproduction of representations constitutes the psychological basis of conscious voluntary activity, as labour – in Marx's definition – is characterised by the fact that the results obtained at the end of a process must exist ideally in the representation of the individual before the start of that process. On the other hand, we have proven that this capability of imagination is acquired owing to the labour activity of humans under the conditions of industrial life.

This exact apparent 'vicious circle in the proof' is repeated when we spoke about the role of language in the exercise of memory and of the formation of the ideational content of consciousness: without language there are no free representations of the imagination, but language in turn is not possible without this ideational content of consciousness.

Don't let this seeming 'contradiction' confuse anyone. This 'vicious circle' speaks in favour of our assertions and demonstrates that human labour, human consciousness and human speech in the process of their emergence were not three independent actors but only separate moments of a single whole – specifically, the social complex. Each of these formations are impossible without the others; the one engenders the other, mutually forming the whole. There is no 'vicious circle' here. Condition and conditioned mutually enclose one another, which constitutes a solid basis for actual development and is the best guarantee of the correctness of the propositions being advanced. In a word, this is the same problem of the dialectic of closed formation we examined above (pp. 47–49).

Labour activity rearranged the consciousness of beasts and elevated it to the level of human reason, and also created the human means of interaction and speech; in turn, human reason and human speech enabled the rearrangement of the forms of human activity and made labour its exclusive heritage. All this, taken together, created the conditions for the tremendous development of humanity in relation both to the means of their activity and to the range and acuity of their consciousness.

---

contrary, we are inclined to think that even the most elementary representations imply the rudiments of a certain generalisation.

Experiments with delayed reactions in animals, which Luria cites, do not in our opinion provided the basis for regarding animals as gifted with imagination. Such actions are fully explainable without this risky hypothesis, simply on the basis of a sense of familiarity that does not require the operation of images at all. Psychologist Nikolai Voitonis, having studied the delayed reactions of animals with us, arrived at results that refuted the hasty conclusions of Hunter and Tinklepaugh on the existence of representations in apes.

Questions about what came first, labour activity or human consciousness, or what preceded what – language or consciousness, and so on – are superficial; before this came the animal state of the humanoids, with the animal activity and animal consciousness peculiar to them.

We will conclude this chapter with the words of Goethe: 'Thinking and doing, doing and thinking – these are the sum of all wisdom. Both must move ever onward in life, to and fro, like breathing in and breathing out. Anyone who makes a law of testing doing by thinking, and thinking by doing will not be mistaken – and if they are, they will soon return to the correct path'.

Preliminary Results

§ 22

Proceeding from what has been said, we will formulate a series of propositions that will be developed in particular in what follows.

What is awareness? What is an idea, a thought?

1. In its elementary manifestation, thinking is already observed in the act of simple sensory perception. Perceiving and distinguishing something means the following: an object – indifferent until that moment and belonging to the uniform, non-partitioned background of consciousness – is shifted into the focus of consciousness, as a result of which the amorphous field of consciousness is partitioned and acquires a definite semantic construction.

Noticing something means restructuring [*perestroit*] the field of consciousness, having isolated a certain part of this field into something partitioned and mutually correlated. The object, until then indifferent to consciousness and having no qualities, is harnessed to a given situation and fills in its gaps, gives meaning to that situation and itself is given meaning owing to the place occupied by it in this context.

Such a semantic alteration of the field of consciousness, such a composition of consciousness around specified data is called perception [*vospriiatie*]. In the majority of cases, moreover, the comprehension [*osmyslenie*] of both the specific item and the entire situation that this item resolves occurs in a single act.

From this point of view, perceiving something means already completing the act of comprehension [*osmyslenie*]. The sensory perception of items is in principle the same problem as thinking and cognition in general.

2. Thus a thought, an idea, even in its elementary manifestation in the act of perception represents a construction of the field of consciousness where every bit of data is related in a given way to the others, and everything together

constitutes a unified, 'articulate' context, an orderly state of consciousness expressing a definite semantic whole.

Thinking, like perception, does not consist of new elements in the form of supplementary images, ideas and representations being added to the content of consciousness, as is usually supposed, but of the material and content of consciousness being rearranged in a given way and taking shape in a new context. A specific 'centre' (a focus) is distinguished in the content of consciousness itself, proceeding from and around which the entire field of consciousness is constructed like a mutually related, self-contained whole. An idea or a concept is precisely this rearranged field.

Philosophers assumed that an idea, apparently existing in the consciousness of the subject as a finished form, takes in the data of the external senses and, using these 'concept vessels', the sensory data is joined to thought. Psychologists believed that perceptions, entering consciousness through the sensory organs, were mechanically bound up with each other and created representations, concepts, ideas and so on, becoming the finished forms of consciousness. An idea, however, is not some kind of special, essentially finished formation that is added to the content of consciousness but only a certain construction of the field of consciousness.

3. Having seized an object with its teeth, an animal has already completed its first experience of the item. But this act of immediately attaining the goal is different from the mediated path of action by which some mediator of action is ultimately conceived of by the subject, and by which roundabout means are perceived.

The perception of a mediator and its inclusion in the order that resolves a situation is at the same time both the perception of the entire situation and its solution. Thus, the mediator itself becomes the means of perceiving other objects, the instrument of the subject's use and of their cognition, extending the radius of human activity and intelligibility. These questions are taken up in Sections 28–30.

4. A more complex form would be the construction of mediating formations in the form of a series of material adaptations that are consciously created and placed by the subject between themselves and the basic target object. In the field of consciousness, the provision of means that could lead to the goal (i.e. the construction of an imaginary series, the working out of a rational context as a project or *plan of action*) is the equivalent of this. The task of using conceivable objects is particularly facilitated by the existence of the ability for imagination.

The idea is thus the mastering of reality in thoughts, in representations. It is an assumption, a plan of action; but for the idea to actually master the object and for the object to rise up to an idea, it is necessary to put this idea into practice and in accordance with it to rearrange the items in practice.

Two simultaneous acts are combined in this process: an idea is put into practice and an item is rationalised, is made a semantic, 'ideal' thing. At this level the idea actually acquires the item – mastering it not only mentally, but also materially; the idea changes the item in accordance with itself and subsides into it in a form defined by the behaviour of this item.

On the path to its realisation, the idea not only masters the item and experiences it, but also experiences itself: the idea experiences objects, but in this way it first experiences itself as valid or invalid, correct or mistaken (see Chapter x).

CHAPTER 3

Material Culture and Thinking

Labour Activity and Thinking

§ 23
Human labour activity is continually creating something new, or putting old relations in another light, continuously producing new relations (i.e. creating a continually renewing social field around people and on the strength of that keeping consciousness in a state of constant vigilance and not letting it be lulled to sleep).

We have indicated the difference between the animal's passive relations of consumption to nature and the productive relations of humans. Relations of consumption are essentially elementary, limited and incapable of creating variety. An object, insofar as it is not the object of industry but simply the object of immediate consumption, is consumed the same way throughout the ages: water, for example, is either drunk or used for bathing. Relations of consumption do not facilitate the development of the forms and objects of consumption. They are conservative; they do not aid in developing the subject themselves or in broadening the sphere of their activity, their wants, and so on. In relations of consumption, objects are not put into ever newer light and the interests of the subject do not diversify, but every time only the very same act is repeated: this constant repetition adapts objects, moulds the organism's needs and abilities and mechanises its relations (i.e. switches them over to the field of unconscious reflexes).

That is why a consumptive consciousness is characterised by a very narrow potential for activity. It is capable only of appropriating what is given, but not creating what is desired. When the form of material necessary for an animal is not found ready in nature, it goes extinct or changes biologically.

Relations of consumption do not enable the rise and the strengthening of consciousness and prepare neither the objective conditions for this (a world of the products of human activity and material culture) nor the subjective conditions (a variety of wants, a diversification of interests and so on).

Human relations are characterised by a high degree of activity in the subject. Humans are not satisfied with the gifts of nature but add life to it, transforming it and themselves creating the conditions for their existence. Here, consumption is conditioned by the preparation of consumable objects.

Insofar as prior changes to the gifts of nature are necessary, the producer inevitably encounters a series of tasks: 1. What changes does the object need to undergo? What functions and qualities must be imparted to it? 2. With what means will it be possible to realise these changes? 3. How can these means be obtained? and so on, and every time the subject is compelled to look for new solutions, continually going beyond the limits of the known sphere, putting items in a new light and turning them in different directions.

In addition, humans – as a component of the social environment – are always found in cooperation with other subjects in the process of production, distribution, exchange and so on, compelled continually to be aware of the present and the future. The social field around an individual, in which numberless individual interests intersect, force the consciousness of individuals to be continually active.

We examined the role of labour in the formation of human society in sections 4–9, and we will now examine the same questions from the view of the problem of thinking.

Humans are active creatures, changing the world. But as living, feeling beings, humans are also limited by the objective world; the objects of their activity exist outside them, as objects *independent* of them, but they are *objects* used for the satisfaction of their *needs*.[1]

Humans need to take these objects, change them and adapt them to their own goals and needs. Here, the object is in opposition to the subject from the very beginning. 'When an object and I meet', Hegel says, 'one of us must lose their quality in order to unite. But I am a living being, in possession of a will, and an actually self-affirming being (*wahrhaft Affirmative*). The object, on the contrary, is a natural something. Hence, it must perish, and through the abrogation of the independence of objects I affirm and preserve myself, by appropriating them. This is the advantage of reason over blind Nature'.[2]

But an item, we must add, does not wholly perish. Only its natural being, not relevant to human needs, disappears; and this only to be reborn and begin its existence 'among men'.

In this *contraversa* (turning into the opposite), the subject occupies the determinative position and is essentially the initial moment. In Hegel's words, 'the object, as something external and a natural entity, does not have its own goals and its own meaning … It must receive all this only from humans and their activity. Appropriating an object, acquiring an object, essentially signifies

---

1 Marks i Engel's 1928–1946, Vol. III, pp. 642–3.
2 Hegel 1911, p. 302.

the manifestation of the primacy of my will in relation to the item and the revelation that the latter is not in itself and for itself; it is not an end in itself. This manifestation of my will and its affirmation over the object is realised in my communicating to the object a different direction than the one it had; I put another soul into it, another meaning; I give it my soul'.[3]

Items involved in the process of labour cease to be simply natural things; they lose their natural properties (if not wholly, then a significant part of them) and acquire other properties, other functions, and other meanings – to be precise, they become items that are useful to humans, they become 'human objects'.[4]

Human activity takes things out of their natural being – out of blind, elemental existence – and communicates rational, useful forms to them; human activity transfers them from the sphere of nature into the sphere of social reality, the sphere of culture. Marx called this process 'making nature into human nature' and showed it to be a process as a result of which 'nature becomes the object of science and of humanity'.

But in overcoming things and subordinating them to one's will and one's needs – in 'humanising objects' – humans simultaneously 'objectify' themselves in these items (*vergegenständlicht sich*); through this act of embodying the individual in the product of labour (which, in Marx's expression, is the realisation of individuality) humans make themselves 'a reality for others' and the reality of others becomes their own.[5]

Humans actively intervene in the life of nature, changing it for their own benefit, creating the conditions for their own existence. But, on the other hand, humans change themselves in this process; nature, changed by them, and the things they are dealing with influence humans and rearrange them. Things change humans not only in the sense, for example, of a military greatcoat and a sabre at someone's side changing their gait and their entire posture up to and including internal self-appraisal; the psychological influence of things is self-evident. An Austrian writer expressed this relation well:

> What you master, masters you –
> What you command, you are servant to.
>   FRANZ GRILLPARZER

---

3 Hegel 1911, p. 298.
4 Marks i Engel's 1928–1946, Vol. III, pp. 626–30.
5 Marks i Engel's 1928–1946, Vol. III, p. 623.

No – the influence of things extends wide and deep. The world of material culture, which constitutes the conditions for human existence, determines and changes humanity in many ways: first, in the process of producing these things; second, in the process of distribution, exchange, and so on; and finally, in the process of immediate consumption, where the product is returned to a person, satisfying their needs, reuniting with and being added to their person, restoring their strengths and abilities (e.g. literally recreating a person).

§24

'The moment of inestimable importance for the rise and strengthening of thinking is the circumstance that inanimate material, having acquired a definite shape and formed in a precise manner by the human hand, begins to serve a certain human purpose and performs work that other beings are able to perform through the means of the inherent organs of the body', Noiré says.[6] We also encounter this argument in Geiger,[7] and Goethe expressed these thoughts even earlier: 'Beginning in the earliest times, thinking and the cognition of reality were stimulated not by internal drives and theoretical motives, but above all by practical interests and the different types of adaptations for achieving certain practical goals' (Goethe, 'The Middle Epoch').

Goethe first set the 'act' against the Biblical 'word' …

> Auf einmal seh'ich Rat.
> Und schreibe getrost: im Anfang war die Tat!

'In the beginning was the Act'. The act, in Goethe's understanding, 'creates itself'. It flows, it is true, from other acts, but itself begins a new series: it is always active.

'With Goethe, everything is an act', Novalis said. Goethe did indeed declare war on purposeless and formless aspirations, recognising only that activity which, in organising things, takes shape itself. This is expressed in the concept of 'act' (Tat, $\pi\rho\alpha\gamma\mu\alpha$).[8]

This thought, cleansed of extraneous motives, enriched by the concept of social experience and raised to the great principle of 'social and historical practice', lies at the base of Marxist doctrine on thinking and cognition.

6　Nuare, 1925 p. 69.
7　Geiger 1872.
8　Likhtenshtadt 1920, p. 69.

'In their research', Engels says, 'naturalists and philosophers have until now completely disregarded the influence of human activity on their thinking; on the one hand, they know only nature, and on the other only thought. But the first, most essential basis of human thinking is precisely *the alteration of nature by humans*, and *not* nature alone as such; human reason developed in proportion to their having learned how to alter nature'.[9]

Dissatisfied with natural reality and the natural properties of things, humans destroy their natural forms in order to construct them anew after their own fashion. In this sense, nature and all its gifts are for humans only the raw material from which they create *their own objects*. But changing things means subordinating them to oneself, 'taming' them. Changing the world also means experiencing that world.

By destroying, creating, building and changing things, the subject communicates to them the properties, functions, and form of a rational existence. But in this process, using things, the subject is compelled to inspect it from all sides; they must, to use Bacon's expression, repeatedly 'dissect things', 'dissect nature' – and, consequently, they are compelled to look into the very nature of things and examine their structure and 'behaviour' closely.

Thus, by producing every type of cross-section in nature – decomposing and assembling, 'tormenting' and testing things – the subject studies and learns about them. They not only command things, but result from things themselves as well.

Things normally do not yield immediately to the intentions of the subject; they are stubborn, and create obstacles. Looking at the matter from this side, it would seem that they are indifferent to the subject. From the point of view of the subject, the objects of labour are the centre of a greater or lesser opposition to their will. Although things are 'helpless' before humans, in their helplessness they prove to be quite persistent, precisely in their opposition.

If objects did not show opposition, nothing would come of the entire undertaking – there would not even be an undertaking. If the desire were immediately fulfilled, like in the stories of the owners of magic wands, then in general wishes would not exist; the beautiful maiden – the thought – would never return to life in this enchanted world. In order for consciousness to awaken, a world full of opposition is needed. The 'obstinacy' of things in relation to the subject is displayed in their passivity. The opposition on the part of things is a great force that facilitates the development and the expansion of the sphere of consciousness.

---

9 Marks i Engel's 1925, p. 25.

Having encountered an obstacle rendered by things, the subject inspects them from all sides, approaches the object by other means, looks for new paths to overcoming it, makes attempts and 'torments' the object until they get the better of the obstacle or are convinced of their impotence; in the latter case, the object does not cease to be a problem and will consequently continually provoke newer and newer attempts by the subject.

In order to subordinate a thing to its will, the subject needs to find its 'weak spot' with which it will easily surrender and display less resistance. Having resisted on all other points and not yielding to other methods, the thing compels the subject to search until a valid solution is found. In this turning into opposites, humans obtain 'what' must be done, 'how' it is to be done, and 'why' it cannot be done another way.

The subject gains experience, knowledge, and mastery. 'Practice makes perfect', as the saying goes.

Humans can only alter things according to their will when they take the laws of these things into consideration and act in accordance with their essence. Creating anything in opposition to the laws of nature is impossible. Even acting against nature, we behave in accordance with its laws and apply their forces. We obey the laws of nature even in the case where we oppose them, and act in concert with nature when we want to act against it. Humanity sets off nature's own laws against its elements.

In reality, it is only possible to command objects by having comprehended their properties. The material itself of a thing suggests the best means of overcoming it and the most rational form of its treatment. Having opposed every interpretation that does not answer to its laws and to every attempt at solution that is not in accordance with the principles of its internal structure, the material itself suggests a rational form of solution.

Humans strive to 'secure the truth of nature' not to satisfy reality itself, but only for themselves, for their interests. Only by this path is objective truth achievable for humanity.

The Materialisation of Ideas in the Process of Labour Activity and the Acquisition of Ideational Content by Things

§25

The subject, in expending his/her [*svoi*] deliberate activity, transferring and investing a part of his/her energy and ability into an object external to him or her, remains in this object as the product of his/her activity after having completed operations upon it, and even in cases where this object passes into the possession and the use of another. It is clear that an artistic work – the Mona Lisa, for example – is the actual manifestation of the individuality of the author that created it and an integral part of the personality of da Vinci, even in cases where this work never belonged to the author and from the very beginning was in the possession of another person, becoming the property of another.

A materialisation and a revelation of the subject occurs in the product. An individual cannot manifest him/herself better or more fully in anything other than in the results of his/her activity.

It is not some sort of abstract will of the subject that accumulates in the product. A concrete goal and specific desire is realised in it; the experience, skill, and intelligence of the subject is materialised and preserved in it. In activity, an idea is 'objectified', receiving a physical, real existence. In the product of labour, a thought acquires material reality. The idea is realised – it materialises. Mediums have sought in vain the manifestations of the soul in the darkness of séances. Every successfully completed action is the reification of an idea – *the materialisation of the soul.*

Animals also act and leave the traces of their own actions; indeed, they are so significant that the entire life of organic nature is conditioned by the changes brought about by them. But as Engels says, 'the changes produced by animals in nature occur without any intent on their part, and in relation to them are somewhat accidental', 'animals use external nature and produce changes in it solely by virtue of their presence'. Changes of this type are not premeditated and represent a blind, elemental result. On the strength of this, these changes are the documents of nature, and not the manifestation of conscious activity.

In all cases requiring mediating actions and the utilisation of means from outside, animals lack the potential for conscious goal-setting and rational voluntary action.

Humans 'in the process of labour not only effect a change of form of what is given to them by nature; in the objects of their activity they also realise a purpose of their own that, like a law, defines the character of their activity, to which he must subordinate their will' (Marx). In this activity, the subject realises what they 'had ideally in their imagination' and takes the idea from the sphere of a subjective state, communicating an external reality to it and giving the idea flesh.

The idea, having been realised, passes into the external world, occupies a specific place in it and performs the job of an object. The significance and force of the product of labour lies in the fact that in it, owing to it, the subjective limitation of an individual's personality is overcome. From now on, the idea is linked with the subject, but not as a subjective idea with its bearer; it relates to the subject as an externally subjective reality, as an object generally is able to relate to a subject.

But what happens with the object at the same time?

Up until human activity engaged it, it constituted only a part of the forces of nature. Its form, content and properties are the product of blind laws; it does not matter where it is located and what it represents.

The external form of gold is as 'important' to nature as its specific weight and inability to oxidise.

An object, as an external physical existence, does not have goals of its own or a meaning of its own. Nature as such needs nothing, wants nothing; whether the sun is shining or has died out does not matter to it. Only human activity takes the objects of nature out of this indifferent reality and communicates that content, those properties and the functions that fully determinate actions can produce, thus imparting to objects a concrete human purpose and meaning.

In the production process, things lose their natural form and properties and acquire qualities that are firmly established by the will and goals of humans. The object is placed in a specific framework; specific functions are imparted to it and it is given a specific direction and meaning.

Falling into the field of rational human activity, the objects of nature become rationally organised *'rational objects'*. In them, human reason actually acquires an objective existence not physically linked with the subject.

Marx said that human activity – human labour – is realised in the product of labour, but in addition to that it means that human intellect has been imprinted on it.

A complex machine, in which all the parts are brought into mathematically precise correlation with each other, is from start to finish a rational complex. Not only is the physical energy of a person woven into it; human reason is also embodied in it. Gigantic screw propellers cast in accordance with precisely calculated curves, levers, couples, flywheels, cam gears – is this transfer of abstract mathematical formulas into heavy machinery that is submissive to the human will really not an obvious indicator of the power of reason over the blind, insensate forces of nature? The instruments of labour are reason materialised – the intellect in its objective existence.

Lenin, while reading Hegel's *Philosophy of History*, emphasised these words: 'Man with his requirements behaves in a practical way in relation to external nature; in making it serve for his satisfaction, he wears it away, thereby setting to work as an intermediary. For natural objects are powerful and offer resistance in many different ways. In order to subdue them, man introduces other natural objects, thus turning nature against itself, and he invents tools for this purpose. These human inventions belong to the spirit, and such a tool must be regarded as higher than a natural object ...'.[10]

Hegel thought that everything real was rational, including nature. This was a very deep idea of rationalist philosophy, finding its fullest expression in the philosophy of the 'Absolute Spirit'. But there is nonetheless no intellect in nature. There is nothing but the rudiments in it, as such; it lacks any rational elements until humans bring them in. The reality of nature is not rational, but a reality created by humans as a result of their conscious activity. The mind has an objective reality only in the world of culture created by humans. Here, it actually lives in external things. We could call it the *objective mind*. Things can preserve the stamp of a mind and become the bearer of an idea.[11] Humans have the ability to objectify their thoughts, which they do continually in the process of their activity. The forms of this embodiment of thought are numberless, and one of the most fruitful forms – according to its historical consequences – is the embodiment of thought in instruments, tools and machines.

Thanks to this rational world of the objects of material culture, the human becomes a being greater than a simple natural being. It becomes a *social* being.

Human reason and human labour find their realisation in the objects of material culture. Objective reality and the rational form are combined in them. 'Reality and thought', Marx says, 'though they are different from each other, at the same time are in unity with each other'.[12] This unity of reality and thinking exists in its most stable form in the objects of material culture, and it is easiest to observe it here.

Insisting thereby on the 'transfer of ideas into objective reality', we can raise the question: is this not Hegelianism? Is the Hegelian philosophy of creating the world through the self-alienation of the Absolute Idea, and so on, not speaking here?

Undoubtedly, much here comes from Hegel, but it is equally indubitable that in the form in which it is developed in Marx represents the most sober and consistent materialism.

Marx's criticism of Hegel's position on this question is highly resolute and highly principled.[13] 'For Hegel the *human being – man* – equals self-conscious-

---

10   Lenin 1931, Vol. XII, p. 158.
11   Nevertheless, the objective mind lives in things only while these things have some kind of use in society and the ideas contained within them find some sort of response in the consciousness of people.
12   Marks i Engel's 1928–1946, Vol. III, p. 625.
13   Marks i Engel's 1928–1946, Vol. III, pp. 640–54.

ness', Marx says. 'All estrangement of the human being is therefore *nothing* but *estrangement* of *self-consciousness*'.[14] This estrangement is regarded by Hegel not as the actual estrangement of humans in objective reality, but is conceived by him as a process, flowing solely in the abstraction of self-consciousness.

Embodied Reason and Its Social Significance

§ 26

The product of labour is not blind physical existence, but is organised rationally and is the bearer of a definite meaning. But it represents not only a thought or an idea; in addition, an external objective reality is inherent in it.

On the one hand, the product of labour is an *object* in the full sense of the word: an external objective existence. It is not, however, an indifferent and meaningless object of nature, because it encloses within its body the material attributes embedded in it by humans. It is a 'human' object – a *rational, subjectivised object*.

Hence, on the other hand, the product of labour is a certain part of the subject (i.e. humans). But at the same time it has not only an existence within the subject, it is also objectified and exists independently from its creator.

A subject reveals his/herself in his/her objects of activity, creating – in a manner of speaking – monuments to him or herself (in this case, it does not matter what kind – glory or disgrace). There is a Russian proverb: 'people live in their own affairs'; individuals actually live in what they create, and only through their deeds can they live in other people and for other individuals.

In the products of activity (deeds), subject and object are found in indissoluble unity, penetrating each other, and mutually expressing each other. Every feat lives in its creator, insofar as it has not yet been brought to completion, and every individual exists only in the works they have accomplished. But the work is not infrequently greater than its author, and a creator is greater than what has already been accomplished.

Insofar as something has already been brought to completion, it begins to exist independently of its author and can have consequences that go beyond the limits of its original purpose. It acquires an objective external existence and acts as a force and a factor independent of its author, often even contravening its original purpose and desires.

---

14   Marks i Engel's 1928–1946, Vol. III, p. 640 and further on pp. 642–52 Marx provides a fundamental criticism of Hegel on this question.

On the other hand, every subject is only what s/he has manifested, what s/he has done. But the subject is more than the sum of the works s/he has accomplished. What s/he has not yet revealed, but is to reveal in the future under other favourable conditions, also belongs to the individual. This aspect, ignored in all past history, now becomes the object of particular attention and the concern of a socialist society. In a country of victorious socialism, where people have been liberated from slavery and oppression, there is a single criterion for appraising an individual: his/her labour (i.e. the full manifestation of their creative ability). Labour does not have a private, personal character for us as it does in capitalism, but is favoured with the highest social appreciation and becomes part of honour and glory; naturally, the strivings of socialist society are directed towards creating all the conditions for the fruitful manifestation of individual gifts.

Subject and object, continually passing into each other in the process of activity, mutually amplify, express, advance and elevate each other in every act of this passing over. The role and significance of the realisation of rational activity in the development of human thinking can be briefly formulated in the following five points:

1. The product of human activity acquires an existence external to it, independent of the individual: a work made by me ceases to be physically linked to me and is not limited by the existence of my will; it acquires an independent existence in space and time. (This independence is only an independence from a certain individual, but not from humanity in general. A product of labour with no reference to humanity or social wants has, of course, no meaning and does not exist as a product.) Consequently, the force of a product of labour lies in the fact that owing to it, the limited existence of the subject is overcome. The thought and intention of the subject, being imprinted and accumulating in the products of activity, acquire in them an objective and historical existence, against which the flow of time acts destructively, but nevertheless with a much slower tempo. A stone, having taken on a certain form, purpose and meaning at the hands of a human – metal, cast and wrought for specific goals; drawings or alphabetical characters drawn on the surface of a material, and so on – do not survive only one generation of people but carry the evidence of human ways of life and thought into future centuries, through the millennia.

Things, passing over from the history of nature into the history of humanity, become documents of humanity. When a subjective intellect dies together with an individual, the intellect objectified in things and works are capable of endless progress in other individuals and generations.

Through the physical shell of a thing, a utensil, a construction, a drawing and so on the work of thought, of a human intellect, that has taken material form in them is visible. They are the objective evidence of human activity, and hence of human thought.

By falling into human hands, the material of nature is transformed from a document of nature into a document of human history, and consequently into *a document of social consciousness*. Therefore, if archaeology wishes to be an actual historical science, and not a painstaking sorter of things according to traditional classificatory schemes; if it wants to occupy itself with things – not for the sake of realogy [*veshchevedenie*], but for the sake of studying history – it must learn how to read these alphabetical characters of things, cut for the most part not in the form of real inscriptions but in the form of the activity and the thought patterns of the people who left these monuments behind them.

'We see how the history of *industry* and the established *objective* existence of history are the *open book of man's essential powers*, the perceptibly existing human *psychology*. Hitherto this was not conceived in its connection with man's *essential being*, but only in an external relation of utility'.[15]

These words, written over ninety years ago – to the shame of our science – have not yet been used and remain acutely topical to this day, not only for archaeology and the history material culture, but for philosophy and psychology as well.

2. In acquiring an independent existence, a product of activity can outstrip the life of a certain individual – and sometimes of entire generations. It is preserved in history and appears as one of its factors.

In imparting an objective external existence to his/her ideas and thoughts (i.e. embodying them in works), the subject makes them accessible to *other* individuals. In these products, the existence of the individual receives a public, 'popular' existence.

Each time, in activity and the products of their labour, the subject *socialises their individual energy, and also socialises his/her own psychic essence* – his/her abilities – and makes them accessible to other individuals. The opportunity to use the abilities of another is created; *the experience of an individual does not remain locked vested within them but becomes accessible for others – it becomes a social experience*.

Individual experience is limited and weak, and has a rather narrow framework for development. Social experience is objective, solid, limitlessly vast and nourishes individual experience.

Only owing to the 'humanised' and 'rational' world of things has communication between people, the exchange of needs, the exchange of thoughts and

---

15   Marks i Engel's 1928–1946, Vol. III, p. 628.

experience become possible. Without it, individuals would not have ideas, and consequently the need for interaction would not arise – as it is with the animals, regarding which Wilhelm Wundt expressed it well when he said that animals do not speak not because they cannot produce articulate sounds, but because they have nothing to say.

In Marx's opinion, the feelings and thoughts of other people become accessible to us through these objective manifestations of human activity.[16]

Thought, being converted into objective reality, acquires at the same time a *social* existence. It becomes the property of many, and therefore *undergoes thorough testing in the works and experience of thousands, receives the corresponding corrections, is improved and gives rise to new problems.*

Of all the things that are necessary for humans, Marx said, the most necessary one of all is another person, the need in the other person. This 'other' person may be given to the individual in a useful form only through his/her material manifestation, through the world of things created by this person (whether it be music, poetry or a building brick). All other relationships are reduced to biological ones – which, however, among humans under the influence of these social relations, were radically altered and acquired historical meaning.

The animal, Adam Smith says, is forced to live a self-contained life. '[It] derives no sort of advantage from that variety of talents with which nature has distinguished its fellows. Among men, on the contrary, the most dissimilar geniuses are of use to one another; the different products of their respective talents ... being brought, as it were, into a common stock, where every man may purchase whatever part of the produce of other men's talents ...'.[17] Every individual, having the opportunity to appropriate the products of another's labour and use the abilities of another, becomes involved in another person's experience, talents and intellect and can add them to their own experience. This way, it becomes possible, for a bit of money, to gain access to the ideational treasury of Shakespeare, Aristotle and in general all the great thinkers, musicians, authors, architects, painters and so on.

The exchange of abilities, experience and mutual achievements constitutes the only ground on which consciousness can grow and develop. The lightning of thought flashes only where it meets with another. The thoughts of another are accessible to us only through their external manifestation, whether it be in an argument, a technical construction, a drawing or in an architectural work.

---

16   Marks i Engel's 1928–1946, Vol. III, p. 626.
17   Marks i Engel's 1928–1946, Vol. III, p. 667.

In encountering the thoughts of another, appropriating the gifts of others and giving one's own – in exchanging experience, abilities and so on – human knowledge grew to colossal sizes and was clarified to exceptional acuity.

This situation cannot be achieved where the objective equivalent of activity – the objective product of labour – is absent: a mongrel dog cannot use the swiftness of the greyhound and add it to the advantages of its own strengths and its own abilities.[18]

It should be emphasised, however, that the process being described here is only an abstract romance of the development of the idea; below (in the second half of the book) we will see that the entire process of the growth and the enrichment of consciousness, historically speaking, progressed in a much more complex manner; that the development of human thinking occurred not in the form of a calm natural continuation of the ideas of preceding generations by subsequent ones but by ruthless social struggle and the violent 'forcing' of production of both the material and the psychic kind from humans by other humans.

3. Insofar as intellect acquires objective existence in things, it can also be preserved and accumulated in them. In its objective existence, thought no longer belongs to the world of psychic phenomena and does not take part in the 'flow of consciousness' as a component of that flow, as something fleeting and transitory.

Human ideas and thoughts, in the act of their realisation, are brought from a changeable, internally subjective mental existence into a world of existence that has already taken place and is objectively anchored, and acquires the solidity of externally material reality.

Hegel spoke of nature as a 'self-alienation of the spirit'[19] (*der sich enthremdete Geist*), and Schelling called nature 'a solidified, petrified intellect' (*eine versteinerte, erfrorene Intelligenz*). However, these formulations do not suit nature as such. No intellect took part in the natural process of the creation of nature, which is why intellect cannot be deposited in it. But these expressions are quite correct in relation to the entire field of culture; it really represents the objective existence of ideas.

Ideas, having acquired objective existence in the objects of material and spiritual culture, can also be preserved and accumulated as the infinite experience of humanity. Thoughts, taken phenomenologically as mental experiences, do not have this possibility. Human consciousness, as a subjectively phenomen-

---

18   Marks i Engel's 1928–1946, Vol. III, p. 666.
19   Hegel 1906, § 247.

ological process, is limited in every moment of its existence as individual consciousness. The sphere and scope of what psychologists call memory is extremely small, and its accuracy is far from perfect. If the existence of thoughts was limited only to the internal mental field and was exhausted only by subjective experience, human consciousness would be as poor as the consciousness of animals. If human consciousness did not surround the external objective world of the intellect – the world of material culture, language and so on – then it would not be an internal intellect; human consciousness would be empty, memory would be absent, no tasks or questions would arise, and goal-setting would be impossible.

The entire world of our representations and ideas is filled precisely with objective content, insofar as these representations concern the objects and relationships of a social order. This alone – concerning their activity – interests humans and occupies their consciousness. In this sense, the world of cultural objects created by human activity is the sole support of human thought, and at the same time the most capacious storeroom of human experience and human activity.

'[T]he history of industry and the established *objective existence* of history are the *open book of man's essential powers*, the perceptibly existing human *psychology*'.[20] Only a thinker of exceptional depth and dimension could say these words.

4. Thus, in the product of labour we have an object raised to the rational form of existence (an 'ideological object') and an idea that has acquired the material form of existence (a reified idea). This movement of thought and its transfer into external reality, and the other way round – the working of objects and their elevation to the level of the idea – represents the only path along which it is possible for human thinking to establish itself, to grow and to develop.

Without this world of cultural values, there would be no human form of thinking and only immediate animal relations would remain, which would run along the paths of instinctively reflexive actions. Thought is aroused by thoughts. The work of a thought begins in the encounter with semantic relationships. Consciousness is kindled only when it comes into contact with objects harnessed by human thought i.e. with objects that have been exposed to human intellectual activity and – owing to this – have acquired a rational meaning. Rationally organised and goal-defined objects, and the world of social relations – that is what gave rise to the work of human thought and provided the impulse for its development (cf. §§ 43, 44). Above all, it is precisely these

---

20   Marks i Engel's 1928–1946, Vol. III, p. 628.

objects that constitute the content of human thoughts. Without this objective content, consciousness would be empty. A thought is a thought when it has objective content (i.e. when a thought works on an object). If there is no objective content in it, then there is no thought as such.

5. And, finally, the object produced becomes the mediator of an action, the instrument and means of further extending the radius of activity, and also of broadening the intellectual horizons of humanity. This moment is found most obviously in the role of the instrument of labour, which is actually the main lever of humanisation and a powerful factor in reorganising the inert consciousness of the animal into active human consciousness.

The Qualitative Particularity of Social Relations

§ 27
'Individuals producing in society – hence the socially determined production by individuals – is of course the point of departure. The individual and isolated hunter and fisherman, who serves Adam Smith and Ricardo as a starting point, is one of the unimaginative fantasies of the eighteenth century' (Marx). The human form of the existence of an individual is possible only on the basis of communication with other individuals. Another person, other people, are necessary for any human existence.

A suggestion is often encountered in the literature that Feuerbach was the first to devise the philosophy of tuism. But the 'you' (*tu*) of Feuerbach is just as abstract a category as his 'I'. From this comes the coarseness of understanding and poverty of ideas that characterise Feuerbach's social views. 'In the form he is realistic since he takes his start from man. But there is absolutely no mention of the world in which this man lives; hence, this man remains always the same abstract man who occupied the field in the philosophy of religion. For this man is not born of woman: he issues, as from a chrysalis, from the god of monotheistic religions. He therefore does not live in a real world historically come into being and historically determined. True, he has intercourse with other men; however, each one of them is just as much an abstraction as he himself'.[21]

'Certainly Feuerbach has a great advantage over the "pure" materialists', Marx wrote, 'in that he realises how man too is an "object of the senses". But apart from the fact that he only conceives him as an "object of the senses", not as "sensuous activity", because he still remains in the realm of theory and

---

21   Engel's 1931, p. 57.

conceives of men not in their given social connection, not under their existing conditions of life, which have made them *what* they are, he never arrives at the really existing active men, but stops at the abstraction "man" and gets no further than recognising "the true, individual, corporeal man" emotionally, i.e. he knows no other "human relationships" "of man to man" than love and friendship, and even then idealised. He gives no criticism of the present conditions of life ...'.[22] Feuerbach examines 'man in general' instead of 'actual historical man'.

Feuerbach completely overlooks the following: for relations between individuals to become possible as *human* social relations, the simple existence of individuals is not enough; it is necessary for these individuals to be linked or separated (which essentially signifies the same thing) by specific *material* interests.

Feuerbach forgot that in order for relations of individuals among themselves to be able to move beyond the boundaries of biological forms and to create a new, particular type of relations – *social* links – more than just 'I' and 'you' are required, and more than just 'cordial bonds', 'love', 'friendship' and similar splendid things (which, however, apart from the preservation of biological appearance – that is, what everything in creation does – create nothing new). In order for *social* relations to arise, the world of material culture (instruments, utensils, etc.) is additionally required, which in turn requires its own conditions in social, technological, ideological and other relations. For this, it is necessary that this 'I' and 'you' *arose* from the beginning as *human* relations. Relations between people, as human relations, became possible on the basis of human labour activity; but, on the other hand, this material culture and means of production themselves become established only as a result of the social relations of individuals and are created by these individuals. Marx formulated this thought as follows: '*Just as* society produces *man* as *man*, so is society produced by him'.[23]

As regards the positions of Feuerbach that were examined, Marx says the following: 'Insofar as Feuerbach is a materialist, he does not deal with history, and insofar as he considers history, he is not a materialist. With him materialism and history are mutually exclusive ...'.[24]

At the turn of the twentieth century, a number of sociologists of the neo-positivist school (De Roberti, Tarde, Ward, Durkheim, Drăghicescu, Cooley, Simmel and so on) insistently advanced a position the 'mental influence' called upon to allegedly explain the essence of every social phenomenon. Mutual

---

22   Marks i Engel's 1933, p. 34.
23   Marks i Engel's 1928–1946, Vol. III, p. 623.
24   Marks i Engel's 1933, p. 34.

mental interaction between individuals, in their opinion, is the formative force of society as such and constitutes a fundamental factor of historical development no less than thinking and speech. 'In the prehistoric stage of evolution', de Roberti says, 'the organic multiplicity, the simple fact of the shared lives of individuals is already striving to go over to a supraorganic, social and spiritual unity through the formation of the first rudiments of a civil union'.[25] However – as far as is known to us – ants 'living shared lives' have nonetheless not created society, a spiritual culture, and philosophy! It is absurd to think that 'mutual mental influence' is given *per se* as a gift of nature in the form of a natural fact. In order for relations between people (including mutual mental influence) to become possible as *human* relations, the establishment of *material mediators in the relationships between individuals* in the form of labour and its products was necessary.

We are talking about the fact that humans became accessible to other humans *in a human way* through their external manifestation in the objects of their activity, through the reification of human thoughts, goals and intentions.

Without this creative activity, consciousness would remain locked within individual people in the form of only the subjective achievements of the particular individual, without the possibility of becoming involved in the experience of others or being accessible to other individuals.

Animals, who 'understand' each other splendidly in everything concerning the instinctive aspects and manifestations of their lives, lack the possibility of taking from each other experience acquired through intellectual means. In Thorndike's and Köhler's experiments, the animals (cats, dogs, apes) were unable to learn the solutions even when these solutions were demonstrated right in front of them. Every individual had to arrive at them independently.

Animals *do not communicate using consciousness*, and that is why – insofar as conscious acts are concerned – the experiences of other individuals is inaccessible to them and they cannot share their experiences with other individuals. No form of *inter-individual experience* arises in the lives of animals; no cultural values are accumulated. The intellectual achievements of particular individuals are not preserved. Intellectual experience is lost both for the individual themselves (as it passes over again into an unconscious, reflexive act) and for others – if, of course, we disregard biological accretions and the inheritance of acquired traits.

Conscious labour activity that creates a world of culture is thus the necessary condition for preserving the intellectual achievements of individuals and

---

25 *Novye idei v sotsiologii*, Book 2, 1914, p. 10.

for the preservation of consciousness in general. Owing to creative labour activity, the following become possible: 1) the transfer of conscious experience of single individuals to others; 2) the preservation of experience temporally – not only through biological inheritance, but through mutual understanding and cultural heritage; 3) hence, social experience is made possible, both in the sense of the sum total of cultural achievements and in the sense of the mutual communication of individual consciousness and *the general basis for the thinking of individuals of a given social circle*; 4) and, finally, the infinite enrichment of human experience and the endless growth of consciousness becomes possible, in relation to both breadth of scope and of depth of understanding.

It should not be thought, however, that human consciousness (like the human means of activity) arose from animal consciousness in a single step and immediately embarked on its own path of development. On the contrary, it must be thought that long after the first gleams, human consciousness was far from human; at the outset it had generally overcome the animal instincts from which, to a certain extent, we are still not yet quite free.

Here, in this transition from the animal to the human, the manifestation of the kind of moment in the life of the *primigenius* that intensified the conscious form of activity – gradually dislodging immediate and instinctive activity – was important. Nature obviously more than once 'attempted' to create humans; perhaps it produced repeated offshoots from the animal into the human that died out and disappeared (and about which some archaeological finds bear witness) until the specific form of humanity survived.

Acting as this historical lever is the instrument of labour that – again, in the context of the confluence of other conditions (the primitive hand, a liberated grasping organ; a diffuse instinct of community, the construction of the hemispheres of the brain, and so on) – could be held, and having been held, marked the firm beginning of humanisation by having made possible the diversity of human activity, the growth of needs and interests and consequently the growth of consciousness.

The Instrument of Labour – the Hand – Reason

§ 28

It was believed that the intellect is the instrument of cognition; Kant was not the only one to think so (on which basis he undertook the truly surprising enterprise of testing this instrument only through discourse about it – an enterprise, as Hegel justly noted, doomed to failure in advance). Nearly all philosophers, insofar as they touched on the questions of cognition, held such a conviction.

Does the intellect know where it is leading? Perhaps the intellect itself does not know where it is going; perhaps something (social conditions) is *leading it*? The position, however, that the intellect is the instrument of cognition is inaccurate and incorrect both historically and in its essence; it must never be forgotten than the intellect is above all *the result and the product* of the mediating objective activity of humans. This question was first clearly advanced theoretically in philosophy by the classical writers of Marxism.

Earlier, we saw that the work itself of consciousness only begins where the subject is capable of goal-setting and action mediated by a third component – that is, by the means for achieving a goal. The striving for a means, the work on means that only on a secondary or tertiary basis aid in achieving the main goal, is the irrefutable evidence of the manifestation of the work of the intellect. The circumstance that an object formed by human hands is placed by them between themselves and nature as a *means* of influencing it is in fact a moment of unprecedented historical importance for the establishment and development of human thinking.

The instrument of labour, this objective medium created by humans and placed by them between themselves and the objects of their influence is a mediator with the help of which humans multiply their strengths and complete every act of work – that is, these instruments reorganised human activity, improved humans themselves and remodelled animal consciousness into human thinking. These thoughts have been expressed many times since Darwin, and in our time scarcely anyone would dispute it. All the more surprising, however, is the carelessness with which these statements are treated in not drawing all the conclusions that flow from it for both psychology and for philosophy and sociology.

Animals are incapable of employing instruments. Being in immediate physical communication with nature around them, animals biologically adapt their organism to the environment. In its external form and character the animal organism is, as it were, an embodied function for specific actions. That is why they do not need instruments.

The instrument, as a mediator and as a means of activity, constitutes the exclusive advantage of humans and humans alone. Disputes about whether animals are capable of employing instruments, and the argument that certain animals (apes, elephants and so on) know how to use objects (branches, rocks, sticks) as instruments is essentially sterile and proves nothing. The question is not whether animals, in exceptional circumstances (in the majority of cases created artificially by humans themselves) get as far as using objects as instruments, but whether such means of activity can become necessary for animals – do they need them? Does the instrument have an advantage for the animal over their natural organs?

In any case, over the course of millennia, animals have never been observed abandoning their natural means of activity and switching over to artificial means, having learned the use of elementary instruments and how to communicate by using them. On the contrary, the facts always indicate the opposite: as soon as animals escape from human custody, they quickly forget all artificial methods and return to their animal nature, to the direct means of activity. This is understandable, since animals are so completely adapted to their normal circumstances with their natural organs that no artificial instruments can replace them.

While an ape can catch on to using a stick as a means, no single animal is ever raised to the level of work on a means that is lacking. Not one animal makes instruments.

The objection may be raised that Sultan, the chimpanzee in Köhler's experiments, independently made one long stick out of two shorter ones by pushing the narrower one into the mouth of the wider one. Hence, animals are also 'tool makers'.

An attentive reader of Köhler's reports regarding this experiments would never come to such a conclusion.[26]

Sultan, of course, had no intention of making an instrumenrt. And he did not do so. The instrument itself was 'made' in his hands, unexpectedly for him.

If Sultan actually knew how to prepare tools, then – no matter the positions of the two sticks in his hands – he would seemingly have to perform the operation of insertion and making a longer stick with no difficulty. But precisely the opposite was observed: when, for example, the sticks in the ape's hands assumed a cross-like formation, Sultan – having frequently repeated the operation of lengthening the stick – became completely perplexed and could not solve the task.

Not only do animals not know how to *make* instruments, they are completely unable to even *use* something as an instrument, in the literal sense of the word. An ape makes use of a stick, a rock, and other objects, it is true, but never as an

---

26 'Sultan takes both sticks, sits on a box and plays with them nonchalantly. Whereupon it came about that he had both sticks in front of him in each hand, in such a position that both lay in a straight line. At that point the ape inserted the narrower one into the mouth of the wider one. And as soon as that happened, he ran to the cage bars to obtain the fruit'. Köhler 1922, p. 91. Insofar as the longer stick accidentally appeared in the ape's hands in this manner – furthermore, clearly by itself – because Sultan in general handled the sticks extremely well.

instrument. It is possible to speak of the actual use of an instrument only in cases where this instrument preserves its functions and its meaning even beyond the limits of the given moment and the given situation. The stick loses meaning for the ape as soon as it exits the field observed simultaneously with the goal; the stick ceases to be a means and loses all its useful functions as an instrument.

The ape strives for a goal, but not for an instrument. It can use an object given in its field of vision as a means; however, the ape never separates it from its immediate sensory environment. The use of a stick is characterised every time by the situation at hand. If something is not required by the situation at hand at the given moment, no animal notices the *possible role* or the useful functions of things. As soon as something exits the animal's field of vision, it ceases to be useful.

If the consciousness and behaviour of an animal are continually conditioned by the sensory field and the animal is not capable of setting any goals whatsoever, then speaking about the use of instruments is of course meaningless.

Animals realise all their needs by means of their own natural organs. They place no mediating objective means between themselves and the objects of their actions.[27]

Humans, on the other hand, almost never act by using only their natural organs. They use artificial instruments.

What advantage does mediated action have over direct, immediate action? What is the advantage of artificial instruments over natural organs?

The advantage consists of the fact that it is possible to perform a multitude of diverse actions with the use of artificial instruments. Animals, commanding only what is given them by nature, are limited in their activity. Natural organs are attached to the body, forming a single whole with them. They cannot be changed arbitrarily as required, they cannot be adapted to other functions and to other types of activity, and it is impossible to replace them with other instruments. Having only natural organs available means having to submit to their capabilities and having to live within the range of activities that do not go beyond the framework of these organs' functions. Animals are excellently suited to only certain activities. Almost no field of activity exists that could not be carried out by some type of animal to a striking degree of perfection. They know how to dig, bore, carve, scratch, fly, and so on. Moles are excellent diggers and

---

27   The apes in Köhler's reports often play with the sticks – teasing each other with them, hitting, poking, and so on – but as soon as it came to serious fights they threw away the sticks and went 'hand-to-hand'.

pikes swim flawlessly, but apart from this 'skill' they are incapable of anything else. The natural conditions of life and the physical constitution of an animal limit its activity to a certain narrow sphere, dooming them eternally to one and the same type of activity. Animals are the slaves of their natural organs.

This eternally uniform activity flows largely along the channel of unconscious activity. Under such conditions, even if flashes of consciousness arise every now and then, the action is always transferred back into the unconscious reflexive field of stereotypical actions.

The advantage of artificial instruments lies in the fact that they are not physically connected to the organism. An instrument is an external object. Arbitrary intentions can be introduced into it, it can be adapted to various kinds of work and various functions, and it is infinitely perfectible.

As an external object, an instrument burdens the hand while it is required for a specific necessity, at the close of which the instrument can be laid aside and replaced by another instrument more suited for the new work. Artificial instruments create the possibility of *manifold activity* itself, permitting the realisation of extraordinarily specialised functions; moreover, the structure of the human body is not changed in any specific direction but remains suitable for every other kind of work.

Thanks to the use of artificial instruments, the *biological closure of the animal form* is overcome; *activity becomes multifaceted and diverse, as do needs*; at the same time, the field of interests and the field of consciousness are broadened.

On the other hand, the instruments of labour as external objects rationally organised by humans that have become the means of their activity, increase the strength of humans and increase their individuality far beyond the limits of their physiological boundaries. Thanks to the use of instruments, Marx says, humans make objects external to them the organs of their activity and, in adding them to their own, thereby extending – despite what the Bible says – their natural organs.

This idea was subsequently developed in a distorted form by Ernst Kapp, who constructed a unified theory on the projection of natural organs externally in the form of the instruments of labour. Natural organs (hands, fingers, teeth and so on), being natural instruments served – in Kapp's view – as the models for artificial organs. 'Human organs served as prototypes, which early humans unconsciously imitated in creating their primitive instruments'.

'A rock with a wooden handle is the primitive imitation of a closed fist', as the prototype of a blunt striking instrument.

'It is not difficult to recognise a simple row of teeth in a saw'. The action of the jaw formed the prototype of the tongs.

'The extended finger with its sharp nail becomes the drill in technical production', and so on. Kapp showed that 'in the instruments of labour, humans always reproduced only themselves in the initial tools and instruments; they put and projected the forms of their organs into them'.[28]

This theory raises too many doubts for it to be acceptable. The more data concerning primitive humanity that accumulates, the more indubitable becomes the statement that the representation of themselves and their organs were worked out in humans significantly later than the needs for primitive instruments (see §§ 44, 45). Speaking about 'unconscious imitation' of the forms of their own natural organs is equally as impossible as the preparation of instruments being an unconscious act. The form and properties of objects themselves defined their use as original instruments which, it should be thought, were not initially worked up but found in finished form, or snapped off or broken off by rough blows. In further development, the manufacture and external appearance of instruments was conditioned by the needs for and purposes of these instruments, and not by the impulse for imitation, by humans' own organs. The path shown by Kapp would be much more complex and difficult for primitive consciousness than the direct adaptation of primitive instruments for the necessary activity.

Kapp's etymological analysis, which had the purpose of showing that 'the Greek word ὄργχνον signified first of all physical organ and only later an instrument'[29] turned out simply to be mistaken. 'Obviously, Kapp was led into an erroneous meaning of this word in German', Ludwig Noiré noted on the subject. 'In the Greek, ὄργχνον means first of all a functional object – that is, a tool of labour, an instrument ... and only subsequently took on the meaning of a bodily organ'.[30]

Indubitably, the use of instruments imparts a colossal power to human activity, broadening its sphere. If the assertion of the naturalists that a spiderweb is an extension of the organism of the spider and the expansion of its natural organs is true, then it is no less true that the world of industry, instruments and secondary stock is the extension of the radius of human activity and the broadening of human individuality into the external world. Individuals do not remain immured within the natural boundaries of their organisms. Physiologically, the arm – for example – ends at a length of about 75cm from the shoulder, but despite that, objects separated from it by many thousands of kilometres are as conveniently reached as anything close by. It is enough to say that

---

28   Kapp 1877.
29   Kapp 1877, p. 40.
30   Noiré 1880 (translated into the Russian as Nuare 1925, p. 210).

the hand of a telegraph operator tapping out specific signs writes on the other side of the earth just as legibly as the hand of a calligrapher. Thanks to the use of instruments, humans have succeeded in overcoming physical space, speeding up time, intervening in the life of nature, relocating the worlds of plants and animals, changing the climate, weighing the planet and so on.

'Whatever forces Nature develops and lets loose against man – cold, wild beasts, water, fire – he knows means to counter them; indeed, he takes these means from Nature and uses them against herself. The cunning of his reason enables him to preserve and maintain himself in the face of the forces of Nature, by sheltering behind other products of Nature and letting these suffer her destructive attacks'.[31]

Thanks to the use of artificial instruments, humans are able to combine in themselves the most *diversified means of activity*; they become the focus of every activity *and all the functions* with which nature endowed other creatures *separately*. They can carry out actions that are biologically contrary to their essence. In the air, in the water, and underground, they feel equally in their element. With the *diversity* of their activities, humans finally overcome the biological limitations of both their physical and their *mental nature*.

By using tools, humans not only alter external nature, but in the process of this alteration they also change themselves, *their needs*, their physical constitution and their natural organs. In particular, this concerns the most important organs in the given relation, which, constantly in direct communication with the instrument, reflect in themselves all of human nature as distinct from that of animals: we are speaking here of the *human mind and the human hand*.

§ 29

Since the time of Darwin, the assertion that the advantage of humans over the animals was created owing to the hand has become generally acknowledged. This remarkable idea was expressed by many even in ancient times. In Greek philosophy, this thought is first encountered in Anaxagoras, and later in an even more eloquent form in Aristotle, who called the hand the 'tool of tools'. We encounter similar views in different variations in many other philosophers: Helvetius, Kant and so on. Kant saw the advantage of the human hand over all the other organs in the fact that 'Nature endowed it, the hand, not with one specific means of activity, but adapted it to perform many varied functions'.[32]

---

31   Hegel 1906, § 245, p. 293.
32   Kant 1799.

What circumstances could facilitate so great and advantage of the hand over the other organs of the body?

Proceeding from specific ecological hypotheses, Lazarus Geiger showed that as a result of life in the trees the ancestors of humanity developed an upright posture and their hands transformed from an organ of movement into an organ of prehension, and that under these conditions the hand gradually lost the functions for moving the body and acquired the peculiarities of a prehensile organ. However, this notion – with which we must reckon with even today – still by no means takes us beyond the boundaries of animal existence: it says nothing about the peculiarities of *the human hand* specifically. Animals know how to grasp and to hold; birds with their talons, for example, and instead of one pair, apes have two pairs of prehensile organs.

As for the thumb, which makes the hand especially suited as an organ for grasping, there is a popular phrase: *le doigt opposable*, the creator of universal history. This assertion can only be considered true with great limitations, insofar as we have in mind specifically *human* use of the hand, and not only the function of grasping.

The forelimbs – while they represent a great advantage for animals as organs of grasping, they are incapable of bringing animals out of their animal aspect. There is a great distance, Engels says, between the prehensile organ of the ape and the human hand. 'The number and general arrangement of the bones and muscles are the same in both hands, but the hand of the lowest savage can perform hundreds of operations that no simian hand can imitate'. The forelimbs of the ape are not yet hands.

'The first operations for which our ancestors gradually learned to adapt their hands during the many thousands of years of transition from ape to man could have been only very simple ones. The lowest savages ... are nevertheless far superior to these transitional beings. Before the first flint could be fashioned into a knife by human hands, a period of time probably elapsed in comparison with which the historical period known to us appears insignificant. But the decisive step had been taken, the hand had become free and could henceforth attain ever greater dexterity; the greater flexibility thus acquired was inherited and increased from generation to generation'.[33]

This constant exercising and perfection of the human hand, as described by Engels, *was possible owing to the variety of labour and on the basis of the use of instruments*. As a consequence, both the physiology of the human hand and *the physiology of the human mind* were altered.

---

33   Marks i Engel's 1925, p. 90.

'Thus the hand is not only the organ of labour, *it is also the product of labour*. Only by labour, by adaptation to ever new operations, through the inheritance of muscles, ligaments, and, over longer periods of time, bones that had undergone special development and the ever-renewed employment of this inherited finesse in new, more and more complicated operations, have given the human hand the high degree of perfection required to conjure into being the pictures of a Raphael, the statues of a Thorwaldsen, the music of a Paganini'.[34]

In the human hand lies the expression of the manifold activity of the subject. Thanks to the use of instruments, it is capable of performing the most diverse functions, it acquires the *universality* characteristic of it alone. It becomes a *universal organ* that no single creature possesses, except for humans. Cicero said about the hand that it was *omnium artium ministra*, the servant of all arts. It is indeed the 'tool of tools', in Aristotle's words.

'What I hold in my hand', Hegel says, 'that magnificent tool which no animal possesses – can itself be a means to gripping something else'.[35] That is why the hand's sphere of action can be extended infinitely. This colossal significance of the influence of the hand has echoed since ancient times in the world view of people and has been preserved in the monuments of material culture, in religious formations, in the creation of myths, in language and so on.

Thanks to the activity of the hand, it became possible for humans to perceive the world, and the reality surrounding them. Humans became aware, above all, of that part of reality that represented the object of their activity.

Human consciousness and intellect do not ascend directly from the hand, but only from the objects created by the hand, from the products of human activity. *The hand was not so much perceived as it aided the process of perceiving the world of objects. The subject, in the process of their activity using their hands, alienates their thoughts, imparting an objective real existence to them. The alienated – and consequently, qualitatively elevated – object* (which is simultaneously a qualitatively elevated idea) *easily penetrates human consciousness, enriching and correcting, conveying experience and posing problems; this object is not simply a natural object but a subjectified one, a thought – a bearer, a 'humanised' object; on the other hand, it is not a subjective thought with its unstable and transient existence, but a thought transformed into objective existence*, objectively palpable.

---

34 Marks i Engel's 1925, p. 90.
35 Hegel 1911, § 55, p. 301.

We are speaking about the fact that *not only objects are accessible to thought through their alteration and subordination, but that thought is accessible to itself through its realisation, through work, through comprehension of an object that has become the embodiment of thought.*

Numerous definitions of humanity are known:

'Man is a social animal' (Aristotle).

'Man is a tool-making animal' (Benjamin Franklin).

'Man is an animal that possesses hands'.

'Man is an animal that speaks, his distinctive properties are intellect and speech, *ratio et oratio*'. '*Homo animal rationale, quia orationale*', Hobbes said. 'Man is a thinking animal because he speaks'. But the opposite could be said just as rightly: Man is a speaking animal because he thinks.

All these definitions and all similar utterances express the same idea in different words. Since humans labour, this unavoidably indicates that they are social and rational creatures, and creatures that possess the capability of speech. If they are social creatures, then all their other traits flow from this with the same inevitability. Each of these definitions draw all the others along behind it, but this means that each of the qualities named include all the others as its condition. Labour, the instruments of labour, the hand, the intellect, speech and so on are inseparably linked with each other; they so firmly mutually condition each other that it is sufficient to wrest just one of these moments out of the historical loop of development for all the others to disappear. It follows from this that they are not isolated realities, but only separate moments of a single unified whole. Labour, the material culture of society, thinking and speech are all components of a single closed formation – a social complex – and insofar as we have a genetic issue in mind, it should not be forgotten that *they could only arise together, all on the same plane.*

We are speaking about a closed formation for – as we shall see further on – these moments, in mutually conditioning each other, create a whole and constitute the living process of the history of human development.

The Cognitive Significance of Mediated Activity

§30

We have seen that human relations to external nature are expressed in labour activity; that humans move towards a formulated goal through a series of roundabout actions, investigating and using a series of means; that the human means of activity (and consciousness as well) are in principle of a mediated character.

The material expression of this mediated relation is the objective mediator that, as Marx said, is created by humans themselves and is placed by them between themselves and the object of action – the instrument of labour in the broad sense of the word.

If this is examined closely, one can be convinced that the entire intellectual wealth of humanity, almost all their knowledge of nature, represents the expression of mediated actions and revolves around the questions of material practice and human relations. At the initial stage, mediating elements, means and instruments of activity focus almost all the energy of human thought activity.

Things interest us and occupy our thinking not according to their nature (or their natural existence) but according to their cultural and historical significance. This is apparently because the world of culture (and not the world of nature) is the flesh of our flesh and the blood of our blood.

All human activity directed at objects is ultimately expressed not so much in the fact that they acted as it is in the fact that they made objects act on each other, being the organiser of this influence. 'In activity', Marx said, 'humans can produce only movement; they only move objects in order to bring them nearer to each other or to separate them from each other; all the rest is done by the properties of the objects themselves'.

The force of human thinking and the secret to the endless growth of its power lie in this mediated activity.

The words of Hegel on this topic are quite brilliant: 'Cunning may be said to lie in the intermediative action which, while it permits the objects to follow their own bent and act upon one another till they waste away, and does not itself directly interfere in the process, is nevertheless only working out its own aims'.[36]

In the process of the mutual interaction of objects, their qualities and their essences are revealed. An object, placed by a human against another object, being exposed to mutual influence and acting in turn, reveals the properties inherent in it, displays its force and its qualities, at the same time disclosing the qualities and properties of other objects or environments in which it was placed by the will of the subject. In the mutual interaction of acid and metal, the properties of both substances are experienced. In this 'confrontation' of objects, both sides show how they behave in relation to one another (what they can and cannot do); they are mutually revealed, displaying their properties and qualities.

---

36   Hegel 1906, § 209.

Here, the subject only has to 'watch' from the side, adding nothing and only noting down the facts the objects themselves are giving an account of in his/her register.

Consciousness does not need to force out or concoct thoughts. They are given by the objects to someone who knows how to compel these objects to reveal their nature and tell the truth about themselves; it is only necessary to know how to notice and to see this.

Discovering the new properties of things, humans find specific uses for them. 'Man', Marx says, 'makes use of mechanical, physical, chemical properties of things in order to change them into tools to act on other things according to his purpose'.[37]

Objects do not have properties and qualities that would be displayed in something on the outside, but all the difficulty of an experiment consists precisely in knowing how to compel an object vividly and graphically to reveal its properties for the purpose of making them accessible for perception, evaluation and measurement.

The task of an experimenting, learning subject is to place the object being studied into conditions under which it loudly expresses the sought-after attributes and qualities. In various changes to these conditions, the object consistently exposes itself not from one, but from many sides, displaying the wealth of its properties. 'Every useful thing', Marx says, 'is a whole composed of many properties; it can therefore be useful in various ways. The discovery of these ways and hence of the manifold uses of things is the world of history'.[38] These properties, as both Lenin and Feuerbach said, can be known only from their actions.[39]

Hence, a learning subject is only required to be a skilful organiser of this 'confrontation' of objects; the objects themselves give an account of all the rest. The high quality and value of the experiment consists in this: we create clear, precise dispositions of objects; we place them in the grasp of exactly specified conditions, and we observe the mutual influence by the one on the other, we observe what happens to them. This is the only true way for the scientist. In this way, cognition penetrates inside the laws of nature and learns the actual properties of objects without inventing its own arbitrary definitions out of itself.

In observing nature both large and small, the question must continually be asked: what is being expressed here, the object or I myself? If, consequently, objects display themselves in interaction with other objects, if they themselves

---

37   Marx 1996, p. 135.
38   Marx 1996, p. 1.
39   Lenin 1931, Vol. XII, p. 37.

give an account of their nature, then what in this case remains of the notorious anthropomorphism of truth, of the assertion of the unknowability in principle of the 'thing in itself' – what remains of the thesis that thinking allegedly imposes its own mechanisms on reality (Kant, Avenarius, Mach, Vaihinger, etc.) or that reality itself is entirely the product of self-presuming cognition 'according to the principles of the unity of *a priori* transcendental judgement' (Cohen, Natorp, Cassirer, et al.)?

We think that all similar idealistic assertions are purely fictive, grounded on absolutely nothing.

§ 31

Since ancient times, philosophers have abused the concept of internal nature and internal essence, opposing this abstraction to the external manifestation of objects and distinguishing the sensory and empirical world from the essential world.

On the basis of this division of the world into two parts – the personal and behind the scenes – an entire range of 'problems' of roughly the following type has arisen before philosophers: is the world of 'things in themselves' accessible to human cognition, or only the world of phenomena? How is the transcendental made immanent for consciousness, and how is the immanent made transcendental? The 'problems' of content and form, material and spirit and so on were advanced.

In the first half of the eighteenth century, the physiologist and poetaster Albrecht von Haller formulated a theory on the impossibility of the transition from the external manifestation of objects to their internal essence in verse:

> Into the core of Nature
> No earthly mind can enter.
> It is happy when it only
> Knows the external shell.[40]

The prominent representatives of Western European bourgeois thought now defend something similar, even in such fields of science as physics. James Jeans, in his 1930 book *The Mysterious Universe* (p. 127) defends the opinion that the

---

40   Haller, *Falschheit der menschlichen Tugend* (1732):
    'Ins Innere der Natur
    Dringt kein erschaffener Geist.
    Glückselig, wenn sie nur
    Die äussere Schale weist'.

phenomenon of our reality is only the shadow of a world unknown to us. Jeans admits as real only the world of the fourth dimension, which can only be known in its entirety to the beings of the fifth.

Any refutations of a logical type are generally powerless against theories of this kind. If someone begins to assert that the entire world consists of thousands of demons that are the causes of every event large and small, but whom no one can observe, then there is no possibility of refuting such an assertion through logic simply because there is no logic in it. No one in the history of philosophy has given proof positive that this is so, if we do not take the attempts of Kant, who saw in his 'antinomies' of the intellect indirect evidence of the existence of a world of *noumena* – that is, a world of inapparent essences of things in themselves. Properly speaking, these 'antinomies' in Kant's system are called on to serve not so much as evidence of the existence of a noumenal world as much as some sort of general *sign* that there is something wrong in the world of noumena.

'Antinomies of the intellect', according to their logical role, are tantamount to Kant's reasoning in the department of transcendental aesthetics, where the divergence between the left and right hand (despite their parity and similarity) when superimposed upon each other must serve – in Kant's opinion – as a sign of the phenomenality of our space and indirect 'evidence' of the fact that everything in the noumenal world is quite different. The celebrated Kantian 'antinomies' prove the existence of the noumenal world just as little as these absurd (from the point of view of geometry) ideas about the left and right hands.

What could a theory like this, that divides the world into empirical and essential, serve? What new problems could it advance for cognition? We dare say that this theory is not only incapable of proposing new problems, but on the contrary it permanently cuts off the development of thought and leads research into an impasse. In this is a sign of the incompleteness of the theory and evidence of its falsity.

The assumption of another, special reality in the form of the inapparent essence of things behind the curtains of real, empirical reality is the act of a cowardly intellect,[41] afraid that the world of hopes that cannot be relied on will be depleted.

---

41 This division of the world into two worlds that absolutely do not interact – the world of phenomena and the world of things in themselves – was of use in allotting to science its sphere (the phenomenal, intelligible world) and to faith and religion its sphere (the world of noumena, absolutely transcendental and inaccessible to human knowledge). The latter is the 'world of truth', however; inaccessible, unprovable, unable even to be promised,

'But, like any cowardice, this is the manifestation of the limitation and shortsightedness of conjecturing a reality so poor that thinking could at some point deplete it entirely'; as every act of cognition reveals a fresh series of new problems, the existence of which people had not even suspected until then.

The internal essence of objects consists only of what it displays, what it *reveals* in relation to other objects. And here once again, as in many other things, a poet who repudiated this superficial scholasticism of 'internal' and 'external' proved to be far more clever and deeper than many philosophers.

Reading *Critique of Pure Reason* about the incomprehensibility of the noumenal kernel of Nature, Goethe noted: 'Analysis and observation of phenomena penetrate nature, and it is impossible to know how far they will come in the course of time'.

To Haller's quatrain cited above, Goethe – at an advanced age – responded with words full of vivacity:

'O Philistine! ... have the grace to spare the dissenter / Me and my kind. We think: in every place / We're at the centre ... Nature has no 'core' or 'shell' / She is rather the whole all at once'.[42] 'Nature has no secrets it does not place naked before the eyes of an attentive observer'.

The internal is always revealed in something; *there is no unrevealed essence in reality*. We apply this principle not only to the object, but to the subject as

---

but nonetheless conceivable, like consolation or duty: the sphere of the freedom of faith – which, however, ethical necessity conceives as the world of immortal souls and a deity.

Nietzsche was correct when he said 'I hold it against the Germans that they were wide of the mark with Kant and his 'philosophy of loopholes', as I call it – he was not a model of intellectual integrity' (*Twilight of the Idols*).

This amicable division of the world, where religion was allotted its sphere and science its sphere with the imperative not to violate the mutual tranquility, is the police force of a cowardly science striving to mark itself off from the pretensions of church and religion, and not to fight. This alone is unworthy of a science that in its essence must always be progressive.

42   'Natur hat weder Kern
     Noch Schale,
     Alles ist sie mit einem Male;
     Dich prüfe du nur allermeist,
     Ob du Kern oder Schale seist!'
     Elsewhere, Goethe says:
     'Müsset in Naturbetrachten
     Immer Eins wie Alles achten
     Nichts ist drinnen, nichts ist draussen
     Denn was innen, das ist aussen'.

well; it is equally good as a criterion for knowledge of the subject. The internal essence of an individual consists of in what and how it is revealed. Hegel developed this thought as follows:

'There certainly may be individual cases where the malice of outward circumstances frustrates well-meant designs, and disturbs the execution of the best-laid plans. But in general even here the essential unity between inward and outward is maintained. We are thus justified in saying that a man is what he *does*; and the lying vanity which consoles itself with the feeling of inward excellence may be confronted with the words of the Gospel: 'By their fruits ye shall know them'. That grand saying applies primarily in a moral and religious aspect, but it also holds good in reference to performances in art and science. The keen eye of a teacher who perceives in his pupil decided evidences of talent, may lead him to state his opinion that a Raphael of a Mozart lies hidden in the boy: and the result will show how far such an opinion was well-founded. But if a daub of a painter, or a poetaster, soothe themselves by the conceit that their head is full of high ideas, their consolation is a poor one; and if they insist on being judged not by their actual works but by their projects, we may safely reject their pretensions as unfounded and unmeaning. The converse case however also occurs. In passing judgement on men who have accomplished something great and good, we often make use of the false distinction between inward and outward. All that they have accomplished, we say, is outward merely; inwardly they were acting from some very different motive, such as a desire to gratify their vanity or other unworthy passion. This is the spirit of envy. Incapable of any great action of its own, envy tries hard to depreciate greatness and to bring it down to its own level. Let us, rather, recall the fine expression of Goethe, that there is no remedy but Love against great superiorities of others. We may seek to rob men's great actions of their grandeur, by the insinuation of hypocrisy; but, though it is possible that men in an instance now and then may dissemble and disguise a good deal, they cannot conceal the whole of their inner self, which infallibly betrays itself in the decursus vitae. Even here it is true that a man is nothing but the series of his actions.'[43]

All this is only the development of Goethe's basic thought, which he expressed with the words: 'A man's actions are the mirror in which he shows his portrait'.

Thus the task of knowing a person, and also of self-knowledge, changes one's attitudes.

---

43   Hegel 1906, § 140.

How is it possible to understand oneself? 'Not through contemplation, but only through action', Goethe responds. 'Attempt to do your duty, and you will immediately find what is in you'.

'If we take the significant dictum 'Know yourself' (Γνωθι σε αυτον), and consider it, we mustn't interpret it from an ascetical standpoint. It does not by any means signify the kind of self-knowledge advocated by our modern hypochondriacs, humorists and self-torturers ... This needs no psychological self-torture ...'. 'Being a hypochondriac is nothing more than being absorbed in the subject', and when 'a person reflects on their inner and moral nature, they usually feel ill'.

'I must admit that I have long been suspicious of that great and important-sounding task: 'know yourself'. This has always seemed to me a deception practiced by a secret order of priests who wished to confuse humanity with impossible demands, to divert attention from activity in the outer world to some false, inner speculation. The human being knows himself only insofar as he knows the world; he perceives the world only in himself, and himself only in the world. Every new object, clearly seen, opens up a new organ of perception in us'.

'The great difficulty about psychological observations is that you always have to look on the inner and outer sphere as being parallel or, rather, as interwoven. There is constant systole and diastole, a breathing in and breathing out of the living organism ...'.

That is why always striving to turn everything that is in us and with us into action remains the most reliable method for understanding humanity and for understanding ourselves as well. When you begin to do, you see the extent to which your ideas are of use and what you yourself are capable of. This corresponds precisely to the subject's internal self-concept; the extent to which a person grows and rises internally when aware of the successful mastery of a great task, and conversely, in the event of failure and being cheated out of results, self-awareness most often fearfully collapses and tends towards an 'inferiority complex'.

The object created by the subject or the work carried out by them, having been given an objective existence and a social reality accessible to others, nonetheless remains 'theirs' and, as such, is the best expression of an individual's essence. Not only is the individual revealed in this, but – as we will see below – society itself is revealed in the individual.

Humans thus understand themselves through the world of a reality created by them. Thus not only objective reality is known, but also the subject; the idea and the thought themselves can also be known only in this manner (i.e. through their realisation, through the objective existence of the thought).

The Tale of How 'the Transcendental Is Made Immanent' and 'the Immanent Is Made Transcendental'

§ 32

Since ancient times, philosophers have essentially laboured on one problem: how objects existing outside the 'ego' in the objective world of reality can be imparted to thinking as a subjective process.

The difficulty for philosophers increased even more owing to the view on the existence of 'two worlds' having taken root. From its very birth, idealist philosophy rested upon this assumption. If the question is to be examined historically, then it would be easy to show that this 'two worlds' theory is the latest philosophical rethinking of ancient animist views; if we go deeper, its roots turn up in the magical world views of primitive society.

Despite the fact that the 'two worlds' theory has been modified in diverse ways throughout the history of philosophy, it continually appears as essentially immutable in idealist systems. The entire matter ultimately leads to acknowledging the existence of a supersensory, metaphysical world apart from the sensual world: 'the world of phenomena and the world of things in themselves'. Φαινγομενα and νοουμενα, phenomenon and essence, *existentia* and *essentia*, material and spirit, finite and infinite, conditioned and unconditional, relative and absolut, transient and eternal – opposed to each other as two alien worlds.

The newest bourgeois philosophy has sought the resolution of these difficulties in two ways:

1) Some have denied in general the transcendental consciousness of the world of reality and admitted that thinking itself creates all their ideas about things from itself; that cognition is in principle incapable of passing beyond its own boundaries and can know only its own definitions (Kant, Cohen, Vaihinger, etc.). But then the question arises: 'How does what is immanent for consciousness become transcendental to it?' (i.e. how does consciousness objectify its own definitions and imagine them as objective, external reality?) In this respect, the same tendency stretches from Berkeley to Kant, to the empiriocritics (Cohen et al.). Moreover, the post-Kantian empiricists, in the name of immanent philosophy, the pragmatists and the *Philosophie des Als Ob* did idealism a disservice when they declared this world of essences, in which idealist philosophy imagined it found the truth and the most solid reality – the actually existing ουσια in the Platonic sense – to be the arbitrary 'fictions' of consciousness, to which nothing in reality corresponds.

2) Others admitted the objective existence of the world of essences, 'truth in itself' and so on (Bolzano, Husserl, Rickert et al.) – but then the ques-

tion arose: how does objective reality, transcendental for consciousness, become immanent for consciousness and accessible to it?

Initially, these philosophers separate reality, in a purely rational manner, into two antagonistic worlds: the ideal world, in principle immanent (the world of ideas, of pure form, of pure essences, and also the mental world) and the world of things, in principle transcendent; and then seek how to link and, no matter what, to unite these two alien and unjoinable worlds, searching for a bridge from subject to object that would simultaneously include the objective definitions of things and the subjective definitions of thinking, and – of course – find nothing of the kind.

Moreover, philosophy was soaring high in abstractions and paid no heed to simple earthly things; or to the fact that, in any activity, humans realise specific ideas, imparting a real external existence to thoughts; or to the fact that an external object, 'transcendental' to consciousness, is made 'immanent' (i.e. 'a human, rational object') and that 'what is immanent to consciousness' (ideas, thoughts) is made 'transcendental' (i.e. objectified).

Irrefutable proof of this is the entire material culture of humanity, which could rightfully rebuke philosophers with the words of a fabulist:

> 'Ungrateful ...
> If you were ever able to raise your snout high,
> It would be obvious to you
> That these acorns grow on me'.

CHAPTER 4

The Problem of Perception in the Field of Marxist Philosophy

The Perspective of Classical Psychology and Philosophy

§ 33
The assumption of the existence of two worlds – the empirical and the supra-empirical – compelled idealist philosophy to form similar conclusions in the field of cognition. The opposition of essence and phenomenon led to the opposition of thinking to perception. Moreover, it was believed that direct sensory perception arises only from the world of empirical existence, which represents surface phenomena and not true essence. It was thought that internal essence was hidden behind these phenomena, accessible not to sensory perception but to thinking, to speculation and to intellectual intuition.

In this connection, the fundamental task of philosophy amounted to seeking the paths for penetrating behind the curtains of the sensory world and grasping, through thought, the actually existing that was hidden behind the phenomena. Thus, metaphysics outlined for itself – as it were – its field of activity (imaginary, of course) and found its proper task, fully corresponding to the term μετα τα φυσικα that had arisen by chance.

It was actually called upon to become the doctrine of the absolute essences that lay beyond the boundaries of the sensory, physical world. The Marxist definition of metaphysics responds precisely to this, because every philosophy of essences as immutable principles is metaphysics in the proper sense of the word.

The philosophy of empiricism, having appeared in history under many names – positivism, sensualism, empiriocriticism, immanentism and so on – started from the premise that information from the sense organs is the basis and source of all cognition. From this circumstance – that the objective world is given to consciousness through sensory perception – empiricists came to the conclusion that nothing more than these subjective sensations is given to human cognition, and that consciousness in principle is incapable of passing beyond the boundaries of the subjective world of its sensations and of knowing anything about the actual nature of the external world.

Similar views were expressed in antiquity by Pythagoras, Heraclitus and others. Locke developed them in the entire doctrine of 'the subjectivity of sensory qualities'. Subsequently, these questions served as the primary object of a philosophical dispute: what is the cognitive value of sensory data; is the world of external reality accessible to consciousness as it is in itself; how is it possible to overcome the subjectivity of cognition; does the external world really exist, or is it a cognitive fiction, and so on. The series of these pseudophilosophical problems is a constant theme of philosophical disputes even today.

Logically, the given problem was brought out in pure form by Descartes, in his 1641 treatise *Meditations on First Philosophy*. In general outlines, it appears as follows: Humans cannot doubt their own existence, since every doubt proves that they exist; otherwise, they could not doubt. Their own experiences of consciousness are in no way refutable self-evidence. The existence of any external object, another person or the entire world outside of me does not have this character of self-evidence, and it is theoretically possible to doubt them.

How do you learn about the existence of these things? Your senses speak to you about them; you see, hear, and feel these things. This is irrefutable, but at the same this means that you are dealing not with the objects themselves, but only with your perceptions and ideas. You *only make inferences* about the existence of objects on the basis of your perceptions and ideas, which are completely subjective.

The same idea has been argued by other means. Having divided perception into the perception of external objects and of internal experiences – into 'external' and 'internal experience' – the idealists asserted that in 'internal experience' we observe our emotional experiences directly and in the original, and in external experience only 'symbolic' knowledge always arises, because here objects are not given immediately, but in translation into the language of perceptions, which are only subjective signs and symbols but not the actual qualities of these objects.

If you wanted to test whether your perceptions corresponded to external objects, you could not do it because the object can appear before you not immediately, but only through your perceptions; consequently, the test would consist of your perceptions being compared by themselves with other perceptions and no matter how you tried, your knowledge would never be able to pass beyond the boundaries of your subjective sensations, perceptions and ideas.

Do these subjective experiences guarantee a correct transmission of the nature and properties of objective things? No! These perceptions depend on the organisation of the sense organs, which are different in different creatures, and in humans – depending on the condition of their health – function differently and indicate the same qualities of things differently. Even in a healthy state, our senses show us the objects not as they are in reality.

In fact, the data of sensory perception cannot even serve as a witness to whether or not the external objective world of objects exists. While dreaming, under hypnosis or hallucinating, we have the same vivid sensory evidence despite the fact that nothing corresponds to reality. Relying on the data of sensory perception, we cannot even know with absolute reliability whether these things exist or if they are only the products of imagination. Sensations, perceptions, ideas and in general the entire field of consciousness is in principle incapable of indicating anything that passes beyond the boundaries of consciousness itself; they have an exclusively subjective significance.

Thus is the 'sophism of idealist philosophy' obtained, which in Lenin's words consists of the fact that perceptions are received not across a link of perception with the external world, but across a partition, a wall separating consciousness from the external world.[1]

The zeal with which philosophers took up the resolution of these imaginary difficulties – purposely improvised, as it were, in the form of some kind of blank jigsaw puzzle – is surprising, though each attempt at a solution brought a new doctrine, system or even an entire philosophical school to life.

Without going into the details of subtle differences, we can break these attempts down into two fundamental types. In idealist philosophy there are two means of resolving the questions of how the external world of objective reality can be known by means of perception:

1. The first solution starts from the proposition that the objective world is transferred into consciousness in the language of subjective experiences, in the form of sensations, perceptions and so on that represent something completely different than the actual properties and qualities of things, but despite that are nonetheless certain 'signals', 'signs', or 'symbols' of these things. On the basis of such subjective data as specific 'symbols' and 'signs', we draw conclusions about things and their properties, the actual nature of which always remains hidden behind these symbols.

Solipsism offers only an extreme variant of this standpoint: what is given to us is only our perceptions and ideas, Berkeley says, and our knowledge in general is incapable of passing beyond the boundaries of subjective data.

'We know only our perceptions', Ernst Mach says, 'and we cannot know anything except them' (*The Analysis of Sensations*). 'Only perception can be conceived as existing' (Richard Avenarius, *Philosophy as Thinking of the World According to the Principle of Least Action*). According to these views, the entire content of consciousness takes shape entirely from perceptions, these basic elements, and all of human experience is only internal experience.

---

1 Lenin 1909, p. 41.

2. The second attempt at a solution consists of the reverse motion of thought. If in the former case, the external objective world in the form of the sum total of perceptions and ideas is transferred into an internal, subjective world, then the latter case starts from the proposition that subjective elements (perceptions and so on) take shape in specific complexes and are *carried* outside by the subject, projected and presumed to be objective things. The object thus is not a real object of external reality, but only an item 'objectified' and presumed in the act of consciousness. Post-Kantian idealist philosophy even invented special terms for this: *objecieren* (Natorp, Cohen) and *objeciendum* (Nicolai Hartmann).

Touching upon these same questions, Schopenhauer said: 'When I probe an object with a stick, then I transfer my own perception to the end of this stick; the same thing occurs in the case of vision, which uses beams of light as tactile feelers. And here, I transfer my own perceptions out into space. This objectification of things and their projection by consciousness externally occurs with such rapidity that it seems to us as if seeing is nothing more than experiencing sensations, while in reality it is an act of constructing consciousness of a body that possesses such-and-such properties. 'Contemplation is only the reverberation of our intellect'.[2]

This standpoint found an even more striking expression in Kant, who contended that experience is made up of two fundamental components: perceptions – which arise externally as formless material – and the *a priori* forms of consciousness, which put sensory data into order and impart spatial and temporal determinations, substantiality, causality and so on to them (i.e. the subjective data of consciousness imparts objective determinations and concreteness).

Neo-Kantian philosophy brought its 'corrections': it liquidated the last remnants of reality in the philosophy of Kant, removing sensations from it as received from outside by consciousness and declaring these sensations to be not given from outside but 'set' by consciousness for itself as 'questions' (*nicht gegeben, sondern aufgegeben*). Sensations, according to the doctrine of Cohen and Natorp, are questions that consciousness asks itself and solves itself.

Classical psychology generally kept to the first method. It was based on the assumptions of the philosophy of empiricism. Associative psychology believed that sensations (alongside simple feelings and elementary volitional impulses) constitute the basic elemental data of consciousness, its mental elements. Sensations are produced for the subject through the sense organs. Entering into consciousness, they are mechanically linked, associated with each other and

---

2 Schopenhauer 1900, pp. 49–62.

form perceptions (Wundt); representations are put together from the association of perceptions in the same way, conceptions from representations and so on.

In general, classical psychology conceived thinking as consisting of two elements: the conglomerate of different types of perceptions and the of the mechanism of associations. Psychology was not interested in the question of whether anything in the objective world corresponded to these ideas. 'Everything that happens outside the boundaries of consciousness, they say, doesn't concern psychologists'.

All these ideas – set forth by us very cursorily in general outline – may have played a positive role in their time, refuting even more scholastic views. But at the current level of knowledge they are so feeble that it seems staggering that they can still constitute the object of serious science.

In the following sections (§§ 34–40) we will attempt to cite general objections against the fundamental assumptions of empiricism and of classical psychology on the question of perception.

Sensation Is Not the Basic Mental Atom

§ 34

Sensation lay at the base of the entire philosophy of empiricism. At one point, Avenarius and Mach even declared them 'the elements of the world'. For classical psychology, in the work of its better representatives (Wundt, Ebbinghaus et al.), sensations were something akin to mental atoms from which human thinking was put together under the mechanical laws of association. Nonetheless, these elementary perceptions of such elemental acts of perception of various qualities never existed in mental reality.

The assumption that, in perceiving things, we allegedly perceive the elemental qualities of these things in the form of sensations and then form a complex of perceptions from them is only an abstract conjecture to which nothing real in mental reality corresponds; on the contrary, everything that occurs in consciousness at the time of the act of perception fully contradicts the assertions of traditional psychology.

Consciousness perceives a thing completely, and not in the form of the sum of separate sensations. Sensations, as the elementary acts of perception of various elementary qualities from which the perception of the whole is allegedly formed, are only abstractions created by psychologists – an abstraction that did not aid psychology but placed obstacles in the path of the development of this science. Believing that genuine elements of consciousness were located in sensations, classical psychology directed all its energy towards their study, and towards the identification of every 'threshold' of irritation, recognition, and so on. Psychology got firmly stuck on the study of perceptions along, but ultimately never learned what these sensations represented.

In reality, it turned out that it was not the various sensations, or even the sum of them, that formed and defined the field of perception, but the opposite: the perception of a certain elementary quality depends on the state of the general field in which this quality is perceived. It is not experience that consists of various sensations, but that things are perceived in conformity with the field of experience in which they are located. Through a series of delicate experiments, the representatives of Gestalt psychology graphically demonstrated that the same quality is perceived differently in different fields.

As concerns the apparatus of associations, that omnipotent tool of classical psychology, it must be noted that with the help of this magical remedy, no problems remain in the field of mental life: sensations are associated in order of their entry into consciousness and form representations. A representation, linked associatively with another representation, forms a judgement (subject plus predicate). A feeling of something pleasant or unpleasant is associated with the things, and we then have ethics and aesthetics. Sounds are associated with meanings, speech results, and so on. Everything immediately becomes 'clear'!

The history of science truly has not created a more fruitless idea than the study of associations. In the final analysis, this study is the rightful heir of empiricist philosophy, tracing its direct descent from Locke's *tabula rasa*. The principle of the absolute passivity of consciousness received its most eloquent expression here. According to this principle, consciousness is a passive recipient in which every type of sensation flows together, coupled and threaded together mechanically. The psychology of Johann Herbart mapped out consciousness in the form of the sum of representations and of the mechanics of their transfer. Classical psychology did not extend that far from it. In Max Wertheimer's apt expression, it saw in humans only 'a sack of sensations'.

Sensation Is Not a Symbol, but the Reflection of Reality

§ 35
Discussions about whether humans are given only subjective experiences in the form of their sensations – and not the actual properties of things – when perceiving them are incorrect.

Also mistaken are all the propositions flowing therefrom on the unknowability in principle of 'things in themselves' and on consciousness in principle being incapable of passing beyond its own boundaries (in rationalist philosophy, this corresponded to the proposition on immanence: Emil Lask's *Satz des Bewusstseins*). The proposition of empiricism on sensations being only 'signs' or 'hieroglyphs', and not the actual properties of things, is incorrect.

It is enough to ask this question: Is object A (e.g. the presence of a magnet) reflected in object B (e.g. a lump of iron) when the former acts upon the latter? It is clear to anyone that it is reflected – and that not only symbolically, but by producing material changes (in the orientation of molecules, in the properties of weight and so on).[3] It is also obvious that in the changes to the state of the lump of iron, the qualities of the other object (the magnet) are *really given* – its strength, position, direction of action and so on. The presence of a magnetic field gives rise to material changes in the lump of iron; consequently, this presence is reflected in it.

All the properties of the magnetic field are really reflected in the lump of iron, which it (the field) displayed in relation to the iron. But this still does not mean that A revealed all its properties, but that what it displayed in relation to B are its actual properties, and together with Leibniz we can say that one thing is reflected in another absolutely correctly and without distortion. We can speak, with some justice, about the *otherness* of one thing in another, about the real presence of the one in the other, which finds its irrefutable expression in those changes which occurred or are occurring in these things.

The advantage of consciousness in perceiving things over the blind but correct reflection just described of things in other things lies in the fact that in the given case, this other thing is a living subject and as such knows about the opposing thing that has some sort of relation to them, and also knows about this reflection.

What is imprinted in consciousness as a result of the perception of things is a direct expression – and in no way a distorted reflection – of the properties of the object, and not conditional signs and symbols, as the empiricists believed.

Of course, these reflections of things in the head of the subject are not the things themselves, and it is clear that our representations of things differ from these things themselves.

In perceptions and sensations, things display their nature and their real properties to the subject. In this sense, Lenin defended materialism from all

---

3   Helmholtz 1962. Similar views on the symbolic significance of sensations were expressed in antiquity (e.g. by Epicurus) and in the Middle Ages by Occam (semiotics, the study of signs).

attempts on the part of empiricists to distort it. Our perceptions, he asserted, are the subjective but correct expressions of the objective world *an und für sich*. Perceptions and representations do not, of course, reflect all the aspects and properties of things, only a certain part – but in this part they are correct reflections of the things themselves.[4] In their manifestations, things are infinite and inexhaustible, and human cognition covers only a certain portion of this infinity, gradually broadening its field and taking in the previously unknown properties of things.

Empiricists on the one hand and rationalists on the other, believed that sensory perceptions distort the actual nature of things and give false representations of them. They sought a way out and saw it in either eliminating the data of sensory perception in general from cognition (the rationalists) or in getting rid of the subjectivity of sensory qualities (the empiricists). They asserted that sensory perceptions give knowledge of isolated things, and not of general laws. If that were so, then no single science could strive for anything more. It is difficult to understand why 'general laws' are necessary to philosophers, if not for the knowledge of various things and of concrete cases. For us, however, it is clear that the evidence of the senses, if only in a message from the eye about the green tint of an object, is insufficient hardly because the object itself is not green. The insufficiency of the evidence of the senses lies not in the fact that the senses purportedly distort reality or provide information about isolated states, but in the fact that the messages left by them are *far too general*. In further concretisation it is ascertained that the general evidence of the eyes about the green tint of an object means that the object absorbs all visible light except green, and the green light is reflected and scattered from it. Hence, in relation to light of different frequencies, this object is receptive to every light except green.

Thus, the evidence of the visual senses proves to be fully correct, but far too general, and its insufficiency lies precisely in its generality and not in the fact that it allegedly provides knowledge about isolated states (i.e. on all points, the matter stands the other way round to what is asserted by the philosophy of empiricism and rationalism).

To (Lenin's) question: is objective reality given to humans in their perception? – we must respond: It is, but in far too general a form; the task of cognition lies in disclosing the concrete meaning of this general data delivered by sensory perception.[5]

---

4   Lenin 1909, pp. 96–9.
5   On the question of how to differentiate hallucinations from reality, praxis – and not logical exercises – provides an exhaustive answer. It cannot be proved by any syllogisms that some-

The evidence of the senses about reality is always correct. What confuses people is not the facts in themselves (in the given case, sensory data) but the dogmas about them and incorrect interpretations of what is sensually given.

§36

Philosophers and psychologists thought that nothing objective was given in mental experiences, and that perceptions are purely internal and subjective phenomena.

Schopenhauer expressed this thought more clearly than anyone: 'For sensation is and remains a process within the organism and is limited, as such, to the region within the skin; it cannot therefore contain anything which lies beyond that region, or, in other words, anything that is outside us'.[6]

When we, with eyes closed, probe an object with a stick, then we feel contact – not in the brain, of course, and not even in the hand, but at the end of the stick: hence, outside our body.

It is clear to anyone that the hear the tapping with our ears – not in the ears but precisely where it is sounding from. We do not take this – our perception – into the space outside us, as the psychologists assert, but actually hear the tap from the origin itself, from outside. The item objectively provides the perception immediately, where it is actually located.

Thus, though perception is a subjective process, the objective properties of the things being perceived are reproduced in it. In this, Lenin saw the fundamental difference of materialism from subjective idealism. 'For the materialist', he said, the 'factually given' is the outer world, the image of which is our sensations. For the idealist the 'factually given' is sensation, and the outer world is declared to be a 'complex of sensations'.[7]

It is meaningless to say, like Mach, that 'we sense our sensations' – this is an empty tautology. Of course, we cannot perceive what in one way or another is not given to our sensory perception. In that tautology, there is no problem. The question lies not in that, but in what we perceive. And by no means do we perceive everything that is accessible to our sense organs – which will be discussed in the following sections.

---

thing exists or that something does not exist. But it does not follow from this that the existence of actual reality can be doubted. The only conclusion that indisputably flows from this is that logic is not fit for such proof, that it should stick to its own business. Logic is far from omnipotent. *Existensbeweiz*, insofar as the matter concerns actual existence, lies beyond the boundaries of the achievements of formal logic.

6 Schopenhauer 1900, p. 46.
7 Lenin 1909, p. 91.

The Relational Dependence of Sense Data

§ 37

The empiricists believed that sensations are the elementary data that are not in need of an explanation and cannot be explained from something else: what a person sees and hears, the specific objects they sense – all this is given together with the physical organisation of humans and their sense organs. In this sense, the 'elementary data of our senses' was believed to be the basic fact of every cognition.

'For me', Feuerbach said, 'the sensual is first in the sense that it is not derivable from something else, but exists through itself and truly'.[8]

This thesis contains one of the fundamental errors of empiricism, and also of all pre-Marxian materialism.

Why do humans only notice objects, and do not perceive other things? Why do they retain certain stimuli, while others are not heeded? Empiricists do not ask themselves these questions. Empiricists and materialist metaphysicians see no problem in the fact that humans perceive objects and phenomena. It seems to them that only having sense organs – vision, hearing, smell and so on – is enough for this.

It was believed that the sense organs were receptors which sensations filtered through by themselves and imposed themselves on consciousness. It seemed to them that, in having these organs, humans perceived everything that was visible and audible – in general, everything that crossed the 'threshold of perception'.

The state of historical science, insofar as it had to do with the history of the origins of thinking, was fully responsible for these views. The picture of the origins of thinking had been painted by positivists in the following colours:

Primitive humans opened their eyes and saw before them a splendid sky, the sun, the stars, the earth and its waters, the plants and animals; they were surprised by these marvellous creations and even surprised at themselves, the phenomena of sleep and death and so on. And they began to ask themselves: What is this, and why is this? They began to think, to solve theoretical problems and became genuine philosophers.

It may seem that these words are an exaggerated caricature; to show otherwise, we will cite no less authoritative an author than Edward Burnett Tylor. 'Evidently', he says, 'two groups of biological processes interested primitive man (the causes of sleep, dreams and death – K.M.). In observing these two groups of

---

8 Feuerbach 1911, p. 94.

phenomena, the early savage philosophers likely came to the obvious conclusion (? – K.M.) that every person has a soul – a phantom, a subtle, incorporeal human form ...'.[9]

Similar, or even stranger, views were expressed by many others (e.g. Heinrich Cunow, *Ursprung der Religion und des Gottesglaubens*).

The fundamental positions of the philosophy of empiricism, having become established in the form of dogmas and preconceptions, acquired such force over minds that they compelled first-class thinkers to make naïve statements. Up to the present, many still believe that having sense organs is enough to see, hear, and perceive everything that is only accessible to them, and that this – according to the theory of empiricism – is enough for the human mind to start working, to ask questions and to solve problems.

Actually, however, primitive humans had no business with the sky, the stars, or many other phenomena. They noticed them as little as animals today notice them.

Primitive consciousness was completely incapable of 'observing' extraneous objects, of 'being surprised' and 'drawing conclusions'. And not only primitive humans – we do not perceive anywhere near all the objects found in the field of our senses. How many objects large and small, located literally before our eyes, we do not notice and let pass by our perception! Are there many people who would know what the buttons on their shirts look like, and how many there are? After all, they 'recount' them at least twice a day: morning and evening, when dressing and undressing.

On the other hand, the observation by Marx and Engels – that animals have sense organs, and that the eye of the hawk can see significantly farther than the human eye but does not notice a hundredth part of what the human eye sees – remains in full force. Dogs, having a significantly more delicate sense of smell than humans, does not discern even a trifling amount of the scents that for humans are known indications of various objects.

The possession of sense organs in no way means that consciousness masters everything that is physically accessible to the perception of these organs.

In his novels, James Fenimore Cooper had the native Americans see things and hear sounds that the Europeans did not detect. And he was correct: the consciousness of the natives was actually oriented differently because it perceived differently; it saw things differently than 'civilised' consciousness.

In the testimony of the explorers of Africa, 'the vision of the San people is simply telescopic'. Speaking of one of the aboriginal peoples of Brazil, Herndon

---

9 Tylor 1899, Vol. II, p. 11.

said they 'possess very keen external senses; they see and hear things completely invisible and inaudible to us'. Of the Abipan peoples, it is said that they can discern things 'that escape the most sharp-sighted Europeans'. But it would be a grave mistake to think that aboriginal peoples perceive the world in a richer and fuller manner than more 'cultured' peoples. Cooper, infatuated with the romanticism of the so-called *Naturvolk* (which, incidentally, never existed in reality), paid no attention to the fact that 'cultural' consciousness perceives objects and phenomena that aboriginals do not notice.

In order to know how to see, hear and perceive even what is immediately given, a great deal of experience – of training – is needed. It is known that under a microscope, the multitude of beings that would escape no microbiologist go unnoticed by the untrained eye. From a lookout, a novice using a viewfinder cannot see the movements of a group of adversaries that would be plain to the experienced eye of a good artillery scout, despite the fact that the retinas of both have precisely identical images, since they are both surveying the same field that has firmly been fixed by the scope.

All the more significant must be the different between the perception of animals and humans, both in relation to what they perceive and in relation to how this occurs.

'My relationship with my environment is my consciousness', Marx said. But the environment of animals is one thing; it is nature – and the natural environment for humans is another: the environment of culture, a social environment. The relation of animals to their environment, and consequently their consciousness, is different than the relation of humans to their industrial and social environment. And because the fact that I perceive as *Homo faber* and *Homo sapiens* – and how I perceive with my sense organs – differs completely from what and how animals perceive.

'Obviously the human eye takes in things in a different way from the crude non-human eye, the human ear in a different way from the crude ear ...'. (Marx).[10] Hegel noted that animals, despite possessing the corresponding organs, do not perceive all object, even if the latter are lying before them, that every type of animal has a specific, quite narrow circle of objects perceived by them, and all the other variety of objects remains indifferent and is not noticed.[11] What is perceived by one type (e.g. the apes) is often completely inaccessible to the perception of others (e.g. dogs or horses).

Köhler spoke about the experiments he carried out on apes, and then on other animals. Food was placed at a certain distance from a cage and tied to

---

10   Marks i Engel's 1928–1946, Vol. III, p. 626.
11   Hegel 1906, §161.

a rope, the other end of which was placed in the cage. Every ape immediately grasped the rope and pulled the food to them. A dog placed in this situation should also have been splendidly able to pull the rope with its paw and teeth; it seemed, however, quite incapable of orienting itself in such a simple situation. 'The dog', Köhler said, '*completely did not notice the rope; it simply did not see it* despite the fact that the rope was literally in front of its nose while it displayed tremendous interest in the goal itself. Dogs (and also e.g. horses) in such a situation could starve to death, incapable of helping themselves, while for the apes there was no difficulty whatsoever here'.[12]

'The dog does not see the rope lying in front of it'. This happens not because the object does not act upon the dog's sense organs. The rope exerts an influence on the dog's organs of vision, casting its image onto the retina of the dog's eyes, but nonetheless is not perceived.

When we say 'the dog does not perceive the wood, the piece of wire' or 'an infant of five months does not perceive separate objects', this does not mean that the images of the given objects do not exist in the field of their vision or on their retinas. This also does not mean that 'perception' of these objects constitutes a part of the variegated chaos of sensations that – as many under the influence of Kant assured us – consciousness later organises and carries outward. Though the perception of an infant represents an undifferentiated field, in no way is it a 'mosaic of a multitude of perceptions'. The child's field of perception is undifferentiated in the sense that it is a uniform, monotonous something; a monoform, indifferent general background similar to the condition of a torpid gaze when a person seems to see everything and nothing at the same time. Of course, this comparison should not be interpreted literally.

In the act of perceiving something from this indifferent, monotonous field of consciousness, a certain part (e.g. their mother's face, for a child) is distinguished as an independent quality, object and so on and shifts into the foreground of consciousness; all the rest is simultaneously perceived as a non-segmented background even if in reality it is quite diverse.

Not every phenomenon and not every event stands out from this indifferent general background and shifts into the focus of consciousness – only some of them that are fully specific to each type of animal. Speaking in the language of the physiologists, not every 'stimulus' irritates an animal, and something that is perceived by one type is not perceived by another. Not all events are equally indifferent to an individual; some phenomena upset them more, some less; to

---

12   Köhler 1922, p. 19.

some they are receptive every time, and to others only sometimes. And there are phenomena to which they are generally indifferent and some they do not notice at all. Indifferent phenomena of this type constitute the largest part of the environment that constantly surrounds animals.

Differentiating a specific quality (e.g. perceiving a specific object or phenomenon) from the 'dead' background of consciousness requires, first, the particular conditions of the environment and, second, the particular *arrangement* of the consciousness – the particular interest of the subject in precisely this part, among the rest of reality that is indifferent to them.

§38

Generally speaking, 'sensual', perceptive consciousness is a biological fact. Animals possess it as well. The perception of animals, however, should be differentiated from human perception. The difference between them is not one of degree, but of essence. Human perception is defined by the conditions and causes of a social order. It takes shape, works and possesses a circle of objects, having little in common with animals' circle of perception. The painstaking attempts of 'well-meaning scientists' to make zoopsychology a propadeutic for the understanding of human psychology therefore miss the mark. Years of experience show that this has only hobbled research, switching the attention of scholars onto the grounds of principles that are essentially foreign to human nature.

Only a specific, quite limited circle of objects, Hegel said, is accessible to the perception of each type of animal. The lion senses the gazelle, and the hawk the rabbit, with extraordinary keenness; other animals can discern roots, grasses and so on very well. Animals can become aroused only by these 'own objects'; it is as if all the rest does not exist for them.

Humans as thinking beings, Hegel continues, make all the objects of nature the subject of their interests.[13]

However optimistic Hegel may have been, humans have come nowhere near making 'all objects' the subject of their interests – but the circle of objects that affect their interests can undoubtedly not be compared with the limited circle of even the most highly developed animal. And this circle, historically speaking, is an ever widening one.

The question arises: why is the circle of objects that occupy animals so limited, and where does this limitless breadth of the circle of objects occupying human consciousness come from?

---

13   Hegel 1906, §161.

Bringing any animal out of the limited field of these 'own objects' and compelling them to also perceive objects alien to them requires – every time – placing the animal in the artificial conditions of an experiment and training them on that object (e.g. fixing the given object, which is usually indifferent to the animal, as a stimulus). Particular work on the animal is needed in order to break off its indifferent relation to the specific objects and arouse *interest* in them, otherwise the animal will not see, notice, or perceive these objects. And as soon as interest disappears, the animal again becomes indifferent to the given object and stops perceiving it.

A curious observation has come out of a cynological laboratory in Moscow. It turned out that dogs, despite their keen olfactory abilities, usually do not perceive at all sharp odours such as that of gasoline or paraffin oil; they cannot discern them, do not notice them, and orient themselves to the scents of living beings. Of course, the point is not that these scents do not stimulate the mucus membranes of dogs' olfactory organs, or that such stimuli do not generally exist in the field of their olfactory perception. The cause here is that these scents play no role in the life of dogs. In order for dogs to begin differentiating (i.e. perceiving) the scent of gasoline or paraffin oil, they must be specially trained in this particular substance, after which they begin differentiating these scents with a finesse that is completely inaccessible to our olfactory capacities.

Stimulating a receptor organ (nerve endings in the retina or the spiral organ of the auditory apparatus) is insufficient for a specific stimulus to reach consciousness and to be perceived; what is necessary is that it brings about a certain shift in the nervous system as such. And this occurs only when the nervous system as a whole is *agitated* in relation to certain stimuli. Whether a certain stimulus provokes a reaction of the central system or if it remains only a local stimulation depends not so much on the intensity of the stimulus (as it seemed to the psychologists devoting their entire energy to researching this aspect) but on the general state of the nervous system, its general predisposition and the general orientation of consciousness – in other words, on the proclivities of the subject's *interests*. When there is a specific orientation of consciousness, the smallest local stimulus of one sense organ or another immediately propagates to nervous system as a whole, provoking certain shifts in it. If the nervous system as a whole is not in this agitated state (i.e. there is no certain interest), even a sufficiently intense irritant, remaining a narrowly local stimulus and not putting the system in motion, is not detected by us.

Noticing something means differentiating it from the general field of specific data, shifting it to the foreground and making it the centre of the framework of the entire field of consciousness. In this sense, knowing how to perceive things to a certain extent means 'discovering' them. Making new discoveries means attaining the ability of looking in a different way, seeing and perceiving something else in comparison with what is usually perceived. Goethe justly believed the ability to see and to notice well to be a great art.

§39

The organs of perception do not, of course, play the final role in the constitution of human thinking, as Engels rightly said: 'The influences of the external world upon man express themselves in his brain, are reflected therein as feelings, thoughts, impulses, volitions – in short, as 'ideal tendencies', and in this form become 'ideal powers'.[14] But it should not be forgotten that the sense organs are only one of the conditions, and in no way the cause of the rise of the human level of consciousness. The answer to human thinking is not found in them (the empiricists saw in them alone the fundamental cause of the human ability for thinking and understanding), but in those causes and conditions that compelled the senses to work and perceive in a certain direction; these causes lie not in sensuousness itself but in the socially material conditions of the lives of people.

In repeating the words of Engels, it can be said: reflecting impressions produced on humans by the external world in the form of feelings, thoughts and impulses, giving them expression in the form of idealistic strivings and thus becoming 'ideal powers' requires, first, that the subject is in a state when they are able (or have to) perceive; second, that the object occupies a perceivable position; the latter, however, is not restricted by the need for it to be on this side of the 'threshold of sensations'.

In order to be in a condition to perceive something, an individual's specific interest in the object is necessary, and consequently that this object be accessible not only to the organ of perception but to a certain degree also to the subject's interests.

In the final analysis, the senses are the sole witness to the external world and serve as a bridge uniting consciousness with the external world, but in order to be a reliable and long-memoried witness, perception needs to be *one-sided* perception, the subject needs to be a one-sided subject, and the object a *not indifferent* object.

The world around us is full of colours, sounds and scents, but we select only those that played a role in our lives. It is said of the Vedda tribe in Sri Lanka that they display a surprising ability in the habit of finding beehives from distant

---

14   Engel's 1931, pp. 52–3.

humming that usually does not reach the hearing of Europeans. 'Where the European is not in a condition to discover absolutely any indications whatsoever, the native shows the tracks of a certain number of negroes, and moreover the exact day they passed by; if the matter occurred that day, then he indicates the hour when it occurred'. William Brett asserts that they 'will tell how many men, women and children passed there, where a stranger could only see faint and confused marks on the path before him ...'.[15]

'Someone who does not belong to our village passed by here, said the Guyanese, looking at the tracks', and Schomburgk, the author conveying this information, noted that the abilities of the natives from this region 'border on the miraculous'.[16]

These and similar facts speak of a certain orientation, or tendency of consciousness.

The *interest* of the subject imparts a specific orientation to their consciousness. Briefly put, the 'one-sided' subject is a necessary condition for any perception, awareness, thinking and cognition. Without this tendency of consciousness, objects do not draw attention to themselves and humans will not see, hear or perceive them.

The field of perception is chiefly limited by the circle of the subject's interests. The solution to the problem of why the perception of animals is limited to a narrow sphere of objects while the sphere of human consciousness is limitless should be sought on this point.

The sense organs are able to perceive something only when they are the senses of an interested person who is concentrating on something in a certain manner.

On the other hand, not every object draws attention to itself and is perceived; only an object that has some sort of relation to the subject and arouses their interest.

Where to look for such objects that are not indifferent to the subject? Where can an 'interested' subject be found? What makes a subject a one-sided subject, and what makes objects not indifferent?

The answer to these questions are given in part in Sections 8 and 25–27, where we examined objective human activity as a two-sided act of 'reifying' the individual and 'subjectivising' the object. Humans had to alter objects and make them 'own objects', transforming them into 'consumer values' in order for these things to gain interest and become accessible to human senses.

---

15   Brett 1868.
16   Schomburgk 1847/48, Vol. 1–3.

Objects, insofar as they have no relation to humans and play no role in their lives, are indifferent for humans and say nothing to them. But an indifferent relation to an object is changed by living interest, *as soon as this object enters into the circle of social interests.*

There can be no doubt that the first objects of human awareness were precisely the objects of their activity, and everything that had a relation to the real needs of life. It is clear that the 'non-indifferent object' is the result of human labour activity and their social lives.

§40

Why do humans take up objects that always remain indifferent to animals?

It is often said that 'need teaches', or 'necessity is the mother of invention', and so on. All this is correct, but the matter cannot rest here. Who invented the need? From where did the necessity appear?

Human needs are in no way a gift or a punishment sent by nature. Natural needs are limited to a very narrow circle consisting entirely of the need for food and the attraction to reproduction. Not one single animal can independently overstep the limits of their natural needs. The words of Hegel stand for all time: 'Animals have a completely limited circle of needs and the means for their satisfaction, whereas the circle of human needs and the means for their satisfaction is actually limitless'.[17] No single animal will ever need a tailor, or matches, or opera glasses, or cigarettes. Even humans may not have a need for matches or electric lamps until these objects are invented and achieve mass distribution. New needs and necessities are themselves the result of the development of human industrial life. '[T]he action of satisfying and the instrument of satisfaction which has been acquired, leads to new needs; and this creation of new needs is the first historical act', Marx says.[18]

The great versatility of human needs and the means of their satisfaction, and hence the infinite versatility of human interest is the result of human labour and social life. They grow with each new branch of production and new social relations.

This versatility of the subject's interest lay at the foundation of the many-sided orientation of human consciousness and of the infinite diversity of their perception. 'All his *human* relations to the world – seeing, hearing, smelling, tasting, feeling, thinking, contemplating, sensing, wanting, acting, loving – in short, all the organs of his individuality ... are in their *objective* approach or in

---

17   Hegel 1911, §190.
18   Marks i Engel's 1933, p. 18.

their *approach to the object* the appropriation of that object. This appropriation of *human* reality, their approach to the object, is the *confirmation of human reality* ... Therefore it is equally as versatile as the essential properties of man and *the forms of his activity*'.[19]

Furthermore, the increase in needs and the means of their satisfaction are closely linked with the division of labour and with the development of diverse human abilities, which in turn played a colossal role in the development of human thinking.

This includes the limitedness of animal 'interests' and the limitlessness of objects that interest or could interest humans, and the corresponding limitedness of animal perception in comparison with the extraordinary versatility of human perception.

In Marx's opinion, the 'feelings' found on the plane of crude natural needs corresponds to this limitedness in natural necessities, and as such they (i.e. the feelings) possess only a *limited* meaning. 'Production thus produces not only the object but the manner of consumption, not only objectively but also subjectively. Production thus creates the consumer'.[20]

'The man who is burdened with worries and needs has no *sense* for the finest of plays; the dealer in minerals sees only the commercial value, and not the beauty and peculiar nature of the minerals; he lacks a minerological sense ...'.[21] This specific tendency of consciousness makes humans capable of perceiving and of being aware of specific aspects of reality, often lacking the ability to perceive other aspects. In this sense, Lenin spoke about the rise of new phenomena for our consciousness when our sense organs – until now indifferent to the given phenomena and not perceiving them – now 'experience an impact from external objects ...'.[22]

The empiricists believed that once humans had sense organs that experience physical stimulation proceeding from objects, then sensory perceptions and sensations were given by themselves – and there was no problem in this. Not only did the empiricists reason this way; so did the rationalists. Even a representative of rationalism such as Ernst Cassirer says: '... *das Sein der Perzeption ist das einzig gewisse, völlig unproblematische Urdatum aller Erkenntnis*'.[23]

Marx says that the fact of physical stimulation of the sense organs is still not at all sufficient to explain sensory perception. Human perception depends on

---

19   Marks i Engel's 1928–1946, Vol. III, p. 625.
20   Marx 1974, p. 60.
21   Marks i Engel's 1928–1946, Vol. III, p. 625.
22   Lenin 1909, p. 84.
23   Cassirer 1929, Vol. III, p. 28.

the general tendency of their consciousness, and *sensation in principle presents the same problem as thinking*.

The empiricists and positivists believed that objects exert influence on passive humans, sensation is imposed on them and, coupled among themselves mechanically, meaning and experience are formed; and that this entire process ran as a mechanical one.

Marx said: objective reality becomes the subject of the human senses and the property of consciousness insofar as humans need it, use objects, construct them, change them and make them human objects.

'... *human* objects are not natural objects as they immediately present themselves, and neither is *human sense* as it immediately *is* – as it is objectively – *human* sensibility, human objectivity'.[24]

'The eye has become a *human* eye, just as its *object* has become a social, *human* object, an object made by man for man'.[25]

'Only through the objectively unfolded richness of man's essential being is the richness of subjective *human* sensibility (a musical ear, an eye for beauty of form – in short, *senses* capable of human gratification, senses affirming themselves as essential powers of *man*) either cultivated or brought into being. For not only the five senses but also the so-called mental senses, the practical senses (will, love, etc.), in a word, *human* sense, the human nature of the senses, comes to be by virtue of *its* object, by virtue of *humanised* nature. *The forming of the five senses is a labour of the entire history of the world down to the present*'.[26]

Thus we see that human senses, the means of their perception and consciousness are the result of the history of human development, and not a biological product of natural history.

Objects enter the field of sensuousness, into people's field of perception and consciousness only to the degree to which they are involved in social and historical praxis. By virtue of this, objects join the field of human interests, drawing human attention to themselves.

The objective world and nature itself are made objects of representation of the human intellect, primarily as objects of human activity and not as physical stimuli of the sense organs.

In order to elucidate the thoughts set forth, we will briefly digress into the field of the history of the perception of colours.

---

24 Marks i Engel's 1928–1946, Vol. III, p. 644.
25 Marks i Engel's 1928–1946, Vol. III, p. 626.
26 Marks i Engel's 1928–1946, Vol. III, pp. 627–8.

From the History of the Perception of Colours

§ 41

In the 1870s, Lazar Geiger[27] drew attention to a curious phenomenon: astonishingly, a number of great ancient literary works completely fail to mention certain such basic colours as blue or green, to say nothing of other more secondary ones.

The *Rigveda*, that enormous epic consisting of more than ten thousand verses in which interest in the sky and in heavenly phenomena was expressed extraordinary clearly, nowhere speaks of a light (or dark) blue sky; in general, no mention of either dark blue or green is encountered in the book.

Green pigments existed around humans, of course, insofar as they were surrounded by the plant kingdom. Nonetheless, none of the ten books of the *Rigveda* once mention green though there is often talk of the earth, trees, edible plants, branches, fruits, pasturable mountains and even ploughed fields and fields of grain.

It was the same, it turned out, with another ancient literary work of the Indo-Iranian world view: the *Avesta*. Interest in the earth and its fertility, and hence in the world of plants, occupies an even greater place in this book than it does in the *Rigveda*. All the more striking is the absence of the colour green in it. The plant world is often described in detail in the *Avesta*; trees are called splendid and fruitful, described as growing high, and sometimes even light golden – but never once are they said to be green.

This circumstance, it turns out, does not constitute a specific peculiarity of Aryan antiquity and the Indo-Iranian world view.

Similar phenomena can be traced in other literary works of antiquity: the *Bible*, in Homer, and so on. The *Bible*, which in its first chapters touches on the heavens and in what follows mentions them 450 times, nowhere says that they are blue.[28] Homeric verses are also striking in the absence of any mention of the colours blue or green.

Faced with the fact of such a widespread 'passing over' of specific primary colours, of course, there can be no discussion of their accidental omission,

---

27   Geiger 1871, pp. 45–60.
28   Colours are often encountered in the Bible: white, black, red, purple, golden and so on, but light and dark blue are not; green is mentioned more than 40 times, but almost always in the meaning of 'greenery', succulent and fresh (the old Hebrew *yachak*, 'greenery, vegetable') in contrast to 'dried out'; in other languages – Georgian, for example – the corresponding places are always translated in precisely the latter meaning of 'greenery' or 'succulent': *nedli, norchi*.

of intentional evasion and the like. They are not mentioned because in those times they were obviously not distinguished; they were not perceived as *qualitatively* primary colours. People had no special names for these colours, and their language did not distinguish these colours among themselves.

If, in general, we approach the literary works of distant antiquity with our repertoire and scales of colours, we will at every step encounter surprises that will shock us with their extraordinary confusion in distinguishing colours.

Homer, for example, says that the hair of Odysseus had the colour of hyacinth, and – as Geiger notes – ancient Greek interpreters, for whom these views were not very foreign, pointed out that he was talking about the colour black.

Pindar speaks about violet ringlets in the same meaning of black, and Homer imputes the colour of violets to iron.

Plants, flowers, fruit and so on are generally characterised more in ancient literary works according to the magnitude of their succulence, shadiness, abundance and fruitfulness than by their colour. Little is said of colours; when they are mentioned, it is in an uncertain and confused manner that makes use of identical expressions for designating the most diverse colours. Homer, for example, attaches the same definition to plants, sand, water, clouds, the night, iron, horses, wine and so on: κυανεος (dark). And the other way round: to one and the same object, he attaches epithets that for our optical senses signify completely different colours.

Even after certain colours were discerned more precisely through scientific observation, they long remained undiscerned among the people and in popular tales, and poets continued to use them as metaphors. Thus, for example, Virgil: 'White (*alba*) privets fall, dark (*nigra*) hyacinths are culled ...'. (*Eclogues* II, 18). Speaking of a face burnt by the sun, Theocritus said: 'For at the same time, violets and hyacinth are black' (Theocr. 10, 28).[29]

One may think that the matter consists not so much in another means of perceiving colours, but in other verbal expressions. Until now, this is what people actually believed. There is an opinion that colours have always qualitatively been perceived by people in precisely the same way as we perceived them now. But since language had not developed accordingly and speech did not have designations for all the individual colours available, one word often served for expressing different colours. Therefore, the linguistic information could lead to confusion if inferences about the perception of colours in the historical past were to be made on that basis.

---

29 We encounter the same in Virgil: 'What if Amyntas be dark? Violets, too, are black and black are hyacinths' (*Eclogues* x, 39).

These beliefs may actually have become irrefutable if history had left testimony only about the designations of colours, but fortunately it also preserved the comparisons of things from the point of view of their colouring. What would it have been like, if Pindar definitely spoke about someone's curls as if they had the colour of violets, and Homer about hyacinth-coloured hair? Did ancient Greeks actually have violet hair, or were the violets of antiquity not actually violet, but black?

The foregoing point of view is insufficient inasmuch as it leads research into a dead end, since the enigmatic question remains: why, in language, *were some colours distinguished and others not?*

This actually constitutes the main problem. Why, at a specific stage of social development, did speech have one designation for black, dark blue, green, violet and even gray, and different designations for red and black?

Remaining silent on these questions or avoiding them means repudiating the research; the belief of the defenders of the standpoint mentioned above – that language did not discern colours, whereas *consciousness* discerned them very well – compels them to this.

The case is somewhat different. Human speech had no special designations for precisely those things that people were simply unable to discern and perceive differentially. Colours were not distinguished in speech because people had no practical foundation for *perceiving* these colours differentially, and in no way because their vocabulary was meagre. To whom would such a rebuke to the *Vedas* and the poems of Homer, striking in their richness of words, images, and comparisons, *not* be unjust?

It is known that when a designation is needed for a new object or new phenomenon, language usually does not prove to be powerless before such a task, immediately creating the necessary word.

If the old poems (*Atharvaveda*, Book 15) speak about a rainbow (the bow of Indra), then its belly is black (literally *nîlas*) and its spine is red (*lohita*), then this means that the colours of the rainbow, from the green band on downward, were only seen as shades of black. This means that dark blue, green and violet were not perceived as qualitatively different, and different shades of black were seen.

As Colebrooke relates, one Indian philosopher of antiquity even solved such a 'problem': what was the reason behind the colour of the sky being black? He responded that the black colour of the eye was imparted to the sky being perceived, much as the eye of a person with jaundice looks yellow to everyone (?!).

Another fact is even more important. The words that now signify dark blue and green – the Greek κυανεος, for example – previously had the meaning of black and genetically represent derivatives of 'black'.

The Greek κυανεος, having the meaning of 'dark navy blue' in Plato's time [Plato (*Timaios* 6, 8) differentiates κυανουν (dark navy blue) from γλαυκος (light navy blue) – a word generally not encountered in the poems of the Homeric epoch], for which Nikolai Marr found parallels in the Japhetic languages, for example the Georgian *m-tvan-e*, the Mingrelian *r-tvan-e* in the sense of 'light blue', and also in different varieties preserved in the meanings of 'sky', 'sea' and 'lake' respectively[30] – this word also had the meaning of 'black' in the more ancient literary works of Greece. Lazar Geiger showed that κυανεος is found in Homer as a description of the colour of Zeus's – and also Hera's – brow. Homer further calls Hector's hair and Odysseus's beard κυανεος. Most probably, he in no way wanted to imply that the hair and beards of these heroes were dark blue.

The relatively funereal vestments of Theseus were described in Homer as: ... καλυμμ' ελε δια θεαων κυανεον του δ'ουτι μελαντερον επλετο εσθος (The goddess took a dark [κυανεον] veil, black like no other vestment),[31] where κυανεος is used in the meaning of deep black.

This word is used to designate the colour of sea sand, and is most often encountered as the description of an overcast sky and the dark colour of rain clouds. At the same time, this word is used for the colour of the sea and of a clear sky, and later, by the time of Plato, had been definitively assigned to dark blue.

Thus, if the work κυανεος simultaneously designated dark blue, green, grey, black, and dark colours in general, then we have the right to say that dark blue was not only called black, but it was perceived as a variety of the colour black and was therefore called as such.

An analogous picture can be traced relative to the Sanskrit word *nîla* (which had the meaning of black, grey, dark blue and light blue, and in the meaning of 'black' is preserved in the Latin *niger*), the Chinese word *hiuan*, which had the meaning of light blue, green and black (and now signifies 'sky blue'), and the Latin *caeruleus*, which long confused philologists with its ambiguity. The word *caeruleus* is encountered in the most contradictory meanings. It was used to describe the darkness of night, rain clouds, an overcast sky and for objects signifying death (e.g. mourning). It had the meaning of 'sky blue' (*caeli caerula*). In Ovid, Propertius and Hellius it is encountered in the meaning of 'green'. In Hellius, *caeruleus* (dark navy blue), *glaucus* (light navy blue) and *caesius* (light blue) are varieties (*species differentes*) of green (*viride*), similar to the way that orange and yellow were once believed to be shades of red. Geiger believes

---

30   Marr 1928a, p. 329.
31   *Iliad*, XXIV, 93, 94.

that the word *caeruleus* went through a number of meanings, beginning from 'black' and going through 'grey' to 'dark blue' and quotes Servius, who reveals the changes in the meaning of this word by direct indication of the fact that in antiquity it was used in the sense of simply black, in contrast to white, corresponding precisely to the meaning of the word *niger* and acting as a synonym for it.

Curious facts in this regard are encountered in the literary works of even those ages when colours had been superbly discerned. In his dictionary, the venerable Georgian lexicographer Saba Sulkhan Orbeliani (1658–1725) formats in detail and reliably defines the entire palette of colours, but in relating the fable 'The Fox Who Became A Monk' (ბერად შემდგარი მელი), he says: 'The fox, having fallen into a crock full of bluing (ლილა), climbed out completely black (მელი შავად შელებილი შეიქმნა). The fox turned out to be stained black.[32] In his dictionary, Orbeliani gives the word *lila* (ლილა) in the meaning of a blue dye – 'bluing' (ლურჯი საღებავი), and in the fable, this dye paints the fox black. This semantic disparity is so striking that professor Aleksandr Tsagareli, when publishing this collection in Russian (*Mudrost' lzhi*), clearly wanted to eliminate the discrepancy and amended the text, translating this as: 'The fox was stained dark blue'.

This, perhaps, was not entirely baseless. It should seem to us, however, that the demands of the topic could not *create* such a discrepancy (bluing that dyes black), but that the topic was fully able to assist in its preservation. Seeing the fox needed to be stained black, the corresponding dye, or soot, or tar or something similar could have been selected first, especially since the latter were no less known – and in any case known no later – than bluing. Bluing was selected, precisely as a variety of black. Time passed, and dark blue began to be qualitatively distinguished from black, but bluing was maintained as an element in the framework of the topic as bluing. According to the topic, the fox's appearance was required to corroborate its assurance that it had turned to the path of religion and become an ascetic. It needed to dress in a black cassock. But bluing, already solidly a part of the topic itself, only dyes blue, and dark blue vestments do not square with the appearance of a monk who abstains. This is why the author, preserving the ancient form of the tale, had to dress the fox in black by means of bluing.

On the basis of a multiplicity of facts from the field of perception of colours and shades, from assessments and judgements on it, it can be said that

---

32   სულ ან-საბა ორბელიანი, სიბრძნე სირუისა "სიმღერის ქვევრი, ლილით საკსკ, ლია დარჩომიჯო. სვლასა აქა-იქა შიბ თურბე ჩავარდა, ამობორტყდა, ამოვიდა. შავაბილი შეიქმნა".

colours were not always distinguished equally by people, similar to the way in which sounds (e.g. certain harmonic combinations of tones) did not always seem euphonious. The sense of harmony and a musical ear in relation to one combination of sounds or another is not naturally given to humans, and what is euphonious for a given stage of development may be discordant for another.

At different stages of human history, the means of perception by people of the most elementary qualities differed to a very large extent.

Geiger thought that the cause of different perceptions of colours among the ancients should be sought on the one hand in the field of the physical properties of light, and on the other in the field of the physiology of vision. The cases cited by Geiger that the historical succession of the perception of colours precisely corresponds to the sequence of their arrangement on the solar spectrum (beginning from red light – with the longest wavelength, allegedly the most active – and ending with the short violet waves, acting the weakest), as if people became aware of light historically in this sequence of arrangement,[33] simply contradicts the facts. According to this theory, orange and brown – and light blue, as well – had to precede violet and dark blue, and moreover they were undoubtedly the last heritage of perception and differentiation.

The assertion that the physiological action of light in the visible spectrum – with the shortest waves weaker than light with longer waves – is incorrect from both a physical and a psychological standpoint. In physics, short-wave light rays are known as the harshest, and from the point of view of psychological activity no one says that yellow light is perceptionally stronger (*sinnlich stärkste*) than dark blue or purple, for example.

On the other hand, Geiger assumed that the cause of the different perception of colours in our ancestors is hidden in the processes of the physiology of vision in past times, and the organisation of the organ of vision in the people of antiquity was different than it is in us. He asked: What must the physiological condition have been of the generation of people who could see the colour of the sky as 'black'? '*Diese Fragen an und für sich sind physiologische Fragen*', he said. And in his report at the assembly of naturalists in Frankfurt am Main in 1867, he proposed the idea of a certain new science: paleophysiology.

It was assumed that due to the imperfection of their retinas, the people of Homer's time were blind to certain colours. A dispute even arose as to whether the 'culturally backward' tribes and peoples whose languages did not distinguish certain primary colours were suffering from individual or general colour blindness. Publications began appearing in print under headlines such as 'The

---

33 Geiger 1872, Vol. II, p. 357.

eyes of 23 Kalmyks'[34] and 'The eyes of 23 Singhalese and 3 Hindus'.[35] The most thorough research into the visual apparatus, however, yielded absolutely no anatomical or physiological evidence of their inability to sense colour.

Of course, the problems are not in the physical properties of the spectrum and not in the particular construction of the visual organ. Similar hypotheses from the same origin send research along a false path, making the correct resolution of the question impossible. The physical processes of propagation, of the refraction of light and the chemical processes on the retina of the eye in humans differ little, even from that of the apes. The image of objects on our ancestors' retinas was the same as it is on ours, but what constituted their interests, and therefore *which* objects they perceived and *what they saw* in these objects – there was the major difference in comparison with our perception. These differences were reflected in the accumulations of language as documents of the history of development of the human means of consciousness and thinking.

People perceived in a different way and did not distinguish certain primary colours not because the chemical processes on the retina progressed differently or because their eyes were constructed in a different way, but because they nurtured no interest in specific qualities that were for them indifferent and useless in practice.

In order to perceive something 'distinctly', one must 'have something to do with it', 'be oriented towards it', or 'have some kind of relation to it'. People did not perceive specific qualities and specific objects because they did not have occasion to use these things and because they did not produce these things. It is known that the Greeks, even in the time of Democritus and the Pythagorists, distinguished only four basic colours: black, white, red and yellow, which Empedocles and Democritus couples with their four elements of the world (earth, air, fire and water). We also know that Greek artists, almost up to the reign of Alexander, were known *for the use of only these four colours* – as Cicero, Pliny and others attest – and were not known for the use of either blue or green paints. *When people began preparing these paints and using the colours in practice, then they began to be qualitatively distinguished from the other colours, and also to be specially named.* And in Herodotus, for example, we meet not four colours but five or six – dark blue among them. Describing seven walls that surrounded the ancient Iranian city of Ecbatana and talking about their colouring, Herodotus named the colours: white, black, red, dark blue and the colour of red

---

34 Kotelmann 1844a, pp. 77–84.
35 Kotelmann 1844b, pp. 164–80.

lead,[36] and in ancient Egypt dark blue had been used since ancient times, but then there *was* a special name for this colour (*qbsd*).

The history of painting provides irrefutable data about the fact that the differentiation of colours went historically hand in hand with the actual use of the corresponding paint. They could only qualitatively distinguish the colour after they began producing or using the corresponding colour in practice.

Until people made and used blue paints, they did not distinguish this colour in their sensory perception, but perceived in 'blue' only a variety or shade of another colour already in use – most often 'dark' or 'black', respectively.

§42

Great confusion as regards colours can be observed in people even today. At first glance, the chaos that obtains in everyday speech in the use of colours seems strange and incomprehensible.

1. Light and dark blue are very often not distinguished as qualitatively different colours from dark and grey, and sometimes from black. We encounter 'dark blue hair' not only in Homer; a common contemporary Russian expression is 'bluish-black hair'; in reality, however, black hair hardly ever has a dark blue shade.

If opinions on the colour of hair can still diverge, then no one would affirm that they have ever seen blue horses, or that blue horses actually existed at some point. In Georgia, however, *lurdzha tskheni* – literally translated, 'blue horse' – generally widespread name for the dark navy blue colour of a horse's coat. This is not some kind of distinctive feature of Georgian vocal perception; it is inherent in very many other languages. The Armenian *kapuytdi* also literally means 'blue horse'. According to Dal's testimony, 'blue horse' is encountered in the Pechersky region as the designation for a certain coat, and 'light blue horse' is a fairly widespread designation for the mouse-grey coat of a horse.

Dal' says that 'among the people, *goluboi* means both dark blue and grey or a dark natural colour ... sometimes the people even call yellow light blue, for example in the Nizhegorodskoi region and others. What is remarkable is that these colours are opposite', he adds. 'If the early squirrel is light blue (?), then spring will be early'. I was severely disappointed at one exhibition, when I was shown the much-praised 'blue fox' – in which I could not find a hint of blue.

Objects that are simply black are often called dark blue, for example gunpowder or poppy seeds ('blue gunpowder', 'blue poppy seeds' – cf. Dal').

---

36 Herodotus, Clip, I, 98.

A specialist in Iranian languages, Vasilii Abaev, informed us of the name of a colour often used in Ossetian: *äqsin*, which has such a multiplicity of meanings that it is impossible to assign it to any specific colour. Some believe that it signifies 'dark navy blue' (Alborov, *Govor osetin-irantsev Mozdokskogo raiona*, 1932), but this word also signifies an indeterminate dark colour. This word is used in the meaning of a colour for large horned cattle, and then according to the material written by Abaev, the Ossetians gave literally the following explanation: 'if the spine is yellow but the ox itself is black, then it's called *äqsin* ...'. How is that to be understood? Like 'varicoloured'? More likely, the original meaning of this word was 'black', since slate grey roofing shale is called *äqsin*.[37]

This is a graphic example of the indefinite apperception of colour in a word that serves as the name of a certain colour and at the same time expresses no *specific* colour. In normal speech, the Ossetians themselves hardly feel any discomfort linked to the use of this word. The multiple meanings of *äqsin*, which surprises us, is not even noticed by them. For them, this word has a fully specific meaning every time.

2. Quite often, people do not distinguish blue and green as qualitatively different colours. Among the people, they are often confused and called blue-green or the other way around.

We have already mentioned that in Hellius, *caeruleus* (dark blue), *glaucus* (light navy blue) and *caesius* (light blue) are subspecies of green (*viride*), and in Propertius and Ovid *caeruleus* is used in the sense not only of dark blue, but of green as well.

Xenophanes discerned only purple, red and yellow in the rainbow. In general, he does not mention green and blue:

Ην τ'Ιριν καλεουσι, νεφος, και τουτο πεφηκε
Πορφυρεον και φοινικεον και χλωρον ιδεσθαι ...

'what they call Iris, this too is cloud, purple, red and yellow to behold' (Eust ad II, p. 27)

In the Turkic languages, this confusion of 'green' and 'blue' is preserved in living colloquial speech even today. Despite the fact that grass has a definite and pronounced green colour, and confusing it with blue seems completely impossible, modern Ottoman says both *yeşiloϑ*, 'green grass', and *goy(g) oϑ* –

---

37   It is significant that the root (*äqz*) in Iranian has the meaning of 'dark blue'. In modern Persian, *äqrär* means 'light blue' and 'dark blue', and in dictionaries as well, the meanings of 'green', 'dark brown' and 'black' are given. The Arabic *äqrär* means 'green' and a dark colour (*de couleur foncée*).

literally 'blue grass'. 'The trees were covered with green leaves' – in Turkish, this idea is conveyed by *ayaϑlar goyadi*, literally 'the trees turned blue'.

On the other hand, green objects are sometimes simply called black (e.g. *chernyi les* 'black forest', *chernoles'e* 'black [i.e. deciduous] forest', *chernaia listva* 'black foliage', cf Dal'). Leaves are hardly ever black.[38]

Thus it can be ascertained that *blue and green are not always perceived as qualitatively different colours*, and only as *different* shades of 'dark' or 'black'. But insofar as they are perceived as varieties of black, then they are called 'black' in the same way.

Concerning the Arawa (a tribe living in southern Papua New Guinea) it is said that they have names for only three colours: black, white and red, but that they use these words for designating blue, yellow and green. In order to distinguish the colours, they use these terms in combination with the names of particular birds that bear the equivalent colouration.

Nevertheless, the confusion of blue and green is most widespread when green objects are called blue and vice versa, when blue objects are called green. The reason for this – as we have shown – lies not in incorrect designation but in the absence of a distinct perception of the colour. If green and blue were perceived as precisely and clearly as the earlier (and more frequently used) colours (e.g. black and red), then there would be no basis for naming them incorrectly. People did not yet know what blue and green were when they already had an understanding of black, white and red.

3. If we go further along this path, deeper into the historical past, we will find a stage when people did not distinguish 'yellow' as a particular colour, believing it to be a shade and variety of 'red'.

The Georgian language bears witness to this; according to the analysis of Nikolai Marr, 'yellow' (*kviϑ-el*) and 'red' (*tiϑ-el*) are from the same archetype *tvϑ\\t̂vϑ – kwϑ*; according to the aspirant group *tiϑ-el* coming from *t̂viϑ-el*, according to the sibilant group *ṭiϑ-a* (– *ṭviϑ-ar*), and in Mingrelian 'red', according to the spirant branch also gives *kwiϑ-el*, and is precisely preserved in this form in the meaning of 'yellow'.[39]

An analysis of even deeper layers might perhaps show that 'red' takes its history from 'black' or 'white', and that originally there was only the differentiation of 'black' and 'white' – or, rather, 'dark' and 'light' coming not from natural col-

---

38 It should be noted that in their historical development, individual colours acquire a particular significance and – as Professor Izrail' Frank-Kamenetskii justly drew my attention to – the extensive problem of the semantics (or symbolism) of colours arises. Dealing with these questions is beyond the scope of this work.

39 Marr 1928a, p. 330.

ourations, but (as we will see below) from the artificial daubing of items of a certain mass (soot, clay and so on).

We meet a suggestion of 'red' coming from 'black' in the Arabic *ahmaru*, 'red', which, however, is encountered in the meaning of 'black'.

The basis of the Russian *chernyi*, 'black', is repeated in *chervonnyi*, 'dark red', having the meaning of 'red' and 'yellow'. This word was preserved in fuller form in the Old Russian *chermnyi*, having the meaning of 'crimson' or 'red'; *vody chermny iako krov'* ('waters as red as blood', 2 Kings 3:22). *Chermnuetsia*, clearing or brightening (of weather, cf. Dal'), *Chermnoe more* – the Red Sea.

The question arises: is it perhaps conceivable that at some point people did not distinguish blue from black, seeing no different at all between the light blue sky of day and the black sky of night? Of course they saw a difference; they did not note the difference in quality of colour, but – let us say – in the 'general mood' of the sky. When, for example, the Roman poets touched upon the sky in verse and wanted to depict it as free of clouds – a clear sky – they very rarely alluded to its colour and more often than not to 'general colouring', speaking of a 'cheerful sky'. The depiction of an 'overcast sky' as 'black', it seemed, had to give cause to describe a 'clear sky' with the opposite colour. But 'light blue' for them was not yet qualitatively different from black, representing only one of its shades, which is why they had to resort to other means – a general description of the sky, and not to its chromatic quality. In these cases, they spoke about the sky as *serenus* (joyous, cheerful), *apertus* (open, i.e. unshaded), *lucidus aethra* (light air) or *sudus* (dry).

Blue and green did not constitute particular colours as we differentiate them; they were only different shades of dark.

At first glance, all this may seem very strange; in fact there is nothing surprising here, considering the fact that even today we perceive certain colours and judge them. And to this day we distinguish colours strikingly poorly, if we keep colloquial speech in mind. The swarthy colour of the human face has nothing in common with 'black' proper; however, we constantly speak of swarthy people and of tanned people as 'black' while the swarthy colour of the skin is qualitatively much more different from 'black' than yellow is from red.

There is a strain of apple, the Pink Reinette, that is encountered everywhere in Georgia under the name *shavi vashli* (and in Mingrelian *uϑa ushkuri*), which is literally 'black apple'; there is decidedly nothing black about it. Sometimes, an apple prevalent in eastern Georgia is called *naϑara vashli*, 'ashen-coloured apple', though it has nothing in common with the colour of ashes; it is a matte orange in hue.

For the great majority of people in our cultural sphere who are not particularly sophisticated about colours, 'light blue' and 'dark blue' are only different shades of qualitatively one and the same colour; for people who deal with paints and have an eye for them, they are *qualitatively* different colours. A painter, for example, cannot hear manifestations of such ignorance without shuddering. They do not realise how, from this dark blue – no matter what degree of its saturation one takes – light blue can be obtained!

I have asked many people: 'What colour is an orange?' and in the majority of cases have received the response 'It's yellow'. Upon further questioning, it became clear that a lemon differs from an orange in that it is 'less yellow', and the orange is 'more deep yellow'. (?!) If a painter were told that orange is only a shade of yellow – 'a richer yellow' – they would marvel at our lack of skill in differentiating colours ...

In all this, it should not be forgotten that colours originally were not perceived separately from objects and, in all likelihood, were not conceived of as definite independent qualities until people 'separated' (differentiated) them from objects, familiarised themselves with the colouration of objects and with the daubing of their surfaces with certain compounds.

It may be that we are indebted to this circumstance by the fact that the earliest colour to become part of our use and our language was black, which could be produced through the application of coal – as data found in the locations of the earliest human dwellings attest.

From this, the fact – very surprising to us – that in many languages 'light' gets its name from 'darkness' (e.g. in the Sanskrit *ràg* 'shine, give light', whereas *rang* signifies dark colours) is explained. Originally, the matter concerned not 'light' and 'dark' as such, but simply the black soot of coal or the mash from clay with which the surfaces of objects were covered.

In a number of languages, the words signifying light have the same basis as 'cover', 'skin' and 'layer'. In Greek, for example, χλωρος, which in Hesiod signified green branches, in Homeric songs signifies exclusively yellow with an alternation and exchange of another word, ωχρος. The Greek root has the meaning of 'colour' in general (χρωμα 'colour', 'dye') and the meaning of 'skin'. Χρως means 'colour', 'skin' and 'surface'.

In Sanskrit, the word *rang* means dark colours, *rakta* 'painted, red', *ragata* 'white', *räg* 'shine, give light', *arguna* 'gold' and so on (this semantic series could be extended indefinitely, especially along the line of Indo-European languages). All these come together around the root *rang*, which in Sanskrit means 'covered' and 'coated' in particular.

It can thus be established that colours take their history from coating objects, and the originally equivalent words did not mean colours but things and objects coated with something, or even the action of coating itself. The names, which subsequently came to signify certain colours, originally did not signify abstract qualities at all but the material realia of existence.

A given quality entered human consciousness and was adapted by language as it became embedded in the custom of human practice. And the object entered human consciousness and human language in precisely the same way as it entered into human use.

4. It would be naive to assume that on one splendid day, humans began reflecting on why the night was dark, the day was light and the moon was yellow. Reflection never arises by itself on its own strengths. In order for humans to begin thinking, they had to be forced into it by the conditions of their lives and their practical interests.

In many early languages, there are no names for a range of colours: green, blue or even yellow. There has already been attention in the literature drawn to the 'mysterious fact' – in the words of one researcher – that there are numerous tribes around the globe that confuse blue with green, designating both with one word. As the collected evidence attests, this case is strikingly concordant among peoples who are far distance from each other both ethnically and spatially.[40] It has been observed, for example, that certain African tribes (the Zozo, Mande and Vai) discern colours poorly, differentiating them mainly by the degree of brightness (dark colours and white); they do not differentiate red and yellow from each other, they also do not discern green and blue, and blue is not distinguished from black. Karl von den Steinen describes analogous facts from the experience of his expeditions among the tribes of central Brazil.[41] In addition, it is curious that they not only confuse the names of colours, but they confuse the colours themselves, making mistakes in discerning them. When, for example, they were given the task of stringing green and blue beads separately, green beads often ended up among the blue, and the other way around – there were blue beads in the green row. But as a rule, this inability to differentiate colours could not be found in locations and among tribes who produced dyes and used them in practice in coating, tattooing, dyeing cloth, embroidery or handicrafts. In these cases, even the least developed tribes manifested a keen sense in differentiating a rather rich palette of colours, moreover using a well developed terminology of dyes.

It has been attested that the inhabitants of the Gazelle Peninsula on New Britain, having prepared and used dyes for every type of painting and draw-

---

40   *Zeitschrift für Ethnologie*, 1878, Vol. x; Andree 1878, p. 326.
41   Steinen 1897.

ing on the face and the body (required in the performance of ritual dances and in time of preparation for war) had around 40 designations for different combinations of colours and lines, and special names for all seven basic colours.

For more frequently used colours, they had not one but several designations corresponding to the quality, tone and material of the dye obtained. For example, they had four terms for the colour red, and for an even more commonly used colour – black – a full six.

5. The history of colours was not, of course, identical everywhere. Not all conceptions of colour arose from the actions of coating something, and the corresponding terms were not everywhere produced from the dyeing of objects. Among many pastoral tribes, ideas about colours were worked out in other ways than through production of dyes and dyeing objects, but preciesly in close connection with stock-raising practices. In primitive stock raising, particular attention was devoted to the objects of animals, and the nomenclature of colours (coats) of domestic animals was introduced into the languages of migrant tribes with an extraordinary detail of shades.[42] Among the most primitive tribes a tremendous multiplicity of names (numbering between 50 and 60, and sometimes more than 100) has been discovered, differentiating all the colours that describe the given types of animals in the most subtle manner. Where colours were not the colours of domestic animals (e.g. blue and green), they were – as it was reported – unable to name them, for example, as regards the pastoral Herero tribe in southern Africa in a survey sent in 1887 to the Leipzig Museum of Ethnography. They said of green objects that they were yellow, and they called blue 'dark'. 'The assertion that these colours needed special names seemed absurd to them', the same survey reports. The main object of concern for the Herero tribe was livestock, and they could differentiate their colours as they differentiated oxen, sheep and goats. Their names for colours were adopted from the word for 'counting livestock', because they differentiated their livestock from that of the others according to colour or coat.

This explains yet another feature in the history of the origin of ideas about colour. In a number of languages where awareness of colours developed in connection with the differentiation of the natural distinguishing features of things (e.g. the coats of livestock), the word for expressing 'colour' does not signify pure chromatic qualities as such, but includes the definitions of 'figure', 'form of a spot' and 'stripes'. Among the Cape tribes, the word *cbala* –

---

42   Andree 1878, Vol. x, p. 332; Radloff 1871, Vol. III, p. 303; Magnus 1880, p. 9.

and *evala* among the Herero – signifies not only colour but also 'pattern of marks', 'figure of a spot', 'stripes' and 'shape'. Muffled echoes of this kind of perception, in which the representation of a chromatic quality has not quite been separated from the objects and is viewed in connection with them, has been preserved in the Georgian word *feri* ('colour', 'colouration'), which has a number of other meanings such as 'likeness', 'general appearance', 'form' and 'means'.[43]

6. If something is not differentiated in perception, it is also not differentiated in speech; if something is perceived as a variety of a specific object (or quality), then it is called by the same term.

Giving an object a special name requires that it is perceived *in particular* (i.e. that it is socially perceived in a particular manner differentiating it from other things). A detailed perception of things and their more detailed differentiation was possible at the primitive stage of development only when these things became the objects and the means of human activity. In order to perceive objects in a differentiated fashion – even if it is colours and dyes – people needed to have something to do with them (association in practice); people needed to use them or *know how* to produce them. When people work on objects, employ them and use them, they learn how to discern these things; they learn how to see what the properties and qualities are, what functions and services these objects perform and how they differ from each other. And despite this, if these objects are perceived as homogeneous (i.e. performing the same work or function, or bearing the same meaning) or as heterogeneous, they are given the same name or different names. Thus, in a certain sense we can even talk openly about the 'homonymous' or 'heteronymous' perception of things.

When perception becomes *general* to a certain degree at a specific stage of social development, the objects perceived remain unnamed no longer. The closest connection between social perception and naming exists on the strength of this. How objects are named depends on how they are perceived and socially given meaning.

This proposition on the correspondence of the means of perception with the means of naming is highly important insofar as the initial unity between 1) practical activity, 2) thinking and 3) speech is formed through this. It helps us orient ourselves in the historical past, to defined the ancient forms of consciousness (i.e. the composition of thoughts), of language (the structure and

---

43   For example, the Georgian *raferi* has two meanings: 'which colour' and 'which' (literally 'which form'), dialectally *rafer* 'by what means', 'how'; *atas ferad*, 'in every possible way'.

order of language) and of practical activity (i.e. 'the composition of things', custom and social relations), if any of these 'parameters' are more or less well known to us.

The history of language thus by and large adequately expresses the history of thinking.

These ideas once attracted Hegel. 'The form of thinking is first of all put down in the language of man', he said. Marx held a similar opinion: 'Language is as old as consciousness, language *is* practical, real consciousness that exists for other men as well, and only therefore does it exist also for me; language, like consciousness, only arises from the need, the necessity, of intercourse with other men'.[44]

Proceeding from the same principle, Lenin – having emphasised the words of Haym – showed that burden of proof in research into the theory of cognition must be shifted from the critique of reason to the criticism of language, to the *task of the critical history of language*. In such a historical study of the development of human thought, Lenin saw the only guarantee of a method capable of giving 'an indisputably conclusive theory of knowledge'.[45]

The Marxist Perspective on the Question of Sensory Perception

§43

The external objective world of reality enters the sphere of the representations of the human intellect through the world of things utilised by humans, primarily as the objects of human activity and not as physiological stimulations and sensations.

Marx contrasted this standpoint with the assertions of the idealist philosophy of rationalism. From this position, Marx criticised old materialist philosophy, including Feuerbachian materialism.

'Feuerbach's 'conception' of the sensuous world is confined on the one hand to mere contemplation of it, and on the other to mere feeling; he posits 'Man' instead of 'real historical man' ... He does not see that the sensuous world around him is not a thing given direct from all eternity, remaining ever the same, but the product of industry and of the state of society; and, indeed [a product] in the sense that it is an historical product, the result of the activity of a whole succession of generations, each standing on the shoulders of the

---

44   Marks i Engel's 1933, p. 20.
45   Lenin 1931, Vol. XII, pp. 307, 315, 145.

preceding one, developing its industry and its intercourse, and modifying its social system according to the changed needs. Even the objects of the simplest 'sensuous certainty' are only given him through social development, industry and commercial intercourse'.[46]

Humanity had already long ago left the state where the objects of its consciousness and the data of its knowledge were limited to the narrow sphere of what was immediately accessible to its natural sense organs. It is absurd to say that in the perception of phenomena, the cognition of objects and the construction of a picture of reality only use the data of their natural sense organs. Engels rightly pointed out that 'the special construction of the human eye sets no absolute barrier to human cognition'.[47]

In his notes as he was reading Feuerbach, Lenin asked the question: 'If man had more senses, would he discover more things in the world?' and answers, 'No'.[48]

Humanity had already long ago grown out of the age at which, in its knowledge, it could rely only on the evidence of its natural sense organs. Humans create the devices with which they see, for example, intra-atomic processes and magnetic fluctuations (i.e. phenomena that even the most complete natural organ of hearing, sight or touch are unable to perceive).

Humans, limited by the physiological boundaries of their sense organs, are in no way limited in their knowledge because of it. Using technological devices created by humans, they extend their perception and cognition infinitely beyond the natural boundaries immediately accessible to their organs of perception.

As a result of humanity's industrial and social life, '[a]part from these direct organs, *social* organs are therefore created in the *form* of society; for example, activity in direct association with others, etc. has become an organ of my *life expression* and a mode of appropriation for *human* life'.[49]

Humans do not remain physiologically limited, they become a *historical* subject and their development is therefore unlimited, as does the development of the objects of their activity and their material culture, which historically is continually created and modified by people.

This historical unlimitedness of development of both the subject and the objects occurs not in accordance with natural laws and does not represent the fruit of naturally biological processes, but is the result of the social and histor-

---

46 Marks i Engel's 1933, p. 32.
47 Marks i Engel's 1925, p. 179.
48 Lenin 1931, Vol. XII, p. 103.
49 Marks i Engel's 1928–1946, Vol. III, p. 626.

ical processes of development. The subject is infinite precisely in the sense of a social being, but as a biological individual they are also limited and mortal, as all other beings are.

Empiricists believed sensations to be naturally given to human consciousness and wanted to explain the essence of the human means of thought on that basis. Many 'Marxists' blindly followed them, as this view was repeated in books, textbooks and systems from generation to generation and acquired the durability of an assertion that could apparently be taken for granted (i.e. the durability of a preconception). This led to psychologism, to biologism and in general to any number of things and, rather than explaining the peculiarity of the human means of thinking, led to the impossibility of its explanation.

All the more should we feel sorry for those who take the principles of sensualism for true Marxism, trailing along being the reactionary philosophy of positivism; there are quite a few of them. And I am not speaking any more about the empiriomonists, the empiriocritics, or Kautsky and the others. Kautsky never stood on the positions of Marxist philosophy. He always stood on the point of view of the reactionary philosophy of positivism, biologism and Malthusianism.[50] More lamentable than anything is that similar views even now echo in the majority of our philosophical publications and textbooks.

Marx showed that sensuousness, as human sensuousness, is not the gift of nature and that the data of human perception is not 'primary, undeductable from other data', as Feuerbach asserted. The sensory perceptions of people is the result of social and historical development, and they differ from each other in different historical periods.

Lucien Lévy-Bruhl believed that primitive consciousness *perceives and sees* as we do, but thinks differently. And we say that Paleolithic humans *not only* think but *percieve in a different way and think differently* that we do *despite the fact* that they look and listen with the *same physiological apparatus* as ours.

Hence, human sensuousness should not be the basis for explaining the forms of human consciousness and thinking; on the contrary, sensuousness needs to be examined from the standpoint of social reality and of history. Sensory perception represents, in principle, the same *historical* problem as thinking, and it should be interpreted from the standpoint of history.

---

50   As confirmation of this, we can quote the philosophical portion of Kautsky's two-volume work *Die materialistische Geschichtsauffassung* (Kautsky 1927); the biological standpoint is reflected even more clearly in his much earlier work, *Ethics and the Materialist Conception of History* (Russian translation Kautskii 1906), in which he attempts to deduce ethical questions from the instincts of animals and ascribes 'consciousness of duty', 'a voice of conscience' and 'remorse' to animals (p. 67).

The founder of experimental psychology, Wilhelm Wundt, displayed a rare breadth of outlook in defending the opinion, in an epoch of universal enthusiasm for natural scientific methods, that the highest mental processes and the complex functions of thinking are social products, and therefore their study should be closely linked with the study of language, folklore, customs and so on. In accordance with this, Wundt divided psychology into two parts: the elementary data of the psyche (sensation, simple feelings, perception, representations) – in his opinion, the natural products of the physical constitution studied by experimental psychology – and the higher mental formations, including the questions of thinking, could be studied as questions of social psychology (*Völkerpsychologie*), to which he dedicated his tremendous multi-volume work.

We must confront these views with the following assertion: not only are the higher functions of the psyche the social products of historical development, but the most elementary functions of the human psyche (sensations, feelings and so on) represent the products of the *history* of society as such and must be studied in general connection with the social and historical development of humanity.

The question of sensuousness is thus put in a completely new light and turned onto another side. The senses and sensory data are in no way the premise of a Marxist theory of cognition and theory of experience but the problem from which humans learn the specific means of sensory perception. The starting point here, as in all Marxist world views, is humanity – not as a natural biological creature, but humanity in its industrial and social existence and in its history.

CHAPTER 5

The Question of a Subject's Self-Awareness

Objects Are Perceived Primarily according to Their Social Significance

§ 44

Human perception began not with the self-awareness of the subject, as the idealists depicted it, asserting that intellectual activity began with self-positing by the subject of themselves as an existing ego, as an absolute subject (Fichte). The consciousness of primitive humans was directed above all towards external objects, and in the beginning it was not privy to its own existence. But primitive consciousness did not perceive all the objects of surrounding reality, but mainly those that constituted the object of its activity. *Natural reality itself entered into people's consciousness through the practical activity of these people.*

Self-Awareness Is Historically a Much Later Phenomenon Than the Perception of Objects of Activity

§ 45

In the process of both objective and intellectual activity, the attention of an individual is directed above all towards the object. The subject is completely occupied with the object, and keeps themselves least in mind. Even when the sense of self-awareness is highly developed in them, in the midst of their activity they most often forget precisely about themselves. At a much lower stage of development (e.g. the animal stage), awareness of self is completely absent. 'For the animal', Marx said, 'its relation to others does not exist as a relation'.[1] Animals never occupy themselves with self-analysis; reflection directed inward is unknown to them. They give themselves no account of their actions or about the work of their organs. When an animal is pursuing prey, they are completely preoccupied with the object. When they are full, they are passive and indifferent.

On the other hand, no reflection inside consciousness, no self-concentration on one's own psyche can reveal anything in it, if consciousness does not have

---

1 Marks i Engel's 1933, p. 21.

its own objective content. And objective content is given to consciousness through the world of things created by labour (cf. §§§ 8–21).

It was not through internal reflection, like the Indian yogis and visionaries of theosophy, that the world was conquered by humans; they were victorious through activity directed outward towards objects. And these objects, transformed into the organs of human activity as instruments and means, imparted strength to humans and enriched their consciousness. The concepts of 'boiling', 'burning' and 'frying' are made possible as a consequence of the mastery of fire, and the concept of 'cutting' first became accessible to consciousness because of the knife.

After all the discoveries, humans 'discovered' their own existence and began to understand themselves through the world of objects they had created and through their means. It has rightly been observed by many that even their own organisms became better intelligible to humans after apparatuses that in their work were reminiscent of the functions of the organs of the human body were devised. Thus, for example, the structure of the eye was studied after the appearance of the *camera obscura* and the invention of the photographic apparatus, and the work of the nervous system became more intelligible to use after the telegraph was invented; *we understand the mechanisms of nature better only after we begin freely reproducing them.*

It would be the greatest error to think that from the very beginning, the subject realised him or herself as an active subject, or that the intellect immediately began reflecting on its own existence. The self – that precondition and the foundation of any activity – long remained in the shadows, emerging only very late into the field of the clear consciousness of the subject. Giambattista Vico was right when he said 'Above all, man exists without realising it'.

Humans needed to discover the continents, cross the seas, measure the universe and to a significant extent transform the ground on which they dwell before they could turn their gaze to their inner psychic world and ask themselves: What am 'I'? How am I doing all this? How do I create my thoughts? And having asked themselves that question (first, in fact, at the philosophical stage of reflection), human consciousness wandered in the dark over the course of millennia; up until now much less was known about the intellect than about any distant star – Betelgeuse, for example; its content, size and temperature have been determined with a great deal of approximation. What society is, what the laws of its existence and development are, what the essence of the processes of consciousness is – humanity knows less about all this than anything else. In any case, there can be no comparison between what science has achieved in the understanding of the essence of physical processes and what has been done in the field of understanding the essences of thought, of speech and so on.

The caustic words of Voltaire about scholars who, with no small amount of precision and in agreement with each other, answered questions about the distances between the planets, about their weight, their volume and so on but were at a loss when asked 'If you know so well what there is outside us, then without a doubt you know even better what is inside us and what you yourselves are. Tell me, what is your consciousness and how do you create your thoughts?' indubitably retain their validity today.

In response to this, these scholarly gentlemen could find nothing better than to cite the most ancient writers: Leucippus, Plato and Aristotle.

'Why are you quoting in Greek?' they were asked.

'Because', the scholars answered, 'what we don't quite understand must be cited in a language that we understand less than any other!'

We can note one thing: awareness by the subject of themselves is a much later fact in the history of thinking, occurring not from direct and immediate perception of the individual self but – as we will see below – arising after a long period of awareness of the subject in the person of and as a collective subject, the 'totemic self'.

An Individual Subject's Perception Was Historically Preceded by the Perception of the Collective Subject

§46

Like all the other animals, even anthropoids cannot recognise themselves in reflective surfaces – for example, the apes, who attempt to catch their reflections in a mirror. It is impossible, of course, to lead any ape to the understanding that they are seeing their own reflection. Self-awareness in primitive humans required a mirror of a completely different type: a 'social mirror', the 'mirror' of social relations.

Primitive humans lived social lives, and therefore their consciousness was social. At this phase of development, the consciousness of the individual self does not yet exist. Consciousness of the *individual*, both one's own and others', is absent. In others like themselves, primitive humans above all saw the embodiment of a specific collective: a totem, a horde, a clan and so forth. Another human was perceived exclusively in the person of the social group to which they belonged. In conformity with this, the relation to this other human was defined as to a person of a 'foreign' or 'hostile' group, or of 'one's own', a 'native' or 'friendly' group.

Something similar can be observed in herd animals. For this reason, Marx was right in saying that the beginning of awareness was as animal as social life at that stage. It was mere herd consciousness.[2]

Humans were never perceived separately from the collective to which they belonged. Particular individual people did not exist at this stage; nor did individual interests isolated from the interests of the collective, and therefore no ideas about the individual self could exist. In themselves, primitive humans also saw only their totem; collective feelings prevailed in their psyches. The remnants of this representation have incidentally been preserved in the custom of blood feuds: it is not the given individual causing the damage who is considered the culprit, but the entire clan (or family) to which they belong. The responsibility for the actions of an individual is borne by the entire collective, and retribution is considered complete if the punishment is suffered by any third party whatsoever belonging to the same family, clan or tribe. Regarding the native tribes of the Congo, Edward Thorndike said they often arrested some poor old woman because a man from her village had committed an offense. 'In such cases, the natives were extremely surprised at the indignation of foreigners. Was the woman really not the guilty party's fellow villager? Did she really not admit his guilt? Collective responsibility is expressed in the fact that it was not one person accusing another for the offence of an individual person, but one village accusing another.[3]

In primitive society, the consciousness of individuals was inseparably fused with the general tribal consciousness. The individual did not differentiate themselves from the collective.

---

[2] Marks i Engel's 1933, p. 21.
[3] Thorndike 1931, p. 143.

PART 2

CHAPTER 6

The Rise of the Idea

§ 47

The fact that views and ideas are always linked to a specific historical epoch and the specific society in which they arise and are applied is empirically known. In tandem with a change of epochs and social structure, some views die out and other, new ones are born. No one, for example, could deny that medieval concepts about the universe, about faith, sin, morals and so on are so far removed from the sphere of thought of Paleolithic humans or from contemporary views that the people of these different times could not easily understand each other. In noting this as an empirical fact, we ask: why do specific views arise and prevail in a specific epoch in a specific society? How do people arrive at certain ideas? How do they create their thoughts?

From our standpoint – as we will see further on (cf. §§ 105, 107) – there is no great difference in principle whether we ask this question in relation to many individuals and the whole of society, or in relation to an independent individual and certain acts of thought. Consequently, the question can be formulated even more simply, and more generally at that: why, and how, are certain ideas born in people's consciousness?

The attentive reader will hardly need to be prompted about the direction in which we will seek the solution to this problem, as we earlier stated the principle we are following: for new ideas to arise, it is necessary that social conditions direct people's interest in such a way that makes a specific understanding of things possible.

The function of thinking is in no way exhausted only by a subjective mental process, by intracerebral activity:

First, thinking expresses not only the subjective condition of consciousness, but concerns the object and expresses the relations of things. The subject's intellectual constructions always have certain objects and their relations in mind. A correct orientation in them requires the individual's ideas correspond to these things to a certain degree. Intellectual activity must reckon with the objective nature of things, in order to correctly express them. Using a more general formula, we can say: intellectual activity does not end within the boundaries of anatomical cerebral space; by its functions, the brain itself – owing to the objective activity of a person – passes outward, stretching into the objective world up to the boundaries of the person's actual influence. There is a great difference between 'anatomical and geometrical' space and 'functional cerebral' space (i.e. the radius of cerebral activity).

This bilaterality of consciousness is completely and fully expressed in a general definition provided by Marx: 'My relationship with my environment is my consciousness'.

Second, the process of cognition does not conclude with the rise of a new idea; it only begins. This is only the initial stage of cognition, *the subjective content of the idea*; it is still *only a plan of activity* and hence the beginning of the following act, which is more important for actual cognition – specifically the *act of realising the idea* (i.e. changing *the relations of reality existing up to then in accordance with the idea*). In this process of realising an idea, humans first actually learn both the essence of an object and the degree of the idea's validity. Thoughts become accessible to themselves through their realisation, through the objective existence of the thought (these questions are examined in §§ 111–116).

Third, in the majority of cases the individual act of thought – an individual's thinking – is only a particular manifestation of mature thought; it is the thinking by an individual of ideas that are formed in the turnover of social relations and consequently historically, and not as a result of only one single individual act of creation (cf. §§ 66, 79, 80).

In light of this, we will attempt to analyse the question of how specific thoughts arise in consciousness twice.

First, from the standpoint of the individual act of cognition, in connection with the question: *what is understanding, what is an idea* (cf. §§ 48–64).

Second, as a social process of the origin and the existence of the idea and its realisation: *the social transformation of ideas and the social phenomenology of though* (cf. Chapters Seven, Eight and Nine).

Comprehension. The Concept

§48

What best gives us an account of what comprehension is and what it was in the historical past is language itself; its data is fuller and more correct than the conclusions of a philosophical school. Here, this word in Russian (*poniatie* [concept]) is found by rights alongside others, fundamentally homonymous with them and close in meaning: *poniat'* ('to understand, comprehend'), *vnimat'* ('to heed') and so on. All these are produced from the Old Russian *imati*, short form *iat'* (as seen in brat' /vziat', 'to take'). These words represent a variety of another Russian word, *imia* ('name', preserved in its fullest form in the genitive *imeni*), which has its prototype in nearly all Indo-European languages: the Latin *nomen* ('name') and *numen* ('will, might'); the Greek ὄνομα ('name, title') and νόμος ('custom, order, law'); the German *Name*; the French *nom*; in these languages they are also accompanied by terms having the meaning of 'take' (e.g. the German *nehmen*, the Greek νέμω ['distribute, appropriate']).

In this case, language faithfully reproduces the meaning of the act of understanding, of comprehension. 'To have an understanding' (*imet' ponimanie*), 'to understand' (*ponimat'*) meant taking, seizing, managing, submitting to one's will, just as knowing the name at a specific degree of the so-called 'magic' world view meant 'having power over things', 'knowing the magic formula with which to subjugate things'.[1]

In the given case, we will not touch on the very old meanings of the common foundation of the words *ponimat'*, *imen*, *nomen* and so forth, which lead into the historical past of the magical world view. Imati, *ponimat'*, *imia*, *imeni*, *numen* and so forth, lying palaeontologically in one semantic series, come from a shared foundation whose original meaning derives from the name of the totem and everything that belonged to it.

We are currently occupied with the history of thought of epochs with world views much closer to ours, when the words *ponimat'* and *poniatie* had acquired the meanings of 'grasping with the intellect' and had begun to signify the mastery of thought (i.e. received an ideological function in the same way that the words *usvoenie* ['learning'] and *osvoenie* ['mastering'], evidently indicating an origin from ownership with the reflexive pronoun *svoi* at their base and now used in both meanings of material and mental appropriation).

The same picture can be traced in the example of the Latin word *capio*: *concipio*, *per-cipio*, *-ceptum-*, having the meaning of 'take', 'seize', 'take possession of', 'perceive with the senses', 'notice' or 'comprehend'; and the German *greifen*: *be-greifen*, *Begriff* with the same meaning; and in examples from other languages.

Of interest to us in connection with the study of the idea is the closest epoch in the development of thinking, when *znat'* 'to know' no longer meant simply 'to see' or 'to hear'[2] and when *myslit'* 'to think' had begun to signify 'to master with the intellect' and 'to grasp intellectually'.

---

1 Vivid remnants of this have been preserved in many ancient folk legends, but the runes of the Kalevala provide particularly rich material in this respect.
2 There actually existed such a period in the development of thinking when знать 'to know' and понимать 'to understand' meant simply 'to see' and 'to hear', respectively. The remnants of this epoch are preserved in the Russian verb ведать 'to know, be in charge of' with its prototype in Latin, Greek and other languages. Among the Greeks, the word σέα – even in Plato's

Carrying out this intellectual operation of embracing things through thinking is possible in the case where the relations of things push the consciousness of people in this direction, and when these objects lie close to people's ideational aspirations.

In other words, objects can be raised to perception, and thinking can form the comprehension of things only in the convergence of two moments: 1. The factor of the object, expressed in the fact that objective relations direct consciousness to specific thoughts, and 2. The factor of the subject i.e. through a specific form of directed or *engaged consciousness*.

Both these factors mutually define each other in the sense that things arrange consciousness in a given way; and a directed consciousness is inclined to perceive and make intellectual comparisons in a certain way, proceeding from correlations which objective relations (*objektive Sachbezüge*) only provide the vaguest hints about.

Comprehension is a form of intellectual operation. 'Intellectual' means mental operations that take into account the material conditions of the situation in which it is performing and acting in accordance with the objective nature of the objects it is using. The comprehension of a thing or a situation is a judgement of its system, its structure, and its place or significance in the system of tasks occupying consciousness. According to this, *comprehension* is the judgement by consciousness of the semantic relation of objects, the law of internal structure or the real significance of the object; in other words, comprehension is nothing other than the 'material world reflected in the mind of man, and translated into forms of thought'.[3]

In philosophy, there is an established tradition of opposing comprehension and representation to each other as if these were two separate domains of abstract categories. Traditional theory attempted to explain the origin of the comprehension of its ideas in a dual manner: either through multiple repetitions of the same representations and the assimilation of forms on an analogy with photographic plates on which several images are captured (psychological theories about 'general representations') or through abstracting 'general signs' i.e. discarding dissimilar signs and preserving similar ones, attempting in its

---

time – meant 'view', 'form' and 'external appearance' as well as having the meaning of image and representation. A similar picture can be observed in Georgian, where შესმენა (*shesmena*) simultaneously means 'to hear' and 'to understand', გესმის (*gesmis*) means 'do you hear' and 'do you understand', and გაიგონე (*gaigone*) means 'listen' (with the ears), 'listen' (in the sense of 'obey'), and 'you know?'. The root of this word, გონ (*gon*) has the simultaneous meanings of 'to see', 'to hear', 'to remember' and 'to think'. გონება (*goneba*) means 'intellect'.

3 Marx 1996, p. 102.

own way to rethink the Aristotelian hierarchy of comprehension: general and particular, specific and generic and so on (the traditional theory of abstraction).

In both cases, it resulted in full-blooded reality gradually losing all its real properties, ultimately resting on an empty abstraction of higher comprehension deprived of all content. A bare, subjective schema – the 'pyramid of conception' – was obtained, ending in the most abstract representations of 'something', under which any intellectual content could be placed.

The question arose: how to find the path back from 'general comprehension' to particular, isolated comprehension? How do the individual and the general relate to each other? How is it possible to infer from the individual case to the general? Philosophers have proposed different paths for a solution: inference by analogy, induction, deduction, reduction (such things existed!) and so on.

We will not tire the reader with an exposition of all these theories, which enjoy such wide dissemination but provide no explanation whatsoever either as regards representations or concepts; let us proceed to the essence of the question.

The Concept and the Notion [*predstavlenie*][4]

§ 49
Philosophers and psychologists have placed a yawning chasm between representational thought and the thinking of the non-figurative – thinking in concepts. Of the psychologists, the works of the Würzburg school – Oswald Külpe, Karl Marbe, Narziß Ach and others – are particularly well known. We maintain that this chasm between visual figurative and non-figurative thinking, between the visual representation and the concept, does not exist.

The ability to retain the visual images of things in the consciousness, what we usually call representations, is nothing other than the ability to reproduce past impressions (visual, auditory, etc.) irrespective of whether it is an image of one object or the image of a whole complex of objects, situations, and so forth.[5]

---

4 [The Russian *predstavlenie* may be translated as notion, presentation, or representation according to the particular nuance it gains in a specific context. As discussed in the introduction, Megrelidze is using the term to specify a category that simultaneously has perceptual and ideational qualities. For this reason the original Russian has been appended to show the use of a single term – ed.].

5 Here, we would emphasise that consciousness moreover does not so much reproduce details as it does a graphic general picture of the object. We almost never remember individual details, despite the fact that we have before us a completely clear, sharp and vivid image. You can imagine the face of your acquaintance very distinctly and vividly, but if you ask your-

If the object of perception represents a continuous whole – a human face or figure, for example – which is impossible to imagine, despite all efforts, as the composition of different parts of of two halves, then in those cases we perceive the object immediately as a definite whole and can speak of a separate *image*.

When the object of perception is no such firm integrated formation but something multipartite, where the separate parts existing independently of one another must be mentally unified, then the perception of such a complex is in principle the same problem as in the first case, but nevertheless the action of thinking and of an intellectual operation is expressed more vividly here. The structure and significance of the object in this case is given to consciousness not immediately through the simple perception of the given objects; they must be sought, thought of or found. Here, consciousness is less associated with the object; it is freer in its intellectual constructions and is not found wholly in the wake of the object.

A mentally constituted context does not always thoroughly reconcile with the data in the perception. Very often a mental logical *order*, established in understanding, has nothing in common with what has been sensuously perceived. In this case, thinking represents a unification of these objects in a definite integral context where all the individual parts would be mutually given meaning along the lines of the task placed before consciousness.

An extreme case of this disconnected (*löse*) formation would be, for example, a simple external additive formation and the operations of summing corresponding to it (i.e. the idea of a simple sum of objects). In practice, we often resort to similar mental operations. To understand the state of some any complex whole – society, for example – or of physical laws in effect in the maelstrom of molecular movements, we formulate certain general laws or establish specific norms of social production and consumption, of mortality and birth rates and so on by summing up in a particular manner the separate phenomena, movements and events, and by comparing statistical data.

Between this means of apperception (disconnected phenomena) and the first case, in which the object of perception is an objectively inseparable whole (for example, it is impossible to imagine a horse as the combination of two halves, something like the way it is described in the adventures of Baron Munchausen) are arranged all the remaining cases according to the degree of optical

---

self, for example, whether they have a birthmark and where, or where they have wrinkles, and so on, you will be amazed not only at the incompleteness of your memory but even by the absence of knowledge of almost all the parts of the face taken separately; the more you think about it, the more your doubts will grow. 'Eidetic' types of memory – discovered by Erich Jaensch – have nothing to do with this, nor do cases where the object is specially studied, for example when sketching.

durability, from the least disconnected formation to the most disconnected (i.e. an individual horse, an entire herd, the sum total of horses in a country or the general number of cigarette butts discarded around the world per day). In these cases, we are dealing with different types of intellectual operations, but for all that it is clear that the reflection of consciousness in the first case is simpler and the work of comprehension is minimal, because in the simple perception of any integrated object, figure or face, consciousness simply 'figuratively' repeats the form of the object given to it and is in maximal independence from the object. In this case, comprehension is a completely elementary act. It is the presence itself of the given form. The question 'What is a spiral staircase?', asked as a joke, will serve a graphic example of the fact that reproducing the visual form of certain things is sufficient for their comprehension. The reaction to this question is stereotypically identical for everyone (besides construction specialists, who think in more precise formulas): 'It's a staircase that ...'. – and here most people halt, immediately putting their finger in motion, shooting upward and describing spirals in the air. No abstract concepts are of help here, where a graphic representation is required for the description of a thing. In the given case, it is actually difficult to provide a 'better explanation' that does without reproducing the image of a spiral passage.

In similar cases, the construction of an object is given to consciousness in the form of the object itself; this is its form, a simple *picture* of the thing. The superficial meaning of the object does not need to be sought, thought of or compared. The meaning of the thing is the thing itself and its external aspect.[6]

In comprehending the context of a more disconnected formation, meaning acts as the law of its composition and of the mutual attribution of the parts. When consciousness has to find the means of connection and compare parts in a definite integral semantic context – hence, when a definite whole is not so much given to consciousness as it is *specified*, when consciousness has to constitute this whole (i.e. compare separate data in an entire context) – in this case the thought work of an encumbered consciousness and the essence of the intellectual process in general (the problem of understanding) appears in much greater relief and more distinctly than in the first case. What do we have, in this case? Is it really the same figurative thinking as in the first case?

---

6   If we wish to seek a deeper meaning of the things visually presented, we place it in some other context where, conducting a semantic function and becoming a cause or a consequence, and so on, it displays its determinations – in other words, we perform on the object of simple representation an act of reflection of the second and higher orders. This is why it may happen that humans have a graphic representation of all the separate parts of the whole (i.e. they do not perceive the complex as a semantic image of a coherent whole); in other words, they have no concept at all.

In principle, both these cases have something in common, since they lie on the same spiral of the human means of perception, representing different stages. But as regards the construction of the field of consciousness, then a difference absolutely exists between them. This includes the fact that in the first case, we have a vivid *image* of a concrete object, simply a *picture* of the object, and in the second case the content of consciousness is not a simple reproduction of the picture, the external appearance and the topographical state of things (or parts) in relation to each other, as far as any part or any moment in this disposition of things serves as a bridge joining the complex into a semantic whole that successfully resolves the situation (i.e. as actually appropriate to the interest of consciousness).

In the latter case, consciousness is not occupied so much with the visual picture of things as it is with the *means of connecting* these things among themselves – the *principle* or *law* of construction of a semantic whole. The question of what this meaning includes is subject to assessment every time, especially in relation to objects: it could be the name of a thing, the specific construction of the complex, the role of the object, the functions, the dependency of cause and effect and so forth.

The difference between notion [*predstavlenie*] and concept thus depends not so much on any essentially different arrangements of consciousness during the act of thought as it does on *the material of thinking and the tasks of comprehension*. Whether consciousness embraces it as a figurative whole or as something subject to comprehension through inclusion in one context or another depends to a significant degree on the material of comprehension. In some cases a graphic representation is needed; in others, the task of comprehension requires judging the laws of connection, the structure of the object, its role, function and name (i.e. not so much the graphic figurative inclusion as much as including the means of connection and the semantic constitution of the closed context). The latter case has to do with the act which in the scientific use of the word is called understanding, or *concept*.

The concept is a particular category of cognition that is permanently equal to itself and always expresses the same thing. On the other hand, the same object *in different contexts is the bearer of different functions and different meanings*; accordingly, *the concepts of it are completely different*.

Both concept and notion [*predstavlenie*] are forms of intellectual activity, but differ from each other in a structural relation. Using a number of simple examples, we will attempt to clarify the difference in the structural relation taken by the field of consciousness in the act of representation and of concept, according to the task before it:

1. The *notion* [*predstavlenie*] of the shift from day to night, periods of cold and warmth, winter and spring and so forth as the simple statement of facts following one another – even three-year-old children have such representations. Night comes after day, after night – day; children at the age of two or three answer this question correctly.

   But in order to understand these phenomena, in order to *have a concept* about them, a simple graphic copying of them is insufficient. To understand them, it is necessary to turn to a third object: the sun: Having considered the rearrangement that consciousness then undergoes, it becomes clear to us that phenomena that were previously *presented* [*predstavliat'sia*] in a simple sequence are now locked in some kind of new cognitive context in which not the shift from day to night, but the movement of the sun or the rotation of the earth now act as the central moment.

   If this latter does not satisfy us and we wish to further comprehend the relation of the sun and the earth, we construct a new context of a much wider scope and make an appeal to, let us say, Kant-Laplace hypotheses about the universe and the solar system, or to some other construction of the same general character.

2. The *notion* [*predstavlenie*] 'the boat floats' (i.e. a reproduction of the image of 'boat on the surface of the water') and the *concept* of the same ('It's not sinking! Why doesn't it sink?') are two different things, both psychologically and cognitively. In order to *understand*, in order to *form a concept* of why a canoe is supported on the surface of the water and does not sink to the bottom, it is insufficient to simply reproduce the given picture ('Landscape with a Canoe'); it is necessary to bring in data about specific weight, the weight relationship of the vessel and the displaced water and to arrange in the mind facts other than the ones used in representing the image of a floating boat.

3. We can have a *graphic notion* [*nagliadnoe predstavlenie*] of an unemployed person in the form of any individual – a person named Meyer, for example. We can know a mass of details describing them: when they lost their job, what hardships they endure, the way in which they were dismissed and so on, but all this does not help us *understand* the essence of the unemployment that has embraced so many people, including Meyer. If we want to really understand the actual reasons for why Meyer has lost her job and cannot find another one, we must appeal to the economic system of capitalism in which she has to live, in which crises and unemployment (i.e. the existence of a market of the unemployed, available for the hire of working hands) is an indispensable component. And having understood what unemployment means in a given economic system of

production and distribution, we will properly understand the the true fate of all the Ernsts, Kuntzes and Meyers languishing in poverty and unemployment.

4. The notion [*predstavlenie*] of a 'table' realised the graphic image of a specific table, real or imagined. The *concept* of 'table' realises in consciousness not the image of a table, but its general principle, its general function, its designation (e.g. 'support, work area' in the broad sense of the word). The concept is not in opposition to the representation, and is not formed from individual representations via their summation and abstraction. The concept of 'table' is not the sum of similar signs of all the tables existing in the world, and is not the result of abstraction; *everything* that could perform the function of a table fits this concept. The function is defined not by some kind of particular essence (in the form of a Husserlian *eidos*) that is supposedly inherent in things but by means of its use – in the given case, in everyday use. Everything that could perform the function of a table has the meaning of a table for people. Even any 'non-table' (e.g. a box, a tree stump, a windowsill and so on) can become a table in concept, if in daily use these objects *replace* a table.

A *concept* is above all understanding (i.e. judgement of the semantic condition of a thing in context with others) and not some category of abstraction, as was in the era of Scholasticism. The concept expresses the object not in its isolated existence, but in one or another semantic attribution. If, for example, someone came up to us and suddenly utters the word 'house' out of all context, we will understand nothing; no concept will arise within us. But it is sufficient to pronounce a few words, even poorly connected grammatically with each other, in order for a given concept to arise: 'What is a house?' Then we will look not for the image of a house, but for a specific semantic aspect of the thing: function, designation and so on. When we want to understand the meaning of any word – 'table', for example – we envisage not the image of one table or another (as the empiricists asserted), but we think above all of the designation of this object: 'for meals', 'for writing', 'for work' and so on.

The concept is a semantic composition in which we correlate objects; it is a semantic combination of objects. The concept expresses not an abstract essence, but a 'layout' of a complete thought. If we realise what we actually mean by the concepts of 'cause', 'goal', 'force' and so on, then we will find no concrete figurative content in our consciousness. We only discover that in these cases our consciousness strives to take a certain general position, a direction, but a specific objective content is absent in it; there are no images and graphic representations. This circumstance misled the psychologists of the Würzburg school, who dedicated vast amounts of research to the question of non-figurative thinking.

If a concept is thus the particular means of intellectually combining conceivable objects, the question then arises: How does it differ from 'free fantasy'?

It must be said that fantasy and the productive imagination are in no way the antipodes or enemy of reason, but only a component of the intellect and an indicator of its strength. The strength of creative consciousness consists of the fact that it can violate established routines, create new combinations and new problems in everyday things. Voltaire was correct when he said: 'Pedestrian opinion considers imagination to be the enemy of reason'. On the contrary, it can function only under conditions of deep thoughtfulness; it endlessly draws up plans, corrects mistakes and erects all its constructions in strict order. Applied mathematics requires the tremendous strength of imagination; in Archimedes it was, if anything, equal to that in Homer.

The role of imagination and of the free combination of presentations [*predstavlenie*] in the process of productive thinking is a tremendous one, as intuition (fantasy) precedes exact calculations, and every implementation is preceded by preliminary construction.

Lenin distinctly highlighted the significance of fantasy in scientific thinking. 'It would be stupid', he said, 'to deny the role of fantasy, even in the strictest science'.

But the concept, in the scientific sense of the word, differs from fantasy in that first, it has to reckon with actual reality and express, with a certain amount of precision, the objective structure of things; fantasy is not bound by this necessity and can be at liberty in its constructions (though historically it is fully conditioned, like every ideological superstructure). Whoever cannot grasp the difference between the hypothetical and the logical, between the fantastic and the real, will find themselves in an unenviable position as a scientist.

The Particular and the General

§ 50

Rationalist philosophy, and the philosophy of empiricism as well, believed notions [*predstavleniia*] to be insufficient for the purpose of cognition on the basis that notions supposedly only provide knowledge of isolated things and separate events, and that in addition knowledge of the universal, which is only supplied with general concepts, is necessary.

It should be noted about this that first, graphic notions [*nagliadnye predstavleniia*] in no way provide knowledge of isolated things, and second, knowledge of an isolated thing is not as poor as it appeared to the philosophers. On the contrary, not only is it not bad, it constitutes the ideal of any knowledge: being capable of fully discerning the individual nature of phenomena (i.e. learning reality) – if human knowledge is not striving for that, then it remains completely enigmatic; what use does humanity have for the general? And if humans could genuinely fully discern the particular nature of phenomena in each particular case, then there would be no point for them in general abstract knowledge of some 'object in general'. There is no problem between the particular and the general in the arrangement that is known to us from the history of philosophy, since the general has no distinctive existence. 'The general', Lenin says, 'exists only in the particular and through the particular. Every particular is (in one way or another) a general. Every general is a fragment (or an aspect, or the essence) of the particular. Every general only approximately embraces all the particular objects. Every particular enters incompletely into the general, etc. etc'.[7]

In bourgeois philosophy, the ancient dispute still continues in a somewhat altered form between the neo-Platonists and the neo-Aristotelians about whether concepts are original essences or if they have existence in things. However, the idea does not represent the essence in either the first or the second meaning. A concept has no other form of existence than that of a judgement by consciousness of the objective relations (or laws) of reality.

The general represents only the expression of the identical behaviour of things. The identical behaviour of things can be conditioned by the identity of the structural foundations of their existence. If an isolated thing did not comprise the universal and did not express this universal, the world would essentially be chaos in which any consistency and conformity to natural laws would be absent. This is why every phenomenon taken individually, reproducing in itself all the foundations of *its* existence, also expresses the *general* law of all similar cases. It is simultaneously *particular* and *universal*. The general and the particular are not opposed to each other: *the particular is the general under various conditions*. Poets have proven to be deeper thinkers on these questions than philosophers: 'What is the general?' Goethe asked. 'An isolated case. And what is the particular? Millions of cases'.

'In order to know what man is (i.e. what is general – км), it is sufficient to know one person – yourself, for example. But in order to know what people are (individual persons, i.e. the particular – км), you must study each of them in isolation', Stendahl said. And this is completely obvious; in other words, fairly exactly the opposite of what traditional logic and all official scholastic philosophy asserts.

---

7 Lenin 1931, p. 325.

The Doctrine of Existence and Concept

§51

In the history of philosophy, every epistemological system is closely linked with specific ontological views and flows from them, exactly as every theory of concepts ultimately rests on ontological questions. The ancient thinkers, not having divided theses fields with an impassable gulf and having begun an account of philosophy from ontological questions, acted more wisely than contemporary European philosophy, which under the influence of Kant limits the tasks of philosophy to the sphere of the logic of cognition, starting from and ending with 'purely epistemological' questions.

Aristotle, Spinoza, Hegel and others intentionally introduced ontological problems and placed them at the foundation of epistemological questions. Post-Hegelian bourgeois philosophy advanced its slogan of a return to Kant, and began considering actual reality to be the absolutely transcendental sphere of metaphysics, inaccessible in principle to cognition, and therefore unworthy of being the object of philosophical investigations. However, each of these philosophical systems is tacitly based on certain ontological and metaphysical premises.

The searches for conformity to natural laws only within the boundaries of cognitive activity, so characteristic of all modern European philosophy (Cohen, Rickert, Husserl, and the entire school joined to them) – it does not matter whether they are in the form of the 'transcendental unity of *a priori* constrictions' (Cohen, Natorp), or of 'consciousness in general' (Schuppe), or of 'regional eidetics' (Husserl), 'the sphere of the significant' (Windelband, Rickert, Lask) – all prove one thing: philosophers held the opinion that the world of material reality lacks regularity, that it is a random chaos of phenomena, and that bringing them into a system and creating a mentally harmonious world constitutes the true task of cognition. But a world thus ordered could not exist in reality but only ideally, in the imagination of philosophers.

Idealist philosophy around the turn of the twentieth century generally dissociated itself from ontological questions. 'We do not care what the theory of cognition leads us to in ontology; ontology must conform with the theory of knowledge, not the other way around',[8] these theoreticians say. As a matter of fact, ontological premises lie at the basis of their epistemological views – the less care taken about them and in checking them, the more mistaken they are.

Since ancient times, two pictures of the world have been opposed to each other in the history of idealist philosophy: one created by empiricist philo-

---

8 Losskii 1906, p. 24.

sophy, and the other created by rationalist philosophy. Along these lines, the doctrine about the concept received essentially different bases and interpretations.

The Doctrine of the Concept in the Empiricists and in Kant

§52

The starting point of empiricism is the proposition that any meaning consists only of the sum of individual sensations, perceptions, representations and so on. This was viewed either as a mechanical coupling of experiences according to the law of association, or as the activity of special 'abilities of the psyche', which supposedly convert the sense data of feelings into ordered experience. Developing further, empiricism gradually grew into a system of rationalist views; the empiricists began to admit that the incoherent data of individual feelings could become experience only through rational processing, which does not present a problem for perception but are the *a priori* forms of consciousness and the intellect. This merging and reconciliation of empiricism with rationalism found its greatest expression in the transcendentalist philosophy of Kant. Experience, in Kant's opinion, consists of two elements: 1) the data of sensory perception (*apprehensia*), which are a formless, uncoordinated chaos of perceptions; and 2) *a priori* categories (i.e. concepts) of the intellect, the synthetical activity of which brings this formless material of sensuousness into a certain order, into ordered rational experience.

Empiricism – which like the transcendental philosophy of Kant can legitimately be called rationalist empiricism – relies on the premise that the world is an incoherent chronicle of events, a random sequence or coexistence of individual events that are in no way connected with each other. Moreover, even the event itself does not exist in reality as some kind of specific whole, since consciousness has (in the form of sensations) only the most elementary individual qualities of something unknown. The world represents the accumulation of singular states, of individual parts unrelated to each other; it is a world of absolute chaos in which chance rules, where there is no consistency and no conformity to natural laws.

In this disordered world, only cognition is called upon to re-establish and to introduce order. *Conformity to natural laws* thus exists not in reality itself as such, but *is only the function of cognition, a method by which it embraces the world and how it imagines this world*. In the system of these views, concepts are only abstract categories of the intellect to which nothing in objective reality corresponds because chaos and sheer confusion rule.

How did philosophers imagine the question 'Where do these concepts, these categories, come from?'

Scholastic philosophy, under the influence of Plato and a falsely interpreted Aristotle, considered these concepts (ideas, representations) to be revelations that were either inborn or acquired.

The philosophy of empiricism, beginning with Locke, sought psychological foundations for the origins of concepts and found them primarily in the fact that individual mental experiences according to the law of associative cohesion are supposedly gathered around a word, forming a sort of permanent mental mass so that in pronouncing the word, consciousness reproduces a number of past experiences associated with it. It is self-evident that this process is purely subjective and the order of links thus established by consciousness is also subjective and cannot to any degree express the objective nature of things.

In the system of transcendental philosophy as it came from the hand of Kant, concepts are considered the *a priori* forms of the intellect. Through them, the formless material of sensations are brought into order. It is even more obvious here that the concept has nothing in common with objective reality. Concepts and intellectual categories represent something similar to the finished form into which the content of experience is poured, like batter. Concepts are given outright by templates that are superimposed on the chaotic world of individual sensations. Cognition is not taken into consideration at all and does not conform to reality; on the contrary, reality must conform to the abstract determinations of consciousness. In the history of philosophy, this false understanding bears the celebrated name of 'Copernican revolution', and was formulated by Kant in the preface to *The Critique of Pure Reason* as follows: 'It has hitherto been assumed that our cognition must conform to objects ... Let us then make the experiment whether we may not be more successful in metaphysics, if we assume that the objects must conform to our cognition ...'.[9]

The Place of the Concept in the System of Rationalist Views

§53

At the foundation of logical rationalist philosophy (Aristotle, Spinoza, Leibniz, Hegel) lies an assumption about the absolute inevitability of everything that has happened – an assumption that everything existing is linked by logical necessity and that nothing in the world happens by chance.

---

9 Kant 1855, p. xxviii.

For the logical rationalist, all of world history flows with mathematical precision and necessity; nothing in it can thus deviate from the unalterably predetermined path. Moreover, the rationalists link everything existing with necessity twice, from both ends.

First, every phenomenon is determined from the preceding moment to the following one: from cause (B) to effect (C), where every cause (B) with all its details is inevitably determined by the preceding state (A) and has just as inevitable consequences (C) and so on from A and B, just as from B to C the process is absolutely determined and the chain develops to infinity so that nowhere does space for chance remain. Laplace examined the world order from this standpoint. 'All phenomena', he said, 'even those which in their insignificant minuteness seem to have no relation to the great laws of nature, are just as much the inevitable consequences of the latter as the rotation of the sun. We must regard the actual state of the universe as the result of its previous state and as a cause having something that will follow. If some kind of ideal intellect knew all the forces acting in nature at a given moment, and the mutual state of all the essences it consists of; and if, moreover, it was sufficiently all-embracing to subject all this data to mathematical analysis, then such an intellect would comprehend in one formula the movement of the greatest heavenly bodies and of the smallest atom'.

Second, every phenomenon is determined from its end (*causa finalis*), since once everything is predetermined, then the end is predicted from the very beginning as a state toward which the process has been directed from the very start and in which it inevitably develops. The end (τέλος) actually existing in every beginning – in rudimentary, embryonic form – for the disclosure of which development serves only as a means, is the ideal completeness of all those forms which the object must inevitably pass through in its development. Every beginning inevitably strives for this end, and in the opinion of the rationalists it represents an internal force compelling reality to move along a predetermined path of development: *entelecheia* in Aristotle, *causa finalis* in Leibniz, *natura naturans* in Spinoza, *sein-sollendes Sein* in Fichte, Absolute Spirit in Hegel and so on.

Leibniz differentiated the creative cause (*causa efficiens*) from the final, teleological cause (*causa finalis*), but this difference was known previously, from the time of Aristotle.

'The creative cause', Schopenhauer said, 'is that *as a consequence of which* something exists, the final cause (*causa finalis*) is that *for which* something exists; thus, phenomena subject to explanation have a creative cause behind them and a final cause before them' (i.e. in the future).[10]

---

10   Schopenhauer 1844, Vol. II, p. 379.

Every phenomenon is thus inevitably linked twice, from two sides – that is, it is pushed on by an inevitable cause behind it (i.e. from the past, the *causa efficiens*) and is drawn forward by an internal entelecheial force, the teleological cause (i.e. to the future, the *causa finalis*). Rationalist philosophy takes all phenomena of reality under the double press of necessity, so that nothing stirs or passes beyond the framework of the eternally established inevitable forms of development. Every particular event, however small, is definitively determined by the last thing immediately adjoining it, but it is no less firmly determined by the future as well. The future not only influences the present, but this future (τέλος) – that is, whatever has to be achieved in the end, the 'idea' or 'entelecheia' – is essentially the actual motive force (κινοῦν) leading from the beginning to the end of the entire process.

This means that everything occurring in the universe, all of world history, *is complete from the very moment of its beginning*, or not even having yet succeeded at beginning, since if everything is absolutely inevitably predetermined in every detail, it means that *what must occur has already occurred ideally and changing anything it it is impossible*. This means that *the past and the future are just as actual* as the present.

When we reflect on past events, we imagine them as something that took place, but which does not exist now. The facts of the past have only an imaginary existence, in the form of a picture of the past, insofar as yesterday no longer exists; they have an existence in reality only insofar as they have left their mark on today, having altered today's things and having been preserved in them. Thus, the actual existence of the past has solely a rational, historical meaning. Or, more simply, the past exists in the present only in a reflected form.

When we think about the future – for example, the future of some city, or the geographical location where it stands – we imagine every possible contour of that city's development, but we never think that this future (say, the year 2933) exists in reality today, or that it is predetermined from here. The future considered to be such insofar as it does not yet exist and must be created. From the proposition about absolute inevitability flows the idea that the world has a single path of development, and that this path is predicted with logical inevitability at any moment and at[11] any point in the course of the process. Everything that follows is determined, and the future is foreordained, by what has gone before; both of them in turn also determine everything that has gone before (i.e. the past) as a norm and programme of the entire process.

---

11   [There is a misprint in the Russian text here, with some repeated text – ed.].

If we thus place sequentially on the abscissa of time all the past states that a city went through yesterday, the day before yesterday, tens of thousands of years ago and so on it must pass through, then every segment of the past and every state of the future, according to the views of rationalist philosophy, will be just as real as the present. There is essentially no difference between them, they are all conceived ideally as having occurred and as completed, and if someone could voluntarily move backward and forward in time, they would simply find both everything that was past and everything that is future in the present. Our ideas of 'before' and 'after', 'at first' and 'afterwards' are only the representations of a limited intellect; these differences do not exist in an actual, teleological world – the future is as real as the present and equally as completed as the past. This means that events do not occur, and that they all occurred long ago and exist eternally. We ourselves are one of the predetermined links of this complete world, and as limited beings are coerced in the process of our lives to run through this previously completed world order; behind us events remain as they were, and ahead of us (i.e. in the future) they stand finished and completed once and for all, as we find them when reaching them.

The foundation of the Hegelian dialectic of being (*Dialektik des Wesens*) and its understanding as *gewesensein* consists of this primordial completeness of the entire future and all of world history. Marx said about Hegel that 'he lets the Absolute Spirit as Absolute Spirit make history only *in appearance*. For since the Absolute Spirit becomes *conscious* of itself as the creative World Spirit only *post festum* in the philosopher, its making of history exists only in the consciousness, in the opinion and conception of the philosopher, i.e., only in the speculative imagination'.[12]

§54

Reality, in all the forms of its manifestation, is rational – so the rationalists assert. 'The order and connection of thoughts is identical to with the order and connection of things', Spinoza said. Hegel paraphrased the same assertion, saying 'What is rational is real, and what is real is rational'. Such a conclusion is inevitable, if we accept the postulate about the absolute inevitability of everything that occurs. In reality, the logical development of the assertion that accidental occurrences do not exist leads unavoidably to absolute existence reality: the pure essences of Aristotle (*entelecheia*), the 'pre-established harmony' of Leibniz, the 'World Spirit' of Hegel – in a word, to a metaphysical essence, to the Absolute, *eo ipsae* to God.

---

[12] Marks i Engel's 1928–1946, Vol. III, p. 110 [Marx and Engels 1975–, Vol. 4, p. 86].

Hegel spoke about the rationality of everything real; historically, this assertion played a great revolutionary role as it meant that everything that occurred was subject to logical inevitability, and thus first revealed the meaning of historical development to the bourgeois world view. The thesis of Hegelian philosophy on the historical conditioning of all social phenomena affirmed the most fundamental assertion – from Aristotle to Spinoza, Leibniz and Hegel – that the world is not an incoherent chronicle of events but a consistent, *logical* whole; that phenomena not only follow one another but flow one from the other; that the basis of the subsequent lies in that which preceded it; and that the subsequent is only the expression of what was given in the unexpanded form of the 'being within Self' of the preceding. This fundamental assertion of all history was elegantly formulated by Leibniz: 'The present is saturated with the past and pregnant with the future' – there is a link of basis and consequence, of cause and effect, between what has passed and what is to come.

This is one of the most fruitful ideas in all the history of philosophy, and the strength of Hegelian philosophy lies precisely in the idea of development, which was first consistently advanced in all the fields of natural phenomena and of society. But in the form of absolute inevitability and necessity it is essentially idealistic, as it brings an inevitable fatalism with it. Once everything is necessary, then the world is complete from its very beginning; nothing can occur in it *and hence there is no history, just as there is no development*. The mysticism of Hegelian philosophy lies specifically in the fact that it admitted the eternal determinacy of everything real. But with this, Hegel only took away everything consistent from, so to speak, the Spinozan understanding of the world. In such a strictly determined, logical world, the participation of God in the process of development is not required, and their role in this world of strict internal necessity is entirely limited: once the basic postulates (e.g. mathematics) have entered force, God has nothing left to do in the multiplication tables. This is exactly why consistent rationalism has always had an inclination towards atheism and materialism (Spinoza, Hegel). God is incapable of changing anything in this system of strict logical inevitability;[13] they cannot interfere in the course of this process, therefore God is *this system itself* and the inevitable logical laws *themselves* are God's laws. Nature, Spirit, τέλος, idea, λόγος – these are the manifestations of the Absolute itself, and therefore no intervention from outside is required. But in such a case this God from the λόγος,

---

13 For example, in Leibniz's system the will of God is completely subordinate to the fatal laws of logic, and therefore the Leibnizian God cannot freely create a perfect world but is fatally compelled only to choose the world of least evils from all the logically possible sinful worlds.

a God from logic, is in many ways stronger than the personal, pre-Spinozan and pre-Hegelian God.

In his doctoral dissertation Marx said 'We might bring up [that] Hegel has turned all these theological demonstrations upside-down, that is, he has rejected them in order to justify them. What kind of clients are those whom the defending lawyer can only save from conviction by killing them himself?'[14] The theological demonstrations of the existence of God prior to Hegel were based on the assumption of the irrationality and randomness of the world: it was believed that the world had no internal logical order – no immanent meaning – and that the world was an open field of lawlessness and happenstance. 'Since the accidental has true being, God exists. God is *the guarantee for the world of the accidental*' (Marx). Since the world is poorly constructed and irrational in itself, then the highest reason and God exist for the induction of order into the 'ill-starred world'. God was internal in relation to the world he created, its highest authority, sovereign and judge (theism).

'Since nature has been badly constructed, God exists. Because the world is without reason, therefore God exists. Because there is no thought (in the material world – *KM*), there is God. But what does that say, except that, *for whom the world appears without reason, hence who is without reason himself, for him God exists? Or irrationality is the existence of God*'.[15]

The God of ordinary theology is thus some kind of contradictory *Notstandsgott* who created an irrational world and then was constantly compelled to personally bother himself about establishing order in it. The God of the rationalists is not the personal God of morals, retribution and so on but a pantheistic god, a diffuse god in the entire universe, a internally immanent reality in all its manifestations great and small. It is the logic of things themselves, the internal law of reality itself; God is this structure and the inevitable logic of the world order.

Hegel inverted all the teleological proofs by rejecting them and setting them off against the completely opposite assertion: since chance does not exist, then God exists – or the Absolute, and this is the logic of reality, the 'World Reason' or 'Absolute Idea'.

If chance does not exist at all in the world, if everything is inevitable and hence the world is rational from beginning to end, then God is completely necessary; it is no coincidence, of course, that Spinoza spoke about God and placed an equals sign between him and Nature: *deus sive natura*. All attempts by interpreters to remove God from Spinoza's system or Hegel's logic are fruitless,

---

14 Marks i Engel's 1928–1946, Vol. 1, p. 104.
15 Marks i Engel's 1928–1946, Vol. 1, pp. 105–6.

since they stand on God and every consistent system of rationalism collapses without God. And if Lenin said that in reading Hegel he usually discarded 'the Absolute', 'god' and the like, he did so not in order to be faithful to Hegel but because of his Marxist reinterpretation. Our current interpreters of Hegel and Spinoza often forget this.

If *deus* in the system of rationalist philosophy is the same as *natura*, so much the worse, because this god is that much stronger and more dangerous.

One of the contradictions metaphysics finds itself prisoner of, in Engels's opinion, is the contradiction between chance and necessity. 'Common sense, and with it the majority of natural scientists', he says, 'treats necessity and chance as determinations that exclude each other once for all. A thing, a circumstance, a process is either accidental or necessary, but not both. Hence both exist side by side in nature; nature contains all sorts of objects and processes, of which some are accidental, the others necessary, and it is only a matter of not confusing the two sorts with each other ... In opposition to this view there is determinism, which passed from French materialism into natural science, and which tries to dispose of chance by denying it altogether. According to this conception only simple, direct necessity prevails in nature. That a particular pea-pod contains five peas and not four or six ... that this year a particular clover flower was fertilised by a bee and another not, and indeed by precisely one particular bee and at a particular time ... these are all facts which have been produced by an irrevocable concatenation of cause and effect, by an unshatterable necessity of such a nature indeed that the gaseous sphere, from which the solar system was derived, was already so constituted that these events had to happen thus and not otherwise. With this kind of necessity we likewise do not get away from the theological conception of nature. Whether with Augustine and Calvin we call it the eternal decree of God, or Kismet as the Turks do, or whether we call it necessity, is all pretty much the same for science.'[16]

The rationalists (such as Spinoza and Hegel) as well as the materialists – both the early ones (Lucretius) and the materialists of the French Enlightenment (La Mettrie, d'Holbach, Diderot and Helvetius) – essentially cannot avoid the fate of acknowledging a singular god, even if a 'Spinozan' one.

Of course, the idea of this deity differs from the Christian one. Here, God is not the subject, existing alongside the world as a second reality. God is found in reality itself, in Nature.

It is significant that materialists before Marx, who vehemently called the personal God into question, always kept a stronger but pantheistic and pan-

---

16 Marks i Engel's 1925, pp. 191–193 [Engels, in Marx and Engels 1975–, Vol. 25, p. 499].

logist God, specifically diffuse throughout the entire universe, 'under their hats' in a sense.

This 'linguistic' God was friendlier than their half-sibling – the sovereign lord of the Jewish religion or the Christian *armes Lämmerschwänschen* (Heine) – but was nonetheless God, moreover a stronger one than all the personal gods in the history of humanity. The internal mainspring of absolute necessity in Nature advocated by Spinoza and Hegel was always God: the pure forms of Aristotle, the *natura naturans* of Spinoza, the 'pre-established harmony' of Leibniz, the 'Absolute Spirit' of Hegel, or 'God' – these are all only variations on the same theme.

The strict logical necessity of everything that occurs constitutes the basis of the pantheistic world view (deism), which in Kant's definition represents a belief in the existence of an original cause, immanent in the world and determining the world order; opposed to it is theism, signifying faith in a personal God and in the existence of Providence. This is the pantheistic God from the *logos* that Voltaire and even Heine believed in, to say nothing of Spinoza, Hegel, Jacobi and others.

This idea of God, whose wisdom is the intellect of Nature itself, who once and for all determines the world order, of course has nothing in common with the ideas of Christian Providence. But providentialism is completely preserved here, in another, stronger form – specifically, in the form of the logically inevitable. The God of Voltaire is the 'primordial and eternal geometer of the world'. Nature, in dialogue with the philosopher, says to the latter 'My poor child, do you wish me to tell you the truth? They have given me a name that does not suit me. They call me Nature, but I am all art' (Voltaire). God is this internal logic of objective reality itself.

And then once again, it seems to come out that 'In the beginning was the Word, and the Word was with God, and the Word was God. The same was in the beginning with God. All things were made by Him, and without Him was not any thing made that was made'.

The most complete system of rationalist idealism was built on similar ontological premises: the philosophy of Hegel, where the idea (or concept) is something that truly exists, 'veritable matter – a matter for which the form is nothing external, because this matter is rather pure thought ... Accordingly, logic is to be understood as the system of pure reason, as the realm of pure thought. This realm is truth as it is without veil and in its own absolute nature. It can therefore be said that this content is the exposition of God as he is in his eternal essence before the creation of nature and a finite mind'.[17]

---

17   Hegel 2015, p. 29. This idea of absolute inevitability and a fatal world received no less clear

From this, no rupture between ontological and epistemological questions exists, nor can it exist. Basic ontological premises and postulates are the same as epistemological ones, and credit must be given to what is completely correct in Hegel's system: 'It is impossible to speak of cognition without speaking at the same time of existence, and if the science of absolute reality is called metaphysics, then the theory of cognition does not precede metaphysics and does not follow it; it is neither the premise of metaphysics nor its task, *it is metaphysics itself*'.[18]

In this system of metaphysics, the concept appears as an objectively existing force of a spiritual type, as the end (τέλος) toward which, as towards a logically inevitable ideal prefiguration, all development strives; which – as an internal maxim, as a law (εντελεχεια) – initially defined the entire path of development from beginning to end.

The concept thus acquires objective existence, independent of the cognising subject and their cognitive activity. Concepts are purely objective existences without any material shell of thought; they are spiritual formations. But they move via reality, the world, and history. Material reality only does the job of the concept, which is why 'all that is real is rational'.

This is why 'for those who regard history in the Hegelian manner the result of all preceding history was finally bound to be the kingdom of spirits perfected and brought into order in speculative philosophy'.[19]

Therein lies the mysticism of Hegelian philosophy, repeatedly noted by Marx, Engels, and Lenin. But the founders of Marxism knew well that this mysticism was the direct consequence of the postulate on absolute necessity, which many of their 'successors' have quietly forgotten about, believing absolute determinism to be one of the fundamental premises of Marxism. In reality, Marx built his philosophy starting from a criticism of the Hegelian idea of absolute necessity and of the absolute concept that flowed from it. In contrast to Hegel he maintained that the concept is not an independent essence ruling over reality; on the contrary, the ideal is nothing else than the material world reflected by the human mind, and translated into forms of thought.[20] In nature, in its natural state, there are no ideas, no eternal predetermination. Reality, while rational human activity has not touched it, is a blind element; though

---

an expression in the East than it did in the West – in the Indian Vedas and Upanishads (particularly in the later interpreters of the ancient texts) as well as in the world view known as Taoism. *Tao* (or *dao*), used simultaneously to mean 'path', 'word' and 'obedience' in philosophical reflections, appears in the meaning of 'rigidly proper' or 'truth'.

18 Windelband 1920, p. 214.
19 Marx and Engels 1975–, Vol. 5, p. 168.
20 Marx 1923a p. XLVIII [Marx 1996, p. 19].

it has its firm natural laws, these laws do not represent logical dependence – as the rationalists thought – and do not act with logical immutability (as is observed in the world of mathematical abstractions), but emerge as the necessity of an event that always has a certain range of individual deviations.

Chance and Necessity

§ 55
Both the one-sided approaches described above (§§ 51–54), leading by different paths (one to subjectivist, the other to objectivist) idealism are the result of theoretical aberrations, believing the casual to be groundless and irregular and placing an equals sign between these concepts.

A false dilemma results: either 1) either chance exists and there is no conformity to natural laws in the world – such conformity is a fiction, a product of the imagination and has a purely *conceptual* existence only in consciousness; or 2) there is no chance in the world – then everything is inevitable, absolutely predestined, and concepts and ideas exist objectively independently of the consciousness of people, being the 'demiurge of reality'.

However, chance in no way signifies the absence of conformity to natural laws, and accidental phenomena should never be considered groundless. The world can be full of the elements of chance, and nevertheless be regular and necessary. It can be a mutually linked whole, and still not be absolutely determined and fatal.

1. Nearly all theoreticians who deny chance identify it with the absence of cause. The error begins here: 'since everything that occurs has its cause, chance is impossible. The accidental does not properly exist, but is only imaginary chance. We call accidental those phenomena whose causes cannot be precisely established and foreseen, as these phenomena in themselves are not accidental but necessary', they say. Hence, the accidental is only a measure of our ignorance. 'Sensible philosophy', Laplace said, 'sees in them [accidental phenomena] only the manifestation of ignorance'. But if we recognise the causes of the accidental, then does chance really stop being such?

That similar reasoning disregards the problem of chance is obvious from the fact that a phenomenon can be called accidental only in relation to another phenomenon through which it is called forth. Chance lies in the fact that the causes giving rise to it are not immutable, but themselves accidental.

Although, for example, a fertilising seed is necessary for fertilisation in the plant or animal world, this seed itself – both in its ripening and in the sense of penetrating a certain spot – is full of the elements of chance, to say nothing of the fact that one of these is far from sufficient for actual reproduction; here, a multiplicity of different conditions are necessary, beginning from the most general climatic factors and ending with the fact that the individual of interest to us did not end up in the belly of some extraneous animal.

It should be said in general, that rationalist philosophy has left us a legacy of a very poor idea of the causal relationship of phenomena. It believed that phenomena are connected with each other like threads, in one linear series from one cause to a sole effect. And so the monstrous legend and ridiculous slander of the world took shape. In the imagination of the rationalists, the material world – so diverse, rich, multidimensional and detailed – became one-dimensional, drawn into a line in the form of separate chains running from definite cause to definite effect. Similar interpretations run counter to the spirit and essence of dialectical materialism, which examines any reality as a certain whole and as the result of the *totality* of causes and conditions. Instead of a linear relationship, the philosophy of Marxism draws the relationship along the totality of conditions – a volumetrical, detailed connection (Lenin) from one state (A) to another (B), and not from one definitive cause to another definitive effect. It costs us tremendous effort in the experiment to artificially impart a one-dimensional, linear character to the process. And we try to achieve it by placing the phenomenon in an artificial vise where we maintain certain conditions without changes and change others in a certain direction, liberating the process from variegated influences and imparting a linear character to it, but we nevertheless do not reach the goal. In this respect it can be said that the interdependence of the phenomena of reality are truly multidimensional; in the traditional understanding of cause-and-effect relationships the world has only one change.

2. On the other hand, the fact that every chance itself is necessary is completely left out of account, but this necessity is of a more general type than absolutely definitive logical necessity.

The necessity of the accidental may be objectively defined, but its occurrence is not anchored with absolute precision in time. The occurrence of every real event depends not on one factor but a multiplicity of them, on the convergence of many conditions among which a direct relationship – or even any relationship – exists. When we speak of the necessity of a specific event, this does not mean that it must appear without fail at a strictly determined moment t, but only in the course of a certain interval (from t to t'), determined according to the objective law of probability. The same should be said of individual details of independent phenomena or events; the general contour and essential features of events may be necessary, but never the full face of a phenomenon in all its separate particular details.

It should further be noted that in the sphere of the atomic world, modern physics is putting forward extraordinarily important clarifications as regards necessity. It points out that precise determinacy relates only to the field of large statistical quantities as objectively more probable states of a tremendous quantity of individual atomic events, and not to the behaviour of an electron taken individually, where there could be any kind of deviation from these norms. Many are now inclined to think the problem of necessity and chance in physics requires a certain rethinking and expansion – but not, of course, in the direction proposed by certain representatives of a completely precise natural science (e.g. Richard von Mises) who demand we forego the principle of causality, thereby bringing confusion into the system of scientific views.[21] All the more colossal do thinkers like Marx, Engels and Lenin seem to us, who for a half-century were at the forefront of science and unerringly posed the problem of dialectical unity and of the interpenetration of the accidental and the necessary. The founders of Marxism first discovered and stated the proposition on *the internal necessity of the accidental*. This is not a deliberate unification of contradictory concepts, but a new concept of *a more universal necessity*, of a necessity of a more general type than the one-dimensional functional necessity that is only an element thereof and – insofar as it applies to real events – represents an abstraction of little value.

Relying on Darwin and his epoch-making work – which was built on extremely broad factual material of chance that caused readers to doubt the former basis of all conformity to natural laws and its metaphysical necessity – Engels showed that chance 'overthrows necessity, as conceived hitherto. The previous idea of necessity breaks down. To retain it means dictatorially to impose on nature as a law a human arbitrary determination that is in contradiction to itself and to reality, it means to deny thereby all inner necessity in living nature, it means generally to proclaim the chaotic kingdom of chance to be the sole law of living nature'.[22]

Engels's thought is quite deep, and moreover it is extremely clear: the accidental is necessary – just not definitive; it is necessary not in a strictly determined moment, but within the boundaries of certain deviations. Thus, on the one hand, 'necessity determines itself as chance' (Engels) – it is only the conformity of the accidental to natural laws, to the extent that every chance, on the other hand, is itself necessary to a certain degree. Such an understanding

---

21 Mises 1928.
22 Marks i Engel's 1925, p. 195 [Engels, in Marx and Engels 1975–, Vol. 25, p. 501].

of chance gives us a broader idea of the problem of conformity to natural laws, and necessity of this kind is a much broader and more universal necessity than absolute determinism.

The findings of Ludwig Boltzmann – who, as is known, advanced an extraordinarily broad theory of the universe – are built on the foundation of this assumption about the regularity of chance as a more universal regularity.

The law of heat loss – the transfer of heat from warmer bodies to cooler ones and the equalisation of temperature – has been known to physics since the time of Sadi Carnot and Clausius. But that still does not mean that the reverse process was generally impossible, or that such a process has no place in reality. Given the existence of two volumes of a gas at different temperatures, it often happens that the molecules of the cooler gas, having greater velocity, penetrate the sphere of the warmer gas; consequently, the temperature to a certain extent transfers from the cooler sphere to the warmer one, but these cases are few and are swallowed up by the incredibly superior number of cases of the opposite process, and as a result the greatest probability remains in the process of the reduction and of the equalisation of temperature states. Since the equality of temperatures is required for the completion of work, then energy in Nature depreciates more and more with this equalisation of temperature states. The growth of heat equalisation signifies a reduction of the value of energy. Mechanical, electromagnetic, chemical and other forms of energy transfer into heat, and the latter strives to dissipate into space. Thus entropy, which expresses the measure of devaluation of the energy of a system; the entropy of the universe strives for the maximum. This means that the world is threatened with what is called 'heat death', a state of full exhaustion of useful energy and the impossibility of any work whatsoever. In other words, it signifies the striving of a system to go over to a more probable (i.e. more constant and less ordered) state. (It is possible that in reality, this is not quite the case: the regeneration of energy occurs together with its devaluation, as a number of authoritative physicians prove; we will not debate this, but take Boltzmann's theoretical construction for convenience.)

Let us assume – Boltzmann says – that the heat death of the universe has come. Is there really no possibility in the universe after this for the appearance of new centres of energy accumulation – that is, of new worlds? If this were so, then nothing more would remain for the theoretical justification of this world than to appeal to divine forces. Though the appearance of a centre, the accumulation of energy from such a dead world – and hence the emergence from chaos of an ordered system – is the least probable event, it nevertheless belongs among the possible; no matter how small the probability, it is nevertheless non-zero. With unlimited time and an eternally continuing shift, any ordered state must necessarily emerge, in the same way that a deck of cards, as a result of infinite shuffling, must in every way assume an ordered state.

Let P signify the probability of the emergence of a specific ordered series out of a random state over the course of one year, where P is an infinitely small magnitude, an infinitesimal fraction.

Then the probability of the non-appearance of this state would be 1-P. Over the course of n years, the non-appearance of this event would be $(1-P)^n$. In an infinitely large space of time, where n→∞, the probability of the non-appearance of this state $(1-p)^n$ would approach zero – $(1-P)^n$→0 – and hence the probability of appearance $[1-(1-P)^n]$ when n→∞ and $\lim(1-P)^n$→0.

This means that the emergence of any ordered state from a random state, given a sufficiently long period of time, is immutable according to the absolute law of chance. Cosmic systems emerge from chaos as inevitable exceptions. But these exceptions are necessary and are themselves regular. Such processes are very rare, but since the universe is infinite, then the extent of these deviations from the most likely state of the universe could be colossal. On the general scale of the universe these deviations are insignificant, but from the standpoint of the terrestrial scale they could be enormous and fully sufficient for the formation of nebulae and entire star systems.

Thus, the existence of chance in the world does not at all require any particular guarantee (in the form of a world idea or divine intention) for the emergence of an ordered system. It emerges necessarily in accordance with the immutable law of chance, since the accident itself is regular and subordinate to fixed laws – the laws of greatest probability, which represent the fully objective relationships inherent in things themselves and not merely the subjective assessment of the occurrence or non-occurrence of events. Only this regularity is of a more general order, more universal than definitive and purely logical necessity.

There is a great difference between the two concepts of reality: do we assume the definite determinacy of phenomena and take them in the order of linear dependence, or do we believe that every event, being formed by a certain key factor, is ultimately the result of the convergence of a multitude of conditions and the actions of many forces?

When, on the basis of the former schema, we construct suppositions about the future, the smallest imprecision in this linear series leads to a tremendous error in the relatively final result.

In the latter case, we take the general sphere of forces of causes and conditions, and outline the most likely distribution of centres of force in it so that whatever particular deviations occur in it, there nonetheless exists a definite maximum of probability that a given general result must occur in the course of a certain amount of time.

When we are dealing with actual reality, where every individual phenomenon is conditioned – apart from the basic key factor – by a multitude of other factors, then the former approach compels us precisely to calculate an endless quantity of individual forces and factors – which is not only impossible in practice, but cannot even be theoretically conceived.

In the latter case, we take the general sphere of conditions and make a judgement about the most likely direction for the process, making no calculation about the separateness of each force component but taking into account *which foci of force* are being formed and what the most likely general direction the entire process as a whole will take. We construct a complex in which the general direction of the process will nevertheless have a fully definite probability of occurrence, whatever individual deviations occur within it.

In the former case we are deprived of the probability of predicting anything, insofar as the matter concerns actual phenomena; in the latter, we forecast with a certain – but quite large – approximation. The former case lacks a position that permits grasping the fullness of all causes and conditions, arranging and theoretically centring the multitude of constituent forces and discerning the most likely general direction of development. In the latter case we occupy just such a position.

If the absolute necessity of the occurrence of some phenomenon at a strictly defined moment and in a precisely defined manner is assumed, then the entire world is placed under the sign of a primordial fatal predetermination. The necessity of actual events is not a definitive necessity, but necessity within the interval of certain limits of deviation. Individual details and particulars almost are almost never repeated precisely. In this sense, a certain moment of chance is present in all the strictest phenomena of reality. *This moment of chance forms the individual character of phenomena.* And this change is not ascribed to things by us, but exists in the things themselves and in their relations. It exists objectively and participates in all the phenomena of reality, which is why there is no place for predetermined fatality and 'providence' in the world. But chance has its own internal regularity, its own solid laws, and by virtue of this the world and its development are not disordered chaos and do not require a particular guarantee in the capacity of a rational, omnipotent soul.

Three Pictures of the World

§ 56
Summing up what has been said in §§ 51–55, we obtain three different pictures of the world.

1. The picture of a world of mechanical causality, where reality is conceived as a mechanical aggregate of individual parts and states, external in relation to one another, internally connected by nothing, where the one runs along the path of its development, gives rise to another and is swept past. The past, of course, cannot be preserved in the present under such externally conglomerative relationships. Every new moment devours the one preceding it, and nothing of the past is preserved in it. At any given moment only the state (a) at hand exists; the next minute it disappears, yielding its place to another state (b). With the appearance of a subsequent state this disappears, and only the latter (c) exists, and so on. The present is thus entirely free of the past. It is determined directly by the immediate moment, and everything preceding it has no relationship to it: knowing today's atmosphere is sufficient for tomorrow's weather, and data about the state of the atmosphere five days or a hundred years ago is of no help. At any given moment the world is as if nothing preceded it, and in every moment of the present it is absolutely 'virginal'. This is the picture of *an essentially ahistorical world.*

It should be noted along with this that absolute determinism, passed down to us from French materialism, leads as Engels said to the assertion of a fatal world in which chance is not explained 'by necessity, but rather necessity is degraded to the production of what is merely accidental'.[23]

2. *The picture of a world of teleological causality*, according to which not only the present actually exists, but the past and the future as well. The series *a, b, c, d, e* ... and so on exists ideally as a completed and immutable world order from time immemorial. Here there is also no history as an actual process of development, since all development from the very beginning is absolutely complete (see §53).

3. The third concept originates from the future, as absolutely determined, does not exist – and still less is there a future as a fact ideally already complete. The future is constantly being created as something new and is created in accordance with the objectively most probable convergence of vectors of force. The past does not disappear without a trace, but is preserved – not in its uniqueness but only in the present. Every new state of the world, abolishing what preceded it, preserves in it in extracted form the entire path travelled, and in its further development is determined on the one hand by the forms already composed, and on the other by new attendant facts. Schematically, this can be depicted as follows:

---

23 Marks i Engel's 1925, p. 193 [Engels, in Marx and Engels 1975–, Vol. 25, p. 500].

*A B*a *C*ba *D*cba *E*dcba and so on.

Here, every new stage of development (e.g. *C*), in abolishing the preceding stage (*Ba*), preserves that stage within it in extracted form, and so forth. Only the present actually exists, but it reflects within it the entire path of its past historical formation. This standpoint reveals before us the true picture of the world in its authentic historical essence.

Concept and Reality

§ 57

Reality, despite the constant presence within it of the moment of chance, is nonetheless regular because chance itself has its own internal laws of greater and lesser chances, sufficiently firm and more universal than purely logical and absolutely definitive necessity.

Reality itself is constructed on the basis of the interaction of internal forces, in certain integral forms (e.g. atoms, molecules, a gaseous or liquid state, or even such forms as the animal and plant worlds and the biosphere in general). Each of these formations has its own internal laws of constitution and its own laws of behaviour, but despite that, there is nothing *logically immutable* in them – not only in the sense that we, as limited intellects, cannot foresee them,[24] but because in them there is no absolute predetermination; hence, even an all-knowing intellect (*intellectus infinitus*) could not foresee what is not in things themselves. 'Unperturbable order everywhere, full consonance in nature' – this, in fact, is a manifestation of lawful blind elements.

In these closed formations of reality that have their own laws, rationalist philosophy saw the *ideological* content of reality – specifically, the objective existence of the concept. In the consistent construction of reality Hegel, for example, saw the result of the activity of the concept. He thought that everything real was linked by absolute logical predetermination, definitively predetermined and subordinate to the idea, that the structure of reality was entirely logical and all of reality in general was rational from beginning to end.[25]

---

24   On the contrary, science often foresees and foretells them, but foresees with a certain amount of approximation; moreover, the degree of precision of scientific approximation has its limits in the objective probability of reality itself.
25   For greater precision, it is necessary to emphasise that Hegel did not completely and fully exclude chance from development. Hegel recognises the existence of accidental phenomena in the world as an empirical fact, but provides the following original clarification:

Hegel's proposition on the rationality of the real and the reality of the rational expresses in different words the same thought as Spinoza's '*ordo rerum idem est atque ordo idearum*'. This means that concepts objectively exist and that material reality is subordinate to the concept.

The empiricists considered concepts to be the purely subjective formations of consciousness. Kant and the Kantians saw the *a priori* categories of reason in them. In both cases, concepts are only purely subjective schemas and intellectual constructions that nothing in actual reality answers to. These concepts do not have their objective equivalence in the objective world of reality.

A standpoint that considers reality to be raw, disordered material that can be grouped and gathered into concepts in any manner whatsoever, and moreover encountering no resistance on the part of the material will find itself in the most blatant conflict with the facts. The sole rational meaning of cognition and concept lies in the fact that consciousness in a certain manner grasps and reflects within itself what is in reality, and the laws and the structure of reality itself. This meaning of the concept vanishes in the traditional doctrine of the empiricists, as well as in the Kantians – for them, concepts are the purely subjective formations of consciousness (even those concepts they call 'generally valid' and 'transcendental').

The great advantage of Hegel – and Spinoza and Aristotle as well – consists of the fact that in the concept, they saw not only the subjective aspect (the free abstraction of the intellect) but also the elements of reality. Developing these views in an excessively one-sided manner, the rationalists arrived at idealism from the other end – but to a more radical (and in particular objectivist) idealism. In the regular formations of reality, Hegel saw ideas put into practice and depicted the matter in such a way that reality itself is a concept (i.e. objectively

---

'So much the worse for facts'. He considers such facts invalid; in his opinion, they are a defect of reality. What is valid in this world is only that which constitutes the genuine fabric of rational existence (i.e. subject to the Concept). From the standpoint of Hegelian philosophy, the genuinely valid world exists in a *uniquely* complete (and perfected) magnificent edition, and this is the immutable realisation of the Absolute Idea; it is the world of true (i.e. ideal) reality, the design of which is drawn in the system of Hegelian logic (which 'paints God as He is in His eternal essence since the creation of Nature until its final breath'). Empirical reality can sometimes deviate from compliance with the laws of reason, permitting 'misprints' and being 'counterrational'. These, according to Hegel, are accidental phenomena, and as such, representing only empty appearances and not truly existing ones, are by no means able to weaken the power of the Concept over the world. By virtue of this, chance – despite its empirical factuality – is excluded from the sphere of the actual, and true science (always being in the element of pure thought) can ignore it.

existing intellect, the manifestation of the World Idea of divine thought). In Hegel's system, concepts exist not only in people's consciousness but in reality itself as well.[26] Hegel often pointed out that the chief art of philosophy lay in considering the substance (object, embodied reality, material) as a subject that develops itself out of itself. The entire history of the world is the realisation of the Absolute Idea in eternally determined and immutable forms. The idea rules hidden in the natural elements, manifesting itself through its laws. The world serves the idea.

The idealism of Hegel on this point has displayed itself most clearly, and this is why it underwent the most radical criticism on the part of Marx. It must be said that Marx always loved Hegel and was drawn to him, but in the early period of his activity he already understood that 'the idea should not be sought in reality itself'. He resolutely refuses to give the concept primacy over objective reality, subjecting its idealist legacy from Hegel to ruthless criticism (*Critique of the Hegelian Philosophy of Right*).

In Marx's opinion, reality in itself is not rational; in it, as such, there is no reason and no goals – either in the sense of deliberate goal-setting or in the sense of the logically inevitable predetermination of an end.

Material existence does not come under the sphere of the logical. Logic is a system of unequivocally determined and mutually attributed ideas. In material reality, we deal with the blind regularity of formations of force and the interrelations of vectors and scalars of force.

There is a system; here are blind elements. There is absolutely unequivocal determinacy and logical necessity; here there is also necessity, but of a different order: relative necessity. There are ideas; here are scalars of force – moreover, the concepts of 'force' and 'vectors of force' mean completely different things, depending on the formation we are dealing with (chemical, mechanical, social and so on).

Actual reality, with its internal necessity, is subordinate to certain laws and is constructed in certain closed formations. But this in no way means that it is subordinate to a concept or serves an idea, or that concepts realise themselves in these formations. The formations of reality, having their own laws of beha-

---

26 'The notion of end as immanent in natural objects is their simple determinateness, e.g. the seed of a plant, which contains the real possibility of all that is to exist in the tree, and thus, as a purposive activity, is directed solely to self-preservation. This notion of end was already recognised by Aristotle, too, and he called this activity the *nature of a thing*; the true teleological methods – and this is the highest – consists, therefore, in the method of regarding Nature as free in her own peculiar vital activity'. Hegel 1906, p. 293 [Hegel 2004, p. 6].

viour, represent no kind of concepts and thoughts; they themselves are neither concepts nor manifestations. Concepts are the products of consciousness, but they can only exist actually in the consciousness of people. They are not in and of themselves inherent in things.

What objectively exist are not concepts as such but those actual formations, expressed using these concepts, that in and of themselves do not constitute concepts. But these closed formations of reality constitute *the objective content and the material foundation* on which every concept *rests*, without which they would be empty abstractions, the play of imagination. A concept does not have an independent force of existence and an independent meaning apart from the force and meaning of the reality that it expresses and reflects.

A concept torn from its objective basis (e.g. from objectively existing relations) is transformed into a meaningless abstraction, into that inexhaustible source of constant falsely philosophical wanderings. Once it is imagined that a concept has its own force of definition – a proper meaning inherent in the concept itself – and once concepts begin being used as self-contained essences that do not imply concrete objective content every time, from that moment scholasticism appears, and dogmatism and the uncontrolled arbitrariness of the play of empty concepts gain a foothold. Many people who are even subjectively convinced of their faithfulness to Marxism, but argue about 'quantity and quality', 'form and content', 'time' and 'space' as if these concepts had a distinct meaning independent of concretely objective content – as if it were possible to use these concepts as essences in their own right, to draw new conclusions from them, to learn the truth and do science – are often guilty of this idealism. The philosophers of the scholastic epoch and Church fathers also thought they were on the true path of scientific knowledge if, proceeding from the essence and meaning of concepts alone as such ('spiritual' and 'corporeal', 'good' and 'evil' and so on) they drew every conclusion via logic about the real existence of the soul, of God and so forth. Clinging to any separate aspect of a fact, giving it a definite name, and then forgetting that it was only an imaginary reality, these philosophers hypostatised abstractions and transformed them into the causes of real events. More than that, they believed these fictions to be reality of the highest order – the internal essence of things, the truly real (*wahrhaft Seiende, essentia* and so on).

As a result of such misunderstandings, some kind of empty abstraction is substituted for the real object of research, and ideas appear to be the origin and essence of reality. The concrete and the real begin to appear external and superficial while the universal and abstract seem more fundamental – the internal essence of reality, from which the matter quickly proceeds to reality in and of itself being taken as dead material and its abstract properties as the internal life-giving soul of the actual process. In similar distortions of the scientific method, Engels notes, initially the *concept* of an object is made from it, and then actual objects are measured with this concept (i.e. reality is measured according to its reflection, the concept). The philosophy of early Christianity and medieval scholasticism often used this method. At first, for example, they classified phenomena into corporeal and spiritual, and then, forgetting about the actual object (humans), they began arguing about how the 'non-corporeal' spiritual) could be connected with the 'corporeal'), and the nature of this connection. Nemesiues of Emesa, in his fifth-century work *De natura hominis*, argued as follows: Let us assume that soul and body are affixed to each other, but it is impossible to affix two bodies so that they match on all points, therefore the body in these points of divergence would be dead. But if they were poured together like two liquids? Water is water and wine is wine, but when they are mixed, both are spoiled and neither water nor wine are obtained! What could be forgiven in the fifth century is in no way forgivable for science in the twentieth. Admittedly, the current representatives of bourgeois philosophy (Martin Heidegger, Benedetto Croce, Hans Reichenbach et al.) have achieved such heights in the acrobatic art of empty concepts that they have outdone even the most refined scholastics of the mediaeval era.

Marx was an implacable enemy of purely abstract ideas – concepts that existed only in abstraction, having no equivalent in reality (i.e. objective meaning). He built the most damning refutations of his opponent on the exposure of these intellectual fictions and illusions of abstract concepts, calling such philosophy 'grandiloquent speculative nonsense'. *The Holy Family* and *The German Ideology* provide the best examples of the criticism of such theories and their champions (Max Stirner, Bruno Bauer, etc.), whom Marx brutally ridiculed, comparing them with the heroes of Cervantes. Marx never tired of ridiculing theoreticians who believed that operating with abstract concepts could provide some sort of knowledge about reality. 'Proudhon', he said, 'shares the illusions of speculative philosophy in his treatment of the *economic categories*; how instead of conceiving them as *the theoretical expressions of historical relations of production, corresponding to a particular stage of development in material production*, he transforms them by his twaddle into pre-existing *eternal ideas* ...'.[27] And further: 'The division of labour is, according to M. Proudhon ... a simple, abstract category. Therefore the abstraction, the idea, the word must suffice for him to explain the division of labour at different historical epochs.

---

27   Marks 1931c, p. 25.

Castes, corporations, manufacture, large-scale industry must be explained by the single word *divide*. First study carefully the meaning of 'divide', and you will have no need to study the numerous influences which give the division of labour a definite character in each epoch'.[28]

On its own strength, nothing flows from the concept itself as an abstract category except empty tautologies. Only that which has been embedded in abstract concepts as such by us ourselves and our imagination can be drawn from them. From this standpoint, Kant's proposition on 'synthetic *a priori* judgements' is a rather doubtful theoretical construction. The distinction between 'synthetic' and 'analytic' judgements advanced by Kant tacitly rests on the arguments for a 'synthetic character' surreptitiously quitting the field of abstract concepts and returning to the thing itself, to the object. But inasmuch as in Kant, the real object constituted just as much a categorical and rational construction as the concept, the object itself represented only the concept and the distinction (between 'synthetic and analytic judgements') remained undecided.

Any conclusions from concepts alone relating to actual reality are impossible. Abstract deductions from abstract concepts will never correspond to anything in reality; philosophers have striven in vain to construct the entire world from one or more logical categories, trying to produce from thin air an entire system from the concepts of 'I', 'the subject' (Fichte), 'the idea' and 'existence and nonexistence' (Hegel). The contemporary bourgeois philosophy of Husserl, Heidegger and others continues along this same path of purely logical deductions.

The concept is not something independent, a pure concept existing in itself, just as 'pure consciousness' and 'pure thought' do not exist. 'The "mind"', Marx says, 'is from the outset afflicted with the curse of being "burdened" with matter'; this concerns not only language, but also the material content of thought. *Consciousness is always the consciousness of definite objects.* 'Consciousness can never be anything else than conscious being' (Marx). *Purposeless consciousness, purposeless thought, is unnatural consciousness, unnatural thought.*

Intellectual reflection every time requires *material* fodder, *objective material* upon which it reflects. Reflection on abstract concepts alone, on ideas and categories, yields nothing except empty rhetoric. Without an object of consciousness, without an object, there is no thought in thinking. *The object is the body of thought*, and without it thought is empty and dead (at the same time, the object can peacefully exist without thought as an unconscious object). Abstract

---

28   Marks 1931c, p. 119 [Marx, in Marx and Engels 1975–, Vol. 6, p. 179].

thinking creates only the semblance of thinking, multiplying tautologies and producing scholastic disputes. The Austrian poet Franz Grillparzer was correct when he wrote:

> I compare the intellect to a mill.
> To make flour, grain is poured in;
> And there is no flour when nothing is poured.
> The grindstone around the millstone – useless friction,
> The movement of the stones yields only dross, sand and dust.

The strength of a concept is not in the concept itself, but in the object that the concept 'expresses', 'represents' and 'reflects' in consciousness. A concept is only a concept of reality when it grasps and expresses the objective structure of reality, and consequently when the concept *by a law* makes a *law of things* for itself. Reality should be addressed, and things – not the concepts about them – should be appealed to every time for an analysis of reality. The task of science, as defined by Engels, consists not of *devising* purely intellectual links between phenomena, but in *discovering* them in the phenomena themselves.

Only those concepts that have an objective equivalent in reality (i.e. expressing definite, actually existing relations of things) are capable of enriching knowledge and being useful to science.

If sciences successfully uses such concepts as atoms, gravitation, cost, social class and so on, this occurs because they are not the arbitrary operations of an intellect that, for example, arranges people purely mentally in specified groups but because these groups and classes actually took shape and exist in society. These concepts express and reflect real and concrete formations that exist independently of the intellectual operations of philosophers, having their own laws of existence and development. Humans, of course, think in concepts; however, they do not always think of concepts but of things. In the act of thought, consciousness is focused not on concepts as such, but is constantly transferred from them to *things themselves* and reflects not on the concepts, but on *those things* the concepts depict.

When Marx says that dialectics unfolds not within the boundaries of concepts alone but that reality itself develops dialectically; that it is not reality that develops in accordance with a concept but that concepts emerge in conformity with reality – in all similar utterances about reality, Marx always means definite, concrete reality: a qualitatively different, closed formation of reality having its own particular laws different from the laws of other formations (e.g. 'a liquid state', 'a gaseous state' or 'tribal society', 'feudal society', 'capitalistic society' and so on).

The empiricists believed that concepts were the result of the skilful operations of the intellect, assembling and arranging phenomena (things, events and individuals) into specific rational groups; they thought that concepts were only the concepts of consciousness, which in reality are in opposition not to the integral formations of reality but to individual, uncoordinated phenomena. The empiricists went even further in their conclusions, believing individual phenomena to be the sum of sensations grouped by consciousness in a certain manner. The concept of 'value', for example, they understood to be the purely intellectually comprised arithmetical average of real prices on a certain type of item; the concept of 'social classes' for the empiricists was a purely intellectual formation that ascribed individuals to specific classes according to certain indications – for example, the extent of their weekly income. All individuals with a weekly income of less than 25 shillings were put into one class, and those with more than that sum into the other (F.G. d'Aeth, Paul Descamps and, in principle, all the advocates of a 'theory of distribution'). Thus it turns out that classes as such in reality do not exist at all; this is only the conditional methods of our theoretical construction – we divide people into classes only in our thoughts, taking arbitrary principles of division and not society itself divided into them. For bourgeois sociologists, of course, there is much to gain from imagining that classes are conditional, purely intellectual categories and not objectively existing sharp divisions of society into separate large groups consisting of individuals actually connected to each other by their position, by the conditions of production and exchange and by objective class interests that compel individuals into combined organisations, into united activity and actually unites people into a specific class whole. Individuals 'assembled', purely mentally, by the idealists into certain conceptual groups are here actually gathered into a specific actual whole, called a class. 'The crudity and lack of comprehension lies precisely in that organically coherent factors are brought into haphazard relation with one another, i.e. into a merely speculative connection' (Marx). Here it is not the concept that completes the arbitrary classification of people but the other way around: the real differentiation of people into classes compels the formation and application of a particular concept, which only reflects and formulates this real whole (a class).

In these cases, the concepts live not only in the imagination of people, but – figuratively speaking – it is as if they are found in objective reality itself. Lenin called Hegel's view that concepts exist in reality 'naive'. "'In nature' concepts do not exist 'in this freedom' (in the freedom of thought and the fantasy of *man*!!) 'In nature' they (concepts) have 'flesh and blood'. That is excellent! But it is materialism. Human concepts are the *soul* of nature – thus is only a mystical way of saying that in human concepts nature is reflected in a *distinctive way* (this NB_ in a *distinctive* and *dialectical* way!!)'.²⁹ This picturesque description of the life of concepts in nature 'in flesh and blood' signifies nothing more than the demands of such concepts – to which qualitatively different formations of actuality would correspond in objective reality – that concepts express the actual sense and laws of such things (in other words, the demand for the concreteness of concepts in contrast to empty abstraction).

The philosophy of dialectical materialism is not satisfied with abstract intellectual categories but demands concrete concepts to which specific *closed formations* correspond in objective reality.

The materialist dialectic extends only to such concepts and to such formations of reality. They alone are capable of real dialectic development and Marx defends the dialectic only as far as such closed formations are concerned, proving that the process of their composition and development is the process of the dialectic of development no longer of a single concept, as Hegel thought, but of material reality itself. Here the concept no longer leads development, but the opposite: it conforms with actual development.

Having gotten rid of actually existing links, we can easily form for ourselves such purely mental concepts as, for example, the sum total of bald people existing at a given moment on the globe, or heavyweight athletes weighing over 100 kilograms. Such concepts will only have an imaginary significance, not a real one, since nothing corresponds to them in reality. They are assembled only in the mind. If a social factor created baldness in humans, organising the bald irrespective of nation, sex, age and so on into some sort of special organisation, or if a person achieving a weight of 100 kilograms changed their physical or social behaviour, then we would actually be dealing with some kind of objective formation. Baldness as such does not unite people into a specific social whole, creates no common interests and so on (if we do not take the rise of the question of hair restoratives into consideration!).

On the subject of Stirner's 'discovery' that 'people are divided into two classes: educated and uneducated', Marx remarked caustically: 'One sometimes divides apes into two classes, the tailed and the tailless'. Marx ridiculed this kind of 'trashy distinction' where theoreticians at first assume chimaeras of some sort of 'purely intellectual or even supraintellectual distinction' and are then astonished, unable to explain to themselves why reality does not harmonise with their illusions. Marx called this kind of philosophy 'cheap moral casuistry'

---

29   Lenin 1931, p. 237 [Lenin 1960–1979, Vol. 38, p. 283].

and 'a triumph of tautology'.[30] In fact, the human mental path can differentiate, group, and divide according to any indication it pleases: colour, weight, age, hair or eye colour and so on – arbitrariness is not limited here but there is little confusion in it if the principle of differentiation is not justified by some sort of *problem* content. Purely mental concepts of this kind contain nothing actual and have no perspectives of development whatsoever, which is why the application of the dialectic to such concepts yields abstract, scholastic cuts of whole cloth. Here, it is not the object that develops and emerges in given forms, but the subject bustles around and about the object, separating it purely intellectually into arbitrary parts and giving them form any which way.

We are dealing with the process of actual dialectic development only where the object is some kind of linked, self-contained whole – be it in social, biological or physical and chemical reality.

The Self-Contained Structure

§ 58

A certain type of self-contained, integral formation (where condition and the conditioned to a certain extent are locked into a single whole) is necessary for any development, hence for the genuine dialectic as well. Moreover, Marx never permits the presence of solely internal causes of development of a self-contained formation, or the existence of an absolutely self-contained system. Completely isolated systems do not exist in nature.

A formation is called self-contained in the event that it is an integrated complex having its own particular laws of structure and behaviour – a formation *qualitatively* different from others. An absolutely self-contained system would be one in which all changes were called forth by causes exclusively endogenous to the given formation, if instead of internal causes the complex experienced no disturbances from within and if the determined and the determinant were absolutely locked into and mutually moved one another. But in this case there would be no development, since the condition and the conditioned, in mutually replacing each other, are incapable of producing something new; the process would revolve on one plane, in one circle, and a progressive spiral of development would be impossible. Absolutely self-contained systems of this kind do not exist in reality – at neither the atomic nor the universal level – as a unified, integrated formation. An absolutely self-contained system, the kind

---

30   Marks i Engel's 1933, pp. 253, 271, 337.

mathematicians imagine, is not a reality but an imaginary category. Formations that have not experienced the influence of external causes, exogenic to the given formation, do not exist in reality.

Moreover, attention should be drawn to one important peculiarity of the self-contained system, expressed in the fact that the action of *every external cause inside a formation is applied in accordance with the internal laws and internal structure of the system* as a connected whole. The causes, hence, must be external, and this *circumstance* magnifies even more those *elements of chance without which* the rich diversity of *development would be fatally complete in advance*. But the action of even these external causes are applied within a self-contained system in accordance with the laws of that formation – or, in other words, the self-contained system reacts to any external cause in accordance with the particular laws of its structure. Every time, a self-contained system draws in and absorbs an external cause in accordance with its internal laws. Thus is created *the historical consistency* without which there would be no real connection between the preceding and the subsequent, without which phenomena would be arranged in an incoherent chronicle of accidental events, and history as a regular sequence and succession of events would be impossible. If every action from without called forth a fundamentally *new* structure of a system every time and nothing of the past remained in it, then the subsequent state would in no way be linked internally with the preceding one (i.e. there would be no history) – that is the first point.[31] Second, no particular states of reality would exist – no self-contained formation and their particular regularity apart from purely mechanical and universal regularity; the world would be absolutely monoform.

Actual development is conceivable only as the mutual relation of a self-contained system and its environment, where the 'external environment' in a certain sense plays the role of the source of causes continually agitating the given formation, bringing into it (this self-contained formation) fresh currents. It is this element of chance that is not foreseeable in the life of the complex, not only from the standpoint of our knowledge but objectively as well, and makes the life of the complex not a fatal and predetermined one, but truly historical.

A self-contained formation is one that at any separate point is determined by the position and state of all its other points, in which each part stands in relation to the entire system as a whole and changes to any of them brings corresponding changes to the whole system; consequently, within a self-contained system a local state does not exist independently in one part, but only in the

---

31   We attempted to describe this image of an ahistorical world in § 56.

general aggregation of the whole. For clarity, we will allow ourselves to cite a simple analogy from the field of physics – which, however, as opposed to Köhler we will ascribe exclusively illustrative (and in no case universal) significance. If, for example, in an unbroken self-contained circuit a current is applied at any single point, then it is applied in all other points and the state of the current in any point taken separately depends on the conditions and states in all the other points. A change at any point brings a change to the entire circuit, however far away it extends.

On the contrary, several such self-contained circuits isolated from each other do not constitute an actual, physically whole formation, however close in proximity they find themselves.

In the first case the grouping, connection and structure of the system forms an objective unity, and it is physically impossible to separately formulate the state at any point without the involvement of the condition of the entire system.

In the second case, the parts of the physical complex form a purely external, additive variety, and acknowledging it as a sum total or not depends on the arbitrariness of our thinking. In this case, laws can only be formulated for each part (of the complex) separately and independently of the other parts. This means that the parts do not constitute an objectively single connected whole; each of them leads their own existence.

Self-Contained Structure and Concrete Concept

§59

The conventional theory of science treats the question of how to study reality extremely lightly. For this, in the opinion of the majority of scientists, it is enough to turn the complex into the sum of simple elements and to explain the life and the laws of the whole by explaining the parts.

If all the wisdom of science consisted only of the study of simple elements, the multitude of separate sciences, the branches of knowledge, the various modes and methods of studying reality would seem superfluous. If the study of simple elements exhausted the entire content of reality, then it would be sufficient to study the nature of the electron, or – in the extreme case – the fundamental chemical elements of which all reality ultimately exists in order to become omniscient using the combinational analysis of their composition.

The positive sciences developed despite these theories. Physicists, chemists, biologists and so on did not work using the methods of mechanically summing up the whole from simple parts; every formation was placed before the court of experimentation and in every individual case the distinctive laws of behaviour of individual whole formations that had nothing in common with the sum of the behaviours of the elements composing it were established.

The diversity of forms of reality and the difficulty of studying it consists of the fact that when, for example, oxygen and hydrogen are locked into a coherent formation (e.g. in a molecule of water, H_2O) this formation begins living a different life than the sum of simple elements composing it (it makes no difference if they are taken together or separately), it acquires particular qualities and displays new laws of behaviour that would be impossible to predict through analysis of the separate elements. These elements, in a coherent form (H–O–H), yield a completely new formation (water) than the free forms do (HHO – detonating gas), and knowing the qualities, functions and laws of behaviour of this new formation requires testing it and studying it in particular.

This problem of a qualitatively new formula, which under the name *Problem der Ganzheit* is now winning greater and greater sympathy among scientists of the most diverse branches of science, was first formulated by Marx in the mid-nineteenth century but without the tint of mysticism that it acquires in the works of many German scientists – to say nothing of those who, hastily bargaining with their consciences, want to use this theory as a support for a 'national united fascist empire'.

The requirements of *concreteness* advanced by the philosophy of dialectical materialism, the requirement of taking into account every time the entire totality of conditions and the qualitative peculiarity of the object, in a philosophical sense here grounds much more deeply and illuminates more clearly the problem of a self-contained formation than all the efforts of contemporary German scientists.

There is nothing supra-real or mystic in a self-contained formation of reality; it represents only a *qualitative* formation and is the basis without which the philosophy of dialectical materialism as a philosophy of concreteness is inconceivable. The concept of the concrete is, of course, only an expression of qualitative specificity.

Correctly studying actual reality means taking objects in their objective regularity, finding the objects of study that constitute some coherent whole or are able to constitute such, and finding the particular structural and behavioural laws of such self-contained formations.

In connection with this arises the problem of general and particular laws of reality. Marx was the enemy of 'abstract, eternal, absolute and universal' laws not only because they yield no useful knowledge but primarily because such laws do not exist in reality.

Absolute, comprehensive laws – except for the general laws of the dialectic of any development – do not exist; nor do the formations of reality themselves exist as absolute. Every actuality is limited by certain conditions. Unconditional existence, as real existence, does not and cannot exist. Every reality – even the most solid one (e.g. the chemical elements) can exist only in the space of certain conditions. Not a single one of our chemical elements is conceivable at temperatures of tens or hundreds of millions of degrees. All the seemingly absolutely solid and unchangeable substances of our earthly reality (atoms, molecules, and so on) under these conditions would cease to exist or be fundamentally altered. In this sense Engels said that '[o]ur whole official physics, chemistry and biology are exclusively *geocentric*, calculated only for the earth ... *The eternal laws of nature* also become transformed more and more into historical ones. That water is fluid from 0°–100°C is an eternal law of nature, but for it to be valid there must be (1) water, (2) the given temperature, (3) normal pressure. On the moon there is no water, in the sun only its elements ...'.[32] Every physical law of nature has an infinite quantity of these 'ifs' (i.e. limiting conditions), the most essential ones of which, playing the most important role, are in practice taken into consideration by science while the rest, which give rise to insignificant deviations, are not taken into account and are discarded in practical calculations. But they do not cease to be participants in the formation of reality owing to the fact that we do not take them into consideration, and the occurrence of every event also depends on these small forces to a certain degree.

The statement of Heraclitus – 'ὅτι πάντα χωρεῖ καὶ οὐθὲν μένει'[33] (everything gives way, nothing stands fast) – has just one meaning in twenty-first century language: there is no unconditional existence. General, abstract laws can be constructed mentally, but they remain only constructions of the imagination and abstractions, in the sense that nothing will correspond to them in reality. Every formation of actuality has its own particular laws of behaviour and development, and the general laws of the dialectic are manifested in them in a specific form, the study of which constitutes

the main task. *Reality in its regularity is always concrete, and every law has significance only in the space of specific limits and conditions.*

---

32   Marks i Engel's 1925, p. 84 [Engels, in Marx and Engels 1975–, Vol. 25, pp. 517–18].
33   Plato, *Cratylus*, 402a.

§60

Cognition can stand on the heights of the understanding of reality only in the case that cognition takes into consideration those delimitations and 'determinations' that reality itself makes by virtue of its blind laws; in other words, if concepts are objective (i.e. every time expressing definite, objectively existing relations). Concrete concepts of this kind deliver science from scholasticism, dogmatism and similar vices of idealist philosophy; they guarantee science a permanent link to reality, imparting to it the riches of concrete content and assuring its fruitful development. This is because with every difficulty, research will appeal not to the sense of the concept itself as such but the real sense of objects that the concept is trying to express. The object itself should never be let out of the field of vision when it is being discussed. It often happens with philosophers that, in discussing an object, they forget about it and begin talking about *its concepts*, drawing conclusions from the sense of the concept and not the object. The abstractions on which consciousness raises the object may be false, but not the object itself.

If concepts, to a certain degree, take the objective formations of reality correctly, the latter themselves indicate the path of their study with regard to both general features and to particulars. Being true to the nature of an object, learning from objects how correctly to know them – this is the only path to comprehending the laws of reality. But this does not mean that the object of cognition itself suggests the path and forms of comprehending and mastering it.

Generalising and classifying facts produced by consciousness does not need to be *only of an intellectual order*. Scientific cognition must take its fundamental principles and determinations not from itself, as the Kantians supposed, but must pay heed to the object and draw those determinations with which reality 'defines' itself, taking the principles and *generalisations occurring in reality itself and existing objectively*, not reckoning with the comforts of the cognising subject.

It is known, for example, how great a role the concept of 'abstract labour' plays in Marx's analysis of the social relations of capitalist society. The scientific fruitfulness of this concept finds its explanation in the fact that abstract labour is not a pure concept, not an abstract category of intellect, but exists *actually* in reality itself. It is not only an intellectual abstraction, expressing abstractly a general quantity of labour, but an actual economic category of reality appearing in the form of exchange value and the ratio of qualitative equivalents of labour.

The concept of 'abstract labour' as a purely intellectual construction, as an abstract qualitative expression of any labour, could be applied to every labour in every epoch, but outside of a commodity-distributing society this concept would have no *actual* significance. The concept would be arbitrarily appended to reality, corresponding to nothing actual and explaining nothing in it.

As an actual economic category, abstract labour appears only after the consolidation of the full-scale form of an exchange economy – specifically, in capitalism – and here it (abstract labour) constitutes the foundation for measuring the exchange value of goods by the quantity of labour time contained within it. 'This reduction [of different kinds of labour to uniform, homogeneous, simple labour] appears to be an abstraction, but it is an abstraction which is made every day in the social process of production' (Marx).[34] In the system of capitalist rationalisation and conveyor-belt production, we have a graphic image of the down-skilling of concrete labour, of the generalisation of the labour process – abstract labour in actuality.

It is not the principles, categories and definitions of the intellect that are valuable for the cognition of reality, but the laws of things and the categories of reality itself. Kant attempted to prove that principles and categories are forms of cognition, and that all scientific knowledge and all human experience are constructed from them. The philosophy of Marxism adheres to the diametrically opposite opinion: cognition occurs not through *a priori* categories and pure thinking, but owing to the fact that thinking adopts its 'categories'; from reality *it takes the principles and laws of reality itself as its definitions.*

Scientific cognition, in the true sense of the phrase, is assured only through such a methodological approach. The concepts and categories of thinking do not need to have any of their own meanings and their own force except for the force and the sense of the objects expressed by them. Abstract thought is feeble and powerless before actual reality, and no matter how much thought

---

34   'The fact that the specific kind of labour is irrelevant presupposes a highly developed totality of actually existing kinds of labour, none of which is any more the dominating one ... The fact that the particular kind of labour is irrelevant corresponds to a form of society in which individuals easily pass from one kind of labour to another, the particular kind of labour being accidental to them and therefore indifferent. *Labour, not only as a category but in reality, has become here a means to create wealth in general, and has ceased as a determination to be tied with the individuals in any particularity*. This state of affairs is most pronounced in the most modern form of bourgeois society, the United States. It is only there that the abstract category 'labour', 'labour as such', labour *sans phrase*, the point of departure of modern [political] economy, *is first seen to be true in practice*. The simplest abstraction which plays the key role in modern [political] economy, and which expresses an ancient relation existing in all forms of society, appears to be true in practice in this abstract form only as a category of the most modern society'. (Italics mine. – KM) Marks 1931a, pp. 74, 75 [Marx, in Marx and Engels 1975–, Vol. 28, p. 41].

thinks of itself as an abstract category and tries to violate reality, nothing worthwhile can come of it.

The cognitive strength of a concept is not in the concept itself but in the degree of correct reflection within it of the object expressed by it. As powerless as abstract concepts are in relation to reality and to the practice of cognition, so are concrete concepts a force. In this sense, Marx said that concepts have cognitive and practical value insofar as they are not only intellectual constructions and rational abstractions but serve as the expression and reflection of the actual process of history. 'These abstractions in themselves, divorced from real history, have no value whatsoever'.[35] Until circumstances emerge as an objective force, theory is only a utopia and an 'improvisation of systems'.[36]

If the theoretician, Hegel says, in not conforming to reality, builds the world for themselves as it ought to be, then similar constructions could exist but only in the imagination, in that pliable sphere where anything at all can be easily created.[37]

On Mathematical Concepts

§ 61

The advantage of the actual formations of reality examined, and of the concrete concepts expressing them, over abstract and purely intellectual concepts lies in the fact that the former reflect definite, objectively existing relations of actuality and the latter (abstract concepts) do not always find their material prototype in reality. Abstract concepts are not so much taken from reality and reflect that reality as they improvise and create for themselves a particular conditional reality that does not actually exist (whole numbers, fractions, geometrical bodies and so on). For the most part, mathematical concepts have only an imaginary, 'hypothetical' existence somehow reminiscent of the existence of the characters in artistic productions, for example Goethe's Mephistopheles or Homer's Odysseus.

Mathematical categories do not exist in nature. There are no numbers in objective reality: no ones, no twos, no halves or tenths – but there are things, plants, animals, buildings and people that we group purely intellectually, con-

---

35 Marks i Engel's 1933, p. 17 [Marx and Engels 1975–, Vol. 5, p. 37].
36 Marks 1931c, p. 117 [Marx, in Marx and Engels 1975–, Vol. 6, p. xx].
37 Hegel 1911, p. 15: 'Gehet seine Theorie in der Tat drüber hinaus, baut es sich eine *Welt, wie sie sein soll, so* existiert sie wohl, aber nur in seinem Meinen, – einem weichen Elemente, dem sich alles Beliebige einbilden lässt'.

ceiving of them in twos and threes, but the things in themselves do not have this determinacy. We thus slip a certain previously generated ideal numeric mesh over reality.

Mathematical concepts do not so much attempt to agree with the structure of reality as they attempt to adapt this reality to themselves, presenting it as consisting of specific numeric groups or of geometrical figures. For example, the actual surface of water or dry land, which mathematically – for the comforts of measurement – is presented as a certain aggregate of triangles or squares, in itself does not consist either of triangles or squares. If we wonder about the numerical determinateness of actually existing objects, we see that numerical apperception relates quite arbitrarily to reality: we can state with equal right about the universe that it is a whole, that it consists of two parts (specifically the northern and southern hemispheres of the night sky), that it is a given quantity of constellations, and finally that it is an infinite multitude of molecules, atoms and so forth.

Hegel rightly spoke about the arbitrariness of mathematical definitions and the impersonality of the material that mathematics uses. Actual cognition usually begins with concrete objects, and all the differentiations that consciousness places on them rely on the data displayed by the material itself. The material of arithmetical and algebraic operations, Hegel says, is 'fabricated' (*gemachtes, gesetztes*), assumed, conditionally accepted and moreover completely abstract and indeterminate; all the specifics of actual relations are erased in them. All mathematical definitions and every subdivision of actual objects performed by consciousness are not characteristic of the objects themselves but are arbitrarily introduced by consciousness and are external to these objects. Such is the principle of every discrete magnitude – units, for example: how units will emerge or be separated in the future depends exclusively on the assumptions of the cognising person. Numerical units of things or separateness has the form of an arbitrary combination or division that is external to them. In general, a magnitude represents a category within which consciousness makes any definitions, but which in itself is indifferent to any definitions or operations applied to it, hence the object of mathematical operations itself has no definitions whatsoever of its own given to it by consciousness itself.[38]

Matters are exactly the same with geometrical operations and proofs. Mathematics imagines every area, every space to be arbitrarily composed of points, lines, triangles and pyramids, in addition not taking into account the object itself and not starting from its real properties.

---

38 Hegel 1923, Vol. II, p. 446; Hegel 1906, § 102.

The arbitrariness of mathematical definitions is even more obvious on continuums – for example, when the degree of heat is represented in the discrete units of degrees Celsius, Réaumur and Fahrenheit, or when time is divided into seconds, minutes, hours and so on.

The concern of mathematical consistency consists not in agreeing with reality but exclusively in not contradicting itself, its fundamental postulates and definitions taken conditionally as original. Thus, any purely mathematical discipline is a system of conditional categories taken hypothetically, mutually connected not by the meaning of actual reality but by meaning conditionally ascribed to them.

Consequently, there are no propositions in mathematics that correspond to anything actual (i.e. there are no truths in the proper meaning of the word, only formally hypothetical truths). Mathematics moves from one proposition to another, relying on the conditional assumption of given basic postulates, the validity or falsity of which mathematics itself does not and cannot establish. It simply takes these propositions as conditional and brings out all the consequents flowing from them: if the Euclidean postulates are accepted, then such-and-such a geometric system is constructed; if the postulate of Lobachevsky or Riemann is accepted, different systems of geometric constructions result. Given certain principles of numbers, there is one system of numeration; given others, there is a different one.

Insofar as certain basic propositions are accepted and specific mathematical postulates come into effect, all further definitions and constructions are predetermined with the absolute immutability of a tautology.

As a consequence of this, the world of mathematical constructions is essentially dogmatic. Actual relations do not exist in mathematics; there can be neither conditions nor conditioned, neither cause nor effect, no chance events. Nothing happens in the world of mathematical dogmatism, nothing occurs; all the conclusions are definitively determined together with the fundamental postulates, regardless of whether or not anyone learns them. Insofar as the principle of differentials has been formulated, the integral of any expression has one or more meanings fully defined, regardless of whether or not this solution is found by anyone, and even if no one ever solves it.

When we are diverted away from actual reality and turn to the sphere of pure possibilities, then not only does actually existing space prove to be logically possible, but also an entire range of other forms of space, the models of which are given in various systems of non-Euclidean geometry. Experience can select those spaces that correspond more to reality (here is where the value of theoretical mathematics lies), but from a purely mathematical standpoint actual space has no advantages over these probable, purely imaginary types of space. Lobachevsky described one of these mathematically possible spaces. But until he formulated the principles of his geometry, this system existed as one of many ideally possible geometries. This means at the same time that absolutely everything can be ideally possible.

In the ideal, and for this reason dead, world of mathematical abstractions, Bolzano's proposition about 'truths in themselves' apparently existing independently in the ideal world outside of any dependence on cognition (so close to the Platonic world view) would be in full force; we only discover them like Columbus 'discovered' the Americas (B. Russell), and then these 'truths in themselves' become 'truths for us'. This is why through the ages, mathematics was the favourite sphere of idealism, constantly serving as the support for every rationalist system. In this lifeless world of abstract categories and identities, the rationalists saw the model of scientific perfection. Of course, it has to be admitted that philosophers had quite a false opinion about perfection.

Presenting an imaginary and nonexistent world, mathematical concepts are pointless and unreal. The concept of existence and existential proofs in mathematics have a completely different meaning that has nothing in common with actual reality. They pursue a single goal: that the system of imaginary, abstract categories is not internally contradictory.

Abstract mathematical concepts and mathematical definitions (e.g. the parallelogram or exponentiation) do not have material content – with the exception of those cases where real events themselves are specifically thus defined, for example, the parallelogram of forces in combining the different vectors of force acting on a point, or the square of distances with a body in free fall.

Expressing only the relations of abstract qualities and not the actually existing relations of things, and not having an element of reality in them, purely conceptual mathematical concepts are themselves incapable of developing and producing something new. Only the cognising subject makes all the delimitations, permutations and groupings in them, and that only intellectually. The object remains indifferent and identical to itself.

The actual formations of reality are a different matter – the state, the law, the plant kingdom, nature in general and so on, for example – all of which themselves develop in accordance with their own laws independent of how they are to be conceived and presented. Moreover, it is not they that adapt themselves to concepts; our concepts and forms of thought have to adapt themselves to the forms and laws of actual development, in order to correctly reflect and express them.

Mathematical abstractions have only an imaginary dialectic – the dialectic of concepts – available to them. In this is revealed the helplessness of dogmatism.

Touching on these questions even in his youth, Marx wrote: 'Here, above all, the same opposition between what is and what ought to be, which is characteristic of idealism ... was the source of the hopelessly incorrect division of the subject-matter ... A triangle gives the mathematician scope for construction and proof, it remains a mere abstract construction in space and does not develop into anything further. It has to be put alongside something else, then it assumes other positions, and this diversity added to it gives it different relationships and truths. On the other hand, in the concrete expression of a living world of ideas, as exemplified by law, the state, nature ... the object itself must be studied in its development; arbitrary divisions must not be introduced, the rational character of the object itself must develop as something imbues with contradictions in itself and find its unity in itself'.

Philosophers have treated the logical force and indisputability of mathematical truths with exaggerated respect. The firmness and coercive force of such truths as $2 \times 6 = 12$ amazed them.

But if there is any kind of indisputability here it ultimately consists of a single tautology, as the object moreover remains invariably the same and nothing in it changes. We only *produce* different permutations and delimitations in it. We take the same object (12 imaginary units) and arbitrarily distribute and assembled them any which way – in pairs, in threes, and so on – obtaining accordingly such truths as $2 \times 6 = 12$, $3 \times 4 = 12$, $5 + 7 = 12$, $11 + 1 = 12$ and so forth; moreover, the reality itself (12 of whatever object you like) is completely indifferent to this entire game: these 12 things remain as they were in relation to all the operations, definitions and subdivisions produced by us.

In this sense, Marx and Engels spoke about mathematics as the fantasy formation of objects and their arbitrary combination in the imagination. The object always remains the same; we only mentally decompose and compose it from different imaginary parts, but nothing occurs with the object itself.

There is no indisputability here, and only the arbitrariness of consciousness, since with the same right and just as adroitly factorise this object (12) and present it in numberless other variations: $4 + 5 + 3$; $\frac{1}{10} \times 120$ and so on.

But if there is something surprising in the fact that $5 + 7$ still necessarily makes 12, and not 10 or 13, then it is the naïveté of philosophers holding the thing, itself hapless in the world, in reverence: these 12, in which some kind of new result is seen, were taken from the very start as such, only in its apperception in two groups of 5 and 7. Moreover, it was forgotten that the units themselves take no part in this operation. They made 12 before their decomposition into parts and remain what they were after their combination. The wisdom of such new definitions is created only by the subject's bustling around the objects. Marx made an excellent point here: 'From the outset an obstacle to grasping the truth here was the unscientific form of mathematical dogmatism, in which the author argues hither and thither, going round and round the subject dealt with, without the latter taking shape as something living and developing in a many-sided way'.[39]

§ 62

Everything that has been said about the abstract concepts of mathematics applies to later stages of development, specifically to the stage of thinking of civilised society with a developed *exchange* economy. From the standpoint of the history of the origin of these abstract concepts about number, quantity and so on, the matter of course stood completely differently.

In the beginning, not only were there not ideas about these abstractions, but it was impossible to even imagine a number *separately* from things, just as it was impossible *separately* to imagine space as such, time, quantity and so on. All these ideas were not separated from the objects being perceived. Concrete things – their aggregations or definite social setting – were always the object of perception, not abstract qualities.

We will not here go into an analysis of the problems concerning the genesis and development of the ideas of number, space, time and so on, particularly as we hope to make this the object of a different publication. Here, we will keep our attention on one issue only.

Despite the great abstraction of mathematical concepts and the arbitrary treatment of objects, this arbitrariness is strictly limited by the objective meaning of the things themselves, the moment the matter touches upon the numeration of actual quantities. When, for example, a mathematician takes actual objects and wishes to perform mathematical operations on them (combination, division, multiplication and so on), they often run up against quite mysterious resistance in the field of abstract numbers, specifically the *resistance of the material* (the object) to forms that do not correspond to its actual nature. Numbers, insofar as we take them as abstract units, can be combined, assembled, divided and so forth in many ways – but when we are dealing not with abstract, but with actual, quantities, these simplest of operations do not always succeed. It is impossible, for example, to divide a specific organic whole in the same way as any abstract unit – it is impossible to speak of half a person without changing the sense of this concept of 'person' – and two dissimilar formations cannot be combined no matter how hard we try.

When asked 'How many are five pears and five apples?' a child of six briskly answered 'Ten'. But when asked 'Ten of what?' he became confused, and after

---

39 Marks i Engel's 1928–1946, Vol. 1, p. 433 [Marx and Engels 1975–, Vol. 1, p. 12].

some hesitation blurted out 'Fruit salad(!)' The child managed to extricate himself from the situation nonetheless. Apples and pears are things that can be combined, all the same, and taken together can make up something actual: specifically 'pieces', 'fruit' or even at the very least 'fruit salad'. Another child – a five-year-old girl – asked the same question could also find a general number for two apples and three plums, but did not know what to call this number and 'solved' the task in her own way, saying 'I'll put them down separately (!)'

The combination of actual things, like any other mathematical operation on actual objects, is only possible when the things have some sort of relation to each other and a general *meaning*, if in reality they possess some sort of *actual 'common denominator'*. In this case, they also have a general term for the given things (i.e. a name as well as a concept in common). Performing the mental operation of combining five pears and five peaches would be completely impossible if for their common number no unifying term or concept existed (i.e. an actual scale of their combined perception such as *'pieces of fruit'* and so on). The objective meaning of things resists mental operations that do not correspond to them.

In Max Wertheimer's words, combining the number of one's own reindeer with the number of one's neighbour is for the Inuits just such a meaningless operation. The Inuits are unable to do so not because of innumeracy or the difficulty of calculation, but because combinations of this kind lack meaning for them: they are objects that cannot be combined, inasmuch as ten of their own reindeer belong to them and five of their neighbour's reindeer are 'their neighbour's reindeer'. No matter how much an Inuit would try to combine them in their head, the task does not change its initial form: 'it would be ten of my reindeer and five of my neighbour's'; they would not arrive at fifteen reindeer 'in general' (i.e. they could not successfully perform the combination, whereas they can manage any numerical operation splendidly inasmuch as the matter concerned homogeneous things).

Any highly cultured consciousness displays such an opinion of combining the seemingly most elementary quantities, every time these quantities in their objective meaning cannot be summed up. No matter how much effort would be put into combining 5 horses and 10 degrees of heat, for example, 15 units cannot be composed from them in any way. The meaning of things resists meaningless operations upon them. Moreover, anything that in objective reality cannot correspond to anything actual (i.e. concepts not having their own objective equivalent in objective reality) are called 'meaningless'.

In this connection, the question arises: How is the practical application of numbers possible? The problem of calculating actual objects – the problem of measuring – crops up.

The point is that as a consequence of the great remoteness of mathematical concepts and categories from the actual and in view of their extraordinary abstractness and emptiness, they cannot simply be applied to real things. 'In order to get any further, we are obliged', as Engels said, 'to bring in real relations, relations and space forms which are taken from real bodies'.[40] When a mathematician appeals to reality, wishing to calculate and compare actual objects, they are obliged every time to assist their abstract concepts by *introducing actual, more concrete determiners of reality itself* in the form of 'pieces', 'persons', or ergs, metres, litres and so on *as specific measures and a scale of things* since it is impossible to express, for example, the quantity of some liquid in the same terms as those in which space and time are expressed.

It should therefore not be surprising if different numbering systems appear among the same peoples in their application to various things, since time requires a different calculation than length or cattle do. We actually find data in the ethnographic literature that is curious in this regard. According to the testimony of Franz Boas, the Tsimshian language of British Columbia has seven different numbering systems used for counting objects belonging to different classes or categories. They resort to the first series when discussing indeterminate objects, the second is used for counting flat objects and animals, the third for round objects and divisions of time, the fourth for people, the fifth for long objects (moreover, the numbers are combined with the word *kan*, 'tree'), the sixth for boats and the seventh for measurements.[41] Richard Parkinson reports that the language of the inhabitants of the Duke of York Islands has different names of numbers for counting fruit, shells used for money, eggs, animals and people.[42]

Human speech everywhere notes a difference in counting diverse objects: people, for example, are not counted like cattle or arrows are; the former can be counted as 'souls' and the latter as 'heads', and numerous other examples. These determiners are a measure, are the scale of things and *they are taken from reality itself*. Mathematics has a single support in reality, and that is measurement. But insofar as these *actual* definitions are taken and applied, the field of 'pure' mathematics is abandoned and the fields of physics and the natural sciences begin. The general tendency of modern mathematics – geometry in particular – must be noted, expressed in the fact that it is developing as a branch of physics (i.e. as actual meaningful mathematics).

---

40   Marks i Engel's 1928–1946, Vol. xiv, 40 [Marx and Engels 1975–, Vol. 25, p. 38].
41   Lévy-Bruhl 1930, p. 130.
42   Parkinson 1907, p. 747.

In measurements, we always have a specific element of *reality* that takes the objective features of things into account. In defining scales and measures, humanity has always started from, and will always start from, the *qualitative* indicators of things. Historically, measurements always find their support in the objective boundaries of the qualitative indicators of things that play a role in social practice: boiling point, freezing point, the time of twilight and dawn, the time for ploughing, harvesting and so on. It is not difficult to guess that every quantitative reflection of consciousness could begin only by starting from such a recognition of reality, and that mathematics – and numerical thinking in general – have their historical support in the ideas of measurement. Measurement is the first quantitative – and at the same time material – indicator of the qualitative peculiarity of reality.

Here, in the problem of measurement, the true historical meaning of mathematical concepts and the character of their origin is revealed; despite all its abstractness, in their genesis mathematical abstractions always have a fully material support in reality. Historically, these concepts were formed in accordance with how reality itself was revealed in social and historical praxis and with the actual combinations and delimitations reality acquired in human praxis.

In connection with this a splendid problem arises: the history of measurements according to the data of material culture, language, speech and thinking. Such a history would paint a full picture of the formation and the development of quantitative thinking.

The origin of the ideas of units, pairs and so on would be impossible if certain integral formations perceived in practice as wholes did not exist in reality. Humans, for example, cannot be conceived as the combination of two separate halves, but only as a single whole; the concept of $2+2 = 4$ would be equally impossible if in every joining of two actual pairs a still newer pair arose; then $2+2$ would not make 4, but 6.

Thus, if we spoke earlier about the 'subjectivity', conditionality and arbitrariness of mathematical definitions, an essential amendment should now be made to say: the arbitrariness and conditionality of mathematical postulates and definitions are far from arbitrary, but are socially and historically conditioned by actual reality and social praxis. 'Purely logical and purely mathematical concepts and definitions' are not fully subjective, but are maximally subjective in the sense that the more distant the concept from reality and the more abstract it is, the more subjectivity and arbitrariness there is in it; in the sphere of consciousness and in the history of thinking, however, we never encounter such ideas – even the most fantastic ones – as would be the result of only subjective arbitrariness and the creation of consciousness from itself, having no support whatsoever in objective reality. The task of theory consists of our being able to understand what appears as only the product of thinking as the products of life, the product of history.

We have brought the reader's attention to mathematical concepts in order, as the greatest abstractions, to show: first, the tremendous difference between a concrete concept leaning on objective reality and the arbitrariness of an abstract concept. As soon as an abstract concept touches upon actual things, the intellectual operation is forced to take the actual definitions of reality itself as help.

Second, in order to show that no abstraction whatsoever is the arbitrary creation of thinking, but is always taken from actual relations and has a material basis in objective reality. 'Like all other sciences', Engels said, 'mathematics arose out of the *needs* of men: from the measurement of land and the content of vessels, from the computation of time and from mechanics'.[43] All mathematical definitions and categories are ultimately imported from the real world; that is only why they are applicable to it.[44]

Consequently, in the abstract sphere of mathematical abstractions, the fundamental proposition remains in force that the construction of thought and of concepts is defined by the structure of reality and of social and historical praxis. The composition and structure of human social experience directs consciousness towards certain objects, and objects – resisting all interpretations that do not correspond to their actual nature – compel us to seek and find more adequate solutions and concepts, and to produce more correct concepts about these things.

---

43 Marks i Engel's 1928–1946, Vol. XIV, p. 39 [Marx and Engels 1975–, Vol. 25, p. 37].
44 'The ideas of lines, planes, angles, polygons, cubes, spheres, etc., are all taken from reality, and it requires a pretty good portion of naive ideology to believe the mathematicians that the first line came into existence through the movement of a point in space, the first place through the movement of a line, the first solid through the movement of a plane and so on. Even language rebels against such a conception. A mathematical figure of three dimensions is called a solid body, *corpus solidum*, hence, in Latin, even a tangible object; it therefore has a name derived from sturdy reality and by no means from the free imagination of the mind'. Marks i Engel's 1928–1946, Vol. XIV, pp. 40–41 [Marx and Engels 1975–, Vol. 25, p. 38].

Generalisation and General Concepts

§ 63

In logic, a concept that does not express a single individual object or several separate objects but their whole class – a concept under which, it is said, 'all conceivable examples of the given type are placed' – is usually called a generic or general concept.

Ancient philosophy debated about how such concepts are formed and what meaning they have. Traditional logic, it must be said, was treated lightly, presuming it was sufficient to take some sort of 'feature' [priznak] and the classification of things would flow by itself; all objects having this feature would go under one concept and those not having it under another.

This was not difficult while matters had not gotten as far as evidence of this magical 'feature'. But the invalidity of the theory manifested itself as soon as defining such a feature was required. Characteristic of any formalism is a naive 'cunning' with which a single unintelligible thing (in this case, a general concept) is turned into another thing even more unintelligible ('the feature') and resting on that.

What is a 'feature'? 'Why are certain features taken up, why were some 'features' taken up in the history of thinking and others not?' The philosophers did not ask themselves such questions because in principle, the theory of cognition occupied antihistorical positions and preferred to soar in the clouds of abstractions. To that extent, '[o]ne of the most difficult tasks confronting philosophers is to descend from the world of thought to the actual world' (Marx).

Classifying things and joining them into 'general concepts' requires, above all, these things actually having some kind of common grounds and it being possible to join them.

People distinguish objects and conceive of them not for the sake of the things themselves but for the sake of their own needs and interests, and to the extent that these things are drawn into the sphere of any given human need. Things are generally conceived of from their actual significance (i.e. as things having a certain sense in human use – practical, ideological or however you like).

Everything that performs the same service and has an identical designation in social custom is placed by consciousness into a single intellectual series and is perceived and interpreted in an identical manner (i.e. placed under a single concept *A*) – this means that it is *generalised*.

In this regard, cases where things that are completely different in their composition, appearance, form and so on are thought of as identical and called with the same name are particularly revealing. Karl von Steinen relates how the Bakairi people, having hung mats of palm thatch they called 'houses' on themselves during masquerades, gave the name to objects unknown to them: shirts, for example, were 'back houses', trousers were dubbed 'leg houses' and hats 'head houses'.[45]

'With striking rapidity, the Bakairi defined objects unknown to them and gave them names they were accustomed to without restrictive additions. The Bakairi cut their hair with sharpened shells or with the teeth of a piranha; my scissors – an exquisite pair – were nicknamed 'piranha teeth' and my mirror was dubbed 'water'. 'Show us the water', they asked, when they wanted to see the mirror. They called the compass 'the sun' and my watch 'the moon''.[46]

Despite the fact that these things for us seemingly have nothing in common with one another, the consciousness of the aborigines placed them under one concept; a pocket watch could be called 'sun' or 'moon' on the basis of the fact that they all serve to determine time.

The interpretation of things and the formation of concepts thus progresses not according to the external resemblance of objects and not according to the proximity of their objectively physical signs, but according to the identity or difference of these objects in human social and historical praxis.

In his notes, Lenin points out the problem that the word always generalises, that in language there is only the universal.[47] Indeed – thought, like language, always generalises the material it is using to a certain extent. This is inherent in every genuine interpretation, out of necessity. Things and phenomena are taken by thinking from their significance or functions; consequently not in isolation but in their reference to other things. Consciousness in the act of thinking assembles and links things (sometimes quite different things) around the specific meaning, role or function of these objects, thereby producing a generalisation and a general concept (i.e. forming specific centres for intellectual comparisons).

A concept is semantic context produced in the experience of thinking that mediates our further cognition, and not at all Kant's finished *a priori* schema or the sum of abstract 'similar signs' as the empiricists believed. Objects encountered in our experience are usually comprehended by attributing them to one or another semantic type (i.e. to a concept) available to consciousness en masse. A single thing attributed to different complexes can correspondingly assume different meanings and be expressed by different concepts. A concept

---

45   Steinen 1894, p. 66.
46   Steinen 1894, p. 75.
47   Lenin 1931, p. 219 [Lenin 1960–1979, Vol. 38, p. 275].

is not always once and for all a given, immutable category of the intellect representing a sum of formal signs, as was the accepted belief in the era of mediaeval scholasticism. Along with the change in the social function of things in social and historical praxis, the concepts about them also change and are reconstructed.

These are explained by the fact that a single natural object at different stages of historical developments is comprehended differently and expressed in different concepts. Water, for example, has physically always been water and will remain water, but its connection with human needs, its industrial use and social functions change from era to era. In the Paleolithic, it had only one social significance, another among the ancient Chaldeans, and a different one in our own time. The problems of hydraulics and the electrolysis of water that we have solved did not exist and could not have existed in those times. Accordingly, the concept of 'water' was different. Despite the fact that superficially the same object of nature appears here, it has different a different social meaning in different historical epochs, puts forward different problems and is fixed in the form of different concepts.

Everything that performs an identical service in social praxis has an identical social designation and is conceived as similar; everything that performs a secondary and partial function that however has a relation to this range will be conceived by starting from here and counting off the 'coordinates' from this. Characteristically, language also assimilates reality in this way.

Every thought and concept thus leads to generalisation – but not at all because people are inclined to generalise, deliberately striving to compose general concepts about things for themselves; generalisation is achieved as an indispensable result of *human* cognition and thinking in contrast to that of animals, and humans are above all interested in things – not the individuality of these things but what they are needed for (i.e. the general). The technique of human thinking and the technique of speech itself lead to generalisation, as they do to the inevitable result of thinking and expression; otherwise it would be impossible to imagine or to express what has been imagined.

But things have consequently been imagined and named differently in different eras and at different stages of development, and concepts have been generalised differently in different places and at different times depending on what the social needs were and how things were used by people in different eras. The task of the history of thinking consists of explaining how and why this occurred.

At the root is a mistakenly widespread opinion that generalisations are not characteristic of primitive thinking. Without a certain amount of generalisation, no thinking – no speech – is possible. Generalisation exists in aboriginal thinking, but *aboriginal* consciousness, relying on its experience, generalises and groups entities, objects and phenomena *in a different way* than 'modern' cognition. Entities and objects that in our praxis have identical names and identical meaning – and thus in our thinking signifying one and the same thing – can in aboriginal consciousness belong to different classes depending on what place these things occupy in social praxis. And vice versa: things that for us have nothing in common with each other can be sorted by aboriginal consciousness into the same class, constituting identical objects in a similar manner; for example, in the testimony of Lumholtz, various sacred plants and feathers were to a certain extent identical in the ideas of the Huichol people. 'What we would have called different', he says, 'were for the Huichol realities that were identical with each other'.[48] But at the base of such generalisations lie the economic and religious significance of these objects for the Huichol, which have already been discredited by 'modern' consciousness.

The remnants of such classifications of entities and objects, strange to us, are preserved in the form of grammatical classes in many North American, African and Australian aboriginal languages, as well as in the northern Caucasus and many other places.

With changes to material culture and social structure, concepts about things also change. *As things change their function and meaning in social use, so change the ideas* about them, and moreover the meanings of the words expressing them become different. Perception of new content occurs on the basis of ideological stock already on hand, but not at all as the formalists taught: 'general concepts' simply receiving new content in a given classificatory heading (subsumation). New content does not crawl obediently into a place of already developed schema and categories that has been prepared for it. Owing to the partial inclusion of new content in the general field of thinking, certain shifts in the structural order occur – sometimes partial, sometimes embracing all of consciousness and changing completely its arrangement (a revolution in consciousness). In the latter case, cognition is constructed anew around new centres of orientation and all the old content appears in a new form.

A reconstruction of consciousness of this kind calls forth new problems, but in the reconstruction both the new and the old content take part. The new content finds expression on the basis of the old ideological stock, but moreover every time changes the structure and direction of thinking as a whole to a greater or lesser degree.

---

48   Lumholtz 1903, Vol. II, p. 233.

The same thing occurs with language. Language does not create a new word *ex nihilo* for a new concept or object, but produces its name from the linguistic stock already at hand. We have already noted that if some kind of outside object fulfils the function of a table, then it is perceived as a table and called one.

At the basis of every idiom always lies some or another objective criteria or specific meaning inherent in the thing itself in human praxis. Without this, every idiom would be arbitrary, and obligatory for no one. The verbal form becomes valid owing to the objective sense of the object, and this sense is defined by the meaning of the object in social use. The communicative function of a word hinges on the fact that the object expressed by the word, with its specific meaning, has entered into social use, and therefore is conceived of and named by the majority of individuals in an identical manner. The word does not rely on the mental content of consciousness – as depicted in Alexander Potebnia, Gustav Shpet and others – but on the realia of human practice and on the objective structure of social and historical experience.

It can be said that generalisation in speech and concept is only produced from the actual generalisation of things in the circulation of social life, and therefore in the consciousness of the many.

The Formation of Concepts

§ 64

Returning to the real formation of reality itself and the concrete concepts corresponding to it, we see that the material of perception (as it is given in social and historical praxis) defines the form and means of its understanding (i.e. the concept). 'It is not enough for thought to strive for realisation, reality must itself strive towards thought' (Marx). If the structure of social reality does not induce consciousness and does not aid in comprehension, then the concept does not arise.

The specific understanding of reality arises owing to the fact that first, in affecting the interests of people, things prompt them in a certain direction; and second, reality itself in the process of development ever more sharply reveals its essential features, internal forces and laws. In the flow of changes undergone by reality, constant forces that form the process and are called most essential by us are preserved in it while everything that is attendant and collateral – called 'external', accidental and immaterial – exerting different influences, mutually destroy their influence.

Thus reality, in the process of its development, gradually cleansing itself of accidental forms and liberating itself from particular states, crystallises in sharper forms that are more easily accessible to consciousness. It more sharply manifests the forms towards which the phenomena are striving in accordance with their internal laws, as towards the greatest possible (probable) state. In the process of their development, phenomena – being put into forms more accessible to an idea – ultimately impose specific thoughts on consciousness.

This conformity of the logical path of cognition with the historical process of the development of reality was what Marx had in mind when he said that the simplest categories of, for example, the political economy of bourgeois society (money, exchange value, abstract labour and so on) existed before capitalism, but only in the appearance of other relations, having other functions and another meaning. They could be imagined as abstract categories, if you like, in their application to capitalist formations, but in that case they would have no real meaning and sense.

'... as a category', Marx said, 'exchange value leads an antediluvian existence. Hence to the kind of consciousness – and philosophical consciousness (here Marx means Hegelian philosophy. – *KM*) is precisely of this kind – which regards the comprehending mind as the real man, and only the comprehended world as such as the real world ... the movement of categories appears as the real act of production ...'.

'But have not these simple categories also an independent historical or natural existence preceding that of the more concrete ones? *Ça dépend*'. 'Money can exist and has existed in history before capital, banks, wage labour, etc., came into being. In this respect it can be said, therefore, that the simpler category can express relations predominating in a less developed whole or subordinate relations in a more developed whole, relations which already existed historically before the whole had developed the aspect expressed in a more concrete category. To that extent, the course of abstract thinking which advances from the elementary to the combined corresponds to the actual historical process'.

'Thus this quite simple category does not emerge historically in its intensive form until the most highly developed phases of society'. 'So although the simpler category may have existed historically before the more concrete category, its complete intensive and extensive development can nevertheless occur precisely in a complex form of society ...'.[49] Classes, for example, existed in society for many thousands of years, long before they were correctly known by people. Despite the fact that the division of society into classes and the class struggle was the mainspring that brought the entire mechanism of history into motion,

---

49   Marks 1931b, pp. 70–73 [Marx and Engels 1975–, Vol. 28, pp. 38–40].

over the course of millennia humanity had no clear idea about them and composed only shadowy legends about 'the lucky and the failures'. A long period of development was necessary in order for the glaringly conspicuous division of society into ownership relations that eradicated all the other differences (class, legal, and so on) that appeared to be natural, established by God and permanent. A cleansing of class relations from extraneous elements and motives of any nature whatsoever besides propertied ones was required in order for this division to be accessible to consciousness. But primarily, the emergence of a class compelled by force of their interests to identify themselves as a class and to consciously united into a solidaristic class whole was necessary for a genuinely correct cognition of the class structure of society and for the realisation of its historic tasks and interests. And this did not happen in the era of slavery, or the era of feudalism.

On this point, Engels wrote: 'But while in all earlier periods the investigation of these driving causes of history was almost impossible – on account of the complicated and concealed interconnections with their effects – our present period has so far simplified these interconnections that it has been possible to solve the riddle. Since the establishment of large-scale industry, that is, at least since the European peace of 1815, it has been no longer a secret to any man in England that the whole political struggle there turned on the claims to supremacy of two classes: the landed aristocracy and the bourgeoisie (middle class). In France, with the return of the Bourbons, the same fact was perceived, the historians of the Restoration period, from Thierry to Guizot, Mignet and Thiers, speak of it everywhere as the key to the understanding of French history since the Middle Ages. And since 1830 the working class, the proletariat, has been recognised in both countries as a competitor for power. *Conditions had become so simplified that one would have to close one's eyes deliberately not to see in the fight of these three great classes and in the conflict of their interests the driving force of modern history – at least in the two advanced countries*'.[50] Thus, social relations themselves can be generalised into specific forms more accessible to thinking.

Generally speaking, *every generalisation* and every classification performed by consciousness is ultimately based on some kind of *objective structure of reality*. Things themselves are 'generalised' in the circulation of social relations. Generalisations are not so much products of the intellect as they are products of those actual generalisations that things undergo in their social existence, social praxis and social use.

---

50   Engel's 1931. P. 70 [Marx and Engels 1975–, Vol. 26, pp. 389–90] (italics mine – KM).

There is a tremendous difference between the general concept of a beginning (the initial state of cognition) and the general concept of an end, which is obtained as a result of more detailed and accurate knowledge. In philosophical literature, for some reason, this question is treated with silence. Moreover, such a distinction is very important for not heaping things that have completely different meanings into a single pile. In the first case, we are dealing with a general concept as an undifferentiated and indistinct idea as a consequence of a lack of detailed knowledge: for example, an person unversed in aircraft types or breeds of horse usually does not particularly differentiate between them; they think of them as identical and designate them with terms such as 'airplane' or 'horse' and so on. In the second case, we are dealing with a differentiated general concept that precisely and in detail depicts concrete reality and goes to the heart of the internal structure of things. We have a concrete concept. For specialists in aviation, there is no airplane 'in general', just as for an expert horse breeder there is not simply 'a horse' but geldings, three-year-old fillies, amblers, trotters and so on. Where horses, deer, sheep and so forth played an important economic role, they had a mass of names. Materials collected by the northern Caucasus linguistic expedition (organised by the *Instutut iazyka i myshlenie* [Institute of Language and Thinking]) report that in the Karachay-Balkar language there are more than 100 names for rams and sheep, distinguishing them by age, sex, colour and other signs (the materials were provided to us by Professor Levon Bashindzhagian, who led the expedition). In Dal's dictionary of the Russian language, we find more than 30 names for distinguishing horses by sex and age, and more than 50 names for various colourations. On the contrary, jackals – which did not play a particular role in agriculture – are not even distinguished by sex. The Arabic language has a few hundred names for camels while Georgian has three, all of which are loanwords (*loini* 'male camel', *dama* 'female camel' and *kozaki* 'young camel', and Russian has one. For physiologists and histologists, 'flesh' is not a general concept but some kind of mundane 'absurdity'. Specialists have extraordinarily concrete and precise knowledge in their fields, and do not resort to such indistinct concepts. Physiologists do not use the term 'flesh' because they conceive the tissues of an organism in a different manner than an ordinary consciousness does – except, of course, in a gastronomic role: physiological concepts then might not even enter their heads.

Every generalisation and every differentiation of an intellectual (and even linguistic) type is only the expression of the actual relations surrounding humanity. But reality is infinitely rich in every relation; why are certain relations of things perceived by people, and others not even noticed at all? The solution is hidden in the structure and direction of human interests (§ 100) that define the content and means of their thinking.

§65

All sorts of ideas and intellectual comparisons can arise in the current of the free flow of an individual's ideas. This fortuity is particularly obvious in children's thinking, where automobiles with their horns could be called dogs (likening the noise to barking), factory smokestacks and even towers could be perceived as trains, and so on. For thinking, however, it is not these transient ideas that have significance but the things that are retained in a certain manner, and socially anchored, in thinking.

Research into the signs of individual thinking (until now studied only by experimental psychologists) does not have that much essential significance, since these transient ideas dissipate the very next moment and only a certain portion of them remain, which is socially anchored and begins playing a certain role. The fundamental question, consequently, lies not in which thoughts enter a person's head, but in which of them are preserved as significant, why are they preserved, and how does this selection out of the colossal mass of the casual flow of consciousness occur?

When we look closely at the formation of concepts from this standpoint, we see that things are generally classified not according to the features of an external observer, or their sensory perception in general, but in the majority of cases *according to their social function.*

A concept is formed as the result of the mental operation of comprehending, understanding and judging the sense relations of reality, as a solution of the task of comprehending objects or the relationships between them. It is formed not only as the result of the multiplicity of acts of repeating the same unexpected flash of inspiration, in the form of discovery. The emergence of a concept has nothing in common with the propositions put forward by the empiricists, who believed that this process occurs through multiple repetitions of the same representations and their mechanical combination. Sometimes *a single act of rational judgement* is sufficient for the emergence of a new idea. Further experience and 'repetitions' function not as the emergence of a concept, but as its verification; furthermore, this verification occurs not by means of innumerable meaningless repetitions of the same thing, but on the basis of several well-considered variations.

Others believed that the concept is the *tool* of cognition, not cognition itself, and as such represents a purely hypothetical and formal category that nothing in actual reality corresponds to. This is the standpoint of formalism. It found its expression in such systems as the philosophy of Hermann Cohen, Paul Natorp, Karl Pearson, Hans Vaihinger, Max Weber and many others.

Above all, a concept expresses the understanding and comprehension of things and their relations; it conveys the semantic expression of the object, its role and its significance as well as the structure and internal law of objects. Hence, it always expresses a certain integrated context, an entire thought, and not a separate class of things taken in isolation. Thus, a concept actually is the 'abbreviated expression of experience', as Marx, Engels and Lenin defined it. It depicts the structure of consciousness at the moment of comprehension, and simultaneously expresses the meaning of a thing, and the law and means of its understanding by the subject. In a word, a concept is *'das in Menschenkopf umgesetzte und übersetzte Materielle'*.

Here, the question on the unity of existence and thinking, put forth by Marxist philosophy as one of its fundamental propositions, is also solved.

'Is there, therefore, an eternal gulf and contradiction between being and thinking? Yes, but only in the mind; however in reality the contradiction has long been resolved, to be sure only in a way corresponding to reality and not your school notions ...'.[51]

'The fact', Engels says, 'that our subjective thought and the objective world are subject to the same laws, and hence, too, that in the final analysis they cannot contradict each other in their results, but must coincide, governs absolutely our whole theoretical thought'.[52]

'Our subjective thought and the objective world are subject to the same laws' only because the laws of comprehension are the same as the laws of things themselves. If consciousness is incapable of approaching reality and cannot make the laws of things its own laws, this means that consciousness has not yet attained the understanding of these things. Insofar as consciousness performs integrated comprehension in the act of thinking of certain things, phenomena or relations and comprehends the mode of communication of the whole, it also anchors this concept in speech by means of a specific expression, term or word. A word, like a concept, expresses an object from the same aspect and in the same manner as understanding and comprehension itself occurred. A word is not a formal appendage to a thing or an idea about a thing; it is not only a sign [*znak*], but also a meaning [*znachenie*]. In its origin, a word expresses an object precisely from the aspect of the semantic condition of this object and its meaning. Marx rightly called language embodied consciousness, 'practically existing, real consciousness'.

In its initial origin, a word expresses a thing from the aspect of its role, its significance, its function, and its practical sense. In its origin, a word defines the aspect from which humans know some object or other, the aspect in it

---

51 Lenin 1931, p. 117 [Lenin 1960–1979, Vol. 38, p. 81].
52 Marks i Engel's 1925, p. 135 [Marx and Engels 1975–, Vol. 25, p. 544].

that interests humans. A word, consequently, expresses first of all *the relation of humans to a thing*, the meaning of a thing *for humans*, and more often than not that meaning that humans have imparted to things in social praxis. A word is a formation that bears meaning, and not a mechanical sign by which the subject conditionally – and often by external means – coordinates a certain complex of sounds with a certain object.

CHAPTER 7

The Sociogenesis of Ideas

The Social Character of Individual Thinking

§ 66
So far, we have examined the problem of the origin of thought from the standpoint of the individual act of perception, in connection with the question of the concept and understanding. But consciousness exists in the world not in the form of isolated single consciousness, but in the environment of other conscious beings. Of all the things that are necessary for humans, Marx said, the most necessary one of all is another person, the need in the other person.

Earlier, we spoke about the fact that cultural values produced by people become the objective mediators of the social connections of individuals; but humans produce not only the world of material culture, and that by means of 'man producing man – himself and other man',[1] and not only in the direct sense of giving birth but in the sense of a social formation, of constant recreation, of 'humanisation'. Humans were created by humans, by culture, by history. Other humans, other people and generally speaking the existence of the individual in a society of those like them constitutes the necessary condition for the existence of humans in the proper sense of the word, and also for the emergence of the human means of activity and the human means of thought.[2] To that extent, thinking inevitably has to reveal itself not only as an individual act but as a social phenomenon. We will keep this task in mind throughout all further exposition.

Although perception is always an individual act performed by any individual subject (it cannot be presented in any other way, insofar as the process of thinking cannot progress anywhere outside a specific neurocerebral system; perception is an indicator of individual orientation, in contrast to herd reflexes), if

---

1 Marks i Engel's 1928–1946, Vol. III, p. 623 [Marx and Engels 1975–, Vol. 3, p. 297].
2 'Man is a *zoön politikon* in the most literal sense: he is not only a social animal, but an animal that can isolate itself only within society. Production by an isolated individual outside society – something rare, which might occur when a civilised person already dynamically in possession of the social forces is accidentally case into the wilderness – is just as preposterous as the development of language without individuals who live *together* and speak to one another'. Marks 1931b, p. 52 [Marx and Engels 1975–, Vol. 28, p. 18].

human thoughts were exclusively individual products, the mutual understanding of people and their mutual communication would be impossible.

The problem of the concept is thus far from being confined to an analysis of individual thinking. The question is posed significantly more broadly: why does an individual consciousness think in one way or another? How is the thinking of individuals conditioned? How are certain concepts historically composed? How are specific ideas created and socially maintained?

In §19, we spoke about the fact that after the rupture of the natural bonds uniting an organism with its environment, consciousness took on the task of the subject's orientation and connection with its environments (i.e. appropriating functions that until then were executed instinctively and automatically, without consciousness). The relation of a subject to its material environment and to other subjects thus acquires the form of intentional relations and actions with a premeditated goal. This means that consciousness appears as a middle term mediating the link between the state of the environment and the final act of the subject's orientation, between the objective situation and the subject. An encounter with a specific situation now does not call forth spontaneous direct action, but places the subject before a problem: tentatively considering the form of action from the standpoint of the end (i.e. of the desired result, the goal) and hence comprehending the situation and resolving it.

This process of *internal reflection* by the subject (i.e. thinking) is wedged like a mediating link between the object of activity and the subject. This reflection of course belongs to the subject; it flows through their neurocerebral apparatus and is the construction of the subject, but it has in mind an object, comprehends the object and to a certain extent is defined by its features.

The act of intellectual reflection is the act of the mutual acquisition of the subject by the object and vice versa – in the act of thinking, the subject acquires the object, finds a path into its core and to mastering it. But in this act, the object also acquires the subject, and its consciousness, in a certain manner. The subject is occupied with this object, and its consciousness is 'possessed' by specific objective content. We say: during the act of thinking, consciousness is immersed in the objective meaning of the task itself, in the meaning of the object itself. And since any act of perception is the thinking of specific content, then perception is linked with the laws of the object and is defined by the objective meaning of reality itself (i.e. the objective content of consciousness). In the latter case, we are dealing with objective, actual, substantive thinking.

But intellectual reflection is not only the mediator between object and subject; it serves simultaneously as the *means of connecting* and of intentional relations *between subjects*, the mediator of interaction between *individuals*. This also constitutes one of the fundamental functions of consciousness. Consciousness could not fulfil this function of communication if the general means of perception in individuals of a specific social circle did not lie at its base. Any mutual understanding and any interaction presuppose the existence of some kind of general *base of understanding*. This common basis is composed of those material and social conditions that define the *interests* of the individuals of a specific society and their thinking (see §§ 100, 105).

The facts of social praxis are often themselves composed in such a way that they direct people towards certain goals and tasks that can be resolved only *in a specific manner*. When certain problems become ripe in society (and this often happens beyond the will and intentions of people), they increasingly frequently affect the interests of many and occupy the consciousness of a multitude of individuals. If 'reality itself strives towards thought' in this way, then what goes unnoticed by some will be noticed by others; what is omitted by one will be grasped by a second, a third, or a fourth. It is enough that just one consciousness prepared in the necessary manner encounters a certain situation or specific task for comprehension to arise, for a specific thought, idea or concept to be born.

The question, consequently, concerns objective socially material conditions that form human thinking in different ways at different stages of its development, independently of individual deviations.

The thinking of individuals is defined by the prevailing social practices of thinking. We thus arrive at the proposition that will be developed in § 87 and § 100: that thoughts are concentrated not only in an individual cranium but fall into an individual brain because they represent the thoughts of a specific era and a specific society.

An independent individual thinks socially composed concepts and ideas. The thinking of an individual is not the result of individual creation but the product of history; it is social thought.

Many were frightened by this standpoint and asked: 'Where is the mental substrate? Where are these social thoughts found? Society does not have an integrated neurocerebral system; it doesn't have any kind of single head at all!'

All the better, if each *individual* head is the organ of *social* thought, *is a social head*. Despite the fact that everyone carries their head on their own shoulders, these heads are nonetheless filed not with thoughts created by these people themselves but with social ideas – both in the sense of a general orientation of the individual consciousness and in relation to the structure of thought as well as of objects (i.e. the content of consciousness).

The objective content of consciousness is nothing other than its social content, since first, specific things become the objects of thinking insofar as historical development puts them forward as problem A, and second, human creation is occupied with objects only *insofar as it thinks and constructs in and through these things on the assumption of relations to other individuals*. From the sum of all thoughts that in general come into the head of a person, take away the thoughts that have a relation to another subject, and see: how much material content remains in their consciousness? Nothing would remain, because there is no other content in it. Consciousness battles with material reality insofar as in these things it has other individuals and relations to them in mind.

In addition, there is no need to look for the abode of social thought in some kind of monstrous common head, when it is scattered among everything large and small that only human activity has touched on and upon which humanity constantly impressed its thinking, in whatever products of their activity this thinking was expressed.

Thus, despite the fact that every act of thinking is always an individual act of understanding, whatever is conceived by an individual (i.e. the problem itself as such) is a social product. The individual act of thought is determined by the conditions and the degree of social development in which an individual has emerged, and above all in which they happen to be thinking and acting. Therefore we say that the thoughts an individual has – how they think and what they think, which includes unbridled fantasy – are social thoughts that emerged historically and circulate in society in all their various forms and their multifaceted manifestations: in items of custom, morals, tastes, language, print and so on.

On the Question of Parallelisms and Convergences

§ 67
Cultural historians, folklorists and ethnographers have long noted the startling fact that in various corners of the world, in the life of societies separated from each other by tremendous distances and expanses of water and having no points of contact with each other whatsoever, it is possible to observe similar formations of the same type in both the sphere of custom and material culture and in the forms of organisation of society, as well as in the sphere of ideological formations, beliefs, mythologies, structures of speech and so on.

Ideas and beliefs are similar to an extremely high degree; extraordinarily strange customs are encountered here and there among tribes in such similar forms that it is impossible not to suppose that they have a common historical provenance or that they are imported. Examples of such analogies and parallelisms have been gathered in tremendous quantities by Tylor, Spencer, Bastian, Post, Frazer, Boas and others.

A cursory acquaintance with the beliefs of various peoples – soul worship, ancestor worship, burial rites – and with the ideas about life after death, forces of good and evil and so on is sufficient to find typological identities in almost every people that had or have these ideas. The keen mind of Voltaire noted before scientists did that 'in almost all the languages of all the peoples, the heart 'burns', courage 'is inflamed', eyes 'sparkle', patience 'runs low', blood 'runs cold', ambition 'puffs people up', vengeance 'intoxicates', blood 'boils' and so on'.

These typological similarities appear with particular expressiveness in the creations of humanity, insofar as we are concerned with the documents of the Paleolithic. The uniformity of forms of all these stone cutters, axes, scrapers, arrows and so on dug up in various corners of the globe, and the identical methods of their production, are staggering to us.

If we make it a goal to look for parallel correspondences, then it is possible to track this typological similarity both in the remains of material culture and in mythology – the settings of thought, language and so on – from the shores of the Atlantic, through Europe and Asia, encompassing the entire Mediterranean basin with its ancient worlds (Egypt, Central Asia, the Caucasus, Persia, the Mesopotamian world), India, China and further on across the Pacific to both North and South America and their aboriginal populations, as well as among the Australian and African tribes. Cultural historians and the theoreticians of comparative mythology have tried to trace this on a larger or smaller scale, but drew only general conclusions about 'the unity of the human intellect' (?!) from this.

Various attempts were undertaken to give a theoretical basis and explanation for these convergences in the stock of ideas, customs and beliefs among the most different peoples and tribes, and a number of theories were put forward that we will briefly investigate here.

The Theory of Dispersion

§ 68
The majority of researchers held to the standpoint that many customs, beliefs and inventions encountered in various countries, constituting the common heritage of all peoples, were inherited from earliest times when the human race inhabited only a small part of the land. The universal features of culture, the inventions and ideas prevailing everywhere were dated by these researchers to the era of initial human successes, achieved in the period preceding the 'universal dispersion' of the human race to all corners of the globe. They believed

that such basic types of activity as the art of acquiring fire, drilling, cutting, chiseling rocks and the like date back to the cradle of humanity, and that having subsequently dispersed, humanity scattered this initial heritage – on the basis of which every people further built their own type of culture – to the ends of the earth.

On the other hand, the same picture of the historical past is drawn by linguists, the adherents of the formalistic school of comparative linguistics who, starting from a certain classification of languages, occupied themselves with questions of the theoretical construction of ur-languages, ur-mythology, ur-peoples and so on.

All these views ultimately rest on a theory of the monogenesis of humanity and on the connected views of a universal dispersion of peoples and culture. However, when dealing with the American continent and the American peoples, for example, the pathos of universal dispersion cools down in the majority of researchers. In the meantime, forms that are similar to each other as regards both the data of material culture and customs, myths and so on are encountered on both sides of the Pacific. And while many of those on the continents of Europe and Asia are explained exclusively by migration, the rights of independent origins and development are put forth on the other side of the ocean.

Academician Ivan Meshchaninov rightly spoke ironically on the method of research according to which, for example, the painted ceramics of Tripoli, Kyzyl-Vank, Annau, Elam and China are taken and thrown together in one pile, tracing the kinship of China with Annau and even Elam, and on that basis looking for the common centre of origin of this art, 'disseminating therefrom to all the other places. All this', Meschaninov notes, 'is possible, since the world tolerates everything. But there is this kind of pottery in the Americas; it has been found in the Pueblo Cranda de Nevada and has been dated to several centuries BCE. And I am afraid that in the general rush of migratory enthusiasm, for example, Nakhichevan pottery will now be 'explained' by parallel lateral East-West comparisons and by the discovery of a single centre from which it moved to the shores of the Aras, whereas the existence of painted ceramics in America will be ascribed to independent appearance and development *in situ*. And out of all the regions indicated, only this one alone will be given such an explanation ... I cannot digest the proposition that only large expanses of water provide the right to the independent development and the manifestation of one cultural form or another in different places'.[3]

---

3 Meshchaninov 1928, p. 226.

On the other hand, there are daredevils of theory whom even oceans do not impede and then, heaping Pelion on Ossa, they launch the migration of peoples across the Bering Strait into the Americas. The majority of authors place the cradle of humanity in Asia,[4] and then scholars lead one branch of this primordial humanity by means of migration to the shores of the Pacific and move them further along the entire eastern Asian seaboard in order to fling them across the Bering Strait onto the American continent and move them along the western shore of North America, thus populating all of North and South America with American peoples introduced from Asia. There is yet another variant, according to which America was united with Europe in the Pliocene and, tearing away from the 'Old World', brought its first inhabitants with it (Ehrenreich).

Resisting all these awkward conglomerations is the simple question: why is it necessary to assume that humanisation has to have arisen, without fail, at some single point? It is impossible to understand what advantage one place (whether it is the Iranian plateau or the Altai) has over many! There are no rational grounds for this, but there are many grounds that contradict this.

If it is even to be granted that people brought the elementary habits of culture – primitive tools; the means to work stone, wood and bone; the acquisition of fire and basic ideological formations – with them from their initial cradle, then research would be faced with even greater predicaments; for in that case it would have to explain why the same methods (e.g. of mastering fire) were not known everywhere. Why did some peoples from this generally necessary initial heritage lose something and consign it to oblivion, and others preserve it?

In addition, parallelisms and correspondences are encountered not only as regards primordial forms, habits and thoughts but also as regards new formations and the latest discoveries – and then this cumbersome general theory of 'a single cradle of humanity and the dispersion of cultures' from a single centre simply cannot explain the facts.

The Theory of Borrowing

§ 69
In aid of the theory of the universal dispersion of peoples, and as a supplement to it, yet another theory is put forward: the theory of borrowing. If the ancestral home of humanity was sought in the previous case, here the question is restric-

---

4 Some are inclined to consider the Iranian plateau to be this place (Tylor 1924), others believe it to be central Siberia (Morgan 1909), yet others prefer the Altai, still others central and western Europe (Wilke 1923).

ted to those looking for the birthplace of one or another idea or discovery (e.g. the site of the beginnings of certain mythological subjects, customs and beliefs) and from there, these ideas settle around the world by way of borrowing from one another.

The Romantic era in particular assisted in turning the gaze of scholars to the countries of the East, which were believed to be the inexhaustible sources of all wisdom and seed beds for all legends, cults and so on.

Typically, the views of many scholars of the time – advocates of borrowing – did not stray very far from the views that dominated back in the preceding century. In his time, Julius Braun also did not doubt that the mythology of all people supposedly was in essence only the repetition of a single ur-mythology; in particular, as an advocate of Egypt, he tried to produce all the parallels from Egyptian myths.[5] The theory of borrowing from one source, in both Julius Braun and Otto Gruppe,[6] rested on the premise that humanity in general was capable of producing a small quantity of ideas, and – having been born in one place – these achievements spread only through borrowing.

It is self-evident that among separate individuals some kind of interaction has always existed, and consequently there was mutual influence and borrowing of every type. If this is our aim, then it is possible to count a great number of individual borrowings that have a place in history. But taking the theory of borrowing as a fundamental principle and methodological premise would be quite mistaken.

First, with such an approach, where the researcher is above all preoccupied with ascertaining the location of the borrowing and not the essence of the object itself, it is possible to find any parallel at all for any object in other parts of the world among different peoples. When a researcher who is well versed in only one certain branch of history produces these comparisons, parallels chiefly to the benefit of that specific cultural sphere fall right into their hands. Characteristic of the hypotheses of borrowing is that at any given moment, that specific sphere of culture presently in the foreground of scientific interest is taken as the starting point and seed bed of legends, beliefs and myths. So, at in the early nineteenth century, India was acknowledged to be this primordial homeland of almost every legend; mid-century it was Egypt; and then Babylon turned up in their place.

Tying in this manner the biased conviction to all historical objects that they were brought from somewhere, they were all heaped into a single pile in which almost nothing remained unborrowed. As a result of this, historical research

---

5 Braun 1864.
6 Gruppe 1887.

concentrated only on one particular kind of specific cultural world that was considered to be some sort of universal breeding ground for the manufacture of all sorts of historical forms and the inexhaustible source of continual borrowings. Thus, certain countries and peoples were elevated to extraordinary suprahistorical heights, and others were denied the ability to create any kind of culture whatsoever. It is this caricature of history that to this day is presented by bourgeois ideologists as a historical science in which all actually existing proportions and relations are distorted.

Second, the advocates of the 'comparative historical method' who believe borrowing to be the main agent of historical creation almost never ask questions about the actual causes of the origin and development of specific historical formations. Many historical explorations leave the impression that the researcher is fully satisfied if they succeeded in replacing one unknown with another, more often than not even greater but further away and much earlier unknown: something Egyptian or Babylonian. Always assuming the borrowing of only finished forms, the researcher never completes work on the important question: why did these forms arise and how did they take shape?

Third, the theory of borrowing is based on the assumption that borrowing presents no difficulties, as if everything that people come into contact with can be mastered by them. Otto Gruppe expressed this opinion in his propositions on 'adaptionism', as if spiritual formations (beliefs, myths and so on), no less than social formations (the state, laws, customs) arose with extraordinary difficulty but, once having arisen, were easily mastered by others. In Gruppe's opinion, these historical formations arose once, and all further history is the history of their alteration over the course of their uninterrupted imitation and 'roaming'.[7]

What is usually left out of account is that every borrowing requires a specific peak of cultural development, specifically a peak that would measure up to the borrowed object. If some nationality achieves the stage of development at which it is capable of borrowing some cultural achievement or other, it can arrive at these forms independently sooner or later.

It need not be thought that people around the world borrowed the means of obtaining fire, animistic ideas, ancestor worship or animal fables from each other. The flimsiness of the theory of borrowing is not in the fact that there are not similar cases in the history of the development of societies, but in the fact that borrowing is not a sufficient explanation and is itself a problem, essentially the same as independent creation.

---

7   Gruppe 1887, Vol. I, p. 267.

The Theory of the Identity of the Human Mind

§ 70

Certain sociologists of the 'neopositivist' school, and representatives of ethno-psychology advanced the following consideration: the intellectual organisation of humans, and the properties of their minds are generally identical around the world and over the entire course of history. Owing to the identity of the human mind, they said, and to the similarity of reactions to internal and external stimuli resulting from this, people everywhere developed in the exact same direction, making similar discoveries and developing similar customs, beliefs and so on.

'If there is a fact firmly established by anthropology', said Wilhelm Wundt, 'it is the fact that the properties of human thinking and feelings and the effects that influence the work of the imagination in all their essential features are identical in people at all latitudes and in all countries. There is no need for the transgressive boundary of any possible argument for the hypothesis of migration in order to explain the similarity of certain mythological ideas'.[8] These similarities were explained by the unity of the human mind in general, and moreover existing local differences were explained by the influence of external causes.

Some believed the coincidence of certain features in the constitution of thinking, in customs, inventions, types of social organisation to be an argument proving the unity of the human mind in general. 'It must be', they said, 'that the laws of human thinking and the structure of the human mind are identical here and everywhere, since such coincidences are encountered independently of each other'.

Others, on the other hand, believed the unity of the mind and the identity of the laws of the human psyche to be the argument proving these coincidences. The constructs of Edward Bennett Tylor, James George Frazer, Andrew Lang – and in general the entire animist school – are based on this.

It is easy to see that the proof in both cases is inadequate. The general identity of the laws of the human intellect, taken by theory as a self-evident premise, is least understood and most in need of explanation. The theoreticians, however, avoid this. The history of human development reveals facts refuting similar opinions and proving that the thinking of the people of different eras and different cultural stages differ radically from one another. The assumption that consciousness has some kind of independent laws and thus –

---

8 Vundt 1913, p. 32.

no matter where it develops – is identical everywhere and always creates identical formations is essentially incorrect. Cognitive activity differs from instinctual and reflexive actions in that it does not blindly repeat the exact same thing, but in each individual case acts in accordance with the sense of the situation itself and in accordance with the requirements of the given task. The act of thought, in contrast to instinctual actions, must precisely be different and not identical. If, despite this, experience shows facts of startling convergences, then the explanation should be sought not so much in the subjective features and laws of consciousness as much as in the objective causes.

Advancing a general proposition about the universal identity of the laws of the human intellect, theoreticians save themselves from the necessity of concrete explanations of specific historical facts (i.e. they abandoned things that were more essential from the standpoint of science).

Considering only convergences, advocates of the comparative method in the majority of cases lost sight of those essential differences which, moreover, were present both with regard to social structures and to ideological formations. There is no doubt, however, that only that theory is valuable and close to reality that is able to explain parallelisms and convergences along with the differences and divergences that are present.

In the system of views of Kantian philosophy, this problem of convergences and parallelisms in thinking generally does not exist. The Kantians guarantee themselves through a special metaphysics: the study of transcendental categories of the intellect, to which – as *a priori* necessary forms of consciousness – all thinking and all experience must submit. But here, the Kantians encounter insurmountable difficulties in the facts: the norms of thinking of the most socially advanced consciousness appeared to be different from the thinking of, for example, the peoples of totemic societies. The Kantians generally avoid raising such questions and try to circumvent them wherever possible. Primarily occupied with the epistemological problems of the physical and mathematical exact sciences, the Kantians are inclined to attribute all other forms of thinking to 'unscientific' and 'pre-logical' forms of thinking, attempting to squeeze them into specific schemas of the 'transcendental conditions of cognition'. Characteristic in this regard is the attempt of Ernst Cassirer.[9] He attempts to prove that mythological thinking represents the first stage of the 'organisation of experience' in the Kantian sense of the phrase, and thus lay a bridge from 'mythological thinking' to scientific thinking. Not that this attempt was crowned with success. A gulf has formed here as a result of the essentially ahis-

---

9 Cassirer 1925, pp. 39–46.

torical arrangement of all Kantian philosophy and, by preserving the fundamental assumptions of Kantianism about the apriority of intellectual categories and the spontaneous self-activity of consciousness, this gulf is impossible to bridge.

The French sociologist Emile Durkheim proposed, as it were, a historical solution to this question by putting forward a theory of the 'social *a priori*'.

Durkheim, as he himself commented on it, accept the general attitudes of apriorism: 'The fundamental proposition of apriorism has it that knowledge consists of a twofold class of elements that are not reducible to each other (from empirical data and *a priori* categories – км). Our hypothesis holds this principle completely'.[10] Moreover, Durkheim insists on only one thing: the social character of these categories of thinking, which Kant and the Kantians believed to be transcendentally *a priori*. As for the rest, he remains in full agreement with the fundamental propositions of Kantian theory. Durkheim's attempt boils down to placing a sociological foundation under the abstractly logical categories and principles of Kantian epistemology, and softening the ahistorical tendencies of rationalist metaphysics of the unchangeable and absolute forms of thinking with sociological corrections and the introduction of historical moments into them.

Durkheim also believed, like Kant, that all thinking is inevitably determined by the *a priori* categories of the intellect. Durkheim only substitutes 'collective ideas' for the transcendental categories of Kant, remaining apart from that on the Kantian standpoint. 'At the base of our judgements', he says, 'there is a certain number of essential concepts that govern all of our intellectual life; philosophers since the time of Aristotle have called them the categories of reason ... They (the categories) are, as it were, the basic frameworks that comprises thought; the latter can be liberated from them only having destroyed itself ... They compose, as it were, the 'backbone of thought''.[11]

From here it is obvious that the beliefs of Durkheim and his followers about the 'social *a priori*' are essentially the same metaphysics as the transcendental apriorism of Kant and the Kantians.

It should be asked, however: are any kind of categories of thinking really necessary in order for the comprehension of things and the resolution of situations to be generally possible? It seems to use that there is no such necessity; in any case this necessity has not been proven by anyone. In order, for example, for a child of eighteen months to make sense of a simple situation and rationally

---

10   Durkheim 1914, Book 2, p. 37.
11   Durkheim 1914, Book 2, pp. 27–8.

solve an elementary task of location, they do not need categories of thinking as they don't have them (like certain animals, judging by the data of well-verified experimenters). The child performs the necessary semantic comparisons on the spot, without the help of any sort of special categories existing in consciousness. 'Categories' of thinking, insofar as they arise and exist as specified patterns and templates (traditions) of thought, do not so much help thinking – as was generally believed – as much as, more often than not, they hinder the ascent of new thoughts. Generally speaking, Francis Bacon's proposition of the *idola* happens to propagate significantly further than was imagined up to now, including into a 'category of thinking'.

Finally, the standpoint presented by Adolf Bastian belongs to this group of theories.[12] In Bastian's opinion, the forms of human thought are homogeneous not only in the cultural spheres of identical degrees of development, but the fundamental identity of the forms of human thought can be decisively observed universally and in all times. Bastian believed that certain specific types of thought exist independently of the conditions under which humans live, and whatever their social relations and the level of mental development are. He described these fundamental forms of thought as 'developing with iron necessity everywhere humans live' and 'elementary ideas'. The human mind is such that these ideas are primordially inherent to it, and no further thought can explain their oirigin, as we ourselves are compelled to think in the form of these elementary ideas. This, the question is transferred into the sphere of the unknown, and the possibility of further research stops.

All similar theories are general and abstract, hardly explaining anything; we understand the facts just as well with them as without them.

The Geographical Theory

§71

Friedrich Ratzel and others saw the general cause of convergences and parallelisms in the influences of natural and geographical conditions in the life of peoples.

We will not dwell on the well-known deficiencies of this ancient theory. This standpoint leaves a most fundamental thing out of account: humans' use of the forces and gifts of nature depends not only on the existence of these gifts in nature.

---

12 Bastian 1860 and 1893.

The valley of the Tigris and Euphrates, despite its natural wealth and geographical amenities, was a sterile plain or arid desert (depending on the season) fatal to the life of the primeval Sumerian tribes with a low level of technology. Only after labour radically changed the nature of the river valley could natural forces become forces useful to humanity. After all, the broadest use of slave labour was required in order for these wretched places to become the richest granaries ('God's garden' – the meaning of 'Babylon' in ancient European) and the luxuriant cultural centre of the ancient world.

It should not be left out of account that the gifts of nature must first become the productive forces of society in order to influence the development of society and condition that development. The initial causes of the development of social forms should therefore be sought not in nature as such, but in the development of the productive forces of social relations. 'As soon as the initial animal state ends, the power of man over nature is always connected with his existence as a member of a commune, a family, a clan and so on, with his relation to other men who condition his relation to nature' (Marx).

The theory of natural conditions does not explain the problem of interest to us, seeing that among people living under identical geographical and natural conditions, sharp differences are very often discovered in the means of production, in social relations, in the forms of culture, customs, beliefs and world views. And vice versa, among peoples inhabiting different geographic settings, social formations of the same time can be – and are – encountered.

Shortcomings of the Existing Hypotheses

§ 72
All the theories enumerated here and the multiplicity of their variations were put forward to explain parallelisms and convergences in the features of the social and spiritual life of peoples.

In order to test their quality once again, try explaining the essence of the question of parallelism to a person who is a stranger to any scientific theories and see what solutions to this question they are able to provide. Tell them that interesting coincidences exist in formations among different peoples, and ask them to try to explain the cause of these coincidences.

Similar attempts we have repeated numerous times in almost every case ended up with the subject, after some reflection, enumerated notions on the spot about a single origin of humanity (theory of dispersion), about the propagation of the same forms owing to mutual influence (theory of borrowing), ideas about the identity of human nature in general (corresponding to psychological theories) and about the influence of the natural environment (geographical theory). Ideas about accidental coincidences were even added to all this. All this was expressed in other terms, but sometimes the formulations directly coincided with the scientists' formulations.

It is extraordinarily characteristic of the state of the theory that scientists who have devoted themselves to the study of these special questions do not wish to go further and cannot show anything better than anything the first layman you meet tells you. What is more, the layman more often than not proves to be more versatile: they state a larger quantity of possibilities, they enumerate almost all the existing theories while the specialists most often see only one favourite path.

On the other hand, we have a very obvious example here of how people can, independently of one another, arrive at the same thoughts and conclusions. In the given case, neither 'settling people elsewhere', nor 'borrowing' from others, nor 'being exposed to geographic conditions', nor calling on the identity of the layman's psychology with the psychology of the scientist for help are necessary. Coinciding opinions about the causes of parallelism were obtained because the problem itself only has a few variations of possible solutions (of course, excluding completely improbable ones of the kind, for example, that some sort of demon whispers the same things to people). And above all, the simplest and most superficial of these solutions are noted. Thus, the solutions of one identical task given to many people will naturally coincide, but not so much around one response as around several, since objectively the task has a certain quantity of possible solutions, of which the most superficial are most often expressed and therefore more often than not coincide. But scientific research and scientific theory must differ from stray thoughts in that they cannot catch hold of the first idea that comes into someone's head, but must stifle such impulses and seek further. 'Good' is the theory that takes as a fundamental principle the first idea that comes to mind and makes it the foundation of all further efforts and scientific constructions!

Questions of Parallelisms in the Marxist Interpretation

§73
Academician Ivan Meshchaninov, taking the question of convergences and parallelisms, notes that similar conditions of economic and social life are the cause of similar forms of cultural creation.[13]

---

13   Meshchaninov 1928, p. 236.

This proposition is correct, but excessively general; it is derived from a certain basic proposition of Marxism about the mutual dependence of the base and the superstructure. But the Marxist method requires that conclusions from general propositions be concretised in their application to individual questions.

First, it remains unexplained how and why these identical conditions emerge, where the similarity of economic and social conditions comes from, or if we agree that these conditions are created by humanity itself.

Second, the development of this general proposition must not lead to the conclusion that identical cultural features always and everywhere must develop under the influence of the exact same causes, and must not lead to the strict identity of the stages of development of all societies. Such an understanding is alien to Marxism. The development of individual societies independently of one another involves similar formations; people often arrive at identical results starting from different goals and prompted by different conditions and causes. The replacement, for example, of matriarchal institutions with patrilineal ones is almost universal, but the exact same causes did not give rise to it everywhere. In some places it occurred under the pressure of settling down from nomadism and the supplanting of the hunt by farming; in others owing precisely to the supremacy of the hunt and so on. Different economic foundations held up communal property in different tribes. Marx noted, for example, that '[t]he first form of property, in the ancient world as in the Middle Ages, is tribal property, determined with the Romans chiefly by war, with the Germans by the rearing of cattle'.[14] The exact same decorative motifs – geometrical forms, for example – could develop from both vegetational ornaments and from the techniques of the work itself (e.g. braiding as it occurred in reality).

Third, the path from identical social and economic conditions to identical ideological formations cannot be covered by a single general proposition, thus circumventing the most essential thing – a concrete analysis of the forms of this dependence. It is necessary to show in more detail how identical social and economic conditions can create an identical way of thinking, and to reveal the internal mainspring and the internal essence of the dependence taking place here. A general question about parallel correspondences should thus, for greater precision, be differentiated into two questions:

1. How is the similarity or difference of tasks that emerge before people explained? Why do similar needs and requirements, and problems of the same type, arise independently of each other?

---

14   Marks i Engel's 1933, p. 52 [Marx and Engels 1975–, Vol. 5, p. 89].

2. How is the coincidence and similarity of type of results, discoveries, achievements and formations at which peoples arrive independently of each other explained?

The formulation given by Meshchaninov touches on the first of these questions but does not deal with the second; it does not explain why identical – and sometimes also heterogeneous – economic conditions and tasks lead to coincident results, achievements, thought formations and so on.

Marx said that humans differ from animals in that they act in accordance with predetermined goals, starting from representations and ideas constructed by them in their heads. *Aber spinnt er weder Zweck noch Mittel aus sich selbst heraus*, similar to the way that the spider spins its web. People's goals and tasks are goals engendered by their needs, which stopped being the biological needs of the animal and became social, historical and economic needs. If human needs were limited only to the biological sphere, there would be just as little concern for their satisfaction as there is among 'the fowls of the air, [who] sow not, neither do they reap ...'. and therefore do not think. This is why the question of the coincidence and of parallel types arises as a problem only as regards people, and never as regards animals. Animals must, with the inevitability of a natural law, be identical: a bee, insofar as it is a bee, can produce only honey and nothing more.

Humanity's means for realising their goals are also not granted by nature. Every generation finds in existence 'a mass of productive forces, capital funds and circumstance, which on the one hand is indeed modified by the new generation, but on the other also prescribes for it its conditions of life and gives it a definite development ...'.[15]

Goals and tasks arise in society independently of the will of separate individuals; they are conditioned by social relations and the forces of production. The maturation of social needs, and consequently of new goals and problems, takes place through objective conformity to the laws of history (see Chapter 9).

The new needs and tasks that arise in this way affect the interests of an ever larger multitude of individuals orienting their consciousness in a certain manner and imparting to it a specific general direction.

Placed before specific needs, requirements and tasks, either do not overcome them (and hence the problem remains, constantly impelling consciousness in a certain direction) or ultimately people solve them in one way or another, and inasmuch as every task of a practical or theoretical type is a relation of data that permits one or several *specific* solutions, then wherever this occurs – in Australia or in the Pamirs – the results will coincide.

---

15 Marks i Engel's 1933, p. 28 [Marx and Engels 1975–, Vol. 5, p. 54].

Thus the question about the parallelisms of thought and coincident formations finds its solution in the identity, or even the difference, of tasks *that have, however, coincident solutions.*

It should not, of course, be thought that one or another discovery or new formation immediately leaps out in finished form, like Athena from the head of Zeus. On the contrary, every achievement – even every individual discovery – occurs as a protracted process of gradual historical preparation *by separate parts and stages,* passing through such a multiplicity of hands and brains that of course the result more often than not is completely impersonal.

Once it was necessary for humanity to deal with a specific material – wood, for example – and to process it, then a certain form of axe became historically inevitable. Thus a stone washed by a current grinding away sharp edges inevitably takes on a rounded shape that is more suited to rolling, only with the difference that here the process runs blindly and spontaneously, while in social activity this 'grinding off edges' and the adaptation of the form of things for their purpose is performed by people. Anywhere urgent needs compelled people to take specific objects for their activity, the material itself to a certain extent suggested the methods of its mastery.

The forms of manifestation of culture and intellect and the forms of activity among people are identical not because the human mind and mental constitution of humanity is identical in general, but because specific social relations, material and social conditions compelled people to a certain type of activity and means of thought, and in accordance with this formulated the identical or different psychology of people, societies and so on.

All the questions of parallel types become significantly easier for us if we consider the *material criteria of determination,* if we take into account the role and meaning of the object, the objective structure of the task of comprehension and of the objects of activity with which humans have to deal.

We of course do not at all wish to say that with this the universal means of explaining all particular cases and separate coincidences – something along the lines of a general formula – has been found; on the contrary, we hold the opinion that any universalism must be cast aside when it is a question of explaining concrete events that were created by concrete causes and conditions. Saying why coincidences of such and such a type exist in spheres of such and such a type is possible only when they are studied separately and actually concrete foundations are brought into the proof.

To clarify what has been said above, we will take a few examples from completely different spheres of experience: the first from the sphere of material culture (§ 74), the second from the sphere of calculating time (§ 75) and the third from the sphere of the typology of thinking (§ 76).

On the Origin of the Tinderbox

§ 74

It is well known that the primitive means of producing fire was the same among almost all peoples. In general, they come down to three basic types: 1) producing fire through friction, 2) through drilling or 3) making sparks by striking flint.

Primitive man could not *invent* friction or drilling as a means of producing fire. This would have meant immediately making *two* gigantic discoveries without any background preparation: first, foreseeing the tremendous benefit of fire without being practically acquainted with it, and second, arriving at the means of producing it through intellectual reflection. There could not be such vast knowledge in a primordial consciousness.

In order to see the link between drilling and the appearance of fire and in order to use this link, both these elements (the practice of drilling and the use of fire) had to be already known separately to humans. They had to already know beforehand the benefit of fire, otherwise they would not have obtained it. Without doubt, humans used fire long before they knew how to obtain fire. Their first acquaintance with fire, Karl von den Steinen said, originates from the use of fire found in nature, where it could arise according to different elemental causes (lightning, the friction of dried branches, volcanoes and so on) and spread as forest or prairie fires.[16]

These assumptions of Steinen's should generally be considered more likely than others. But starting from here, Steinen drew unlikely conclusions about the first discoveries of the means of obtaining fire. 'Humans noted', he said, 'how during powerful storms and winds, dry tree branches and boughs rubbed against each other and caught fire. Without analysing this phenomenon, they began imitating it ... they sought out dry pieces of wood and began rubbing one on the other ... It is quite possible, having noted that rubbing wood heats it, they understood that friction produces a high degree of heat – i.e. fire(?!). In all likelihood, the discovery that wood began to emit smoke and finally glow gladdened them immensely'.[17]

Here, the consciousness of early humans is ascribed the force of speculative reflection, surpassing everything known to us up to that time in its brilliance! Primitive humans could not arrive at drilling or friction through reflection. Primitive consciousness was not occupied with the observance of nature and

---

16   Steinen 1897, p. 212.
17   Steinen 1897, pp. 217–18.

the theoretical search for the causes of this or that phenomenon. *There could be no invention here.* Praxis itself had to bring consciousness to this idea and put *right into the hands* of primitive man the means of obtaining fire, otherwise no keen intellect would have been able to reach such a colossal discovery. Evidently, the process did not run from the goal (fire) to the search for the means and techniques of obtaining it (friction, drilling), but in the opposite order: the praxis of drilling wood and its polishing was often accompanied by unforeseen collateral phenomena – light smouldering or even the ignition of the piece of wood being worked on.

We actually find material in the ethnographic literature that thoroughly confirms this proposition. It covers, for example, drilling holes in the ends of bows using wooden sticks, which is widespread among Australian, African and many other tribes.

According to the account of Leo Frobenius, the 'Omulungi (a tribe living in what is now western Tanzania) attach a bow string to the bow, having drilled a hole each on both ends. To do this, they lay the bow on the ground and hold it with their knees. They then take a stick of hard wood, place it perpendicular to the place where the hole is to be made, and begin twisting the stick between their palms in one spot until the bow has been drilled through. When this work – which often requires several days – is done, the spot is rubbed with oil. When a traveler gave them an iron nail and suggested doing the work with that tool, they refused the offer with a derisive smile, noting that the bow, when being tightened later, could crack – if it did not happen earlier during the drilling of the hole. Almost every African and Madagascan tribe, and all the peoples of the Pacific, drill small holes in the same manner as these people'.[18] During such actions, the wood naturally can smoulder and catch fire slightly at the drilling spot.

The entire question is why people paid attention to these cases – how could they understand their significance, use and hold on to them? It presents difficulties, the size of which is now not easy for us to judge after the 'cart of history' has already traveled this entire path of development. According to the testimony of certain scientists, quite recently there were tribes who did not themselves know how to obtain fire and only put all their art into preserving it. Frobenius pointed out one such tribe in Papua New Guinea.[19] Wilhelm Schmidt cites information about the Adamanese tribe: *'Zwar besitzen die Andamanesen jetzt, das Feuer, aber immer nur an einem schon vorhandenen Feuer angezündet;*

---

18   Frobenius 1910, p. 310.
19   Frobenius 1910 p. 306.

überall, im Hause, auf dem Schiff bei Seefahrten, wird sorgfältig ein Feuer oder Feuersglut lebendig erhalten; im Falle des Erlöschens wären sie nicht imstande, selbst ein neues Feuer zu entzünden ...'.[20]

If everything that humans happened to face in the course of their lives could be kept and rationally used, then all the great discoveries of history would perhaps have been made during humanity's very first steps. Having no idea about the benefit of fire, humans would not know how to use these occurrences (of easy ignition during drilling); they would try to eliminate them as phenomena injurious to their goal (the preparation of a bow) – that is, they would act fully against the discovery.

Second, in order to make use of the occurrences of the appearance of the faint signs of fire, a great deal of experience in the handling of fire is needed. Try lighting a campfire from weakly smouldering tinder – it requires a great deal of ability and a particular technique. Humans had to learn all this in the period preceding the ability to obtain fire. When people made use of fire but did not know how to obtain it, they naturally had to apply all their efforts to preserving a fire and not letting it go out. A fire dying out under these conditions was evidently a great misfortune. A primitive horde then had to take fire from other tribes, which in turn was connected with particular difficulties (the complexity of carrying fire over long distances, the cultural significance of often not permitting fire to be given to others, and so on). In general, fire had to be protected.

The remnants of such a vigilant relationship to fire has been preserved in many places among many peoples: the custom of preserving an undying hearth, the cult of the vestal virgin (special priestesses whose role included constantly sustaining a religious flame), tales of 'unquenchable fire', even up to such rites as the widespread 'unquenchable vigil light' hanging in front of icons in the services of the Christian cult that came down to us having evidently passed through a long series of different interpretations. One interesting custom is preserved in many places in the Caucasus, where when a family moves to another location, fire from the old hearth is taken and carried to the new one. We encounter similar customs almost everywhere among different peoples. The ancient Greeks, resettling in distant colonies, carried fire from their hearths with them. The expressions 'extinguished hearth' (თამყრალი კერა, *thamqrali kera*) or 'cold hearth' (გათივებული კერა, *gathivebuli kera*) in Georgian

---

20 Schmidt 1910, p. 63. [Although the Andamanese now possess the fire, it is always only lit from an already existing fire; everywhere, in the house, on the ship during sea voyages, a flame or blazing fire is carefully kept alive; in case of extinction, they would not be able to kindle a new fire themselves – ed.]

signify the death of a family or clan. 'May your hearth die out' (დაგეფსოს კერა, *dagephsos kera*) is one of the most terrible curses in Georgian speech. The myth of Prometheus must be connected here. The basic motif of the legend of Prometheus, who stole fire from the gods for humans, most likely traces its roots back to the world view inherited from the era when people made use of fire but could not obtain it. The necessity of stealing fire from the heavens somehow does not tie in with the ability to freely reproduce fire when it is first needed.

A lengthy period, over the course of which humans had to constantly see to the maintenance of a fire and protect it in every way possible, inevitably had to produce a sufficiently complex technique of using fire: humans became familiar with easily inflammable substances and with materials that smouldered slowly and kept a flame for a long time (decayed wood, different types, hard wood and so on); they had to excel in the skill of carrying fire during their constant moves from place to place, in the art of lighting a fire from little smouldering sparks, and so on.

All this is only the first series of conditions: people had to be prepared through experience and the technological equipment for perceiving fire that accidentally manifested itself. The second series of necessary circumstance is linked with the objective situation: fire has to *emerge precisely in human hands in the process itself of their activity*, otherwise they cannot test the link that exists here between friction and the phenomenon of ignition. It is very difficult to assume that early man, observing the friction of dried branches from the wind, understood that friction engenders flame.

Only owing to the coincidence of the two series of conditions indicated could humanity make use of these cases of the unforeseen manifestation of fire in the process of their economic activity and arrive at the 'discovery' of the tinderbox.

It must be emphasised that this discovery could occur only in the process of economic activity. We find striking evidence of this in the ethnography of culturally primitive tribes. In Micronesia, for example, Frobenius said that the *device for obtaining fire serves* other goals simultaneously, specifically *as an augur* for drilling shells. Sufficiently frequent coincidences of these tools are encountered in many other places: the tools for obtaining fire are simultaneously used simply as a drilling apparatus.

This proposition is further corroborated by the fact that in certain places *the same people engage* in both handicrafts. 'The drilling itself, among the Omulungi', according to Frobenius's evidence, 'is believed to be an art that not everyone can manage. Among the Omulungi, the same people who are occupied with lighting fires produce this'.

Consequently, an important fact is established: fire is obtained by precisely the same means with which the work of drilling is performed, and more often that not this operation is performed by the same people and the same tools.

But fire could arise in humans' hands not only when drilling (see page xxx, Fig. 1); it also arose in connection with performing other primitive work: when sawing something in two, for example, by using the sharp edge of one stick of bamboo on another (Fig. 2), when smoothing sticks or pieces of wood on each other (Fig. 3), or when *laying* grooves through rubbing the end of a hard stick on a much softer plank (Fig. 4), when striking two stones together, when chipping rocks, when chopping bamboo with a stone axe, the surface of which is rich in the flint that gives rise to sparks III – it is from here that the means of making fire through striking stones got its start.

All these primitive methods of work are historically attested, and each of them could inspire people to a specific means of obtaining fire with just as much success as drilling. Indeed, all existing means of obtaining fire repeat the description of form. Fig. 2 depicts the means by which Australian tribes obtain fire. Fig. 3 depicts the tinderbox of the East Indian archipelago. Fig. 4 is the means of obtaining fire in New South Wales. In Fig. 5, the tinderbox prevailing in Polynesia, and also encountered in the Congo, is presented. The means of making fire through striking rocks exists to this day everywhere in the Caucasus and in many other places.

The majority of scientists hold the opinion that three basic means of obtaining fire developed one from the other such that the process of development passed sequentially through all stages from friction to drilling, finally achieving the summit: the art of making fire. We believe that there was no such necessity in a sequential development of this kind, and that this process occurred differently.

The transition from friction to the idea of drilling is an insuperable path of development for the intellectual reflection of early man.

And to arrive at the idea of making fire from drilling is much more difficult than directly discovering the former when splitting stones or chopping bamboo. For this, it had to be known that drilling is also friction, a certain type of friction. But such broad generalisations are inaccessible to primitive consciousness; it was incapable of drawing such conclusions.

There are facts attested in ethnography saying that once a specific form of obtaining fire is proven (e.g. friction), then it is persistently held on to and is not replaced by other means (e.g. drilling) until all these primitive means are supplanted by means, such as matches, that cannot be competed with.

All the methods of obtaining fire listed above can fully emerge *independent of one another* and, most likely, this is how it occurred in reality. Historic-

Figure 2

Figure 3

Figure 4

Figure 5

ally, obtaining fire did not have one origin and no one line of development, but *several independent* sources and variants. In different parts of the world, people discovered one method or another, and developed them, independently of each other. And no matter how many objectively likely possibilities for the emergence of fire in the praxis of human activity there were, they were all found by people living under different conditions.

If these methods of obtaining fire at the various ends of the earth coincide, then this occurs in accordance with the principle that the task itself objectively always has a few variants of possible solutions. In a primitive economy, *only a few* paths for the emergence of fire exist; whether they were found in Africa or the Americas, everywhere they were the same. Insofar as people arrived at the discovery of fire, they ran across one of these possible variations, and hence the coincidences inevitably had to be grouped *around several* objectively possible types.

Parallelisms in the Sphere of Calculating Time

§ 75

The concept of time has historically always been linked with its practical calculation. Having some kind of idea of time means knowing how to count it somehow. Until the emergence of counting time, humans did not, and could not, have had an idea of it – like the animals, which although they possess some kind of instinctive sense of time do not have any conscious idea of it.

For contemporary thinking, time is like a one-dimensional linear continuity, monotonous at all points. Needless to say, primitive humans could not have had ideas about such an abstractly monotonous continuum. For primitive consciousness, time existed rather in separate segments, which were occupied with events or activities that were more or less important to it – and these intervals were far from uniform. It was as if time did not exist among these separate segments, but was some kind of 'indifferent state'. For us, it is now impossible to imagine conceiving the existence of 'gaps' or breaks in the temporal sequence in which time is absent. Primitive consciousness did not imagine that time existed everywhere and that it was always *uniform*.

The remnants of such partial ideas of time have been preserved up to the present. 'Certain African tribes', according to Bosman's information, 'distinguish time in a quite amusing fashion, specifically into lucky and unlucky time …'. Between 'the greater and lesser lucky periods' they count seven unlucky days, over the course of which they do not travel, hike or undertake anything significant, spending them doing nothing. Here, it is easy to detect the classical division into lucky and unlucky days, as with the Romans[21] (*dies nefasti*, 'ominous days' in contrast to the usual ones, *dies fasti*). To this day, Monday is in many places considered to be an unlucky day. In Georgian, such days have a special designation: კვიმატი დღეები (*k'vimati dgeebi*, which means 'hard or evil days'), corresponding to the classical *dies nefasti*.

Without a doubt, people formed the first ideas about time for themselves only after time actually began to play a certain role in their economy and under its influence. One idea or another about time was produced in conformity with what role time played in the distribution of specific economic concerns and actions. In Georgian, for example, we encounter the designations 'month of haying', 'month of reaping' and 'month of harvesting grapes'. In the Chukchi language, the division of time into months is interpreted exclusively from the standpoint of animal husbandry, in which the deer plays the main role among the Chukchi. January is called 'the time of the stubborn bull deer', February is 'the time of the shivering deer udder', March is 'the time when the udder sheds its hair', April is 'the time of the birth of calves', August is 'the time when the deer scrape their horns', and so on.

Insofar as the change from day to night, periods of warmth and cold, and periods of rain, snow and sunny weather all existed, people were not free in the selection of time and were compelled to structure their activity in conformity with these objective indicators of time.

Everywhere and among all peoples, since humans began counting time and formed some sort of idea about it, certain habits of the measurement and of the form of its calculation by days, weeks, years, economic periods, heavenly phenomena, by the moon (by the phases of the moon – the division into months occurred from this, as the analysis of the meaning of this work in many languages shows), by the sun and so on were produced. They are repeated universally, and it should not be thought that these are only accidental coincidences lacking support in objective reality. If these calculations of time did not inherently have a certain objective content in the praxis of social reality, then their frequent coincidence would have to be considered a miracle.

---

21   Lévy-Bruhl 1930, p. 286.

It should be thought that *arbitrary measurements of time have never existed in the history of humanity*. The division of time has historically always been conditioned by certain economic determiners. *Economic activity, forming and being grouped around certain points of time, lay at the basis of one or another division and calculation of time* that – in the majority of cases – was later anchored in a religious order. The ripening of certain fruits, the time of the hunt, the time of putting livestock out to pasture, the change of cold and warm periods, the flooding of rivers, the change of the characteristic winds or the alternation of periods of rain and dry weather all served as such points in different places and at different stages of the development of time, insofar as all this was closely linked with specific economic undertakings. Subsequently, the calculation of time was mainly built on the movement of heavenly bodies.

It has now been historically established that the Egyptians, back in deep antiquity, counted 365 days in the year, and the ancient Mayan culture of Mexico also had 365 days in the year, but here it is impossible to speak of some sort of borrowing. When these peoples worked out their calculations of time, they did not know of each others' existence. If borrowing occurred, then it would have had to also extend to the determination of months, the number of days in them and so on, whereas the Egyptian calendar has 12 months of 30 days each plus five extra days to make 265, but in the Mayan calendar there were 18 months of 20 days each plus five interstitial days.

Marx said that the astronomy and the calendar of the ancient Egyptians were created out of the necessity of calculating the flooding periods of the Nile. It was important to the ancient Egyptians to determine the periods of the year when the flooding of the Nile began (coinciding with the time of the solstice) in order to regulate their agricultural activities.[22] The coincidence in the number of days is, of course, conditioned by the fact that the year actually consists of 365.25 shifts of day and night. And when peoples achieved the degree of development at which it was necessary for them, in accordance with their agricultural needs, to take account of the entire period of a full revolution around the sun, then sooner or later each of them *in their own way* approached reality.

---

22   Marx 1923, p. 452 [Marx and Engels 1975–, Vol. 35, p. 515].

Convergences in the Realm of Types of Thinking

§ 76

The same principle remains in force if we take the most general case of parallelism, where coincidences concern not only individual details but the type of thinking in general. As an example, let us take magical thinking. It prevailed at a certain stage of development in almost all peoples, and can be observed among certain culturally less developed tribes even today. Lévy-Bruhl described this type of thinking in detail in a number of his well-known works.[23]

Lévy-Bruhl was inclined to explain such thinking by the fact that the consciousness of primitives was full of 'collective ideas', and under their influence it followed the path of 'mystical' connections and comparisons.

But thinking that is typologically similar with magical thinking is sometimes observed in the praxis of contemporary thinking, for example, in the form of everyday superstitions that quite educated people are sometimes disposed towards: artists, scientists, political figures and so on, about whose consciousness it cannot be said that they are guided by the 'collective ideas' of early humans. For them, a black cat crossing their path is a symbol of misfortune, and a broken mirror a great deal of unpleasantness. They have 'lucky' and 'unlucky' things they believe in, and which they carry with them as amulets.

If we look closely at where, and in which circles, superstitions are most often encountered, we note as a general rule that they are predominantly linked with certain professions and widespread in specific social circles. More often than not, they are encountered among hunters, sailors, people devoted to games of chance (cards, roulette, betting), in the world of the theatre among actors, stockbrokers, thieves and so on. In general, among all those professions where chance plays an important role.

This type of thinking – magical thinking – finds its support in specific spheres of experience, above all in the sphere of activity where success is subject to accidental fluctuations and depends not on the efforts of the subject but on alien forces and circumstances that humans can neither predict nor prevent; where there is no certainty that a certain action will without fail lead to a specific goal, where no result provided for in advance exists.

Such conditions objectively represent 'the conditions of fate' and a 'conjectural state'. Experience, in these cases, is something highly incoherent. No single datum of such experience provides a person with confidence in specific consequences. During the hunt, a small bush thrusting its way into the course

---

23   Lévy-Bruhl 1922; 1927; 1923.

of business could make a muddle of everything.[24] The structure of the experience is such that it provides no specific indications of what success depends on, and it is not known what relates to what. If the entire affair had been created by human hands and the entire series of dependencies had been constructed by people themselves, then it would be known which of the data relates to the essence of success and which does not. But in fact, this is not so. On the contrary, in all such cases consciousness is faced with the chaos of chance (i.e. faced with facts that objectively have no relation to each other). But consciousness must orient itself among them, must interpret and correlate facts that are in no mutual dependency whatsoever (i.e. interpret an objectively meaningless complex). Under these circumstances, only the arbitrary links of phenomena are possible. Consciousness thus acts, establishing links between things not on the place of actual dependencies, but on the plane of equivalences according to signs and omens – in a word, imagining magical correspondences and magical links between things.

Under conditions of the predominance of unforeseen hostile forces, humanity lived through a very long period that served as the actual basis for the emergence of the magical mode of thinking. Magical thinking predominated over a very long period of time, beginning with the era of primitive hunting society with a totemic world view and the stage of animistic representations and going through all of ancient history, through the Middle Ages with its demonology, angelology and so on, having been reduced to fragments up until our time as various religious beliefs.

Primitive humans were *constantly* surrounded by hostile forces, under conditions of the inconstancy of fate; this supported their magical thinking. But now people sometimes fall into a 'lucky situation' – more often than not people connected with a certain branch of activity, for example, gamblers, amateur hunters and so on, and then the inclination towards magical thinking revives; people begin to tell fortunes, make up superstitions, devise amulets and so forth.

Tellingly, superstitions are localised around a specific complex: hunters, for example, are superstitious in spheres related to hunting; but in everything else he may not be superstitious. Among gamblers, superstition is localised around the complex of the game, and outside the boundaries of this sphere they are usually fully rationally thinking people with a good sense of the real.

---

24 Here, of course, we have in mind not modern rationalised hunting – trawler fishing, for example – where chance plays an insignificant role, but primitive hunting and amateur sport hunting.

This serves as a striking confirmation of the proposition that the mode of thinking depends on the material of thinking, that the objective composition and structure of experience defines the form of thinking.[25]

Insofar as chance predominates in the life of people, so does cultural consciousness begin to manifest an inclination towards magical thinking, since in this case a certain field of experience is created that serves as a source feeding every type of superstition and keeping consciousness in a state of superstitious anxiety and fear.

When such a situation is eliminated and people become dependent on their activity, when they are made the masters of their fate and the creators of all the conditions of their life and not the playthings of the whims of a self-willed lord or the chance of the market, then superstition falls away and the inclination towards unreal imaginary links is ejected from consciousness, just as the basis for mythological thinking and myth creation in general is eliminated.[26] This thought is formulated with extraordinary imagery in Marx: 'Is the conception of nature and of social relations which underlies Greek imagination and therefore Greek [art] possible in the age of self-actors, railways, locomotives and electric telegraphs? What is Vulcan compared with Roberts and Co., Jupiter compared with the lightning conductor, and Hermes compared with the Crédit Mobilier? All mythology subdues, dominates and fashions the forces of nature in the imagination and through the imagination; it therefore disappears when real domination over these forces is established'.[27]

Social Existence and Social Consciousness

§ 77
When in the science of Marxism we are talking about the material and socially historical conditionality of forms of thinking and social consciousness, it seems to many that here there is a dependency of such an order that consciousness directly takes the organisational forms characterising the given society and makes them the norms of thinking. It was thought that, by analogy, there

---

25 We have looked into this question in greater detail in Megrelidze 1935c.
26 Or magic formulas and motives of superstition are switched and re-examined in such a way that they contain nothing magical in them. For example, the custom of covering one's mouth when yawning (and later making the sign of the cross over the mouth), which was at one point a preventive gesture against evil spirits or sickness that could rush in through an open mouth now has a rationalised meaning: 'it is impolite to show a wide-open mouth in society'.
27 Marks 1931b, p. 81 [Marx and Engels 1975–, Vol. 28, p. 47].

was a direct correspondence between social structure and the structure of thought. The theoretical constructions of Émile Durkheim and Marcel Mauss, for example, rest on such views.[28] Durkheim believed that people think in forms taken by analogy from the social structure, creating categories of thinking in the image and likeness of the organisational forms of society. Moreover, theoreticians concerned themselves only with establishing purely external resemblances between the organisational forms of society and the forms of thought. Many – like Aleksandr Bogdanov, for example – attempted to interpret the subordination and hierarchy of generic and specific concepts in the study of traditional logic as a direct transference of the feudal class hierarchy into the sphere of thinking.

Despite the fact that here, generally speaking, the possibility of some kind of correspondence is not excluded, such reasoning is incorrect since at issue in the given case are two spheres, the dependence between which in no way becomes more comprehensible from a formal analogy being established between them. It is possible to build such parallels anywhere by means of external comparisons with a certain strained interpretation, but this does not move us a single step forward in understanding the actual essence of the dependency at hand here.

Such theories grossly oversimplify and distort the ideas of Marxism. If the forms of thinking were only a simple repetition of the organisational forms of society, then consciousness would be a dead apparatus, pointlessly reproducing forms alien to it. It would not aid in the correct orientation of individuals, but would confuse them.

In Marx's opinion, the forms of thinking and of social consciousness depend on the development of the forces of production and on the relations of production in the sense that the latter determine people's needs and requirements, arrange them in a certain fashion, unite interests around certain tasks that divide or unite people in specific social forces, form opposing castes, classes, groups and so on, place before them certain tasks and stimulate their thoughts and actions in a certain direction.

Not only does the subject of history (humans and society) change in the process of historical development, but objects change as well; things, their roles and their meanings change and the objective content and actual meaning of the objects themselves becomes different. Moreover, the historical development of society gives birth to completely new objects never before seen, new types of plants and animals and new objects of industrial, economic and even

---

28   Durkheim and Mauss 1913.

theoretical interest. Synthetic rubber, the problems of nitrogen and the stratosphere could not always have been the object of human praxis and the objects of their thinking. They are brought forward by specific social and historical conditions, similar to the way in which the tasks of the proletariat as a class and hegemon, and the questions of subatomic energy and high voltage and so on could not arise in either the ninth century or the sixteenth.

Insofar as consciousness is compelled to solve them, new objects and tasks dictate the specific forms and methods of comprehension to it. In all these cases, thinking does not *simply reproduce one or another social structure* – this would be pointless – but *acts every time in accordance with the meaning of these objects and makes mental constructions that solve the given tasks*. Even quite recently, the development of new branches of mathematics and new methods of calculation were required in order to approach the solution of the questions of atomic physics and wave mechanics.

Material conditions, social relations, and the class struggle are thus the causes that form social consciousness, insofar as they determine the *interests* of people, put forward certain tasks, themes and problems and impart to consciousness a specific purposefulness. '[N]ew superior relations of production', Marx said, 'never replace older ones before the material conditions for their existence have matured within the framework of the old society. Mankind thus inevitable sets itself only such tasks as it is able to solve, since closer examination will always show that the problem itself arises only when the material conditions for its solution are already present or at least in the course of formation'.[29]

Insofar as historical development actualises specific objects of activity and of comprehension and sets up tasks and problems, and insofar as the latter have only *specific* solutions, then their solutions – and hence the means of thought within certain limits – will coincide, and the similarities can exist without any borrowings. '*Même nature*', said Marx, quoting Pierre Trémaux, '*mêmes facultés, renaîtront sur un même sol*'.[30]

---

29   Marks 1931a, p. 87 [Marx and Engels 1975–, Vol. 29, p. 263].
30   Marks i Engel's, Fridrikh 1928–1946 Vol. XXIII, p. 374 [Marx and Engels 1975–, Vol. 42, p. 305].

The Individual and Society

§78

When we say that objective conditions place people, independently of their wills and desires, into specific groups and classes, centring people's interests around certain goals and tasks; when we say that in the course of historical development, specific problems come to a head and certain tasks arise – that does not mean that all thoughts and actions of an individual taken separately always start from these shared goals, having to do specifically with them. On the contrary, in the majority of cases, people – living as a rule with their own closest interests – at first hardly notice these historical tasks and shared goals.

The directions of thoughts and actions of separate individuals is motivated by the most diverse circumstances and are different. The great number of chance stimuli compel individuals to think and act in their own way. Each separate individual has his/her own personal means of solving conflict; each person has his/her own personal 'logic' dependent on their personal qualities.

But such individual acts and phenomena do not organise social forces around themselves and do not create social opinion. In order for individual phenomena (or the acts of an individual person) to develop to the level of a social event, it is necessary for many people to be interested in it, for the interests of the masses to converge around this individual phenomenon or for the opposing interests of many to intersect at this point.

The most diverse ideas can be conceived in the brains of separate individuals, but this is not enough for the idea to acquire a *social* existence. An idea becomes a social idea only when it answers the interests of many individuals who readily pick it up.

Insight, the force of reason or talent alone is too little for an individual to be in a condition to assimilate, discover or invent something; people invent new ideas or assimilate ones already worked out on the basis of certain cultural accumulations. This accumulation is created by previous development and is the achievement of preceding generations, on whose shoulders every new generation stands. Each generation receives from the preceding one a certain sum of historically accumulated experience, a certain heritage of both spiritual culture and material means. It is clear that without differential calculus and Newtonian physics neither modern physics or modern chemistry would be possible, just as without the primitive steam boiler, the modern engine would be inconceivable.

Second, it is necessary that the problem itself (crystallising and being revealed with great precision in the course of development) frequently touches on the interests of people and induces their consciousness in a certain direction. As a result, the circle of people who are occupied with the given problem will gradually widen. The work of each on some aspect contributes to a solution, and the solution as a whole is prepared gradually in separate parts from various ends. In the history of humanity, not one major problem of a technological or theoretical type has been solved right from beginning to end by someone alone. Usually, every great problem is solved from different sides, in parts, by the work of many individuals besieging the question from different points, often not even suspecting the existence of the problem in all its scope.

The existence of a shared problem is realised owing to the fact that separate individual achievements, being arranged in a certain order and objectively being coordinated among themselves, gradually close up into some sort of whole.

Sometimes, all these preparatory conditions and partial solutions prepare the idea so much that all that remains on the part of an individual inventor or thinker is to take up what is lying there, almost fully prepared. Here, it most often happens that some people reap the fruit sown and painstakingly grown by others. Often, an individual researcher needs to make the final stroke for everything that was prepared before them to close up into a single harmonious order and the colossal idea comes into existence seemingly at once. But nonetheless, how difficult that final, concluding stroke can be!

Apart from everything else, any understanding requires that the general direction of consciousness answers the demands of the task, otherwise its meaning is not revealed to consciousness and understanding does not set in. The psychology of the moment a solution occurs, of the emergence of a thought, of the birth of an idea, is interesting: a thought, continuously and imperceptibly working somewhere in the depths of an excited brain, now suddenly flares up so clear and sharp in consciousness that one is astonished at its simplicity and clarity. This is often prepared without our intentional assistance, as some kind of 'underground work' of consciousness running in the background and preparing a change in the general field of consciousness in a certain manner. As soon as consciousness – favourably situated for the desired solution – encounters a specific situation leading to a solution, the solution arises immediately and unexpectedly. Sometimes, the activity of consciousness consists of a series of tests (as has been observed, for example, while solving various riddles, rebuses and so on); consciousness tries on, 'takes aim at' and attempts to place the given object in one semantic context or another until suddenly the solution comes to light. This means that the field of consciousness assumed a position in which the desired object is freely harnessed to a context with others in such a way that it constitutes a specific semantic whole that solves the situation (i.e. it interprets the whole entire circle of things); the object itself is also interpreted in this complex owing to its place and position in it.

In order to conceive, decide, and draw certain conclusions, for the individual as such it is necessary that the problem takes shape as the result of the work of many minds and the activity of a great number of other people, and that the objective composition and structure of the task is revealed more sharply in the course of social life. Thus, the role of a separate individual in the process of composing social thoughts is more or less accidental.

It is in this sense that statements about the era as the bearer of specific ideas should be understood.

§79

Ultimately, in the individual everything is social, and this applies above all to their thoughts. The quantity of ideas belonging exclusively to a person is insignificant in comparison with the ideas that they share with certain social spheres and with all their contemporaries in general. Individual consciousness lives through what is found in continual interaction with others, *continually assimilating social thoughts and alienating their own.*

Social reality is the basis for the life and the activity of a separate individual; social consciousness serves as the source that nourishes individual thinking. To a significant degree, social consciousness determines not only the direction of individual thinking (objects, materials, themes and tasks) but also imposes the predominant habits of thinking upon it.

Once upon a time, the broad minds of the ascending young revolutionary bourgeoisie understood this very well, but the ideologists of the doomed, reactionary bourgeoisie has stopped understanding it. Many people, Goethe said, see a historical personality 'as their Hercules – and they are perfectly right. But they forget that even the Colossus consists of individual parts, and that even the Hercules of antiquity is a collective being – a great supporter of his own deeds and the deeds of others. But, in fact, we are all collective beings ... For how little *have* we, and *are* we, that we can strictly call our own property? We must all receive and learn both from those who were before us, and from those who are with us. Even the greatest genius would not go far if he tried to owe everything to his own internal self. But many ... do not comprehend that; and they grope in darkness for half a life, with their dreams of originality. I have known artists who boasted of having followed no master, and of having to thank their own genius for everything. Fools! As if that were possible at all; and as if the world would not force itself upon them at every step, and make something of them in spite of their own stupidity'. '[V]ery little of me would be left, if I could but say what I owe to my great predecessors and contemporaries'.

When, in the course of time, we become acquainted with one historical figure or another – when, for example the system of Aristotelian, Hegelian, or Newtonian thought rises in all its magnificence before our mental gaze – we are amazed and dispirited by the grandeur of the thinker, the person, the creator and often cannot find the answer to the question: how was such a colossal personality possible? But it is worth becoming more closely acquainted with the eras in which these giants lived and worked, with the historical facts and the world of ideas immediately surrounding them, as it becomes clear that they alone did not create all this *ex nihilo*.

Hegel's famous *Aufhebung*, which amazes us even now with its immensely deep meaning, was simply current in that era: Schelling spoke of 'potentiation'; in connection with the questions of periodicity and cyclicality, called the same idea *Stegierung*. Hegel only developed, refined and formulated this idea to the thorough fullness that the idealist standpoint was capable of, and coined *Aufhebung*, an expression much more appropriate for the idea. Now, there are few who remember the other attempts and achievements.

If such achievements of the physical sciences such as Newton's principle of relativity in classical physics, Riemann's geometry, Gauss' teachings about curvilineal coordinates, Minkovsky's four-dimensional continuum and Michelson's and Morley's experiments were brought together in one observable series, and if we tried from this standpoint to comprehend Lorentz transformations, then the path along which Einstein could go to his famous discovery of the theory of relativity, which he let us understand in a masterful exposition in his book 'The General and Specific Theory of Relativity' would actually become accessible. An extraordinary sharpness, keenness and broadness of mind would be required, however, in order to make these comparisons and to see the physical meaning of Lorentz's formulations in precisely this light. This is what the excellence of Einstein consists of.

Only because our historical knowledge is limited and quite fragmentary, and we regard individual thinkers in isolation, are we unable to not exaggerate the achievements of major personalities, writers, thinkers and masters. In this, in part, is the reason why, insofar as historical personalities continue to excite minds, their glory grows with the centuries to legendary proportions. But it is worth becoming acquainted in detail with, for example, Goethe and his milieu in order for Goethe to cease amazing and overwhelming us. It is sufficient to become acquainted with Spinozism, Johann Gottfried Herder, and so on for Goethe to become more comprehensible and accessible to us. We begin to understand that these thoughts flared up repeatedly, carried everywhere in vague form. 'Certain attitudes and thoughts', Goethe said, 'are often carried in the air, such that many people can catch them. The air is like a common spirit belonging to everyone, by the means of which everyone is in mutual interaction. This is why many astute and passionate minds immediately apprehend what others are thinking, out of the atmosphere. Or, speaking less mystically: certain ideas mature over the course of a certain period, just as fruit in different gardens fall from the tree at the same time'.

Such thoughts have generally been expressed more than once, but the philosophy of Marxism first gave these facts a scientific explanation. At the base of all mental life, it places material criteria: social and historical praxis and existing social relations.

'Ideas are carried in the air' – these words and all such expressions have no other meaning than that the conditions and facts of social reality themselves take shape in such a way that they burst into consciousness and compel people to conceive things in a certain manner, in accordance with their actual interests. These facts and relations of things themselves are in no way ideas; but rising into the consciousness of people, they acquire their equivalent in mental existence.

Insofar as all these preliminary conditions of cognition are met and the material and social conditions have sufficiently matured, then the question of which individual completes the act of discovery of one idea or another and who first expresses it is not important, since if one person passes by it and does not notice it, the second or the tenth will. We have no grounds to think that without Aristotle or Euclid, the world would have no logic or geometry. One historian rightly noted: 'Columbus 'discovered' the Americas, of course. But if there had been no Columbus, would the Americas have remained undiscovered? ... Would the Pythagorean theorem be unknown, if there had been no Pythagoras or his school? And if there had been no Newton, would we have no idea about the law of gravity? And would everyone still be riding around in stagecoaches, if Stephenson had not invented the locomotive? I do not think this requires an answer. Insofar as the conditions for a certain scientific discovery or technological invention were ripe, then the discovery would be made, and it makes no difference who does so. That is why every argument about personal priority is petty and offensive'.[31]

In the period of maturity for certain tasks and problems, a multitude of individuals are occupied with them; they are assaulted by more than one consciousness, now independent of each other and not knowing about each other, now mutually urging and contradicting each other, mutually exciting and inspiring each other until finally the matter falls into the hands of a capable

---

31 Beloch 1924, Vol. I, pp. 2–3.

and talented, or even simply lucky person who expounds everything more or less coherently. And these thoughts and ideas are usually assigned to whoever was able to do this earlier and better than the others, though of course they do not belong to them alone.

Thus, talent and gifts are only the midwife in the social process of the birth of a social idea. The actual parents, the mother and father of these ideas, are social conditions and social praxis, which create them and give them 'a start in life'. 'I am the secretary of society', Balzac said. 'Time commands, and I write'.

Thoughts and ideas are not the product of free individual creation, but – like the individual themselves – are the product of society and social relations. And therefore, when the issue is human thinking, the stages of thinking and the means and forms of the composition of human thought, their solution cannot be sought either on the path of logical investigations or in the labyrinth of traditional psychology, but *above all one should ask about the sociogenesis of these ideas.*

One individual or another is only the 'accidental' mouthpiece of socially mature social ideas. These ideas are not arbitrarily invented by individuals; on the contrary, individuals are placed under conditions where certain ideas and means of thinking are imposed on them by things and people formed by relations and social interests. Separate individuals are only the narrators or bearers of certain ideas, insofar as they are social ideas. People need to be regarded as the children of their age. Otherwise neither the essence of society nor the essence of thinking can be understood.

These, however, do not solve the question of the role of the personality in history, and the foregoing does not at all intend to understate this role. On the contrary, we are certain that the widespread opinion belittling this role must necessarily be reconsidered and several corrections must be made to the relevant statements of Plekhanov on this subject. It is enough to recall the series of names of great thinkers (in the spheres of both science and art), whose ideas inspired humanity over the course of many centuries, to understand all the injustice of a theory that rejects the role of the personality. All the more significant must be the role of the prominent personality at much shorter historical distances on the order of twenty to forty years.

The Social Genesis of Ideas

§ 80

It is interesting to trace the process itself of the birth and social consolidation of ideas. The affair usually begins with a certain shared intellectual ferment – vague, scantily formed and timid manifestations of certain attitudes, inclinations, tastes and so on. In a period of maturation for specific ideas, this theme does not affect a few; many approach it from different sides. There are often presentiments of the idea, sounded out here and there by many; it is found in a diffuse, wandering, indistinct state. And above all, it by no means receives its hazy expression in science but in separate manifestations of attitudes and inclinations, in tastes, fashions and so on, that in capitalist society – for example – find their immediate reflection in the market of art, ready-to-wear items, and so on. From here, by all appearances, new moods flow into art – at first in mass forms (fashionable songs, sayings, current humour and so on), then manifesting itself in the works of the artists of the word, of paint and of sounds, and only as a result forcing their way, in a much clearer and rational form, into science. Of philosophy's share, as Hegel said, there remains only 'twilight'. 'Only one word more concerning the desire to teach the world what it ought to be. For such a purpose philosophy always comes too late. Philosophy ... does not appear until reality has completed its formative process'.[32]

It is important to remember that in the historical process, the prominent role is played not by isolated events (even the most dramatic and outstanding), but specifically everyday ones, 'the most common and everyday ... encountered billions of times', which, as Lenin said, constitute the actual elements and force of history.

'An excellent picture of history: the sum of individual passions, actions, etc. ('everywhere something akin to ourselves, and therefore everywhere something that excites our interest for or against'), sometimes the mass of some general interest, sometimes a multitude of '*minute forces*' an infinite exertion of minute forces which produce a tremendous result from what appears insignificant'.[33] From this 'common and everyday' our requirements are revealed; our tasks, ideas and representations crystallise.

In the process of this mass ferment, ideas break through more and more frequently, come to the surface and percolate in many places and from many sides, ultimately finding their more or less clear expression. There are few who pay attention in the beginning; the majority do not notice them. Then, having taken notice, they react to it with approval or hostility. The idea begins to acquire enemies, and along with them friends. Will it gain acceptance and trust, will it

---

32   And further, 'When philosophy paints its grey in grey, one form of life has become old, and by means of grey it cannot be rejuvenated, but only known. The owl of Minerva takes its flight only when the shades of night are gathering'. Hegel 1911, p. 17.
33   Lenin 1931, pp. 155, 324.

conquer or be defeated – that depends on the way in which the idea touches upon the interests of people, whose interests it represents and who gains the upper hand in the given social struggle.

Having gained acceptance and widespread dissemination, the idea becomes better visible in all its good and bad, all its strength and weaknesses; it is rejected or becomes generally accepted and commonplace.

This process of the ascent of a thought from its timid beginnings to being an everyday idea known to all is described in a somewhat strange but picturesque form by a Russian poet:

> In the beginning a thought, embodied
> in the concise poem of a poet.
> Like a young maiden, obscure
> to the inattentive world.
> Then, having dared, she
> is already shifty, talkative,
> in all her aspects visible
> as a sophisticated woman.
> In the free prose of the novelist
> an old chatterer. Then,
> raising an impudent cry, she
> multiplies in the polemics of magazines,
> already long known to everyone.
>
> YEVGENY BARATYNSKY

CHAPTER 8

The Process of the Social Circulation of Ideas

The Propagation of Ideas

§ 81
We have spoken about individuals being only the bearers of social ideas and attitudes, and about thoughts, the conditions for the origin of which in one way or another matured in society, finding expression through individual consciousness, through the mouths and hands of separate individuals.

But an individual is capable of being a particular messenger of the shared state of minds only because they are a part of this whole, its product, because they exist as an individual only in society and think social thoughts.

Individual consciousness moves in social conditions and lives by them; the individual appropriates social ideas and participates in the form of one of the elements of force in the formation of social consciousness. Everything that an individual consciousness achieves as an individual consciousness is socially conditioned; it achieves based on social inheritance and existing relations.

But what an individual achieves as a separate personality does not remain walled up within the boundaries of their individuality and does not remain only individual, but continually passes beyond these boundaries, becomes social and is included in social existence; others the achievements of an individual, accept them or reject them, approve of them or condemn them – in a word, everything individual somehow, in one form or another, is socialised and collectivised.

A discovery made by one individual or another, the thoughts they express, even their separate acts or products of activity become the property not of them alone, but of others. Thoughts and acts meet with sympathy or hostility, approval or condemnation, acceptance or rejection; they are criticised, fought for or against, and so on.

The products of an individual consciousness thus enter into a more or less wide circle of social circulation and interaction, becoming a component of social consciousness and a known factor of social reality.

In order for an idea to enlarge the sphere of its circulation and of its influence and to conquer wider social opinion, the following are necessary:

First, that actual interests support it so that it is linked with the vital interests of people and finds support among them. The success of ideas, Marx said, depends on the extent to which the masses are 'interested' in certain goals and the extent to which these goals rouse their enthusiasm. 'The 'idea' always disgraced itself insofar as it differed from the 'interest'.[1] Theory is capable of capturing the masses when it argues *ab hominem* (Marx), and it argues *ab hominem* when it is linked to specific social interests and serves these interests.

Second, in order for the idea to find a response in specific social spheres, it is necessary for the idea to be accessible to them. Karl von den Steinen recounts how the natives he was studying displayed no interest whatsoever in such things as a camera. These things were far too distant from their sphere of things and the sphere of their thoughts. They were *weber Hand – noch – Kopfrecht*. But 'objects, the origins of which they could form some kind of idea, occupied their imagination more strongly than the others ...'.[2]

In order to reach the consciousness of the masses, an idea must not be too far from their mental requirements. Nevertheless, it should not be forgotten that the social conditions that give birth to an idea in society at the same time rearrange the brains of these people, adapting them to a certain understanding.

If the conditions for the manifestation of an idea are not socially prepared, then it will be very difficult for a new idea to clear a path to consciousness. Ideas that are ahead of their time, moving beyond it, experience a terrible situation in society. 'The history of philosophy, of the sciences and of religion all show that opinions spread in great quantities, but the ones that are comprehensible, that is, commensurate with the human intellect at its present stage of development, always predominate'. (Goethe)

'The idea', Stendahl said, 'must be two or three degrees higher than the general level of intellect so as not to be boring. If it is higher than eight degrees, then the heads of that society begin to hurt'. There is undoubtedly a grain of truth in these aphorisms. The tragedy of new inventions, discoveries and ideas that are ahead of their time lies in the fact that humanity, which every time is only the society of a specific era, assimilates them with great difficulty. From that it is understandable why new ideas encounter opposition and a hostile reception in society. The proposition expressed by Gauss in his time about the curvature of space, appearing isolated and independently of other ideas and facts discovered only later on, found itself in such obvious disagreement with all the other prevailing ideas that it could not meet with approval; Gauss, as he himself admitted in private correspondence, 'fearing the screams of the Boeotians', preferred to abstain from publishing his discoveries. So it was with many others – Giambattista Vico, for example, whose *New Science* was not noticed by

---

1 Marks i Engel's 1928–1946, Vol. III, p. 105 [Marx and Engels 1975–, Vol. 4, p. 81].
2 Steinen 1897, p. 74.

his contemporaries and passed by its own time, while centuries later, in Hegel's time, the ideas that were in many regards similar to the ones expressed by him enjoyed great fame and general acceptance.

The active organisation of social and educational work, which permits the rapid reconstruction of consciousness and, with the assistance of teaching, facilitates the mastery of the most difficult ideas and intellectual habits is another matter.

But the primary cause of the success or failure of specific ideas ultimately lies not in the intellectual level of people and not in the value or truth of the ideas themselves, but in existing social relations, in the arrangement of social forces and interests. New ideas, especially revolutionary ones, encounter the organised or blunt resistance of their enemies not only because of obstinacy or intellectual backwardness, but because these ideas contradict the vital interests of some and serve others well. Both hostile camps live for a time with the old (i.e. prevailing) ideas and manage with them in one way or another. New ideas have to prove themselves in defiance of the old ones, therefore they can break through only with struggle. But the force of ruling ideas lies in the fact that they sit firmly in the heads of people, occupying all the positions of social opinion by tradition, by routine, and most importantly owing to the active support of the ruling class through schools and the million-headed hydra of the printed word – in short, through the entire apparatus of mental influence.

Moreover, one part of society (the privileged classes), whose interests the ruling ideas actually serve, succeeded in adapting themselves to them and recognising their interests in them, while the other part (the oppressed classes), living with the old ideas and often coming into conflict with them, though vaguely feeling their hostility but nonetheless not clearly recognising their own position, their own interests and the paths to overcoming the old, are often compelled to think their thoughts using concepts that are foreign to the ruling views. Hence, the one and the other,[3] until a certain time move in a ring of old ideas that is difficult to break. A tremendous underdevelopment of people's views from their social way of life, the tempos of the development of material culture and social relations is often observed in history. The conservative aspect of ideology, mentioned numerous times by the classical writers of Marxism, finds its expression in this.

---

3 To characterise the struggle of social opinion, we speak of two parts of society for the sake of the simplicity of the exposition; in reality there are more – to be precise, just as many as there are social classes, groups, and layers linked by objective class or group interests.

The victory or defeat of some ideas or others ultimately depends on the social direction of the historical process of development. In the long run, the ideas win whose actual bearers are a progressive class, capable in their social position of appearing as *the new creative force of history*. We can therefore say that the origin and rule of certain views and ideas in a specific era are just as inevitable as a change in the development of productive forces and social relations. These propositions were clearly formed in Marx in his famous *Introduction to the Critique of Political Economy*.

Social Circulation of the Products of Mental Creativity

§ 82

Something that has been completed is no longer subordinate to the agent, just as the arrow is no longer subordinate to the archer once it has been shot from the bow and a word no longer belongs to the person speaking it after it has flown from their mouth – and more so when it is scattered around the world in print.

Thus, in entering the sphere of social relations, interaction and circulation, the idea, the thought, the word – like any other product – begins its own 'journey to the people', so to speak. The idea is applied, it is tested in different relations, on the most varied materials and under the most varied conditions from the most diverse aspects.

In becoming the object of use for many, travelling from hand to hand, testing itself on different materials, flying from mouth to mouth and being run through the prism of a multitude of minds and through the experience of many, an idea is subjected to changes, thorough processing, criticism, corrections, distortions or improvements, and so on.

In the process of social interaction, a result is thus obtained about which it is already impossible to say that it is an individual production, since it is the universal result of the actions of a multitude of individual, and often of many generations. This final result consists of the additions and supplements of the mind, and of the creative activity of of many. The simple and lapidary form of a popular proverb hides the collaboration of such a large multitude of nameless authors that the product becomes genuinely impersonal.

All mental formations, as well as the material culture of humanity, represents the result of historical layers of experience of a series of generations, the product of general selection, often even a full semantic reversal, the product of endless supplementing and individual additions, filtered in diverse ways through the prism of reflection and the experience of a vast multitude of people. In these products it is as if we are actually dealing with some kind of *combined history of the human mind*.[4]

In this process of the social life of an idea and its social interaction, the exposure of its good and bad aspects, its veracity or falsity, is completed in part. Hence in this regard, as the classical writers of Marxism noted, the historical movement of thought moves along the path of approaching an ever more adequate cognition of objective reality. As we will see below (Chapters 9 and 10), a fuller inspection of the idea and the exposure of its essence occurs in the praxis of its implementation and in the process of the social struggle for its realisation. Praxis shows that what is true is true because, in correctly reflecting reality, it leads in its development to the correct results, and the false leads in the majority of cases to a dead end. In this sense it is possible to say that errors and truth spring from the same source, but ultimately truth belongs to humanity and errors belong to the times. But the path of the adequate understanding of reality lies deeper, and finding it is more difficult than seeing the mistake, which in the majority of cases consists of one-sidedness and lies on the surface. It is ridiculous and naïve, however, to think that truth itself is capable through its logical force of overcoming established opinions if the organised force of people of the advanced social class, of a party, does not act as its advocates.

On Popular Creativity

§ 83

There is a quite widespread, but extremely mistaken opinion about folklore, folk tales, legends, songs and so on that they were originally the product of the individual creativity of independent authors that passed on to the masses and are therefore considered to be of the people. This is not only a simplification and a superficial understanding, but a complete distortion of the actual essence of folklore. Such an interpretation is by no means in line with the overwhelming majority of folkloric material, but is artificially imposed on it.

Albert Wesselski, who published his *Versuch einer Theorie des Märchens* [An Attempt at a Theory of Fairy Tales – ed.] in 1931, believes that the first cre-

---

[4] The perfection and the high level of quality we find in the best examples of popular creativity, popular poetry, epics, popular songs and so on finds its explanation precisely in this. The perfection of the form, the grandiosity, the majestic simplicity and brevity, the minimum of means of expressiveness and the maximum of meaning encountered here is the result of the interaction and the long process of selection reflected in these examples, which have gone through millions of hands, mouths and minds.

ators of *Natursagen* were primarily independent priests and that myths owe their existence to the personal creativity of various prophets, priests or poets who supposedly freely improvised these subjects, 'answering the questions that arose among the inquisitive and rejoicing at the gullibility of the audience'. 'The collective, the people', Wesselski says, 'cannot be regarded as the author, the keeper, or the disseminator' of these tales, mythological subjects, stories and so on.[5] In the opinion of a number of theoreticians, the people only disseminate, deforming or demolishing (*zersagt*) the stories, legends, and so on but do not create them; the actual creators of every folkloric motif and subject are individual personalities. 'The people', in Wesselski's words, 'do not produce but only reproduce' the stories and legends, and moreover corrupt these products of the creation of independent authors. Wesselski attempts to convince us that the stories of folklore, passing over to the mouths of the people and changing from storyteller to storyteller, are distorted and degrade during these wanderings.

We believe that it is precisely in the process of this journey of the simplest traditional motifs (at one point having a paradigmatic, cultural or magical meaning) *that these stories and legends are first composed in all their multifarious variations and alternate versions.* These simple motifs, in the process of their social circulation and their general mass use accumulate an entire mass of layers and are joined with other, identical simple motifs, ultimately acquiring certain plot lines, schemas and so on.

Philosophers and psychologists have excessively simplified the question, believing that the human mind is capable of joining all sorts of things in the imagination and creating any miracle of fantasy they like. The facts, however, tell us that people's fantasies are strictly historically limited. Even the most brilliant visionary has never succeeded in creating a genuinely new fantastic form that was not the repetition of older, traditional ones that were already known. People are not at all free in the play of their imaginations. Every flight of fantasy leans on some sort of plot outline that is already known and on basic motifs that have historically already been produced and exist traditionally. In this sense, fantasy is always subordinate to some sort of schemas and norms that are already known and follow a specific traditional outline.

Like specific means of thinking, basic motifs and basic forms are not the creation of an individual consciousness. They are composed as a result of a multitude of convergences, mutual influences and layers one upon the other, of

---

5 'Das Kollektivum, das Volk kommt weder als zubereitend, noch als erhaltend, noch als vertreibend in betracht'. Wesselski 1931, p. 178.

the thoughts and views of many generations. They are created over the centuries, by the centuries-old accumulation of separate motifs and characters, and represent the most complex historical mass. The historical meaning of these ideas completely evaporates in the attempt to understand them as the work of individual creativity.

In the formations of spiritual culture, as with those of material culture, every boundary between the individual and the social is so obliterated that it is impossible to distinguish where the individual ends and the social begins. We cannot definitively show what in them belongs to an individual personality and what is owing to treatment by many, as each thing, even every detail, was actually made by someone, but of course every product of an individual is the result of not only individual experience and individual creation, but at the same time the product of historical and historical experience and the layers of activity of many.

In the body of a product (any product of labour, whether material or ideological), all this is fused into a single whole. In it, as a specific social and historical formation, these differences are obliterated and levelled into the indistinguishable whole of the object (material or ideal), which in turn is subject to subsequent generations of further treatment and changes.

Marx says that '[a] critical history of technology would show how little any of the inventions of the eighteenth century are the work of a single individual. Hitherto there is no such book'.[6] By the same right, this proposition is applicable to all theoretical discoveries in general, and Marxist philosophy consistently applies it to the entire field of ideological creation and of theoretical and ideological achievements; the dishes we call ideas are never under any conditions cooked outside the communal kitchen.

More importantly, this confluence of the individual and the social and the absence of perceptible boundaries between them takes place on even deeper foundations. In fact, this boundary generally does not exist in the nature of social reality, not only in the formations of material and spiritual culture but also in humans themselves. Insofar as this refers to the human personality, it is impossible – as we have already noted – to draw this boundary and show where within it the personal ends and the social begins.

When theoreticians spoke about the individual and the social, about the relation between personality and society, they mainly argued about priority: is the individual determined by society or, on the contrary, do personalities determine the development and fate of society? The former position

---

6 Marx 1923, p. 317 [Marx and Engels 1975–, Vol. 35, p. 375].

was occupied by the adherents of the sociological school: Moritz Lazarus, D. Drăghicescu, Émile Durkheim, Lucien Lévy-Bruhl and others. The latter position was occupied by the individualists: Georges Palante, Gustave Le Bon and others. An extreme representative of the latter standpoint was Thomas Carlyle, who in his book *On Heroes, Hero-Worship, and the Heroic in History* formulated the widespread opinion on history as follows: the history of humanity is the biography of great people. Carlyle's aphorism expresses the standpoint of the annalist historians, for whom Greek history beyond Alexander the Great was not visible and the personality of Napoleon Bonaparte overshadowed the social reality and actual relations of French society and European states.

In general, Marx rejects setting society off against the individual. As a theoretical premise, he takes the indisputable fact: everything social exists only on the strength of the fact that and to the extent that their makers, creators and bearers are concrete individuals. Conceiving any social phenomenon whatsoever outside of concrete personalities is impossible. The life and activity of people and the thinking of individuals is possible only insofar as individuals draw everything out of society, insofar as they continually appropriate social products of both a material and an ideal type, hence, insofar as *the individualisation of the social* continually takes place. In the process of production, distribution, exchange and consumption, everything social is continually turned into the individual. But on the other hand, every individual product, whether material or ideal, every individual manifestation does not remain only individual and persona, but is joined to the more or less broad circle of social existence and becomes the property of others; it becomes *social. The individual is continually socialised.*

'But also', Marx says, 'when I am active *scientifically*, etc. – an activity which I can seldom perform in direct community with others – then my activity is *social*, because I perform it as a *man*. Not only is the material for my activity given to me as a social product (as is even the language the language in which the thinker is active): my *own* existence is social activity, and therefore that which I make of myself, I make of myself for society ...'.[7]

Thus, the individual and the social are not disconnected and separate metaphysical categories or entities; no actual boundaries exist between them. The social is continually converted into the individual and is performed through living people, specific personalities, and the individual in turn is continuously socialised. *Both of them (the individual and the social) exist in each other and through each other.* The classical writers of Marxism – Marx, Engels, and

---

[7] Marks i Engel's 1928–1946, Vol. III, p. 624 [Marx and Engels 1975–, Vol. 3, p. 298].

Lenin – repeatedly warned against the metaphysical interpretation of these questions. 'Above all we must avoid postulating 'society' again as an abstraction *vis-à-vis* the individual. The individual is *the social being*. His manifestations of life – even if they may not appear in the direct form of *communal* manifestations of life carried out in association with others – *are* therefore an expression and confirmation of *social life*. Man's individual and species-life are not *different*, however much – and this is inevitable – the mode of existence of the individual is a more *particular* or more *general* mode of the life of the species, or the life of the species is a more *particular* or more *general* individual life'.[8]

On Borrowing

§84

In both cases – the case of the appropriation by an individual of what is socially given (regardless of whether material or ideal) and in the case of the return by an individual of their achievements (i.e. the socialisation of the individual) – the existence alone of the objects of borrowing is insufficient. Appropriating something and using it requires not only being in need of the given objects or wanting to borrow them, but actually being capable of and being in a position to borrow.

Quite often, when disputing the value of some idea or another or in wanting to play down the significance of some thinker, people speak about the repetition of old ideas or borrowing from others. The superficiality and inconsistency of such an understanding should now be obvious to anyone. In his time, even Goethe sharply rebuffed such superficiality, and Heine rightly scolded one philosopher who complained that another philosopher had stolen from him. '... [P]oor Schelling, a fallen, mediatised philosopher, wandered mournfully among the other mediatised gentlemen in Munich. I once saw him there and could almost have wept tears at the pitiful sight. And what he said was the most pitiful thing of all; it was an envious railing at Hegel, who had supplanted him. As one shoemaker talks about another whom he accuses of having stolen his leather and made boots of it, so I heard Mr. Schelling, when I once saw him by chance, talk about Hegel, about Hegel, who had 'taken his ideas'; and 'it is my ideas that he took, and again 'my ideas' – this was the poor man's constant refrain. I assure you, if the shoemaker Jakob Böhme once talked like a philosopher, the philosopher Schelling now talks like a shoemaker. Nothing

---

8   Marks i Engel's 1928–1946, Vol. III, p. 624 [Marx and Engels 1975–, Vol. 3, p. 299].

is more absurd than ownership claimed for ideas. Hegel did, to be sure, use many of Schelling's ideas for his philosophy, but Mr. Schelling would never have known what to do with these ideas anyway. He always just philosophised, but was never able to produce a philosophy. And besides, one could certainly maintain that Mr. Schelling borrowed more from Spinoza than Hegel borrowed from Schelling'.

No matter how savage these words, they are correct, since 'stealing ideas' is not as simple as it might seem at first glance. Great thoughts and great ideas, despite their immateriality, are not such light material that anyone can pick them up and carry them into life or literature. Above all, this requires having the most favourably endowed head and a gigantic heart, and knowing how to ascend to the heights of these ideas. 'Thou art like the spirit thou canst comprehend'.

Only those who are genuinely capable of seizing an idea and putting it into action – consequently, those to whom these ideas arguably belong – can evaluate, take, 'steal' and use it. In this sense, all the great minds have sinned against the Sixth Commandment – since no single person has created a culture, an independent science or an independent idea on their own. Herein lies the remarkable problem of cultural continuity. What is a new invention, a new discovery, but nothing more than the successful use of ideas, things and achievements created by the labours of thousands of generations and hundreds of thousands of fellow citizens? 'What does discovery mean, and who can say that he has discovered this or that?' Goethe asked. 'After all, it is pure idiocy to brag about priofity; it is simply unconscious conceit not to admit frankly that one is a plagiarist'.

The world of ideas, in Heine's opinion, should not be protected by the law of the European elder. 'Nothing is sillier', he said, 'than this charge of plagiarism ... The poet dare help himself ... wherever he finds material for his work. He may even appropriate entire columns with their carved capitals, if the temple he thus supports be a beautiful one. Goethe understood this very well, and so did Shakespeare before him. Nothing could be more absurd than the demand that the writer create all his subjects himself, because that is what originality consists of. I remember the fable in which the spider caught the bee in the act of plagiarism, reproaching her with the fact that from thousands of flowers she gathers material from which she then prepares her honeycomb and honey: 'But I', he noted in triumph, 'weave all my cloth from original thread that I produce myself'.

The proposition put forward remains in force not only as regards borrowing of the individual type, but also in the sphere of social borrowing – tribal, national and so on. It must be understood that borrowing requires certain preconditions: it is possible only if the borrowing society is equal to the given material and spiritual requirements (i.e. equal to the objects borrowed).

Once a society adopts, or even inherits, some formation or another of spiritual or material culture, tools of production, or forms of organisation, it follows that it has reached a certain stage in its development and, lacking the opportunity to borrow, it would have independently sought out these forms and created them. Borrowing is not a simple mechanical transfer of ready-make cultural acquisitions or habits, but a creative adoption. Cultural values or concepts as a result of borrowing are subject to a certain – sometimes even radical – revision and to changes.

Among bourgeois historians, archaeologists, ethnologists, linguists and cultural historians there is a widespread but false admonition that believes borrowing to be the main factor in the history of a society's development. For many theoreticians it was sufficient to discover a similarity of mythological subjects, ornamental motifs, lexical or even morphological formations in language in different parts of the world to draw an immediate conclusion about borrowing by some from others, about affinity, about a community of origin or immediate vicinity in earlier times and about the subsequent separation of these peoples,[9] or to throw the borrowed forms from some countries into others through extraordinary adventures, often arriving at general conclusions about the existence of some 'ur-mythology', 'ur-language', 'ur-folk' and their 'ur-motherland' – views that distort and confuse all the historical maps and the actual historical relations of peoples. Many of these opinions can be considered as already overcome, but as unspoken premises and prejudices they are nonetheless 'vestigially' preserved in the heads of many researchers, leading their work astray.

The weaknesses of the theory of borrowing should be thoroughly taken into account; one should not be 'naïve', discussing how other peoples absolutely borrowed from cultured peoples and how the latter cultivated the former. Unfortunately, the history of peoples so far has yielded precisely the opposite proof. The educational role of 'civilised' peoples in relation to the 'less cultured' during the period of the entire class history of society has been expressed over the centuries as the latter being mercilessly cultivated as slaves; this did not at all occur on the basis of some sort of racial hostility but by virtue of the parasitic

---

9 Finding traces of a base six counting system in European languages (by sixes, by the dozen, by the gross and so on), for example, was enough for Johannes Schmidt to draw a conclusion about the birthplace of the Indo-Europeans in Asia near Babylon, where a base six system also existed (among the Semitic peoples) and from here the Indo-Europeans could only borrow it! Schmidt 1890.

classes knowing well how to dress up their private, proprietary interests in the toga of 'national', 'race' and 'universal' interests.

Social Consciousness

§85

What conclusions follow from the above? What is social consciousness? Does it actually exist, or is it only our purely mental representation of the simple mechanical aggregate of individual people's opinions?

As is known, this term ('social consciousness', 'forms of social consciousness') is often encountered in Marx, and in the *Introduction to a Critique of Political Economy* he formulates the general principle of the dependency of social consciousness on the state of the material forces of production and the development of productive relations.

Among bourgeois ideologists, the term 'national consciousness' or 'national spirit' (*Volksgeist*) first appeared on the scene in Schelling and Fichte. The German 'school of history' in the person of its main representatives, Friedrich Carl von Savigny (1779–1861) and Georg Friedrich Puchta (1798–1846) produces the doctrine of 'national spirit' as a fundamental metaphysical force, supposedly lying at the base of all social processes and creating all social institutions and as the starting point of its construction in the sphere of the theory of law and the state.

These concepts have become more fashionable since the founding of *Zeitschrift für Völkerpsycholgie und Sprachwissenschaft*, published by Moritz Lazarus and Heyman Steinthal in the 1860s and 1870s. The above authors, having availed themselves of the traditions of the German 'school of history' – particularly the Hegelian concept of World Spirit and its particular manifestation in the history of the development of individual peoples in the form of a 'racial' or 'national spirit', joined these ideas with Herbartian psychology and made the principle of 'national spirit' and 'national psychology' the universal principle of history. Moreover, Lazarus and Steinthal laid psychometaphysical premises at the foundation of their views.

By 'social intellect', 'social soul', 'national spirit', '*l'ésprit publique*'[10] they meant purely psychological content. 'The people' or 'the nation', in Lazarus's opinion, is above all a 'spiritual whole'.[11] This 'national spirit' exists as gen-

---

10   *Zeitschrift für Völkerpsychologie und Sprachwissenschaft*, Vol. III, p. 7.
11   Lazarus 1917, Vol. I, p. 372.

eral for all the individuals of a given people and makes a national whole out of them. The state, law and all other social formations are the natural manifestations of the 'social intellect' and the 'products of organic discovery, of the national spirit'. In Lazarus's opinion, finding the originality of a 'national intellect' requires seeking out the shared portion and shared features in the consciousness of individuals. Social life, in the opinions of these authors, is a mental process that does not, however, lead to the sum of separate psyches but possesses its own particular behaviour and particular laws. It is not subordinate to the general law of causality but has its own special causality – specifically, a 'mental causality'. From this, in fact, first came the most absurd division of the sciences into the natural sciences (the sphere of the rule of physical causality) and the mental sciences (the sphere of the rule of 'mental causality'). The task of the psychology of peoples, according to Lazarus and Steinthal, consists of studying the behaviours of 'national consciousness' in general and the 'soul' of individual peoples in particular.

Though others – Wundt, for example – criticised these metaphysical sets, in their theoretical constructions they remained essentially in the positions of consistent psychologism. Psychology was considered the basic foundation of social science.

Wundt, in his multi-volume work *Völkerpsychologie* (published between 1900 and 1906) calls not the 'national soul', not the 'national spirit', but above all such mental formations of social life as language, beliefs, customs and so on the object of national psychology. Wundt considers these phenomena to be the exclusive products of the mental life of people and of the mental communication between them. Language, beliefs, art, and morals, in Wundt's opnion, are the 'generally valid products of the collective *mental* activity of people'. The task of social science, in his opinion, therefore consists of 'the analysis of the mental acts lying at the base of this activity'.

'What binds people into a certain social whole? How, and on what ground does a certain 'social unity' and 'social ego' arise out of separate individual consciousnesses?' asked the advocates of the psychological standpoint, and answered: on the ground of individuals' mutual *mental* communication. That said, some of them understood the 'mental communication' between individuals as conscious communication and conscious imitation (Gabriel Tarde), others as unconscious and instinctive (Vladimir Bekhterev, Scipio Sighele). On the ground of mutual mental infection through shared emotions and of mutual imitation (conscious or unconscious), people begin to live, they said, through shared experiences, thoughts and emotions, whereby precisely those emotions that at a given moment unite people – vengeance, anger, ecstasy and others – come to the fore.

The social links of individuals are regarded by many as exclusively mental. Moreover, they often pointed precisely to the facts of the instinctive mutual infection of individuals with shared emotions. The adherents of the organic school (Herbert Spencer, René Worms and others) spoke about it, all the psychologists including Durkheim alluded to it, the representatives of the biosocial hypothesis expressed identical views, and so forth. Tarde, Sighele, Le Bon and others devoted social research to this question.[12] In the Russian literature, we note two authors as far from each other as Nikolai Mikhailovskii and Vladimir Bekhterev.[13]

These scientists were inclined to see the manifestation of social consciousness in such facts, for example, as the phenomenon of 'mental contagion' enveloped in the certain conditions of people not unlike reflexive contagious movements such as yawning or mass 'mental infection' during the ceremonial St. Vitus's dance (Bekhterev). Social consciousness is thus understood to be phenomena having purely physiological bases and proceeding as unconscious and reflexive movements. Many armed with this principle of 'mental contagion' went so far that they wanted to explain most social movements with its help. Briefly put, by the concept of social consciousness sociologists meant such phenomena by which people to a certain extent ceased being people and became animals controlled only by reflexive and instinctive acts. There have been such 'sociologists' who portrayed major social events and revolutionary movements in the same light as a fit of yawning. The great French Revolution, for example, was characterised as a 'storm of passions' and 'a thirst for equality' that suddenly seized the population of France in 1789.[14] The 'good intentions' of this movement of scientists reached a point where they wanted to see the manifestation of the unconscious animal instincts in humans – similar to those that manifest in a time of mass panic – in all the major social revolutionary movements.[15]

To be sure, for those who did not learn to distinguish biological reflexes from the manifestations of human consciousness as 'socially historical formations',

---

12   Tarde 1898; Sighele 1901; Le Bon 1895.
13   Mikhailovskii 1882; Bekhterev 1921.
14   'It is possible to cite numerous examples of the storm of human passions owing to the mutual mental infection of people', said one of these 'sociologists'; 'such, for example, was the thirst for equality that enveloped France around 1789. Such was the passion for freedom of trade in England in 1846. In the American Union, abolitionism around 1860 became the passion of the Northern States ... and finally, we see that in France a new passion is being born: the passion for decentralisation and so forth'. Novicow 1893.
15   Mak-Daugol 1916.

the essence of social phenomena and the form of social consciousness will be an inaccessible treasure behind seven seals.

Bourgeois sociology, beginning in the second half of the nineteenth century, and all its theoretical constructions primarily rested upon psychological principles. Psychology was called upon to explain history. The relations between people were conceived only as relations of a mental type, as mental relations. Only psychological content was sheathed in the concept of social phenomena; in any case, the collective psychical formations of a mental type were seen in them. Even such institutions as the state and law were and are considered mental formations, and they are ascribed 'mental content' and psychological meaning. In the relations between people, only mental and psychological communication is factored in, and no one asks what these mental relations rest on. 'Society is a mental whole', bourgeois scientists repeat with one voice, attempting to cover the yawning gap between the antagonistic classes of capitalist society with a curtain of words. Even the bourgeois social scientists (like Werner Sombart, for example) who sharply condemn in rhetoric the psychologist positions in sociology do not abandon this opinion.

Sombart, in one of his later publications, *Soziologie: Was sie ist und was sie sein sollte* [Sociology: What it is and what it should be – ed.],[16] complaining about the existence of the immense multitude of separate sociological theories and attempting to classify them into six basic groups, warns in the beginning that he repudiates all existing theories in order to put forward yet another one – his own. On the question of society, Sombart says, our starting position is people's mutual *mental* links. '*Ausgangspunkt unserer Betrachtung ist die Tatsache der Verbundenheit der Menschen, ihres Mit-Für-Gegeneinander*' ['The starting point of our contemplation is the fact of the connectedness of people, of their with-for-each other' – ed.]. On the question of what the peculiarity of people's social interdependence is, Sombart replies: '*Die dem Menschen eigene Art der Verbundenheit ... ist die geistige; die Menschen sind im Geiste verbünden ... Im Geiste verbunden sein bedeutet: verbunden Sein durch Sinnzusammenhänge wie sie vor allem die Sprache schafft (Wie sie auch Symbole herstellen können). Sinnzusammenhänge werden geschaffen durch Ausdrucksmittel, die eine "Bedeutung" haben, d. h. einen abstrakten, objektiven, aus eimen bestimmten Kausalzusammenhang herausgehobenen Sinn. Die Griechen benannten diesen Sachverhalt in wundervoller Hellsichtigkeit mit dem einen Wort λογος, das bedeutet*: 1. *Wort*, 2. *Sinn*, 3. *Geist* (*nur nicht* "*Tat*")'.[17] Hence, in Mr Sombart's

---

16 *Sitzungsberichte der Preussischen Akademie der Wissenschaften, Philosophisch-historische Klasse*, 1936, II–V.

17 *Sitzungsberichte der Preussischen Akademie der Wissenschaften, Philosophisch-historische*

opinion, people in society are linked by purely mental means – by words and by thoughts, only not by actions and deeds. This is repeated several times in Sombart, and is especially emphasised in the form of an aphorism: *Alle Gesellschaft ist Geist, und aller Geist ist Gesellschaft* [All society is spirit, and all spirit is society – ed.].

When such a widely acknowledged authority among bourgeois social scientists as Mr. Sombart, advancing a certain standpoint, calls it a new theory (*Entwurf einer Noo-Soziologie als selbständige Wissenschaft*), then it is improper to doubt or object to it in scientific circles. In a zealous reading, however, we did not succeed in discovering new elements in the fundamental propositions advanced by Mr. Sombart, and in its essential parts the theory appeared old. By way of a personal opinion, we note that at the end of the nineteenth century, similar sociological improvisations by Wilhelm Dilthey on Hegelian motifs turned out somewhat more lively and talented, especially if we take into account the experience of tremendous social change endured since that time, which obviously remains pointless for Werner Sombart, Hans Freyer,[18] Nikolai Hartmann[19] and other bourgeois social scientists.

The Composition and Content of Social Consciousness

§ 86

By social consciousness, Durkheim and Lévy-Bruhl mean that certain social ideas, and customs as such are instilled and imposed on each individual as 'collective ideas' that are created not by individuals but formed socially and make up supraindividual social traditions. Beliefs, customs, language and so on are such 'collective ideas'. In the opinions of the above authors, they are not created by individuals ('collective ideas do not depend on individuals for their existence', Lévy-Bruhl says) but are transmitted from generation to generation as socially established traditions and are forcibly imposed on people.

Klasse, II–V, pp. 67, 68. [The kind of connectedness peculiar to man ... is the spiritual; people are allied in spirit ... To be connected in the spirit means to be connected by means of the contexts of meaning such as those which language above all creates (as you can also create symbols). Contexts of meaning are created by means of expression that have a 'meaning', i.e. an abstract, objective sense, which is distinguished from a causal context. The Greeks named this state of affairs with wonderful transparency with the single word λογος, meaning: 1. Word, 2. Sense 3. Mind (just not 'act') – ed.]

18   Freyer 1930.
19   Hartmann 1933.

It should be noted that this compulsion as regards the individual, according to Durkheim's conviction, is distinguished by the special feature of every generally social phenomenon.[20]

'The consciousness of primitive humans was thoroughly socialised', Lévy-Bruhl says. In his opinion, this means that a personality is entirely under the power of collective ideas, i.e. ideas that, first, are independent of individual psychology; second, are *imposed* on individual personalities from the very earliest age; and third, are transmitted from generation to generation.

In our opinion, the sociological interpretation of the questions of thinking and the forms of social consciousness cannot rest only on the 'mental communication of individuals' or on the factor of tradition, on the transmission of the same forms from generation to generation according to tradition.

Starting from these assumptions, it is impossible to explain developed thinking and the change to the forms of social consciousness. When psychological causes and the mental communication of people are considered to be factors of historical development, then the development and modification of forms of thinking are depicted as the spontaneous development of consciousness out of itself. This was, and remains, the standpoint of idealist philosophy.

For us it is clear that if the forms of thinking undergo specific changes in the history of the development of society, then these changes must rest on something actual in practice; consequently, real forces that call forth these changes arise in society.

These forces are above all new material and new social relations that are not 'mental'. It is these (the material causes and social relations) that break the old habits, old forms and traditions of thinking and move the consciousness of people forward or backward and creating new forms and new means of thinking or reviving forgotten ones.

When the history of thinking is based only on the factors of traditions, what is meant by this is that all *new relations* arising in society are always conceived only in the customary forms and old patterns of thinking.[21] This means that changes in social reality bring nothing new to the consciousness of people and cannot give rise to any changes whatsoever in them. Thus, they reach

---

20 Durkheim 1902.
21 Up to a certain point, this does actually occur. New things and new relations are conceived using old means and old habits until new forms of understanding take shape. New forms of thinking are born not from old ones (on the contrary, in the majority of cases traditional concepts oppose the rise of new ones) but from new relations of reality, and are affirmed against the forces of tradition precisely as new forms of thinking, hostile to the old ones and contradicting them.

an absurd conclusion in which the fact of the development of thinking remains beyond explanation.

The point is not that the ruling thoughts are imposed on an individual (the representatives of the French school of sociology – Durkheim, Lévy-Bruhl, de Saussure – had this alone in mind) and not that humans, from their very infancy, are 'stuffed' with certain ideas, that specific established habits, views, ideas and so on loom over an individual – that is obviously a fact that goes without saying, which nobody is arguing against; the point is that if these ideas do not find actual support in life experience and in the actual interests of individuals, they will constantly be inclined towards 'keeping the course'. In parallel with these embedded ideas, another series of thoughts will arise in people that are more relevant to their actual interests, and these actual thoughts will gradually force out the traditional ones.

If they do not correspond to the actual interests of individuals in society, the traditional ideas they assimilate through education, propaganda and so on will always 'roll like water off a duck's back'. In light of this, the bourgeoisie and bourgeois ideologists do not always succeed in imparting the bourgeois structure of thinking to the proletariat, despite the grandiose means of mental oppression being in the hands of the ruling class of capitalists: the press, the scientific institutions, the entertainment centres, the schools and the entire ideological arsenal in general with all its strength employed for the dulling of the class consciousness of the proletariat. In defiance of all these difficulties, the proletariat has taken and is taking *its own* path of consciousness, working out *its own* ideology, at heart hostile to the bourgeoisie and rebutting all previously existing and traditional views.

The question of cultural and historical succession consists not only of the inheritance of certain forms, but of the creation of new ones. Together with material culture and social relations, of course, each generation also inherits certain ideas – a sum of ideas and views – but if actual relations and social interests will not support these traditional ideas, or if these views begin to contradict people's current interests, then people begin to repudiate old ideas and create new ones for themselves.

Only thus is the development and alteration of thinking possible, and the constant overcoming of traditional routine with new intellectual forms, habits and means. Changes and shifts in the world of ideas is based on real progress occurring under the material conditions of the life of society and of social relations.

Old thoughts and traditional habits are demolished *not by new ideas, but by life and new facts that intrude into this life*. New ideas are not born in people's heads on their own strength, but are driven into these heads by the strength of social interests and under the influence of new facts; they are driven out the same way.

The incursion of new facts and new relations demolishes routine forms and traditions of thinking, and construct new paths, new habits and means of thinking in people's consciousness. It should be specified, of course, that people do not get rid of old views and habits immediately; they can be preserved for a very long time through constant reexamining.

On the other hand, de Saussure's linguistic conceptions correspond to Durkheim's sociological views. de Saussure, proceeding from the assertion that at present no direct rational link exists between a signified object (*signifié*) and the sound complex signifying it (*signifiant*), arrives at the obviously fallacious conclusion that language is an entirely traditional phenomenon and that the life of a language is subject only to the force of tradition.

Although de Saussure admits that language changes, he adheres to the opinion that the people who speak it do not change it and cannot change it.[22] Saussure, for example, notes that 'shifts between the idea and the sign', 'between the signifying and the signified', and the most diverse 'shifts in the meaning of words' and so on takes place but on the question of why they take place and which forces compel this, he gives no answer. Moreover, Saussure does all he can to prove that these changes are in no way grounded, but only accidental.[23]

It is beyond doubt, however, that these shifts must have a material basis. The meaning of words and the sense of things do not change arbitrarily or by accidental whim, but because things *actually change* their purpose and their functions, because the objective meaning and everyday significance of these things change *and our relations to them change*.

The changes to our ideas and concepts about things always rests on the actual changes to these things in social use and social relations. This lies at the foundation of all shifts occurring in the sphere of language, both as regards semantics and as regards morphology and phonetics.

The conception of the advocates of the 'sociological school' about the essence of social consciousness is based wholly on psychological assumptions; this is where the fallaciousness of their positions lie. They believe that mutual influence – the links and relations between people – is a phenomenon of only a mental type, that social consciousness is based only on mental links and is created on the basis of the spiritual and mental communications between people.

---

22 Saussure 1933, pp. 81–4.
23 Saussure 1933, pp. 94–5.

The adherents of the sociological school do not take into account that mental communication between individuals became possible on the basis that material and social relations between them had been established in contrast to corporeal and biological relations that prevail in the animal world (see § 27).

Not only mental and spiritual elements, but above all material conditions and the social relations of people, take part in the formation of social consciousness. Material conditions and social relations: these are what take part in the formation of one form of social consciousness or another. And this is why, in consciousness, a dual content – social relations and material reality – is reflected.

It *must always* be remembered that mental aspirations and ideas bind and separate people not on their own, but only insofar as these ideas are the expression of specific social needs and interests. The ideas themselves can exist in society and be a social force only insofar as they actually express some kind of social interests. In the opposite case, ideas are not only chimeras, but they can even exist as chimeras.

There is a tremendous difference, when analysing social phenomena, in whether we start off from ideas and the 'mutual mental influence' of individuals or from actually existing relations between people and their interests, which create these mental and ideal aspirations and transform them into a social force or devalue them. In the first case, we will wander in the sphere of the abstract maxims of idealism; in the second, standing on the firm ground of reality, we will study this reality itself and not the products of sheer imagination.

Social consciousness is not only a traditional formation, it is continually created and re-created anew by people in accordance with new social needs and interests.

What Marx said about the nature of the creation of history is also fully applicable to the development of social consciousness: each new generation stands on the shoulders of the preceding one; in existence, it finds a certain sum of productive forces, some historically creative relation of people to nature and to each other; all this, however, on its part is also subject to change. Our understanding of history shows that 'circumstances make men just as much as men make circumstances'.[24] But once 'men are the producers of their conceptions, ideas, etc.'. and once 'the production of ideas, of conceptions, of consciousness is at first directly woven with the material activity and the material intercourse of men' (Marx), then people do not only inherit an old stock of ideas, habits, means of thinking and so on but continually change them and create new forms corresponding to new needs.

---

24   Marks i Engel's 1933, p. 29 [Marx and Engels 1975–, Vol. 5, p. 54].

As regards the individual, they are not only 'compelled to think as others think, in traditionally established forms' (Durkheim, de Saussure, Lévy-Bruhl), but on their part they themselves to a certain extent *compel others to think differently*. They not only perceive traditionally generated forms, but also take part in the creation and re-creation of these forms.

Quite apart from the conscious influence of an individual on social life, they take part in it even when they are not thinking about it. The participation of an individual in the process of forming social consciousness (in speech creation, the creation of social opinion, of tastes, of habits, of morals and so on) is expressed in the fact that the individual, living in society and communicating with others, acts in a certain manner, reveals certain thoughts, expresses their opinions and so forth. If their deeds, thoughts and statements do not diverge from the generally accepted ones, a separate individual enables the affirmation and canonisation of certain norms with them; consequently, they take part in the process of strengthening specific norms, thinking, language and so on. If they depart from generally established norms and diverge from the latter, then the individual is making *an attempt at innovation*; whether it is intentional or unconscious does not matter.

There is an infinite multitude of such attempts, conscious and unconscious, on the part of separate individuals. The afterlife of a thought that an individual has let slip, or of a separate expression, does not depend on the idea or expression itself.

Falling into general circulation, an idea or word becomes dependent on the conditions of the given social environment. Here is where it is kept or lost; it depends on the disposition of the general sphere of social consciousness: is the mood of people in favour of acceptance of this particular attempt or not, to what extent is the consciousness of a multitude of other individuals inclined to take these ideas, and to what extent they actually perceive these new formations.[25] In turn, the mood depends on the material conditions of social existence and of social relations. But once there is a great multitude of

---

25   As an illustration, we will cite one simple example from the memoirs of Pëtr Gnedich, *Kniga zhizni* (Gnedich 1929, p. 245) about the origins of the genre of theatrical satire known as 'vampuka'. 'Its author, Mikhail Volkonskii', Gnedich recounts, 'had written a grotesque against theatrical affectations and manners. This was the origin of the name. Volkonskii once told a story of how there was a celebration at the Smolny Institute in honour of the aged Duke of Oldenburg, and the chorus of pupils, bearing flowers, sang to him with the famous motif from *Robert*:

Vam puk, vam puk, vam puk tsvetov podnosim ... (Here's a bunch for you, a bunch for you, a bunch for you, of flowers we bring ... [here there is a play on the word *puk* <fart> and *puchok* <bunch>] – ed.)

these particular attempts coming from different people, then taken all together, attempts that are comparatively more successful and closer to the interests of one social group or another gain an advantage.

It should be added that identical attempts are made independently of each other by different people, and of course they are more often repeated rather more expressively. Consequently, more successful attempts gain an advantage not only owing to their quality but as a consequence of the fact that they crop up more often (i.e. owing to the mass of repetitions that also enable their affirmation).

The social environment represents the arena where constant interweaving, clashes, selection and struggle takes place for a spot in the social consciousness. Social consciousness is thus *in a continual process of formation*. It is formed through the participation of concrete individuals making their contribution to the shared process of creating social opinion, tastes, means of thinking and so on, where each individual is a greater or lesser but nonetheless known component of force.

§ 87

Marxism proceeds from the proposition that social consciousness does not exist outside of its concrete bearers and creators, outside of living individuals, in the same way that history – in the form of a self-sufficient essence that constructs and raises itself, pursuing its goals and realising its ideas, as was assumed in Hegel – does not exist. In reality there is no history that people themselves – specific, concrete individuals – have not created.

One girl, hearing this story, asked: 'Is that really a name, Vampuk?' At first no one understood. But then they figured out that the girl had combined two words into a proper noun. Volkonskii answered her:

'Really? You don't know? Vampuk is a common name. There's a feminine version, too: Vampuka. Very sonorous names!'

Then it dawned upon him. Turning to me, he added: 'Eureka! I've found the name for the heroine of my parody: she will be Vampuka'. And that is how this sobriquet was created, and gained its wings – and now nothing can remove it from theatrical practice ... From Vampuka came the adverb *vampukisto*, and even the verb *navampuchit'*.

This nonsense word, which accidentally sprang into existence, would not of course have been kept if the parody had had no effect. Social acceptance of this particular attempt was obviously prepared by the rebellion of the spectators against the prevailing manners of the stage. Having been affirmed socially, an idea, word or term is no longer subordinate to its author, but has its own fate determined by social laws: the author named the heroine of the parody 'Vampuka', but socially this name was assigned not to the heroine, and not even to the show, but to an entire genre.

Marxism rejects attempts to interpret social consciousness in the spirit of a 'collective social ego', 'public self-consciousness' or 'national consciousness'; it considers these concepts to be false.

In a society torn by class contradictions, there is no unified social opinion nor can there be any. There are antagonistic classes here, and each class has its own class aspirations, tasks and goals, hence its own consciousness, its own class ideology.

Social consciousness (as we will see below, §§ 98–100) implies *a community of interests* of a certain circle of people; where there is no such community of interests, there is no social consciousness. Consciousness always rests on concrete interests that unify or separate people. Therefore it is impossible to speak (at any rate, while a society of class antagonisms exists) of a 'public', 'national' or 'racial' consciousness; this is an empty sound, a pseudo-concept to which nothing in actual reality corresponds.

Where the centralisation (consolidation) of people's actual interests around shared goals, tasks and interests is impossible, no social consciousness exists.

'Within every national culture', Lenin said, 'we can distinguish at least two cultures'. It is obvious that the consciousness of the German proletariat as a class, and its interests, have nothing in common with the social consciousness of the German bourgeoisie and its interests. The interests and ideal aspirations of the German worker are in general the same as the French, English, Polish or American workers, and quite far from the social ideals of their own national German bourgeoisie.

In a society in which class antagonism prevails, social consciousness is above all class consciousness resting on class interests, expressing these interests and acting as their advocate. Class consciousness necessarily exists insofar as the opposition of class interests, which sooner or later must inevitably be realised, exists. The vanguard of a class, a party that organises the will of that class and conducts the struggle, is called upon to accelerate the process of awakening class self-consciousness.

CHAPTER 9

The Social Implementation of Ideas

The Material Support of Ideas

§ 88
Up to now, we have examined the process of the *emergence and circulation of ideas*, touching only upon the way in which certain phenomena, things or events make a path into consciousness. So far, only the question of how phenomena are raised to consciousness and to the stage of ideal existence in the thoughts of subjects, how things are embraced by consciousness and, on the other hand, how consciousness takes hold of objects and is filled with material content have been addressed.

But this is still nowhere nearly sufficient to understand the actual role and essence of intellectual activity.

An idea is the understanding of a situation, the mastery of tasks, the comprehension of objects. However, this is only the first and initial stage of mastering objects in thought and the 'ideation of things'. For an idea truly to master things, and for things actually to become 'ideal things' (hence, in order for people to actually master their thoughts as well as their objects), *putting the idea into practice* and reconstructing matters and things in accordance with the idea is necessary (i.e. reconstructing reality, which lacks ideas, so that it is a mutually linked rational context with definite goals).

Here, in a single act, an idea is put into practice; it is materialised, it receives an objective existence, and things become infused with certain goals – rational objects bearing the meaning of ideal things. At this stage the idea actually acquires flesh and masters the thing *not only in thought*, but also in practice, as it changes this thing in accordance with itself and materially subsides into it, defining the laws and behaviour of this thing. In converting thoughts into action, people learn the value of an idea on the one hand and the actual nature things on the other (see §§ 110–14).

The subjective state of thought is the initial stage of the idea in the exact sense that in this form the idea has an as yet incomplete existence; it exists only in the imagination. In this form, the idea is still only on the threshold of all its future transformations – only on the threshold of its further social and historical phenomenology. It is not yet full-fledged; it is not yet an action, but only the beginning of an action. Though thought, as Marx said, exists ideally in the ideas of a subject, as a project of action and as a result foreseen in advance, it exists as such an ideal concept in the human head only in order to be used for something, to pass over into action. 'Thought strives to be transformed into reality', (Marx), otherwise it is futile and useless. And until the idea has begun this transition into action, in its subjective existence it represents only the beginning of the subsequent act.

Heine once said it was frightening to think that the objects we created required our souls. But it is even more frightening to have created a soul that demands a body from you and chases you with these demands. Thoughts born of us in our minds are just such souls; they do not leave us in peace until we have given them bodies, until we realise them in a tangible and real phenomenon. Thoughts strive to become actions, word wishes to become flesh; in this sense the world actually is the external manifestation of the word!

These mystical-sounding words contain nothing enigmatic, of course, if the poetic liberty is cast aside and 'the world' is understood to be the world of industry, of agriculture, of culture and social relations constantly created by humans themselves and not nature in general – the one in which Hegel, for example, wished to see the manifestation of Absolute Spirit, the noumenal Idea or the Word of God.

In this sense, it is only for humans to 'express and implement their ideas – and the waters are divided from dry land, darkness and light are created, or even new beasts and new vegetation appear'.

In §§ 25 and 26 we described the process of implementing thoughts in action in the labour activity of humans, in production; there, we examined the issue mainly from the standpoint of the separate activities of an individual.

This is insufficient for the complete image, as the individual realisation of thoughts is not something that drives itself; it is conditioned by social factors and is only an element of the social life of ideas and of the social realisation of social ideas.

The goal of further exposition, according to this, consists of examining precisely this aspect of *the social phenomenology* of ideas, of the social transformation of ideas into action, historical events, cultural values and so on.

§ 89

Ideas as such (as 'existing ideally in the ideas of man' – Marx) cannot create anything real; in and of themselves they are powerless and dead despite all the attempts of the idealists to endow them with omnipotence and to draw all creative forces out of them via deduction.

The subjective existence of an idea alone is not sufficient for the conversion of thought into action. In order for something to come out of an idea, real forces are needed that would begin to act in the same direction in for the benefit of the idea. The only bearer of a deliberate vital force in history is humanity. The active intervention of people is required in order for history to accomplish anything.

In a paroxysm of divine consolation, many frequently spoke of the axiomatic triumph of truth and the fall of evil, as if history served the idea and was the realisation of the idea of justice. 'In order to triumph', as Anatole France stated ironically, 'just causes need force quite as much and even more than unjust causes require it'.

'Ideas *cannot carry out anything at all*', Marx said. 'In order to carry out ideas men are needed who can exert practical force'.[1] For people to raise their hands and display an effort, it is necessary that they are induced to this by real motives and want to change what exists. People cannot be prompted only by any given human stimuli. If an idea does not have real support in these vital human interests, in the objective striving of social interests, it has no future and is fruitless. In this case, not only can the idea not be realised, but it is even rarely born as a fantasy.

Marx particularly emphasised the role and significance of *interest* in the field of cognition, of thinking in the structure of people's views and ideology. In the theses on Feuerbach, he expressed this thought as the demand that reality be examined not only 'in the form of the *object*' but 'subjectively, as *sensuous human activity*' in the form of 'practice'.[2] He expressed this same thought more clearly and more graphically elsewhere in his writings. 'The 'idea'', he said, 'always disgraced itself insofar as it differed from the 'interest''.[3] In Lenin's notebooks, these words are copied out, underlined and fitted with a *nota bene*.

Social interests in the broad sense are the real source that impels and fertilises people's intellectual activity; on the basis of interests, thoughts are born and take shape; social interests serve as the real support for the existence of ideas, being the only force pushing these ideas through to life and transforming them into reality.

The same social forces that create, organise and reconstruct general needs and interests also create, form and reconstruct the thoughts of people and their entire mental and ideal world in accordance with these interests.

Owing to this formulation of the question, the classical writers of Marxism were the first in the entire history of philosophy to *carry the problems of epistemology out of the narrow sphere of individual cognition and raise them*

---

1   Marks i Engel's 1928–1946, Vol. III, p. 589 [Marx and Engels 1975–, Vol. 4, p. 119].
2   Marks i Engel's 1933, p. 18 [Marx and Engels 1975–, Vol. 5, p. 3].
3   Marks i Engel's 1933, p. 23 [Marx and Engels 1975–, Vol. 4, p. 81].

to the heights of the problems of social consciousness, linking thought to the schema of economic formations and to the development of social and class interests.

So, what do social interests represent? What are they based on, and how do they take shape?

Needs and Interests

§ 90
When speaking about human needs, human interests, social interests and so on, it should always be remembered that 'humans in general' do not exist, but always only humans from a specific time and society, just as society is not 'society in general' but a specific society located at a certain historical stage of development.

Human needs are not a table of needs given once and for all; they are not inborn natural and biological needs. Ideological sociology, proceeding from 'human essence' and 'their natural needs', forgets that owing to the development of productive life, what is natural for humans has become the great multitude of such needs: fire, electrical lighting, books, theatre and so on, which have nothing in common with the limited sphere of natural and biological needs.

After humans quit the feral mode of life and entered on the path of industrial development, their needs and their interests far outgrew the sphere of natural biological needs and became *historical* in the proper sense of the word: these needs were created and destroyed, took shape and were modified depending on material conditions and social relations.

Marx considered this formation of human needs and their constant modification to be one of the main causes for a boundary being placed between animal and human existence.

The industrial life of humans constantly engenders new needs and changes old ones: 'the action of satisfying and the instrument of satisfaction which has been acquired, leads to new needs; and this creation of new needs is the first historical act'.[4]

Needs and interests are engendered by the social conditions of production. People's interests are defined by their position in the system of productive relations that has been created and the placement of people in the social process of production, distribution and exchange.

---

[4] Marks i Engel's 1933, p. 18 [Marx and Engels 1975–, Vol. 5, p. 42].

Over the course of all of human history, the relations of people, their placement in the social system of production and distribution, and consequently *the fundamental vital interests of people have been defined by the existing forms of property*.

The form of property, the division of labour, the placement of people in the social process of production and distribution: these are all only different expressions of one and the same thing. Marx said: 'Division of labour and private property are, after all, identical expressions: in the one the same thing is affirmed with reference to activity as is affirmed in the other with reference to the product of the activity'.[5]

The form of property, and property relations, can thus be taken as fundamental (and defining all other social relations), on the basis of which people's interests – general and private, collective and individual, group, class and so on – take shape.

Property in general has always and will always exist as long as humans exist. A given form of property inevitably accompanies the history of a society in all the stages of its development. Moreover, property as such – in Marx's opinion – is constantly created in every act of production. 'All production', Marx said, 'is appropriation of nature by the individual within and by means of a definite form of society. In this sense it is a tautology to say that property (appropriation) is a condition of production'. It is clear that '... it is tautological to say that where no form of property exists there can be no production and hence no society either. Appropriation which appropriates nothing is a *contradictio in subjecto*'.

Scholars of the ideology of the parasitic classes, having permitted no thoughts of the possibility of other forms of property besides the private, have always understood property to be only private property. Marx proved that these two concepts (property as such, which has always been and always will be, with private property, which arises at a certain stage of social development and is overthrown in the next) should never be confused. 'It is ridiculous', he said, 'to make a leap from this to a definite form of property, e.g. private property (this is moreover an antithetical form, which presupposes *non-property* as a condition, too). History shows, on the contrary, that common property (e.g. among the Indians, Slavs, ancient Celts etc.) is the earlier form, a form which in the shape of communal property continues to play a significant role for a long time'.[6]

---

5   Marks i Engel's 1933, p. 23 [Marx and Engels 1975–, Vol. 5, p. 46].
6   Marks 1931b, pp. 55–56 [Marx and Engels 1975–, Vol. 28, p. 25].

The Construction of Social Interests

§91

All production assumes the existence of two fundamental agents in its composition: material and personal conditions of production (in other words, the means of production and labour power). In order for people to be able to produce the objects necessary for their lives – simply put, in order for living to be possible – certain material means of production must first be available and, second, these means must be somehow accessible to the producers and workers.

There was no rupture between these fundamental factors of life and production in the first stages of the development of society, when the collective form of property was prevalent, because the all conditions of labour belonged to society. The owner was the community as such: that is, all the members of the primitive horde, or later of the primitive community, were both the owners of all the means and conditions of production and the immediate producers. Here, a direct unity between the material and the personal conditions of production took place. In other words, *the means of production were not alienated from the immediate producers; there was no mediator between them*, separating them and conditioning their association. The primitive community (i.e. all the members of the community) were the immediate possessors and masters of all the material conditions of labour and the means of production at their disposal, being themselves the producers at the same time.

The division of labour, to the extent which it existed at this stage of development, was only a technical, natural, half-mature division of labour; it proceeded from the interests of the individuals themselves and at the same time served the general interests of all the members of the community.

Society intentionally regulated general production, and that is why it had to divide labour based on the interests of all the members of the community. The place of each individual in society in the entire process of production was thus defined by the interests of the entire collective, and hence, of each member. In conformity with this, the division of the products of labour also took place based on the general interests of the entire collective.

Equal participation in social labour in conformity with one's own abilities, and equal participation in the distribution of products, collective property, collective division of labour and collective distribution: on these grounds within the community, the contradiction of the private interests of the members of the community among themselves could not and did not exist. Personal interests had no material preconditions and no material support.

Under such a social structure, the interests of separate individuals could not contradict each other and the general interests of the entire community, but constituted a single whole with them. *The contradiction between private and general interests did not exist*: what worked in favour of the community or was injurious to it also worked exactly to the benefit or to the detriment of any member of that community, and vice versa – whatever was injurious to the separate individual also weakened the collective as such.

There is no individual interest here that did not touch upon others and did not extend to the interests of the entire collective. The general interest of the collective does not exist in abstraction, as the arbitrary sum of separate private interests, but is found in reality as a whole. Individual and general interests here are not separate, but actually constitute a single whole.

At a certain stage of the development of the productive forces of society, these primitive communist relations collapse. As material conditions and the means of production become the objects not of communal or tribal ownership but the objects of ownership by private individuals or individual families in the person of the head of these families, *the means of production are alienated from the direct producers* and a rupture between the material conditions of labour and labour power ensues.

'Whatever the social form of production', Marx said, 'labourers and means of production always remain factors of it. But in a state of separation from each other either of these factors can be such only potentially. For production to go on at all they must unite. The specific manner in which this union is accomplished distinguishes the different economic epochs of the structure of society from one another'.[7]

If in primitive communist society there was a unity between these two factors, then the emergence and consolidation of the institution of private ownership and private property means that the owner, in possessing the material conditions of production (the means of production), bars them from the producers and separates these two necessary conditions of production. Private owners, wedging themselves between these conditions as an extra condition, '… prevent[ing] the coming together of the material and personal levers of production … forbid[ding] the means of production to function, the workers to work and live' (Engels).

After such a rupture, the means of materially uniting these two necessary elements changes. Their unity is regulated not by society but by private owners proceeding not from the interests of the collective but from their own proprietary interests. Having seized production, the owners defend their position as

---

[7] Marx, *Kapital* Vol. II, p. 12 [edition not given- ed., Marx and Engels 1975–, Vol. 36, p. 42].

mediator – persons who condition production (i.e. the unity of labour power and the means of production). They claim that as the owner of the material conditions of production, they are also a necessary condition of production – and, moreover, the main condition. They confirm themselves as owners, as *the third agent of production*. The owners become mediators conditioning the unity of the actual factors of production (labour power and the means of production), hence they become a force defining the entire process of social production – in other words, they become the mediators of all life.

With the consolidation of the rule of private property, all social wealth passes into the hands of private owners; the totality of productive forces torn from the direct producers is concentrated in their hands. Having seized the conditions of production, and defining the unity of labour power with the means of production, private owners become the masters of all social life and the lords of the situation.

Social wealth, in the form of the conditions of production, are transformed into the wealth of the owners, and therefore the owners are invested with forces that until now were not inherent in individual persons. They regard social production as their property. They are, in fact, the masters and lords of all production, land, forests, raw materials – all the sources of life in general.

At the same time, the means of the division of labour also change. Henceforth, the division of labour does not depend on the will of the individual, proceeding from the interests of society, and does not serve them, but is subordinated to the will of the owners and answers to the interests of private proprietors. The free and equal division of labour is replaced with a forced, unequal division. After a *division of the conditions of labour* of this kind has occurred, in which some become the owners of the material conditions and the means of production, and others are deprived of property, equality is impossible; in the same way both the place of the individual in the social process of production and their place in the distribution of the revenue is decided, since whoever owns something takes part in the process of production and in accordance with this receives a share in the distribution. The welfare of the individual and their social position are defined not by *labour* but by *property*. If you are a landowner, and consequently you take part in production using landed property, rent falls to your share out of the general revenue. If you are a capitalist and your capital is tied up in production, you receive profit. And for those taking part in production using their labour as labourers, serf-owners or slaves, there are wages, a few days off, and simple upkeep through food.

The consolidation of the rule of private property gives a certain part of society the opportunity to take part in the distribution of the revenue and to appropriate the labour of others without themselves having to labour. Individuals are now not required personally to take part in production: their property, their plot of land, their capital or their tools of production do so, whereby they take the lion's share of the social revenue. And whoever does not have property – are they a worker? A worker, from the standpoint of the capitalist, is also an owner: they are the owner of their labour power (!) and can also take part in the process of production with their 'property' and accordingly receive 'their share' of the revenue. The concept of property is thus distorted. If in the former case, with regard to the possessing classes, property is understood to be private property and the ownership of the material wealth of society, then in the latter case (as regards workers) property is understood to be the fact that they have arms and legs and physical gifts (?!) in general.

The means of production, being converted into private property, become the source of fraudulent gains. The owners, in capturing the social wealth and accumulating social labour, direct it towards their own wealth and turn it through the implement of the further exploitation of the masses to their own goals and interests.

With the infiltration of personal property, primitive communist relations collapse. With the breakup of collective property into personal ownership, the means of the division of labour and the means of the distribution of the results of labour and so on change. A 'division of labour' of the kind becomes possible where pleasure and labour, production and need fall to the share of various individuals.

Private property, finding its soil and wedging itself into social relations, grows, capturing ever broader social relations and ever more deeply breaking society down into haves and have-nots, into rulers and oppressed, into the privileged and the powerless. From this point, the history of society becomes the history of property relations, the history of the struggle for property, and the entire history of society unfolds as the history of the replacement of one form of private property by others. In a word, from this time the history of all society becomes the history of class struggle.

Under the rule of private property, of course, there is no social interest as *a single whole*, nor can there be one. With the breakup of collective ownership and of social property, *social interest is broken up into a sum of private interests*. Society is not united by interests that are common to all its members. Social interest no longer exists; instead the uncoordinated interests of individual owners, of the haves and have-nots and so on emerge – interests opposed to and contradicting each other. *Individuals are not united in society by interests common to them all; they are linked by interests that are opposed to and contradict each other*. This is first the contradiction of private property, the opposition of interests of separate owners among themselves, and second the contradictory class interests of the haves and the have-nots, the consolidation of the interests of the parasitic classes against the enslaved and so on.

If the *unity* of society, the *community and unity* of interests, corresponded to collective property then the decomposition of community property and the consolidation of private property relations implies the *breakup* of the common interest.

Henceforth, the position of the separate individual in society – and consequently the *interests* of the individual – are not defined by the individual him or herself and not by the collective will, but by the elemental forces that have seized social relations. Right from their very emergence into the world, individuals find themselves in circumstances not created by them, at a place not chosen by them, in much the same way as they did not choose their parents. They find themselves in a society standing at a specific stage of the development of productive forces, with a certain previously established distribution of social goods and the means of production, and with established social relations.

It does not depend on the individual whether s/he inherits capital, enterprises and landed property or if s/he was born into a proletarian family, no silver spoon in the mouth. Right from birth, individual persons are shown their place in society, and even specific professions are imposed on them. The place and position of an individual in society is thus defined by existing social relations created owing to a certain distribution of the means of production and the material conditions of life.

The placement of people in society and in the social process of production is the result of property relations created around the material conditions of production. In fact, labour power – like the material means of production – can be regarded in two ways: on the one hand, as a factor of production, and on the other as the source of revenue. The latter property always flows from the former. The source of revenue does not exist that could not also be an agent of production. If capital, land or labour power are not participants in production, they cannot be sources of the revenue.

As a result of the consolidation of private property, not every individual possessing labour power has the material means of production at his/her disposal. And labour power is then useless to him or her; it can only feed him or her in the event the individual participates in production belonging to another person, taking the place in that production indicated by the master of the enterprise. Thus, the dependence of labour on the material conditions and means of labour takes the form of the dependence of the labourer (the 'owner' of labour power) on the proprietor (i.e. the owner of the material conditions of production).

The owner, having the material conditions of production and the conditions of the distribution of labour in his/her hands, acquires the power of a master, the function of an administrator and of a boss, and has property as the source of the revenue; the proletarian, having only labour power, becomes subordinate to the boss and has his/her labour as the source of their existence. Marx said: 'To the single individual distribution naturally appears as a social law which determines his position within [the system of] production in which he produces; distribution thus being antecedent to production. The individual starts out with neither capital nor landed property. He is dependent by birth on wage labour as a consequence of social distribution. But this dependence is itself the result of the existence of capital and landed property as independent agents of production'.[8]

The place of an individual in society, like the sphere of their real interests, is thus defined wholly *objectively*. They flow from the position of these individuals in the system of production and distribution, completely independent of the individuals themselves.

The Domination of Fetishistic Relations

§ 92
Property relations, the relations of property, become basic and fundamental insofar as the placement of people in society, the division of labour, the place of individual, the distribution of the members of society in accordance with the various sorts of production, the distribution of products and so on all depend on them. Nevertheless, in Marx's opinion, all the moments enumerated above are the same as property. They are identical expressions, where in one case the same thing is affirmed with reference to the means of activity as is affirmed in the second with reference to the activity, and in the third with reference to the products of activity.[9]

'[T]he division of labour also implies the contradiction between the interest of the separate individual or the individual family and the common interest of all individuals who have intercourse with one another. And indeed, this common interest does not exist merely in *the imagination, as the 'general interest', but first of all in reality, as the mutual interdependence of the individuals* among whom the labour is divided ... And finally, the division of labour offers us the

---

8   Marks 1931b, p. 64 [Marx and Engels 1975–, Vol. 28, p. 33].
9   Marks 1931b, p. 63 [Marx and Engels 1975–, Vol. 5, p. 46].

first example of the fact that, as long as man remains in naturally evolved society, that is, as long as a cleavage exists between the particular and the common interest, as long, therefore, as activity is not voluntarily, but naturally, divided, man's own deed becomes an alien power opposed to him, which enslaves him instead of being controlled by him'.[10]

'This fixation of social activity, this consolidation of what we ourselves produce into a material power above us, growing out of our control, thwarting our expectations, bringing to naught our calculations, is one of the chief factors in historical development up till now'.[11]

With the consolidation of the rule of the capitalistic form of private property, all social relations are distorted and appear in an inverted form. Instead of being subordinated to people, property subordinates them. Things begin to rule over people, dictating their relations among themselves to them; people are depersonalised. In becoming owners, people are turned from independent persons having a will into the abstract representatives of their property, becoming its appendage and its tool. The weight and position of an individual in society depends on the 'weight' of their property. It is not a person, but their property speaking and acting for them. People begin to have their value as the value of their possessions (the value of a landowner is only the value of their land, and the value of a holder of capital is the extent of their capital). People's fates begin to depend on the fates of their capital. People depend on things which it seems they possess, but which possess them. Marx called such distorted relations 'fetishistic', describing them as follows:

As a result of the capitalist division of social wealth and labour, '[t]he social power, i.e. the multiplied productive force which arises through the co-operation of different individuals as it is caused by the division of labour, appears to these individuals, since their co-operation is not voluntary but has come about naturally, not as their own united power but as an alien force existing outside them, of the origin and goal of which they are ignorant, which they thus are no longer able to control, which on the contrary passes through a peculiar series of phases and stages independent of the will and the action of man, nay even being the prime governor of these'.[12]

What meaning would private property have, however, if it did not serve as a means of profit? Why would property be needed, if it did not provide, in Marx's words, 'the opportunity to command the labour of others'? The owner defends their right to control the material conditions of production, and by virtue of

---

10   Marks i Engel's 1933, p. 232 [Marx and Engels 1975–, Vol. 5, pp. 46, 47] (italics mine – KM).
11   Marks i Engel's 1933, p. 24 [Marx and Engels 1975–, Vol. 5, pp. 47–8].
12   Marks i Engel's 1933, p. 24 [Marx and Engels 1975–, Vol. 5, p. 48].

that they subordinate people and rule over them not for the sake of amusement and the pleasure of being a master. 'They only enslave people', Engels said, 'in order to prevent them from working for their own benefit'.

How can one person benefit from the work of another, if the latter is unable to produce more than what is necessary to preserve their own life?

'The subjugation of a man to make him do servile work, in all its forms, presupposes that the subjugator has at his disposal the instruments of labour ... In all cases, therefore, it presupposes the possession of a certain amount of property, in excess of the average. How did this property come into existence? In any case it is clear that it may in fact have been robbed, and therefore may be based on *force*, but that this is by no means necessary. It may have been got by labour, or it may have been stolen, or it may have been obtained by trade or by fraud. In fact, it must have been obtained by labour before there was any possibility of its being robbed'.[13]

But at what stage of historical development does private possession and private property become possible? It is clear that this is possible only after the productivity of labour attains a level where the labour of the worker can create a general quantity (S) of the means of existence that, in covering the most necessary requirements of the producer (S_1) yields a certain surplus (M): S-S_1 = M.

Private ownership and private owners have in mind precisely this *surplus of products* remaining over and above needs, *which can be alienated from the immediate producer* while preserving their miserable existence. This is what private property rests on, in fact; its meaning is in squeezing this additional working time and labour surplus out of people for the benefit of the owner.

If we ask what the struggle over the course of all past human history was around, what the subject of the constant discord was, what all the groupings of social interests took place around and are taking place around; if we ask for what reason has all of human history developed and continues to develop as the history of the most brutal conflicts, of class struggles, civil wars, imperialist wars and so on – we must answer all these and similar questions with this: the mainspring of history was the struggle for the consolidation of one form of property or another, and the bone of contention was the possession of material goods (i.e. the source of social accumulation). Without this, the history of society as the history of culture and civilisation would be impossible.

---

13   Engels 1921, pp. 166, 167 [Marx and Engels 1975–, Vol. 25, p. 149].

Surplus Product and Private Property

§93

In Sections 8, 19 and 27 we described the role of the product of labour, which – placed as a mediator of relations between humans and nature and between individuals – shattered the natural and biological links and relationships, consolidating in their place intentional links and economic and social relationships (i.e. ones that emerged not as physical and biological relationships but began with regard to production and the appropriation of material goods).

But the mutual relations of individuals became truly social relations capable of development only at that stage of the industrial life of humanity where products are not simply products but surplus product, and the relations of individual begin taking shape not simply around extraction and production of immediately necessary products but *around production and appropriation of 'surplus product'* (i.e. when the problem of expanded reproduction and the problem of accumulation arose) and, consequently, the productivity of labour attains a level of development that ensures making a surplus above the necessary minimum.

Until that point (i.e. before the possibility of making a given surplus permanent, and not accidental or episodic) people's relations are separate from those of the animals, but only slightly. People produce the necessary products and immediately consume them; if food is scarce, they eat each other or die out. At this stage there is no accumulation, growth of productive forces, or expansion of development; there is no development when society lacks a free product suitable for circulation and for the mutual relations of people (exchange, agreement and so on) or when production goes immediately from hand to mouth – operation with products, and the social relations of distribution, exchange, circulation and so on are quite limited.

At the stage of the economy where human labour – when all one's time is spent on it – can in the best case create the minimum necessary for the preservation of life, the use of other people is otherwise impossible other than as a participant in the process of labour on an equal foundation and in the equitable distribution of product. At the given stage, it is impossible for humans to produce economic profit from another person for one's own benefit, and it is impossible to appropriate another person's labour, hence accumulation – social or private – is impossible. Consequently, expanded production does not exist, and there is no economic life in the real meaning of the phrase. This 'economy' scarcely differs from that of the animals. At this stage, humans have not come far from the animals, since *it is impossible to use the energy of humans and to draw economic profit from it without encroaching on their physical exist-*

ence. The only means of profit that people could produce from other people was the one destroying the other, in much the same way as occurs in the animal world. The natural form of appropriation of the energy of another is the other creature being eaten or – which is essentially the same – the last bite, without which they could not live, being taken from them.

Production of a certain surplus above the necessary minimum for the means of existence (let us call it 'surplus product' or a labour surplus, as Marx called it) first creates the possibility of such relationships where the use of another person and the appropriation of a share of the products produced by them is possible without the physical destruction of that other person, precisely on the basis of preserving their miserable life for the appropriation of the products of their labour.

The surplus product that a person is capable of producing under the corresponding conditions has since then been the mainspring of all social development and the material foundation of all history.

'If the labourer', Marx says, 'wants all his time to produce the necessary means of subsistence for himself and his race, he has no time left in which to work gratis for others. Without a certain degree of productiveness in his labour, he has no such superfluous time at his disposal; without such superfluous time, no surplus labour and therefore no capitalists, no slave-owners, no feudal lords, in one word, no class of large proprietors'.

'If each man's labour were but enough to produce his own food, there could be no property' – private property could not exist.[14]

But humans do not stop producing this surplus without a particular reason; they certainly do not produce it for the pleasure of the process of labour itself. All the discussions of moralists about humans in every social structure being selfless toilers or about the instinct of accumulation inducing them to it like bees or ants and so on is empty, tedious chatter.[15] People are not so stupid as to produce a surplus without a particular need and a particular compulsion towards it, furthermore knowing that this surplus goes into the hands of their enemies and exploiters. Free of all the rest, they will produce exactly as much as will be sufficient for consumption. On the other hand, human needs are not so limited that they could not consume everything they produce. The development of society has not yet reached the level of productivity where humans could create a quantity of products they would be up to their ears in and still have a great deal left over. The surplus of products we are talking about is not

---

14   Marx 1923, p. 450 [Marx and Engels 1975–, Vol. 35, p. 512] (with quote from Ravenstone).
15   Mak-Daugol 1916.

at all an *absolute surplus of products but a relative one* (i.e. what is obtained as a result of the maximum limitation of consumption and the preservation of a quantity of products sufficient to satisfy only what is absolutely necessary).

Hence, in order for there to be a surplus from the labour of individuals above their needs, what is necessary on the one hand is *limiting their consumption of the absolutely necessary and keeping them in poverty*, and on the other *compelling them to produce a maximum* only of what can support the human organism.

In all of the preceding history of humanity, the accumulation of riches never took place on the free will of those whose labour was actually accumulated. If something was accumulated in society, whether it is the social process of accumulation in pre-class society or private accumulation in class society, it occurred in only one way: people forcibly wrung out this labour surplus from other people. This compulsion is, in the first place, compulsion of a social and economic type, in a society of class antagonism it rests on property relations that are most clearly revealed in the capitalist means of production and distribution. And if anyone produces material accumulations, then it is only with the goal of making it the source of the revenue (i.e. in order to rule over others and to appropriate the labour of others).

A private owner, in seizing the material means of production, separating the immediate producers from the conditions of labour and standing between them as a mediator has in mind nothing other than this surplus of products; their goal is organising production so that the immediate producers are compelled to produce the maximum surplus of products for the benefit of the owner.

Only after the development of productive forces makes the production of surplus product possible is the history of the primitive horde first transformed into the actual history of the development of society. Starting from here, people's relations took shape around the production and the appropriation of this surplus product.

Under collective property, accumulation was a social affair proceeding from general interests and serving society. In the tribal structure, social accumulation sometimes achieved – as is now becoming clear – significant proportions. After the disintegration of tribal society and the consolidation of private property, the deflation of surplus product is organised by the owners for the purposes of increasing their own wealth. The surplus product becomes the object of private care, appropriation and accumulation. Social accumulation is thus replaced by private, appearing in the form of private accumulation. The private owner organises production only for the goal of gaining the maximum of surplus labour from others. Since that time, the entire history of society has developed as the history of antagonism over the possession of this sole source of wealth, for the right of appropriation, for the right to participate in the distribution of this product and so on. In a word, the entire history of society becomes the history of the forcible compulsion of people to produce a surplus that is placed at the disposal of the parasitic classes.

The development of production and culture, and the development of humanity in general, moved at such a snail's pace towards the possibility of accumulation that nearly no changes were detected over the course of millennia. Many culturally less advanced tribes, not having reached any form of social accumulation, are to this day still stuck at the most primitive level.

At each stage of the historical development of human society, surplus product and the means of its production and appropriation have taken the most varied forms. In tribal societies, it is the background of tribal accumulation; in slave-owning societies, it appears in the form of absolute property over all means of production, over people (slaves) and everything they produce; in feudal society, in the form of the *corvée*, and subsequently of quitrent; and under capitalistic relations in the form of surplus value, profit and rents (of an industrial, land or loan percentage). Common to all of them is that every development of the productive forces of society and the expansion of production is possible only on the basis of accumulation; no development of society is possible without it. Properly speaking, accumulation, the development of productive forces, the expansion of the productive base and the development of society in general are only different expressions of the same process.

Of course it would be absurd to argue about whether private property in general is good or evil irrespective of what epoch and what stage of the development of society is being discussed. It is naïve to think that the history of humanity accidentally developed along the paths of private property due to an unfortunate mistake,[16] that it could have developed as the history of industry, culture and civilisation to the current stage not on the basis of private property but as part of the tribal structure, for example. In criticising Proudhon,

---

16   Thus, for example, the case was presented by Jean-Jacques Rousseau, who portrayed the origin of private property as society's first fall from grace.
    Rousseau considered 'the first man who, having fenced in a piece of land, said "This is mine" and found people naïve enough to believe him' to be the true founder of a civil society based on property relations. 'From how many crimes, wars, and murders, from how many horrors and misfortunes might not anyone have saved mankind by pulling up the stakes or filling up the ditch, and crying to his fellows: "Beware of listening to this impostor; you are undone if you once forget that the fruits of the earth belong to us all, and the earth itself to nobody"'. Rousseau 1755.

Marx noted: '[T]o obtain this development of productive forces and this surplus left by labour, there had to be classes which profited and classes which decayed'.[17]

'If Saint Sancho (here referring to Max Stirner – KM) ... had once looked at this private property in its empirical existence, in its connection with the productive forces of individuals, then all his Solomon's wisdom, with which he will now entertain us, would have been reduced to nothing. Then it would hardly have escaped him ... that private property is a form of intercourse necessary for certain stages of development of the productive forces; a form of intercourse that cannot be abolished, and cannot be dispensed with in the production of material life, until productive forces have been created for which private property becomes a restrictive fetter'.[18]

But it is even worse to think and hope that once the relations based on private property at some point enabled the growth of the productive forces of society, then at any time thereafter they could also enable the development of society. Only people blinded by reactionary ideology cannot see today that private property and social relations based on it have changed into pernicious chains for any development of society, that they must be burst and actually destroyed by a revolution on a vast section of the world economy.

Proprietary Alienation and Its Liquidation

§ 94

In Sections 25 and 26, we spoke of the alienation that occurs in any human labour activity as the implementation by humans of their premeditated goal into the external existence of a product through conscious activity. This type of alienation, defined by labour, is the expression of labour activity and as such is in Marx's words 'a necessary condition, independent of all forms of society, for the existence of the human race; it is an eternal nature-imposed necessity'. This *alienation* is at the same time *appropriation*, the sole form of actual appropriation by humanity of the substances needed for their lives. The appropriation that became established with the emergence of private property, appearing in the form of alienation by some individuals of the share of labour and the products of others for their own benefit, is of a different type entirely. This type of alienation is based not on the principle of labour, but on *the principle of*

---

17   Marks i Engel's 1928–1946, Vol. v, p. 356 [Marx and Engels 1975–, Vol. 6, p. 159].
18   Marks i Engel's 1933, p. 339 [Marx and Engels 1975–, Vol. 5, p. 355].

property and with the development of capitalist relations it grows, becomes universal and – like all similar definitions of social life – acquires a distorted character. Alienation no longer signifies the working appropriation by the producers themselves of the means of their existence; on the contrary, it is the gratuitous appropriation by the parasitic sector of society (the owners) of the products of the labour of others on the basis of the appropriation of all the social means and sources of life. Owing to this a situation is created where on the one hand 'we have a totality of productive forces, which have, as it were, taken on a material form and are for the individuals themselves no longer the forces of the individuals but of private property, and hence of the individuals only insofar as they are owners of private property ... On the other hand, standing against these productive forces, we have the majority of the individuals from whom these forces have been wrested away, and who, robbed thus of all real life-content, have become abstract individuals ... Labour, the only connection which still links them with the productive forces and with their own existence, has lost all semblance of self-activity and only sustains their life by stunting it'.[19] But insofar as the latter (the have-nots) necessarily need access to the means of production, they must enter into mutual relations with the owners of the conditions of labour. '[T]he wage-worker', Marx said, 'has permission to work for his own subsistence, that is, *to live* only insofar as he works for a certain time gratis for the capitalist ...'.[20] Therefore a 'division of labour' of this kind becomes possible where intellectual and material life, pleasure and labour, production and need fall to the share of various individuals; insofar as individuals entering into mutual relations enter into conflict with one another at the same time.

This circumstance also lies at the base of 'alienation' acquiring the most varied social and fetishistic forms, appearing as something universal: 'Estrangement is manifested not only in the fact that *my* means of life belong to *someone else* ... the inaccessible possession of *another*, but also in the fact than everything is itself something *different* from itself – that my activity is *something else* (activity that is foreign to me – KM) and that, finally ... all is under [the sway] of *inhuman power*'.[21]

Under the rule of private property, 'the productive forces appear as a world for themselves, quite independent and divorced from the individuals, alongside the individuals; the reason for this is that the individuals, whose forces

---

19   Marks i Engel's 1933 p. 57 [Marx and Engels 1975–, Vol. 5, pp. 86–7].
20   Marks 1933, p. 38 [Marx and Engels 1975–, Vol. 24, p. 92].
21   Marks i Engel's 1928–1946, Vol. III, p. 662 [Marx and Engels 1975–, Vol. 3, p. 314].

they are, exist split up and in opposition to one another', and the productive forces of society are in opposition to them as the forces of private property.[22]

Thus, in contrast to what we said in Sections 25 and 26, alienation under the conditions of an antagonistic society appear as proprietary alienation, as alienation of a person's own forces, rights, interests and conditions of their life from them into the property of *another* and at the disposal of *another*. 'Private property, insofar as within labour it confronts labour, evolves out of the necessity of *accumulation*, and is in the beginning still mainly a communal form, but in its further development it approaches more and more the modern form of private property. The division of labour implies from the outset the division of the *conditions* of labour, of tools and materials, and thus the fragmentation of accumulated capital among different owners, and thus, also, the fragmentation between capital and labour, and the different forms of property itself. The more the division of labour develops and accumulation grows, the further fragmentation develops'.[23]

The meaning of private property ... is in the gratis alienation of surplus labour in the immediate producers. The owner's aspiration consists of taking the accumulation into their own hands and *organising all social accumulation as their own property*. The private owner henceforth becomes the mediator of all life; all the wealth created by the direct producers, doomed to miserable lives in poverty, flows to them. The owner organises production with the goal of appropriating the surplus product, organises social accumulation as their own property – private property; in a word, pursuing their private interests and having only their personal profit in mind, they direct the social economy as their own, private economy.

'[B]y the overthrow of the existing state of society by the communist revolution ... and the abolition of private property which is identical with it, this power (alienation. – KM), which so baffles the German theoreticians, will be dissolved ...'.[24]

Alongside the abolition of private property and the socialisation of the means of production, the distorted relations consolidated under capitalism will be abolished, and alienation in the latter sense (i.e. proprietary alienation) will also be abolished. After the liquidation of private property, it will not be private individuals but society itself in charge of production, distribution, exchange and all social life. The social position of an individual will no longer be defined by property, but by labour. From an object of exploitation, labour will become a

---

22   Marks i Engel's 1933 p. 56 [Marx and Engels 1975–, Vol. 5, p. 86].
23   Marks i Engel's 1933, p. 56 [Marx and Engels 1975–, Vol. 5, p. 86].
24   Marks i Engel's 1933 p. 27 [Marx and Engels 1975–, Vol. 5, p. 51].

matter of honour.[25] The labourers of a socialist society will not enrich the owners – the parasites – with their labour, but themselves, their collective farms, their society, providing for their prosperous cultural life in doing so. The problem of accumulation (no longer private capitalist, but socialist, accumulation) will here not only not be removed, but become one of the main branches of the socialist project, insofar as the appropriation by an individual of the full product of their labour for the purposes of their consumption is out of the question over the course of the entire socialist period. Moreover, this cannot be so in a communist society; there is little consolation in the kind of communism where society has to remain stuck at a stage of development that will one day be achieved, and this is inevitable if we adopt the 'right to the full product of our labour'[26] widely proclaimed by numerous petty-bourgeois ideologists, since this would mean depriving society of every source of accumulation and fully paralysing its development.

Communist society differs from socialist society in that under a socialist economy, economic compulsion still exists on individuals (but the compulsion is not on the part of the private owner, but a social and state compulsion) stimulating them to produce above the quantity of products consumed by them a certain share that will go into the socialist accumulation fund of society. The principle of the socialist distribution of labour and of products among individuals says: Each person, after the deduction of a share going to the fund for the socialist project, will receive in proportion to his/her labour. What an individual gives to society thus constitutes his/her individual labour share. '... what

---

25   Labour, the only full-blown manifestation of human life, is not even considered life in capitalist society, only the means to it. If only they are able, a worker must sell his/her life activity (labour) in bits and pieces to the capitalist or languish among the army of the unemployed. '[The worker]', Marx said, 'works in order to live. He does not even reckon labour as part of his life, it is rather a sacrifice of his life'. The worker's twelve exhausting hours of labour that enrich their oppressor and abase their human dignity to the state of a beast of burden, is for them not life but a kind of nightmare. Labour as such has no meaning for the worker 'but as *earnings*, which bring him to the table, to the public house, into bed'. They live in consumption, and not in labour that inspires the creative life of humanity. 'Does [the worker] consider this twelve hours' weaving, spinning, drilling, turning, shovelling, stone-breaking as a manifestation of his life, as life? On the contrary, life begins for him where this activity ceases, at table, in the public house, in bed'. Marks 1932, p. 21 [Marx and Engels 1975–, Vol. 5, pp. 202, 203].

26   Proudhon advanced the demand for 'the full product of labour' as a 'socialist' principle, and Ferdinand Lassalle – as is known – insisted on the formulation of the 'undiminished proceeds of labour'. Marx and Engels subjected these theories to annihilating criticism. Cf. Marks 1933 [in Marx and Engels 1975–, Vol. 3] and Engels's *Zhilishchii vopros* [*The Housing Question* (Engels 1942), Russian edition not specified -ed].

the producer is deprived of in his capacity as a private individual benefits him directly or indirectly in his capacity as a member of society'.[27] The portion of labour that individuals give to society in one form returns in another much more useful form to them.

In a communist society, the development of the productive forces assumes the growth of the cultural level of the workers and the possibility of automating all the processes of labour to such a degree that the human share remains, for the most part, *creative* labour. Here, humanity is completely liberated from every compulsion: they can occupy themselves with whatever actually fascinates them. The opposition of mental and physical labour disappears. Labour, being creative labour, 'becomes not only a means of life, but life's prime want' (Marx). And whatever humans occupy themselves with under these conditions, they will always be producing values many times greater than they are capable of consuming to cover all their personal needs. No matter the extent to which the personal consumption of humanity increases, personal consumption always has certain limits that the individual cannot exceed (this is particularly demonstrably obvious in the spheres of food, drink, clothing and so on), whereas the possibility of the growth of productive social labour under communism is not bound by any limits. From here flows the principle of communist society: from each according to their ability, to each according to their needs.

In accordance with this, a society is communist in which '*surplus product*' is produced by individuals not by means of any sort of compulsion, but as the results of the high cultural level of the technology of a communistically organised society, in which *surplus product* is not so much a premeditated goal as it is *the necessary property of labour-saving work, where we will be dealing with an absolute surplus over and above maximum consumption* and thus in which the process of accumulation – and consequently the colossal growth of the forces of society – will themselves flow from the free labour of individuals.[28] The output in excess of consumption in communist society will be obtained not as a result of the limitation of the personal consumption of individuals but of their maximum satisfaction, not on the basis of the economic compulsion of individuals to produce but on the basis of the full freedom of occupation.

---

27 Marks 1933, p. 25 [Marx and Engels 1975–, Vol. 24, p. 85].
28 We are not trying to portray the people of communism as some sort of ideal, selfless beings (though they actually are such); we are noting the simple fact that insofar as the issue is creative labour, and consequently the direction of forces towards which an individual has an actual calling and is attracted to, people are always prepared to give all their time and power the matters that occupy them the most. Thus the concern of a future society arguable becomes not how to *force* people to work; on the contrary, it becomes how at times to *tear them away* from work and to organise their rest so as to preserve their health.

In a socialist society, economic compulsion (more precisely, the true economic stimulation of socialist labour) and a certain 'inequality' will remain and serve socialist accumulation (i.e. the creation of the foundation for communist society). These questions are taken up comprehensively in Lenin[29] and we will not dwell on them at greater length.

Since the time of Adam Smith, there has been debate about what is meant by productive labour and how to distinguish productive labour from unproductive.

Marx adheres to the standpoint that every economic category is a historical formation and that no definitions valid for all historical epochs and formations exist. In particular, he considered the distinction between productive and unproductive labour as a category of capitalist society and – as is known – provided the following definition: from the standpoint of capitalist economy, only labour that creates capital, labour exchangeable for capital and, consequently, labour that produces this capital is considered productive. Any labour immediately exchangeable for the revenue of society or for services and does not produce surplus value – regardless of whether or not that labour is useful – should be considered unproductive.

From the standpoint of the capitalist, any labour used by a *third* party, which enriches them as an entrepreneur or mediator (i.e. labour exploited by capital and serving capitalist accumulation) is considered productive. In a capitalist economic system the labour of a tailor, for example, who comes home, sews a suit and makes his earnings directly from the customer is unproductive labour, and the tailor is an unproductive worker. If the tailor receives the same order as a wage worker through the owner of a tailoring workshop, then the labour is productive labour and the tailor is a productive worker, since in this case a certain share out of the sum of value created by the tailor goes without compensation to the owner of the workshop in the form of profit (i.e. serves capitalist accumulation). It makes no difference from the standpoint of the consumer, since in both cases the product is the same. But in the first case the tailor creates only consumer value for the client; the tailor earns and entirely consumes all the revenue. In the second case, 'the tailor produces not only a coat, he produces capital; therefore also profit; he produces his master as a capitalist and himself as a wage labourer'.[30]

That is why, Marx says, in the capitalist system of production, '[t]o be a productive labourer is ... not a piece of luck, but a misfortune'.[31]

---

[29] Lenin 1919.
[30] Marks 1923, Vol. 1, p. 262 [Marx and Engels 1975–, Vol. 31, pp. 192–3].
[31] Marx 1923, p. 448 [Marx and Engels 1975–, Vol. 35, p. 510].

In a socialist economy, the concept of 'productive labour' acquires a completely different content and a different meaning. From the standpoint of a socialist economy, productive labour – or, if we discard this term of capitalist relations and speak more plainly, *socialist* labour – is labour that is socialistically organised (i.e. takes part in the social process of socialist accumulation in a socialist project). Any social and state wage labour is such, no less than taking part in socialised and collectivised labour, insofar as the individual takes part in socialist accumulation in this fashion. On the other hand, any labour that takes part in private accumulation and serves private accumulation, is non-socialist labour (for example, the labour of a self-employed farmer) or anti-socialist and inimical to socialism (for example, labour that enriches wealthy peasants, private entrepreneurs and so on). Non-socialist labour is also any labour not linked to socialising a source of revenue or that seeks an independent source of revenue, i.e. any private labour that *immediately and independently earns* all its revenue and thus stands aside from socialist accumulation. If a writer, for example, having written a book, publishes it by themselves and earns all the revenue, their labour is 'non-productive' from the standpoint of a socialist economy; it is non-socialist labour even in the case where the content of the book is superb and aids the socialist project in every possible way, since the labour in this case is not socialistically organised, circumvents the channel of socialist accumulation, and does not materially take part in this accumulation. In accordance with this, a situation where the labour may not be socialist but the product of labour is, and vice versa, where the labour may be socialist but the product is not for example, the labour of a bad workman who, though it is organised as socialist in form, results in anti-socialist and harmful production in content.

§95

In summing up Sections 93 and 94, we can say that only at the stage of social development where the production of a certain relative surplus above the necessary maximum becomes possible does history become the actual history of the development of society as we know it up to now.
1. Beginning with this stage of development, human labour must be accumulated as the aggregate of the means of production and material goods passed from generation to generation. History as *the history of the continuity of humanity's material and intellectual culture* thereby became possible.
2. Only in this case is a share of the products liberated from the sphere of immediate consumption for the purposes of circulation, exchange, bargaining, contracts, the means of profit, economic domination and so on,

and consequently can lie at the foundation of specifically social relations in contrast to biological relations. On the basis of, and owing to, surplus product, the economic utilisation of people by people became possible. At this stage of development, individuals can relate to each other not only as biological individuals but there is the possibility among them of economic and industrial relations, of the division of labour, of exchange and so on. The large-scale form of human relations as social relations (*do ut des, do ut facias, facias ut des, facio ut facias*), in contrast to immediate animal relations, becomes possible.

3. At this stage of development the creation of wealth that can go to improving and expanding the means and methods of human industrial life (i.e. the development of society) is possible.

Starting from this time, all human history takes shape and progresses as the history of the struggle for property, for the mastery of the productive forces of society, as the history of wars, of oppression, of domination and subjection – in a word, as the history of class enmity. Past history was not made voluntarily by the conscious and selfless labour of individuals, but through enslavement, domination and compulsion. All the past history of society unfolded as the history of the struggle for the mastery of accumulated social wealth and around the problems of social accumulation. And the question now posed by history in all its sharpness is also the question of whose hands social production and accumulation lie in: is it to be private capitalist any longer or must it become social and socialist – a question to which history has already given a decisive answer over a tremendous stretch of the globe, where the invincible foundations of a new era in human history have been laid.

The Concept of the Collective Social Field of History

§ 96

The history of society is deliberately created by no one, but it is made by everyone on a daily and hourly basis. Every person inevitably takes part in this general process, whether they want to or not. Merely by the fact of their existence, an individual, whoever they are – infant, disabled, or full-fledged worker, bringing with them a sum total of needs and concerns – necessarily takes part in the general process of creating history and moreover takes part in every moment of their lives, asleep or awake, working, resting or amusing themselves.

The significance and specific weight of each person in the process of creating history is quite different, but we are taking the mass of people who are, ultimately, the true creators of any history. The individual interests, aspirations and behaviours of people motivated by the most varied causes, the individual actions, mutual relations and particular events seemingly having no direct links with one another – all this multiplicity of individual phenomena scattered across space and time nevertheless occurs in society, and hence in social reality all this, being interwoven, is gathered together to form *one general sphere of action*. All these individual phenomena, particular states, minor local events that in the majority of cases are do not *directly* depend on one another, we can imagine as *a single whole*, as *a general sphere of force*, as a unified process. A single overall sphere of the confluence of every possible major and minor social force of action is created, even though they emerge independently of each other; a sphere of encounters, interweaving and various rearrangements of individual scalars and vectors of force acting in society.

At any given moment in time, social reality can thus be regarded as something whole, as a single overall sphere of all forces acting simultaneously, of individual behaviours, states, and so on. At the same time, it is an image of the general state of history at the given moment, the ratio of all social forces at hand at the present moment. In other words, it is the image of the momentary state of the general volatile sphere of history. The construction of this social whole is always defined by the prevalent form of property, and its material features and its laws vary under different social and historical formations. In class society, the structure and laws of the movement of this whole are defined, as we will see below, by the essence and mutual relation of two fundamentally opposed and competing classes.

Though the general social sphere is not objectively perceived or felt by us, it exists in reality as a specific whole consisting of the mutual relations of the enormous multiplicity of individual forces large and small, defining the current history at any given moment.

All the changes and historical progress occurring in society can therefore be regarded as certain displacements of the relations of force within this general social sphere, progressing – depending on size – as a particular and local change or as a fundamental change that seizes the whole and changes all the fundamental relations of force (i.e. the entire structure of society).

Though this general social sphere is a known continuity, the mutual connectivity and mutual conditionality of its separate elements cannot be identified with a self-contained formation such as an organism, a nervous system or physical field of force, for example, in the experiences of surface tension, where the mutual link is so solid that the state of the system as a whole firmly depends on its state at all the individual points, and the smallest local changes alter the state of the entire field. The general sphere of actual history resembles this image somewhat; as we will see below, here the change of the whole does not depend so much on the individual particular phenomena or the behaviours of separate individuals as it does on *the mass condensation of forces* and the formation of general mass centres of force of aspirations and interests.³² Therefore, drawing an analogy with an organism or physical phenomena and taking the mechanical principle of the violation and restoration of equilibrium is impossible without entirely distorting the entire Marxist conception.

The process of creating history is thus the general labile field of history, one general continuous process in time in which everyone takes part. On the part of its factual content, of course, this general social field consists of the actions of separate individuals. The 'anatomical' content of the actual history really presents itself as the accumulation of the behaviours and actions of individual persons, since everything that is done in history is of course done by people; without the participation of individuals, nothing could happen in it.

But if we begin to examine historical changes from the standpoint of the individual persons taking part in it, and if to comprehend the general picture we begin to trace the movements of each person in isolation from each other, then the whole presents itself to use as the chaotic conglomerate of accidental collisions, lacking regularity. If, in this general sphere of the interaction of every possible individual force, we succeed in mapping out a few centres around which the actions of large multitudes are grouped, then the general image of the mutual relations of force become clearer; we understand that the behaviour of the social whole depends on the mutual relations of *these few centres of force* and that the general process will develop in the direction of action of the centres that are strengthening. The true and final causes of historical events, in Engels's words, are not the impulses of separate individuals but the stimuli that set broad masses and entire people into motion; these latter appear in the person of individual groups or classes that arose on the basis of the economic organisation of the given society. Here, stimuli that call forth not fleeting, transitory outbursts but persistent movements leading to great historical changes are important.³³

§ 97

In the life of society, each person as a rule acts on the basis of their position and in pursuit of their goals. Individuals, Marx said, have always started out from themselves, and could not do otherwise. They always pursue only their

---

32 Lenin said that Marx's dialectical method obliges us to look at society 'like a living organism in its functioning and development'. An individual phenomenon is only one of the branches of certain social relations belonging to a certain social and historical formation.
33 Engel's 1931, p. 69.

own interests.[34] This manifests especially clearly after the decomposition of collective property, after the collapse of the common interest into the sum of private interests of individual owners, when the actions and behaviours of individuals are defined by their position as owners.

Under the rule of private property, the interests of individuals appear as separate, particular and differently directed interests. The accumulation of individual, differently directed interests existing in society constitutes a certain *general sphere of mutual relations and the struggle of interests*.

The interests of people represent the only living force that sets the mechanism of every history into motion. All the social changes and historical shifts are carried out by the force of collision and the mutual relations of interests, and progress as certain shifts occurring in the general sphere of social interests. Thus the image of the history of antagonistic society is the spontaneous result of the collision of particular forces and the various intersections of the individual vectors of force of particular, individual interests.

But if we examine the social and historical process only from the standpoint of the private interests and actions of individual people taking part in it, then the history of society appears to us in the form of a confusion of uncoordinated behaviours and acts, in no way connected with one another, of separate individuals, history as a whole appears to be an incoherent chronicle of accidental events and individual particular states, in the succession of which there is no regularity whatsoever.

If, apart from the particular states, individual conditions and motives defining the actions of individuals, no general forces existed that directed the actions and thoughts of many in a certain direction and along certain *general channels* through the prism of individual interests and behaviours, then conformity to the laws of history would be only transient and fictitious.

If the particular interests of separate individuals remained only particular, without affecting other individuals and shared interests, if they were not gathered into certain general centres of interests and thus did not form the *centres of force* of actual history, social and historical regularity as such would be simply impossible. But the facts show that this is not so, that certain general stimuli and real interests compel people and drive them: some to mutual convergence, unification and solidarity, others to mutual hostility and antagonism.

Particular interests, as they take shape beyond the will and desires of individuals, also develop independently of them and take shape in general or opposing group and class interests. 'Individuals have always ... proceeded *from*

---

34   Marks i Engel's 1933, pp. 24, 66, 226, 426 [Marx and Engels 1975–, Vol. 5, p. 246, *inter alia*].

themselves', Marx said, 'but since they were not *unique* in the sense of not needing any connections with one another, and since their *needs*, consequently their nature, and the method of satisfying their needs, connected them with one another ... they *had to* enter into relations with one another. Moreover, since they entered into intercourse with one another not as pure egos, but as individuals at a definite stage of development of their productive forces and requirements, and since this intercourse, in its turn, determined production and needs, it was, therefore, precisely the personal, individual behaviour of individuals, their behaviour to one another as individuals, that created the existing relations and daily reproduces them anew'.[35]

Therefore '... *personal interests always develop, against the will of individuals, into class interests, into common interests which acquire independent existence in relation to the individual persons*, and in their independence assume the form of *general interests* ... as such they come into contradiction with the actual individuals and in this contradiction, by which they are defined as *general* interests, they can be conceived by consciousness as *ideal* and even as religious, holy interests'.[36]

In Lenin's *Philosophical Notebooks* we find the following important stroke in the description of the character of conformity to the laws of history: 'An excellent picture of history: the sum of individual passions, actions, etc. (everywhere something akin to ourselves, and therefore everywhere something that excites our interest for or against), sometimes the mass of some general interest, sometimes a multitude of *'minute forces'* which produce a tremendous result from what appears insignificant'.[37]

The existence of this 'mass of general interest', and the gathering of 'minute forces' of individual interests and actions into the masses of general interests and to create something immense, requires objective conditions to direct individual interests into certain general channels and the actions of separate individuals to be objectively gathered and accumulated into some form of *general centres*.

If the historical process consisted only of uncoordinated, differently directed individual vectors of force of the collision of individual actions and particular motives, stimuli and interests, then in colliding they would erase and level each other without by doing so creating *general centres of mass interest*, a solid

---

35 Marx and Engls 1927–1935, Vol. v, p. 418 [Marx and Engels 1975–, Vol. 5, p. 437].
36 Marx and Engls 1927–1935, Vol. v, p. 226 [Marx and Engels 1975–, Vol. 5, p. 245] (italics mine – KM).
37 Lenin 1931, p. 155 [Lenin 1960–1979, Vol. 38, pp. 307–8].

volitional mass of interests that, owing to their colossal dimensions and power alone, are the true levers of history and of human changes.

The question is, which forces in this society that has dissolved into private interests and private relations, are capable of forming centres of general interests, are creating social consolidation, unions, groups, classes and so on, and with that are, in a certain manner, creating and organising the opinions of people as solidaristic or opposing opinions? Putting the questions of thinking in this light and placing a robust materialist foundation under them, Marxism indicates at the same time the path of their solution: the development of the productive forces of society and the forms of property corresponding to them, the placement of people in the social process of production and exchange constitutes the real bases on which the specific grouping of interests takes place. The relations of individuals to the means of production, and consequently to the material conditions of life and the specific place occupied by individuals in society resulting from it – their position in the system of social production, distribution, and exchange – inevitably centres the interests of some individuals around certain tasks and goals, and the interests of other people around other tasks and goals.

Personal and particular interests can form a compact historical force only in cases where, in unifying around specific points, goals and tasks beyond the will and desires of people, they strive *objectively* for certain *centres of general mass interests* that are decisive in all major historical movements.

Otherwise, we would be dealing with a decentralised, uncoordinated state of vectors of force in which the mass of minute forces erasing each other would be unable to form powerful centres of general forces, and therefore every historical event would appear only as an accidental result of a chaotic process deprived of laws and consistency.

The thoughts and behaviours of separate individuals stimulated by numberless particular circumstances and motives are different, and it is impossible to predict how, in some instances, an individual will behave in the general sphere of social relations. If, apart from these particular stimuli and accidental actions of separate individuals, no general causes *that impel people en masse* (as if they did not think and behave in individual circumstances and act in a private capacity) and condition their aspirations towards identical goals, shared tasks and actions existed, then history would be an arena of occurrences devoid of any general regularity.

But owing to the fact that a given division of labour exists, the placement of people in society and the placement of interests proceeding from it; owing to the fact that the personal and particular interests of individuals do not remain particular, but affect – even beyond their will – the interests of others, developing into common interests and forming common centres of mass, group and class interests, the historical process is the process of the mutual interaction of these *centres of force* of history. History is thus a regular sequence that is not forcefully violated by separate individual and particular deviations.

It could be said that an individual as such, in many respects, is for science still an unsolved riddle, but people in general are becoming the axiom. We can never guess what some individual person will do, but we can say with some accuracy how people in certain circumstances will act. This is understandable, since insofar as the separate individual and isolated phenomena in general are at issue, they can vary within the boundaries of sufficiently large deviations and 'take on values' that are so far from each other than it is impossible to speak of a correct sequence and the strict regularity of the process. The 'pivot' around which the vast majority of cases would group as around a specific centre of the greatest possibilities – a *Häufungspunkt* (limit point), so to speak – is absent in the phenomena. When we are dealing not with a single separate individual, but with a large number of them, and examine a society of people as a large multitude of individuals linked by their positions and specific social relations, then despite all the separate deviations the thoughts, aspiration and behaviours of people tend in general towards a specific general type, forming certain general channels.

This specifically is where the character of social and historical conformity in capitalist society, which Marx defined as a social regularity, being implemented with the inevitability of a natural law, as a *natural and historical regularity*.

'Communist theoreticians ... are distinguished precisely by the fact that they alone have *discovered* that throughout history the "general interest is created by individuals who are defined as private persons". They know that this contradiction (of general and private interests – KM) is only a *seeming* one because one side of it, what is called the 'general interest', is constantly being produced by the other side, private interest, and in relation to the latter it is by no means an independent force with an independent history – so that this contradiction is in practice constantly destroyed and reproduced. Hence it is not a question of the Hegelian 'negative unity' of two sides of a contradiction, but of the materially determined destruction of the preceding materially determined mode of life of individuals, with the disappearance of which this contradiction together with its unity also disappears'.[38]

---

38   Marks, i Engel's 1933, p. 227 [Marx and Engels 1975–, Vol. 5, p. 247].

Class Interests

§ 98
Since the interests of individuals depend directly on their social position (i.e. on the existing prevalent forms of property) and since individuals find themselves, independently of their will, placed in specific social groups and classes depending on what place they occupy in the social process of production and distribution, the both generality and the fragmentation and opposition of their interests flow from this.

Identical relations to the means of production (i.e. to the material conditions of life) and the identical positions of individual in society (in the system of production and distribution) resulting from this create interests common to these individuals.

The opposing positions occupied by individuals as a result of a given distribution of the means of existence create general opposing interests of individual social groups and classes.[39]

The first circumstance (identical position and commonality of interests) lies at the foundation of class solidarity, serving the cause of the internal cohesion of individuals and the creation of a specific social whole as a class.

The second circumstance (opposing positions and general opposing interests) form the basis of class antagonism, class hostility and the class struggle and is the sole force and sole path of development of a society consisting of antagonistic classes.

Thus, the means of production and form of property are inevitably linked with certain groupings of social interests and condition them; and vice versa, a certain structure of social interests maintains and constantly recreates specific forms of social life, production and exchange. The opposition of class interests and the class struggle are only an expression of the contradictions that develop within the process of social production.

---

[39] Marx says about capitalist society that here 'separate individuals form a class only insofar as they have to carry on a common battle against another class; in other respects they are on hostile terms with each other as competitors. On the other hand, the class in its turn assumes and independent existence as against the individuals, so that the latter find their conditions of life predetermined, and have their position in life and hence their personal development assigned to them by their class, thus becoming subsumed under it. This is the same phenomenon as the subjection of the separate individuals to the division of labour and can only be removed by the abolition of private property'. Marks, i Engel's 1933, p. 44 [Marx and Engels 1975–, Vol. 5, p. 77].

From this standpoint, a class interest is nothing other than the fundamental task of the given class resulting necessarily, objectively and unambiguously from the position of that class in the given system of social relations.

A class interest is thus a fully *objective and real something*, and not a subjective definition. Subjectively, interests inimical to a person may seem to them to be their own interests, but objectively these interests do not become theirs because of it. The existence of a class interest does not depend on whose consciousness it may be, and does not depend on whether or not their bearers are conscious of these interests. If the existence of a class signifies the existence of individual occupying a certain place in the social process of production, distribution and so on, it means that a real social formation exists and that the class interests of these individuals, as a system of tasks for this class, are instead defined completely *objectively* and independent of the consciousness, will and desires of these people. It is possible that individuals are not conscious of their own interests, that class interests remain generally unrecognised by their class as a subject of history (as, for example, with slaves or with impoverished peasants before the proletarian revolution) but the interests of these people do not cease to exist; they exist inevitably on the strength of the actual position of things as a result of specific social relations.

Marx had this objective character of a social interest in mind when he said that 'common interest does not exist merely in the imagination, as the 'general interest', but first of all in reality, as the mutual interdependence of the individuals among whom the labour is divided ...'.[40]

Class interests have a real existence even when they are not yet recognised by a class, in the same way that the class interests of the proletariat actually existed before the proletariat recognised itself as a class. These interests are defined by the position of the proletariat in the capitalist means of production and by the laws of development of capitalist economy.

The immortality of the cause of Marx and Engels is not only in the fact that through their works they first revealed the class interests of the proletariat and presented them in undisguised form, and in so doing assisting in awakening the class self-consciousness of the proletariat in their universal historical tasks, but their great service before history also includes the fact that they first brought a historical science absorbed entirely in grandiloquent phrases and pharisaical maxims about morals out of the sphere of subjectivism and placed historical cognition on the firm foundation of objective reality.[41]

---

40 Marks, i Engel's 1933, p. 23 [Marx and Engels 1975–, Vol. 5, p. 46].
41 Cf. Lenin 1926–1935, Vol. I, pp. 60–63 [Lenin 1960–79, Vol. 1, pp. 137–9].

'... [C]ommunists do not oppose egoism to selflessness or selflessness to egoism, nor do they express this contradiction theoretically either in its sentimental or in its highflown ideological form; they rather *demonstrate its material source, with which it disappears of itself*. The communists do not preach *morality* at all ... They do not put to people the moral demand: love one another, do not be egoists, etc.; on the contrary, they are very well aware that egoism, just as much as selflessness, *is* in definite circumstances a necessary form of the self-assertion of individuals'.[42] Marxism builds its social ideals not on abstract principles and general didactic wishes, but on the real data of history itself. We are building a communist society on the basis not of ethical assumptions and moralistic demands, but by establishing the material conditions of life in such a way that people do not have to fight like dogs for possession of a bone and that some do not live at the expense of others.

The nucleus of Marx's sociological concept, in Lenin's definition, consists of the fact that 'Marx put an end to the view of society being a mechanical aggregation of individuals which allows all sorts of modification at the will of authorities (or, if you like, at the will of society and the government) and which emerges and changes casually, and was the first to put sociology on a scientific basis by establishing the concept of the economic formation of society as the sum total of given production relations, by establishing the fact that the development of such formations is a process of natural history',[43] that the historical development of society is subject to inevitable objective laws and that the desires, intentions, aspirations and opinions of people are themselves defined by their position and objective social forces. In Engels's words, nothing happens in the history of a society 'without a deliberate intention, without a desired aim. But this distinction (between the history of society and the history of nature – KM), important as it is ... cannot alter the fact that the course of history is governed by innate general laws'.[44]

Class interests represent the ideal of a social structure that most meets the position of a given class and is objectively most advantageous for it. It is the ideal of society outlined from the standpoint of the objective position of that class.

Until the oppressed class is clear about its own position and recognises its interests, it is not united by the consciousness of solidarity. Despite this, the struggle nonetheless occurs, but it is conducted as a disorganised elemental class struggle since the movement at this stage of development does not yet

---

42 Marks, i Engel's 1933, p. 227 [Marx and Engels 1975–, Vol. 5, p. 247] (italics mine – KM).
43 Lenin 1926–1935, Vol. I, 62–63 [Lenin 1960–79, Vol. 1, p. 142].
44 Engel's 1931, p. 67 [Marx and Engels 1975–, Vol. 26, p. 387].

have a common recognised goal or common programme; hence, the movement is not a unified whole, it has an episodic character, the struggle is disorganised and scattered in time and space, and separate particular movements are not subordinate to the general class goal.

After a class recognises its position, its tasks and interests, it not only elementally but consciously represents a unified whole and its struggle becomes an organised struggle for the realisation of its tasks and ideals. Now, the movement creates for itself a guiding centre (a party), it has a programme, strategy and tactics, and on the strength of this it possesses a deliberate purposeful orientation. Henceforth, individual particular movements pursue not only local goals and serve not only local interests; they thus do not disperse class energy, but each particular movement serves a shared class goal and is the bearer of shared class tasks, ideas and causes. In Lenin's definition, the role of the party as vanguard consists of awakening class consciousness, uniting the masses, organising and leading them into battle, guiding the movement as a whole, subordinating each particular movement to the general and raising it to the heights of the general interests and tasks of the working class.

Ideas Are Derivatives of Social Interests

§ 99
Insofar as what is at issue is the history of society, of changes to the forms of social life, and the evolution of views and the shift of ideas, it should be remembered that interests are the living force impelling people to carry out these changes. Whatever history represents and however it progresses, it remains incontrovertible that no one but people themselves make it. People can be moved only by their needs and interests, and not by some kind of motives standing outside their lives. But as noted, these interests are defined by the existing forms of property, the division of labour, of production and of exchange.

All the actions and behaviours of people in society are defined and directed by a certain distribution of their interests. But people, forced by their position to act in a certain manner and to pursue certain goals, also possess consciousness; and their consciousness also takes part in this process of life in that it serves as a tool of rational orientation, making goals pursued by people with conscious goals.

The position of people in society and the interests resulting therefrom thus define all their ideas and representation, the orientation of their consciousness, all the content of their thoughts and the means of thinking.

'Consciousness (*das Bewusstsein*) can never be anything else than conscious being (*das bewusste Sein*), and the being of men is their actual life-process'.

'The production of ideas, of conceptions, of consciousness, is at first directly interwoven with the material activity and the material intercourse of men – the language of real life. Conceiving, thinking, the mental intercourse of men at this stage still appear as the direct efflux of their material behaviour'.

'The ideas which these individuals form are ideas either about their relation to nature or about their mutual relations ... *It is evident that in all these cases their ideas are the conscious expression – real or illusory – of their real relations and activities, of their production, of their intercourse*, of their social and political conduct. The opposite assumption is only possible if in addition to the spirit of the real, materially evolved individuals a separate spirit is presupposed'.[45]

The interests of people in the broad sense, in whatever form they appear and however the moralists assess them, are the sole impulses arousing people to action (i.e. they constitute the only living force of any act of historical creation). Objective social interests define the intentions and goals of individuals and create social opinion and social ideals; they aid in the realisation of these ideals and set the boundaries of this realisation.

What, from this standpoint, do ideas, thoughts, ideals and all the formations of consciousness in general, the entire sphere of thought as such, represent?

All these ideal formations in the brains of people, in Marx's words, are the necessary sublimates (products) of their material life process,[46] and are only a reflection of the life interests of people. They are, *above all, their own interests raised to consciousness and having received a certain expression in the consciousness of people*. Ideas and conceptions, Marx said, if they are to be examined cut off from their material and social basis, are only 'whimsies or fixed ideas'.[47]

We thus arrive at the further clarification of the definition of the idea itself and of the essence of thought. *The idea*, in accordance with the above, is nothing other than the *false or true, correct or mistaken reflection and perception by people of their illusory or actual interests.*

The idea is only the *subjective* expression of interests, *the subjective aspect of an interest*. From the objective side, interests are the objective content of tasks that are necessarily given together with the material conditions of existence of a given class, independent of people's opinions and desires.

---

[45] Marks, i Engel's 1933, p. 16 [Marx and Engels 1975–, Vol. 5, p. 36] (italics mine – KM).
[46] Marks, i Engel's 1933, p. 17 [Marx and Engels 1975–, Vol. 5, p. 41].
[47] Marks, i Engel's 1933, p. 139 [Marx and Engels 1975–, Vol. 5, p. 160].

Ideas and thoughts are thus *one of the particular forms of the manifestation of human interests* that aside from their *subjective* manifestation in people's consciousness have in addition a multitude of other manifestations in the social, economic, legal and political life of a society.

Conceptions, ideas, thoughts and in general all the ideal formations in people's brains are certain *derivatives from social interests* and to that extent, like all other forms of the manifestation of these interests (such as legal, political, etc.), are dependent on material conditions and social relations.

People's thoughts and views, their ideology, religion and philosophy, like law, politics, familial forms, and the state do not exist on their own, but on the strength of the social relations and material conditions that arrange people in society in a specific manner and building their interests in accordance with this. The regularity of their development is only the *reflected regularity of the development of the material motive forces of history*.

'Morality, religion, metaphysics, and all the rest of ideology (also law, the state, politics and so on – км) as well as the forms of consciousness corresponding to these, thus no longer retain the semblance of independence.[48] They have no history (of their own, spontaneous – км), no development; but men, developing their material production and their material intercourse, alter, along with this their actual world, also their thinking and the products of their thinking. It is not consciousness that determines life, but life that determines consciousness'.[49] 'The philosophers', Marx says, 'have only to ... realise that neither thoughts nor language in themselves form a realm of their own, that they are only *manifestations* of actual life'.[50] They are the expression of social interests.

We can now tentatively recapitulate what has been said about the paths of cognition. In defining epistemological problems, the founders of Marxism took a radically different position from all preceding philosophy, in particular from the lines of Kantian philosophy prevailing in Europe. Above all, Marxism seeks the solution of the questions of the theory of cognition in the history of cognition. In the opinions of the bourgeois philosophers, the forms of thinking are given *a priori* in the form of unchangeable, eternal categories and have significance independently of time, social affiliation and so on. For Marx, the forms of cognition are something that change over the course of historical development, depending on the development of social interests and on the content (i.e. the objects) of cognition.

---

48 'It must not be forgotten', Marx says, 'that law has just as little an independent history as religion'. Marks, i Engel's 1933, p. 54 [Marx and Engels 1975–, Vol. 5, p. 91].
49 Marks, i Engel's 1933, p. 17 [Marx and Engels 1975–, Vol. 5, pp. 36–7] (italics mine – км).
50 Marks, i Engel's 1933, pp. 434, 435 [Marx and Engels 1975–, Vol. 5, p. 447].

As opposed to Kantian philosophy, which considered the question 'How is cognition possible?' (*Wie der Erkenntnis*) fundamental to epistemology, Marxism advances another, more fundamental question: 'what (which phenomena specifically) do humans make the object of their thinking?' (*Was der Erkenntnis*). These two questions must be examined in unity, not separately. Cognition is the reflection of reality, and that is why the means of thought (the forms of thinking, the *Wie der Erkenntnis*) depend on the objects of cognition and the tasks of comprehension (on the content of thinking, on the *Was der Erkenntnis*). And vice versa, the general orientation of consciousness defines the objective content of thinking. Pre-Marxist philosophy, believing that the content of thinking is naturally given to humanity insofar as they have sensory organs, did not notice any sort of problems here.

Marxism puts the question of the object of cognition and of the subject in a new light. The cognising subject, for Marx, is not an isolated 'human atom' (Engels: *lumpiges Einzelindividuum*). In this role, humans act in their social existence – class – and their vanguard – the party – at the same time being the *real subject of history*.

Not every individual at every time is capable of correctly reflecting reality in their cognition, independently of their social affiliation. The realisation of correct cognition depends on the existence or manifestation of particular conditions for cognition. These conditions not only rule over the subject, but also extend over the objects. Which objects are perceived and which are ignored depends on the structure of social *interests and the actualisation* of objects in social and historical practice.

Cognitive activity, regardless of its active character, requires a push from outside in order to be put into motion. These stimuli should be sought in social causes. For the emergence of new ideas, new social relations, new objects of thought or the need for new comprehension of old relations – more precisely, two main conditions – are needed:

1. The active orientation of consciousness on specific objects and
2. The tendency of objects, their aspiration towards thought.

The first of these conditions is expressed in the general form of the concept of the interest. The interest of the subject defines the orientation of consciousness on particular tasks, themes and objects. The second condition is defined by the meaning of objects and their real significance in social and historical praxis. Objects, falling into the centre of attention and of individuals' activity, suggest specific methods and forms for their understanding that gradually approach increasingly adequate cognition. Here, we have the increasing convergence noted by Lenin of the historical path of cognition with its logically valid one.

3. Going over to the social existence of an idea, we put the concept of *social interest* as an *objective* category to work, appearing in class society in the form of objective class interests. The concept of *social interest* contains within it both the moments noted above, synthesises them and defines both conditions of cognition. On one hand, a social interest activates the consciousness of the large mass of people, imparting a specific orientation to it. On the other hand, the significance and real meaning of objects in social praxis depends on it (on the social interest). The social interest moves specific objects into the foreground, actualising them and moving others back.

Formulating these conclusions in other words, we can say: the structure of thought depends first on the tasks of comprehension, and second on the material (the objects) of thought. Both the one and the other are defined by social praxis and by a given structure of objective social interests. The material of comprehension is formed by social and historical praxis, by which the tasks of comprehension are defined.

How people arrive at consciousness of their interests, how their interests become conscious interests – the answer to these questions naturally issues from the above.

The existence in a society of specific views, opinions, convictions and ideas would be impossible if they did not find a certain support in social interests. Ideal formations are bound by their emergence and existence to particular manifestations of human interest (past or current) and are more or less truthful or distorted reflections of particular social interests in people's consciousness. *From this standpoint, ideas and thoughts are certain stages on the path of the full and correct perception by people of their actual interests.*

The Character of Conformity to the Laws of History in an Antagonistic Society

§ 101

Basing themselves on the fact that people place specific tasks before themselves, pursue specific goals and aspire to realise their intentions, the idealists put together and extremely simplistic representation of the character of the historical process. They attempted to present history as the realisation by people of their previously outlined goals and desires, as the conscious realisation by them of their tasks and ideas outlined in advance. They depicted the process of historical creation as a premeditated process, as if people in the history of their development had arrived at previously thought-out results. This orientation was presented by a broad circle of such names as Wilhelm Windelband, Heinrich Rickert, Hermann Cohen, Paul Natorp, Rudolf Stammler, Karl Vorländer, Georg Simmel and others.

Others, joining immediately to the Hegelian interpretation of 'Absolute Spirit', imagine the matter as if history, serving a specific eternal idea, is the realisation of a certain logic fulfilling the plans and intentions of a World Spirit and the world manifestation of the *Logos*.[51]

As a variation on the same theme, they attempt to present history in the form of some sort of super-real subject, capable of pursuing its own goals and of moving through events, in addition using humanity only as means and material.[52]

All similar theories – which have many a representative in contemporary philosophy – while differing among themselves in certain particulars, agree on a fundamental point: specifically, that history, in contrast to natural history, is ostensibly the science of ideas (human or divine) freely believed by people and realised by them. In other words, history is the realisation of rational intentions and moral goals, and forming judgements about it is possible only based on *evaluative relations to it, subjectively, axiologically*. In keeping with this, they placed a teleological principle, instead of the principle of causality, at the base of history. They based it either on ethics (Hermann Cohen, Paul Natorp, Franz Staudinger et al.) or on psychology (Lester Ward, Gabriel Tarde, Georg Simmel, and so on).

1. Ideological historiosophy, proceeding from assumptions that ideas govern history and that people create their history in accordance with their own goals

---

51   Dilthey 1922 and 1927; Freyer 1923 and 1930.
52   This, for example, is what one of the prominent representatives of contemporary bourgeois philosophy, Richard Kroner, having recently declared his sociological views at a philosophical congress in the United States, wrote: 'The idea holds sway over the entire world, being nothing other than existence itself, inasmuch as it manifests in a mental form'. 'History is the service of the idea, the struggle for the idea'. 'The struggle in history is conducted not for the fate of people, races, or nations; here, the fate of the idea, and therefore also the fate of the world, is decided. Every historical conflict is, to a much smaller degree, the struggle for possession of the world, rather than the struggle for the possession and development of the mental appearance of the world'. 'The idea acquires the content of the gigantic struggle that history serves – the imposing spectacle in which races, nations and individuals, like actors, play a role intended for them by the idea'. Kroner 1936, pp. 204–12. It seems highly strange to us that Kroner advances these propositions on his own behalf when they have such a well-known author, which for some reason is not mentioned even once in the report of this neo-Hegelian. The neo-Hegelians obviously decided to rest on Hegel's laurels with the conviction that the nineteenth century had completed and exhausted all the development of science. But in this case, is it worth making statements on your own behalf?

and intentions, forgot that these goals and desires do not fall from the sky and that people's ideals do not come by chance.

People's desires and intentions are not given to them from on high, are not the emanation of a World Spirit; 'pure thought, freely supposing itself out of nothing' (Cohen) is not woven out of itself. Though people themselves create their ideas and their representations, just as they themselves are the creators of their history,[53] the direction in which people begin to desire, think and act and the direction in which they will create their own history does not depend on them. The society in which individuals find themselves placed – even the fact itself of their birth – does not depend on the individuals; they inherit the state of productive forces and social relations from the preceding generation. In the same way that the social position and interests of particular individuals are not selected by them, they are also not free in choosing their ideas, in working out their representations and in planning their goals. Humans, of course, always desire and strive for what they consider good and useful, correct or advantageous. But what will seem so to them – will they, and can they, believe one thing or another to be correct, good and useful – is not in any way dependent on them.

All prior history is evidence that people are far from free in having their convictions and views, and in disposing of their opinions as they like; they cannot imagine, desire and think whatever they like. I am no longer speaking about political control of a state. Thoughts, desires, feelings and moral principles are imposed on people by their social existence. The same people who – beyond their will – form social relations in conformity with their material means of production, *are compelled* to also form all principles, ideas and categories in conformity with their social relations and objective social interests.[54]

Vulgar materialists, when they speak about freedom and determinism of the will, are limited chiefly by examining only the physiological aspect of the question. They reduced the unfreedom and determinacy of the will and of human behaviour to determination by their physical causes and physiological data. This standpoint is extremely crude and incomplete; it is incapable of explaining neither human behaviours nor human thoughts. The cause of specific views and behaviours cannot be seen only in human physiology. People think, act and

---

53   So as not to leave room for any ambiguity, Marx noted in his criticism of Stirner: '*History* does *nothing*, it "possesses *no* immense wealth", it "wages *no* battles". It is *man*, real, living man who does all that, who possesses and fights; "history" is not, as it were, a person apart, using man as a means to achieve *its own* aims; history is *nothing but* the activity of man pursuing his aims'. Marks, i Engel's 1928–1946, Vol. III, p. 118 [Marx and Engels 1975–, Vol. 4, p. 93].
54   Marks 1931c, p. 93.

behave in one way or another not from physiological determinacy, but above all owing to the social conditions in which they have to live. The difference in the thoughts, aspirations and behaviour from the convictions and aspirations of a bourgeois is not at all owing to the different physical determinacy of their psyches and the differences of their physiological constitutions. Change the social conditions of individuals and you will see what changes occur in the broad masses, with the same physical and physiological constitution, as regards their world-views and convictions.

Insofar as the subject of discussion is humanity, real historical humanity, it should be clear that freedom and unfreedom of opinions, wills, desires and behaviours is above all a social question, not a physiological one. It is especially apparent in those cases where mass opinion, mass aspirations and the behaviour of a vast group of people – social classes – are concerned, where it is quite absurd to draw the physiological determinacy of the will in for help.

2. In a society where private property and private interests prevail, the historical process of development cannot be a conscious realisation of the specific ideas and interests of all of society, simply on the basis of the fact that such an interest common to all and uniform ideas that unite all the forces of society do not exist. Here, individuals are prompted not by interests and ideals common to them all, but by opposing aspirations. The historical process thus does not have the form of coordinated actions, but turns out to be the spontaneous result of the struggle and clash of countless individual interests and of particular aspirations, forces and actions. Though the actions of particular individuals pursue a specific conscious goal every time, the results that occur in the meeting, intersection and clash of these particular desires and conscious goals are often far from desirable.

'History', Lenin says, 'does not begin with a conscious aim ... What is important is that which appears *unconsciously for mankind* as the results of its action ... *In this sense* "Reason governs the world"'.[55]

3. Even in those cases where, in creating their history, people realise their interests, they are not always capable of controlling the forces they intentionally called to life. The feats accomplished by people often exceed the intentions of those people, being at odds with their original desires and frustrating the original plans.

The actions of people realising their interests produce in history something above and beyond what they strive for and achieve. '[People] gratify their own interest, but something further is thereby brought about, which was latent in

---

55   Lenin 1931, p. 153 [Lenin 1960–1979, Vol. 38, p. 306].

their interest, but which was not in their consciousness or included in their intention'.[56] A thing, inasmuch as it is made, and an event, inasmuch as it is complete, acquires objectively historical existence and as such they become agents in their own right, independent of the will and desire of their creators. They can play a role and acquire a significance and an objective meaning that no one intended and that no one put into them when creating them. If the prophet Isaiah said 'You turn things upside down, as if the potter were thought to be like the clay! Shall what is formed say to the one who formed it, "You did not make me"? Can the pot say to the potter, "You know nothing"?' – however strange it may be, it sometimes turns out just that way, and – what is more amusing – truth is on the side not of the Old Testament prophet, but of the pot. A thing made, a feat accomplished, having taken its place in the objective world and in history, begins somehow to live its own life and can lead to results directly opposed to the desires and intentions of their creators. In this sense, what has been done often outgrows the authors and agents themselves in its significance and its force.

Each victory we achieved is fraught with consequences that are impossible fully to account for, especially in the current state of society and human knowledge. 'Each victory, it is true', Engels said, 'in the first place brings about the results we expected, but in the second and third places it has quite different, unforeseen effects which only too often cancel the first. The people who, in Mesopotamia, Greece, Asia Minor and elsewhere, destroyed the forests to obtain cultivable land, never dreamed that by removing along with the forests the collecting centres and reservoirs of moisture they were laying the basis for the present forlorn state of those countries ...'.

'When the Arabs learned to distil spirits, it never entered their heads that by so doing they were creating one of the chief weapons for the annihilation of the aborigines of the then still undiscovered American continent. And when afterwards Columbus discovered this America, he did not know that by doing so he was giving a new lease of life to slavery, which in Europe had long ago been done away with, and laying the basis for the Negro slave trade. The men who in the seventeenth and eighteenth centuries laboured to create the steam engine had no idea that they were preparing the instrument which more than any other was to revolutionise social relations throughout the world. Especially in Europe, by concentrating wealth in the hands of a minority and dispossessing the huge majority, this instrument was destined at first to give social and political domination to the bourgeoisie, but later, to give rise to a class struggle

---

56   Lenin 1931, p. 153 [Lenin 1960–1979, Vol. 38, p. 306].

between bourgeoisie and proletariat which can end only in the overthrow of the bourgeoisie and the abolition of all class antagonisms'.[57]

People cannot take into account all the consequences of their actions; in particular, this concerns people living in a society torn by class antagonisms and proprietary interests.

The ruling proprietary classes never made it their aim to move history forward; the development of productive forces and the growth of cultural power were in no way among the intentions of the possessing classes who had seized all the sources of social life: the land, the mines, the banks, industry and transport. These people strove for, and are striving for, profit; they have attempted to increase their revenue, and history turned out to be a collateral, unintended result of realising these interests of private property.

§ 102

Even if all the activities carried out in history by particular individuals are conscious, the historical process as a whole still does not become a conscious realisation of goals.

People's aspirations and ideas, of course, are realised in history, but they are not realised through people's agreements, pacts and combined and unanimous activities that previously took into account the universal beneficial nature of these ideas but as the result of the clash of differently directed interests, through struggle. Thus, the realisation of ideas is the process of a social order, and in class society it is not the attainment of specific, previously outlined and conscious goals but the result of the clashes of various opinions, contradictory interests and the relentless struggle of classes.

Engels described this elemental character of historical creation thus: '[E]ach person follows his own consciously desired end, and it is precisely the result of these many wills operating in different directions and of their manifold effects upon the world outside that constitutes history'. In addition, the most varied motives, aspirations, and incentives move particular individuals. 'Thus the conflicts of innumerable individual wills and individual actions in the domain of history lead to a state of affairs quite similar to that prevailing in the realm of unconscious nature.[58] The ends of the actions are desired, but the results which actually follow from these actions are not desired ...'. '[People's] motives, there-

---

57   Marks i Engel's 1925, pp. 102, 103 [Marx and Engels 1975–, Vol. 25, pp. 461, 462].
58   In Engels's words, the following situation prevails in unconscious nature: 'In nature – in so far as we ignore man's reverse action upon nature – there are only blind, unconscious agencies acting upon one another, out of whose interplay the general law comes into operation', Engel's 1931, p. 67 [Marx and Engels 1975–, Vol. 26, p. 387].

fore, in relation to the total result are likewise only of secondary importance',[59] what is important is what comes out at the end as a general social resultant.

The viciousness of the idealistic understanding of history consists of the fact that the process of history is considered to be intentional; the idealists believe that history is created by people in accordance with previously thought out goals and ideas, that history is the conscious result of freely set and realised goals (e.g. the family, the state, and the law in the understanding of the majority of bourgeois ideologues). Even more vicious are the views of the sociologists who imagine history as the realisation of a certain logic, as a logical chain of succession of certain links along the path of development of the 'Absolute Idea'.

Against these maxims and abstract mystical representations, Marxism sets off the sober propositions of a truly scientific philosophy: consciousness does not exist on its own, and thoughts and ideas do not arise through spontaneous generation from the depths of pure consciousness. People are not free to improvise their thoughts through 'the free act of the self-positing of thinking', as Hermann Cohen thought.

In order to imagine something, people must be compelled to it by objective social causes and interests. The social conditions of life are involuntarily imposed both as objects (i.e. the content of thinking) and as the means of thinking. Ideas and thoughts are brought into people's heads insofar as they find support in the actual lives and interests of these people.

It is not ideas that move history; on the contrary, it is people compelled by the state of their productive forces to change the conditions of their existence and also compelled in accordance with this to construct and reconstruct their thoughts and their views. 'In direct contrast to German philosophy which descends from heaven to earth, here it is a matter of ascending from earth to heaven. That is to say, not of setting out from what men say, imagine, conceive ... but setting out from real, active men, and on the basis of their real life-process demonstrating the development of the ideological reflexes and echoes of this life-process. The phantoms formed in the brains of men are also, necessarily, sublimates of their material life-process, which is empirically verifiable and bound to material premises'.[60] 'This conception of history ... has not, like the idealist view of history, to look for a category in every period, but remains constantly on the real *ground* of history; it does not explain practice from the idea but explains the formation of ideas from material practice, and accordingly it comes to the conclusion that all forms and products of consciousness cannot be dissolved by mental criticism ... but only by the practical overthrow of the

---

59   Engel's 1931, p. 68 [Marx and Engels 1975–, Vol. 26, p. 388].
60   Marks, i Engel's 1933, p. 16 [Marx and Engels 1975–, Vol. 5, p. 36].

actual social relations which gave rise to this idealistic humbug; that not criticism but revolution is the driving force of history, also of religion, of philosophy and all other kinds of theory'.[61]

Both the origin of certain ideas and their realisation are thus not an individual act but above all a phenomenon of a social type; ideas are inseparably linked with social processes and flow from them. This is why the task of Marxist philosophy in the spheres of thinking and the history of ideology consists of our understanding 'what seems to [us] to be a product of *thought*' to be 'a product of *life*'.[62]

The 'social intellect' that develops in all past history is not the premeditated realisation of specific ideas and the organised fulfilment by society of its shared goals (there are no such common ideas, shared goals and common will in an antagonistic society) but the result of the clash of particular interests and class aspirations. The given forms of social, economical, political and ideological life are not consciously established, but emerge spontaneously in the process of the social struggle of interests, becoming the tools of class rule. Not only the political and legal forms, but the fates of ideas – technological, moral, artistic, scientific and so on – depend directly or indirectly on the blind laws of an anarchic economy and market, that arena for the clashes of private interests and state actions.

In light of this, all of preceding history had the character of a blind, spontaneous process, in many respects reminiscent of the condition prevailing in unconscious nature where regularity paves the way in the form of the blind result of the clashes and mutual influence of various forces.

The Social Implementation of Ideas

§103

The material conditions and social relations that are the motive forces of history also govern the life of ideas of a society, yielding a fertility of ideas in certain historical periods and a drought of ideas and idiocy in others.

As we have said, ideas and representations – insofar as they have emerged and exist in people's consciousness, expressing specific interests – strive to leave their imaginary existence and pass over into deed; they strive to reconstruct things in their own image and in them acquire a real existence in the flesh.

---

61   Marks, i Engel's 1933, p. 28 [Marx and Engels 1975–, Vol. 5, p. 54].
62   Marks, i Engel's 1933, p. 226 [Marx and Engels 1975–, Vol. 5, p. 246].

But the transformation of ideas into deeds requires first, the existence of certain material preconditions, and second, that the ideas capture the masses, inspiring them and rousing them to action. Every realisation of an idea is possible only because in these ideas, people *realise – or it seems to them they are realising – their interests.*

Thoughts, convictions, ideas – inasmuch as people achieve them through hard work, of course – are also motive forces and stimulations. In this sense, it would be possible to use the words of Virgil: *mens agitat molem* – mind moves matter. But the acquisition of ideas, like their realisation, is defined socially: social conditions place limits on both the awareness of these ideas and on their realisation. Ideas can capture the masses, and the masses will strive for their realisation only in the event that these ideas express specific social interests and if *the realisation of these ideas is at the same time the realisation of the vital interests of the masses themselves.*

If ideas cannot acquire a mass character and if, consequently, they do not lean on social interests (i.e. they do not have real social forces under them), then they have no significance, even if they are expressed hundreds of time: they lead to nothing. In and of themselves, ideas are impotent. *'In order to carry out ideas men are needed who can exert practical force'.* (Marx).[63] To lead to anything, ideas need people who are interested in them, who see their interests in them and have put effort into their realisation.

From this standpoint, what is theory and what is practice? What does their difference consist in?

From this standpoint, what is theoretical is what has existence only in thought, and practical is what has passed over into deed, has been realised or is in the process of realisation.

'[T]heory also becomes a material force [and hence a practical force – KM] as soon as it has gripped the masses' (Marx). In order for certain ideas and intentions to seize the masses, it is necessary for these ideas to touch upon the interests of the masses and form certain centres of general mass interest.

Marx said: 'Theory is capable of gripping the masses as soon as it demonstrates *ad hominem*', and this only occurs when it touches upon the interests of the masses and is an expression of these interests.

Starting from this, we can formulate the same question of theory and practice somewhat differently, using the words of Feuerbach: 'Theoretical is what is still hanging about only in my head; practical is what is found in the heads of many. What unites many heads, forms a mass and spreads, and with that wins

---

63   Marks, i Engel's 1928–1946, Vol. III, p. 147 [Marx and Engels 1975–, Vol. 4, p. 119].

a place in the world'.[64] Only in this case is the transition to reality secured for an idea, since the efforts of a few single people in the swamp of decaying social life will be futile.[65]

Marx never tired of expressing the thought that an idea always leans on certain interests of people, that everything in history happens only as a result of the struggle of social interests, beginning from the earliest years of his literary activity until the end of his life, in thousands of different variations and formulations. All the more striking that many who consider themselves 'experts' on Marx, touching upon the Marxist theory of cognition, forget this basic point and forget that any cognition is a fact of a social type, a historical fact leaning on a certain arrangement and objective construction of social interests. These 'experts' prefer to construct a theory of cognition according to the old traditional canvas of empiricism, on the basis of the irritation of the sensory organs and the accumulation of the simplest sensations.

For their realisation, ideas require certain material preconditions. These preconditions are, on the one hand, real conditions, and on the other, people's interests; the latter are a living material force that conditions people's thoughts and aspirations, moving both the history of thinking and the entire history of a society.

'Theory can be realised in a people only insofar as it is the realisation of the needs of that people'. The question is can, and will, 'theoretical needs be immediate practical needs? It is not enough for thought to strive for realisation must itself strive towards thought'.[66]

Insofar as the idea is revealed and exposes itself in people's consciousness as their actual interests, it no longer has to be forced out of one's head and to compose a theory on the basis of 'the self-positing of pure consciousness'; *it is enough to take the actual definitions of reality and actual generalisations that reality itself makes in the process of its development, and to make this data of reality itself into the principles of cognition and action.*

---

64   Marks, i Engel's 1928–1946, Vol. 363 Letter from Ludwig Feuerbach to Arnold Ruge, June 1843. Feuerbach 1903–11, Vol. 18, pp. 342–43.
65   'The Marxist', says Lenin, 'proceeds from the same ideal; he does not compare it with "modern science and modern moral ideas, however" but *with the existing class contradictions*, and therefore does not formulate it as a demand put forward by "science" but by such and such a class, a demand engendered by such and such social relations (which are to be objectively investigated), and achievable only in such a way in consequence of such and such properties of these relations. If ideals are not based on facts *in this way*, they will only remain pious wishes, with no chance of being accepted by the masses, and hence, of being realised'. Lenin 1926–1935, Vol. 1, p. 289 [Lenin 1960–1979, Vol. 1, pp. 416–17].
66   Marks, i Engel's 1928–1946, Vol. 407 [Marx and Engels 1975–, Vol. 3, p. 183].

'Just as the *economists* are the scientific representatives of the bourgeois class, so the *socialists* and *Communists* are the theoreticians of the proletarian class. So long as the proletariat is not yet sufficiently developed to constitute itself as a class, and consequently so long as the very struggle of the proletariat with the bourgeoisie has not yet assumed a political character, and the productive forces are not yet sufficiently developed in the bosom of the bourgeoisie itself to enable us to catch a glimpse of the material conditions necessary for the emancipation of the proletariat and for the formation of a new society, these theoreticians are merely utopians who, to meet the wants of the oppressed classes, improvise systems and go in search of a regenerating science.

But in the measure that history moves forward, and with it the struggle of the proletariat assumes clearer outlines, *they no longer need to seek science in their minds*; they have only to take note of what is happening before their eyes *and to become its mouthpiece*. So long as they look for science and merely make systems, so long as they are at the beginning of the struggle, they see in poverty nothing but poverty, without seeing in it the revolutionary, subversive side which will overthrow the old society. From the moment they see this side, science, which is produced by the historical movement and associating itself consciously with it, has ceased to be doctrinaire and become revolutionary'![67]

The significance of these words has not yet properly been assessed. They speak about the demands of a true science: not to invent abstract, purely intellectual definitions and advance them as doctrine, but to take as principles of cognition the actual definitions of reality itself, making them the law for thinking. Scientists can only be the mouthpieces of actual events in their undisguised form insofar as they are the ideologues of a revolutionary class. Marx and Engels formulated their relation to theory thus, in the *Communist Manifesto*: 'The theoretical conclusions of the Communists are in no way based on ideas or principles that have been invented, or discovered by this or that would-be universal reformer. They merely express, in general terms, actual relations springing from an existing class struggle, from a historical movement going on under our very eyes'.[68]

---

[67] Marks, i Engel's 1928–1946, Vol. v, p. 377 [Marx and Engels 1975–, Vol. 6, pp. 177–8] (italics mine – KM).

[68] Marks, i Engel's 1928–1946, Vol. v, p. 495 [Marx and Engels 1975–, Vol. 6, p. 498].

§104

Ideas (political, technological, moral, aesthetic or whatever you like), having grown out of social needs, create an entire world (technological, literary, the world of cultural values, etc., according to the content of these ideas) in the direction of the vector of their activity. *Ideas, in thus acquiring objective existence* and the solidity of fact, are harnessed to a series of already completed and objectively existing entities and take part in them as components of this objective sphere of history. This is the world of objective history, forming with all the parts of its material and intellectual history into a certain unified whole together with the people whose behaviour (and mutual relations) are defined by the laws of this whole. Everything new that enters into this social complex is assimilated by the latter and subjected to its laws; simultaneously, the social whole itself adapts to this new thing, in part or in whole, and commensurate with it undergoes changes of a particular or more general type.

These objectively created social relations, in defining people's interests and formulating their aspirations, ideas and the entire world of ideas of a society, promote or hinder the realisation of certain interests and ideas.

If, in Section 25, we spoke about the conscious setting of goals and the intentional realisation of ideas in the act of production and communication, then it now turns out that the intentions of people are conditioned by social relations, *that each act of production and communication into which individuals have to enter is only the particular manifestation of the given general social structure,* that the existence in individuals' consciousness of certain ideas, like the realisation of these ideas and interests, is a process *of a social type* and in all preceding history this process progresses in the form of social conflicts.

§105

The unity of aspirations and the generality of opinions corresponds to the unity of interests. The fragmentation of interests gives birth to the variety of goals and the difference of views. The opposition of views and of principles is only the reflection of antagonistic interests that are tearing capitalist society apart and serving as the mainspring of class struggle. But the oppressed classes being aware of their position and their interests requires active intervention by the vanguard and conscious part of the class – specifically the active educational work of the party, rousing class self-awareness among the proletariat and organising its struggle against the existing structure.

In class society, all social movements – like ideological ones – occur through the clash of class interests and the class struggle. The composition of any ideology, the strengthening of each world view, like all the changes and shifts in people's thinking, occurred not through spontaneity but at the price of a relentless struggle of specific social groups, classes and parties.

If specific ideological foundations and a specific means of though and representation correspond to a specific means of production,[69] then the bearers, subjects and implementers of these principles and ideas are always given social groups or classes. Class 'subjectivism' not only does not exclude the objective truth of cognition, it is the core condition for achieving it. The advocate of objective truth is precisely the class whose interests are aimed at uncoupling and maximally developing the productive forces of society, and consequently is the bearer of a much higher means of production and therefore a much more advanced means of thinking. A reactionary, obsolescent class is compelled to mask the actual state of affairs in favour of its own interests. The interests of a revolutionary class require an accurate prognosis, i.e. a true understanding and exposure of surrounding reality. Not only is the true face of reality not frightening to the revolutionary class, but a true understanding of this reality is the sole guarantee of its success.

§ 106
To realise its interests and pave the way to its ideas and aspirations, a class must win power and establish its rule. 'No class of civil society', Marx says, 'can play this role (of the overthrow of the old social, political and ideological foundations. – KM) without arousing a moment of enthusiasm in itself and in the masses, a moment in which it fraternises and merges with society in general, becomes confused with it and is perceived and acknowledges as its *general representative*; a moment in which its demands and rights are truly the rights and demands of society itself; a moment in which it is truly the social head and the social heart. Only in the name of the general rights of society can a particular class lay claim to general domination. For the storming of this emancipatory position, and hence for the political exploitation of all spheres of society in the interests of its own sphere, revolutionary energy and intellectual self-confidence alone are not sufficient. For the *revolution of a nation* and the *emancipation of a particular class* of civil society, to coincide, for *one* estate to be acknowledged as the estate of the whole society, all the defects of society must conversely be concentrated in another class, a particular estate must be the general stumbling-block, the incorporation of the general limitation, a particular social sphere must be looked upon as the *notorious crime* of the whole of society, so that liberation from that sphere appears as general self-

---

69 See Marks 1931c, second and fifth observations.

liberation. For *one* estate to be *par excellence* the estate of liberation, another estate must conversely be the obvious estate of oppression. The negative general significance of the French nobility and the French clergy determined the positive general significance of the immediately adjacent and opposed class of the *bourgeoisie*'.[70]

The class coming to power must find help and support in other oppressed classes in order to mobilise all the forces of society against the ruling class for the overthrow of the existing structure. To get support among the masses, the class that is rising to power or already ruling is compelled to proclaim its class interests as the common interests of all of society. '[E]ach new class', Marx says, 'which puts itself in the place of one ruling before it is compelled, merely in order to carry through its aim, to present its interest as the common interest of all the members of society, that is, expressed in ideal form: it has to give its ideas the form of universality, and present them as the only rational, universally valid ones'. This portrayal by the parasitic classes of their own class interests as the highest ideals was, in all of preceding history, only the organised deception of the mass of people, insofar as class structure and oppression – changing only its form – remained stable. Only the proletariat, which overthrows every subjugation and sees its ideal in a classless communistic society, has the actual right to affirm that it represents the interests of all labourers and of exploited humanity and, in liberating itself, it liberates all humanity from the chains of slavery of private property and from the parasitic classes.

In speaking about social ideas and their realisation through social struggle, we of course have in mind the central questions of social consciousness and and the ideological formations that are cardinal on the paths of the development of history. But, *mutatis mutandis*, the same applies to every individual act of understanding and of the formation of thought, and to every individual setting and establishment of goals. We want to emphasise again that the laws of individual thinking in general are the same as the laws of the social composition of thought. But it does not flow from this at all, that the study of society should begin with the study of the nature of humanity, as bourgeois sociologists believed. On the contrary, it is impossible to understand human beings without having studied the society in which they are formed and in which they live. People's individual thinking among the general mass is conditioned by the same factors and is subject to the same general laws as social consciousness in general. Both here and there, thinking is supported and nourished by the move-

---

70 Marks, i Engel's 1928–1946, Vol. I, p. 409 [Marx and Engels 1975–, Vol. 3, pp. 184–5].

ment of people's real or illusory interests, and is only the expression of those interests in the broad, and not narrowly mercantilist sense of the word.

Class Consciousness

§ 107
In view of the above, class ideology is only the expression of the interests of a given class. These are the interests of a class raised in one form or another to the awareness of individuals of that class, having found reflection in their consciousness.

The ideology of the ruling parasitic classes represents the ruling material relations expressed in the forms of consciousness through the ideas and views of that class (i.e. the ideal expression of those relations that make this class the ruling one, and its thoughts the ruling ideas). *It is the expression of the interests of the ruling class, developed by the ideologues of that class in a direction that gives class interests the apparent form of universal interests and portrays them not only as the interests of the ruling class but as the interests of the whole of society.*

In order to consolidate its rule, defend its property and secure its rights and interests, it proclaims them as a universal good, an inevitable world order, the highest perfection, the absolute truth and so on.

There is no better description or more comprehensive account of the essence of class consciousness than the one Marx gave us, which is why we are citing here these places from *The German Ideology* in their entirety, despite their length.

'The ideas of the ruling class are in every epoch the ruling ideas; i.e., the class which is the ruling *material* force of society is at the same time its ruling *intellectual* force. The class which has the means of material production at its disposal, consequently also controls the means of mental production, so that the ideas of those who lack the means of mental production are on the whole subject to it. The ruling ideas are nothing more than the ideal expression of the dominant material relations grasped as ideas; hence of the relations which make the one class the ruling one, therefore, the ideas of its dominance. The individuals composing the ruling class possess among other things consciousness, and therefore think. Insofar, therefore, as they rule as a class and determine the extent and compass of an historical epoch, it is self-evident that they do this in its whole range, hence, among other things rule as thinkers, as producers of ideas, and regulate the production and distribution of the ideas of their age: thus their ideas are the ruling ideas of the epoch. For instance, in an age and in a country where royal power, aristocracy and bourgeoisie are contending for domination and where, therefore, domination is shared, the doctrine of the separation of powers proves to be the dominant idea and is expressed as an 'eternal law'. The division of labour, which we already saw above as one of the chief forces of history up till now, manifests itself also in the ruling class as the division of mental and material labour, so that inside this class one part appears as the thinkers of the class (its active, conceptive ideologists, who make the formation of the illusions of the class about itself their chief source of livelihood), while the others' attitude to these ideas and illusions is more passive and receptive, because they are in reality the active members of this class and have less time to make up illusions and ideas about themselves. Within this class this cleavage can even develop into a certain opposition and hostility between the two parts, but whenever a practical collision occurs in which the class itself is endangered they automatically vanish, in which case there also vanishes the appearance of the ruling ideas being not the ideas of the ruling class and having a power distinct from the power of this class. The existence of revolutionary ideas in a particular period presupposes the existence of a revolutionary class; about the premises of the latter sufficient has already been said above.

If now in considering the course of history we detach the ideas of the ruling class from the ruling class itself and attribute to them an independent existence, if we confine ourselves to saying that these or those ideas were dominant at a given time, without bothering ourselves about the conditions of production and the producers of these ideas, if we thus ignore the individuals and world conditions which are the source of the ideas, then we can say, for instance, that during the time the aristocracy was dominant, the concepts honour, loyalty, etc., were dominant, during the dominance of the bourgeoisie the concepts freedom, equality, etc. The ruling class itself on the whole imagines this to be so. This conception of history, which is common to all historians, particularly since the eighteenth century, will necessarily come up against the phenomenon that ever more abstract ideas hold sway, i.e. ideas which increasingly take on the form of universality. For each new class which puts itself in the place of one ruling before it is compelled, merely in order to carry through its aim, to present its interest as the common interest of all the members of society, that is, expressed in ideal form: it has to give its ideas the form of universality, and present them as the only rational, universally valid ones. The class making a revolution comes forward from the very start, if only because it is opposed to a *class*, not as a class but as the representative of the whole of society, as the whole mass of society confronting the one ruling class. It can do this because initially its interest really is as yet mostly connected with the common interest of all other non-ruling classes, because under the pressure of hitherto existing conditions its interest has not yet been able to develop as the particular interest of a particular class. Its victory, therefore, benefits also many individuals of other classes which are not winning a dominant position, but only insofar as it now enables these individuals to raise themselves into the ruling class. When the French bourgeoisie overthrew the rule of the aristocracy, it thereby made it possible for many proletarians to raise themselves above the proletariat, but only insofar as they became bourgeois. Every new class, therefore achieves domination only on a broader basis than that of the class ruling previously; on the other hand the opposition of the non-ruling class to the new ruling class then develops all the more sharply and profoundly. Both these things determine the fact that the struggle to be waged against this new ruling class, in its turn, has as its aim a more decisive and more radical negation of the previous conditions of society than all previous classes which sought to rule could have.

This whole appearance, that the rule of a certain class is only the rule of certain ideas, comes to a natural end, of course, as soon as class rule in general ceases to be the form in which society is organised, that is to say, as soon as it is no longer necessary to represent a particular interest as general or the 'general interest' as ruling.

Once the ruling ideas have been separated from the ruling individuals and, above all, from the relations which result from a given stage of the mode of production, and in this way the conclusion has been reached that history is always under the sway of ideas, it is very easy to abstract from these various ideas 'the Idea', the thought, etc. as the dominant force in history, and thus to consider all these separate ideas and concepts as 'forms of self-determination' of the Concept developing in history. It follows then naturally, too, that all the relations of men can be derived from the concept of man, man as conceived, the essence of man, Man. This has been done by speculative philosophy. Hegel himself confesses at the end of the *Geschichtsphilosophie* that he 'has considered the progress of *the concept* only' and has represented in history the 'true *theodicy*'. Now one can go back again to the producers of 'the concept', to the theorists, ideologists and philosophers, and one comes then to the conclusion that the philosophers, the thinkers as such, have at all times been dominant in history: a conclusion, as we see, already expressed by Hegel. The whole trick of proving the hegemony of the spirit in history (hierarchy, Stirner calls it) is thus confined to the following three attempts.

No. 1. One must separate the ideas of those ruling for empirical reasons, under empirical conditions and as corporeal individuals, from these rulers, and thus recognise the rule of ideas or illusions in history.

No. 2.   One must bring an order into this rule of ideas, prove a mystical connection among the successive ruling ideas, which is managed by regarding them as 'forms of self-determination of the concept' (this is possible because by virtue of their empirical basis these ideas are really connected with one another and because, conceived as *mere* ideas, they become self-distinctions, distinctions made by thought).

No. 3.   To remove the mystical appearance of this 'self-determining concept' it is changed into a person – 'self-consciousness' – or, to appear thoroughly materialistic, into a series of persons, who represent the 'concept' in history, into the 'thinkers', the 'philosophers', the ideologists, who again are understood as the manufacturers of history, as the 'council of guardians', as the rulers. Thus the whole body of materialistic elements has been eliminated from history and now full rein can be given to the speculative steed ...

Whilst in ordinary life every shopkeeper is very well able to distinguish between what somebody professes to be and what he really is, our historiography has not yet won this trivial insight. It takes every epoch at its word and believes that everything it says and imagines about itself is true'.[71]

Ideological Changes and Social Changes

§108

When, in Marxist science, people speak about the contradictions that arise in social life – about social contradictions – this should always be understood to mean the contradictions of people's *interests*. When, for example, the classical authors of Marxism portrayed the contradictions between the state of the forces of production and the existing relations of production, they always portrayed it as the contradictions of people's *interests*, and not at all as contradictions between things. The relations taking place here are not physical but social, precisely in that because of them, social interests prove to be arranged in such a way that they cause conflicts between people, and not things. The contradictions in society exist not among things, but among people with regard to these things (their production, distribution, exchange and so on). Things could easily reconcile themselves with one another, if only people could reconcile themselves with one another concerning these things.

For historical science, the position conquered by the classical authors of Marxism – consisting of the fact that every change and shift in the ideological

---

71   Marks, i Engel's 1933, pp. 36–40 [Marx and Engels 1975–, Vol. 5, pp. 59–62].

currents of a society can occur only on the basis of a specific arrangement of social interests, and owing to the redistribution and regrouping of the interests of people, 'real, active men, as they are conditioned by a definite development of their productive forces and of the intercourse corresponding to these' (Marx) – is of paramount importance.

Over the course of all preceding history, nothing has changed in social life and in social consciousness other than through struggle and social conflicts. The consolidation or disappearance of specific beliefs, views, customs and so on is always linked with certain social shifts that occur in a society, with the victory or defeat of certain social layers, groups or classes.

Behind every change in the composition and structure of a language, of beliefs, customs, ideas and views are hidden certain social shifts, the social movements of people, the redistribution and other centring of social interests; social conflicts, the shift of social forces, political powers and so on are brought to light.

From this flows a position of tremendous methodological significance for historical science: in the fixed forms of language, of myths, customs and so on, and on the back of those changes that have occurred and are occurring in them, we must look for concrete social forces in the form of collectives of people carrying out specific social shifts. *We should always look for specific social conflicts of a historical type on the backs of ideological formations.* The data of mental culture, of language, of folklore and so on are thus the documents of a historical past, more often than not more dependable than the evidence of historians who – intentionally or otherwise – suppressed or distorted actual history for the benefit of the politically dominant classes.

CHAPTER 10

Testing Ideas in the Process of Their Implementation

What Is Experience

§109
To explain certain views or stocks of thought, theoreticians of the formalist school use a few favourite but rather questionable methods. In these cases, they usually seek out analogous ideas in some individual thinker from their predecessors or contemporaries. The question of the cause and genetic roots of ideas is considered as having been explained if it can be successfully found that at some point, similar ideas were expressed by someone and, by drawing a comparison, the scientific investigation is considered complete. Bourgeois theoreticians believed that ideas themselves flow from other ideas as a result of their purely logical development. In not asking about the actual instigating forces of the movement of thought, idealists never passed beyond the sphere of the world of ideas in their explanations and did not even ask questions that suggested themselves: why certain ideas were forgotten over the centuries and arose anew, why the most varied – and often even directly contradictory – conclusions were drawn from the exact same ideas, and so on.

In Marx's opinion, ideas flow not only from preceding ideas, but are produced from social relations, the alignment of people and the differentiation of their interests. It is not so much the heritage of ideas that has decisive significance for the development of thought as it is how social interests take shape. Transitioning from certain ideas to others requires that definite material forces come into effect and that ideas rest on actual interests. Moreover, it must be remembered that the origin of an idea, as well as its realisation, is not just the fruit of individual efforts but is a social process.

In realising an idea and reconstructing reality in accordance with our ideas, we impart an objective material existence to our thoughts and simultaneously make things rationally organised and ideal. Human reason thus becomes objective and acquires a material shell of *external existence*, manifesting its content and its essence in the entire immense world of culture created by human will and labour.

Human experience is thus *social and historical experience* existing not only in the form of subjective experience, knowledge and the habits of separate individuals but *objectively*, as the world of social relations, as the world of material and mental culture.

The empiricists and positivists attempted to construct their theory on the basis of purely subjective elements, starting from psychological premises and believing that only the data of the sensory organs play a decisive role in the formation of human experience and that experience represents the mechanical aggregate of associations and mental experiences.

The rationalists – particularly the followers of Kant – constructed their theory of experience on *a priori* principles, drawing completely away from the material world and believing concepts to be the transcendental forms of every perception, thought and cognition.

In the former case, ideas represented accidental associative cohesions of certain subjective experiences; in the latter, ideas – alien to every actuality – created their own particular world of abstract categories and 'pure logic', having no relation to objective material reality. If in the former case thinking was explained starting from narrowly mental laws of association, in the latter case the activity of thinking was considered to be the spontaneous development of 'pure thought from itself'.

Marxist philosophy asks the question about thinking on a different plane. It carries the problem of thinking and the questions of epistemology out of both the narrow sphere of individual cognition and the sphere of abstractly logical exercises and *elevates them to the heights of the problems of social consciousness and of ideal formations*, and in doing so placing the questions of cognition on a solid historical foundation and linking them to the concrete historical development of society.

Marx carefully draws the general schema of social and historical experience as follows: 1) the social causes and material basis for the origin of certain representations, views and ideas; 2) the struggle for ideas as the struggle for specific interests; and 3) the realisation of ideas through struggle. And here, the theoretical and cognitive significance that this struggle has for the realisation of ideas should be particularly emphasised.

Testing Ideas by Experience, Practice

§ 110

In its first manifestation in the world, an idea is usually vague, obscure and abstract. In its abstract generality, it lacks the concrete fullness of content, and as such can conceal in itself tawdry motifs that feed deceptive hopes. In dealing with 'pure ideas' torn from reality in their ambiguity, a certain hypertrophy either on the side of underestimation or on the side of overestimation is almost always inevitable. But further development reveals the actual sense and true content of these ideas. In the process of realisation, everything false and deceptive contained in them is inevitably revealed, and – on the other hand – so is the true and valuable connected with them. '[I]t is easy to understand', Marx said, 'that every mass-type "*interest*" that asserts itself historically goes far beyond its real limits in the "*idea*" or "*imagination*" when it first comes on the scene and is confused with *human* interest in general'.[1]

As an illustration of this, Marx points to the French Revolution of 1789, whose widely broadcast ideas about universal liberty, equality and fraternity, having declared the coming of the kingdom of reason, justice and eternal right and having appeared so dazzling in their time, were unable to not reveal themselves in essence as the liberation only of the bourgeois class, achieving not freedom as such but only the freedom of trade and private enterprise. 'We know today', Engels said, 'that this kingdom of reason was nothing more than the idealised kingdom of the bourgeoisie; that this eternal Right found its realisation in bourgeois justice; that this equality reduced itself to bourgeois equality before the law; that bourgeois property was proclaimed as one of the essential rights of man ...'. In a word, it was revealed that 'the most numerous part of the mass, the part distinct from the bourgeoisie, did not have its *real* interest in the principle of the Revolution, did not have a revolutionary principle of its *own*, but *only* an '*idea*', and hence only an object of momentary *enthusiasm* and only seeming *uplift*'.[2] And if the French craftsmen and workers, convinced at the beginning that they were fighting for universal liberty, took part in the overthrow of the monarchy and cleared the path for the political rule of the bourgeoisie, then they inevitably had to end with the conviction that they were not fighting for their own cause and that only the bourgeoisie were reaping the fruits of victory.

Or let us take another example: the fascist idea of the 'corporatist state', emerging as a desperate attempt by reaction to save the general foundations of a decaying capitalism unable to be supported on the basis of bourgeois democracy, is in essence the expression of the political bankruptcy of bourgeois ideas. But for the seizure of power, the mass of petty bourgeois needed to be deceived with false slogans, which is why the idea of 'national socialism' poured out in bombastic promises of the struggle against the evils of capitalism, including the assurances of realising paradise within the borders of

---

[1] Marks, i Engel's 1928–1946, Vol. III, p. 105 [Marx and Engels 1975–, Vol. 4, p. 81].
[2] Marks, i Engel's 1928–1946, Vol. III, p. 105 [Marx and Engels 1975–, Vol. 4, p. 82].

the German Empire over the course of two four-year periods, of raising the material well-being of the masses and of leading the nation to the highest economic prosperity. However, on the second day after the seizure of power, these masses – having suffered the full weight of fascist oppression – had to understand that the conscious portion of the German proletariat had long known about 'national socialism' and the blatant reactionary character of fascist ideas in their Hitlerite 'edition'.

The false is inevitably revealed in the realisation of ideas, and the correct is differentiated from the mistaken. The idea of socialism has drifted around Europe over the course of a number of centuries in the form of a more or less obscure ideal of the future. But the immaturity of this idea corresponded to undeveloped social relations and the uncertainty of the mutual position of classes. Only the limitations of the existing social structure were obvious; not knowing how to remove them, obscure and confused solutions were offered in the guise of socialist ones. Such, for example, was the idea of petty bourgeois 'socialism' and of the independent personality on the basis of scattered small-scale ownership and land allotments propagandised by anarchists and revealing themselves in essence as contradictory nonsense leading once again to social stratification and the rebirth of the same relations of social inequality against which they had been directed.

In the ideas of the great utopian thinkers (Saint-Simon, Fourier and Owen) socialism is the expression of absolute truth, reason, and right, and in their opinion it was worth revealing this idea so that it conquered the whole world under its own strength; '[a]nd as absolute truth is independent of time, space, and of the historical development of man, it is a mere accident when and where it is discovered' (Engels). In order to abandon this diffuse and obscure state, the idea of socialism – in Engels's words – had to be placed on real ground. Scientific socialism differs from all such abstractions in that 'socialism [is] no longer an accidental discovery ... but the necessary outcome of the struggle between two historically developed classes – the proletariat and the bourgeoisie' (Engels).

And even after the idea of scientific socialism took full shape and was put into literary shape in the works of the classical authors of Marxism, it still nevertheless seemed somewhat schematic to many. Early on in the twentieth century, socialism was to a certain extent only a 'concept', and few then imagined all the concrete forms that have now become materially tangible, demonstrable and obvious. But what a long and complex struggle was needed to make this flesh and blood of socialism self-evident; what difficulties and obstacles had to be overcome, what quantities of enemies had to be dealt with and what masked forms of political banditry had to be restrained in order, after having trained its advanced citizens in the struggle, to mobilise all the energy of a great country for the fulfilment of Leninist ideas.

§ 111

In the process of realising ideas, people who have certain insights and attempt to transform reality in conformity with them have to see and be convinced of facts to the extent that their assumptions were correct and in which a part of them were mistaken. On the strength of this, they are compelled to introduce corresponding changes and correctives into their original concept and structures of thought. In this way, an idea is tested and justified or its falsity is revealed. In Lenin's opinion, people come to an idea, as they come to the *truth*, through their practical rational activity. Lenin showed the way along which people go 'from the subjective idea ... towards objective truth'.[3] This path, in his opinion, runs through praxis. 'Nature is reflected in the human brain. By checking and applying the correctness of these reflections in his practice and technique, man arrives at objective truth'. '[M]an by his *practice* proves the objective correctness of his ideas, concepts, knowledge, science'.[4]

§ 112

In the process of the social realisation of an idea, difficulties are revealed that previously were not visible, new problems requiring special solutions come forward, and new series of ideas are born.

In the searches to justify certain propositions or technical ideas, it often happens that one thing is sought but something different is found. When discovering new technical ideas, in the majority of cases there is no suspicion of all the enormous consequences flowing from them that are only gradually revealed in the further process of the *mastering* of the given ideas. Otto von Guericke, having constructed his 'Magdeburg hemispheres' device in 1654, only wanted to prove the possibility of empty space as disputed by philosophers, but in the course of his experiments discovered the force of the pressure and elasticity of air.

The steam engine originally began to occupy minds with the goal of solving the task of pumping water out of mine shafts using the force of its own vapor, and the first steam mechanism was designed only for that purpose. Only further experiments introduced into this idea the entire wealth of content of a universal steam engine.

---

3   Lenin 1933, p. 184 [Lenin 1960–1979, Vol. 38, p. 201].
4   Lenin 1933, pp. 184, 193 [Lenin 1960–1979, Vol. 38, pp. 201, 191].

When in 1820, Hans Christian Ørsted finally succeeded in detecting the influence of an electric current on a compass needle, no one could have foreseen the consequences which, as a result of this discovery, appeared in the form of an entire branch of electromagnetic phenomena and all of radio technology.

In their experiments, Michelson and Morley wanted to understand the law combined velocities in the field of the propagation of light, and as a result had to repudiate all the nearly fundamental postulates of classical physics and reconstruct all our ideas about movement, time, space, mass, gravity and so on.

§ 113
The struggle for an idea and its realisation is the expression not of raw practicalness, but represents a deep creative process in which theoretical and cognitive activity take to the highest flight.

No matter how complex and difficult it was for thought to reveal the mainspring of the fall of capitalism and to formulate the sociopolitical ideas and historical tasks of the proletariat in their universal significance, it was even more difficult and theoretically complex to find the concrete path for their realisation, to organise the struggle of the masses, to lead them from victory to victory and actually put these ideals into practice. Here, it is not enough simply to be armed with a sum of ideas and quotations from Marx; it is necessary to know oneself how to create new ideas at every step, using them to illuminate the path of praxis and enriching Marxism with new theoretical achievements. This is the path along which humanity gradually broadened and deepened its cognition, approaching an ever more adequate cognition of reality. '[M]an by his practice proves the objective correctness of his ideas, concepts, knowledge, science', Lenin said.[5]

Pragmatism and Marxism

§ 114
The followers of the new positivist school in philosophy, who call themselves pragmatists, also proclaim praxis to be a criterion of truth. But nevertheless, Marxism and pragmatism are as different as night and day. For the pragmatists, truth is purely subjective; in their opinion, it has no objective significance. Everything that is useful is true, the pragmatists say. 'Pragmatism', in the words of one of the founders of the theory, 'at the outset, at least ... stands for no par-

---

5   Lenin 1933, p. 184 [Lenin 1960–1979, Vol. 38, p. 201].

ticular results'.[6] The most contradictory statements find justification in pragmatism; from the standpoint of the pragmatists, all theories are of equal worth. Pragmatists are prepared to consider even the most timid and clumsy assumptions as truth, if these hypotheses help anyone with anything or even simply serve as consolation. If the existence of God is the idea of an idle head, but '[i]f theological ideas proved to have a value for concrete life, they will be true for pragmatism', James says, 'in the sense of being good for so much'.[7]

Developing their views further, pragmatists provide the following definition of truth: ideas must agree not with objective reality, but with other ideas. Whatever helps our ideas agree with one another is true. Our ideas about things, in the opinion of the pragmatists, cannot agree with external objects and be controlled by them, since – as we know from the words of Schiller – 'The world, then, is essentially ὕλη (not yet having a material form), it is what we make of it. It is fruitless to define it ... by what it is apart from us'.[8] Truth, in the definition of the pragmatists, is only the agreement of our ideas with other of our ideas. 'A new opinion', James says, 'counts as 'true' just in proportion as it gratifies the individual's desire to assimilate the novel in his experience to his beliefs in stock. It must both lean on old truth and grasp new fact; and its success ... in doing this, is a matter for the individual's appreciation'.[9]

As we see, truth for the pragmatists (as for many other bourgeois philosophers) is a purely subjective category. That is why the pragmatic conception is closely linked with the doctrine of such representatives of subjectivism as Hans Vaihinger,[10] for whom truth appears in the role of pure fictions, of fictional assumptions. The pragmatists and the fictionalists, in denying the existence of objective truth, must inevitably arrive at solipsism in the subsequent development of their basis propositions.

---

6   Dzeims 1910, p. 39 [James 1921, p. 54].
7   Dzeims 1910, p. 52 [James 1921, p. 73].
8   Schiller 1902, p. 60.
9   Dzeims 1910, p. 44 [James 1921, p. 63]. A similar subjectivist concept of truth has become generally accepted for the majority of bourgeois thinkers. We could cite here a great many definitions given by bourgeois theoreticians working in the most varied fields of theory, but they all essentially repeat the same thing. For example, one of the most visible representatives of the now fashionable neorealist school, Hans Reichenbach, says: 'Darum bedeutet Wahrheit für die Naturwissenschaft *nicht* Übereinstimmung mit dem Ding – das wäre eine unmögliche Fordernug – sondern innere Widerspruchslosigkeit dieses Begriffssystems'. [Therefore truth does not mean for Natural Science conformity with the thing – that would be an impossible demand – but inner contradiction of this conceptual system – ed.] (Reichenbach 1922, p. 348).
10 Vaihinger 1920.

The pragmatists assert that truth has no independent content, and that the essence of truth consists only of the *process* of validation.[11] This is why the pragmatists have *no objective criteria* of truth. James attempts to dispute this proposition,[12] showing that they (the pragmatists) supposedly possess the most irreproachable criterion of truth; at the same time, however, he declares that they do not recognise *objective* truth as such.[13] What is the purpose, in this case, of the most absolute criterion if what is measured by this criterion does not exist?! Praxis may be the criterion of truth, if objective truth somehow or other exists. If it does not, the dispute over criteria becomes comical.

The principal difference of the Marxist tenet consists of the fact that the pragmatists deny objective existence, and the Marxists base all their theoretical constructions on the existence of the external material world and of objective truth. Cognition is cognition insofar as to one degree or another it expresses this objective truth. Praxis in and of itself is not truth, as the pragmatists assert, but it leads there. Verification through praxis only shows us whether we have in our hands a proposition that accurately reflects objective truth or an error.

A Thesis on Practice in Its General Philosophical Meaning

§ 115

In the philosophy of Marxism, the concept of social praxis in the broad sense not only plays a role as criterion of truth, but has a much more general significance. We have discussed this theme throughout the course of this book. Here, we will briefly and schematically formulate only the general conclusions in three basic points:

1. Social praxis and objective social interests put intellectual activity into motion and serve as the actual basis for the emergence of new ideas. Social interests turn the consciousness of people in one direction or another and direct thinking to specific things, tasks, goals, and objects. And these latter, with objective compulsoriness, define the means of their comprehension.
2. Social interests are the source of the forces impelling people to struggle for the *realisation* of their ideas.
3. In realising its ideas, thinking not only masters reality and experiences it, but also gains experience over itself: cognising and changing objects,

---

11 Dzeims 1910, p. 134 [James 1921, p. 201].
12 Dzeims 1910, p. 143 [James 1921, p. 233].
13 Dzeims 1910, p. 145 [James 1921, p. 235].

thinking at the same time cognises itself, learning from its mistakes. *Thoughts become accessible to themselves through their realisation, through the objective existence of the thought.* In the process of the conscious realisation of ideas (i.e. the practical use of ideal achievements), people, *in verifying the degree of truth of their concepts*, arrive at new ideas, discover new problems, and consequently further broaden and deepen their knowledge of reality.

At the same time, this path of activity and cognition depicts, in general strokes, the entire theory of social and historical experience in the interpretation given in the system of Marxist philosophy.

This is why we say that it would be one-sided to examine the question of praxis in its narrow meaning only as a problem of the criterion of truth, since in the interpretation established by the classical writers of Marxism this principle plays a role not of a *particular* but of a more *general* principle, representing one of the constitutive principles of the dialectic of cognition.

Concluding Observations

§116

In investigating the fundamental questions of the sociology of thinking, we have in this book only touched upon a limited period in the history of the development of human thinking, specifically the period of pre-socialist social relations. In a socialist society, specifically in a communist society as a result of the destruction of class differences and the destruction of the opposition between town and country, of the difference between mental and physical labour, almost all the definitions and *fundamental tenets of the sociology of thinking change dramatically*. This constitutes the object of particular research. In the relations of a socialist and communist society, for example, it is impossible to completely apply even such a fundamental principle of Marxism as the proposition that social existence defines consciousness, in the sense this proposition has in a society of class antagonism where the process of historical creation essentially runs in the form of an elemental (natural) process. Blind elemental forces do not dominate in the development of a socialist society; on the contrary, the history of society together with the world of nature surrounding humanity, which humanity subjugates and domesticates, becomes a rational world and a rationally directed history.[14] At this level of development

---

14 'With the seizing of the means of production by society ... the mastery of the product

the conscious will of the free citizens of a socialist society and scientifically balanced solutions define the direction of the entire historical process: *social consciousness* defines existence, and not the other way around.

From this standpoint, we could formulate the entire tremendous difference between Hegel and Marx as follows:

In Hegel, the world originally came from reason; in Marx, it only moves towards reason, to a rational form – to communism.

---

over the producer [is done away with]. Anarchy in social production is replaced by systematic, definite organisation. The struggle for individual existence disappears. Then for the first time man, in a certain sense, is finally marked off from the rest of the animal kingdom and emerges from mere animal conditions of existence into really human ones. The whole sphere of the conditions of life which environ man, and which have hitherto ruled man, now comes under the dominion and control of man, who for the first time becomes real, conscious lord of nature, because he has now become master of his own social organisation. The laws of his own social action, hitherto standing face to face with man as laws of nature foreign to, and dominating him, will then be used with full understanding, and so mastered by him. Man's own social organisation, hitherto confronting hum as a necessity imposed by nature and history, now becomes the result of his own free action. The extraneous objective forces that have hitherto governed history pass under the control of man himself. Only from that time will man himself, with full consciousness, make his own history – only from that time will the social causes set in motion by him have, in the main and in a constantly growing measure, the results intended by him. It is the humanity's leap from the kingdom of necessity to the kingdom of freedom' (Engel's 1932, p. 63 [Marx and Engels 1975–, Vol. 25, p. 270]).

SUPPLEMENT

Nikolai Iakovlevich Marr and the Philosophy of Marxism[1]

Translated by Craig Brandist

It would be in vain to hope that one author could to any degree to grasp the entire significance of such a multifaceted scientist and profound thinker as Nikolai Iakovlevich Marr, particularly in conditions when the old ideas still persist, when the ideological legacy of the old world still oppresses the consciousness of scientists, making it difficult to think and work in new ways.

Despite all the efforts that we are currently making to measure and evaluate Marr's activities, we must say that we are not yet able to grasp the full breadth of this great thinker. We will only reveal the enormous fruitfulness and the depth of the ideas Marr raised gradually, in the course of our hard work on specific questions of Marxist philosophy, Marxist sociology, linguistics, history, and a range of other disciplines.

The following statement does not claim fully to account for all the philosophical problems raised by Marr's theory. We select just a few little islands from Marr's vast ideological legacy and focus the reader's attention on them.

Marr's first and basic scholarly activity as a social scientist, linguist, historian of material culture and historian of thinking, consists in that at the very beginning of his scientific activity he adopted a concrete-historical approach in contrast to the quasi-historical positions of traditional linguistics and the false historical point of view of bourgeois historiography, as a counterweight to the anti-historical positions of idealist philosophy and the ahistorical attitudes of the dominant bourgeois science in general.

This quasi-historical attitude of bourgeois linguistics is expressed, for example, in the fact that time as such is considered a factor in the evolution of language; as if the simple passage of time changes language like the natural processes of weathering or the formation of crystals. Bourgeois linguistics does not understand that the passage of time itself is not history, and that a language changes not under the influence of time as such, but under the influence of

[1] A lecture delivered at an evening dedicated to the memory of N. Ia. Marr at the USSR Academy of Sciences, 27 February 1935.

specific material content of time, due to the real shifts taking place in society and in social relations – shifts that change the material conditions of people's existence, forcing them to change their views and concepts.

Indo-European linguistics, in its philosophical premises, assumes a certain self-sufficient essence of language, as if dependent on the eternal laws of the psyche, or – according to the latest fascist discoveries – on the 'national spirit', and allegedly having an independent history. Bourgeois scientists cannot or, rather, do not want to understand that the psyche of people, human thinking and social consciousness, are not just a product of nature.

Despite ingrained scientific traditions, from the first steps of his scientific activity, Marr stood on the ground of actual history. This, it seems, was facilitated by the social conditions of heavy national oppression and class battles, in which Marr's scientific views were formed, at first still on the paths of traditional bourgeois science. There is no denying the significant role played by the influence of his teachers and mentors V.R. Rozen and A.N. Veselovskii, bourgeois thinkers and scholars who had a very broad historical outlook.

Having taken the path of actual history, Marr developed his teaching in the direction of Marxism, first spontaneously under the pressure of living material, and then, in the post-October period, having mastered the Marxist methodology in the course of his work, even more confidently than before. In contrast to the naturalistic understanding of man, Marr put forward the proposition about the social essence of language, the historicity of forms of human thought and the consequent need for the historical study of language in connection with production, material culture, social relations and thinking as a single historical-creative process of humanity.

Positivistic philosophy and the point of view of naturalism consider man as a simple continuation of natural and biological relations. Marxism, in contrast to idealist views and vulgar materialistic understanding, considers social reality as an area governed by laws that are qualitatively different from physical or biological laws.

The nature of the relationship of individuals with the environment and with other individuals in social reality is qualitatively different from the nature of biological relationships. The latter exist as direct, bodily relations of mutual eating or mutual benefit produced by animals without any conscious intent. Man became man in so far as, instead of the natural conditions of the environment, he created an artificial environment around himself by his production activities. In contrast to animals, man creates his own conditions of existence.

The product of labour and the material culture produced by man and placed by him between himself and the natural environment *become the intermediary of relations between individuals*. From this time on, the relations of individuals cease to be only bodily-biological, and all relations of individuals are woven around these third objects – the conditions of labour and the products of labour; the relations of individuals are formed as human relations concerning the production, possession, appropriation, and distribution of these material goods. This thereby makes possible, for the first time, relations of alienation, exchange, contract, oppression, agreement, etc., i.e. social relations in the proper sense of the word, unthinkable in the animal kingdom. At the same time, the objective world of material culture produced by man makes it possible to accumulate both material goods and reason and human experience, and serves as the main lever of the historical development of mankind.

These new social relations, different from any biological relations, are at the same time conditions for the humanisation and consciousness itself, conditions for the origin of the human way of thinking and the human way of speech. The human stage of thinking and human language are products of social relations, the result of the historical development of man.

Marx pointed out that consciousness, language, and thought, like law and all other types of superstructure, do not have their own development, their own history.[2] The history of their development is only a reflected force of the history of society and social relations.

Following this materialist methodology, Marr comes to the following conclusion: 'Japhetic theory teaches that language and sound speech are not a simple gift of nature at any stage of their development or in any part ... Humanity created its language in the process of labour *in determinate social conditions* and recreates it with the advent of actual new social forms of life and everyday life, in accordance with the new thinking in these conditions ... The roots of inherited speech are not in external nature, it is within us, within our physical nature, but in *sociality*, in its material base, economy and technology [*tekhnika*]'.[3]

The approach of empiricism, on the one hand, and rationalism, on the other, led human thinking to be presented in an un-historical fashion; as if it had no past history and no prospects for future development. The forms of human thought were assumed to be given once and for all time. Philosophy began with the obligatory norms of logical thought as 'pistol shots'.

Empiricists considered human thinking to be a natural phenomenon, a natural function of the work of the senses and the mechanism of association. The human mind was represented as a product of certain natural laws and an object of natural scientific research.

---

2   Marks i Engel's 1933, pp. 17, 54, 435.
3   Marr 1928c, p. 18 (my emphasis – KM).

Rationalists, however, began philosophy with reason taken in abstraction, with absolute and eternal logical categories, as if representing the inner essence of all being and existing even before the 'emergence of material reality'.[4] In both cases, thinking was absolutised, and the thinking of a certain historical epoch, the norms of thought of a certain society and a certain class were imposed on the entire history of mankind as beyond doubt.

In contrast to such views, the classics of Marxism put forward the demand for a truly historical understanding of thinking. They opposed the idealistic tendencies of empiricism from below and the mystical tendencies of rationalism from above to the position of socio-historical practice, the arrangement of social interests as the basis for the formation of our ideas, concepts, our intellectual activity in general, and all our knowledge.

According to the Marxist-Leninist understanding, reason is not a ready-made eternal form. Forms and ways of human thinking are formed historically and are modified in the process of social development. At the same time, human consciousness historically did not begin with the subject's self-consciousness, as the idealists, who believed that mental activity began with the subject's self-recognition of himself as a thinking subject assumed, as if the first act of consciousness was the awareness of his own self (Fichte). The consciousness of primitive man was primarily directed at objects, and at first he was completely unaware of his own existence.

The world was not conquered by man by internal reflection, like the Hindu yogis and visionaries from theosophy, but by activity directed at external objects. These very objects, transformed into organs of human activity as its means and tools, were the first objects of understanding, those objects that really enriched the human consciousness with real knowledge. The concepts of 'boil', 'burn', 'fry', etc. are made possible by the possession of fire, and the concept of 'cut' becomes available to consciousness for the first time thanks to the appearance of the knife.

The achievements of the new theory of language, which comprehensively support this position by palaeontological analysis of the oldest layers of language, should be considered the greatest conquest of Marxist thought. On the basis of rich material from the field of linguistics, mythology, monuments of

---

4 'Logic', Hegel said, 'should be understood as a system of pure reason, as the realm of pure thought. This realm is the truth, as it is without cover in itself and for itself. We can therefore say that this content is the image of God (Logos, or the idea – км), as he is in his eternal essence before the creation of the world and the finite spirit', Hegel 1923, Vol. 1, p. 31. This formula expresses the highest ideal of the rationalistic worldview and for all post-Hegelian idealistic philosophy and remains unsurpassed.

material culture, Marr was able to establish extremely important data about the first steps in the history of human thinking. He came to believe that man made the discovery of his own existence later than all his first historical discoveries, and that he began to understand himself through the world of things that he created in the process of social production. At the same time, the self-consciousness of the subject historically began not with the awareness of the individual self, but with the collective subject. This undifferentiated consciousness of the individual subject in the collective is based on the undifferentiated nature of society itself, on the collective economy, on the unity of interests and the actual absence of the individual at this stage of development. At this stage, the individual exists only in his totem and identifies him or herself entirely with his/her group, with his/her totem. This consciousness, as Marx said, is still 'herd, tribal consciousness'. 'And this ... "tribal consciousness" is further developed by increased productivity, increase of needs, and what is fundamental to both of these, the increase of population. With these develops the division of labour ...'[5] and this has played a crucial role in man's awareness of himself as an individual.

Marr's research fully confirmed these positions. The realisation of the individual self was preceded by a long period in which man conceived himself as a 'communal [*sobornoe*] subject' as a 'totemic I'. Marr proves that the isolation of personal subject becomes a fact later in the history of thought, and that consciousness of an individual I historically went hand in hand with the development of ownership, first personal and then private.

Traditional philosophy assumed that the mind is its own instrument of knowledge and that man develops cognitive activity by virtue of his natural curiosity and natural desire for ideal truth. But the philosophers forgot that the human mind is primarily the *result* and *product* of mediating the objective activity of man, and that the theoretical aspirations of reason are only the expression and reflection of certain of man's practical interests. Marx said: 'The production of ideas, of conceptions, of consciousness is at first directly interwoven with the material activity and the material intercourse of people, the language of real life. Conceiving, thinking, the mental intercourse of men, appear at this stage as the direct efflux of their material behaviour ... People are the producers of their conceptions, ideas, etc., real, active men, as they are conditioned by a definite development of their productive forces and the intercourse corresponding to these, up to its furthest forms'.[6]

---

5   Marks i Engel's 1933, p. 21.
6   Marks i Engel's 1933, p. 16.

These fundamental principles of Marxist philosophy found their consistent development and refinement in Marr's work on concrete material. 'Awareness', says Marr, 'was not created natural-historically, by the mere fact of finding an object in the physical environment, but in the process of it being worked on using technical means, taken not from nature, but from production'.[7]

Marr's analysis clearly shows that the external objective world of reality entered the circle of representations of the human mind through the world of things that were mastered by man, primarily as objects of human activity, and not as sensations.

Nature itself, as such, was recognised by people through their production activities. It was conceived by consciousness not as distinctive nature, but in its apperception as 'carried out' [*sodeiannoe*], 'co-created'. This is indicated by the analysis of archetypal meanings of the words 'natura' and 'cultura', which go back to the meanings 'produced', 'made', and 'hand'.[8]

The objects of nature – the moon, stars, sun, etc. – were recognised by man as a measure of time or as beneficial forces that promote growth, only because and after the 'sun' resp. 'weather', seasons, in general – 'sky' began to play a role in his economy (pastoral or agricultural).

Moreover, palaeontological analysis reveals that at an early level of consciousness, even the concept 'to be' was absent, the concept of original existence was absent, as well as the word 'is' that corresponds to it. And when a need for its expression arose, what was used was the word that serves to denote the action 'to have', 'to control', i.e. the name 'hands', since, according to Marr, 'there was no notion of an independent being, *what was recognised was only the existence of what was under control, under the power, or use of the collective*'.[9]

Here we are faced with a number of the most important problems of Marxist philosophy. This is primarily a new theory of awareness and understanding. How did an awareness of reality come to be historically and how does man become aware of reality? How are our notions and concepts of things formed? This raises the problem of a new, truly Marxist theory of concept formation.

Here we are given certain outlines that guide us to the correct Marxist path of scientific research.

First of all, it should be noted that people distinguish objects and use them not for their own sake, but for the sake of human interests, and inasmuch as these things are drawn into the sphere of real human needs. Things are learned

---

7   Marr 1928c, p. 84.
8   Marr 1928c, pp. 84–89.
9   Marr 1928b, p. 18.

in the process of drawing them into the field of social practice, into everyday economic activity and social relations.

A person knows things: 'stone', 'wood', 'metals' or 'entities', 'dog', 'deer', 'horse' or 'camel' not in their completely objective essence, but primarily from the point of view of the relationship of these objects to a person, from the point of view of their social significance. The 'essence of things' from this point of view is, if you will, anthropomorphic, but anthropomorphic in the objectively social meaning of the word. In this sense, not only our ideas about things are anthropomorphic, but also the things themselves, because man, actively intervening in the life of nature, changes the nature of things, leaves the stamp of his rational activity on them, *'humanises'* them, makes them *'reasonable'*, human things. The essence of things is thus determined by the actual relation of these things to human needs, in accordance with the role, function, and service they carry out in social and historical practice. Therefore, things are thought by a person based on their real significance in human usage (practical, ideological, or whatever).

Our concepts, from this point of view, do not mean any special categories of abstraction that represent the sum of formal features, as has been thought since the time of scholasticism. The concept does not express things in their isolated existence, but in some semantic [*smyslovoi*] correlation with other things. One and the same object, the same thing in different contexts is the bearer of different functions, and accordingly, the *concepts* of it are completely *different*. The context in which objects are given to us is determined by the social function of these objects in social reality.

This explains the fact that one and the same object can historically be understood quite differently and represent different concepts. Physically 'water', for example, has always been water and will remain so, but socially 'water' in the palaeolithic era, in ancient Egypt and for us – are completely different things. The problems of hydraulics and the electrolysis of water, solved by us, were not and of course could not be posed at that time. Despite the fact that outwardly the same object of nature (H_2O) appears here, it has different social significance in different epochs, constitutes different objects of thought, puts forward different problems and expresses different concepts.

A concept is a semantic [*smyslovoi*] context in which we relate objects; it is a scheme for combining conceivable objects. Consciousness in the act of thinking centres (sometimes very different) things around a certain meaning [*znachenie*], role, or function of these objects. At the same time, it is also an act of generalisation, i.e. the formation of a well-known centre for mental correlations. A concept is a point to which all other data are projected and from which these data are measured – a kind of coordinate system of reference, and not a ready-made Kantian a priori scheme or a sum of similar abstract features, as the empiricists thought.

Everything that performs the same service and has the same purpose in social usage, is located by the consciousness in one thought series, is perceived and understood in the same way, i.e. it is summed up under one concept. In this respect, what is especially significant are those cases when things that are completely different in their composition, appearance, form, etc., are thought in one concept and called by the same name. 'The Bakairis', says Karl von Steinen, 'cut their hair with the teeth of a piranha fish, and my scissors were called, without much thought, "piranha teeth". 'They called the mirror water – "show us the water" – they asked when they wanted to see the mirror'.[10]

Despite the fact that these objects are very different from each other, they are appercepted [*appertsepiruiutsia*] into one concept; and pocket watches can be called the sun on the grounds that both serve to determine time.

In a letter to Engels, Marx said 'Since the middle of the seventeenth century almost all great mathematicians, in so far as they have concerned themselves with the theory and practice of mechanics, have taken the simple, water-driven flour mill as their point of departure. Indeed, this was why the words *Mühle* and mill, which came to be used during the manufacturing period, were applied to all driving mechanisms adapted for practical purposes'.[11]

In another letter, Marx even more clearly articulates his thought: 'But what would old Hegel say, were he to learn in the hereafter that the *general* [*das Allgemeine*] in German and Nordic means only the communal land, and that the *particular*, the *special* [*das Sundre, Besondere*] means only private property divided off from the communal land? Here are the *logical categories coming damn well out of "our intercourse"* after all' (my emphasis – K.M).[12]

This assessment of the formation of concepts applies not only to the historically past stages of thinking, but also extends to the present: 'In organic chemistry', says Engels, 'the significance of a body, hence also its name, is no longer determined merely by its composition, but rather by its position in the *series* to which it belongs. If we find, therefore, that a body belongs to such a series, its old name becomes an obstacle to understanding it and must be replaced by a *series name* (paraffins, etc.)'.[13]

The semanticisation [*osmyslenie*] of things and the formation of concepts occur in this way not on the basis of the external similarity of objects and

---

10 Steinen 1894 (1930, *Sredi dikikh narodov Brazilii*, Russian translation).
11 Marx, letter to Engels, 28 January 1863.
12 Marx, letter to Engels, 25 March 1863 [actually 1868 – ed.].
13 Engel's 1933, p. 501.

not because of the proximity of their objective-physical features, but because of the identity or difference of the functions of these objects in social and historical practices. This is proven by the entire brilliant chapter of Marr's teaching on functional semantics. If, for example, metals are ordered according to their appearance (bronze, copper, iron, etc.) apperceived as 'stone' and the name of 'stone' (stone tool, 'axe') is transferred to metal tools, this is not because the stone itself is similar to metal, but because the metal began to carry out the same service in social reality as was carried out by the stone. As a result of this, they were perceived and interpreted in the same way, and therefore they were also designated by the same name. The same thing is observed with the change and transfer of the name 'dog' to 'deer', 'horse' to 'camel', etc. The zoological nature of these animals plays a very secondary role for thinking. Thinking is mainly focused on the social significance of these objects.[14]

By tracing the history of the word in this way, we can establish previous forms of human thought that even the most advanced bourgeois scientists (such as Lévy-Bruhl) consider to be fundamentally inaccessible to our knowledge.

This point explains the associations that occur in the practice of the so-called primitive consciousness that are strange from the point of view of our thinking. If certain items performed the same service, e.g. they have the same type of cult meaning, they are treated identically, even if in all other respects they had nothing in common with each other. For example, 'for the guichel', as reported by Lumholz, '"wheat", "deer", and "gikuli" (a sacred plant) are in a sense identical'.[15]

These positions concerning cognitive activity and the formation of concepts, established by Marr on the basis of the analysis of specific material from the field of language, the history of material culture, cult remnants, etc. overturn all the suggestions of the empiricists who begin the work of knowledge with the senses and elementary sensations, and deprive many lost 'Marxists' who are entangled in the networks of vulgar empiricist philosophy of their soil.

Moreover, Marr does not confine himself to a new theory of awareness, a new theory of the concept; he poses the problem on a much broader scale. In complete agreement with Marx and Lenin, a new theory of sense perception is advanced. It turns out that not only is our knowledge and thinking socially conditioned, but also that all the work of our sensory organs is also socially conditioned.

---

14 Cf. Marr 1926, p. 32.
15 Lévy-Bruhl 1930, p. 84.

Empiricist philosophy based all its constructions on direct data of sense perception. Sensations were considered the primary, simplest, absolutely reliable and self-explanatory elements. It was believed that it is enough to have eyes and ears to see, hear and perceive everything that is generally available to our organs of perception.[16] The sense organs were supposed to be those receivers open to external stimuli through which the sensations of the external world continuously enter the consciousness. Here they are combined by the mechanism of association and are formed into representations; concepts arise from representations in the same way as associations, judgements arise from concepts, and so on.

The classics of Marxism, in contrast to these weak positions, established that it is not enough to have eyes and ears to be able to see, hear and perceive everything that is physically accessible to the perception of our organs, everything that crosses the notorious 'threshold of irritation'.

If this by taking simple way we solved the problem of thinking, then as Engels notes,[17] sense organs are also present in animals, the eagle eye sees further than the human eye, but does not notice a hundredth part of what the human eye sees. Many animals, though having finer senses than man, do not distinguish a hundredth part of the odours that are features of various things to man.

Marx notes that physical stimulation of the sense organs is far from sufficient to explain human sensory perception. So many such large and small phenomena, things and events that go unnoticed, despite the fact that they occur in the field of our perception! Things and phenomena that do not affect our interests are usually not noticed by us, we often look at them, but do not see them.

We must not forget that the sense organs are only one of the conditions for the emergence of the human stage of consciousness, and not its cause. The key to human thinking is not in them, but in the causes and conditions that made the senses work and perceive in a certain direction, and these causes are not in sensuality itself. These conditions and these causes are the conditions and causes of the social order. The eye, as Marx said, became the human eye because of the social existence of man. 'For not only the five senses, but also the so-called spiritual senses, the practical senses (will, love, etc.), in a word,

---

16   Even Ernst Cassirer, a philosopher distant from empiricism says '… das Sein der Perzeption ist das Einzig gewisse völlig unprolematische Urdatum aller Erkenntnis' [the being of perception is the only certain, completely unproblematic primal datum of all cognition – ed.], Cassirer 1929, p. 28.
17   See Marks i Engel's 1925, p. 95.

the human sense, the humanity of the senses – all these come into being only through the existence of their objects, through humanised nature'.[18]

We see, therefore, that both the feelings of man and the path of his perception are the result of social and historical life, and not the product of nature and natural history. 'The cultivation of the five senses is the work of all previous history' says Marx.[19]

A person begins to perceive objects only in so far as they are drawn into the sphere of human use and into the circle of social relations.

If, for example, we take the question of the history of colour differentiation, we find a curious fact. In a number of large ancient literary monuments there is absolutely no mention of some primary colours. In the *Rig Veda* and the *Avesta*, we find neither blue nor green throughout their entire length. These same colours are absent from the Bible, Homeric songs, and other ancient monuments. Approaching with our colour concepts and scales, we find in Homer and other ancient writers an incredible 'confusion' in distinguishing colours: according to Homer, Odysseus' hair is the colour of hyacinths, Pindar's hair is also the colour of violets, while on the other hand, violets are said to be black (!!). Where blue [*sinii*] objects are described, such as the sky, they are called black, and so on.

As a result of detailed analysis of similar facts, it is found that there was a time when blue [*goloboi*] and blue [*sinii*] did not differ as qualitatively distinct; these colours were considered shades or varieties of black.[20]

It turns out that in Greece, for example, green and blue [*sinii*] colours were not distinguished qualitatively from each other *until people were familiar with the use of appropriate paints*. When they began to produce these colours and practically apply them, they also began to distinguish them qualitatively from other previously recognised colours, and already in Herodotus' descriptions of the seven walls surrounding the city of Ekbatan, we no longer find just four colours (black, white, red, yellow), but seven, and blue [*sinii*] among them.[21]

If you go even deeper into the historical past, we will find a stage when yellow was not distinguished as a special colour, but rather was considered a shade and variety of red. Marr shows this is evidenced by the Georgian language. *Ts'it-*

---

18   Marks i Engel's 1928–1946, Vol. III, p. 626 [*Economic and Philosophical Manuscripts 1844*, Third Manuscript – ed.].
19   Marks i Engel's 1928–1946, Vol. III, p. 627.
20   [In Russian two shades of blue are designated as different colours rather than varieties of the same colour. The difference is a matter of hue rather than lightness, so '*sinii*' is closer to violet and '*goluboi*' to green – ed.]
21   Herodotus, *Clio*, I, p. 98.

eli 'red' and *q'vit-eli* 'yellow' are derived from the same base, in the archetype *t'vit-ar*, or *t'vit-ar* by whistling and hissing groups[22] and *q'vit-eli* by the spirant branch.

Going even further, we see that there was a time when even the 'red' colour did not differ from black. Historically, 'red' is a derivative of 'black'. In relation to this, the data are also preserved in the Russian language, where 'chermnoe' with the same basis as 'black' [*chernoe* – ed.] has the meaning of 'crimson-red' ('the waters of chermny like blood', *The Book of Kings*).

Taking all these facts into account, we are convinced how profound Marx's insight was, when he argued that sensuality, as *human* sensuality, is not a gift of nature, that the data of sense perception are not 'primary, not deducible from another, data', as the empiricists claimed. People's sense perception is the result of socio-historical development and it is not the same in different historical periods.

Back in the 60s of the last century, L[azar] Geiger noted the fact that information about some of the main colours were absent from many ancient literary monuments, and came to the conclusion that the structure of the visual organ of man in ancient times was different from that of us. These questions seemed to Geiger to be questions of physiology, and He proposed the idea of a specific science – palaeophysiology.[23] Now we are well aware that the problem is not in the different physiological structure of the eye, but in the different orientation of consciousness and interests of people in different communities. The physiology of the eye, ear, and other organs of our ancestors is not much different from ours, but there is a big difference in what and how these organs perceived in different epochs.

Lévy-Bruhl believed that primitive consciousness perceives and sees in the same way as our own, but *thinks* differently; we believe that Paleolithic man not only *thinks*, but also *perceives differently and sees differently than we do, despite the fact that he looks and listens with the same physiological apparatus as our own.*

Lenin, enumerating 'the fields of knowledge from which the theory of knowledge and dialectics should be built', emphasises language and gives it a special note 'very important'.[24] In the materialist study of the history of the formation of language as a 'real human consciousness' (Marx), Lenin saw the only the possibility of building a Marxist theory of knowledge on a truly historical basis.

---

22   In Mingrelian ti-da is 'red'.
23   'Diese Fragen', said Geiger, 'sind an und für sich physiologische Fragen'. Geiger 1871.
24   Lenin 1933, p. 315 [Lenin's *Philosophical Notebooks* – ed.].

Lenin emphasised Haym's words with particular attention and pointed out that 'the critique of reason must become the criticism of language'.[25]

'Thousands of years have passed' says Lenin 'since the time when the idea was born of 'the connection of all things', 'the chain of causes'. *A comparison of how these causes have been understood in the history of human thought would give an indisputably conclusive theory of knowledge*'.[26]

Lenin thus pointed out to us a new, unbroken path, following which we can build a genuine Marxist theory of knowledge. Marr, armed with a wealth of knowledge and the power of extraordinary talent, worked hard to pave this path. He discovered and put into our hands a powerful scientific weapon – the paleontological method in its Marrist sense.

In the last years of his work, Marr came close to the specifically philosophical problems of his teaching. These years, which – we can safely say – were the most fruitful in his scientific work (so he believed himself), were almost entirely devoted to the solution of precisely those questions that are so clearly outlined by Lenin. Not only the most ancient forms of activity and speech, but also the most ancient beliefs, forms of worldview, and the ways of thinking of the most remote epochs have been preserved in the historically deposited formations of language, customs, material culture, and so on. The subsequent historical development, creating new historical forms, at the same time continues a continuous chain of historical reinterpretation of old terms, representations and concepts. Taking these forms, which are given to us in our present experiences, we establish their past meanings through analysis and discover the previous historical forms of language, worldview, and thinking.

In the person of Marr the palaeontology of language found a brilliant master and all-round scholar. In his hands, the dead, fossilised survivals of vocabulary, morphology, grammar come to life, science in them resurrects the fragments of worldviews of epochs, seemingly completely lost in the abyss of oblivion, and builds up from these fragments a picture of the history of past forms of thought.

Thus, on *the same plane as the questions of the palaeontology of speech, there is a problem of great scientific significance, the problem of the palaeontology of thinking*, the task of excavating the most ancient layers and survivals of the forms of development of human thinking.

The general scheme of the development of worldviews has so far been understood as the development of one form of belief from another, in a process of natural continuation of previous ideas by the subsequent generation, the

---

25 Lenin 1933, p. 145.
26 Lenin 1933, p. 307.

self-development of an idea until all its internal potential has been exhausted. This scheme turned out to be false. The transition from one idea to another requires certain material forces operate in a specific direction of development and that ideas are based on certain social interests of people. Marxist philosophy considers all shifts in the world of ideas as derived from social conflicts and real social shifts.

Behind the back of all the linguistic changes in vocabulary, in meaning, in morphology, phonetics, and so on, Marr demanded the ability to see determinate social shifts. These latter are the real causes of changes in thinking, worldview, and language.

At the same time, and in full agreement with the basic principles of Marxism-Leninism, Marr puts forward the extremely fruitful principle of stadial shifts in the development of language and thinking. The concept of stage expresses a qualitatively defined step in the development of the social mode of production, social relations, along with worldview and ideological formations. Each stage in its development prepares the next and transitions into it due to changed social conditions, by the force of a clash of social interests, and through a series of revolutionary explosions from within. All the changes and shifts that occur in social and ideological forms are brought about by social conflicts. This constant social struggle is the living force of every historical process, which later, at the stage of class society, takes more concrete forms of the clash of private property interests and the struggle of classes.

This Marxist concept, which opens up an extremely profound understanding of the meaning of history and the nature of historical lawfulness, represents the starting point and the main theme of Marr's last works.

Marr provided the first general outlines of the most ancient stages of language development. He established a number of stages, nodal historical points of development (stages of totemic, cosmic, microcosmic, technological, etc. worldviews), where speech creativity was based on certain motifs of worldview and where the norms of thought were determined by the material conditions of production and social relations.

Expanding and deepening his research on the way to reveal the stages of worldview and the stadial development of thinking, Marr placed another problem of great significance for the philosophy of Marxism before us.

In the light of Marr's the teaching we are faced anew with the problem of the entire history of philosophy and, first of all, with the question of understanding the history of ancient philosophy. We can safely say that the history of philosophy has not made a step forward in the hands of bourgeois ideologists since the time of Hegel, who first laid the foundation for this discipline as a systematically coherent whole.

But Hegel still understood that 'every philosophy is the son of its time'. Later epigones often forgot this and presented the history of philosophy as a gallery of individual heroes of the thinking mind, or as a history of philosophical textbooks and a collection of biographies of their authors. At the same time, the official history of philosophy begins with Greece, ignoring the rest of the world and considering the entire East an alien world of exoticism, devoid of mental potenial. And if some people try to draw the countries of the East into the circle of problems of the history of philosophy, then they are stuck with the biased categories and arbitrary definitions of the modern bourgeois-European worldview.

It is not only the philosophy of the Eastern countries that is subjected to this fate (bourgeois modernisation), but all ancient Greek philosophy is also interpreted and explained within the limits of modern concepts of bourgeois philosophy.

Even Plato, and partly Aristotle, not to mention the pre-Socratics, are trimmed and combed according to the concepts of modern idealistic views. Plato, as presented by P. Natorp or N. Hartman, for example, present vivid examples of such distortions.[27]

Marx did not regard any philosophical system as the result of individual reflection by individual philosophers. Ideas do not fall from the sky and philosophers do not produce their ideas from their imagination, like a spider weaving its web out of itself. The philosopher draws his opinions from society, and therefore the ideas expressed in the philosophical system are only reflections of the views and interests of certain strata, groups, or classes.

In the Marxist scientific approach, *the history of philosophy is conceived on the same plane as the history of the forms of social consciousness, the history of ideology and the history of worldviews in general.*

According to Marx, 'philosophy is first worked out in the religious forms of consciousness'[28] and mythology, and so today, when we consider ancient Greek philosophy, for example, it cannot be divorced from the surrounding ideas and the fundamental worldview from which its notions grew, unless we want to distort the true history. They are closely connected with the mythological outlooks that are common not only in Greece, but also throughout the world, because at a certain stage worldviews with the same basic motifs meet everywhere.

The fragments of Thales of Miletus or Anaximenes, in which statements like the following occur: 'water is the god of all, water is the foundation of all', 'the

---

27 Natorp 1921; Hartmann 1909.
28 Marks 1923, Vol. 1, p. 42.

origin of all things is air', etc. cannot of course be interpreted in the sense that 'water' and 'air' were understood at that time as spiritual principles, as categories of essence or substance, from which all other particular forms of being are derived, as is represented by the later rationalistic philosophy.

Even when Anaxagoras has such a seemingly abstract concept as νοῦς [nous], we have no reason to interpret it as 'mind', 'spirit' or 'soul', nor to translate it into these terms, if we do not want to radically distort the actual historical facts. The concept of 'mind' in the proper sense, purged of magical and 'cosmogonic' concepts, did not yet exist. Anaxagoras' νοῦς [nous] acts only as a force that connects and separates things. Diogenes Laertius, summarising the first Chapter of the book of Anaxagoras, formulates his views as follows: 'all things were together (i.e. mixed), then came νοῦς [nous] and set them in order'.[29] It is Impossible to interpret this νοῦς [nous] as a comprehensive principle of regularity in the later rationalistic sense of the word.

Essentially Anaxagoras' νοῦς [nous] is only a variation of the same ideas that we find in Empedocles. In Anaxagoras νοῦς [nous] acts as a force of attraction and repulsion, exactly the same as Empedocles' sympathy (love) of Φιλία [filia] and strife νεῖκος [neikos].

When in one fragment of Anaxagoras it is said 'it (νοῦς [nous]) is the thinnest of all things and the purest, and it has all knowledge (γνώμη [gnómi]) about everything and the greatest strength; and νοῦς [nous] has power over all things, both greater and smaller, that have life (ψυχὴν εχει [psychí échei)'.[30] Γνώμη [gnómi] meant something distant from 'knowledge' and 'comprehension' in our sense. At this stage, the word had the meaning 'to be possessed', 'to participate', 'to participate physically', and so on. Like the word λόγος [logos] it shared the meaning of magical symbiosis, which is why we find fire in the meaning of both reason and λόγος [logos] in Heraclitus. 'Reason', 'word', 'λόγος [logos]', 'spirit' and 'soul' are still emerging from economic-cosmogonic notions in this period and are not yet differentiated from 'fire', 'air' and even 'water'. This is clearly evidenced by the fragments attributed to Heraclitus, where 'fire' is the world-forming [beginning] – 'the whole world is an eternally living fire' and where the same fire also plays the role of 'reason'. According to Hippolytus[31] 'he (Heraclitus) claims that 'fire' is rational ([phronimon]) and is the cause of the world order'. Heraclitus often refers to fire as the name of the deity Zeus, which according to linguistic analysis actually had the meaning of 'fire' resp. 'sky' (cf

---

29   'πάντα χρήματα ἦν ὁμοῦ: εἶτα νοῦς ἐλθὼν αὐτὰ διεκόσμησε', Diog. L. II, 6 [actually III, 6 – ed.].
30   H. Diels, *Die Fragmenter der Vorsokratiker*, 1922. Vol. 1, p. 44. [Anaxagoras fragment 12 – ed.].
31   Ibid, p. 385.

Latin *deus* and Sanskrit *deva*). But even more often in Heraclitus 'fire' is called λόγος [*logos*] and γνώμη [gnọ̄mi̱], where the term λόγος [*logos*] is understood in two ways: on the one hand, 'word' or 'truth', uttered by the sage, and on the other hand, the 'life-giving power', that is spread throughout nature. 'Everything in the world happens according to this λόγος [*logos*] that is, 'fire''. Everything that is done through the participation of this power is good and beautiful, even if people do not understand it. The inner force that animates a person, represented by the later worldview in the form of the 'soul', is identified in Heraclitus with 'fire', resp. 'air', 'wind', 'breath', which are only derivatives of 'fire' and its varieties.

According to Sextus Empiricus 'Heraclitus definitely says that not only man is a rational being, but the whole surrounding world is animate'.[32] 'According to Heraclitus, we absorb this universal reason (λογικόν [*logikon*]) with our breath and thus reach consciousness ...'.[33] The more of this global 'fire' the soul contains, the wiser it is; – 'a dry soul is wisest and best' (the word dry here does not have a metaphorical, but a physical meaning). 'If a person gets drunk, he is unsteady on his feet and can be led by a child, and he does not know where he is going, because his soul has become wet', i.e. darkened. (Here we have the curious fact of a later physical reinterpretation of older magical motifs).

If all this is compared with the views that are reflected in legends, myths and monuments such as the ancient *Vedas* and the *Avesta*, then we will see that we are dealing – typologically with the same worldview motives, where 'mind', 'spirit' and 'soul' are understood bodily and are only derivatives of 'fire' or 'air' or 'water'.

Johannes Hertel, one of the most competent specialists, comes to the following conclusion based on a huge critical re-evaluation of the entire European-theological understanding of ancient *Vedic* and *Avestan* literature: 'All Aryan literature serves as proof that the concept of 'immaterial' was completely absent among the Aryans at their primitive. Everything that we call abstractions appeared to the Aryans to be materially corporeal. This matter, which made up all things, was *fire*, whether in the form of its luminous resp. dark variety, or colourless manifestation'.[34] In the *Rig-Veda* and the *Avesta*, everything that is alive and active is fire. In the *Atharva Ved*, this view is expressed in a hymn (XII, 119) as follows: 'Fire is in the earth and in plants, water also contains fire, fire is in rocks, fire is inside people. Horned animals and horses have fire within them. Fire pours from above from the bright sky. The fire of the Devas belongs to

---

32 Sextus Empiricus, *Adversus Mathematicos*, VIII, 286.
33 *Adversus Mathematicos*, VII, 129.
34 Hertel 1927, p. 48.

the second intermediate space (between heaven and earth) ... O earth, whose clothing is fire, whose knees are black, make me bright and sharp'.[35]

The same fire burns in the human heart, and in general within man, as in the sky, and this fire gives life to man. 'Soul' and 'knowledge' at this stage of development of thinking are still a kind of 'fire'. The concept of 'soul' and 'spirit' develops from the notion of 'fire'.

According to Hertel's research, many types of 'fire' are distinguished in ancient Aryan literature. There is a 'fire of knowledge (Avestan *daēna* –, *cisti* –, *bao'ah* –, *manah* – etc.) the fire of health, the fire of military prowess, the fire of political power (*xvarenah*), even the fire of wealth (*aši* –, *ərət* – etc.), fire producing (or rather, the power of growth – K.M.) – the fire of the soul (*cidra* –), etc'.[36] 'Reason' and 'intellect' (*mazdah*), 'soul', 'knowledge', 'spirit' are still only separate types of 'fire' at this stage of development. Notions about these things are derivatives of 'fire'.

The notion of 'fire' as a life-giving force, developing into the concepts of 'wisdom', 'reason', 'spirit', 'soul', does not break ties with 'water', or with 'air' (resp. 'wind'). According to the views of both the *Rig-Veda* and the *Avesta* water and wind represent only different manifestations of the same 'fire'. Fire (*Agni*) is called the 'grandson' or 'son of the waters' (apām, napāt).[37] 'The waters, stones, and wood contain the germs of fire ...'. (Rg. v. VI, 48, 5). 'It is carried in the womb of plants, trees, and the earth' (Rg. v. VII, 4, 5).

The cultic drink *Soma* (in the *Avesta*: *Naoma*) was represented as fire in a liquid state. Taking this drink, according to their perspective a person increased their 'inner fire', acquired wisdom and the magical power of knowledge. Rain falling from the sky also contained fire, and therefore had the power of fertilisation. Generally speaking, rivers and waters are the sisters of Agni, or, in other words, water. – it is only a manifestation of fire in another form. In one of the songs of the *Rig-Veda* (I, 65) about fire, it is said that it is 'related to the waters, as are brother to sisters'.

Such representations we meet with concerning 'the earth'; the earth, as Hertel establishes, was represented as having arisen from fire radiated from the heavens (*Avesta*, V, 6.49–51) 'since, – says Hertel the as stars have light, i.e. fire from which the earth is produced'.[38]

Turning now to ancient Greek philosophy, we find that Heraclitus, for whom 'fire' also acted as the rational principle of 'spirit', 'soul', etc. again did not break

---

35   Hertel 1927, p. 50.
36   Hertel 1927, p. 44.
37   Hertel 1927, p. 58.
38   Hertel 1927, p. 24.

its connection with 'water'. Fire is characterised here through the concept of fluidity and the similarity with the fluidity of water. Moreover, in Heraclitus 'water' and 'earth' are produced from 'fire' by cooling and solidifying the latter. The transformation of fire first yields water, but through solidification water turns part into earth, part back into fire.

It should be noted that in Heraclitus, fire directly turns into water, and not by passing through the preliminary state of 'air'. In a series of stages of the transformation of 'fire' Heraclitus does not mention air specifically, since 'air' (resp. wind) is, according to his perspective, the same as 'fire'.

We can thus establish that Heraclitus's 'fire' is essentially the same as Anaximenes' 'air' and Anaxagora's νοῦς [*nous*].

Comparing these data with the results of linguistic analysis, with the motifs of folk tales, and data from material culture, etc., we get a definite picture. It is not accidental that in the Russian language we find a coincidence of such terms as '*voz-dukh*' [*vozdukh* = air] and '*dukh*' [spirit], or when the fricative spirant *kh* in sibilant *sh* is completely normal for the Russian language, '*dush-a*' [*dusha* = soul] and '*dyshat"* [to breathe], '*dykh-anie*' [*dykhanie* = breathing];[39] or even the Greek names ψύχρός [*psukhrós*] -cool, as well as in the meaning of 'water' and air space, and ψυχή [*psūkhḗ*] – with the meaning of 'breath', 'life force' and 'soul'.

Voltaire noted the very curious fact that in almost all languages and among all peoples 'the heart is aflame', 'courage lights up', 'eyes sparkle', 'blood boils', 'the soul burns', and so on. – These expressions, which we now understand only as poetic metaphors, are linguistic remnants that indicate an ancient belief about the existence of an 'inner fire', and, of course, they did not contain anything metaphorical at that time. These things and phenomena were once really perceived in such a direct objective meaning.

Very common throughout the East is the motif in which a person, through asceticism,[40] i.e. abstinence from spending spiritual energy – fire, reaches such inner strength and wisdom (i.e. The internal accumulation of fire), that fire sometimes breaks through and blazes over his head.

The Vedic *Agni*, Avestan *Mithra*, *atman* (breath, internal fire, life force), *prana* (with the same meanings as *atman*), brahman (inner fire, fire of the soul, fire of the heart), ascetic fire, shining through the human body, radiance around the head in Christian iconography, the 'fire' of Heraclitus, Anaxagoras'

---

39 Marr 1931a, pp. 48, 49.
40 As Hertel shows, the Hindi word for asceticism, *tapas*, means 'heat' (Glut, fervour), the ascetic is designated by the word *tapasa*, which means 'possessed by heat', i.e. fire (Glutwesen, Glutmensch), Hertel 1927, pp. 7, 60.

νοῦς [*nous*] and so on – all these are facts of the same worldview order. 'Fire', 'air', 'spirit', 'soul', 'word' [*slovo*], 'λόγος' [*logos*], 'reason' are palaeontologically arranged in one semantic series.[41]

Thus – 'water', as well as 'air' resp. 'fire', 'spirit', 'soul', etc. – have the strongest touch of magical notions and cultic sense in ancient Greek philosophy. One cannot, of course, fail to note the following evidence, provided by Aristotle in his summary of Thales: 'Some think that even the ancients who lived long before the present generation, and first framed accounts of the gods [εολογησαντας],[42] had a similar view of nature; for they made Ocean and Tethys the parents of creation, and described the *oath of the gods as being by water*, to which they give the name of Styx; for what is oldest is most honourable, and the most honourable thing is that by which one swears'.[43] and in Homer we meet an indication that the Ocean (Ὠκεανός [*okeanos*]), which surrounds the whole world and from which all heavenly bodies arise and descend, is the beginning (the father) of all the gods, 'Oceanus, from whom the gods are sprung' ([*Iliad*] II. XIV, 201) 'Oceanus, from whom they all are sprung' ([*Iliad*] XIV. 246).

Thales' 'water', Anaximenes' 'air', Heraclitus' 'fire', Pythagoras' 'magic number', Empedocles' four elements – these are basically the same cult-magical elements, or perhaps primitive 'categories of thinking', so widely spread across

---

41 The motifs of Greek philosophy held in common with the mythological views of Eastern countries could not, of course, remain unnoticed by historians of philosophy; but the facts of such coincidences were interpreted by them completely erroneously; on these facts they built hypotheses about borrowing, about the migration of peoples, or drew up a scheme of a common Indo-European proto-language, *ur*-mythology, etc. For instance, in Gladsich (1852) it seemed that the pre-Socratic philosophy is only a repetition of the views of the five main peoples of Asia; Pythagorean philosophy allegedly repeated the Chinese worldview; Herodotus – the Persian, Eleatic – the Hindu, in Empedocles – the Egyptian and Anaxagoras – the Jewish. Eduard Röth (1846) tried to convince us that all pre-Socratic philosophy is borrowed from Egypt and revolves in the circle of Egyptian religious and philosophical ideas. Zeller builds his conception on the premises of the dominant Indo-European history, the Indo-European *ur-Volk* and that the Greeks brought perspectives common to all Aryans with them from Asia. 'Die Griechen stamen mit den übringen indogermanischen Volken aus Asien, und sie müssen aus dieser Ihrer altesten Heimat schon ursprünglich zugleich mit ihrer Sprache mitgebracht haben' [The Greeks came with the other Indo-European peoples from Asia, and they must have brought their language from this their oldest homeland at the same time – ed.], Zeller 1869, Vol. 1, p. 23. The inconsistency of such views should be obvious if we pay attention to the fact that we find the same perspectives not only among the Indo-European peoples, but Also among the Chuvash, Georgians, Svans, etc.

42 It stands to reason that this word (Θεολογία [*theologia*]) has a completely difference sense and significance than that which it acquired in the middle ages.

43 Aristotle, *Metaphysics*, book 1 part 3.

the face of the earth in folklore, fairy tales and myths; these are the same motifs that are so clearly reflected in such literary monuments as the *Bible* (the legend of the creation of the world from 'water'), the *Vedas*, the *Avesta*, and the ancient Chinese and the Hindu philosophers, and even the Aramaic philosophers of the middle ages, etc.

All these notions and concepts of ancient philosophy are directly related to the stage of the cosmic worldview and Marr considered them in this regard.[44]

Marxist science is thus faced with a new task: reconstructing the entire history of philosophy and restoring a correct picture of the past forms of worldview and perspectives of ancient philosophers in the light of real, rather than fictional history.

Moreover, this way, we will find that a considerable number of basic concepts and categories of later and even modern bourgeois philosophy, such as 'spirit', 'soul', 'substance', 'Logos', 'idea', etc., are only later reinterpretations of the notions of the cosmic and totemic stage of thought. Palaeontology of the concept of 'truth' [*istina*] (resp. the word for 'truth') leads us to 'sun' and 'sky'; palaeontology of the concept 'spirit', 'soul' – to 'fire', resp. the 'sun' or 'sky', and the palaeontology of the word 'god' – leads to totemic views and to the 'cultic dog' or even to the 'cultic pig'. The Georgian *ğmerd* 'god', preserved in a more complete form in the Mingrelian *ğor-mod* and in the Svan *ğer-med* is traced by Marr to the cultic dog, resp. 'pig': *do-ğor* – dog in Mingrelian, and *ğor-ond* in Georgian – pig.[45]

Marr does not consider only a person's language and thinking in respect of their historical formation and social essence; it turns out that even such manifestations of life as joy, sorrow, the sense of beauty, song, dance, games, as far as the human capacity for jollity, sorrow, etc., is concerned, have nothing in common with biological manifestations. They are all products of social life, not of the biological nature of man. Man does not sing as birds sing. The human song has a different, non-biological origin, and a different meaning, namely, a social one. The manifestations of human mirth and sorrow have nothing to do with the frolic and lethargy of animals. *They are associated primarily with certain social institutions of jollity or sorrow.* There are certain traditional norms, 'templates' or even organisational forms in which human fun, grief, games, etc. are manifested. these Forms were developed socially and historically and at the beginning had a completely different meaning and purpose, referring mainly to the complex that Marr called 'labour-magical actions' [*trud-*

---

44 Marr 1931a, p. 48.
45 Marr 1931a.

magicheske deistviia]. In later stages, they changed their meanings, but they still contain many formal and survival elements, through the analysis of which we discover their previous meanings.

All these various aspects of human life have, therefore, the same history of stadial development and historical reinterpretation, as thinking, speech and the data of material culture.

Marr tries to grasp the development of language, thinking and material culture, and all other manifestations of human life, activity and cultural creation in one common historical process. Human thinking, language, graphic speech, fine arts, songs, music, games, institutions of fun and sorrow, mummery, mysteries, drama, religious education, religious beliefs, customs, material culture, etc., etc. All this is included in one common flow of mutually determined historical development with stadial shifts and the consequent reinterpretation of all corresponding concepts.

All these areas which, for science, are still scattered, find the unity of explanation in the expanded system of historical science outlined by Marr. Marr seeks to present the entire history of the world as one common historical process, the development of humanity, the inner spring of which is the development of the productive forces and the relations of production of society. This concept of expanded historical science is the concept that Karl Marx first put forward in its entirety.

Science does not yet recall such a colossal picture of history, and yet this is the real history of society that Marx, Engels, and Lenin opened up and developeded and that our socialist state demands of us. Marr provides only the first sketches of this grandiose history, which, as a whole, can only be built up in a future socialist society by the hard work of several generations of scientists of a new type, with new, completely socialist concepts. As they work scholars will be more and more surprised and admire the magnitude of the theoretical work that this penetrating mind was able to raise and managed to outline.

Assessing Marr's work, many have often spoken about his unconscious, spontaneous materialism. However, for greater accuracy, it is necessary to emphasise that if in Marr's early works we were really dealing with a manifestation of spontaneous materialism, then this is already out of the question in relation to the last stage of development of the theory.

Starting in 1924, Marr consciously developed his teaching based on Marxist methodology. This, in the main, explains the tremendous progress made by his theory in the last ten years of the life of this remarkable scholar. Marr himself was well aware of the role the October Revolution played in the development of his theory, liberating so many oppressed languages and nationalities in the most multi-tribal and multilingual country. In his public speeches, he repeatedly said that without the October Revolution there would have been no new theory language.[46]

We well remember the words of another major scholar – the Bolshevik M.N. Pokrovskii, 'If Engels had lived among us, Marr's theory would now have been studied by every Commissar, because it would have been included in the iron inventory of the Marxist understanding of the history of human culture'.[47] What M.N. Pokrovskii expressed as his private opinion and desire in 1928, we can now establish as an undisputed conquest: Marr's theory has firmly entered the iron inventory of Marxist science.

Marr's new theory of language is the brainchild of the October Revolution, and let everyone, both our friends and our enemies, know that we will defend it with the same determination as all the main gains of the working class and the socialist state.

No matter how much we talk about the extraordinarily intensive development of the natural sciences and the gradual approach to the ideal, when, according to M. Planck grasping all the fields of physical science in one whole would crown all the constructions of theoretical physics, – it is necessary to say that the success of the social sciences of our socialist homeland has irrevocably overtaken all the advanced countries of the hostile capitalist world, and in the field of historical sciences has made it quite possible to achieve the ideal that physicists still only dream of.[48]

We have no doubt that the younger generation, honouring the memory of Nikolai Iakovlevich Marr throughout the Soviet Union and being the most active fighter for new revolutionary ideas of science, will pave the most difficult paths of history. They were outlined in the fire of the proletariat's class battles under the leadership of Marx, Engels, Lenin and Stalin – these lights of the new era of human history.

---

46   Marr 1931b, pp. 3–6; Marr 1931c, p. 8.
47   *Izvestiia TsIK*, no. 118 (3352), 23 May 1928.
48   Planck 1922.

Glossary of Names

Abaev, Vasilii Ivanovich (1900–2001) Russian linguist. An advocate of Marr's 'new theory of language' in the 1920s–40s. Among his works are publications about Ossetian and Persian etymology, Ossetian folklore, Iranian studies and general linguistics.

Ach, Narziss (1871–1946) German psychologist and university lecturer who worked in Königsberg and Göttingen. A member of the Würzburg School, he is known for his introspective experiments on mental processes.

Alborov, Boris Andreevich (1886–1968) Ossetian philologist and one of the founders of the Ossetian Historical-Philological Society. He worked on the development of Ossetian language and literature. He was arrested during Stalin's purges and was twice exiled to Siberia.

Anaxagoras (c. 510–c. 428 BCE) Pre-Socratic Greek philosopher.

Anaximenes of Miletus (c. 586–c. 526 BCE) Ancient Greek Pre-Socratic philosopher.

Augustine of Hippo (aka Aurelius Augustinus Hipponensis and Saint Augustine, 354–430 CE) Roman African, Manichaean, early Christian theologian and Neoplatonic philosopher.

Avenarius, Richard Ludwig Heinrich (1843–1896) German-Swiss philosopher. His radical positivist theory was generally known as 'empirio-criticism'.

Bacon, Francis (1561–1626) English philosopher and statesman whose works played a significant role in the development of the scientific method.

Balzac, Honoré de (1799–1850) French novelist and playwright.

Bashindzhagian, Levon Gevorkovich (1893–1948) Georgian linguist, specialist in Caucasian studies and poet. A close colleague of Nikolai Marr at the *Institut iazyka i myshleniia* (Institute of Language and Thinking). He was a prominent propagandist of Marr's ideas.

Bastian, Adolf Philipp Wilhelm (1826–1905) German polymath best remembered for his contributions to ethnography and anthropology.

Bauer, Bruno (1809–1882) German rationalist philosopher, historian, and theologian.

Becher, Erich (1862–1929) German philosopher and psychologist. A proponent of psycho-vitalism who held that supra-individual psychological forces operate from the most primitive levels to the entirety of human culture.

Bekhterev, Vladimir Mikhailovich (1857–1927) Russian neurologist and pioneer of objective psychology, best known for showing the role of the hippocampus in memory, the study of reflexes, and a type of arthritis subsequently called Bekhterev's disease.

Berkeley, George (1685–1753) Irish philosopher whose work is often characterised as 'subjective idealism'.

Boas, Franz Uri (1858–1942) German-born American anthropologist. Sometimes called the 'Father of American Anthropology'. An acknowledged influence on the ideas of Nikolai Marr.

Bogdanov, Aleksandr Aleksandrovich (pseudonym of Aleksandr Aleksandrovich Malinovskii, 1873–1928) Russian philosopher, author, physician, revolutionary and leading member of the Bolshevik faction of the Russian Social Democratic Labour Party until 1909. He remained very influential on Soviet thought despite his high-profile disagreements with Lenin. His 1922 book, *Tektologiia*, is now regarded as a forerunner of systems theory.

Boltzmann, Ludwig (1844–1906) Austrian physicist and philosopher. He invented statistical mechanics, the theory which connected the properties and behaviour of atoms and molecules with the large-scale properties and behaviour of the substances of which they were the building blocks.

Bolzano, Bernard (1781–1848) Bohemian mathematician, logician, philosopher, theologian and Catholic priest of Italian extraction. His anti-Kantian philosophy was an important influence on the development of phenomenology.

Bosman, Willem (1672–1703) Dutch merchant in the service of the Dutch West India Company who spent much time in the Dutch Gold Coast, which he described in his 1704 book *Nauwkeurige beschrijving van de Guinese Goud- Tand- en Slavekust* (An accurate description of the Guinean gold-tooth and Slave Coast).

Braun, Julius (1825–1869) German historian of art, culture and religion. He argued that the fundamental principles of art and religion were derived from ancient Egypt and were transmitted, through the Semites, Greeks and Romans to the Germanic and other 'northern' peoples.

Brett, William Henry (1818–1886) British missionary in British Guiana. Published *Legends and Myths of the Aboriginal Indians of British Guiana* in 1890.

Bühler, Karl Ludwig (1879–1963) German psychologist and linguist. Professor and Head of the Psychology Department at the University of Vienna 1911–1938 before moving to the United States. His work develops Gestalt psychology, and he was one of the founders of the Würzburg School of psychology. He made important contributions to the philosophy of language, especially his 'organon model' of communication and his treatment of deixis as a linguistic phenomenon. He influenced a number of early Soviet thinkers, including Valentin Voloshinov and Lev Vygotskii.

Calvin, John (b. Jehan Cauvin, 1509–1564) French theologian, pastor and reformer in Geneva during the Protestant Reformation.

Carlyle, Thomas (1795–1881) British historian, satirist, essayist, translator, philosopher, mathematician, and teacher. In *On Heroes, Hero-Worship, and The Heroic in History* (1841), he advanced the thesis that the actions of the 'Great Man' play the key role in history, and that history 'is but the biography of great men'.

Carnot, Nicolas Léonard Sadi (1796–1832) French mechanical engineer in the French Army, and a military scientist and physicist, often described as the 'father of thermodynamics'.

Cassirer, Ernst Alfred (1874–1945) German-Jewish philosopher who began as a member of the Marburg School of neo-Kantianism but later developed his thought by incorporating aspects of Hegelianism and phenomenology. His three-volume *Philosophy of Symbolic Forms* (1923–1929) was influential on a number of early Soviet thinkers, including Marr, Frank-Kamenetskii and Mikhail Bakhtin.

Cervantes, Miguel de Cervantes Saavedra (c. 1547–1616) Spanish writer regarded as one of the world's greatest novelists, best known for *Don Quixote*, published in two parts between 1605 and 1615.

Clausius, Rudolf Julius Emanuel (1822–1888) German physicist and mathematician. One of the main founders of the science of thermodynamics.

Cohen, Hermann (1842–1914) German-Jewish philosopher, one of the founders of the Marburg school of neo-Kantianism.

Colebrooke, Henry Thomas (1765–1837) English orientalist and mathematician. He was one of the first major Sanskrit scholars in Europe.

Cooley, Charles Horton (1864–1929) American sociologist perhaps best known for his contention that a person's self emerges from interpersonal interactions in society and the perceptions of others, often referred to as the 'looking-glass self'. These were developed in his *Human Nature and the Social Order* (1902) and *Social Organisation* (1909)

Cooper, James Fenimore (1789–1851) American writer of historical romances depicting frontier and Native American life from the seventeenth to the nineteenth centuries.

Croce, Benedetto (1866–1952) Italian idealist philosopher, historian and politician.

Cunow, Heinrich (1862–1936) German Social Democratic Party politician and Marxist theorist who wrote on primitive society and the history of the French Revolution. The second volume of his major philosophical work, *The Marxist Theory of the Historical Process of Society and the State* (vols. 1–2, 1920) was published in Russian translation in 1930. The first volume of his four-volume study *History of Economy* (1926–31) was published in Russian translation as

GLOSSARY OF NAMES 401

The Economy of Primitive and Semi-civilized Peoples, in 1929.

D'Aeth, Frederic George (1875–1940) British social administrator, lecturer and author of works on social issues such as the alleviation of poverty.

Dal', Vladimir Ivanovich (1801–1872) Russian lexicographer particularly well known for his landmark *Explanatory Dictionary of the Living Great Russian Language*, which was published in four volumes in 1863–1866.

Descamps, Paul (1872–1946) Belgian sociologist.

De Roberti, Evgenii Valentinovich (1843–1915) Russian sociologist, positivist philosopher and economist. A prominent liberal and member of the Kadet Party, as well as a leading Russian Free Mason.

D'Holbach, Paul-Henri Thiry, Baron (1723–1789) French-German author, philosopher and encyclopaedist. He was prominent figure in the French Enlightenment.

Diderot, Denis (1713–1784) French philosopher, critic, and writer, particularly known as co-founder, chief editor, and contributor to the *Encyclopédie*. He was a prominent figure during the French Enlightenment.

Dilthey, Wilhelm (1833–1911) German philosopher best known for the way he distinguished between the natural and human sciences. He held the natural sciences seek to arrive at law-based causal explanations, while the human sciences should pursue the understanding of the organisational structures of human and historical life.

Diogenes Laërtius (fl. 3rd century CE) Biographer of the ancient Greek philosophers.

Drăghicescu, Dimitrie (1875–1945) Romanian politician, sociologist, diplomat and writer. He studied in Paris at the Collège de France under Emile Durkheim, Gabriel Tarde, and Henri Bergson. He taught sociology at the university of Bucharest and wrote a textbook on the discipline. A number of his essays that were translated and published in Russian periodicals.

Driesch, Hans (1867–1941) German biologist and philosopher, who worked in experimental embryology and developed a neo-vitalist philosophy of entelechy.

Durkheim, David Émile (1858–1917) French sociologist who formally established the academic discipline of sociology.

Ebbinghaus, Hermann (1850–1909) German psychologist who pioneered the experimental study of memory, He is credited with outlining the 'curves' of learning and of forgetting.

Edinger, Ludwig (1855–1918) German anatomist and neurobiologist.

Ehrenreich, Paul (1855–1914) German anthropologist and ethnologist. After extensive fieldwork in Brazil, North America, Mexico, India and East Asia his work focused on comparative mythology and linguistic studies.

Einstein, Albert (1879–1955) German-born theoretical physicist who developed the theory of relativity, a major pillar of modern physics.

Empedocles (c. 494–c. 434 BCE) Greek pre-Socratic philosopher.

Euclid (*Eukleídēs*, aka Euclid of Alexandria, fl. 300 BC) Greek mathematician, often called the 'founder of geometry'.

Feuerbach, Ludwig Andreas (1804–1872) Post-Hegelian German philosopher, who played an important role in the transition from idealism to various forms of naturalism, materialism and positivism.

Forel, Auguste-Henri (1848–1931) Swiss neuroanatomist, psychiatrist, entomologist and eugenicist, known for his investigations of brain structure. He is considered a co-founder of neuron theory, and is also known for his early contributions to sexology and psychology.

Fourier, François Marie Charles (1772–1837) French philosopher, early socialist thinker and one of the founders of utopian socialism.

France, Anatole (1844–1924) French poet, journalist, and novelist. A member of the *Académie française*, who won the 1921 Nobel Prize in Literature.

Frank-Kamenetskii, Izrail' Grigor'evich (1880–1937) Lithuanian-born Russian-Jewish Orientalist, philosopher, biblical scholar and linguist. One of the most talented collaborators of N. Ia. Marr, whose ideas he imbibed selectively. He was personally acquainted with Megrelidze at the *Institut iazyka i myshleniia* (Institute of Language and Thinking).

Frazer, James George (1854–1941) British social anthropologist and folklorist, an influential figure in the development of modern studies of mythology and comparative religion. He is best known for *The Golden Bough* (1890), which catalogues the similarities among magical and religious beliefs around the world. Frazer's work was translated into Russian and widely received.

Freyer, Hans (1887–1969) German sociologist and philosopher. He argued history develops through three stages, which repeat themselves in a cycle: *Glaube, Stil,* and *Staat* (belief, style, the state).

Frobenius, Leo Viktor (1873–1938) German ethnologist and archaeologist. He was a major figure in German ethnography, especially for his work on African history.

Gauss, Johann Carl Friedrich (1777–1855) German mathematician and physicist who made significant contributions to many fields in mathematics and science.

Geiger, Lazarus (or Lazar, 1829–1870) German Jewish philosopher and philologist. He is best known for his *Ursprung und Entwickelung der menschlichen Sprache und Vernunft* (Vol. 1, Stuttgart, 1868), in which he asserted that the evolution of human reason is closely bound up with that of language. He also maintained that

GLOSSARY OF NAMES 403

the origin of the Indo-Germanic language is to be sought in central Europe rather than in Asia.

Gnedich, Pëtr Petrovich (1855–1925) Russian writer, dramatist, translator and historian of art. Megrelidze refers to his memoirs *Kniga zhizni. Vospominaniia 1855–1918* (Leningrad: Priboi, 1929).

Goethe, Johann Wolfgang von (1749–1832) German polymath, writer and statesman.

Grillparzer, Franz Seraphicus (1791–1872) Austrian writer mainly known for his dramas.

Gruppe, Otto (1851–1921) German compiler and commentator on myth, chiefly remembered for his *Griechische Mythologie und Religion-Geschichte* (1906), which summed up nineteenth-century readings of Greek mythology.

Guericke, Otto von (1602–1686) German scientist, inventor, and politician. He established the physics of vacuums, discovered an experimental method for demonstrating electrostatic repulsion, and advocated the reality of 'action at a distance' and of 'absolute space'.

Guizot, François (1787–1874) French historian, orator, and statesman.

Haller, Albrecht von (1708–1777) Swiss anatomist, physiologist, naturalist, encyclopaedist, bibliographer and poet. Often regarded as the 'father of modern physiology'.

Hartmann, Paul Nicolai (1882–1950) Baltic German philosopher who began as a Marburg School neo-Kantian but moved towards phenomenology and 'critical realism'.

Haym, Rudolph (1821–1901) German philosopher who wrote biographies of Wilhelm von Humboldt (1856), Hegel (1857), Schopenhauer (1864), Herder (1877–1885) and Max Duncker (1890).

Heidegger, Martin (1889–1976) German philosopher best known for contributions to phenomenology, hermeneutics, and existentialism.

Heine, Christian Johann Heinrich (1797–1856) German poet, writer and literary critic.

Helvétius, Claude Adrien (1715–1771) French philosopher and freemason. He defended a materialist theory of human nature in which all human action is determined by the surroundings.

Heraclitus of Ephesus (c. 475 BCE, fl. 504/3 BCE–501/0 BCE) Pre-Socratic Ionian Greek philosopher.

Herbart, Johann Friedrich (1776–1841) German philosopher, psychologist and founder of pedagogy as an academic discipline.

Herder, Johann Gottfried von (1744–1803) German philosopher, theologian, poet, and literary critic.

Hertel, Johannes (1872–1955) German Indologist who specialised in the study of narrative literature such as the *Panchatantra* and the *Vedas*.

Hochheimer, Wolfgang (1906–1991) German psychologist. A student of Max Wertheimer, Kurt Goldstein and Adhemar Gelb.

Husserl, Edmund Gustav Albrecht (1859–1938) Moravian Jewish philosopher, founder of the phenomenology movement.

Jacobi, Carl Gustav Jacob (1804–1851) was a German mathematician who made fundamental contributions to a range of problems in the discipline.

Jaensch, Erich Rudolf Ferdinand (1883–1940) German philosopher and psychologist.

James, William (1842–1910) American philosopher and psychologist. One of the founders of the philosophical school known as pragmatism, and of functional psychology.

Jeans, Sir James Hopwood (1877–1946) British physicist, astronomer and mathematician.

Kapp, Ernst Christian (1808–1896) German philosopher of technology and geographer. He was prosecuted for sedition in the late 1840s and was subsequently forced to leave Germany.

Kautsky, Karl Johann (1854–1938) Czech-Austrian philosopher, journalist, and Marxist theoretician. Kautsky was recognised as the most authoritative representative of 'Orthodox Marxism' between the death of Engels in 1895 until the outbreak of World War I in 1914.

Koffka, Kurt (1886–1941) German psychologist. He worked alongside Max Wertheimer and Wolfgang Köhler to develop Gestalt psychology, which he pursued into areas such as visual perception, sound localisation, developmental psychology, and experimental psychology.

Köhler, Wolfgang (1887–1967) German psychologist and phenomenologist who, along with Max Wertheimer and Kurt Koffka, was one of the founders of Gestalt psychology. Köhler's work on the mentality of apes was a landmark in the psychology of thinking in illustrating how the influence of a number of external conditions exerted an important influence on the development of higher animals.

Kroner, Richard (1884–1974) German neo-Hegelian philosopher, best known for his book *Von Kant bis Hegel* (1921/24), a history of German idealism.

Külpe, Oswald (1862–1915) German psychologist. One of the founders of experimental psychology.

La Mettrie, Julien Offray de (1709–1751) French materialist philosopher and physician. He is best known for his work *L'homme machine* (*Machine Man*, 1747).

Lang, Andrew (1844–1912) Scottish man of letters and specialist in folklore, mythology and religion. Like Tylor, he explained the seemingly 'irrational' elements of mythology as survivals from more primitive forms.

Laplace, Pierre-Simon, marquis de (1749–1827) French scholar and polymath whose work contributed to the development of several disciplines, including mathematics, physics, astronomy, engineering and philosophy. In his *magnum opus*, the five-volume *Mécanique Céleste*

(*Celestial Mechanics*, 1799–1825) he summed up and extended the work of his predecessors.

Lask, Emil (1875–1919)   German philosopher. A student of Heinrich Rickert at Freiburg, he was a member of the Baden (Southwestern) school of neo-Kantianism but drew close to phenomenology.

Lazarus, Moritz (1824–1903)   German philosopher and psychologist, founder, with Haymann Steinthal, of *Völkerpsychologie* [cultural psychology], and, in 1860, the journal *Zeitschrift für Völkerpsychologie und Sprachwissenschaft*. He was an outspoken opponent of anti-Semitism.

Le Bon, Charles-Marie Gustave (1841–1931)   French polymath whose interest encompassed anthropology, psychology, sociology, medicine, and physics. He travelled widely in Europe, Asia and North Africa, carrying out nascent anthropological analyses of the civilisations he encountered. His essentialist approach to humanity informed his work on the psychology and sociology of crowds as psychological entities determined by their 'racial unconscious'.

Leibniz, Gottfried Wilhelm (1646–1716)   German polymath. A prominent and influential logician, mathematician and natural philosopher.

Lévy-Bruhl, Lucien (1857–1939)   French scholar trained in philosophy who furthered anthropology with his contributions to the nascent fields of sociology and ethnology. His primary field of study involved 'primitive mentality', the main texts of which were published in Russian translation.

Lindworsky, Johannes (1875–1939)   German psychologist who aimed to describe and explain the psychic elements underlying the experience and their connection. He influenced the development of Gestalt psychology.

Lloyd Morgan, Conwy (1852–1936)   British ethologist and psychologist, generally remembered for his theory of emergent evolution, and for the experimental approach to animal psychology.

Lobachevsky, Nikolai Ivanovich (1792–1856)   Russian mathematician known primarily for his work on hyperbolic (non-Euclidean) geometry.

Locke, John (1632–1704)   British empiricist philosopher and classical liberal thinker.

Lorentz, Hendrik Antoon (1853–1928) was a Dutch physicist who, with Pieter Zeeman (1865–1943) won the 1902 Nobel Prize in Physics for the discovery and theoretical explanation of the Zeeman effect, splitting of a spectral line into several components in the presence of a static magnetic field. He also worked out the transformation equations that were to underpin Albert Einstein's theory of special relativity.

Lucretius (Titus Lucretius Carus, 94 BCE–c. 55 BCE)   Roman poet and philosopher. Author of the philosophical poem *De rerum natura*, about the tenets and philosophy of Epicureanism. Translated into English as *On the Nature of Things*.

Lumholtz, Carl Sofus (1851–1922) Norwegian explorer and ethnographer. Investigated the indigenous cultures of Mexico and Australia.

Luria, Aleksandr Romanovich (1902–1977) Pioneering Russian neuropsychologist. He was one of the founders, with Lev Semenovich Vygotskii (1896–1934), of 'Cultural-Historical Psychology', and a leader of the 'Vygotskii Circle', also known as 'Vygotskii-Luria Circle'.

Mach, Ernst Waldfried Josef Wenzel (1838–1916) Austrian physicist and philosopher, who made significant contributions to physics, philosophy, and physiological psychology.

Manteifel', Petr Aleksandrovich (1882–1960) Russian zoologist and naturalist who won the Stalin prize in 1941.

Marbe, Karl (1869–1953) German psychologist, one of the founders of the Würzburg School.

Marr, Nikolai Iakovlevich (1864–1934) Georgian philologist and archaeologist, an academician from 1912, and a prominent figure in early Soviet academic life. He was personally acquainted with Megrelidze as director of the Leningrad Public Library and as director of the *Institut iazyka i myshleniia* (Institute of Language and Thinking), where Megrelidze worked while researching what would become *The Fundamental Problems of the Sociology of Thinking*. From 1932 until June 1950 Marr's controversial ideas in linguistics, known as 'Japhetic theory' and, from 1923, the 'New Theory of Language', were given official support.

McDougall, William (1871–1938) British psychologist. Author of influential textbooks on the theory of instinct and of social psychology.

Meshchaninov, Ivan Ivanovich (1883–1967) Russian linguist, archaeologist and ethnographer. An academician from 1932. A close colleague of Nikolai Marr, he took over the directorship of the *Institut iazyka i myshleniia* when Marr died in 1934.

Michelson, Albert Abraham (1852–1931) American physicist and Nobel Laureate (1907) known particularly for his work on measuring the speed of light and especially for the 1887 Michelson-Morley (with Edward Williams Morley) experiment aiming to detect the existence of the 'luminiferous aether', a supposed medium permeating space that was thought to be the carrier of light waves.

Mignet, François Auguste Marie (1796–1884) French journalist and historian of the French Revolution.

Mikhailovskii, Nikolai Konstantinovich (1842–1904) Russian literary critic, sociologist, writer on public affairs, and a theoretician of the Narodnik (Russian populist) movement.

Mises, Richard Edler von (1883–1953) Austrian-born American mathematician, engineer, and positivist philosopher who notably advanced statistics and probability theory.

Morley, Edward Williams (1838–1923) American chemist and astronomer famous for his extremely precise and accurate measurement of the atomic weight of oxygen and, with Albert Auguste Michelson, for the Michelson-Morley experiment aiming to detect the existence of the 'luminiferous aether', a supposed medium permeating space that was thought to be the carrier of light waves.

Müller, Johannes Peter (1801–1858) German physiologist and comparative anatomist, regarded as one of the great natural philosophers of the nineteenth century.

Natorp, Paul Gerhard (1854–1924) German philosopher and educationalist. A co-founder and prominent member of the Marburg School of neo-Kantianism.

Nemesiues of Emesa (fl. c. 400 CE) Christian philosopher, bishop of Emesa (now Ḥimṣ, Syria) and the author of the treatise *De Natura Hominis* ('On Human Nature'), regarded as the earliest extant handbook of theological or philosophical 'anthropology'.

Noiré, Ludwig (1829–1889) German philosopher of language known especially for his theory that language, reason and labour emerged simultaneously. He was influenced by Arthur Schopenhauer's 1818 work *The World as Will and Representation* and by his close friend, the philologist Friedrich Max Müller. His works were widely received in the USSR in the 1920s and 1930s, having a significant influence on, *inter alia*, Nikolai Marr and Aleksandr Bogdanov.

Orbeliani, Saba Sulkhan (1658–1725) Georgian writer and diplomat. He compiled *The Georgian Dictionary*, which combines the functions of both a lexicon and an encyclopaedia.

Ørsted, Hans Christian (1777–1851) Danish physicist and chemist who discovered that electric currents create magnetic fields, the first connection found between electricity and magnetism.

Owen, Robert (1771–1858) Welsh textile manufacturer, philanthropist and social reformer, a founder of utopian socialism and the cooperative movement.

Palante, Georges Toussaint Léon (1862–1925) French philosopher and sociologist. A strident aristocratic individualist whose ideas in some ways resembled those of Nietzsche and Schopenhauer, he vocally opposed Durkheim's holism in favour of methodological individualism.

Parkinson, Richard Heinrich Robert (1844–1909) Danish explorer and anthropologist.

Pavlov, Ivan Petrovich (1849–1936) Prominent Russian physiologist best known for his work on reflexes and classical conditioning.

Pearson, Karl (1857–1936) English mathematician who has been credited with establishing the discipline of mathematical statistics.

Planck, Max Karl Ernst Ludwig (1858–1947) German theoretical physicist who won the Nobel Prize in Physics in 1918 for his discovery of energy quanta.

Plekhanov, Georgii Valentinovich (1856–1918) Russian revolutionary, philosopher and a Marxist theoretician. A founder of the social-democratic movement in Russia.

Pokrovskii, Mikhail Nikolayevich (1868–1932) Russian Marxist historian, particularly influential in the USSR in the 1920s. An official campaign of denunciation of his alleged errors was initiated in January 1936.

Post, Albert Hermann (1839–1935) German anthropologist who pioneered the study of the legal relations of indigenous peoples.

Potebnia, Aleksandr Afanasevich (1835–1891) Russian philosopher and linguist, professor of linguistics at the University of Kharkov. Best known for his 1862 book *Mysl' i iazyk* (Thought and Language).

Proudhon, Pierre-Joseph (1809–1865) French libertarian socialist and journalist whose ideas were foundational for later radical and anarchist theory. He was the target of criticism in Karl Marx's 1847 book *The Poverty of Philosophy*.

Puchta, Georg Friedrich (1798–1846) German jurist noted for his works on ancient Roman law.

Pythagoras of Samos (c. 570–c. 495 BCE) Ancient Greek philosopher whose political and religious teachings influenced the philosophies of Plato, Aristotle, and, through them, Western philosophy. Certain numerological theories are ascribed to him, though scholars today debate whether they were actually the work of his followers.

Ratzel, Friedrich (1844–1904) German geographer and ethnographer. He is now best known as the first person to use the term *Lebensraum* in the sense later adopted by the Nazis, though his interpretation was primarily spiritual and racial rather than economic and political.

Reichenbach, Hans (1891–1953) German philosopher and educator who was a leading representative of the Vienna Circle and founder of the Berlin school of logical positivism. He moved to the United States in 1938.

Ricardo, David (1772–1823) British political economist, one of the founders of classical economics.

Rickert, Heinrich John (1863–1936) German philosopher, a prominent member of the so-called Baden, or 'Southwestern' School of neo-Kantianism.

Riemann, Bernhard (1826–1866) German mathematician known particularly for his contributions to analysis, number theory, and differential geometry.

Rozen, Viktor Romanovich (1849–1908) Russian Orientalist and Arabist. Academician of the St. Petersburg Academy of Sciences (from 1890). A leading figure in establishing late imperial oriental studies, Rozen was one of the teachers on Nikolai Marr.

Russell, Bertrand Arthur William (1872–1970) British philosopher, logician mathematician, historian, writer, essayist and Nobel laureate. He was also a social critic and political activist.

Saint-Simon, Claude Henri de Rouvroy, comte de (1760–1825)   French political and economic theorist whose thought exerted an influence on politics, economics, sociology and the philosophy of science.

Saussure, Ferdinand de (1857–1913) Swiss linguist and semiotician whose work is widely considered foundational in the development of twentieth-century linguistics.

Savigny, Friedrich Carl von (1779–1861)   German jurist and historian who argued law is part and parcel of national life and that the theory and practice of jurisprudence must be studied as a unity.

Schelling, Friedrich Wilhelm Joseph (1775–1854)   German philosopher who, along with J.G. Fichte and G.W.F. Hegel, was one of the three most influential thinkers in the tradition of 'German Idealism'.

Schiller, Johann Christoph Friedrich von (1759–1805)   German poet, philosopher, physician, historian and playwright.

Schmidt, Johannes Friedrich Heinrich (1843–1901)   German linguist who developed the so-called *Wellentheorie* (wave theory) of language development, according to which innovations of a language spread from a central point in progressively weaker concentric circles. He held that this should result in convergence among dissimilar languages.

Schmidt, Wilhelm (1868–1954)   German anthropologist and Roman Catholic priest who was a leading figure in the cultural-historical European school of ethnology.

Schomburgk, Moritz Richard (1811–1891)   German botanist and curator of the Adelaide Botanical Garden. Author of *Versuch einer Zusammenstellung der Flora und Fauna von Britisch-Guiana* (1848).

Schopenhauer, Arthur (1788–1860) German philosopher, best known for his 1818 work *The World as Will and Representation*, in which the phenomenal world is presented as the product of a blind and insatiable metaphysical will.

Schuppe, Ernst Julius Wilhelm (1836–1913)   German positivist philosopher and advocate of the idea of conscious immanence, according to which the subject and object form a unity.

Sextus Empiricus (c. 160–c. 210 CE) Pyrrhonist philosopher and a physician.

Shpet, Gustav Gustavovich (1879–1937) Ukrainian and Russian philosopher, psychologist, theorist of art, and translator.

Sighele, Scipio (1868–1913)   Italian sociologist and criminologist who approached the theory of crowds from the direction of criminology.

Simmel, Georg (1858–1919)   German sociologist, philosopher, and critic. One of the first generation of German sociologists. His neo-Kantian approach laid the foundations for anti-positivist, cultural sociology.

Sombart, Werner (1863–1941) German economist and sociologist, leader of the so-called 'Youngest Historical School'. He is chiefly remembered for his magnum opus, *Der moderne Kapitalismus*, which was published in three volumes 1902–1927.

Smith, Adam (1723–1790) British economist, philosopher, author and moral philosopher. A pioneer of political economy and a key figure during the Scottish Enlightenment.

Spencer, Herbert (1820–1903) British philosopher, biologist, anthropologist, sociologist, and prominent classical liberal political theorist. Much of Spencer's work was translated into Russian and widely received in the late imperial period, and his Lamarckian evolutionary theories, as applied to society, had an influence on many thinkers, including Marr.

Spinoza, Baruch (1632–1677) Dutch, and Sephardic Jewish philosopher of Portuguese origin. Considered one of the great rationalist thinkers of seventeenth-century philosophy.

Stammler, Karl Eduard Julius Theodor Rudolf (1856–1938) German philosopher of law who distinguished the purely formal concept of law from the ideal, the realisation of justice.

Staudinger, Franz (1849–1921) German high school teacher, philosopher, and activist in the consumer cooperative movement.

Steinen, Karl von den (1855–1929) German physician, ethnologist, explorer, and anthropologist. Contributed important work to the study of Indian cultures of Central Brazil, and the art of the Marquesas.

Steinthal, Haymann (1823–1899) German philologist and philosopher. Joint founder, with his brother-in-law Moritz Lazarus, of *Völkerpsychologie* [cultural psychology] and, in 1860, the journal *Zeitschrift für Völkerpsychologie und Sprachwissenschaft*.

Stendahl (Marie-Henri Beyle 1783–1842) French writer, particularly known for the realist novels *Le Rouge et le Noir* (*The Red and the Black*, 1830) and *La Chartreuse de Parme* (*The Charterhouse of Parma*, 1839).

Stephenson, George (1781–1848) was a British civil and mechanical engineer renowned as the 'Father of Railways'. Megrelidze may also refer to Stephenson's son **Robert** (1803–1859) who built on the achievements of his father.

Stirner, Max (pseudonym of Johann Kaspar Schmidt, 1806–1856) German philosopher, widely regarded as one of the forerunners of nihilism, existentialism, psychoanalytic theory, and individualist anarchism.

Strassen, Otto Karl Ladislaus zur (1869–1961) German zoologist. A follower of Darwinism, who focused primarily on biological morphology and developmental mechanics.

Tarde, Gabriel (1843–1904) French sociologist, criminologist and social psychologist. A pioneer of the idea of the 'group mind' or the psychology of the crowd, in which he foregrounded the importance of imitation and innovation as explanatory concepts.

Thales of Miletus (c. 625–546 BCE) Greek mathematician, astronomer and pre-Socratic philosopher.

Thiers, Marie Joseph Louis Adolphe (1797–1877) French statesman and historian.

Thierry, Jacques Nicolas Augustin (1795–1856) French liberal historian.

Thorndike, Edward Lee (1874–1949) American psychologist, whose work on comparative psychology and the learning process led to the theory of connectionism and helped lay the scientific foundation for educational psychology

Trémaux, Pierre (1818–1895) French architect, Orientalist photographer, and author of numerous works of a scientific and ethnographic character.

Tsagareli, Aleksandr Antonovich (aka Alexander Anton von Zagareli, 1844–1929) Georgian linguist, professor at Saint Petersburg State University and co-founder of Tbilisi State University.

Tylor, Edward Burnett (1832–1917) British anthropologist, the founder of cultural anthropology. A typical nineteenth-century cultural evolutionist, whose works *Primitive Culture* (two volumes, 1871) and *Anthropology* (1881), defined the context of the scientific study of anthropology, based on the evolutionary theories of Charles Lyell. Tylor's works were translated into Russian and published in the late imperial period and exerted a significant influence on Russian and early Soviet thought.

Vaihinger, Hans (1852–1933) German philosopher, generally known as a scholar of the work of Kant.

Veselovskii, Alexander Nikolaevich (1838–1906) Russian literary theorist who laid the groundwork for comparative literary studies. One of the teachers of Nikolai Marr.

Vico, Giambattista (1668–1754) Italian political philosopher and rhetorician, historian and jurist. His *magnum opus*, the book *La Scienza Nuova* (*The New Science*, 1725) arguably inaugurated the modern field of the philosophy of history.

Voitonis, Nikolai Iur'evich (1887–1913) Russian zoologist and comparative psychologist.

Volkonskii, Mikhail Nikolaevich (1860–1917) Russian writer and dramatist, author of historical novels and parodies. He gained renown for his libretto to the parodic opera *Vampuka, nevesta afrikanskaia, obraztsovaia v vsekh otnosheniiakh* (Vampuka, the African bride, exemplary in all respects).

Voltaire (*nom de plume* of François-Marie Arouet, 1694–1778) French writer, historian, and philosopher. A key figure in the French Enlightenment, he is renowned for his wit, his criticism of the Roman Catholic Church, and of Christianity more generally. Known also as a vocal advocate of freedom of speech, of religion, and of separation of church and state.

Vorländer, Karl (1860–1928)   German neo-Kantian philosopher who published various studies and editions of the works of Kant, including studies of the relation between Kantian and socialist thought, and of the influence of Kant on the work of Johann Wolfgang Goethe.

Ward, Lester Frank (1841–1913)   American botanist, palaeontologist and sociologist who played an important role in the establishment of sociology as a discipline in the United States.

Watson, John Broadus (1878–1958)   American psychologist who popularised the scientific theory of behaviourism and established it as a psychological school.

Weber, Max (1864–1920)   German sociologist, philosopher, jurist, and political economist.

Wertheimer, Max (1880–1943)   Austro-Hungarian-born psychologist. One of the founders of Gestalt psychology, along with Kurt Koffka and Wolfgang Köhler. He is known for his book, *Productive Thinking*, and for conceiving the 'phi phenomenon'.

Wesselski, Albert Franz Maria (1871–1939)   Austrian Journalist, Translator, literary scholar and folklorist based in Prague. Renowned especially for his study of Latin narratives, comparative mythology and fairy tale research.

Windelband, Wilhelm (1848–1915)   German philosopher. A prominent member of the so-called Baden, or 'Southwestern' School of neo-Kantianism.

Worms, Renè (1869–1926)   French sociologist, often considered a member of the organismic school of sociology, who founded both the *Revue internationale de sociologie* and the Institut International de Sociologie.

Wundt, Wilhelm Maximilian (1832–1920)   German physician, physiologist, philosopher, and one of the founders of modern psychology. He is widely regarded as the 'father of experimental psychology' for founding the first formal laboratory for psychological research in 1879, at the University of Leipzig. He believed, however, that language was crucial to all higher mental functions, which were outside of the scope of experimental research. Instead these needed to be the object of *Völkerpsychologie*, which employed historical and comparative methods.

Ziegler, Heinrich Ernst (1858–1925)   German zoologist who specialised in developmental history, genetics, behavioural research and animal psychology. He was an advocate of race hygiene and eugenics.

References

The following bibliography refers both to the editorial apparatus and Megrelidze's original text. In the case of references to Marx and Engels, Megrelidze uses a variety of editions available at the time. Where the original passage cited has been found the translation and reference refers to the latest, and still incomplete English language edition. Where this has not been possible the text cited by Megreidze has been provided. There are cases in which Megrelidze's references are incorrect or incomplete and it has been necessary to provide an annotation where this is needed.

Alpatov, V.M. *Istoriia odnogo mifa: Marr i Marrizm*. Second edition. Moscow: URSS.
Andree, Richard 1878, 'Über den Farbensinn der Naturvölker', *Zeitschrift für Ethnologie*, 10: 323–34.
Ash, Mitchell G. 1998. *Gestalt Psychology in German Culture 1890–1967: Holism and the Quest for Objectivity*. Cambridge: Cambridge University Press.
Bastian, Adolf 1860, *Der Mensch in der Geschichte*, Leipzig: Wigand.
Bastian, Adolf 1893, *Kontroversen in der Ethnologie*, Berlin: Weidmann.
Becher, Erich 1911, *Gehirn und Seele*, Heidelberg: C. Winter.
Bekhterev, Vladimir 1921, *Kollektivnaia Refleksologiia*, Petrograd: Kolos.
Beloch, Karl Julius 1924, *Griechische Geschichte*, Strassburg: Trübner.
Bhaskar, Roy 1998 [1979], *The Possibility of Naturalism: A Philosophical Critique of the Contemporary Human Sciences*, London: Routledge.
Bogdanov, A.A. 2010 [1910], *Padnie velikogo fetishizma*, Moscow: URSS.
Brandist, Craig 2011, 'Semantic Palaeontology and the Passage from Myth to Science and Poetry: The Work of Izrail' Frank-Kamenetskij (1880–1937)', *Studies in East European Thought*, 63, no. 1: 42–61.
Brandist, Craig 2015, *The Dimensions of Hegemony: Language, Culture and Politics in Revolutionary Russia*, Leiden: Brill.
Braun, Julius 1864, *Naturgeschichte der Sage. Rückführung aller religiösen Ideen, Sagen, Systeme auf ihren gemeinsamen Stammbaum und ihre letzte Wurzel*, München: Bruckmann.
Brett, William H. 1868, *The Indian Tribes of Guiana*, London: Bell and Daldy.
Bühler, Karl 1918, *Die geistige Entwicklung des Kindes*, Jena: Fischer.
Bühler, Karl 1921, *Die geistige Entwicklung des Kindes*, Jena: Fischer.
Bukharin, N.I. 1926 [1922], *Historical Materialism: A System of Sociology*, London: Allen and Unwin.
Bukharin, N.I. 2005 [1937], *Philosophical Arabesques*, London: Pluto Press.
Cassirer, Ernst 1925, *Philosophie der symbolischen Formen*, Vol. II, Berlin: B. Cassirer.
Cassirer, Ernst 1929, *Philosophie der symbolischen Formen*, Vol. III, Berlin: B. Cassirer.

Cherchi, Marcello and H. Paul Manning 2002, *Disciplines and Nations: Niko Marr vs. His Georgian Students on Tblisi State University and the Japhetidology/Caucasology Schism*. (= Carl Beck Papers in Russian and East European Studies number 1603).

Dilthey, Wilhelm 1922, *Einleitung in die Geisteswissenschaften*, Berlin: Teubner.

Dilthey, Wilhelm 1927, *Der Aufbau der geschichtlichen Welt in den Geisteswissenschaften*, Leipzig: Teubner.

Driesch, H. 1903, *Die Seele als elementarer Naturfaktor*, Leipzig: Engelmann.

Driesch, H. 1905, *Der Vitalismus als Geschichte und als Lehre*, Leipzig: Johann Ambrosius Barth.

Driesch, H. 1921, *Philosophie des Organischen*, Leipzig: Engelmann.

Dzhioev, O.I. 1980a, 'Net v mire bogatsva, ravnogo chelovecheskoi zhizni ...', *Literaturnaia Gruziia*, 12: 174–82.

Dzhioev, O.I. 1980a, 'Net v mire bogatsva, ravnogo chelovecheskoi zhizni ...', *Literaturnaia Gruziia*, 1980b, 'Aktual'nost' sotsiologii myshleniia K.R. Megrelidze', *Filosofskaia i sotsiologicheskaia mysl'*, 2: 86–93.

Dummett, Michael 1993, *Origins of Analytical Philosophy*, Cambridge, MA: Harvard University Press.

Durkheim, Émile 1902, *La division du travail social*, Paris: F. Alcan.

Durkheim, Émile 1914, *Novye idei v sotsiologii*, Book 2, St. Petersburg: Obrazovanie.

Durkheim, Émile and Marcel Mauss 1913, *Les formes élémentaires de la vie religieuse et le système totémique en Australie*, Paris: F. Alcan.

Dzeims, V. [James, William] 1910, *Pragmatizm*. St. Petersburg: Shipovnik.

Engel's, Fridrikh [Engels, Friedrich], 1931, *Liudwig Feuerbach i konets klassicheskoi nemetskoi filosofii*, Moscow: Gos-sots.-ekon Izd.

Engel's, Fridrikh [Engels, Friedrich], 1932 *Razvitie sotsializma ot utopii k nauke*, Mocow: Partizdat.

Engel's, Fridrikh [Engels, Friedrich], 1933, *Dialektika prirody*. Moscow: Partizdat.

Engels, Friedrich, 1921, *Herrn Eugen Dühring's Umwdlzung der Wissenschaft*, Stuttgart: Diets.

Engels, Friedrich, 1942, *The Housing Question*, London: Lawrence & Wishart.

Feuerbach, Ludwig 1903–11, *Sämtliche Werke*, Stuttgart.

Forel, Auguste 1910, *Das Sinnesleben der Insekten*, München: E. Reinhardt.

Frank-Kamenetskii, I.G. 1932, 'Itogy kollektivnoi raboty nad siuzhetom Tristana i Isol'dy', in *Tristan i Isol'da. Ot geroini liubvi feodal'noi Evropy do bogini matriarkhal'noi Afrevrazii. Kollektivnyj trud Sektora semantiki mifa i fol'klora pod redaktsei N. Ia. Marra*, Leningrad: Izd. ANSSSR, pp. 261–76.

Freyer, Hans 1923, *Theorie des objektiven Geistes*, Leipzig: Teubner.

Freyer, Hans 1930, *Soziologie als Wirklichkeitswissenschaft. Logische Grundlegung des Systems der Soziologie*, Leipzig-Berlin: Teubner.

Friedrich, Janette 1993, *Der Gehalt der Sprachform. Paradigmen von Bachtin bis Vygotskij*, Berlin: Akademie Verlag.

Friedrich, Janette 2006, 'Les traces de N. Marr dans le livre de K. Megrelidze "Osnovnye problem sociologii myšlenia" (1937)', *Cahiers de l'ILSL*, 20: 109–25.

Frobenius, Leo 1909, *The Childhood of Man: A Popular Account of the Lives, Customs and Toughts of the Primitive Races*, London: Seeley.

Frobenius, Leo 1910, *Detstvo chelovechestva*, St. Petersburg: Lukovnikov.

Geiger, Lazarus 1871, *Vorträge zur Entwicklungsgeschichte der Menschheit*, Stuttgart: Cotta.

Geiger, Lazarus 1872, *Ursprung und Entwicklung der menschlichen Sprache und Vernunft*, Stuttgart: Cotta.

Gibson, J.J. 1979, *The Ecological Approach to Visual Perception*, Boston: Houghton Mifflin.

Gladsich, August 1852, *Die Religion und die Philosophie in ihrer Weltgeschichtlichen Entwicklung*, Breslau: Hirt.

Gnedich, Pëtr 1929, *Kniga zhizni*, Moscow: Priboi.

Gruppe, Otto 1887, *Die griechischen Kulte und Mythen*, Leipzig: Teubner.

Hartmann, Nicolai 1909, *Platos Logik des Seins*, Giessen: Töpelmann.

Hartmann, Nicolai 1933, *Das Problem des geistigen Seins*, Berlin: De Gruyter.

Hegel, G.W.F. 1906, *Enzyklopädie der philosophischen Wissenschaften im Grundrisse*, Leiden: Herausgegeben von Bolland.

Hegel, G.W.F. 1911, *Rechtsphilosophie*, edited by G. Lasson, Leipzig: Meiner.

Hegel, G.W.F. 1921, *Phänomenologie des Geistes*, Leipzig: Meiner.

Hegel, G.W.F. 1923, *Wissenschaft der Logik*, Leipzig: Meiner.

Hegel, G.W.F. 2004, *Hegel's Philosophy of Nature*, edited by A.V. Miller, Oxford: Oxford University Press.

Hegel, G.W.F. 2015, *The Science of Logic*, edited and translated by George Di Giovanni, Cambridge: Cambridge University Press.

Helmholtz, Hermann von 1962, *Treatise on Physiological Optics*, New York: Dover.

Hertel, Johannes 1927, *Die Sonne und Mithra im Awesta*, Leipzig: Haessel.

Hochheimer, Wolfgang 1932, 'Analyse eines "Seelenblinden" von der Sprache aus', *Psychologische Forschung*, 16, no. 2: 1–69.

Husserl, Edmund 1973 [1900], *Logical Investigations*, London: RKP.

Ilizarov, B.S. 2012, *Pochetnyi akademik Stalin i akademik Marr*, Moscow: Veche.

James, William 1921, *Pragmatism*, New York: Longmans, Green and Co.

Kant, Immanuel 1799, *Anthropologie in pragmatischer Hinsicht abgefasst*, Frankfurt and Leipzig: Publisher not given.

Kant, Immanuel 1855, *The Critique of Pure Reason*, translated by J.M.D. Meiklejohn, London: Henry Bohn.

Kapp, Ernst 1877, *Grundlinien einer Philosophie der Technik*, Braunschweig: Westermann.

Kautskii, Karl [Kautsky, Karl] *Etika i materialisticheskoe ponimanie istorii*, St. Petersburg: Iakovenko.

Kautsky, Karl 1927, *Die materialistische Geschichtsauffassung*, Berlin: Dietz.

Kazanskii, N.N. (ed.) 2013, *Trudy Instituta lingvisticheskikh issledovanii: Acta Linguistica Petropolitana*, Vol. IX, St. Petersburg: Nauka.

Koffka, Kurt 1921, *Die Grundlagen der psychischen Entwicklung*, Osterwieck: Zickfeldt.

Koffka, Kurt 1935, *Principles of Gestalt Psychology*. New York: Harcourt, Brace.

Köhler, Wolfgang 1918, *Nachweis einfacher Strukturfunktionen beim Schimpanse und beim Haushuhn*, Berlin: Königl. Akademie der Wissenschaften.

Köhler, Wolfgang 1921, *Intelligenzprüfungen an Menschenaffen*, Berlin: Springer.

Köhler, Wolfgang 1922, *Intelligenzprüfungen an Menschenaffen*, 2 Auflage, Berlin: Springer.

Kotelmann, Ludwig 1884a, 'Die Augen von 22 Kolmücken', *Zeitschrift für Ethnologie*, 77–84.

Kotelmann, Ludwig 1844b, 'Die Augen von 23 Singhalesen und 3 Hindus', *Zeitschrift für Ethnologie*, 164–80.

Kroner, Richard 1936, 'Philosophy of Life and Philosophy of History', *The Journal of Philosophy*, 33, no. 8: 204–12.

Lazarus, Moritz 1917, *Das Leben der Seele*, Berlin: Dümmler.

Le Bon, Gustave 1895, *Psychologie des foules*, Paris: F. Alcan.

Lenin, V.I. 1909, *Materializm and Empiriokrititsizm*, Moscow: Zveno.

Lenin, V.I. 1919, *State and Revolution*, London: Allen & Unwin.

Lenin, V.I. 1926–1935, *Sochineniia*. Moscow and Leningrad: Gosizdat.

Lenin, V.I. 1931, *Leninskii sbornik*, vol. XII. Moscow and Leningrad: Institut Lenina.

Lenin, V.I. 1933, *Filosofskie tetrady*, Moscow: Partizdat.

Lenin, V.I. 1960–1979, *Collected Works*, Moscow: Foreign Language Press.

Lévy-Bruhl, Lucien 1922, *Les fonctions mentales dans les sociétés inférieures*, Paris: F. Alcan.

Lévy-Bruhl, Lucien 1923, 'La discussion. La mentalité primitive', *Bulletin de la Société française de philosophie*, 23, no. 2: 2–48.

Lévy-Bruhl, Lucien 1927, 'L'âme primitive', Paris: Alcan.

Lévy-Bruhl, Lucien 1930, *Pervobytnoe myshlenie*, Moscow: Gos.soz.-ekonom.

Lindworsky, Johannes 1922, 'Umrisskizze zu einer theoretischen Psychologie', *Zeitschrift für Psychologie*, 89, 313–43.

Likhtenshtadt, V.O. 1920, *Goethe*, Moscow: Gosizdat.

Lloyd Morgan, Conwy 1909, *Instinkt und Gewohnheit*, Berlin: Teubner.

Losskii, Nikolai 1906, *Obosnovanie intuitivizma*, St Petersburg: Stasliuvich.

Lumholtz, Carl 1903, *Unknown Mexico*, London: Macmillan.

Magnus, Hugo 1880, *Untersuchungen über Farbensinn der Naturvölker*, Jena: Fischer.

REFERENCES 417

Mak-Daugol, V. (McDougall, William) 1916, *Osnovnye problem sotsial'noi psikhologii*, Moscow: Kosmos.
Marks, Karl [Marx, Karl] 1923, *Teoriia pribavochnoi stoimosti*, Vol. 1, Petrograd: Priboi.
Marks, Karl [Marx, Karl] 1931a, *K kritike politicheskoi ekonomii*, Moscow: Gosizdat.
Marks, Karl [Marx, Karl] 1931b, *Vvedenie k kritike politicheskoi ekonomii*. Moscow: Sotsekgiz
Marks, Karl [Marx, Karl] 1931c, *Nishcheta filosofii*. Moscow: Gosizdat.
Marks, Karl [Marx, Karl] 1932, *Naemnyi trud i kapital*. Moscow: Partizdat.
Marks, Karl [Marx, Karl] 1933, *Kritika Gotskoi programmy*, Moscow: Gosizdat.
Marks, Karl i Engel's, Fridrikh [Marx. Karl and Engels, Friedrich] 1925, *Arkhiv K. Marksa i F. Engel'sa*, Vol. 2, Moscow: Gosizdat.
Marks, Karl i Engel's, Fridrikh [Marx. Karl and Engels, Friedrich] 1928–1946, *Sobranie sochinenii*, Moscow and Leningrad: Gosizdat.
Marks, Karl i Engel's, Fridrikh [Marx. Karl and Engels, Friedrich] 1929, *Izbrannye proizvedeniia*, 3 volumes, Moscow: Gosizdat.
Marks, Karl i Engel's, Fridrikh [Marx. Karl and Engels, Friedrich] 1933a, *Nemetskaia ideologiia*, Moscow: Gosizdat
Marr, Nikolai Iakovlevich 1926, *Sredstva peredvizheniia. Orudie samozashchity i proizvodstva v do-istorii. (K yviazke iazykoznaniia s istoriei material'noi kul'tury)*, Leningrad: Akademiia nauk.
Marr, Nikolai Iakovlevich 1928a, 'Iafeticheskie nazvaniia krasok i plodov v grecheskom', *Izvestiia GAIMK*, 2: 325–331.
Marr, Nikolai Iakovlevich 1928b, *Aktual'nye problemy i ocherednye zadachi iafeticheskoi teorii*, Moscow: Izd. Komakademii.
Marr, Nikolai Iakovlevich 1928c, *Iafeticheskaia teoriia*, Baku: AzGIZ.
Marr, Nikolai Iakovlevich 1931a, *Iazyk i myshlenie*, Moscow: Ogiz.
Marr, Nikolai Iakovlevich 1931b, *Iazykovaia politika, iafeticheskaia teoriia u udmurskii iazyk*, Moscow and Leningrad: Izd. Narodov SSSR.
Marr, Nikolai Iakovlevich 1931c, *K semanticheskoi palaontologii v iazykakh neiafeticheskikh system*, Leningrad: Akademiia nauk.
Marx, Karl 1923, *Das Kapital*, Vol. I, Berlin.
Marx, Karl 1974, *Grundrisse*, Berlin: Dietz.
Marx, Karl 1996 [1887], *Capital: A Critique of Political Economy*, Vol. 1, in Marx and Engels 1975, Vol. 35, Moscow: Progress Publishers.
Marx, Karl and Friedrich Engels 1927–1935, *Marx-Engels Gesamtausgabe*. Moscow and Leningrad: Partizdat.
Marx, Karl and Friedrich Engels 1934, *Ausgewählte Briefe*, Moskau-Leningrad.
Marx, Karl and Friedrich Engels 1975–, *Collected Works*, Moscow: Progress Publishers; London: Lawrence and Wishart.

Matthews, W.K. 1950, 'Soviet Contributions to Linguistic Thought', *Archivum Linguisticum*, 2: 1–23 and 97–121.
Medvedev P.N. 1983 [1926], 'Sociologism without Sociology (On the Methodological Works of P.N. Sakulin)', in *Bakhtin School Papers*, edited by Ann Shukman, Colchester: University of Essex, pp. 67–74.
Megrelidze, Konstantin Romanovich 1935a, 'N. Ia. Marr i filosofiia marksizma', *Problemy istorii dokapitalisticheskikh obshchestv*, 3–4: 70–89.
Megrelidze, Konstantin Romanovich 1935b, 'N. Ia. Marr i filosofiia marksizma', *Pod znamenem Marksizma*, 3: 35–52.
Megrelidze, Konstantin Romanovich 1935c, 'O khodiachikh sueveriiakh i "pralogicheskom" sposobe myshleniia', in *Akademiku N. Ia. Marru*, Moscow: SSSR, pp. 461–96.
Megrelidze, M.K. 1989, 'Dva slova ob otse', *Filosofskaia i sotsiologicheskaia mysl'*, 2: 93–105.
Meshchaninov, Ivan Ivanovich 1928, 'O doistoricheskom pereselenii narodov', *Vestnik Kommunisticheskoi akademii*, 29.
Meshchaninov, Ivan Ivanovich 2010 [1929], 'Introduction to Japhetidology: Theses', in *Politics and the Theory of Language in the USSR 1917–1938: The Birth of Sociological Linguistics*, edited by Craig Brandist and Katya Chown, London: Anthem Press, pp. 175–9.
Mikhailovskii, Nikolai 1882, 'Geroi i tolpa', *Otechestvennye zapiski* 1, 2 and 5.
Mises, Richard von 1928, *Wahrscheinlichkeit, Statistik und Wahrheit*, Berlin: Springer.
Morgan, Jacques de 1909, *La première civilisation*, Paris: Leroux.
Moss, Kevin 1984, *Olga Mikhailovna Freidenberg: Soviet Mythologist in a Soviet Context*, Cornell University: UMI Dissertation Services.
Müller, Johannes 1840, *Handbuch der Physiologie der Menschen für Vorlesungen*, 2 volumes, Coblenz: J. Hölscher.
Mulligan, Kevin (ed) 1987, *Speech Act and Sachverhalt: Reinach and the Foundations of Realist Phenomenology*, Dordrecht: Nijhoff.
Mulligan, Kevin (ed) 1995, 'Perception', in *The Cambridge Companion to Husserl*. Edited by Barry Smith and David Woodruff Smith, Cambridge: Cambridge University Press.
Natorp, Paul 1921, *Platos Ideenlehre*, Leipzig: Meiner.
Nikonova, A.A. 2003, *Problema arkhaicheskogo soznaniia i stanovlenie otechestvennoi kul'turologicheskoi mysli (20–30-e gody XX v.)*, Kandidatskaia dissertatsiia: St. Petersburg SPbGU.
Noiré, Ludwig 1877, *Ursprung der Sprache*, Mainz: von Zabern.
Noiré, Ludwig 1880, *Werkzeug und seine Bedeutung in der Geschichte der Menschheitsentwicklung*, Mainz: von Zabern.
Noiré, Ludwig 1917, *The Origin and Philosophy of Language*, Chicago: Open Court.
Novicow, Jacques 1893, *Les luttes entre les sociétés*, Paris: F. Alcan.

Nuare, Liudvig [Noiré, Ludwig] 1925, *Orudie truda i ego znacheie v istorii razvitiia chelovechestva*, Kharkov: Gosizdat Ukrainy.

Parkinson, Richard 1907, *Dreissig Jahre in der Südsee*, Stuttgart: Strecker & Schröder.

Pavlov, I.P. 1923, *Dvadsatiletnii opyt ob'ektivnogo izucheniia visshei nervnoi deiatel'nosti zhyvotnikh*, Moscow and Petrograd: Gosizdat.

Perlina, N. 2002, *Olga Freidenberg's Works and Days*, Bloomington: Slavica.

Philipse, Herman 1995, 'Transcendental Idealism', in *The Cambridge Companion to Husserl*, edited by Barry Smith and David Woodruff Smith, Cambridge: Cambridge University Press, pp. 239–322.

Planck, Max 1922, *Einführung in die Theorie der Elekrizität und des Magnetismus*, Leipzig: Hirzel.

Plekhanov, G.V. 1941, *Fundamental Problems of Marxism*. London: Lawrence and Wishart.

Radloff, W. 1871, 'Haustiere der Kirgisen', *Zeitschrift für Ethnologie*, 3: 285–313.

Reichenbach, Hans 1922, 'Der gegenwärtige Stand der Relativitäts-Diskussion', *Logos*, 10: 316–78.

Rollinger, Robin D. (ed.) 1999, *Husserl's Position in the School of Brentano*, Dordrecht: Springer.

Röth, Eduard 1846, *Geschichte unsere abendländischen Philosophie*, München: Bassermann.

Rousseau, Jean-Jacques 1755, *Discours sur l'origine et les fondements de l'inégalité parmi les hommes*, Amsterdam.

Saussure, Ferdinand de 1933, *Kurs obshchei lingvistiki*, Moscow: OGIZ.

Schiller, F.C.S. 1902, *Personal Idealism*, London: Macmillan and Co.

Schmidt, Johannes 1890, *Die Urheimat der Indogermanen und das europäische Zahlsystem*, Berlin: Abhandlungen der Königlichen Akademie der Wissenschaften zu Berlin.

Schmidt, Wilhelm 1910, *Die Stellung der Pygmäenvölker in der Entwicklungsgeschichte des Menschen*, Stuttgart: Strecker & Schröder.

Schomburgk, Richard 1847/48, *Reisen in Britisch Guiana*, Vol. 1–3, Leipzig: Weber.

Schopenhauer, Arthur 1844, *Die Welt als Wille und Vorstellung*, II, Leipzig: Brockhaus.

Schopenhauer, Arthur 1900, *O chetveroiakom korne zakona dostatochnogo osnovaniia*, Moscow: Kushnerev.

Schuhmann, Karl and Barry Smith 1985, 'Against Idealism: Johannes Daubert vs. Husserl's "Ideas" I', *The Review of Metaphysics*, 38, no. 4: 763–93.

Shilov, L.A. (ed.) 1995, *Sotrudniki Rossiiskoi natsional'noi biblioteki – deiateli nauki i kul'tury: biograficheskii slovar'*, St. Petersburg: Izd. RNB.

Sighele, Scipio 1901, *La foule criminelle*, Paris: F. Alcan.

Smith, Barry 1988, 'Gestalt Theory: An Essay in Philosophy', in *Foundations of Gestalt Theory*, edited by Barry Smith, Munich: Philosophia Verlag, pp. 11–81.

Smith, Barry 1994, *Austrian Philosophy: The Legacy of Franz Brentano*, Chicago: Open Court.
Spenser, G. [Spencer, Herbert] 1898 *Osnovaniia sotsiologii*. St. Petersburg: Sytin.
Spencer, Herbert 1912 [1898], *Principles of Sociology*, New York: D. Appleton & Company.
Ste Croix, Geoffrey de 1981, *The Class Struggle in the Ancient Greek World*, London: Duckworth.
Steinen, Karl von den 1894, *Unter den Naturvölkern Zentral-Brasiliens*, Berlin: Reimer.
Steinen, Karl von den 1897, *Unter den Naturvölkern Zentral-Brasiliens*, Berlin: Reimer.
Tarde, Gabriel 1898, *Études de psychologie sociale*, Paris: Giard and Brière.
Teilor, E.B. [Tylor, E.B.] 1899, *Pervobytnaia kul'tura*, Vol. II.[1]
Thomas, Lawrence 1957, *The Linguistic Ideas of N. Ia. Marr*, Berkeley: University of California Press.
Thorndike, E.L. 1898, *Animal Intelligence: An Experimental Study of the Association Processes in Animals*, New York: Macmillan.
Thorndike, E.L. 1913, *Educational Psychology*, New York: Teachers College.
Thorndike, E.L. 1931, *Kongo*.[2]
Tihanov, Galin 2012, 'What was "Semantic Paleontology" and What Did it Have to Do with Literary Studies', *Stanford Slavic Studies*, 39: 288–311.
Trautmann, Thomas R. 1997, *Aryans and British India*, Berkeley: University of California Press.
Tsigler, E. (Ziegler, Heinrich Ernst) 1914, *Instinkt*, Petrograd: Soikin.
Tuite, Kevin 2011, 'The Reception of Marr and Marrism in the Soviet Georgian Academy', in *Exploring the Edge of Empire: Soviet Era Anthropology in the Caucasus and Central Asia*, edited by Florian Mühlfried and Sergey Sokolovsky, Halle: LIT Verlag, pp. 197–214.
Tylor, John M. 1924, *The New Stone Age in Northern Europe*, New York: C. Scribner's Sons.
Vaihinger, Hans 1920, *Die Philosophie des Als Ob*, Leipzig: Meiner.
Vasil'kov, Iaroslav 2001, 'Tragediia akademika Marra', *Khristianskii Vostok*, 2: 390–412.
Vundt, V, [Wundt, Wilhelm] 1913, *Mif i religiia*, translated by V. Bazarov and P. Yushkevich, St. Petersburg: Brokgaus-Efron.
Watson, J.B. 1914, *Behaviour, an Introduction to Comparative Psychology*, New York: Holt, Rinehart and Winston.
Wertheimer, Max 1925, *Über Gestalttheorie*, Erlangen: Philosophische akademie.

---

1 It appears Megrelidze's reference is incorrect. The book was first published in 1872 and then again in 1896 and 1897 with parts that questioned Christian views removed. It was published without such incursions in 1939.
2 Megrelidze's text lists a translated 1931 work by Thorndike work called Kongo, but this does not appear to exist. The only translated book from 1931 is *Psikhologiia obucheniia vzroslykh*, Moscow and Leningrad: Gos. Uchebno-pedagogicheskoe izd.

Wertheimer, Max 1961, *Productive Thinking*, London: Tavistock Publications.
Wesselski, Albert 1931, *Versuch einer Theorie des Märchens*, Reichenberg: F. Kraus.
Wilke, Georg A. 1923, *Kulturbeziehungen zwischen Indien, Orient und Europa*, Leipzig: Kabitzsch.
Windelband, Wilhelm 1920, *Einleitung in die Philosophie*, Tübingen: Mohr.
Zedania, Giga 2014, 'Konstantin Megrelidze's Theory of Consciousness', *Identity Studies*, 5, no. 1: 77–86.
Zeller, Eduard 1869, *Die Philosophie der Griechen Entwicklung*, Leipzig: Fues.
Zur Strassen, Otto 1908, *Die neuere Tierpsychologie*, Leipzig: Teubner.

Archival References

Peterburgskoi filial arkhiva rossiiskoi akademii nauk (PFA RAN):
Fond # 77 Institut iazyka I myshleniia im. N. Ia. Marra.
Fond # 800 Marr, Nikolai Iakovlevich.

Index

The index mainly shows the names of persons mentioned in the text, with the exception of certain texts and themes not mentioned in Megrelidze's extensive table of contents.

Abaev, Vasilii I.   162
Ach, Narziß   182
Alexander the Great   292
Anaxagoras   121, 390, 393–394
Anaximenes   389–390, 393, 394
Aristotle   109, 121, 123, 124, 175, 190, 192, 193, 209, 256, 281, 389, 394
Augustine   198
Avenarius, Richard   127, 136, 138
Avesta   385, 391–395

Bacon, Francis   101, 257
Bakhtin, Mikhail M.   xii, xxi
Balzac, Honoré de   282
Baratynsky, Yevgeny   284
Bashindzagian, Leon G.   xi, xiii, 241
Bastian, Adolf   248, 257
Bauer, Bruno   212
Becher, Erich   44
Bekhterev, Vladimir M.   297, 298
Berkeley, George   132, 136
Bhaskar, Roy   xvi
Bible, The   154, 385, 395
Boas, Franz   231, 248
Böhme, Jakob   293–294
Bogdanov, Aleksandr A.   xxiv, xxv, 275
Boltzmann, Ludwig   204–205
Bolzano, Bernard   132, 227
Bonaparte, Napoleon   292
Bosman, Willem   270
Braun, Julius   252
Brett, William   150
Bühler, Karl   49, 73–74
Bukharin, Nikolai I.   xiv

Calvin, John   198
Carlyle, Thomas   292
Carnot, Nicholas   85, 204
Cassirer, Ernst   127, 152, 255
Chikobava, Arnold S.   xiii
Cicero   123, 160
Clausius, Rudolf   204
Cohen, Hermann   127, 132, 137, 190, 242, 347, 348, 352

Colebrook, Henry   156
Columbus, Christopher   281, 350
Cooley, Charles   113
Cooper, James F.   144–145
Croce, Benedetto   212
Cunow, Heinrich   144

D'Aeth, Frederic   215
Dal', Vladimir I.   161, 241
Darwin, Charles   44, 116, 121, 203
Deborin, Abram M.   xi
Democritus   160
De Roberti, Evgenii   113–114
Descamps, Paul   215
Descartes, René   135
Diderot, Denis   198
Diogenes Laertius   390
d'Holbach, Baron (Paul-Henri Thiry)   98
Dilthey, Wilhelm   300
Dondua, Karpez D.   xiii
Drăghicescu, Dimitrie   113, 292
Durkheim, Emile   5, 113, 256, 275, 292, 298, 300–303, 305

Ebbinghaus, Hermann   138
Edinger, Ludwig   75
Ehrenreich, Paul   251
Einstein, Albert   280
Empedocles   160, 390, 394
Engels, Friedrich   xviii–xix, xxiv–xxvi, 3, 6, 36, 62, 101, 103, 122–123, 144, 149, 170, 198, 200, 203, 207, 212, 221, 228, 231, 233, 240, 243, 292, 314, 320, 328n26, 334, 340, 341, 345, 350, 351–352, 356, 367, 368, 382, 384, 396, 397
Euclid   281

Feuerbach, Ludwig   19, 112–113, 126, 143, 169–170, 171, 354–355
Fichte, Johann G.   173, 193, 213, 296, 378
Forel, Auguste   41
Foucault, Michel   xxv
Fourier, François   368
France, Anatole   310

INDEX

Frank-Kamenetskii, Izrail' G.   xxii, 163n38
Franklin, Benjamin   124
Frazer, James   5, 248, 254
Freidenberg, Ol'ga M.   xxii
Freyer, Hans   300
Frobenius, Leo   264, 266

Gauss, Johann   280, 286
Geiger, Lazar   xxii, 23, 100, 122, 154–161, 386
Gestalt psychology, *Gestalt* theory   xvi–xviii, xx, 62–66, 139
Gibson, James J.   xviii
Gnedich, Pëtr   305–306n25
Goethe, Johann   94, 100, 129–131, 149, 189, 224, 279, 280–281, 286, 293, 294
Grillparzer, Franz   99, 214
Gruppe, Otto   252, 253
Guericke, Otto von   369
Guizot, François   240

Haller, Albrecht von   127, 129
Hartmann, Nikolai   137, 300, 389
Haym, Rudolf   387
Hegel, Georg   28–29, 35–36, 40, 98–99, 104–106, 110, 115, 123, 125, 130, 145, 147, 151, 190, 192–201, 208–210, 216, 224, 225, 280, 283, 287, 293–294, 306, 309, 362, 374, 382, 388–389
Heidegger, Martin   212, 213
Heine, Heinrich   199, 293–294
Helvetius, Claude   121, 198
Heraclitus   134, 221, 390–391, 392–393, 394
Herbart, Johann   139
Herder, Johann   280
Herodotus   160–161, 385
Hertel, Johannes   391–392
Hesiod   165
Hippolytus   390
Hobbes, Thomas   124
Hochheimer, Wolfgang   88–91
Homer   155, 156, 157, 161, 188, 224, 385, 394
Husserl, Edmund   x, xvi–xviii, xx, 132, 187, 190, 213

Jacobi, Carl   199
Jaensch, Erich   182–183n5
James, William   371–372
Jeans, James   127–128

Kant, Immanuel   xix, 115, 121, 127, 128–129, 132, 137, 146, 186, 191–192, 209, 213, 223, 235, 256, 366
Kapp, Ernst   119–120
Kautsky, Karl   171
Koffka, Kurt   xvii, 55, 57–58, 75–76
Köhler, Wolfgang   x, xvii, 50–59, 65, 66–69, 71–73, 114, 117–118, 145–146, 219
Kroner, Richard   347n52
Külpe, Oswald   182

La Mettrie, Julien   198
Lang, Andrew   254
Laplace, Pierre-Simon   186, 193, 201
Lasalle, Ferdinand   328n26
Lask, Emil   140, 190
Lazarus, Moritz   292, 296–297
Le Bon   292, 298
Leibnitz, Gottfried   140, 192–198
Lenin, Vladimir I.   xxv, 31, 36, 104–105, 126, 136, 140–141, 152, 169, 170, 188, 189, 198, 200, 202, 203, 215–216, 235, 243, 283, 307, 310, 330, 334n32, 336, 341, 342, 345, 349–350, 355n65, 369, 370, 383, 386–387, 396, 397
Leont'ev, Aleksei N.   xxi
Leucippus   175
Lévy-Bruhl, Lucien   5, 171, 272, 292, 300–302, 305, 383, 386
Liebert, Albert   x
Lindworsky. Johannes   69–70
Lobachevsky, Nikolai I.   226, 227
Locke, John   134, 139, 192
Lorentz, Hendrik   280
Lucretius   198
Lumholtz, Carl S.   237, 383
Luria, Aleksandr R.   xxi, 92–93n62

Mach, Ernst   127, 136, 138, 142
Marbe, Karl   182
Marr, Nikolai Ia.   xii–xiv, xix, xxi–xxv, 25, 157, 163, 375–397
Marx, Karl   xviii, xxiv–xxvi, 6, 7–10, 14, 18–19, 22, 24–34, 37, 38, 41, 59, 61, 62, 65, 71, 81–83, 99, 103–106, 109, 112–113, 119, 125, 126, 144, 145, 151–153, 169–170, 171, 173, 176, 179, 195, 197, 198, 200, 203, 210, 212–217, 220, 222–224, 228–229, 234, 238–239, 243, 258–261, 271, 274–

Marx, Karl (cont.) 276, 285–286, 288, 291–293, 296, 304, 308–320, 322, 325–330, 334–336, 338, 339–346, 348n53, 354–356, 358–363, 364, 365–67, 370, 374, 377, 382, 383, 385–385, 386, 389, 396, 397
Mauss, Marcel 275
McDougall, William 79n50
Medvedev, Pavel N. xxi
Megrelidze, Iosif V. xii, xiii xxix
Megrelidze, Konstantin R. ix–xxvii, xxix–xxxi
Meshchaninov, Ivan I. xi, xxiii, 250, 259, 261
Michelson, Albert 280, 370
Mignet, François 240
Mikhailovskii, Nikolai K. 298
Minkovsky, Hermann 280
Mises, Richard von 203
Morgan, Lloyd 45
Morley, Edward 280, 370

Natorp, Paul 127, 137, 190, 242, 347, 389
Nemesiues of Emsa 212
Nietzsche, Friedrich 128–129n41
Newton, Isaac 280, 281
Noiré, Ludwig xix–xx, 37, 100, 120
Novalis (Georg Philipp Friedrich Freiherr von Hardenberg) 100

Orbeliani, Saba 158
Ørsted, Hans Christian 370
Ovid 157, 162
Owen, Robert 368

Palaeontology, semantic xxi–xxv, 179–182, 235–238, 288–291, 364, 378–396
Palante, Georges 292
Parkinson, Richard 231
Pavlov, Ivan P. 42
Pearson, Karl 242
Pindar 155, 156, 385
Planck, Max 397
Plato 10, 157, 175, 192, 389
Pliny 160
Plekhanov, Georgii V. xxiv–xxv, 282
Pokrovskii, Mikhail N. 397
Post, Albert 248
Potebnia, Aleksandr A. 238
Proudhon, Pierre-Joseph 324–325, 328n26

Puchta, Georg 296
Pythagoras 134, 160, 394

Ratzel, Friedrich 257
Reichenbach, Hans 212
Ricardo, David 112
Rickert, Heinrich 132, 190, 347
Riemann, Bernhard 226, 280
Rousseau, Jean-Jacques 234n16
Rozen, Viktor R. 376
Russell, Bertrand 227

Saint-Simon, Claude 368
Saussure, Ferdinand de 303, 305
Savigny, Friedrich Carl von 296
Schelling, Friedrich 110, 280, 293–294, 296
Schiller, Johann 371
Schmidt, Wilhelm 264–265
Schomburgk, Moritz 150
Schopenhauer, Arthur xix, xxv, 137, 142, 193
Schuppe, Ernst 190
Sextus Empiricus 391
Shakespeare, William 109, 294
Shpet, Gustav G. 238
Sighele, Scipio 297, 298
Simmel, Georg 113, 347
Smith, Adam 109, 112, 330
Sombart, Werner 299–300
Spencer, Herbert 13–14, 44, 248, 298
Spinoza, Baruch xix, 190, 192–199, 209, 294
Stalin, Iosif V. xii, xxiv, 397
Stammler, Rudolf 347
Staudinger, Franz 347
Steinthal, Heyman 296–297
Stephenson, George 281
Strassen, Otto 61
Steinen, Karl von 166, 234–235, 263, 286, 382
Stendahl, Haymann 189, 286
Stirner, Max 216, 325, 362

Tarde, Gabriel 113, 297, 298, 347
Thales of Miletus 389–390, 394
Theocritus 155
Thierry, Jacques 240
Thiers, Marie 240
Thorndike, Edward L. 42, 48–50, 53, 60, 114, 176
Trémaux, Paul 276

Tsagareli, Aleksandr   158
Tylor, Edward Burnett   5, 143–144, 248, 254
Tymianskii, Grigorii S.   xi

Vaihinger, Hans   127, 132, 242, 371
Vedas   154, 156, 391–395
   Rigveda   154, 385, 391
Veselovskii, Aleksandr N.   376
Vico, Giambattista   18, 174, 286
Virgil   155, 354
Voloshinov, Valentin N.   xxi
Voltaire (François-Marie Arouet)   175, 188, 199, 249, 393
Vorländer, Karl   347
Vygotskii, Lev S.   xxi

Ward, Lester F.   113, 347
Watson, John   42
Weber, Max   242
Wertheimer, Max   x, xvii, 58, 139, 230
Wesselski, Albert   289–290
Windelband, Wilhelm   190, 347
Worms, René   298
Wundt, Wilhelm   109, 138, 172, 254, 297
Würzburg school   182, 187

Xenophanes   162

Ziegler, Heinrich   45

Printed in the United States
by Baker & Taylor Publisher Services